Gospel Interpretation and Christian Life

Francis J Moloney, SDB

Scholars Collection

1. *Opening the Scripture*, 2014, Antony Campbell SJ

2. *Amplifying that Still Small Voice*, 2015, Frank Brennan SJ

Gospel Interpretation and Christian Life

Francis J Moloney, SDB

Adelaide

Text copyright © 2017 remains with the Francis J Moloney for all papers in this collection. All rights reserved. Except for any fair dealing permitted under the Copyright Act, no part of this book may be reproduced by any means without prior permission. Inquiries should be made to the publisher.

Unless noted otherwise, the Scripture quotations contained herein are from the New Revised Standard Version of the Bible, and the Revised Standard Version of the Bible copyright © 1989, and are used by permission. All rights reserved.

National Library of Australia Cataloguing-in-Publication entry
Creator: Moloney, Francis J. (Francis James), 1940- author.
Title: Gospel interpretation and Christian life
 / Francis J Moloney.

ISBN: 9781925643091 (hardback)
           9781925643107 (ebook : epub)
           9781925643114 (ebook : pdf)
           9781925643084 (paperback)

Series: Scholars collection.
Notes: Includes bibliographical references and index.

Subjects: Bible. Gospels--Criticism, interpretation, etc.
 Christian life.
 Theology, Practical.

Cover art work DUCCIO DI BUONINSEGNA, *The Calling of the Apostles Peter and Andrew* (1311). National Gallery of Art, Washington, DC, USA. Cover design by Raghava Rao Tulluri.

Layout, in Minion Pro 11, by Extel Solutions, India.

Published by:

An imprint of the ATF Press Publishing
Group owned by ATF (Australia) Ltd.
PO Box 504
Hindmarsh, SA 5007
ABN 90 116 359 963
www.atfpress.com
Making a lasting impact

For my many colleagues
at
Catholic Theological College
1976–1998, 2006–2017

Table of Contents

Foreword	ix
Acknowledgements	xiii
Introduction	**1**
1. The Story Behind the Book	3
Gospel Interpretation	**13**
2. Mark 6:6b-30: The Twelve, Mission, and Failure	15
3. Following Jesus into Radical Discipleship: A Reading of Mark 8:14-9:29	47
4. Marriage and Wealth: A Study of Mark 10:1-31	77
5. Literary Strategies in the Markan Passion Narrative: Mark 14:1-15:47	93
6. "He is going before you into Galilee." Mark 16:6-8 and the Christian Community	117
7. God's Gift of Servant Discipleship in the Gospel of Mark	131
8. Matthew 5:17-18 and the Matthean Use of "Righteousness"	147
9. Luke 22:14-38: Eucharist and Mission	171
10. When is John Talking about Sacraments?	191

Christian Life   **219**

11. Sacred Scripture and the Magisterium: A Restless Relationship?   221

12. Sacred Scripture at Vatican II   237

13. The Gospel of Creation. A Biblical Response to *Laudato Si'*   259

14. A New Testament Hermeneutic for Divorce and Remarriage in the Catholic Tradition   283

15. On the Writing of *The Gospel According to Judas*: Some Theological and Pastoral Reflections   309

16. The Word of God, Jesus Christ, and the Eucharist: Christian Hope in a Secularized World   329

17. The Word in the World: Then and Now   349

Bibliography   **371**

Indices

    Index of Authors   399

    Index of Biblical References   405

Foreword

The introduction to this collection ("The Story Behind the Book"), sharing something of the story that generated exegetical and pastoral reflections from 1983 till the present, offers me the possibility to explore something of the personal and academic journeys that lie behind the essays that make up this volume. I am thus able to limit this foreword to expressions of gratitude, some technical clarifications, and an explanation of the dedication.

I am most grateful to the editors, editorial boards and publishing houses that published the original versions of the following essays. Without exception, they generously and enthusiastically supported further publication. They are indicated in detail in the list of acknowledgements that follow. Reflecting my recent scholarly activity, these publishers are located in Rome, India, the USA, Australia, and the Philippines. On the whole, the essays appear almost exactly as they were originally published.

The major alteration made to the typescripts has been the unification of the scholarly style-sheet. I have used the current Society of Biblical Literature Style-Sheet (2014), with two notable exceptions. In the first place, I have avoided scholarly abbreviations for journals and series that are normally found in scholarly essays. My reader need not search in a list of abbreviations to find my sources; they are reproduced in full in the text and in the footnotes. Secondly, only since 2014 has the Society of Biblical Literature asked for the full Christian name of authors and editors. All essays published prior to that date have maintained the use of initials. Here and there I have retouched, and sometimes updated, an older essay. Such alterations are very few, always obvious, and never change the course of the original argument. As I will explain in my "Introduction," I have undertaken some major rewriting for the oldest essay in the collection "When is John Talking About Sacraments?" (1982). But even there the argument pursued remains unchanged, however much updated.

I am very grateful to Hilary Regan, the Chief Executive Officer of ATF Theology Press, who suggested this collection. It is one of several such collections of the work of Australian scholars that Hilary has initiated. Such volumes are a source of recognition and personal satisfaction for Australian theologians and biblical scholars. We often receive considerable acclaim overseas, but go unnoticed in our native Australia. This experience is largely due to the secular nature of Australian society, and the well-established local tradition of the "tall poppy syndrome." Hilary Regan and ATF Theology offer an important service to Australian theological activity. We are all grateful to Hilary and the quality publication house he directs at the Australian Theological Forum Limited. I am personally grateful that Hilary approached me, enabling the further publication, in a book form, of a number of articles that are regularly sought after, but sometimes difficult to locate.

The book is dedicated to the many people who have accompanied me at my long-term academic home in Melbourne. It calls for some explanation to non-Australians, and indeed even to Australians who are not aware of the ever-shifting Melbourne theological scene. The explanation is best expression via a potted history. I returned to my home in Australia, after 11 years of study, research, and teaching, in 1976. I immediately took up my post as a Lecturer in New Testament at Catholic Theological College (CTC), then located in Clayton, Victoria, close to Monash University. The academic authority and setting of the College was provided by the ecumenical Melbourne College of Divinity (MCD).

The MCD was founded in 1910, authorized by Victorian State Parliament to grant degrees from undergraduate to doctoral level, largely to students from a number of Protestant traditions, although the Jesuit Theological College was established in Parkville in the late 1960's, and Jesuit academics and students frequented the facilities there. In 1973 CTC (along with the Jesuit Theological College and the Yarra Theological Union) was admitted as an associated teaching institute within MCD. This was a major step in Catholic theological education resulting from the post-Vatican II desire to improve the human, spiritual, and academic formation of the Catholic population, especially those preparing for ministry as Priests, or educators in Catholic schools. It had been approved by the Catholic Bishops in 1972. In those early days, CTC was closely associated with the many seminaries located in the city of Melbourne. Those early years were also marked by large numbers of lay students and Religious men and women. Most major courses were taught during the day for the seminarians, and in the evenings for lay people and Religious.

In 1994 I was appointed the Foundation Professor of Theology at the newly-founded Australian Catholic University. Located on the University's campus at Chadstone, close to Clayton, I continued to teach and direct research at CTC until 1998. From 1976-1998 I was privileged to serve under five Masters of the College: Rev. Dr (now Professor) Austin Cooper, OMI (twice), Rev Dr Gerard Diamond, Rev Dr (now Professor) Norman Ford, SDB, Rev Dr John Begley, SJ (RIP), and Rev Dr (now Archbishop) Mark Coleridge.

In 1999 I took up the position of the Professor of New Testament at the Catholic University of America, Washington, DC. I returned from that ministry in the USA to assume the role of the Superior of the Australia-Pacific Province Salesians of Don Bosco in 2006. By this stage, CTC had relocated to its current fine facilities in East Melbourne, adjacent to the Melbourne campus of Australian Catholic University. In 2012 the Melbourne College of Divinity became part of the national tertiary education system as the specialized University of Divinity (UD). The Provincial Superior of my Religious Congregation, I resumed teaching and directing research at CTC in 2006. I have continued to do so since then, even though I was re-employed as a Senior Professorial Fellow at ACU from 2012-2016. Appointed a Senior Fellow of Catholic Theological College in 2009, in 2017 I resumed my presence at the College as a full-time member of CTC/UD.

I have already mentioned the Masters of the College from 1976-1998. But I wish to acknowledge here the many other people, past and present, academics, administrators, and students, alive and deceased, with whom I have shared my ministry at CTC. Among the deceased I would like to single out Barbara Stead, RSM, John Begley, SJ, Ian Murdoch, SDB, Margaret Brady, and Rod Doyle, CFC. Apart from the years in Washington, DC, I have been part of Catholic Theological College, in one way or another, for almost 35 years. We are blessed by the ongoing presence of Professor Austin Cooper, OMI. Professor Norman Ford, SDB, has very recently been appointed an Emeritus Professor of the University of Divinity, and is still an important presence to the College. My long association with CTC has generated many reasons for the dedication of this book to the people who have been part of my life for such a long time. Not least among them is the warm reception I was given in 2017 as I resumed my full-time presence here, supported and encouraged by the current Master, Dr Shane Mackinlay, and Deputy Master, Dr Frances Baker, RSM.

Francis J. Moloney, SDB, AM, FAHA
Catholic Theological College
University of Divinity
Melbourne, Victoria, Australia

Acknowledgements

In order to provide a time-line for original publication of the essays gathered in this volume, the following acknowledgements are listed in chronological order, from the earliest (1982) to the most recent (2017). Their order as chapters in the volume depends upon the location of a text in the New Testament (Gospel Interpretation), or the relevance of a particular biblical-theological theme (Christian Life).

"When is John Talking About Sacraments?" *Australian Biblical Review* 30 (1982): 10-33.

"'He is going before you into Galilee.' Mark 16:6-8 and the Christian Community." Pages 108-21 in *Be My Witnesses. Essays in Honour of Dr. Sebastian Karotemprel SDB*. Edited by Jose Varickasseril and Matthew Kariapuram. Shillong: Vendrame Institute Publications, 2001.

"The Twelve, Mission and Failure in Mark 6:6b-30." Pages 159-89 in *Prophecy and Passion. Essays in Honour of Athol Gill*. Edited by David Neville. ATF Series 5. Adelaide: Australian Theological Forum, 2002.

"L'Écriture Sainte et le Magistère: une relation mouvementée." Pages 493-505 in *La Responsabilité des Théologiens. Mélanges offerts à Joseph Doré*. Edited by F. Bousquet, H.-J. Gagey, G. Médevielle, and J.-L. Souletie; Paris: Desclée, 2002. [Translated as "Sacred Scripture and the Magisterium: A Restless Relationship?" for this volume].

"Literary Strategies in the Markan Passion Narrative (Mark 14:1-15:47)." *Studien zum Neuen Testament und seiner Umwelt* 28 (2003): 5-25.

"On the Writing of *The Gospel According to Judas:* Some Theological and Pastoral Reflections." *Australasian Catholic Record* 85 (2008): 337-50

"God's Gift of Servant Discipleship in the Gospel of Mark." *Lantayan: A Pastoral-Theological Journal* 8 (2009-2010): 7-24.

"The Word in the World: Then and Now." *Pacifica* 23 (2010): 337-54.

"Matthew 5:17-18 and the Matthean Use of Δικαιοσύνη." Pages 33-54 in *Unity and Diversity in the Gospels and Paul. Essays in Honor of Frank J. Matera*. Edited by Christopher W. Skinner and Kelly R. Iverson. Early Christianity and Its Literature 7. Atlanta: SBL, 2012.

"Following Jesus into Radical Discipleship: A Reading of Mark 8:14-9:29." Pages 76-104 in *Priest, Poet and Theologian. Essays in Honour of Anthony J. Kelly, CSsR*. Edited by Neil Ormorod and Robert Gascoigne. Melbourne: Mosaic Press, 2013.

"A New Testament Hermeneutic for Divorce and Remarriage in the Catholic Tradition." *The Australasian Catholic Record* 92 (2015): 269-88.

"The Word of God, Jesus Christ, and the Eucharist: Christian Hope in a Secularised World." *The Australasian Catholic Record* 93 (2016): 310-25.

"The Gospel of Creation. A Biblical Response to *Laudato Si'*." *Salesianum* 78 (2016). 583-605.

"Sacred Scripture at Vatican II." *Toronto Journal of Theology* 23/2 (2016): 183-200.

"Marriage and Wealth. A Study of Mark 10:1-31." Pages 151-58 in *The Bible and Catholic Theological Ethics*. Edited by Yiu Sing Lúcás Chan, James F. Keenan, and Ronald Zacharias. Maryknoll, NY: Orbis Press, 2017.

Introduction

1
The Story Behind the Book

A glance at the titles of the essays, as they are listed in the Table of Contents, will inform my reader (or a prospective buyer of the book!) that the following collection of essays is evenly divided. It opens with studies of the four Gospels, with a particular concentration on the Gospel of Mark.[1] These exegetical essays give way to more general, sometimes more hermeneutically focused, reflections upon Christian life. This formal division is somewhat artificial. If my own assessment of what I have written over the past few decades has any value, I would suggest that my interpretations of the Gospels address Christian life, and my essays on the Christian life lean heavily on an interpretation of the Gospels! Of course, I am not the one who should make that judgment. That has always been my aim for my published work, but the essays published here no longer belong to me; they are the property of anyone who wishes to make of them what they will.

Generally, the essays devoted to specific texts from Gospel of Mark, and themes that are drawn from its story as a whole, come from the first decade of the third millennium, a period of intense focus upon that Gospel. After my theological education (1966-1970: STL) and basic formation in Biblical Studies (1970-1972: SSL), I proceeded to doctoral studies at the University of Oxford (1972-1975). My research there was focused upon the Christology of the Gospel of John. From the completion of those Studies (D. Phil.: 1976), to my publication of my Sacra Pagina commentary in 1998 (reprinted

---

1. I will use the traditional names Mark, Matthew, Luke, and John to refer to the four Gospels, and to their authors. The names were added to the texts late in the second century to ensure the distinctiveness of each account. We do not know the names of the historical author(s) of the Gospels.

many time since), John's Gospel remained my main area of scholarly interest.[2] Teaching in Australia (Catholic Theological College and Australian Catholic University) and Rome (Salesian Pontifical University, Gregorian University, Pontifical Biblical Institute) and Israel (*l'Ecole Biblique et Archéologique Française*) had necessarily expanded my areas of interest but the Fourth Gospel remained my major area of ongoing research and scholarly publication.

In 1998 I was appointed the Professor of New Testament, and then the Katharine Drexel Professor of Religious Studies, at the Catholic University of America, Washington, DC. I had been teaching the Gospel of Mark at various levels for some years, and was fascinated by the potential for an imaginative interpretation found in the differences, yet similarities, between what was most likely the first canonical Gospel of appear (Mark: 70 CE?) and the last (John: 100 CE?). Given my change of university and academic context in 1999, I decided to focus scholarly attention on the Gospel of Mark. During my time in Washington, I regularly gave doctoral seminars on the Gospel of Mark, and maintained my contact with the Fourth Gospel by teaching a full course on John to the Masters students (M. A.; M. Div.) every year. Thus, I never abandoned my first love, but allowed my years of familiarity with that text, and its interpretation simmer. Good students, at whatever academic level, always ask questions and issue challenges that make me think and re-think many of my interpretations. This was certainly the case for me in Washington, DC, where many of my firmly held positions were called into question. They were rich years, accompanied by a group of outstanding scholars (Joseph Fitzmyer, SJ [RIP], Raymond Collins, Frank J. Matera, and Frank Gignac, SJ [RIP]), exceptional doctoral students, all of whom have gone on to significant academic positions in the USA, and supported by wonderful library facilities.

---

2. My doctoral research was first published as *The Johannine Son of Man*, Biblioteca di Scienze Religiose 14 (Rome: LAS, 1976). It was reprinted, with an appendix, in 1978, and appeared in a second edition in 2007 (Eugene, OR: Wipf & Stock). The commentary appeared as *The Gospel of John*, Sacra Pagina 4 (Collegeville, MN: The Liturgical Press, 1998). It had been preceded by *Belief in the Word: Reading John 1-4* (Minneapolis, MN: Fortress, 1992), *Signs and Shadows. Reading John 5-12* (Minneapolis: Fortress, 1996), and *Glory **not** Dishonor. Reading John 13-21* (Minneapolis, MN: Fortress, 1998).

This period is strongly reflected in the essays dedicated to the Gospel of Mark in the collection that follows. They were generated by relevant background work into the early Church and the turbulent years that led to the Jewish War (66-70 CE) and initial, sometimes experimental forays, into the Markan world and the narrative it produced. Some of these essays were "testing the waters." They generally led to further enriching debate, and were very instrumental in the eventual publication of a commentary on Mark in 2002 (reprinted in 2012).[3] Other essays on Mark, written and published after 2002, stretched original insights further than I had suggested in the commentary.

All the essays demonstrate my fascination with the Markan portrayal of the disciples in the Gospel, and one of them is dedicated entirely to a sketch of their performance across the story, understood as a unified narrative articulation of early Christian Theology, Christology, and Discipleship. This aspect of my work has sometimes been criticized. Some reviewers and colleagues think that I am "too harsh" on the disciples. My only defense is to claim that what I have tried to uncover is *what Mark says about the disciples in the story, right down to the fear, silence and failure of the women in the final verse of the Gospel (Mark 16:8)*. But there is more. If I have an "agenda" running in my analysis, it comes from the title of this book. My experience (maybe I am alone in this?) is that Christian life is regularly marked by failure. Of course, it is also marked by wonderful moments of love and joy. But am I the only one who regularly "gets it wrong"?

I am convinced that Mark and his early Christian community, faced with false hopes of an imminent return of the Lord (see Mark 9:1; 13:9-13), and suffering for their belief in Jesus as the Christ and the Son of God (1:1; 14:62; 15:39), experienced the failure generated by fear and flight (see 14:50; 16:8). I think that the historical disciples of Jesus of Nazareth did much better than the way Mark reports their performance. But what we find in the Markan narrative comes from a post-resurrectional theological perspective. Mark did not tell his story to tell us "how things were back then," but to address Christians who hear and read his Gospel. A critical interpretation of the role of the disciples in the Gospel of Mark directly addresses all forms of

---

3. Francis J. Moloney, *The Gospel of Mark. A Commentary* (Peabody, MA: Hendrickson, 2002). Reprinted in a paperback edition in 2012 by Baker Academic (Grand Rapids, MI).

Christian life. My guess is that is why it was accepted into the Christian canon from the start, despite its neglect in the early centuries. Since the middle of the nineteenth century, once its role as the chronologically "first" of the Gospels was recognized, it has become one of the most commented upon New Testament books.

Coming to this collection, I could not possibly omit something on the Gospel of John, and the choice to publish a study on the presence or absence of Sacramental material in the Fourth Gospel was easy and obvious. The essay "When is John Talking About Sacraments?" is the oldest essay in this collection. It goes back to a lecture given at the 1981 Melbourne Scripture Seminar, published in *Australian Biblical Review* in 1982. There are two significant reasons for the current re-publication of this Johannine essay, even though it is 35 years old. In the first place, despite the brashness of its tone, reflecting the immaturity of a 42 year old (young among biblical scholars!), its published version continues to be widely cited in secondary literature dedicated to the Gospel of John. In my advanced years, I am surprised when I see it regularly mentioned in the never-ending and yet to be resolved discussion of the presence or absence of Sacramental hints in the Gospel of John.

Some find Sacraments at every turn, and others claim that the Gospel of John is rejecting any such human participation in the communication of God's gifts. A small group of influential commentators suggest that texts that obviously reflect the Sacramental practices of the early Church were added to the original Gospel, to make it more "Catholic." Between these three extreme positions, there are various shades of opinion. My early attempt to steer a "middle-path" through this debate still appears to garner interest, as it focused upon both the text and the world that produced and received it to develop some "criteria" that might guide us. Whatever its contemporary value, I am glad to make it more available, given the continued interest and frequent reference to it.

Over the past decade I have published two collections of my shorter Johannine work, but this essay is available only in the 1982 volume of *Australian Biblical Review*.[4] Its publication in this col-

---

4. For my collections of earlier Johannine essays, see Francis J. Moloney, *The Gospel of John. Text and Context*, Biblical Interpretation Series 72 (Boston/Leiden: Brill, 2005), and Idem, *Johannine Studies 1975-2017*, Wissenschaftliche Untersuchungen zum Neuen Testament 372 (Tübingen: Mohr Siebeck, 2017). The details of the 1982 publication of the essay on Sacraments in John can be found above, in the Acknowledgements.

lection remedies that lacuna. Although this 1982 study has been updated and rewritten more than anything else in this collection, nothing has changed in the argument. I have added more recent bibliography and toned down some of the rhetorical writing of the original that reflected my academic immaturity and the "public lecture" setting of an address at a Seminar. However, it retains its goal of a search for possible "criteria" that might guide commentators in their reflection of possible Sacramental background to some Johannine narratives (e.g. John 6:1-15; 13:21-38; 19:34-35) and discourses (e.g. 6:51-58).

The essay on the Lukan last supper narrative has not appeared in this form anywhere else, but it also has a history, associated with my own academic interests. It depends heavily upon my long-time interest in New Testament Eucharistic texts, and especially on the chapter on Luke in the third edition of my *Body Broken for a Broken People*.[5] It is included to round off the selections from my work on all four Gospels. I chose to rework my earlier study of Luke 22 because most Christian readers, and churchgoers, are not aware of the *very different* record of the events of Jesus' final night with his disciples. The words of Institution during the celebration of the Eucharist in most Christian traditions, and certainly in the Catholic tradition, are a blend of what is found in 1 Corinthians 11, Mark 14, and Matthew 26. Luke *subordinates* the so-called words of Institution to his wider concern: Jesus' farewelling and commissioning his Apostles. It is a superb example of Luke's genius and originality, shaping an established tradition to speak directly to a missionary Church. This addition to my focus upon Mark, and to a lesser extent Matthew and John, reflects my deep concern for the poverty of the biblical literacy of most believing and practicing Christians. This is not the place to enlarge upon that question, but when I am told that something is found "in the Gospels," most are surprised when I ask: "Which Gospel?" This widespread poverty is the result of a lack of

---

5. Francis J. Moloney, *A Body Broken for a Broken People. Divorce, Remarriage, and Eucharist* (Melbourne: Garratt, 2015). The first edition, with the title *A Body Broken for a Broken People. Eucharist in the New Testament* appeared in Melbourne in 1990 (Collins Dove). Both editions have been published in the USA (Hendrickson/Paulist) and the UK (DLT).

exposure to the richness and the diversity of our four-fold Gospel tradition.[6]

In this brief telling of the story that has produced the book that follows, I wish to focus upon the people to whom several essays were dedicated. There are many other people who have accompanied on my journey, academically and otherwise, but by sheer happenstance essays found in this book were originally dedicated to significant people. I have retained reference to these colleagues as each of them, in his own way, reflects part of that story: my long presence in Australian theological education (Anthony J. Kelly, CSsR and Athol Gill), my ministry of teaching and research at the Catholic University of America (Frank J. Matera), and my service to the universal Catholic Tradition as a member of the International Theological Commission to then Holy See (Sebastian Karotemprel, SDB and Joseph Doré, SS).

Foremost among them is my long-standing friend and colleague, Anthony J. Kelly, CSsR. Tony and I have worked in theological education in Australia for the best part of 40 years. We worked together immediately after the Second Vatican Council in the ecumenical setting of the Melbourne College of Divinity. When I departed these shores for Washington, DC, he was my successor as the Professor of Theology at Australian Catholic University in 1999.[7] We have forged an even closer relationship since I came back to ACU in 2012. We were fortunate to hold positions as Senior Professorial Fellows, with a major focus upon research in the University. His balanced and pro-

---

6. Over the years I have attempted to address this problem. Most recently, see Francis J. Moloney, *The Living Voice of the Gospel. The Gospels Today*, 2nd ed. (Melbourne: John Garratt, 2006 [first edition in 1986]); Idem, *A Friendly Guide to the New Testament* (Melbourne: Garratt, 2010); Idem, *A Friendly Guide to the Gospel of Mark* (Melbourne: Garratt, 2012); Idem, *A Friendly Guide to the Resurrection of Jesus Christ* (Melbourne: Garratt, 2016); Idem, *Reading the New Testament in the Church. A Primer for Pastors, Religious Educators, and Believers* (Grand Rapids: Baker Academic, 2015). After 40 years of teaching, research, and publication I sense that I have failed to communicate very widely the fundamental truth about understanding the Gospels: they are not primarily *historical narratives*, but inspired statements, *in a narrative form*, of what God has done for humankind in and through Jesus Christ. The vast majority of clergy and people still read them as "stories about Jesus," despite my efforts.
7. We maintained our close personal and academic relationship from 1999-2005, evidenced by the highly-respected study that we co-authored at that time: Anthony J. Kelly and Francis J. Moloney, *The Experience of God in the Johannine Writings* (New York/Mahwah, NJ: Paulist, 2003).

found understanding of the Christian Tradition, coupled with his sparkling interpretation of it, have helped my own work across those decades, especially across the past five years of our close association at Australian Catholic University.[8]

Another Australian scholar mentioned in these pages is Athol Gill, who passed away suddenly in March 1992. Athol was a remarkable and important figure in the presence of the Baptist tradition within the Melbourne College of Divinity. He had many passions, and one of them was the Gospel of Mark. The essay in this volume recalls that passion, but in Athol's life it spilled over into his Christian life. Many of us in Melbourne Christian circles owe much to his inspiration as a teacher, preacher, leader, radical disciple of Jesus Christ, and reformer.[9] I deliberately chose the theme of the Markan Jesus' never-failing presence to his struggling disciples, as that was a feature of Athol's life and ministry among the less-fortunate in society, typified by his establishment of the community of the Gentle Bunyip in Clifton Hill, Victoria. Continuing a long-standing Baptist tradition of social awareness, Athol embodied Jesus' care for the apparent "failures" in our society.

The essay on "righteousness" in Matthew was written to honour a dear friend and colleague during my Washington, DC, days: Frank J. Matera. Frank's doctoral work had been on the Gospel of Mark.[10] We shared a keen interest in literary and narrative-critical approaches to the Four Gospels. My arrival at the Catholic University of America in 1999 coincided with a decision on Frank's part focus more broadly on New Testament ethics, Christology, Theology, and the Letters of

---

8. Evidence for the ongoing influence of Tony Kelly's thought on my work can be found in the essay, "The Gospel of Creation. Biblical Reflections on *Laudato Si*'" on pp. 259-82 of this volume, and especially in Francis J. Moloney, *Eucharist as a Celebration of Forgiveness* (New York/Mahwah, NJ: Paulist, 2017), 83-99.
9. For striking evidence of Athol's use of the Gospel of Mark to challenge contemporary Christianity, see Athol Gill, *The Fringes of Freedom: Following Jesus, Living Together, Working for Justice* (Homebush: Lancer Books, 1990), and Idem, *Life on the Road: The Gospel Basis for a Messianic Lifestyle* (Homebush: Lancer Books, 1992).
10. Frank J. Matera, *The Kingship of Jesus. Composition and Theology in Mark 15*, Society of Biblical Literature Dissertation Series 66 (Chico, CA: Scholars Press, 1982).

Paul.[11] Academically, I was on the receiving end of a gentlemanly and respectful association with everything I wrote. No scholar could have asked for more. Above all, however, I appreciated his support in difficult times. In 2003 the then Dean of the School of Theology and Religious Studies, Rev. Prof. Stephen Happel, died suddenly. He had begun an unpopular restructuring of the School, and I was asked to step in, initially as the acting Dean, and then formally as the Dean of the School. Frank's long experience as an academic at the Catholic University of America, his down to earth wisdom, and supportive presence saw me through challenging days from 2003-2005. I trust that the presence of *both* of us at CUA in those challenging years helped its School of Theology and Religious Studies to become the formidable center of learning that it is today.

Finally, I make mention of two significant scholars with whom I worked in the setting of the Pontifical Theological Commission. A majority of essays in the second half of this book, under the general title "Christian Life," focus upon the balance that a contemporary Catholic scholar must maintain while attempting to push frontiers, yet always respecting the caring role of the Church's Magisterium. Nowhere else is this call for "balance" needed that in the service rendered to the Catholic Church than in the Pontifical Biblical Commission and the Pontifical Theological Commission. I was privileged to serve on the Theological Commission from 1986 till 2002. Essays are dedicated to Sebastian Karotemprel, SDB, and Joseph Doré, SS, two significant conversation partners within the Theological Commission. They were fine examples of the challenges and the potential richness that can emerge from creative tension between the theologian and the Magisterium.

Rev. Professor Sebastian Karotemprel, my fellow-Salesian, had dedicated his life to the crucially important dialogue between the

---

11. Frank J. Matera, *New Testament Ethics. The Legacies of Jesus and Paul* (Louisville: Westminster John Knox, 1996); Idem, *New Testament Christology* (Louisville: Westminster John Knox, 1999); Idem, *New Testament Theology. Exploring Diversity and Unity* (Louisville: Westminster John Knox, 2007); Idem, *Galatians*, Sacra Pagina 9 (Collegeville, MN: The Liturgical Press, 1992); Idem, *Romans*, Paideia Commentaries on the New Testament (Grand Rapids: Baker Academic, 2010).

Catholic Tradition and the Religions of India.¹² His long teaching career in India and Rome led to his being appointed to the Pontifical Theological Commission at a difficult time. Inter-religious dialogue was being sidelined, after the publication of the statement from the Congregation for the Doctrine of the Faith, *Dominus Jesus*, affirming the absolute centrality of Jesus Christ in a way that underestimated the work of Sebastian, and others like him.¹³ Parallels between the Catholic theological tradition and other religions had long been suggested as a pathway to greater understanding and a creative reciprocity between all concerned. *Dominus Jesus* led to difficulties in this dialogue. In the ten years that I worked with Sebastian, despite the difficulties of the Roman theological climate, he argued courageously for the ubiquitous presence of the divine mystery in other religions, and yet always showed respect for a Magisterium that could not always be persuaded.

An essay on the difficult interface between Scripture and the Magisterium, is dedicated to Joseph Doré, SS. Joseph came to the Commission after a long and distinguished career. A Sulpician Priest, charismatically committed to seminary education, he was the Director of the *Grand Séminaire de Nantes* (1965-71), until he took up the position as the Director of the *Séminaire des Carmes*, the seminary attached to *l'Institut Catholique de Paris*. He was the Dean of the Fac-

---

12. Among many published works, see Sebastian Karotemprel, *Albizuri among the Lyngams: A Brief History of the Catholic Church among the Lyngams* (Shillong: Vendrame Institute Publications, 1985); Idem, *Volti Africani, Latinoamericani e Asiatici dello Stesso Signore* (Bologna: EMI, 1997); Idem, *Meeting Christ on the Indian Road* (Shillong: Don Bosco Centre for Indigenous Cultures, 2000). Perhaps of greater significance than his writings, however, was his establishment of the Don Bosco Centre for Indigenous Culture in Shillong, with its library (the Otto Hopfenmüller Library), museum, and his founding of the significant journal *Indian Missiological Review* (now *Mission Today*).
13. *Declaration "Dominus Iesus" on the Unicity and Salvific Universality of Jesus Christ and the Church* (Rome: Congregation for the Doctrine of the Faith, 2000). The most notorious victim of this declaration was the Jesuit theologian Jacques Depuis, author of the rightly famous *Towards a Christian Theology of Religious Pluralism* (Maryknoll, NY: Orbis Books, 1997). Subsequent to *Dominus Jesus*, his work was singled out by the Congregation for the Doctrine of the Faith in 2002 as dangerous because it "raised as many questions as it seeks to answer." A deeply committed Catholic Priest, the Jesuits at the Gregorian University suggested that his premature death (2004) was brought on by this formal condemnation of his life's work.

ulty of Theology at *l'Institut Catholique de Paris* from 1988-1994.[14] In 1994 he was appointed the Archbishop of Strasbourg. His long history of ecclesiastical leadership, from 1965 until his retirement from his episcopal role in 2007, was always marked by a powerful awareness of the delicate relationship that exists between Catholic scholarship and the Magisterium. It was only fitting that his career closed with his magisterial leadership at Strasbourg. The essay in this volume, dedicated to Archbishop Joseph Doré, addressing the relationship between the work of the Biblical scholar and the Magisterium, was first published in a volume of essays to honour Joseph, with the fitting title: *The Responsibility of Theologians*.[15]

The remaining essays could be regarded as "occasional," but they have their story. My role in supporting the notorious British novelist, Jeffrey Archer, in writing *The Gospel According to Judas* generated considerable heat from some parts of the Catholic world.[16] Many suggested that I had "lost the plot" in associating myself with such a figure, and suggesting that Judas Iscariot may have had a positive understanding of Jesus, despite his act of betrayal. The essay included in this collection is a response to that criticism, and in some ways further develops the theme of the relationship between the theologian and the Magisterium. The final essays are recent. They have a strong focus upon the Word of God, and were originally delivered for major events: the Centenary celebration of the Melbourne College of Divinity in 2010, and the International Eucharistic Congress in Cebu, the Philippines, in 2016.

All the essays, reflecting a long and very blessed academic career, have their setting. My friend and colleague, Mark (now Archbishop) Coleridge, once said to me: "Text without context is pretext." I have long treasured those words and my students at every level are tired of hearing me repeat them. I trust that this brief situating of all the essays in this collection in their respective "contexts" is interesting for a reader, and a helpful guide to the opinions and sentiments expressed in what I have written over the past 30 years.

---

14. See Joseph Doré, *À cause de Jésus* (Paris: Éditions Plon, 2011); Idem, *Peut-on vraiment rester catholique?* (Paris: Éditions Bayard Culture, 2012).
15. F. Bousquet, H.-J. Gagey, G. Médevielle, and J.-L. Souletie, eds., *La Responsabilité des Théologiens. Mélanges offerts à Joseph Doré* (Paris: Desclée, 2002), 493-505.
16. Jeffrey Archer and Francis J. Moloney, *The Gospel According to Judas* (London: Macmillan, 2007). Some of the discussion this book generated is documented in the essay. See below, pp. 319-23.

Gospel Interpretation

2
Mark 6:6b-30: The Twelve, Mission, and Failure

In memory of Athol Gill (1937-1992)

It is with a sense of gratitude and privilege that I pen this study in memory of Athol Gill (1937-1992). There were many sides to Athol, and I have chosen to reflect upon a passage in the Gospel of Mark (6:6b-30) for reasons associated with a few of the more obvious of them. Athol Gill had a serious professional interest in the Gospel of Mark, but never read a Gospel purely because of his "professional interest." One of the reasons this Gospel attracted his interest was its focus upon the disciples of Jesus, a theme that he often used to challenge contemporary Christian individuals and communities.[1] But Athol was not only interested in issuing challenges. He was keenly aware that the best of "Christian achievers" were those who realistically accepted the brokenness present in their own lives, and who turned to offer a fragile hand to those who, often through no fault of their own, are forced to the margins of Australian society. He had a deep concern for those judged by our society as "failures." In many ways, the community of the Gentle Bunyip "institutionalized" his concerns.

It is thus, to the Gospel of Mark, the disciples in that story, and their failure, that I would like to turn. The Twelve are authorized for a mission, instructed on their attire, their possessions and their behavior. The mission meets with great success (vv. 7-13). Without notice, the account of the death of John the Baptist follows (vv. 14-29), and only after that episode has been told in its entirety do the ones who were sent out, gather around Jesus again (v. 30). My study of this

---

1. See Athol Gill, *The Fringes of Freedom: Following Jesus, Living Together, Working for Justice* (Homebush: Lancer Books, 1990), and Idem, *Life on the Road: The Gospel Basis for a Messianic Lifestyle* (Homebush: Lancer Books, 1992).

intriguing Markan passage is an inadequate word of gratitude to the memory of Athol Gill, exponent of the Gospel of Mark and disciple of Jesus.

The Setting

The Gospel as a whole

The Gospel of Mark traces the God-directed passing of time, systematically articulated in the larger blocks of material and the smaller episodes that unfold within them, according to a logic that leads inevitably toward the cross. The reader is led further into a story whose ending is known, yet is surprised on the way – and at the end. The plot as a whole is shot through with hints that look forward to the end of the story. The Gospel of Mark is unique among the Gospels because, unlike most narratives (including Matthew, Luke and John), the crises that emerge during the course of the narrative are not resolved through a *dénouement* at the end of the story (Mark 16:1-8). Much is resolved, but a further crisis emerges which cannot be resolved by the story itself (see 16:7-8). This suggests that it might be resolved in the lives of the people reading the story.[2]

In a good story the reader is told enough to be made curious, without ever being given all the answers. Narrative texts keep promis-

---

2. The statement of this paragraph reflects the radical shift that has taken place in Markan studies. Mark was early classified as the follower and abbreviator of Matthew (Augustine, *De consensu Evangelistarum*, I,2; PL 34:1044: "Marcus eum [Matthew] subsecutus, tamquam pedissequus et breviator eius videtur"). This classification was accepted down to the modern era, but Mark is now understood as a story-teller of great subtlety. For a succinct history of the reception of the Gospel of Mark, see D. E. Shildgen, *Power and Prejudice. The Reception of the Gospel of Mark* (Detroit: Wayne State University Press, 1999). On Mark's literary subtlety see, among many, F. Kermode, *The Genesis of Secrecy. On the Interpretation of Narrative* (Cambridge, MA: Harvard University Press, 1979); J. D. Kingsbury, *Conflict in Mark. Jesus, Authority, Disciples* (Minneapolis: Fortress, 1989); R. M. Fowler, *Let the Reader Understand. Reader-Response Criticism and the Gospel of Mark* (Minneapolis: Fortress, 1991); D. Rhoads, Joanna Dewey and D. Michie, *Mark as Story: An Introduction to the Narrative of a Gospel*, 2nd ed. (Minneapolis: Fortress, 1999); Kelly R. Iverson and Christopher W. Skinner, eds., *Mark as Story. Retrospect and Prospect*, Society for Biblical Literature Resources for Biblical Study 64 (Altanta: Society for Biblical Literature, 2011).

ing the great prize of understanding - later.³ The "later" of the Gospel of Mark, I suggest, is the "now" of the Christian reader. If this is true, then the single parts of the story, in our case Mark 6:6a-30, might helpfully be read in the light of the "now" of the Christian reader as we begin the third Christian millennium.

As the plot of the Gospel of Mark unfolds there are signs within the narrative that the readers and the listeners encounter.⁴ They indicate major turning points in the story as a whole. These textual markers show that the author is "up to something." There are six major moments when the reader meets significant turning points in the story. The "good news" begins (1:1), Jesus initiates his ministry in Galilee (1:14-15), he announces his forthcoming death and resurrection for the first time (8:31), he enters Jerusalem (11:1-11), a decision is made that Jesus must be arrested and killed (14:1-2), and women discover an empty tomb (16:1-4). We have domesticated the Gospel story to such an extent that we are not sufficiently aware of the dramatic nature of these turning points. As has been obvious since the days of Wilhelm Wrede, Albert Schweitzer, and Karl-Ludwig Schmidt, this "framework" was devised by the Evangelist Mark, and its appearance in the first early Christian "gospel" was intentionally a theological statement.⁵ *Whatever the first readers knew of the life-story*

---

3. See S. Rimmon-Kenan, *Narrative Fiction: Contemporary Poetics*, New Accents (London: Methuen, 1983), 125.
4. The Gospel of Mark was no doubt written to be read. However, the experience of Alex McCowen, who proclaimed the King James Version of the Gospel to packed houses in both London and New York, demonstrates that it remains a powerful listening experience. Perhaps too much has been made of the radical change (and even betrayal) which takes place when an oral text becomes a written one. See especially W. Kelber, *The Oral and Written Gospel. The Hermeneutics of Speaking and Writing in the Synoptic Tradition, Mark, Paul, and Q* (Philadelphia: Fortress Press, 1983). See the helpful remarks of Fowler, *Let the Reader Understand*, 48-52, and the developing importance of what is called "performance criticism." For a fine study of this development, see Kelly R. Iverson, "Performance Criticism," in *The Oxford Encyclopedia of Biblical Interpretation*, ed. Steven McKenzie, 2 vols. (New York/Oxford: Oxford University Press, 2013), 2:97-105.
5. Wrede was the first to show that the Gospel of Mark is a theological document, Schweitzer stressed further the distance between the life of Jesus and the Gospel accounts, and Schmidt demolished the earlier suggestion (especially from H. J. Holtzmann) that the Gospel of Mark provided a "framework" (in German: *der Rahmen*) for the life of the historical Jesus. See W. Wrede, *The Messianic Secret*, trans. J. C. G. Grieg (Cambridge and London: James Clark, 1971 [Original German

of Jesus of Nazareth was subverted by the Markan story. The Markan plot of Jesus' presence in Galilee, his journey to Jerusalem, the cross, the resurrection and the silence of the women was not familiar to the early Christian world. Such a "plot" saw the light of day *for the first time* when Mark invented it, and it was accepted by Matthew and Luke as the basic story-line for their accounts of Jesus' life, death and resurrection. It is this *radical newness* of the Markan story that must be kept in mind.⁶ It is an original way of telling the story of Jesus, and its author must be credited with an equally original "point of view" which led him to plot the story in this way.⁷

Mark's plot is designed to lead the reader to a surprising re-telling of the story of the death and resurrection of Jesus to which she or he could not remain indifferent. On the basis of the major textual markers that I have identified, one can trace the following temporal and geographical strategies.⁸

---

in 1901]); A Schweitzer, *The Quest of the Historical Jesus*, trans W. Montgomery (London: A. & C. Black, 1910 [Original for this translation in 1906]); K.-L. Schmidt, *Der Rahmen der Geschichte Jesu. Literarkritische Untersuchungen zu ältesten Jesusüberlieferung* (Darmstadt: Wissenschaftliche Buchgesselschaft, 1964 [Original in 1919]).

6. See the important essay by E. Schweitzer, first published in 1964: "Mark's Theological Achievement," in W. Telford, ed., *The Interpretation of Mark*, Issues in Religion and Theology 7 (Philadelphia: Fortress, 1985), 42-63. Kelber, *The Oral and Written Gospel*, pushes this to the limit. He rightly argues that Mark took a vivacious and living oral tradition and created something quite different with his "writing" (see pp. 44-139). But he argues that the movement from oral tradition to written Gospel created a written text that contradicted what went before. The thesis is overstated, but further highlights the radical newness of the Gospel of Mark. For a more acceptable use of Kelber's insights, see C. Myers, *Binding the Strong Man. A political Reading of Mark's Story of Jesus* (Maryknoll: Orbis Books, 1990), 91-109.

7. It is possible that the Johannine "framework" is closer to what actually took place in the life of Jesus of Nazareth. Maybe Mark has radically altered a relatively well-known framework. For some suggestions along these lines, see F. J. Moloney, "The Fourth Gospel and the Jesus of History," *New Testament Studies* 45 (1999): 42-58.

8. For a similar focus on "textual markers" (which he calls "text signals"), see B. van Iersel, *Reading Mark* (Collegeville: The Liturgical Press, 1989), 18-30. Van Iersel follows the earlier work of B. Standaert, *L'Evangile selon Marc. Composition et Genre Littéraire* (Brugge: Sint-Andreisabdij, 1978), which uses textual markers to trace a chiastic structure across the Gospel of Mark and within its single sections. See also A. Stock, *Call to Discipleship. A Literary Study of Mark's Gospel*, Good News Studies 1 (Wilmington: Michael Glazier, 1982), 47-53.

1. Mark 1:1-13 serves as a prologue to the Gospel, and provides the reader with a great deal of information about God's beloved Son.
2. Through Mark 1:14-8:30 the words and deeds of Jesus' ministry increasingly force the question: who is this man (see 1:27, 45; 2:12; 3:22; 4:41; 5:20; 6:2-3, 48-50; 7:37)? Some accept him, some are indifferent and many oppose him, but the question behind the story is: can he be the Messiah? In 8:29 Peter, in the name of the disciples, resolves the problem by confessing: "You are the Messiah." The guessing has come to an end. This section of the Gospel can be called "The Mystery of the Messiah," although it closes surprisingly with Jesus' warning Peter not to tell anyone of his confession of faith (8:30). Peter's understanding of Jesus' messianic identity may not be the whole truth about Jesus.
3. Mark 8:31-10:52 reports Jesus' journey to Jerusalem, largely focussed upon Jesus' teaching of his oncoming death and resurrection (8:31; 9:31; 10:32-34) and his instruction of increasingly recalcitrant disciples.
4. He enters Jerusalem (11:1-11), brings all Temple practice to an end (11:12-24), encounters and silences Israel's religious authorities (11:27-12:44), and prophesies the end of the Holy City and the world (13:1-37).
5. The ministry is over as Jesus enters his passion and death (14:1-15:47). Although the textual markers indicate that 8:31-15:47 is made up of three major sections, there is a sense in which the three sections work together to form a "second half" of Mark's literary and theological presentation of the story of Jesus. If 1:14-8:30 made it clear that Jesus is the Messiah (8:29), but suggested that this may not be the whole truth (8:30), the second half of the Gospel goes further. Jesus is a suffering Messiah, the Son of Man (8:31; 9:31; 10:32-33). In 15:37 a Roman centurion confesses: "Truly this man was God's Son!" The suffering Son of Man is truly the Son of God. Mark 8:31-15:57 can be called "The Mystery of the Son of Man."
6. Many questions raised by the story remain unresolved. The disciples have fled (see 14:50) and Jesus has cried out: "My God, my God, why have you forsaken me?" (15:34). Jesus' question is resolved in the concluding story of women visiting an empty tomb. In 16:1-8 the reader learns that God has not forsaken his Son. He has been raised (see 16:6). But the solution to the problem of

failing disciples lies in the future. They are to go into Galilee, there they will see him (v. 7. See 14:28). The women, frightened by what they have seen and heard, flee and say nothing to anyone (v. 8). This open ending to the story matches its beginning. It can be regarded as a epilogue.

These major blocks of material emerge from close attention to the textual markers in the Gospel. The artistry of Mark the Evangelist cannot be fully appreciated without a more detailed analysis of this overall literary structure.[9] For the purposes of this essay, we need to examine more closely the wider context of Mark 6:6b-30, the Mystery of the Messiah (1:14-8:30).

Mark 1:14-8:30

I have already suggested that the Evangelist designed the first half of his Gospel in response to the question, "Is this man the Messiah?" and the second half in response to the question "How can this man be the Messiah, but also the suffering Son of Man?" These two "halves" of the plot, however, overlap. Narrative units are not separated by brick walls. One episode flows into the other, looks back to issues already mentioned, and hints at themes yet to come. Peter's confession of faith in Mark 8:29 and Jesus' response in v. 30 might mark the closure of "The Mystery of the Messiah," but a theme of "blindness" has emerged in 8:22-26 in the strange story of a blind man at Bethsaida who has his sight restored in stages. This theme will be resumed in 10:46-52 where a further story of a man coming to sight is reported: the story of blind Bartimaeus. Between these two miracle stories, where blind men are cured, Jesus speaks of the oncoming death and resurrection of the Son of Man (see 8:31; 9:31; 10:32-35) and instructs increasingly obtuse disciples who will not or cannot understand what it means to follow Jesus (see 8:32-33; 9:33-37; 10:36-45). An earlier accusation of blindness also comes into play. After the second multiplication of the loaves and fishes (8:1-10) Jesus asks his dull disciples: "Do you not

---

9. Since the original publication of this essay, I have attempted such a close reading in F. J. Moloney, *The Gospel of Mark. A Commentary* (Peabody: Hendrickson, 2002). It was reprinted in a paperback version by Baker Academic (Grand Rapids) in 2012.

yet perceive or understand? Are your hearts hardened? *Having eyes do you not see*, and having ears do you not hear?" (8:18).[10] These few examples of overlapping themes, equally significant textual markers for the reader, although not as *structurally* important as 1:1, 1:14-15, 8:31, 11:1-11; 14:1-2, and 16:1-4, are further indications of Mark's artistic skill. As "the Mystery of the Messiah" (1:14-8:30) comes to a close, "the Mystery of the Son of Man" (8:31-15:47) is being prepared by the theme of blindness in 8:14-26.

"The Mystery of the Messiah" (1:14-8:30) establishes relationships, as well as raising questions concerning the person of Jesus. The Gospel of Mark is not only about Jesus, Son of God and Christ. It is equally about the challenge of "following" him to Jerusalem – and beyond. On three occasions across Mark 1:1-8:30 the narrator makes a general statement (generally called a "summary") about Jesus' ministry, which introduces a series of events illustrating that activity (see 1:14-15; 3:7-12; 6:6a). There are, of course, other similar general statements or summaries of Jesus' ministry in the Gospel (see, for example, 1:39, 45b; 4:33-34; 6:53-56; 9:30-31; 10:1).[11] What is unique about these three, however, is that each of them is immediately followed by material which deals with disciples and discipleship (1:16-20; 3:13-19; 6:6b-13). Episodes follow until, serving as a climax, three different audiences respond to the words and deeds of Jesus. Two of the responses are negative (3:6 [the Pharisees and the Herodians]; 6:1-6a [people from "his own country"]), and the third is a misunderstanding (8:29 [Peter, responding on behalf of the disciples]). The three summaries each begin a narrative block, lead directly into passages which deal with disciples, and each of the three responses conclude that section of the story. These three sections unfold as follows:

In 1:14-15 we read a summary of the ministry of Jesus: "Now after John was arrested, Jesus came to Galilee, proclaiming the good news of God, and saying, 'The time is fulfilled and the kingdom of God has come near, repent and believe in the good news.'" This summary is immediately followed by the account of the vocation of the first disciples (1:16-20). Jesus then exercises his ministry in Galilee, chiefly at Capernaum (1:21-3:6), until representatives of the Jewish people, the

---

10. See Myers, *Binding the Strong Man*, 110-11.
11. For a study of the Markan "summaries," see E. Best, *The Temptation and the Passion: The Markan Soteriology*, Society for New Testament Studies Monograph Series 2, 2nd ed. (Cambridge: Cambridge University Press, 1990), 63-102.

political leaders and the religious authorities, respond to him: "The Pharisees went out and immediately conspired with the Herodians against him, how to destroy him" (3:6). This narrative unit (1:14-3:6) can be entitled: *Jesus and the Leaders of Israel*.

1. In 3:7-12 we find a lengthy general statement about Jesus' Galilean ministry. It concludes with the following summary: "He had cured many so that all who had diseases pressed upon him to touch him. Whenever the unclean spirits saw him, they fell down before him and shouted, 'You are the Son of God!' But he sternly ordered them not to make him known" (3:10-12). This summary leads into the account of Jesus' institution of the twelve (3:13-19). But the wonder of Jesus' ministry meets opposition from his family and from Israel (3:20-35). He teaches them through parables (4:1-34) and a stunning series of miracles (4:35-5:43). Returning to his home town, his own people reject him: "Is not this the carpenter, the son of Mary and brother of James and Joses and Judas and Simon, and are not his sisters here with us?' And they took offence at him" (6:3). Jesus was "amazed at their unbelief" (6:6a). This narrative unit (3:7-6:6a) can be entitled: *Jesus and his own*.
2. Immediately following Jesus' rejection in his home-town, we find another brief general summary about his ministry in Galilee: "Then he went about among the villages teaching" (6:6b). This is immediately followed by Jesus' sending out the Twelve on a mission which parallels his own (6:6b-13). The narrative is now marked by increasing hostility between Jesus and the Jews (see 7:1-23), and a deeper involvement of his disciples, his new family, with his ministry (see 6:7-13, 30-44; 8:1-10). It draws to a close as the question which has been lurking behind the narrative from 1:14 is broached two questions asked by Jesus: "Who do people say that I am?" (8:27) ... "Who do you say that I am" (v. 28). Peter responds: "You are the Messiah" (v. 29). The reader has known throughout that Jesus is the Messiah. The narrator informed the reader of that in 1:1. However, the characters in the story, and especially the disciples, have had to stumble to this point on the basis of Jesus' words and actions. The "mystery of the Messiah" has been resolved. There is a sense in which Peter is correct, but the report of Jesus' warning to the disciples ("them") sounds a warning bell, and opens the door to the second part of the Gospel:

"He charged them to tell no one about him" (8:30). As we have already suggested, the second half of the Gospel, "the mystery of the Son of Man," will show that Peter - and all the disciples - still have a long way to go. This narrative unit (6:6b-8:30) can be entitled: *Jesus and the disciples.*

We are now in a position to consider Mark 6:6b-30, a passage which opens the third and final sub-section of the "Mystery of the Messiah" (1:14-8:30). This sub-section is highlighted by an intense focus upon the disciples of Jesus. Thus, I will suggest, despite the presence of the long presentation of the death of John the Baptist in 6:14-29 (and indeed, because of it) our passage concerns itself with the close association of the disciples with the mission of Jesus ... and their failure!

The literary structure of Mark 6:6b-30

One of the features of Markan style is the use of so-called "sandwich" constructions. Another term for this literary technique is "intercalation." Mark regularly begins a narrative, then breaks into it with another narrative, and closes the narrative that he had begun earlier. Two of these "sandwich" constructions are very well known. Earlier in the story the reader finds the intercalation of the curing of the woman with the flow of blood between Jairus' request that Jesus cure his daughter, and Jesus' coming to Jairus' home and raising the young woman (5:21-24a [Jesus and Jairus], 24b-34 [Jesus and the woman], 35-43 [Jesus raises Jairus' daughter]). Later, after his arrival in Jerusalem for the first and only time (11:1-11), as Jesus walks with his disciples from Bethany to Jerusalem, he curses a fig-tree, brings all activity in the Temple to a stand-still, and the next day the disciples notice the dead fig-tree (11:12-14 [Jesus curses the fig-tree], 15-19 [all Temple activity is brought to an end], 20-21 [the fig-tree has withered]). But there are a number of such passages in the Gospel of Mark (see also 3:20-35; 4:1-32; 6:21-35; 14:17-31; 14:53-72).[12]

---

12. See J. R. Donahue, *Are You the Christ? The Trial Narrative in the Gospel of Mark*, Society for Biblical Literature Dissertation Series 10 (Missoula: Society of Biblical Literature, 1973), 58-63; H. C. Kee, *The Community of the New Age. Studies in Mark's Gospel* (London: SCM Press, 1977), 54-56; Kermode, *The Genesis of Secrecy*, 128-34; J. R. Edwards, "Markan Sandwiches. The Significance of Interpolations in Markan Narratives," *Novum Testamentum* 31 (1989): 193-216;

The expression "sandwich" is opportune, as very frequently in these simple but effective literary structures, the passage "in the middle" has a determining influence on the meaning of the passage as a whole. It is what is in the middle of a sandwich which determines whether it is a ham and cheese sandwich or, to use an expression which has become almost symbolic of Australians since the hit-song of "Men at Work," a vegemite sandwich. If, therefore, this is the case in the passage we are considering, then the death of John the Baptist is not a foreign body which had to be fitted in somewhere, and hardly suits its present context. On the contrary, it is the report of this martyrdom which indicates to the reader the deeper significance of the association of the disciples with the mission of Jesus (vv. 6b-13) and guides the reader toward a correct understanding of the report of their return in v. 30.[13]

But the majority of commentators do not see Mark 6:6b-30 as a Markan sandwich. Many link v. 30 with the bread miracle which follows in vv. 31-44.[14] Others see it as a part of a bridge passage from the account of the death of the Baptist into the bread miracle.[15] Those

---

R. M. Fowler, *Loaves and Fishes. The Function of the Feeding Stories in the Gospel of Mark*, Society for Biblical Literature Dissertation Series 54 (Chico: Scholars Press, 1981), 114-16; Fowler, *Let the Reader Understand*, 147-54; T. Shepherd, "The Narrative Function of Markan Intercalation," *New Testament Studies* 41 (1995): 522-40.

13. As Edwards, "Markan Sandwiches," 200, remarks: "The middle story provides the hermeneutical key for the understanding of the whole."

14. See, for example, M.-J. Lagrange, *Évangile selon Saint Marc*, Études Bibliques (Paris: Gabalda, 1920), 158-59; B. H. Branscomb, *The Gospel of Mark*, The Moffatt New Testament Commentary (London: Hodder & Stoughton, 1937), 111-12; D. E. Nineham, *The Gospel of St Mark*, Pelican Gospel Commentaries (Harmondsworth: Penguin Books, 1963), 182; E. Lohmeyer, *Das Evangelium des Markus*, 17th ed.; Meyers Kommentar 1/2 (Göttingen: Vandenhoeck & Ruprecht, 1967), 122-23; H. Anderson, *The Gospel of Mark*, New Century Bible (London: Oliphants, 1976), 170-71; R. Pesch, *Das Markusevangelium*, 2 vols., Herders theologischer Kommentar zum Neuen Testament II/1-2. (Freiburg: Herder, 1977), 1:345; J. Gnilka, *Das Evangelium nach Markus*, 2 vols.; Evangelisch-Katholischer Kommentar zum Neuen Testament II/1-2 (Zürich/Neukirchen-Vluyn: Benziger/Neukirchener Verlag, 1978-79), 1:254-55; R. Guelich, *Mark 1-8:26*, Word Biblical Commentary 34a (Dallas: Word Books, 1989), 336.

15. See, for example, V. Taylor, *The Gospel according to St. Mark* (London: Macmillan, 1966), 318-20; E. Schweitzer, *The Good News According to Mark* (London: SPCK, 1971), 131-32; W. L. Lane, *Commentary on the Gospel of Mark*, The New International Commentary on the New Testament (Grand Rapids:

who do link v. 30 with vv. 6b-13 sometimes understand the use of οἱ ἀπόστολοι in v. 30 as a rare use of this expression, outside the Luke-Acts and the Pauline Letters where it is common, as a title of honor.[16] They thus regard their report to Jesus as entirely positive: "The description corresponds to the two basic facets of Jesus' ministry and that of the early Christians. Like Jesus, the apostolic Church spread the gospel not in words alone, but in deeds."[17] Whether or not this understanding of the disciples' report is correct remains to be investigated, but its positive nature is largely determined by the optimistic assessment of the Markan use of οἱ ἀπόστολοι in v. 30. A closer look at the link between vv. 6b-13 and v. 30 indicates that this description of the disciples as "apostles," the only place outside Luke-Acts and the Pauline Literature where such a description is to be found, may not be as exalted as some suggest. Indeed, it may be one of the more important indications of the literary link between vv. 6b-16 and the potentially negative assessment of the disciples in v. 30.

After the summary statement of v. 6b, the narrator reports: "And he called to him the Twelve, and began to send them out (καὶ ἤρξατο αὐτοὺς ἀποστέλλειν) two by two" (v. 7a). The remainder of v. 7 recalls the earlier association of the Twelve with Jesus in 3:13-14, and in vv. 8-9 the narrator continues to report explicit instructions on what they are to take on the mission. As we will see below, these instructions associate the Twelve on their mission with the person and mission of Jesus. Vv. 10-11 are marked by a change from the narrator's report to the direct speech of Jesus. He gives instructions on how they

---

Eerdmans, 1974), 223-36; M. D. Hooker, *The Gospel according to St Mark*, Black's New Testament Commentaries (London: A. & C. Black, 1991), 162; K. Stock, *Boten aus dem Mit-Ihm-Sein. Das Verhältnes zwischen Jesus und den Zwölf nach Markus*, Analecta Biblica 70 (Rome: Biblical Institute Press, 1975), 97.

16. See, Stock, *Boten aus dem Mit-Ihm-Sein*, 98-99; J. Painter, *Mark's Gospel*. New Testament Readings (London: Routledge, 1997), 103-104; Hooker, *St Mark*, 162. E. LaVerdiere, *The Beginning of the Gospel. Introducing the Gospel According to Mark*, 2 vols. (Collegeville, MN: The Liturgical Press, 1999), 1:169, comments: "It has already become traditional among early Christians." This is hardly the evidence of Mark, Matthew and John.

17. LaVerdiere, *The Beginning of the Gospel*, 1:169. See also H. C. Waetjen, *A Reordering of Power. A Socio-Political Reading of Mark's Gospel* (Minneapolis: Fortress, 1989), 124-25; Painter, *Mark's Gospel*, 103-104.

are to behave in a concrete missionary situation.[18] In vv. 12-13 the narrator's voice returns to report the success of those who were sent out in v. 7. These remarks open with the words, "So they went out (καὶ ἐξελθόντες)" (v. 12a). No longer "with Jesus" (see 3:14), they scatter to do the things that Jesus has done (6:12b-13). The section on the death of the Baptist is then inserted (vv. 14-29). In v. 30, themes from the beginning (v. 7a) and the end (v. 12a) return. Both passages are from the narrator and, most likely, indicate a Markan redaction of earlier tradition. The "going out" is reversed as the narrator tells the reader that they "returned" (καὶ συνάγονται). Indeed, more than a simple return to the geographical place which they had left earlier is implied by this verb. They do not simply return, but they come back to gather around Jesus again (see 3:14). Jesus' action of "sending out" (v. 7a: ἀποστέλλειν) is recalled as those who return are described as the "sent ones" (οἱ ἀπόστολοι). There is no need to associate the use of the noun οἱ ἀπόστολοι in v. 30 with the widespread use of this title of honor in Luke-Acts and Paul. In the light of the rest of the Gospel of Mark, the word cannot bear the weight of such dignity.[19] The Twelve are called ἀπόστολοι (v. 30) because they were the ones whom Jesus began to send out (v. 7a: ἤρξατο αὐτοὺς ἀποστέλλειν). It is an appropriate noun to use as the story-teller returns, in v. 30, to recall the beginning of his "sandwich" in vv. 7-13.[20]

An initial suggestion concerning the literary structure of Mark 6:6b-30 can thus be proposed:

> vv. 6a-13: The association of the disciples with the mission of Jesus, as they are "sent out." They are scattered as they go, two by two, to their successful missionary activity (vv. 12-13).
> vv. 14-29: The death of John the Baptist.

---

18. This change of literary form, from a narrator's report to Jesus' direct speech, is a first hint that vv. 6a-13 is composite, formed by pre-Markan traditions (vv. 8-9), material from the earliest missionary experiences (vv. 10-11), and the redactional hand of the Evangelist (vv. 6a, 7, 12-13).
19. See the succinct, but accurate survey by J.-A. Bühner in his two articles, "ἀποστέλλω" and "ἀπόστολος" in *Exegetical Dictionary of the New Testament*, eds. H. Balz and G. Schneider, 3 vols. (Grand Rapids: Eerdmans, 1990), 1:141-46.
20. See Schweitzer, *Mark*, 125. With reference to v. 7, he comments: "It is still clearly a designation of their ministry and not a regular title." Thus also, among others, Taylor, *St. Mark*, 319; Anderson, *Mark*, 171. See a similar use of the word in John 13:16.

v. 30: The return of those "sent out" to make their report to Jesus. They "gather" and tell Jesus what they have said and done.

This "initial suggestion" must be tested by a closer reading of the text.[21] However, one must notice the presence of the key words which state Jesus' initiative in sending out disciples so that they might do what he has done thus far in the story and their scattering to perform this mission (v. 7a: sending out; v. 12a: they went out). The sending out and the scattering serve as a frame around the beginning and the end of vv. 7-13. The "coming back" (συνάγονται) of "those sent out" (οἱ ἀπόστολοι) opens v. 30, in a deliberate *reprise* of vv. 7-13.

One final element in support of the literary structure suggested above is to be found in v. 31. If v. 30 looks back to vv. 7-13 for its interpretation, in the light of the report of the death of John the Baptist (vv. 14-29), how does v. 30 relate to v. 31? Given the obvious relationship that exists between v. 31 and the account of the bread miracle (v. 31 leads directly into v. 32), commentators are notoriously concerned about the relationship between v. 30 and v. 31.[22] I am suggesting that v. 30 concludes vv. 6b-29. It is the final statement in a sandwich construction which makes 6:6b-30 a literary unit. This does not mean that it is entirely unrelated to v. 31. Narratives flow from one scene to another. In a good narrative one episode is not separated from another by a solid brick wall. Clearly, there is a relationship between v. 30 and v. 31. It is to "the Twelve" of v. 30 (see v. 7) that Jesus addresses the words of v. 31 (καὶ λέγει αὐτοῖς). But a new theme is introduced in v. 31. The Evangelist prepares for a new moment in the story by his request that the disciples come away so that they might be alone

---

21. Interestingly, although not common in traditional commentaries, scholars who have focussed attention upon Markan intercalations regularly see 6:6b-30 as an example of this technique. See, for example, Donahue, *Are you the Christ*, 59; Kee, *Community of the New Age*, 54; Kermode, *The Genesis of Secrecy*, 128-31; Fowler, *Loaves and Fishes*, 114-32; Edwards, "Markan Sandwiches," 198, 205-206; Shepherd, "Markan Intercalation," 530-31; 534-35, 539. In a most unlikely division of the material, C. E. B. Cranfield, *The Gospel according to St Mark*, The Cambridge New Testament Commentary (Cambridge: Cambridge University Press, 1959), 197-98, 204-205, makes a major division between 6:13 (closing a section running from 3:7-6:13: "Later Galilean Ministry") and 6:14 (opening a section running from 6:14-8:26: "Jesus goes outside Galilee").
22. See above, notes 13-16.

(v. 31a). It is a brief calm before the storm. However much preachers may have focused upon that element in Jesus' words (the need for quiet time and space), the trigger for what follows in the narrative is found in v. 31b: "For many were coming and going, and they had no leisure even to eat." There is very little resting in a lonely place (v. 31a) in the Gospel of Mark! The "coming and going" of great crowds (see 6:33-34, 44, 54-56; 8:1-4) and the theme of "eating" (see 6: 36-44; 7:2-5, 14-15, 18-20, 26-28; 8:1-10, 14-21), introduced in v. 31b, will dominate 6:33-8:21.[23]

Reading Mark 6:6b-30

I have already made a number of affirmations concerning the literary structure of vv. 6b-30. They need to be tested by a closer reading of the text, both within the limited context of the sandwich structure suggested above, and also in the light of all the reader has learnt about Jesus and the disciples to this point in the narrative (1:1-6:6a).[24]

Mark 6:6b

The reader has already encountered major summary statements in 1:14-15 and 3:7-12 which opened sub-sections of the first half of the Gospel (1:1-8:30). The first summary opened a sub-section (1:14-3:6)

---

23. I can only make these affirmations at this stage. However, it is widely recognized that the reports of the feeding of the milling crowds in the two bread miracles (6:31-44 and 8:1-10, with its aftermath in 8:11-21) serve as "bookends" around disputes which have much to do with the theme of "eating" in 7:1-23. The miracle of 7:24-30 continues the theme of "eating" but introduces a new theme, further developed in 7:31-37. The first half of the Gospel (1:14-8:30) asks, "who is Jesus?" and 7:24-37 serves to introduce the Gentile world into this discussion. See Francis J. Moloney, *Mark: Storyteller, Interpreter, Evangelist* (Peabody, MA: Hendrickson, 2004), 73-81, and Fowler, *Loaves and Fishes*, 91-147, especially pp. 116-19.
24. With this statement I am taking a methodological stance. Newer methodologies were another great interest of Athol Gill. This is not the only way one might read a Markan text, but I am using a modified form of narrative-criticism. I say "modified" because, unlike a number of contemporary narrative critics, I still ask historical questions. It is dishonest to describe the impact an ancient text makes upon a contemporary reader without asking questions about the origins and the original setting of the text in question. On this method, see F. J. Moloney, "Narrative Criticism of the Gospels," *Pacifica* 4 (1991): 181-201.

leading to the decision, on the part of Jewish leaders, that Jesus must die (3:6). Indeed, 1:14-3:6 can be described as an encounter between Jesus and the leaders of Israel. The second summary opened a further sub-section (3:7-6:6a) during which Jesus preached the parables of the Kingdom (4:1-34) and worked miracles (4:35-5:43). But framing this activity he chooses a "new family" (see 3:13-19, 34-35) over against the family of his flesh and blood (see 3:20-21, 31-35), his nation and his home town (see 3:22-30; 6:1-6a). Mark 3:7-6:6a can be described as Jesus and his own (see 3:34-35; 6:1-6a). The summary statement of 6:6b opens a further sub-section. In a few succinct words it describes Jesus' ongoing personal commitment to the task of moving from village to village, teaching. A passage from earlier in the story comes to mind: "Let us go on to the next towns, that I may preach there also; for that is why I came out" (1:38). For all its brevity, the statement of 6:6b indicates that Jesus relentlessly commits himself to the reason for his "coming out." As well as serving as a textual marker (a summary statement followed immediately by discipleship material), it has a function within its own immediate context. Jesus' ongoing commitment to his mission is closely associated with his sending out the Twelve on a parallel mission reported in vv. 7-13.[25]

Mark 6:7-13

Some introductory remarks to this complex passage are called for. The summary statement in v. 6b may have been already in the pre-Markan tradition, but its present setting comes directly from Mark's hand.[26] It is an indication of his careful insertion of this part of the

---

25. Most would accept that v. 6b leads into the association of the disciples with the mission of Jesus. As LaVerdiere, *The Beginning*, 152, comments on v. 6a and its context: "Until now, Jesus dominated Mark's literary stage. Now the Twelve remain with him at the center." Against this, however, see Lagrange, *Saint Marc*, 143-44; Stock, *Boten aus dem Mit-Ihm-Sein*, 83; Guelich, *Mark*, 313-14. They associate 6a and 6b as the final verse in the unit of 6:1-6.
26. See Pesch, *Das Markusevangelium*, 1:325-26. For a survey of possible relationships between tradition and Markan activity in 6:6b-13, 30, see E. Best, *Following Jesus. Discipleship in the Gospel of Mark*, Supplements to the Journal for the Study of the New Testament 4; Sheffield (JSOT Press, 1981), 190-93; Idem, *The Temptation and the Passion*, 75-76; Lohmeyer, *Markusevangelium*, 113. I regard vv. 6b, 7 and 12 as Markan, with redactional touches in other verses. See Gnilka, *Markus*, 1:236-38.

narrative into a larger literary design. His hand is also present in the close association of what follows in vv. 7-13 with v. 6b by means of the regular (and inelegant) use of καί. Each statement, either from the narrator or from Jesus himself, is linked to what went before by means of "and." The technical description of this element in Markan style is the "paratactic καί."[27] The conjunction καί appears no less than seven times in seven verses. However inelegant (and even forced), the repeated use of the link-word καί joins elements of vv. 7-13. It makes clear to the reader that what is said and done to the disciples in vv. 7-13 associates them with Jesus' own ongoing mission, succinctly described in v. 6b. We are dealing with a deliberate Markan construct in vv. 6b-13, elements of which may have had different origins before they were placed side by side in the Gospel of Mark. There are three constituent elements in vv. 7-13:

> vv. 7-9: The giving of authority and the external signs of the missionary are reported. Much of v. 7 could be from the hand of Mark, but the rest of the passage came to Mark from earlier traditions.
> vv. 10-11: Jesus instructs the Twelve on the behavior of the missionary in a concrete situation. The experience of early Christian missionaries is reflected in this passage.
> vv. 12-13: A report from the narrator, largely composed by the Evangelist, closes the passage, telling of the success of the mission of the Twelve.

Each of these sections has its importance, and their being connected by the Markan paratactic καί indicates that they are to be understood as a unified message on the mission of the disciples.

(a) Mark 6:7-9

Instructions for missionaries parallel to those found in Mark 6:8-9 are found in Q (see Matt 10:8-10; Luke 10:4). Such instructions were already a part of Christian tradition, reproduced in different con-

---

27. See F. Blass, A. Debrunner and R. W. Funk, *A Greek Grammar of the New Testament and Other Early Christian Literature* (Chicago: The University of Chicago Press, 1967), 239 § 458. On Mark's use of parataxis, see Fowler, *Let the Reader Understand*, 134-40.

texts by Mark, on the one hand, and by Matthew and Luke (Q) on the other. Scholars regularly point to the instructions – no bread, no bag, no money, and only one tunic[28] – as a deliberate attempt on the part of the early Christian missionaries to separate themselves from the wandering Cynic preachers who were allowed such trappings.[29] Crucial, however, for the Markan context is Jesus' giving authority to the Twelve over the unclean spirits (v. 7).[30] This authority, up to this point of the narrative, belonged only to Jesus (see 1:27). It was earlier promised to the Twelve, appointed to be with him (3:14: καὶ ἐποίησαν δώδεκα ἵνα ὦσιν μετ'αὐτοῦ) "to have authority to cast out demons" (3:15: καὶ ἔχειν ἐξουσίαν ἐκβάλλειν τὰ δαιμόνια). This promise now becomes reality as the disciples are formally given a share in Jesus' authority over the demons.

The unique Markan contribution to the tradition on the sending out of the missionaries is the indication of their sharing in the mission of Jesus. This is particularly clear when one looks back to the establishment of the Twelve in 3:14-15. The intimate association of the Twelve "with Jesus" is what authorizes them to do what, up to this point, only Jesus has done. Jesus is the one who was sent out to preach (see 1:14-15, 27, 38-39; 2:2, 13) and to have authority over demons (see 1:21-28, 32-34, 39; 3:11-12). The Twelve are promised a share in this mission in 3:14-15, and in 6:7-9 they are authoritatively commissioned to begin this activity. The fundamental element, however, in the Twelve's sharing in the mission of Jesus is that they "be with him … so that they might …" (3:14-15: καὶ ἐποίησεν δώδεκα ἵνα ὦσιν μετ'αὐτοῦ … καὶ ἔχειν ἐξουσίαν). Grammatically (and theologically) their being sent out to preach and their having authority over demons in 3:14b-15, depends upon the ὦσιν μετ'αὐτοῦ v. 14a.[31]

---

28. Lagrange, *Saint Marc*, 146-47, insists that two tunics were a sure sign of excessive wealth. One tunic was all that was necessary, given the urgency of the situation. A second tunic may also have served as a temporary shelter for the wandering preacher.
29. See Pesch, *Das Markusevangelium*, 2:326-28; Guelich, *Mark*, 324.
30. A Matthean version of this passage is found in Matt 10:1 used as the opening of Jesus' missionary discourse (10:1-11:1), picking up on earlier uses of this passage in Matthew (see 4:23-24; 9:35). In Matthew it is not immediately connected with the sending of the Twelve in 10:5-10. There is no parallel in Luke.
31. On this, see the important study of Stock, *Boten aus dem Mit-Ihm-Sein*. On 3:14-15, see pp. 15-27. Stock concludes: "Alles ist konzentriert auf die Person Jesu. In

The reader of Mark 6:7-9 recalls the crucial relationship between the "being with" Jesus and the participation in the mission of Jesus, programmatically spelt out in the appointment of the Twelve in 3:14-15. One could state the Markan affirmation negatively as follows: associated with Jesus, the Twelve have authority to preach and cast out demons, but separated from Jesus, all such authority will cease. It no longer has its source in the relationship initiated and established by Jesus. The negative sense of Mark 3:14-15 has been accurately translated into the Johannine Jesus' remark to the disciples in John 15:5: "Without me you can do nothing" (χωρὶς ἐμοῦ οὐ δύνασθε ποιεῖν οὐδέν). *He* appointed the Twelve (3:14: καὶ ἐποίησεν δώδεκα), *he* calls them (6:7a: καὶ προσκαλεῖται τοὺς δώδεκα), *he* began to send them out (v. 7b: καὶ ἤρξατο αὐτοὺς ἀποστέλλειν), and *he* charged them (v. 8a: καὶ παρήγγειλεν αὐτοῖς). The initiative of Jesus can even be traced in his sending them out two by two (v. 7b). Not only does this recall the familiar Old Testament legislation concerning witness (see Deut 17:6; 19:15), and reflect early Christian practice (see, for example, Paul and Barnabas, Peter and John, in Acts). It also looks back to Mark 1:16-20 where Jesus called the first disciples in pairs (v. 16: Simon and Andrew; v. 19: James and John).[32]

In the light of this background from earlier stages in the narrative, the traditional sayings commanding the missionary to go without bread, bag, money and a second tunic may insinuate a further Markan message. This becomes even more likely when one considers that only in the Markan version of this saying are the Twelve *permitted* to take a staff and to wear sandals (6:8-9. Contrast Matt 10:10; Luke 10:4). One of the features of the Markan narrative is the presentation of Jesus as a preacher and a miracle worker who is forever on a journey. Until such time as Jesus arrives in Jerusalem, almost every pericope begins with a verb of motion (see 1:12, 14, 16, 19, 21, 29, 35; 2:1, 13, etc.). When these verbs of motion are read in conjunction with the breathlessly regular Markan use of the adverb εὐθύς

---

seiner Gegenwart sollen sie sich aufhalten. Von ihm empfangen sie Sendung, Vollmacht, Inhalt und Befähigung für ihr Wirken" (p. 27).

32. For a detailed collection of this and further material on the need for two or three witnesses, see Stock, *Boten aus dem Mit-Ihm-Sein*, 86-87. Lohmeyer, *Markusevangelium*, 113, suggests that it might come from Qoh 4:9: "Two are better than one, because they have a good reward for their toil."

("immediately"),³³ the reader receives the impression of an unconditional response to a divine urgency which marks this charismatic wanderer. The staff and the sandals are symbols of this lifestyle, and the disciples, devoid of all other necessities, are permitted to join Jesus in his missionary journey.³⁴ This is a creative use of tradition that also gives theological weight to the command that the disciples take none of the necessities. All they are commissioned to do is to be resourced by their dependence upon Jesus (3:13-14), by their being "followers" of Jesus (1:16-20), joining him in his response to a God-directed journey. There may have been an attempt to differentiate Christian missionaries from wandering Cynics in pre-Markan tradition. But in 6:7-9 Jesus authorizes the Twelve to join his missionary journey, and thus they have the signs of a person on such a journey. Their taking nothing else is a further sign: they depend totally upon him. "Messengers are not to be believed if they rely upon their own resources (material or spiritual) rather than on the One whom they proclaim."³⁵

The conclusion to this analysis of vv. 7-9 can be stated simply: *the Twelve are commissioned to associate themselves with the mission of Jesus*. However, a further essential component to the mission of the Twelve is apparent to the reader in the light of earlier parts of the narrative. Disciples have been chosen by Jesus (see 1:16-20; 2:13-14; 3:13) and from among them, Jesus has further "instituted" the Twelve (3:14: ἐποίησεν δώδεκα). The disciples, and thus also the Twelve are to be followers of Jesus (1:16-20; 2:13-14). They are intimately associated with him (3:14) and it is from this intimate association that

---

33. As is well known, Mark uses this adverb more times in his 664 verses (42 times) than the rest of the New Testament put together (12 times).
34. For Pesch, *Das Markusevangelium*, 1:328-29, the exception in Mark is explained by the antiquity of the tradition. It takes into account the rough and dusty nature of Palestine, the original setting of the Christian mission. See the similar remark in Hooker, *St Mark*, 156. I would regard the Q tradition as more original, and thus see a Markan theological point of view emerging here. LaVerdiere, *The Beginning*, 1:154-56, associates the staff and the sandals with Exod 12:11, and comments: "Their Christian journey would be a new exodus, a personal passage from slavery to freedom" (p. 155). This link is somewhat forced, despite the attractive parallel with Exod 12:11.
35. Schweitzer, *Mark*, 130. See also Lagrange, *Saint Marc*, 145. Lohmeyer, *Markusevangelium*, 114, rightly comments: "Es handelt an den Zwölfen mit Gottes Gewalt und an Gottes Statt."

their mission flows (3:14b-15). *The Twelve are missionaries of Jesus only in so far as they respond to the initiative of Jesus, remain with him, recognize that their authority to preach and cast out demons is from him. They remain at all times "followers" of Jesus, and never self-reliant agents.*

(b) Mark 6:10-11

The instructions on the behavior of the missionaries in any given situation reflect the experience of the earliest missionary activity of the Christian communities.[36] The literary form changes, from the report of vv. 7-9 into the direct speech of vv. 10-11.[37] There are parallel instructions in Matt 10:11-15 and Luke 10:5-12 which may each reflect an independent tradition (M and L).[38] Mark is using a tradition that came to him from the setting of early Christian missionary practice. All three Synoptic Gospels, when they come to deal with the question of mission, place these instructions in the mouth of Jesus to establish some principles that might guide the wandering missioners. Two basic points are made, one a warning and the other a recognition of the importance of the task of the missioner, associated with the spreading of the Kingdom of God.

It appears that there were been difficulties in the early missionary activities of Christian communities. As well as the evidence in the three Synoptic passages just mentioned, there are clear warnings in *Didache* 11.1-12. Missioners were to stay in the first house that offered them accommodation. To arrive in a village, begin preaching the gospel, but then be seen to move from house to house – perhaps in pursuit of better lodgings or more congenial company – would make a lie of the gospel the missionary was preaching.[39] Thus, Jesus warns: "When you enter a house, stay there until you leave the place"

---

36. This should be said for the whole of vv. 7-13 (see Pesch, *Das Markusevangelium*, 1:325-26), but it is particularly clear in vv. 10-11.
37. See Pesch, *Das Markusevangelium*, 1:326.
38. On the difficulty of being certain over the nature of the history and the relationships of the traditions in vv. 7-13, see Stock, *Boten aus dem Mit-Ihm-Sein*, 95-96. LaVerdiere, *The Beginning*, 1:153, comments: "Mark's account is the oldest, that is, written prior to the other two. However, the accounts of Matthew and Luke, while written later, refer to a historical context that is older than the one in Mark." See also Pesch, *Das Markusevangelium*, 1:325-26.
39. See Schweitzer, *Mark*, 130.

(v. 10. See also *Didache* 11:3-6). It is on Jesus' authority that missioners are now warned that they must live the gospel they claim to preach. This is an early Christian recommendation to put one's life where one's words are.

Jesus' second recommendation is linked to a practice reported in later Jewish literature. The Lukan redaction of this instruction shows that there was need for further explanation for this practice to make sense in a Gentile setting, once it was removed from an audience familiar with Jewish practices (see Luke 10:10-11).[40] The shaking off the dust from the feet comes from the belief that Israel was God's "holy land." Returning from the impure lands which surrounded Israel, travelers would shake the dust from their feet. This gesture indicated the impurity and godlessness of the land they had just left, and the holiness of the land they were entering (see, from the Mishnah, *Oholoth* 2.3; *Tohoroth* 4.5; and from the Babylonian Talmud, *Shabbath* 15b). Within the early Christian mission this gesture takes on an eschatological significance. The place that did not receive the missioner, or would not hear the proclamation of the gospel, was to be judged as "godless" by means of a symbolic shaking of the dust from the feet of the missionary.[41] In a symbolic sense, they no longer belong to God's chosen people. This was to be a sign, a witness (v. 11: εἰς μαρτυρίαν) against all who rejected the opportunity offered by the Christian message.[42] The missionaries who put their lives where their words were, proclaimed the gospel in both word and deed (v. 10). They thus had authority to indicate to that place which rejected (μὴ δέξεται) the missionary and the message that they were brought judgment upon themselves (v. 11).[43] As with vv. 7-9, however, it is not the missioner who is rejected. They are only "witnesses" to the message.[44] Although not as obviously linked to the earlier Markan

---

40. See Pesch, *Das Markusevangelium*, 1:330.
41. The verb δέχομαι (to receive) is a technical term, used to indicate the reception of the missionary and her or his message (see 9:37; 10:15).
42. There is a possibly link between the sending out "two by two" in v. 7 and the need for two witnesses to act appropriately in v. 11.
43. Hooker, *St Mark*, 157, makes an interesting link with the rejection of Jesus by his townsfolk in 6:1-6a: "These words indicate the urgency of the situation. Jesus' words read ominously, coming so soon after the story of his own rejection in his home town."
44. See Gnilka, *Markus*, 1:240: "Die Ablehnung der Boten ist die Ablehnung der Botschaft, die in Gericht zu retten vermag."

passages on the choosing of disciples (1:16-20; 2:13-17; 3:13) and the sending of the Twelve (3:14-15), it is as *emissaries of Jesus* that the missioners have authority to proclaim judgment. Despite its origins in the missionary practice of the early Church, the Markan paratactic καί links vv. 10-11 with vv. 7-9 and the more obvious connections found there with 3:14-15. The missionaries have authority because of their "being with him" (3:14).

(c) Mark 6:12-13

The concluding report of the immediate and apparently universal success of the mission does not present great exegetical difficulties. What Jesus said *would* happen, *does* happen. This is not surprising. However, what must be noted is the inclusion in this report of activities that were not part of the commission in v. 7. They were given authority over the unclean spirits. However, in vv. 12-13a, as well as casting out demons, they also preach conversion (ἐκήρυξαν ἵνα μετανοῶσιν). 3:14-15 has again played a formative role in the construction of this passage. As the Twelve were appointed they were promised authority to preach and to cast out demons (3:14b-15), flowing from their "being with him" (3:14a). However, the nature of their preaching is further specified in 6:12. They "preach that people should convert." This preaching of conversion reaches even more deeply into an association with the mission of Jesus. His entire ministry was placed under the rubric of preaching conversion in the opening summary of 1:14-15 (κερύσσων τὸ εὐαγγέλιον τοῦ θεοῦ … μετανοεῖτε καὶ πιστεύετε ἐν τῷ εὐαγγελίῳ).

The healing of the sick is a further association of the missionary activity of the Twelve with the ministry of Jesus up to this point in the narrative (see 1:29-31, 34, 40-45; 2:1-12; 3:1-6, 10; 5:25-34; 6:5). The link between the successful mission of the disciples and their healing of the sick (v. 13: πολλοὺς ἀρρώστους), reported in such close literary proximity to Jesus' failed mission in his own town (6:1-6a), where all he could do was heal some of the sick (6:5: ὀλίγοις ἀρρώστοις), is ironic. In terms of the unfolding argument of the narrative, the new family of Jesus (see 3:34-35) takes over and expands the mission of Jesus beyond the boundaries imposed upon him by those who could not transcend the limitations of his human origins (see 6:2). The practice of anointing with oil was widespread in the Hellenistic world, and by the time of the writing of the Gospel of Mark had probably become part of Christian practice (see especially Luke 10:34; James 5:14).⁴⁵

Much of what was said in conclusion to the analysis of vv. 7-9 returns. *The Twelve are commissioned to associate themselves with the mission of Jesus.* That was already very apparent in vv. 7-9, but it has been further reinforced by means of the instructions on the authority of the missioners in v. 11, and especially in the deepening of the relationship between the mission of the Twelve and that of Jesus in vv. 12-13. Indeed, they are more successful than Jesus had been in the immediately previous scene: Jesus in his home town (6:1-6a). Earlier parts of the narrative continue to act as intertext to the reading experience. Disciples have been chosen by Jesus (see 1:16-20; 2:13-14; 3:13) and from among them, Jesus has further "instituted" the Twelve (3:14: ἐποίησεν δώδεκα). The disciples, and thus also the Twelve, are to be followers of Jesus (1:16-20; 2:13-14). They are intimately associated with him (3:14) and it is from this intimate association that their mission flows (3:14b-15). Like Jesus, they go out, preach conversion (v. 12; 1:14-15), drive out demons and heal the sick (v. 13; 6:5). The conclusion to vv. 7-9 must be firmly restated: *the Twelve are missionaries of Jesus only in so far as they respond to the initiative of Jesus, remain with him, recognize that their authority to preach conversion, to cast out demons and to heal the sick is from him. They remain at all times "followers" of Jesus. Without him, they can do nothing* (see 3:14-15. See also John 15:5).⁴⁶

Mark 6:14-29

Given the limitations of this paper, and its focus upon the disciples, I will make general remarks about the report of the death of John the Baptist. Morna Hooker has accurately described majority opinion about its location in the Gospel of Mark:

> Between the account of the sending out of the Twelve and that of their return, Mark inserts an account of Herod's reaction to the rumours about Jesus, together with the story

---

45. For a full discussion of this issue, see L. T. Johnson, *The Letter of James*, Anchor Bible 37a (New York: Doubleday, 1995), 330-32
46. See especially Stock, *Boten aus dem Mit-Ihm-Sein*, 82-97.

of his beheading of John the Baptist.⁴⁷ There seems no logical connection between the two themes, but the somewhat artificial insertion provides an interlude for the disciples to complete their mission.⁴⁸

This study suggests that this is not an appropriate understanding of the Markan story. The framing of vv. 14-29 with vv. 6b-13 and v. 30 provide a very "logical sequence to the two themes." Indeed, it is the death of John the Baptist (vv. 17-29), prefaced by a brief discussion over Jesus (vv. 14-16) which serves as the central section of the "sandwich," providing meaning to the flanking passages on the sending out and the return of the Twelve.

There are two parts to the report on the death of the Baptist.⁴⁹ Herod's concerns over Jesus are reported in vv. 14-16. This passage is christological, but the figure of John the Baptist is entwined with Herod's assessment of Jesus at every turn. The first reason given for the increasing fame of Jesus is the suggestion on the part of "some" that John the Baptist has been raised from the dead (v. 14).⁵⁰ The resurrection of John the Baptist may point to an expected eschatologi-

---

47. The Herod in question is Herod Antipas, who was the tetrarch over Galilee and Perea (east of the Jordan) from 4 B.C.E. till 39 C.E.
48. Hooker, *St Mark*, 158. Compare Pesch, *Das Markusevangelium*, 1:344: "Als günstiger Platz bot sich die Position zwischen Aussendung (6:7-13) und Rückkehr (6:30) der Zwölf an." The theological and literary questions are well summed up by LaVerdiere, *The Beginning*, 1:153: "Our biggest challenge is to see how Jesus' identity and John's death and burial are related to the mission of the twelve." Edwards ("Markan Sandwiches," 206 n. 37) rightly points to the further need to relate "the Baptist's martyrdom to the twelve as well as to Jesus' impending crucifixion."
49. Pesch, *Das Markusevangelium*, 1:332, 338-40, suggests that vv. 14-16 had been added to the non-Christian folkloric tale of vv. 17-29, prior to Mark. This accounts for the presence of the passage in the Gospel. The link between vv. 14-15 and 8:28 is clear. See Gnilka, *Markus*, 1:244-45. Pesch further claims that vv. 17-29 is a mixture of traditions of Jewish martyrdom and oriental dinner-parties, influenced by the Book of Esther. See also J. P. Meier, *A Marginal Jew. Rethinking the Historical Jesus*, 5 vols. Anchor Yale Bible Reference Library (New York/New Haven: Doubleday/Yale University Press, 1991-2016), 2:173-74. On the possible history of the tradition, see Gnilka, *Markus*, 1:244-47.
50. There is strong textual support for the singular form of the verb here: "and he (Herod) said" (ἔλεγεν). However, the plural (ἔλεγον) is to be retained. The singular was probably transferred from the report of Herod's opinion in v. 16. See Painter, *Mark's Gospel*, 100. In support of the singular, but translating it as

cal prophet, and Jesus, John the Baptist *redivivus* would thus be the prophet of the end time, possessing great powers (v. 14).[51] Perhaps there is no need to make such a dramatic link between John the Baptist and Jesus. As Hooker remarks, "It is not clear what is meant by the suggestion that John the Baptizer has been raised from the dead; if such a rumour ever circulated, then the idea of an individual being raised was not incredible in popular imagination."[52] The opinion expressed in v. 14 may be as simple as that. Thus it may not be very different from the opinion of "others" who suggest that Jesus is one or other of the several expected prophetic forerunners to the messianic era: Elijah (see Mal 4:5-6), or one of the prophets from of old (with possible links to Deut 18:18?),[53] found in v. 15. The reader, instructed by the prologue (1:1-13) and the narrative to this point, knows that all suggestions miss the point, but the question, "who is Jesus" continues to be raised by the characters in the story.[54]

"Und man sagte," see Pesch, *Das Markusevangelium*, 1:333. See also Lagrange, *Saint Marc*, 149 ("on disait").

51. The reference to resurrection and the possession of great powers (v. 14) has led K. Berger and R. Pesch, to identify Jesus as the expected eschatological prophet who would rise from the dead and be a miracle worker. This suggestion has served as a basis for E. Schillebeeckx's understanding of the resurrection of Jesus as something that was already part of the pre-Easter expectation of his followers. For a discussion of this, see F. J. Moloney, "Resurrection and Accepted Exegetical Opinion," *The Australasian Catholic Record* 58 (1981), 191-202. For all its faults, one should consult the work of Berger for a rich analysis of Jewish and Christian speculation on the eschatological prophet. See K. Berger, *Die Auferstehung des Propheten und die Erhöhung des Menschensohnes. Traditionsgeschichtliche Untersuchungen zu Deutung des Geschickes Jesus in frühchristlichen Texten*, Studien zur Umwelt des Neuen Testament 13 (Göttingen: Vandenhoeck & Ruprecht, 1976). For its application to this context, see Pesch, *Das Markusevangelium*, 1:333-37. But see J. P. Meier's bald assessment: "There seems to have been no idea in pre-Christian Judaism about Elijah returning to prepare the way for a messiah" (*A Marginal Jew*, 2:226).
52. Hooker, *St Mark*, 159. In 9:11-13, however, Jesus is again linked with John the Baptist. In an interesting suggestion, L. T. Johnson, *Religious Experience in Earliest Christianity* (Minneapolis: Fortress, 1998) 77-78, suggests that v. 14 reflects beliefs associated with necromancy: "Was it possible that the beheaded John the Baptist was more powerfully at work in this man whom he had baptized?" (p. 78).
53. There may be no contact between Deut 18:18, where Yhwh promises to raise up a prophet like Moses, and "the prophets of old" in v. 6. The simplest interpretation is that many regard Jesus as belonging to the line of Israel's great prophets. See Lohmeyer, *Markusevangelium*, 116-17; Gnilka, *Markus*, 1:249.
54. See LaVerdiere, *The Beginning*, 1:156-60.

Herod takes the former option. He decides that Jesus must be the risen John the Baptist, whom he beheaded (v. 16). These words from Herod ("John, whom I beheaded") allow the Evangelist to pick up the tale of John's martyrdom, reporting it in a lengthy flashback in vv. 17-29. For the reader, the issue has been raised of the relationship between John the Baptist and Jesus, and with it the awareness that as the Baptist went to death, so also must Jesus. There are important differences between the reports we have of John the Baptist's death in the Gospels (basically Mark 6:17-29, repeated in an abbreviated form by Matt 14:3-12 and pared down to a brief statement in Luke 3:19-20) and in Josephus (*Antiquities* 18.5.2). This is not the place to discuss the differences,[55] and Mark has made some glaring errors of fact.[56] It is helpful to be aware that, for Josephus, Herod killed the Baptist because he was afraid of a rebellion by the people. This enables us to see the Markan theological focus more clearly.[57] The christological issues raised in vv. 14-16 lie hidden underneath the folkloric narrative of vv. 17-29.[58] For Mark, John the Baptist is put to death by a ruler who recognized that he was "a righteous and holy man" (v. 20. See also v. 26), but who succumbed to public pressure (see vv. 22-26). The Baptist would not give in weakly to pressure, even from one who recognized his virtues. He stood by his God-given task preaching repentance and forgiveness of sins (see 1:4). For Mark, John's judgment of Herod's marriage is a public call that sinfulness be recognized (see 6:17-19).[59]

There is much in this Markan version of the story, the only episode in the Gospel that does not have Jesus at its center, which points

---

55. For a good discussion, see Meier, *A Marginal Jew*, 2:56-62. See further, H. W. Hoehner, *Herod Antipas. A Contemporary of Jesus Christ* (Grand Rapids: Zondervan, 1980), 110-72.
56. It was incorrect to call Herod Antipas a "king," and Philip was not married to Herodias, but to her daughter, Salome. Herodias had previously been married to a half-brother of Antipas, known simply as Herod. See Meier, *A Marginal Jew*, 2:172.
57. See Meier, *A Marginal Jew*, 2:171-76. Meier rightly argues against any attempt to harmonize Mark and Josephus, insisting that, "Josephus is to be preferred for history; Mark is to be mined for tradition history and theological intent" (p. 175).
58. On the "foreign" nature of vv. 17-29 within the Markan text, see Lohmeyer, *Markusevangelium*, 117-21.
59. For background on the Jewish martyr as an advocate of the law before the authorities, see 2 Macc 6:18-31; 4 Macc 5:1-6:3. See Guelich, *Mark*, 331.

forward to Jesus' death. He too is put to death by a ruler who recognizes his goodness (see 15:9-10, 12, 14), but who succumbs to public pressure (see 15:10. 14-15). Jesus does not give in to such pressures, not even to save his life, but announces the present and future coming of God as King (see 14:58, 60-62). Yet there is a difference between John and Jesus. After the slaying and the ghoulish presentation of the head upon a dish (vv. 27-28), Mark's account of John the Baptist's death closes as his body is taken by his disciples and laid in a tomb (v. 29). According to vv. 14-16, rumors of the resurrection of the Baptist are in the air; but they are only rumors. The Christian community reading this story believes that Jesus has been slain, buried, and has been raised from the dead (see 16:1-8).[60]

Once this is clear, then the theological and literary function of vv. 14-29 within the context of vv. 6b-30 emerges. Mark uses his traditions concerning the death of John the Baptist for at least two reasons. John the Baptist is the messenger of God (see 1:2-3), the one who announces Jesus (vv. 7-8). He has an unswerving commitment to his God-given mission: to preach a baptism of repentance for the forgiveness of sins (1:4). It has cost him his life (6:17-29). Secondly, his life and death have close parallels with the life and death of Jesus. A deal of information about discipleship has been provided for the reader in the narrative thus far (1:16-20; 2:113-14; 3:13-19, 20-35; 4:10-11, 33-34). The disciples have had a moment of weakness in the stormy sea (4:35-41) to which we shall briefly return. The reader is aware that *unconditional commitment to God's design and being a follower of Jesus* should mark the life of the Twelve, at present out on their mission (vv. 7-13). It is also made clear for the first time, by means of this interlude, that discipleship will cost no less than everything (see 8:31-9:1). As followers of Jesus, they are called to share in the destiny of Jesus (see 8:34-35), proleptically acted out in the martyrdom of John the Baptist.[61] "John's martyrdom not only prefigured Jesus' death, it also prefigures the death of anyone who would come after him!"[62] We turn to v. 30 with this message ringing in the ears of listener and in the mind and heart of the reader.

---

60. For a good summary of the links between Jesus and John the Baptist, see LaVerdiere, *The Beginning*, 161-63. See also Myers, *Binding the Strong Man*, 214-17.
61. See Gnilka, *Markus*, 1:252.
62. Edwards, "Markan Sandwiches," 206.

Mark 6:30

Those who were sent out in v. 7 return, and gather around Jesus. The use of the verb συνάγω indicates more than a simple return. The returning Twelve adopt a physical position around Jesus (πρὸς τὸν Ἰησοῦν) which is reminiscent of the ὦσιν μετ'αὐτοῦ of 3:14.[63] That context (3:14-15) was very present in Jesus' commissioning and sending out the Twelve in vv. 7-9. It returns in the first seven words of v. 30a. But the final nine words indicate that they have not understood what has happened to them, and what they have done. They "announce" (ἀπήγγειλην) their achievements to Jesus. This is a strong verb, generally used in contexts of public revelation (see, for its only other uses in Mark, 5:14, 19).[64] They are the masters of the situation, as they come back to proclaim to Jesus πάντα ὅσα ἐποίησαν καὶ ὅσα ἐδίδαξαν (v. 30b). What must be noticed is the Twelve's transferal of the authority for what they have done and said *to themselves*. Despite the focus upon Jesus as the one who authorizes and sends in vv. 7-13, they report in v. 30 "everything" that *they* did and everything that *they* said.[65] This is to miss the point of their being *sent by Jesus* on a mission (3:14b-15; 6:7-13) which will only be an effective proclamation of the Kingdom (however "successful" it might appear) if they are "with Jesus" (3:14a).

They were authorized to do and say things by Jesus. Separated from him, acting as their own agents, they are no longer behaving as disciples of Jesus. There is deep irony in the fact that the returning missionaries report to the one who authorized them, who gave them ἐξουσία (see 3:15; 6:7), telling him all the things that "they" have done and said. The reader knows that their missionary activity depends entirely upon the one to whom they are joyfully announcing their success. The essential qualities of a true disciple have been made clear by means of the episode of the death of the Baptist (vv. 14-29: the

---

63. See Stock, *Boten aus dem Mit-Ihm-Sein*, 99.
64. It is also used in the longer ending of Mark (see 16:10, 13). The solemnity associated with the verb is obviously also found there.
65. Stock, *Boten aus dem Mit-Ihm-Sein*, 100, comments, "Das πάντα ὅσα eine Totalität (cf. Mk 11,24; 12,44) heisst es 'sie haben restlos alles berichtet.'" In his careful analysis, however, Stock does not comment sufficiently on the subject of the verbs ἐποίησαν and ἐδίδαξαν. He commented earlier (p. 27) on 3:13-14: "Mit-ihm-Sein und Ausgesendet-Werden sind aufeinander bezogen. Das Mit-ihm-Sein befähigt sie zur Fortführung des Wirkens Jesu." Is this happening in v. 30?

middle of the sandwich). Not only are they authorized by Jesus, but like the Baptist, they are to accept the destiny which the following of Jesus necessarily brings. There is nothing of this in the report of the Twelve as they come back from their mission. They are unable to recognize that they have associated themselves with Jesus in a mission that has to do with the reigning presence *of God* (v. 6b), cost what it may (vv. 14-29). They come back flushed with their success, yet show that they have failed as disciples of Jesus.[66]

Conclusion

It has been claimed that this section of the Gospel of Mark reflects haphazard editing. The author wanted to include teaching on the mission, so that those of the Markan community involved in such activities would have a "Jesus-word" to direct them, but it makes little sense in its present context.[67] Mark also wished to tell the story of the death of the Baptist, but its present location in the narrative is judged as an "artificial insertion."[68] For some, therefore, there is little rhyme or reason why these two traditions were placed side-by-side at this stage of the Gospel. I trust that the above study indicates the rhyme and reason for the location and the strategic articulation of the traditions now found in Mark 6:6b-30. True to their call which comes to them from God through Jesus (1:16-20; 3:13-19), and like the Baptist, the disciples are to commit themselves unflinchingly to the mission for which they have been empowered by their association with Jesus (6:7-13). As with the Baptist, it will cost them no less than everything (vv. 14-29). They fail. They return to Jesus, the source of all that they do and say, with whose mission they are privi-

---

66. A disturbed textual tradition (the uncials of Alexandrinus, Leningrad and Oxford, and the Gothic translation) suggests that the Twelve tell Jesus about the death of the Baptist ("and they reported everything to him and what they had said and taught"). See Gnilka, *Markus*, 1:258. Perhaps the earliest interpreters (the scribes) saw the problem. But, to the best of my knowledge, I am alone in making this suggestion. It can be found, however, in P. J. Flanagan, *The Gospel of Mark Made Easy* (New York: Paulist Press, 1997) 69, with a note on p. 84, indicating that he has taken the idea from my lectures.
67. See, for example, Nineham, *Saint Mark*, 167-69
68. Hooker, *St Mark*, 158.

leged to be associated (6:6b-7), to tell him everything *they* have said and done (v. 30).[69]

As Jesus stilled the stormy seas, he questioned the faith of his disciples: "Why are you afraid? Have you no faith?" (4:40). This was the first indication of the limitations of the fragile human beings called to be disciples of Jesus. Up to this point they have responded unflinchingly to his call (1:16-20; 2:13-14; 3:13-19), and accompanied him on his wandering mission as healer, preacher and wonder worker (1:17-4:34). But after the calming of the storm, filled with awe and puzzlement, they ask one another, "Who is this then, that even the wind and sea obey him?" (4:41). They are not able to understand *who Jesus is*. More miracles follow (5:1-43), and Jesus own townsfolk ask the right question: "Where did this man get all this?" (6:2), but they are not able to go beyond his local trade, his mother and his siblings (v. 3). But what of the Twelve, instituted by Jesus (3:14-19), what of the "new family" of Jesus (see 3:34-35)? The elegant Markan sandwich construction of 6:6b-30 takes the dramatic presentation of the disciples and the Twelve one step further. Now the Twelve, chosen from among the disciples (see 3:13), are not able to understand *who they are!*[70] Dennis Nineham missed the point when he wrote of 6:6b-13: "We may say, in fact, that this incident, which might have been expected to be so important, plays no vital part in the structure and development of the Gospel."[71] Within its immediate context of 6:6b-30, and within the broader narrative canvas of the Gospel as a whole, it plays a strategic role. It leads the reader from the disciples' initial

---

69. Against Stock, *Boten aus dem Mit-Ihm-Sein*, 97-102. Anxious to make the connection between vv. 7-13 and v. 30, Stock develops an entirely positive portrait of the Twelve in v. 30. Stressing the importance of their being ἀπόστολοι, an ongoing office in the community, he concludes that they have succeeded in carrying further the work and teaching of Jesus. See also LaVerdiere, *The Beginning*, 168-69. I would submit that the Twelve have not measured up to the criteria established by Stock in his analysis of 3:14-15 (see *Boten aus dem Mit-Ihm-Sein*, 27).
70. Fowler, *Loaves and Fishes*, 116-19, has correctly pointed out that the command to have no money and no bread in 6:6b-13 (see v. 8) is not obeyed. In 6:37-38 they have five hundred denarii, five loaves and two fishes (see also 8:5-7). Fowler remarks: "The virtue enjoined upon them in 6:8 has now become a vice in their eyes" (119). Fowler does not see 6:30 as a possible further initial indication of their failure, but his suggestions add weight to my argument that their movement into failure is under way in 4:41 and 6:30.
71. Nineham, *St Mark*, 168. But see Gnilka, *Markus*, 1:244.

successes (see 1:16-20; 2:13-14; 3:13-19; 6:6b-13), through their doubt (see 4:41), via the account of the death of the Baptist (6:14-19), into failure (6:30).[72]

But this is not the end of the story. That can only be found somewhere in Galilee, in a meeting between the risen Lord and the disciples (see 14:28; 16:7). There they will see him, as he promised, despite the failure of everyone in the story, including the women who had accompanied him from Jerusalem, through the Cross and into an empty tomb (15:47; 16:1-4). No matter how dramatic even their failure at the tomb might appear to be (see 16:8), they (we) will see him (see 14:28; 16:7). But that, of course, is a story which reaches beyond the bounds of Mark 1:1-16:8.[73]

---

72. A plotted movement of the disciples' response to Jesus - from unperceptiveness through misconception to rejection - was identified by T. J. Weeden, *Mark – Traditions in Conflict* (Philadelphia: Fortress, 1971) 26-51. For a response to Weeden, see F. J. Moloney, "The Vocation of the Disciples in Mark," in *"A Hard Saying." The Gospel and Culture* (Collegeville: The Liturgical Press, 2002), 53-84.
73. For further reflection upon this statement, see the essay "'He is going before you into Galilee.' Mark 16:6-8 and the Christian Community," on pp. 117-30 of this volume.

3
Following Jesus into Radical Discipleship: A Reading of Mark 8:14-9:29

In Honour of Anthony J. Kelly, CSsR.

All four Gospels highlight the relationship that existed between Jesus and his disciples, albeit in different ways. In the Synoptic tradition, this is even the case where Mark, Matthew and Luke are working with the same narratives which each author nuances in a unique fashion. The Gospel of John has its own way of describing this relationship.[1] Despite their differences, only one word can be used to capture what Jesus asks of anyone who wishes to follow him in all four Gospels: "radical." The call of Jesus cuts across boundaries of family, culture and religious traditions, asking that others join him in a God-given mission to bring in the reigning presence of that God among men and women. For John, they are to love as Jesus has loved them so that the world might recognize Jesus as the sent one of the Father, and thus come to eternal life (see John 13:34-35; 15:12, 17; 17:2-3, 18-20, 21, 23; 20:21-23).[2]

It is clear that driving both Jesus and the Gospels is the design of God, and this design questions many accepted absolutes. Indeed, all four Gospels show that to follow Jesus will cost no less than everything. The consistency of the radical nature of what it means to respond to the call of Jesus Christ across the Gospels is a sure sign

---

1. For an excellent recent study, see Rekha M. Chennattu, *Johannine Discipleship as a Covenant Relationship* (Peabody, MA: Hendrickson, 2006). For an older, but still valuable study, see Marinus de Jonge, *Stranger from Heaven and Son of God: Jesus Christ and the Christians in the Johannine Perspective* (trans. J. E. Steely; Missoula, MT: Scholars Press, 1977), 1-27.
2. See Francis J. Moloney, *Love in the Gospel of John: An Exegetical, Theological and Literary Study* (Grand Rapids, MI: Baker Academic, 2013).

that this goes back to the very first followers of Jesus of Nazareth.[3] It is with a sense of privilege that I offer this study of Christian discipleship to my long-standing dear friend and colleague, Anthony J. Kelly, CSsR, on the occasion of his seventy-fifth birthday. Tony has lived a unique response to that call within the Catholic tradition that has guided and inspired many, myself included.

Introduction to a Critical Reading of Mark 8:14-9:29

The radical nature of Christian discipleship finds eloquent expression in the Gospel of Mark, most likely the earliest of the Gospels (written about 70 CE). Although this Gospel is a carefully constructed narrative, one senses the passion and urgency of Jesus of Nazareth in his desire to associate others with him in his mission and destiny. Matthew and Luke, who no doubt looked to the earlier Gospel of Mark for guidance, continue that urgency, albeit with different nuances.[4] At a critical moment in the "good news" according to Mark, Jesus asks his disciples who they think he is (Mark 8:29. See also Matt 16:15; Luke 9:20), and uses their reply to initiate a process of direct instruction on what is required of them, if they wish to follow him (Mark 8:34-9:1. See also Matt 16:24-28; Luke 9:23-27). It begins a series of encounters

---

3. There are a number of "criteria" that have been developed to test whether or not a tradition goes back to the historical Jesus, and is not the product of preaching/teaching of the early Church. For a very clear presentation of them, see John P. Meier, *A Marginal Jew. Rethinking for Historical Jesus*, 5 vols., Anchor Yale Biblical Library (New York/New Haven: Doubleday/Yale University Press, 1991-2016) 1: 167-95. Two of them, *dissimilarity* with anything else at that time and the *coherence* of the theme across various traditions and literary forms, are strongly present in the radical nature of Christian discipleship in all four Gospels. It certainly goes back to Jesus' demands of his original disciples. Nowadays (2017), this approach is under severe criticism. See, for example, Chris Keith and Anthony Le Donne, eds., *Jesus, Criteria, and the Demise of Authenticity* (London/New York: T. & T. Clark, 2012).
4. This sentence accepts the hypothesis that Mark was the first Gospel, and developed a story of Jesus from traditions that came to him. Matthew and Luke were independent of one another, but they knew and used the Gospel of Mark, as well as other early traditions that came to them from a number of other sources, among them the so-called "sayings source" known as Q. For a very clear presentation of this hypothesis, see John S. Kloppenborg, *Q, The Earliest Gospel. An Introduction to the Original Stories and Sayings of Jesus* (Louisville, KY: Westminster John Knox, 2008), 1-40.

between Jesus and his disciples that runs from 8:22-10:52. Mark has deliberately set this section of his Gospel between the strange miracle of the curing of the blind man at Bethsaida (8:22-26), and the healing of another blind man, Bartimaeus (10:46-52). Between these two miracles, Jesus tells of his forthcoming death and resurrection on three occasions (8:31; 9:31; 10:32-24).

This reflection focuses upon the section of the Gospel of Mark widely regarded by interpreters as directed to the "formation of disciples." Jesus' exclusive attention to his disciples, and what is asked of them, dominates the story that is "framed" by the two healings of blind men in 8:22-26 and 10:46-52. There are further textual markers that show literary sub-divisions in this passage, especially the three passion predictions of 8:31, 9:31 and 10:32-34. Mark designed 8:22-9:29, 9:30-10:31 and 10:32-52 as distinct literary units, to present Jesus' preparation of his disciples for the challenges that lie ahead, both in the paschal events, and in the Christian experience after that unique event. As disciples struggle with their "blindness" (8:22-26; 10:46-52), they must face the fact that they have been called to follow a Messiah who is a suffering and vindicated Son of Man Messiah. He will call them to the way of the Cross (8:27-9:29), to service and receptivity (9:30-10:29), and then repeat, in more immediate terms, the same call to service, receptivity and Cross (10:30-45). This instruction of the disciples closes with Jesus' powerful words, in which he points to himself as the one who leads the disciples along the way of service and self-gift unto death: "For the Son of Man also came not to be served, but to serve, and to give his life as a ransom for many" (10:45).[5]

Another theme finds a threefold repetition across 8:22-10:52. Each time Jesus speaks of his forthcoming death and resurrection, he asks his disciples to follow him down the same "way" (8:27; 9:33, 34; 10:17, 32, 46, 52). *Never* do the disciples accept this challenge. Each passion prediction is systematically followed by the disciples' failure to understand or accept what Jesus is saying (see 8:32-33; 9:32-34; 10:35-37, 41). They either do not or will not accept that they have committed themselves to follow a crucified and risen Christ. However, their fail-

---

5. See the careful work of Gian Paolo Peron, *Seguitimi! Vi farò diventare pescatori di uomini*, Biblioteca di Scienze Religiose 162 (Roma: LAS, 2000), 131-75. Peron entitles this section of Mark's Gospel: "Jesus educates the disciples."

ure is always accompanied by Jesus' patient taking his disciples to himself and teaching them that they must reach beyond their hopes and expectations (8:34-9:29; 9:35-10:31; 10:38-40, 42-45).[6]

This rapid overview of the narrative and thematic rhythms of Mark 8:22-10:52 indicates that there are three moments in the story during which Jesus devotes himself to the instruction of his followers on the nature of true discipleship: 8:22-9:29, 9:30-10:31 and 10:32-52. But stories are not static. They depend upon what has already been told, and look forward to what is yet to take place. These literary "sections" are not separated by brick walls, as the ebb and flow of the text throws light on what is yet to come, or looks back to what has already been said or happened. For that reason I am reaching back to the passage that immediately precedes 8:22-9:29. Mark 8:14-21, a passage which looks further back in the narrative to the bread miracles of 6:31-44 and 8:1-9, also looks forward to the "blindness" of the disciples in 8:22-9:29, and beyond.[7]

The "prologue" to the Gospel (1:1-13), a passage addressed only to the story's readers and listeners, is even more important for an understanding of the meaning and message of Mark. What is learnt in the prologue determines the reading, hearing and understanding of all that follows, from 1:14-16:8. As we reflect upon the call to radical discipleship in 8:14-9:29, everything that has been said and done in 1:1-8:13 has prepared the reader/listener for Jesus' teaching and instruction, and the readers and hearers of the story, who are aware of what was said about Jesus in 1:1-13 are specially privileged. They *know* what the people in the story *do not know*.

On arrival at 1:14-15, as Jesus bursts onto the scene with his preaching of the Kingdom, the reader/listener has been informed that

---

6. The identification of this central section of the Gospel of Mark, specifically aimed at the formation of disciples, the followers of Jesus *who are characters in the story* and the followers of Jesus who are *readers of the story*, was first identified by Norman Perrin, "The Christology of Mark: A Study in Methodology," *Journal of Religion* 51 (1971): 173-87.

7. For a more detailed description of the literary design of the Gospel of Mark as a whole, see the essay "Mark 6:6b-30: The Twelve, Mission, and Failure" on pp. 16-20 in this volume. For a recent fine study of Mark 8:27-9:13 as a "turning point" in the Markan narrative that has a "Janus-character," looking both back to what went before, and anticipating which will follow, see Gregg Morrison, *The Turning Point in the Gospel of Mark. A Study in Markan Christology* (Eugene: OR: Pickwick Publications, 2014).

Jesus is the Christ, the Son of God (1:1), the Lord (v. 3), the "stronger one" (v. 7), who baptizes in the Holy Spirit (v. 8). In his baptism at the hands of John the Baptist, signs of a new creation appear in the dove (v. 10), and a voice from heaven announces that Jesus is the beloved Son of God, in whom God is well pleased (v. 11). Now possessed by the Spirit he is driven into the desert, only to be nourished by the angels, in the company of the wilds beasts, as were Adam and Eve before they turned away from obedience to God. In Jesus, God's original creative design for human beings, in intimate relationship with him and the rest of creation, has been restored (vv. 12-13. See Gen 2:18-20; Isa 11:6-9). Armed with this knowledge, the reader/listener enters a narrative that will have many turns, some of them surprising.[8] One of these surprises is the cost of discipleship. Mark 8:14-9:19 is a key passages directing the reader/listener to "learn" what it means to follow Jesus. It reveals the uncompromisingly radical nature of discipleship, and the never-failing presence of Jesus with his fragile disciples.

They had forgotten to bring bread (Mark 8:14-21)

We begin our reflection with Jesus and the disciples crossing the Sea of Galilee in a boat, after the second multiplication of the loaves and fishes, reported in 8:1-9. Several themes emerge in vv. 14-15, indicating that the discussion about bread that follows serves as a conclusion to themes, especially about "eating," that have been running through the narrative for some time (see 6:31-44; 7:1-23, 24-30; 8:1-9). But it also looks forward, to the issue of the disciples' blindness and lack of understanding. The narrator reports that, once in the boat on the lake, the disciples had forgotten to bring bread, and then seems to contradict that statement by immediately affirming that they had one loaf (Greek: ἄρτος = "bread") with them (v. 14). But the backward-looking link with the accounts of the multiplication of the loaves is obvious (6:31-44; 8:1-9). On both occasions there is insufficient food to feed the multitudes, but there were five loaves (6:38) and then seven loaves (8:5). The theme of "bread," present across this section of the narrative (see 6:31-

---

8. For a detailed analysis of Mark 1:1-13, and an explanation of the function of this "prologue" as a key to the reading of the rest of the Gospel, see Francis J. Moloney, *The Gospel of Mark. A Commentary* (Grand Rapids, MI: Baker Academic, 2012), 27-41.

44; 7:1-23, 24-30; 8:1-9), continues into v. 15. Jesus warns the disciples against the "leaven" of the Pharisees and the "leaven" of the Herodians (v. 15).[9] The warning is very severe and recalls Jesus' immediately previous encounter with the Pharisees in 8:11-13. That encounter looks back, in turn, to the hostile encounter Jesus and the Pharisees and the Scribes, reported in 7:1-23. Even there the discussion, initially between the Pharisees and Jesus, and then with Jesus speaking to the crowds and his disciples, was about "eating" (see 7:2, 3, 4, 5, 14-15, 18-19).

The association of the Herodians with the Pharisees in 8:15 adds a note of violence. The Pharisees and the Herodians had earlier decided that Jesus must be slain (3:6), and it was the weak Herod who had bowed to peer-pressure to give Herodias the head of the slain John the Baptist (6:14-29). The disciples, who have been with Jesus throughout all that has been told from 6:6b to this point in the narrative, are warned against the superficiality of the Pharisees, who will not accept who Jesus is and what he is able to do. They are also warned that such an approach to Jesus leads to an association with the deeper agenda of the Pharisees and the Herodians: Jesus' death. But the disciples had begun to stumble as Jesus told the parables (4:1-34), and their superficiality and lack of understanding have increased since then (see 4:35-41; 5:16, 31; 6:7-30, 35-36, 45-52; 7:17-18; 8:4). The disciples have witnessed Jesus' gift of "bread" (6:31-44; 8:1-9) but they are warned, lest they run the danger of falling victim to the "leaven" of the Pharisees and the Herodians (8:15) who were unable to recognize who Jesus is, and were planning to rid themselves of him (3:6). Such warnings are called for at this turning point of Jesus' story. The first passion prediction is looming (8:31).

The disciples do not seem to remember Jesus' multiplication of the loaves and fishes in 6:31-44 and 8:1-9. They discuss among themselves Jesus' saying on the leaven. Unable to make any link with leaven as they are without bread (v. 16), they are ignoring Jesus' warnings about the leaven of the Pharisees and the Herodians. Jesus, aware of the discussion, asks why they show such concern. They should know better, but they do not. He accuses them of lack of perception and understanding, and hardness of heart (v. 17). Earlier in the story the disciples have already shown lack of perception (see 7:18) and under-

---

9. As well as its link with the "bread" theme, there is evidence that the ancients regarded "leaven" as an element of corruption. On this, see among many, Joel Marcus, *Mark*, 2 vols., Anchor Yale Bible 27-27A (New York/New Haven: Doubleday/Yale University Press, 2000-2009), 1:506-507.

standing (see 4:12; 6:52; 7:14). In their hardness of heart they have joined the Pharisees (3:5; 6:52). The use of prophecy to accuse them of blindness and deafness is more subtle, but also recalls an earlier episode in the narrative. Jesus accuses them in the words of Jeremiah (5:21) and Ezekiel (12:2), "Having eyes do you not see, and having ears do you not hear?" (Mark 8:18ab).

This allusion to the disciples' blindness and deafness looks back to Jesus' restoration of hearing and speech to the Gentile man in 7:31-37. Gentiles greeted that healing with an allusion to the Old Testament, in 7:35: "He has done all things well; he even makes the deaf hear and the dumb speak" (see Isa 35:5-6). None of this seems to have made any impression on the disciples, and no such acclamation has accompanied their constant presence with Jesus, no matter what wonders they witness or words they hear. They are not even able to remember the actions of God, done in and through Jesus (v. 18). Two elements in Jesus' accusation are new: blindness and the need to remember. The need to overcome blindness will play a major theological and literary function in the section of the Gospel which follows (8:22-10:52), and the story-teller is writing a story so that disciples of all times and places might "remember."[10]

The fragility of the disciples is laid bare as they are interrogated about immediate past events in the narrative: the multiplication of five loaves of bread for the 5,000 and the twelve baskets that remained (v. 19; see 6:31-44), and the multiplication of seven loaves of bread for the 4,000 and the seven baskets that remained (v. 20; see 8:1-9). This is what they should remember, as they manifest their concerns about the lack of bread in the boat.[11] They are running close to the agenda of

---

10. See the valuable study of Kelly R. Iverson, "Incongruity, Humor and Mark: Performance and the Use of Laughter in the Second Gospel (Mark 8:14-21)," *New Testament Studies* 59 (2013): 2-19. Iverson reconstructs a "performance" of this scene, with its play upon the obtuse (and amusing) misunderstanding of the terms associated with bread. See especially pp. 14-19 where he shows how such an analysis "forces the audience to recognize their fidelity with the Twelve" (p. 17).
11. This interpretation relates vv. 14-21 and the "one bread" of v. 14 with the fact that Jesus has already made much out of very little, and thus provided nourishment in 6:31-44 and 8:1-9. It is not necessary to argue that the "one bread" is the Eucharistic bread for all the nations or even to interpret the "one bread" Christologically: Jesus is sufficient for all their needs As Robert Guelich rightly remarks, with reference to 6:31-44 and 8:1-9: "We have then in 8:14 the ingredients (need, limited resources) for another Feeding miracle" (Robert A. Guelich, *Mark 1-8:26*, Word Biblical Commentary 34a (Dallas, TX: Word Books, 1989], 422).

the Pharisees who argued and tested Jesus in vv. 11-12, unable to see the signs of the kingdom of God in the presence of Jesus. God's reigning presence has been liberally manifested to them in the two bread miracles, and the "fragments" from those feedings are still available to Jew and Gentile (see 6:43; 8:8). But they seem to have no recollection, as they wonder about the lack of bread.[12]

Jesus' stinging question to them, "Do you *not yet* understand?" closes the episode (v. 21). It also closes a long section in the narrative that has never been far from the theme of bread (6:31-8:21). The use of "not yet" glimmers with a hope that there will come a time when they will understand. But read in tandem with the narrator's harsh words to these same disciples after the first bread miracle (see 6:52: "for they did not understand about the loaves but their hearts were hardened"), the question of v. 21 reflects a problem behind the narrative. The bread miracles have contacts with the Eucharistic practice of the Markan community (see 6:41; 8:6). The disciples have been commanded to feed the hungry from their table (6:37) and they were responsible for the distribution in both accounts (6:41; 8:6). The feeding of the multitudes, both Jewish and Gentile, is a task the disciples must perform. The two bread miracles (6:31-44; 8:1-9), each with its subsequent critical encounter between Jesus and the disciples (6:45-52; 8:14-21), are set within Jesus' sending out of the disciples on their mission (6:13-30), Jesus' angry rejection of Israel's ritual table practices (7:1-23), and his subsequent presence among the Gentiles (7:25-37). Feeding and bread were recurrent themes (see 7:2, 3, 4, 5, 15, 18, 19, 27, 28). But the disciples' hearts are hardened (6:52; 8:17) and they do not understand about the bread (6:52; 8:17-18). They would prefer that the people look after themselves (6:35-36; 8:3-4).

Now involved in their Gentile mission, post-resurrection Markan Christians, with this story of Jesus as their guide, wondered about sharing the table with others. Their Jesus-story instructs them that they are to "remember" (v. 18c). They must share in the universal mission of Jesus, cost what it may (see 6:14-19). An important part of that mission was table fellowship, and the closely related Eucharistic fellowship. The community was to provide bread for many different people, Jews and Gentiles, as the bread provided by Jesus was still

---

12. The Greek for "fragments" is κλάσματα. It was the word used in the early Church to refer to the Eucharistic species. See, for example, *Didache* 9:3, 4.

available in the "fragments" gathered after his feeding of Jews (6:31-44) and Gentiles (8:1-9). A story has been told of an original group of disciples who would have preferred to exclude some people from the table. Such an approach to the sharing of the bread provided by Jesus reflects lack of understanding and hardness of heart (6:52; 8:17-18). The problem of table-fellowship in the early Church was understandably widespread (see Acts 10-11; Gal 2:11-21), and the members of the Markan community, who originally read or listened to this story, were not free from such problems. The increasing focus upon the fragile relationship between Jesus and his disciples *in the narrative* addresses disciples *hearing or reading the narrative*. The members of all who are reading or listening to this passage in the Gospel of Mark audience are asked: "Do you not remember? ... Do you not yet understand?" (vv. 18c, 21).

A Blind Man (Mark 8:22-26)

The boat trip concludes as Jesus and the disciples come to Bethsaida, where "some people" lead a blind man to Jesus and beg him to touch him (v. 22). A totally blind man, who cannot walk by himself or speak for himself is presented to Jesus. Much in this account parallels the miracle that closed the first bread cycle, the curing of the Gentile deaf mute reported in 7:31-37. But there are important differences between the two miracles. Jesus responds to the request of v. 22 by gesture and word, *but the cure is not effected* (vv. 23-24), and Jesus must again touch the man, who only then sees clearly (v. 25). The usual Markan command to secrecy closes the episode (v. 26). Both Matthew and Luke, who follow the Markan narrative closely at this point of their stories, omit this episode (see Matt 15:1-16:20; Luke 9:10-36), as it seems to set limits on Jesus' capacity as a miracle worker.

Such a judgment, however, undervalues Markan theological and literary strategies. The brief miracle story of 8:22-26 plays an important literary and theological role in at least two ways:

1. Following an episode during which Jesus accused his disciples of blindness (see v. 18a), the miracle tells of a man who moves from no sight (v. 22), to a limited vision (vv. 23-24) to full sight (v. 25), before being dismissed from the scene (v. 26). The passage looks back to the blindness of the disciples (v. 18) and forward to the

episode which follows, closing the first half of the Gospel, where two of these stages of "sight" will be realized (8:27-30). It also opens the door upon the second half of the Gospel (8:31-15:47), during which the nature of "full sight" will be explained by the teaching and the death of Jesus.

2. The "overlap" between the first and second major sections of the Gospel begins with 8:22-26. As the first half of the story draws to a close, the destiny of both Jesus and the disciples has become central. For the first time the disciples have been described as blind (8:18a) and the three-staged cure of a blind man follows. On arrival at 10:46-52, after a section of narrative devoted to Jesus' journey to Jerusalem, speaking of his oncoming death (8:31; 9:31; 10:32-34) and instructing his disciples on the destiny of anyone who wishes to "follow" Jesus, the reader meets another cure of a blind man, Bartimaeus. Thus, as the literary and theological agenda of 1:14-8:30 draws to a close, to be concluded in Peter's confession and Jesus' warning in 8:29-30, the second half of the Gospel has already begun in 8:22-26. There is a deliberate "framing" of a series of episodes and Jesus' teaching between 8:22-26 and 10:46-52.

With one notable exception, the actions of a traditional miracle worker are provided in considerable detail in v. 23abc. Initially, Jesus takes the man by the hand and leads him out of the village. This movement sets the scene for Jesus' final command to the man in v. 26 not to go back into the village. Once outside, however, the spitting and laying on of hands are *what one would expect* in a curing of a blind man. There is evidence of parallel activities from the ancient world.[13] In answer to Jesus' question concerning his sight (v. 23d), the man regained sight, and reported that he saw human beings, but they looked like walking trees (v. 24). The point of this report is that the man sees, but he does not see properly, an initial response to a curing activity also found in the Hellenistic world. Jesus' initial intervention, using expected miracle working practices, has produced only partial sight. Thus, in a second moment Jesus lays his hands upon the man's

---

13. For example, Tacitus, *Histories* 4.81; Suetonius, *Vespasian* 7.2-3, and Dio Cassius 66.8, all report Vespasian's healing of a blind man in Alexandria in this way. See further information in Moloney, *Mark*, 164 n. 240.

eyes. The spitting ritual has been omitted. This action results in an intense gaze from the man, total cure, and fullness of vision (v. 25). The man has made a journey from "no sight" (v. 22) to "partial sight" (v. 24) to "full sight" (v. 25). He can be dismissed from the story, but prohibited from going back into the town, lest false messianic expectations be aroused. The Markan defense of Jesus' messianic identity is now urgent, as the story-teller draws to the close of a section that consistently raises the question of Jesus' identity. Throughout 1:14-8:21 many wonder about Jesus' identity (1:27, 45; 2:12; 3:22; 4:41; 5:20; 6:2-3, 48-50; 7:37). That mystery will shortly be partially resolved in Peter's confession in 8:29, and finally resolved on the cross (see 15:39). The climax must not be anticipated, and thus the man disappears from the scene entirely (v. 26).[14]

Jesus' accusation of the disciples in v. 18a leads into this miracle story. The reader has followed the increasing blindness of the disciples. They have moved from their initial unconditional response to Jesus' call (see 1:16-20; 3:13-19) into lack of understanding (4:10, 13, 23; 5:16, 31; 6:7-30, 37; 8:4), unbelief (4:40-41), hardness of heart (6:52), and a dangerous closeness to the leaven of the Pharisees and the Herodians (8:11-21). Jesus' accusations in 8:17-21 are well-grounded! But in 8:21 he asked whether they did "not yet" understand. There is hope that they may still move from the blindness of their unfaith into true sight. The miracle story of 8:22-26 is a paradigm of that possibility. It plays an important literary function in setting the agenda for the rest of the Gospel, and continues to ask questions to readers and disciples of all times.

The Confession at Caesarea Philippi (Mark 8:27-30)

Jesus' journey with his disciples from Bethsaida to the region of Caesarea Philippi is geographically possible (v. 27a), but the main point that Mark wishes to make as he introduces this episode is that "on

---

14. These few brief words respond to the problem of the so-called "messianic secret." Jesus of Nazareth was careful about the emergence of false messianic hopes. The Gospel of Mark turns that memory into a theme across the Gospel, holding back any explicit confession of Jesus as Messiah and Son of God until he suffers and dies (see 14:61-62; 15:26-32, 39). But in terms of what characters in the story actually do and say, as has often been said, the so-called Markan "messianic secret" is the worst-kept secret of all time.

the way" (v. 27b) Jesus interrogates his disciples. Jesus and his disciples are still in the northern reaches of Palestine. But a theme of "the way" has been introduced. A journey has begun. It leads from Caesarea Philippi, via the mount of transfiguration, back to Galilee (9:30). From Capernaum (9:33) he travels through Judea and the Transjordan (10:1), to Jericho and from there to Jerusalem. Jesus and his disciples' being on "the way" will be mentioned regularly in the second half of the Gospel (see 10:17, 46, 52; 11:8; 12:14), especially in association with the three passion predictions (see 8:27; 9:33, 34; 10:32). As he begins this journey Jesus asks the question which has been lurking behind the narrative since 1:14. The reader, having read the prologue of 1:1-13, knows who Jesus is, but characters in the story do not. To them Jesus poses the question: "Who do people say that I am?" (v. 27c).

The staged movement from blindness to sight, recorded in the miracle story of vv. 22-26, immediately after Jesus' accusation that the disciples were blind (v. 18), is partially repeated in the response of, first the disciples (v. 28), and then Peter (v. 29).[15] The disciples' description of the opinion of many highlights Jesus' prophetic charism, with possible hints of his being the expected precursor of the messianic era. Some say that he is John the Baptist, others Elijah, and yet others one of the prophets (v. 28). Herod has already suggested that Jesus was John the Baptist *redivivus* (6:16), and the reader is aware that the disciples report accurately what has already been said about Jesus in 6:15: "It is Elijah. ... It is a prophet, like one of the prophets of old." For Christian readers, John the Baptist was also Jesus' precursor (1:2-3, 7-8). There was Jewish speculation that Elijah would return to bring in the messianic era (see Mal 4:5) as also that Isaiah and Jeremiah (see 2 Esdras 2:18) or an eschatological Mosaic prophet might usher in the eschatological age (see Deut 18:18). Whether people are suggesting that Jesus is another prophetic figure, or even giving him the dignity of the expected messianic precursor, the reader knows that, in the light of 1:1-13, they are wrong. *This understanding of Jesus matches the complete blindness of the man in 8:22.*

---

15. The parallels between vv. 22-26 and vv. 27-30 were highlighted by Robert H. Lightfoot, *History and Interpretation in the Gospels*, The Bampton Lectures 1934 (London: Hodder and Stoughton, 1935), 90-91, and have been accepted, with variations, by many scholars since then.

Jesus turns to the disciples, and asks his fragile followers who they think he might be. Despite their failures, they are the ones to whom the secret of the Kingdom has been given (4:11), and it is as specially privileged "insiders" that Jesus asks them the question. Peter, speaking in their name, replies: "You are the Christ" (v. 29). There is a sense in which this confession of faith is correct. Jesus was called "the Christ" in 1:1, but more was said of Jesus in the prologue (1:1-13). Especially important were the words from heaven: "This is my beloved Son, in whom I am well pleased" (v. 11). The story has already indicated that the mystery of Jesus' messiahship will involve suffering and death (see 2:20; 3:6), and for that reason the narrator closes the first half of the Gospel by reporting that Jesus "warned them severely to tell no one about him" (v. 30).[16] Jesus' warning to the disciples, who have come to a partial understanding of who Jesus is in v. 29, is not a negation of their confession. It is a warning that it is not the whole truth, and thus must not become the basis of their proclamation. *It thus matches the second stage of the blind man's journey, when he saw once again, but did not see properly (see vv. 23-24).* As Jesus' initial laying on of hands and spitting applied traditional healing medical methods, but only produced partial sight, so also Peter's confession of Jesus as "the Messiah" is an acceptance of a culturally, religiously and historically conditioned meaning of that expression.[17] The disciples' confession, subsequent to Jesus' accusing them of blindness in v. 18, indicates that they are capable of arriving at a stage of partial sight: partial and imperfect belief. While we may not be sure of the precise contours of messianic expectation in the First Century, later elements in the narrative make it clear that the disciples wish to follow a figure on his way to Jerusalem in glory, surrounded by powerful people on his right and his left (see 9:34; 10:37).

---

16. The Greek verb (ἐπιτιμάω) carries a strong sense of "rebuke," and is surprisingly powerful in this context. It has been used in 1:25 and 3:12 to silence unclean spirits.
17. There is little agreement on what first century messianic hopes might have been. There is almost universal agreement that there was no *uniform* messianic expectation. For an indication of the discussions, see James H. Charlesworth, *The Messiah. Developments in Early Judaism and Christianity*, The First Princeton Symposium on Judaism and Chistian Origins (Minneapolis: Fortress, 1992). See also the briefer, but excellent study of Paula Fredriksen, *From Jesus to Christ. The Origins of the New Testament Images of Jesus*, 2nd ed. (New Haven: Yale University Press, 2000).

Peter is correct when he confesses, in the name of the disciples, that Jesus is the Christ (see 1:1). But, like the blind man (see vv. 23-24), he is only partially correct; his eyes are not fully open to the truth about Jesus. There is a deeper mystery to the messianic status of Jesus of Nazareth, whom the disciples are following. They are yet to come to full sight, matching the final experience of the blind man, seeing everything clearly (v. 25). After commanding them to silence, he immediately broaches that deeper mystery, announcing in the first prediction of his forthcoming passion, that the Messiah is the Son of Man who must go up to Jerusalem to be slain and to rise from the dead (v. 31). These words open the second major section of the Gospel of Mark, dedicated to the story of the crucified Christ and Son of God, the suffering and finally vindicated Son of Man. The confession at Caesarea Philippi begins the disciples' further response to the paradigm of a movement from blindness to full sight. Peter's confession, followed by Jesus' warning (vv. 29-30), shows that they have arrived at partial sight. Their difficulty is understandable. They have not read the Prologue (1:1-13), and have witnessed the ominous increase of tension between Jesus and the leaders of Israel (see 2:1-3:6; 7:1-23; 8:11-13, 15). The slaying of John the Baptist (6:14-29) adds to the atmosphere of impending violence and Jesus has warned that the day will come when he will no longer be with them (2:20). The remaining half of the Gospel will indicate that true faith and fullness of sight are possible when one accepts that Jesus is Messiah and Son of God (see 1:1, 11; 8:29; 9:7), the Son of Man who must suffer, die and rise in Jerusalem (see 8:31; 9:31; 10:32-34). The stage is set for the reading of 8:31-15:47 where this presentation of Jesus unfolds, along with the story of the disciples' struggles to come to fullness of sight.[18]

---

18. Beyond the possibilities of this paper, it is important to be aware that the disciples all fail, abandoning Jesus in fear in 14:50. They never again appear as a group in the story. However, they are promised restoration at the empty tomb, especially in the words of the young man, telling them to go to Galilee, where they will see Jesus (16:7), words which repeat the promise of Jesus to his fragile disciples at the Last Supper (14:28). Jesus never fails the failing disciples. See Moloney, *Mark*, 339-54, especially pp. 349-54. See also the essay "God's Gift of Servant Discipleship in the Gospel of Mark" on pp. 131-46 in this volume, and Francis J. Moloney, *Mark: Storyteller, Interpreter, Evangelist* (Peabody, MA: Hendrickson, 2004), 159-81.

The Way of the Son of Man: the Cross (Mark 8:31 - 9:29)

The paradigm of the three-staged journey from blindness to full sight (8:22-26) has led to a presentation of the blindness of "the people." They saw Jesus as a prophet and perhaps the one who was to usher in the messianic era (vv. 27-28). Better than this, but still only partial sight, the disciples confessed that Jesus was "the Christ" (v. 29). The limited nature of this confession leads Jesus to charge them to tell no one about him (v. 30). This warning links the conclusion of the first part of a narrative (1:14-8:30) with the second (8:31-15:47). Mark 8:22-30 has both provided a response to the question of the identity of Jesus (v. 29), and introduced the second half of the story: if Jesus' warning about Peter's messianic confession indicates that it reflects only partial sight, what more is required?

The passion prediction (8:31)

In 8:31-15:47 Jesus, the Christ, Son of God and vindicated Son of Man will be made known to the reader, by word and deed. Mark immediately introduces the first passion prediction: "And he began to teach them that the Son of man must suffer many things, and be rejected by the elders and the chief priests and the scribes, and be killed, and after three days rise again. *And he said this plainly*" (8:31-32a). For the first time in the Gospel, Jesus speaks clearly of who he is, the Son of Man, and he describes the destiny of the Son of Man: suffering, rejection, killed and risen. The use of "must" (Greek: δεῖ = "the Son of Man *must* ...) indicates that the future suffering, dying and rising of the Son of Man will not fall upon him as some inevitable and unavoidable tragedy; it forms part of God's design for Jesus, the Christ, the Son of Man. In a deliberate contrast to v. 30, where the disciples were severely warned against speaking about Jesus as "the Christ," Jesus proclaims his message on the Son of Man for the first time: "and he said this openly" (v. 32a). Jesus is not a powerful, royal Messiah (v. 29). Such an understanding of Jesus is not to be spread abroad (v. 30). His messiahship is to be found in his future as the Son of Man. That future will involve rejection, suffering, death and resurrection after three days (v. 31). *This is true sight, a fullness of vision. Such fundamental truth must not be hidden; it must be openly proclaimed.* The reader is led further into the mystery, as Jesus tells of his forthcoming death, and ultimate victory through resurrection, revealing himself, slain and raised, as the Son of Man. To be a disciple of Jesus means to join him in this experience.

The Disciples' failure (8:32-33)

Peter, in the name of the disciples, vigorously opposes Jesus' first self-revelation. He was ready to confess that Jesus was the Messiah (v. 29), but talk of death and resurrection was not a part of his scheme. Thus Peter "took hold" of Jesus and began to rebuke him (v. 32bc). The roles of master and disciple, clearly established in 1:16-20; 2:13-14 and 3:13-19, have been reversed. Peter the disciple, rather than accept the warning of Jesus in v. 30, attempts to impose a messianic expectation that has no place for suffering and death upon Jesus. The physical "taking hold" and the reversal of who should warn whom (see vv. 30, 32) indicate that Peter fails to accept Jesus' self-revelation as the Son of Man (v. 31).

Jesus' reaction does not focus only upon Peter: "Turning and *seeing his disciples*" (v. 33a). Peter has spoken in v. 29, and acted in v. 32, in the name of the disciples. Jesus' words to Peter are directed to all the disciples. Using a Greek word which has its background in Aramaic, right order is established as Jesus rebukes Peter (v. 33b), addressing him as "Satan." The master is once again determining the narrative, and the expression "Satan," while primarily linking Peter with the designs of Satan, briefly described in 1:12-13, also carries with it the meaning of "stumbling block" (see Matt 16:23, where Simon Peter is called "Satan" and "stumbling block"). Jesus and the disciples are "on the way" (see v. 27), but Peter is blocking that way, holding Jesus back, and rejecting Jesus' acceptance of God's plan. The vocation of the disciples is recalled as Peter, and all the disciples, are told that they must take their correct place: "get behind me" (v. 33b. See 1:16-20; 2:13-14). There is a blend of angry reproof in the use of "Satan" and a command that disciples keep their place "behind" Jesus, and not block his path to Jerusalem with their all-too-human understanding. The spatial and the theological are involved in Jesus' indication to Peter (and the disciples) that they are not on the side of God, but on the side of human beings (v. 33c). Standing in Jesus' way, blocking his journey, continues the idea of Peter's being a "stumbling block," out of his correct place "behind" Jesus. However, Jesus' journey is not mere geography. It is a response to the design of God. Thus, their being "out of place" also means that they are opposing God's design. The rejection of Jesus' prophecy of his oncoming suffering and death as Son of Man is a rejection of God's plan for the Messiah (v. 29 and v. 31).

Jesus instructs the failing disciples: the cross (Mark 8:34-9:1)

The discourse that follows in 8:34-9:1 is made up of formal instruction. The author opens the possibility of discipleship to others, beyond the group that has come to be identified as such in the narrative thus far. Jesus' calling the multitude, as well as the disciples (v. 34a) addresses the readers and listeners of all times. *Anyone* who wishes to be a follower of Jesus (v. 34b) is addressed by the words that follow. The disciples *in the story* and the readers *of the story* hear the words of Jesus.[19] Typical didactic forms pile on top of one another: "anyone who .." (v. 34), "whoever …"(v. 35a), "whoever …" (v. 35b), rhetorical questions (vv. 36-37), "whoever …" (v. 38). In 9:1 the teaching comes to a climax.

Based upon the predicted experience of the Son of Man (v. 31), a disciple is called to renounce himself, take up his cross, lose his life for Jesus and the gospel (vv. 34b-35), never to be ashamed of Jesus and his words (v. 38). As Jesus rejects the expected messianic glory and embraces the destiny of the suffering Son of Man, so must the disciple. Jesus' coming and the gospel are closely associated (see 1:14-15). *The disciple must be prepared to give all for Jesus and the gospel.* Life itself is at stake. One can have all the glory of this world (see v. 29), but lose one's life (v. 36), for which there is no substitute (v. 37). Jesus' call to discipleship is paradoxically a call to self-gift unto death and a summons to life. Crucial to this paradox is the identity between Jesus and the suffering Son of Man vindicated in resurrection (v. 31). The vindicated suffering and dying Son of Man will come "in the glory of his Father with the holy angels" at the end of time (v. 38). Rejection of the way of the Son of Man, Jesus and his words by

---

19. The portrait of the disciples in the Gospel of Mark is written for "anyone who wishes to come after" Jesus. See Elizabeth Struthers Malbon, "Disciples/Crowds/Whoever. Markan Characters and the Readers," in *In the Company of Jesus. Characters in Mark's Gospel* (Louisville, KY: Westminster/John Knox, 2000), 70-99.

"this adulterous and wicked generation," will lead to rejection when the same Son of Man comes in glory (v. 38). The Son of Man will exercise his authority.

For the first time in the narrative, some light is shone upon the puzzle of Jesus' use of "the Son of Man" in 2:10 to declare his authority to forgive sin, and his use of the same term to declare his authority over the Sabbath in 2:28. The appearance of the expression "the Son of Man," used by Jesus to affirm his authority in two conflicts with those who reject him, and ultimately seek his death (see 3:6), has created "a gap" in the narrative. It cannot be explained within its immediate context, but the reader waits until the author provides further information – later in the story - which may explain why Jesus, the Son of Man, has authority over sin and over the Sabbath. The promise of his future coming in power with the angels in the glory of his Father, to exercise his authority in the rejection of those who were ashamed of Jesus and the gospel, goes a large part of the way. Yet the promise of 8:38 still requires fulfillment. The reader/listener waits for the remaining parts of the narrative for further information on the authority of the Son of Man (see especially 14:61-62).

This first section dedicated to Jesus' instruction of his failing disciples closes with an enigmatic saying that may have had a long and complicated history in the tradition. It is open to a number of interpretations, but must be understood in the light of v. 31d: "and after three days rise again." There is solemnity in Jesus' opening words, "Amen, I say to you," indicating to the reader that something climactic is about to be said, after having asked for commitment to the cross, self-loss, the word of Jesus and the gospel (vv. 34-38). He promises the gathering of disciples and the crowd that some of them will not die before they see the kingdom of God come with power (9:1).

The future of Jesus, Messiah and Son of Man (8:29, 31), is fundamental to the future of the disciple who takes up the cross, lays down his life, and is not ashamed of Jesus. Jesus has told the disciples that he will be slain, "and after three days rise again" (v. 31). This is what the "some who are standing here" will experience. The crucified yet risen Christ will be the guarantee of the truth of Jesus' teaching. The Son of Man will be slain, but his loss of self in death will be vindicated in resurrection. There are some standing there hearing Jesus' words who will experience the apparent failure of the crucifixion, overcome by God's power in the resurrection. The resurrection of Jesus will be the kingdom of God coming in power. This will be true sight: an acceptance of a discipleship which responds to the teaching of Jesus in 8:34-38 (cross, loss of self, and ultimate vindication), empowered by the presence of the risen Jesus, the kingdom of God come in power. As the story-teller looks back upon the world within the text, he singles out this privilege for "some who are standing here" in the time of the narrative. However long past it may have been, the Markan community and its Gospel, along with all subsequent Christian communities who possess that Gospel as the Word of God, exist because of the experience of some who were standing there (9:1). They have experienced the paschal event, the transformation of suffering into power. It can only be "some" because, as has already been indicated to the reader/listener, Judas will have abandoned and betrayed Jesus by that stage of the story (see 3:19). The witness of these foundational disciples lies behind the Markan narrative and lives on in the Christian Church, and in all Christian communities, as a saving Word of God.

The transfiguration as instruction: glory through death and resurrection (Mark 9:2-13)

Six days separate the initial teaching of all who would be disciples of Jesus (8:34-9:1) and Jesus' taking the "inner circle" of the Twelve, Peter, James and John (see 3:16-17), on to a high mountain where they could be by themselves. The "after six days" may be an indication that the event about to be reported took place on the seventh day, and would thus have a sense of fulfillment. It also recalls Exodus 24:16, where Moses, accompanied by Joshua, spent six days on the mountain until, on the seventh day, Yhwh called to him from the cloud. It also creates a temporal link between 7:2-13 and the preceding 8:27-9:1. The location on the mountain marks what follows as akin to a theophany. In the Bible, mountains are regularly the places where the divine and the human touch. Mark reports "he was transfigured before them." The self-contained narrative of 9:2-8 was shaped by the story-teller and inserted into this place in the narrative to continue the double-pronged message being developed here: the significance of Jesus' relationship to God (vv. 1-4, 7) and the fragility of the disciples (6-5, 8).²⁰ The aftermath (vv. 9-13) continues these themes. Jesus further informs the privileged disciples about his resurrection and his relationship to Elijah (vv. 9, 12-13), but they are not able to understand this information (vv. 10-11).

An important narrative strategy is at work here. The reader/listener is aware of Jesus' relationship to God, as this has been made clear in the prologue (see especially 1:1-3, 9-11), but none of the *characters in the story* have been given this information. It is revealed to Peter, James and John on the mountain. In a parallel fashion, the reader is also aware of Jesus' relationship to the Elijah figure of John the Baptist from the prologue (see 1:4-8), but only as Jesus and the disciples come down from the mountain is this relationship made known to *characters in the story*. The reader follows the response of the disciples, armed with the knowledge provided by the authoritative voices of God (1:2-3) and the narrator (1:1, 4-13). How will the disciples respond to this crucial information?²¹

The description of Jesus' transformation uses language associated with the appearance of heavenly beings: the impression of a bright and intense whiteness (v. 3a. See Dan 7:9), beyond anything that could be generated by human hands (v. 3b). What is most surprising about the scene, however, is the introduction of Elijah with Moses, talking to Jesus (v. 4), especially the naming of Elijah before Moses. Traditionally, these two figures have been explained as representatives of the Law (Moses) and the Prophets (Elijah). But the two figures are introduced in the reverse order. Also, if reference to the Law and the Prophets were intended, there was no need to go

---

20. The narrative of the transfiguration existed before the Gospel of Mark, but it has been notoriously difficult to discover a *Sitz im Leben* for the development of the account. But, as Morna D. Hooker, *The Gospel according to St Mark*, Black's New Testament Commentary (London: A. & C. Black, 1991), 214, remarks: "In his (Mark's) God-filled universe, a heavenly confirmation of Jesus' identity would have seemed no more out of place than the acknowledgement of his identity by the unclean spirits." See also the fine study of Dorothy A. Lee, *Transfiguration*, New Century Theology (London/New York: Continuum, 2004), 1-37.
21. Every detail of the story insists upon its instruction of the disciples: he was transfigured *before them* (v. 2), there appeared *to them* Elijah with Moses (v. 4), the cloud overshadowed *them* (v. 7a), *you* listen to my beloved Son (v. 7b); only Jesus was *with them* (v. 8). "The whole event, from first to last, takes place solely for the sake of the three disciples" (Robert H. Lightfoot, *The Gospel Message of St Mark* [Oxford: Clarendon Press, 1950], 44).

beyond Moses, regarded by Jewish tradition to be the first and the greatest of all the prophets (see Deut 18:15-18), as well as the figure who mediated God's gift of the Law. There are probably two elements involved. In the first place, both Elijah and Moses were figures who had experienced theophanies on a mountain (see Exod 19:16-25; 1 Kings 19:11-18) and more importantly, both were celebrated in Jewish tradition as having been transported into heaven. This is clear for Elijah in 2 Kings 3:9-12, and subsequent Jewish reflection (see Sir 48:9; 1 Macc 2:38; *1 Enoch* 89:52; 93:8; Josephus, *Jewish Antiquities* 9.28). Even though Moses' death is recorded, the place of his burial is unknown (Deut 34:5-8), and subsequent tradition associated Moses with exaltation to heavenly glory (see Josephus, *Jewish Antiquities* 3.5.7; 4.8.48; Philo, *Life of Moses* 2.288, 291-292).

Once this link is made, then the conversation between Jesus, Elijah and Moses is to be linked to Jesus' words in 8:38. Like Elijah and Moses, Jesus will be transported to heaven, and thus take his place as the Son of Man, in the glory of his Father and the holy angels (8:38). The scene, therefore, is an anticipation of the glorification of Jesus that must take place by means of his suffering, death and resurrection into glory (see 8:31). However, it is Elijah who is named first because he has been so important in the surrounding narrative. In 8:28 the disciples reported that some people regarded Jesus as Elijah, and in the scene which immediately follows, as Jesus descends the mountain with Peter, James and John, it is again the figure of Elijah who is discussed (9:11-13). The close association of "what is written" of Elijah, and the slaying of John the Baptist (6:14-29) as an anticipation of what will be done to the Son of Man, determines his position before Moses at the transfiguration. As with the Jesus' teaching in 8:34-9:1, it is the Christology of the passion prediction in 8:31 which determines the meaning of Jesus' further dealings with the disciples.

But the disciples fail. Once more speaking in the name of the other disciples, Peter, addressing Jesus as "Rabbi," suggests that the theophanic experience be held in perpetuity (v. 5). The setting up of three booths to make a permanent shrine of the transfigured Jesus, along with his heavenly companions, is a further flagrant rejection of Jesus' words on his destiny as the Son of Man (8:31) and his invitation to all who would be his disciples to share in that destiny (8:34-9:1). The narrator's comment for the reader makes it clear that such is the case. He was ignorant, and he was frightened (v. 6). These two qualities have already been part of the disciples' response to Jesus. As we have seen in our reflection on 8:14-21, their ignorance was the subject of Jesus' harsh words to them in 8:17-18, and it will not disappear as they journey with Jesus to Jerusalem. This is not the first time that the disciples have experienced fear. On two earlier occasions it was a prelude to the disciples' lack of faith (see 4:41; 6:50), and the expression will return regularly across the second half of the story, until its final dramatic occurrence as the Gospel's second last word (see 16:8: "for they were frightened." Greek: ἐφοβοῦντο γάρ). Privileged yet failing disciples are wrapped in a cloud, which recalls the experience of God's intervention into the life of Israel at Sinai, a theme which returns regularly to speak of God's presence to the people (see, for example, Exod 13:21-22; 24:16; 33:7-11; 34:5; 40:34-35; Ezek 1:28; 11:23). From the cloud comes a voice which repeats for the disciples what had previously been made known only to the reader: "This is my beloved son" (v. 7b. See 1:11). While the word from heaven in 1:11 looked back to Psalm 2:7 and Genesis 22:2, 12, 16, to speak of God's pleasure in his Son, here the words are aimed at the disciples. They are instructed: "Listen to him" (v. 7b). They must listen to the word of the beloved son. The words of God to Israel in Deuteronomy 18:15, 18 come to mind: "The Lord your God will raise up for you a prophet … him you shall heed."

Disciples have confessed that Jesus is the Messiah (8:29), but the opening moments of the mystery of the Son of Man have been marked by Jesus' prediction of his suffering and death (8:31). He has asked all who would follow him to share this destiny (8:34-9:1). The disciples have resisted this invitation (8:29, 32-33; 9:5-6). Who has the authority to make such demands? Three of them now have the response to that question from the most authoritative voice in the Gospel: the voice of God tells them that they have gathered around the Son of God and that they must listen to him. Imperceptibly, the major Christological categories of the Gospel of Mark have been introduced across the center of the Markan narrative: Messiah (8:29), Son of Man (8:31), and Son of God (9:7). It appears that Jesus' sonship is the interpretative key for understanding the messianic Son of Man. The reader has now heard the voice of God twice announce the sonship of Jesus (1:11; 9:7), *but this is the first time God has spoken such authoritative revelatory words to characters in the story.* However troublesome the words of Jesus have become, and however difficult his demands will become as he leads them to Jerusalem, the disciples must listen to him, Christ (8:29), Son of Man (8:31) and Son of God (9:7). The same collection of Christological titles will appear, ironically, as Jesus goes to his death (see 14:61-62; 15:31-39).

For the moment, however, there is more of the story to tell, and the situation is transformed as the disciples look around confusedly. The only person they now see is Jesus, without the trappings of glory (v. 8). There is no sign that the disciples have overcome the partial sight expressed by Peter in 8:29, and further indicated by their unwillingness to accept Jesus' agenda in 8:32-33, and God's agenda in 9:5-6. Yet, they are not abandoned. The authoritative word of God has assured them that they are followers of his beloved Son, and are to listen to him. The reader/listener wonders: will they?

As in earlier situations in the Gospel, Jesus instructs the chosen but confused and failing disciples (vv. 9-13. See 4:10-25; 7:17-23; 8:14-21). They are not to speak of their experience of the Son of Man coming in the glory of his Father with the angels (9:2-4. See 8:38) until Jesus, the Son of Man has crossed the essential threshold of the cross and the resurrection. Both elements are involved in the narrator's report of Jesus' words: "until the Son of Man should have risen from the dead" (v. 9). There will be no resurrection without violent death, and the return in glory, prefigured in the transfiguration is fundamentally dependent upon the fulfillment of the passion prediction of 8:31. For once, it appears that this command is obeyed, and they keep the matter to themselves, but they wonder what rising from the dead might mean. The categories of 8:31, repeated in various ways in Jesus' teaching (8:34-9:1) and the transfiguration (9:1-8), continue to puzzle the disciples. The idea that the proximate death of Jesus, the Son of Man, would be overcome by a resurrection from the dead is beyond them. They will not "listen" to the voice of the beloved Son (see v. 7), as they attempt to puzzle things out in their ongoing ignorance. They do, however, have something of an answer in the tradition of the scribes that Elijah must first come (v. 11). The Jewish tradition, already reflected in the juxta-positioning of Malachi 3:1-2 and 4:5-6, that Elijah would return to introduce the messianic era is something they would like to investigate further. Is this the meaning of "rising from the dead"? It might be, but their puzzlement seems to be with the notion of the resurrection of the Son of Man (8:31; 9:9). What is the relationship between the Son of Man and Elijah?

They have much to learn, but Jesus does not abandon his disciples as they flail about in their ignorance. The hint of the possible identification of John the Baptist and Elijah, provided for the reader in 1:4-6, is now clarified. It is true that Elijah comes before the messianic era to restore all things, but there is a twist to the story. The problem that must now be faced and resolved is that the Messiah (8:29) is also the suffering and dying Son of Man (8:31). It is "written" that the Son of Man "should suffer many things and be treated with contempt" (v. 12). This claim looks to Daniel 7:13. "The holy ones of the Most High," whose experience is described in Dan 7:15-27, is one of suffering, rejection and death as they remained faithful to the God of Israel under Antiochus IV. The "one like a son of man" in 7:13 is the personification of these "holy ones." When Jesus takes over that expression, and speaks of himself as "the Son of Man," he indicates – to himself and to his listeners – that he must also undergo, persecution, suffering and death. It has been written in the vision of Daniel 7 that the Son of Man should suffer.[22] And the forerunner, Elijah, who has come in the person of John the Baptist (see 1:4-6), puts everything in order.

This description of the role of John the Baptist as the Elijah *redivivus* is obscure, but its explanation is that there *first* had to be the Baptist and his experience, and *then* the Son of Man. By means of this sequence everything is "put in order." The order referred to is the order of God's design. John the Baptist has accomplished his mission successfully, even though, as the reader is aware, they have done to him whatever they pleased (see 6:14-29). The forerunner, Elijah-John the Baptist, and the Messiah-Son of Man, Jesus, must undergo suffering. The Elijah-like figure is a forerunner of the Son of Man in every way. What was written has already taken place in the experience of the Elijah *redivivus* (see 6:14-29), and is yet to take place in the experience of the Son of Man (v. 13. See 8:31). The Son of Man coming in the glory of his Father and with the holy angels (9:2-8. See 8:38) will make sense only in the light of his prior death and resurrection (vv. 9-13). Subsequent to the wonder of the transfiguration, Jesus has led the thoughts of Peter, James and John back to the message which has begun (see 8:31-9:1) and will continue to dominate 8:31-15:47: there can be no glory without the cross.

---

22. Not all would agree with this link between the Son of Man as a vindicated suffering figure, in both Daniel 7 and the Gospel of Mark. For the discussion, and a presentation of the above position, see Francis J. Moloney, "Constructing *Jesus* and the Son of Man," *The Catholic Biblical Quarterly* 75 (2013): 719-38.

The epileptic boy: instruction on the need for God (9:14-29)

A close temporal link is maintained between the transfiguration (v. 2: "and after six days"), the discussion between Jesus and the three disciples (v. 9: "and as they were coming down the mountain"), and their subsequent rejoining the other disciples (v. 14: "and when they came to the disciples"). The account that follows was originally a miracle story, but it has been transformed into instruction for the disciples.[23] The traditional description of the ailment (vv. 17-18, 20-22a), Jesus' rebuke of the unclean spirit (v. 25), the cure (vv. 26ab-27) and the response of the crowd (v. 26c), provide the basic account. Elements directed at the disciples have been inserted into the traditional cure: the gathering of the disciples, the crowd and the questioning scribes (vv. 14-16), the inability of the disciples to effect a cure (vv. 18c-19) and Jesus' explanation of why they failed (vv. 28-29). This "mixed form" of healing and teaching provides a conclusion to a series of encounters between Jesus and his fragile disciples (8:32-9:29) that have followed the first passion prediction (8:31) in which they have shown that they have not progressed beyond "partial sight" (see 8:24).

In vv. 14-15 the crowd acts as an intermediary. Disciples and scribes are arguing as Jesus, Peter, James and John approach them. The "great crowd" (ὄχλον πολύν) initially gathered around the argument between the disciples and the scribes (v. 1), are "greatly amazed" (ἐξεθαμβήσαν) and they run from the argument toward Jesus (προστρέχοντες ἠσπάζοντο αὐτόν). The highly charged language, already hinting at unresolved frustration, sets the scene for Jesus' asking what was being discussed. This allows one of the crowd to provide the initial material required for the miracle story: the description of his son's ailment (vv. 16-18ab). Addressing Jesus as "Teacher" (v. 17b), the unnamed member of the crowd describes an illness that resembles what modern society would call epilepsy: seizures, falling, foaming at the mouth and grinding of the teeth (v. 18ab). But he regards the illness as possession by a dumb spirit (v. 17c). His initial desire was to bring the sick boy to Jesus (v. 17b), but in the absence

---

23. The passage has a number of odd features. Most likely, it has been the Markan rewriting of a traditional miracle story to insert it into his unfolding presentation of the relationship between Jesus and the disciples which has created the oddities. See the summary, coming to this conclusion, in Meier, *A Marginal Jew*, 2:653-56.

of Jesus, he asked the disciples to cast out the spirit, but they were not able to do so (v. 18c).

The reference to the disciples' inability to effect a cure leads to Jesus' harsh words which are directed to the disciples (v. 19). He has earlier addressed the Pharisees as "this generation" (8:12) and further described the world hostile to him and his disciples as an "adulterous and sinful generation" (8:38). The danger that the disciples might draw close to this generation (see 8:15) is becoming a reality. It is their lack of faith which frustrates, and leads Jesus to wonder just how much more time he must spend with them in their increasing failure. This is an important question and it remains with the reader/listener as the narrative proceeds further. As failure increases, one might expect Jesus to declare, "enough." *But this never happens.* Although expressed in different words, Jesus called the Twelve to be "with him" in 3:14-15, to share his life and ministry. The same idea is present here, but stated from Jesus' side of the relationship. The brief expression of anger and frustration, which prepares for Jesus' response to the disciples in v. 29, does not lead to Jesus' abandoning the disciples. Nor does it influence his decision to help the member of the crowd (v. 19c). Both the rhetorical question of v. 19 and the action that follows in vv. 20-27 serve as *instruction for failing disciples*.

The boy is led to him and the initial conflict between Jesus and the demon takes place (v. 20. See 1:24; 5:7-10). There is a brief interlude, breaking into the rhythm of the traditional miracle story, as Jesus asks how long the boy has had this condition, and is informed that he has been like this since childhood (v. 21). This interlude enables the second description of the ailment in v. 22a. The repetition (see vv. 17, 18ab) serves as an introduction to the man's earnest initial statement of faith: "If you can do anything, have pity on us and help us" (v. 22b). The theme of faith, already raised as Jesus scolded the unfaith of the disciples who could not cure the boy (vv. 14, 18, 19), returns. There can be no question of Jesus' capacity to have pity and help, as all things are possible for the one who believes. There is a double meaning to this famous expression.[24] The context demands that "the one who believes" is, in the first place, Jesus. He has been asked to

---

24. See Christopher D. Marshall, *Faith as a Theme in Mark's Narrative*, Society for New Testament Studies Monograph Series 64 (Cambridge: Cambridge University Press, 1989), 118-20.

help, if he can (v. 22b), and as one who believes, Jesus responds to the man's hopes. His immediacy with God is the source of his miraculous authority. But the believing subject quickly becomes the father. The disciples, who have become increasingly arrogant in their self-understanding (see 6:7-30; 8:32-33), have not been able to work this cure, despite Jesus' earlier promises (3:14-15) and their initial successes (see 6:13, 30). In contrast to the arrogance of the disciples, the man proclaims his belief … and his littleness of belief (v. 24b). The example of the Syrophoenician woman (7:24-30) is recalled. She was prepared to admit that she brought nothing to her request of Jesus, except her belief that the dogs might be fed by the crumbs from the table (see 7:26-28). This is a fundamental issue in the Markan understanding of faith, and an explanation for the ongoing failure of the disciples. They are beginning to impose their designs upon Jesus (see especially 8:32), and regard discipleship as something they can determine (see 6:7-30). For this they are regarded as a "faithless generation," not prepared to admit their failure (see v. 19). The father of the possessed boy recognizes his lack of faith, and crying out, asks Jesus to help him in failure. The author exploits this gap between the lack of faith of the disciples (v. 19) and the faith of the man from the crowd (v. 24). There is no sign that the disciples turn to Jesus in their need.

The man from the crowd has turned to Jesus in nothingness and, as with the Syrophoenician woman (see 7:29-30), Jesus effects the cure of his son (vv. 25-27). Much of the traditional story is found in the report of the cure: the running together of an excited crowd (v. 25a), the rebuking of the spirit (v. 25b) by means of a firm command (v. 25c). As with earlier healings, the spirit leaves in a convulsion of the possessed boy (v. 26a. See 2:26) and an impression is left that the boy is dead (v. 26b. See 5:39). But this is a false impression! Jesus takes the boy by the hand and raises him up (v. 27). The Christian language of resurrection rings out as the miracle story comes to a close.[25] But the Markan purpose for the telling of this tale is yet to be finalized. Reflection on the failing disciples has been part of the story throughout (see vv. 18, 19, 24), and they return to the action in vv. 28-29. The

---

25. As Hooker, *St Mark*, 225: "The vocabulary will have reminded many of Mark's readers of the greater miracle of resurrection, and will have encouraged them with the belief that Jesus will one day raise those who appear to unbelievers to have died."

end of the episode provides the reader with the reason for its inclusion at this stage of Mark's story.

Following a pattern now regular in the Gospel, the disciples use their privileged association with Jesus, asking him privately "when he had entered the house" (see 3:20; 4:10-12, 33-34; 7:17), why they had been unable to drive out the demon. Many themes have emerged across this miracle story. Among them we find Jesus' opening statement on their lack of faith (v. 19), the key to his ability to work the miracle because of his oneness in faith with God (v. 23), and the man's openness to Jesus (v. 24), articulated at the center of the passage. All these themes come to a climax in the explanation of v. 29: "This kind cannot be driven out by anything but prayer."

It is not *the disciples* who drive our demons, but God. As all things are possible for Jesus because of his immediacy with God (v. 29; see 1:1, 11, 35-39; 3:28-29; 6:2), they must learn to turn to God in faith and prayer if they hope to be successful *disciples of Jesus*, whose mission is to announce and inaugurate the reigning presence *of God* (1:14-15; 4:10-12). As the disciples will shortly be told: "All things are possible with God" (10:27). The correction of Peter (8:33) and the subsequent instruction on the need for all disciples to share in the cross of Jesus, and thus come to glory (8:34-9:1), has made no impact. Peter, James and John have failed to understand the transfigured Jesus as, full of fear, they ask to set up tents to "hold" this moment in a time and a place (9:5-6). They then remain puzzled about what glory through death and resurrection might mean (9:10-11). Not only Peter, James and John fail. All the disciples in the story fall under the accusation of Jesus: "You are not on the side of God, but of men" (8:33b). Yet, importantly, even though Jesus has asked the frustrated question: "How long am I to be with you? How long am I to bear with you?" (9:19), he is still *with them*, instructing them as they journey to Jerusalem.

Conclusion

With this passage, the first act of Jesus' preparation of his disciples for what lies ahead in Jerusalem, comes to an end (8:27-9:29). Disciples who are readers and listeners *of the story* have read and heard the prologue (1:1-13). They are aware that Jesus is God's beloved Son (1:11). They have now heard the voice from heaven announce further that the disciple must "listen to him" (9:7). But they are reading and listening to a story of disciples *in the story* that do not recognize Jesus as God's Son, nor are they listening to him. The characterization of the disciples has arrived at a stage where they are presented as becoming increasingly self-sufficient. They were called to "follow" Jesus (1:16-20; 2:14-15), to "be with him" in order to be able to cast out demons (3:14-15). They were sent by Jesus and succeeded in their mission of casting out demons (6:7-13), but returned to Jesus, to report all the things *they had done* (6:30).[26] They have decided that Jesus is the Christ (8:29), but they will not accept that he is also the Son of Man who must go to Jerusalem, suffer, die and rise (8:32). Their lack of faith (4:41), hardness of heart (6:52), increasing blindness, and lack of understanding (8:17-18) have brought them to a critical stage, recorded in the episode of 9:14-19. They are no longer able to perform as disciples *of Jesus* (9:18, 28) because they do not share his closeness with God (v. 29; see 1:1, 11, 35-39; 3:28-29; 6:2). In the light of what they have achieved earlier in the story (see 6:7-13), they raise their frustrated question: "Why could *we* not cast it out?" (9:28). This is why Jesus tells them to focus their attention on God, and not on themselves: "This kind cannot be driven out by anything but prayer" (v. 29).

Mark's narrative strategy leads him to stress the failure of the disciples *in the story*, so that he might instruct later disciples, readers and hearers *of the story*. Following Jesus is such a radical commitment that Mark has chosen to lead his readership into a better understanding of their vocation to be followers of Jesus Christ through a portrait of very fragile original followers. Called to "follow" (1:16-20; 2:13-14) and to "be with him" so that they might continue his mission (3:14-15), they have begun to falter. No doubt disciples of all time have had the same experience, and that is why Mark made this narrative decision. The Jesus that disciples are following is a suffering and risen Son of Man (8:31). As he took up his cross, a disciple must take up his or her cross (8:34-38). If there is doubt about the authority of Jesus to make such radical demands, then they are cleared away by their vision of the transfigured Jesus and hearing the voice from heaven, telling disciples that Jesus is God's beloved Son, and they must "listen

---

26. For this interpretation of Mark 6:6b-30, see the essay "Mark 6:6b-30: The Twelve, Mission, and Failure," on pp. 15-45 of this volume.

to him" (9:2-7). But their puzzlement continues (vv. 8-13) and their arrogance remains in place (vv. 14-28). To be "with Jesus" (3:14), the disciples must not only follow him down the way of the Cross, but join him in his oneness with God (9:29). Precisely because of the challenge of this radical call, Mark has chosen to portray the disciples in the story in all their fragility. Disciples of all times experience similar fragility. The call remains radical, and disciples remain fragile.

Jesus never abandons the failing disciple. This is a central message that Mark 8:14-9:29 communicates to disciples of all times. The paradigm of blindness, partial sight and fullness of sight (8:22-26) is acted out in the faith experience of the disciples. To this stage in the Gospel, they are not able to reach beyond their own hopes and expectations (8:32-33; 9:5-6, 11, 29). Mediocrity in Christian life, to which we all contribute, indicates that these Gospel-problems remain with us. But despite his frustration with his disciples (9:19), he calls them for instruction (8:34), he promises that they will be the foundational members of a future community, based on the power of the kingdom established in and through the paschal mystery (9:1), he manifests himself to them in his glory (9:2-4), instructs them further on the meaning of his death and resurrection (9:12-13), overcomes their failure to help a believer, the father of an epileptic boy (9:19-27), and finally instructs them on their need for God (19:29). The positive message for a life of radical discipleship, dramatically set in a narrative that tells of fear and fragility, is clear: take up your cross (8:34), lose your life for Jesus' sake and for his Gospel (v. 35), never be ashamed of Jesus and his word (v. 38), "listen to him" (9:7), and at all times turn to God in prayer (v. 29).

Finally, and most importantly, if you fail in your dream to live out these radical demands, do not despair, as Jesus never fails the failing disciple. This does not mean that failure does not matter; it means that God and his love for us matters even more than our failure.

4
Marriage and Wealth: A Study of Mark 10:1-31

The legal and prophetic traditions of what Christians call the Old Testament, the Jesus of the Gospels, and the recommendations of Paul and the other writers of the Christian New Testament, have always been at the heart of the liturgical life and much of the preaching of the Christian Churches. But a long tradition of systematic reflection upon ethical or moral traditions, until recent times, has looked elsewhere for its inspiration and justification. Largely determined by medieval European history, a more biblically and sacramentally inspired tradition, nourished by the Fathers of the Church, faded into the background in the eleventh century, as Papal authority struggled with the secular princes. A more juridical, less biblical, theological, and sacramental self-understanding of Christianity emerged.[1]

Outstanding theological contributions, inspired by biblical, patristic and liturgical traditions, continued to appear, singularly represented by Thomas Aquinas (1225-1274). But a more juridical tradition of ethical thought gradually emerged in the development of an area of Christian reflection that came to be known as Moral Theology.

---

1. The development of a more juridically structured Western Church owes much to the reforms of Pope Gregory VII (1073-1085), during a period of intense conflict between secular and religious authority. The authority of the Pope over the secular Princes was dramatically acted out in the submission of Henry VII (Holy Roman Emperor) to Gregory VII at Canossa in 1077. For a brief summary of this period, and its effects upon the Catholic Church's self-understanding, see Francis J. Moloney, *Reading the New Testament in the Church. A Primer for Pastors, Religious Educators, and Believers* (Grand Rapids: Baker Academic, 2015), 5-7. For a stimulating reflection upon the role of Gregory VII in European and Catholic history, see Eamon Duffy, *Ten Popes who Shook the World* (New Haven: Yale University Press, 2011), 59-69.

It had little to do with the Gospel roots of the Christian phenomenon, except to refer – uncritically, piecemeal, and in a proof-text fashion – to biblical passages that might be applied to one or other moral "case." The history of modern Catholic Moral Theology has sometimes been marred by bitter factional divisions that have led this theological discipline a long way from its biblical roots.

That era is thankfully behind us, as Moral Theologians and Ethicists working in the Christian tradition have returned enthusiastically to a consideration of the role of the Word of God in their reflections and research. In the Catholic tradition, Vatican II stated unequivocally that Sacred Scripture must lie at the heart of all Theology (see *Dei Verbum* 24; *Optatam Totius* 21). The following study is dedicated to a critical reading of a passage from the Gospel of Mark (10:1-31) where one finds Jesus' teaching on marriage and wealth.[2] Not surprisingly, the interpretation of this passage across different Christian traditions has led to contrasting ethical conclusions on marriage and divorce, and the role of evangelical poverty.

The Structure and Message of Mark 8:22-10:52

Scholarly commentary recognizes a literary frame of two cures of blindness around 8:22-10:52 (8:22-26; 10:46-52).[3] The cure of a blind man at Bethsaida (8:22-26) leads into the confession at Caesarea Philippi (vv. 27-30) and brings the first half of the story to a close (1:14-8:30). But it also creates a literary "overlap" with the following section of the Gospel. Between the two miracles where Jesus heals blindness, he predicts his passion three times (8:31, 9:31; 10:32-34). The three passion predictions, framed by two stories of blindness transformed into sight, are directed to the disciples as they journey toward Jerusalem. The two miracles are closely linked with Jesus' question of the disciples in the earlier harsh words he had with them in the boat after the second bread miracle (see 8:1-9): "Are your hearts

---

2. Throughout this study I will use the term "Mark" to refer to the author(s) of this Gospel, without claiming to know the identity of the historical author.
3. For more detail on the frame, see Francis J. Moloney, *The Gospel of Mark. A Commentary* (Grand Rapids: Baker Academic, 2012), 162-64; 171-72, and on 10:1-30, see pp. 192-203. See also "Following Jesus into Radical Discipleship: A Reading of Mark 8:14-9:29," on pp. 47-66 of this volume.

hardened? *Having eyes do you not see,* and having ears do you not hear?" (8:17-18).

Across 8:27-10:45, more than anywhere else in the Gospel of Mark, Jesus directs his attention and his teaching toward the disciples. The disciples are *always* at the center of the action. On only three occasions, other characters appear (9:14-27; 10:2-9; 10:17-22). The father in 9:14-29 is used as a narrative ploy to highlight the failure of the disciples. But the Pharisees (10:1-12) and the rich man (10:17-31) are active agents.

> 8:22-26: The cure of a *blind man* at Bethsaida
> > 8:27-33: The *first passion prediction* and the failure of Peter.
> > 8:34-9:29: The *first instruction* of the disciples:
> > > 8:34 to 9:1: *The Cross* and the disciples
> > > 9:2-13: The instruction of the transfiguration
> > > 9:14-29: The lesson of the boy the disciples could not heal
> > 9:30-34: The *second passion prediction* and the failure of the disciples
> > 9:35-10:31: The *second instruction* of the disciples:
> > > 9:35-50: *Service and receptivity* as marks of a disciple
> > > 10:1-31: The practice of discipleship
> > > > a) 10:1-12: in marriage
> > > > b) 10:13-16: through *receptivity*
> > > > c) 10:17-31: in one's attitude to wealth and possessions.
> > 10:32-35: The *third passion prediction*
> > > vv. 36-40: The *failure* of James and John. Their *instruction* on the *Cross*
> > > vv. 41-44: The *failure* of "the other ten." Their *instruction* on *service*
> > > v. 45: The Christological motivation for the teaching on cross, service and receptivity.
> 10:46-52: The cure of a *blind man*: Bartimaeus.

At the center of this carefully designed narrative (9:30-10:31) Jesus instructs his disciples on a God-directed understanding of marriage (10:1-12) and wealth (10:17-31). The disciples are challenged to be "receptive" (see 10:13-16) in a way that questions culturally accepted norms and practices. Jesus' teaching is as counter-cultural today as it was in the time of the early Church. The ecumenical discussions that continue over the interpretations of these passages by different Christian traditions are an indication of their ongoing relevance.

Mark 10:1-31: Disciples, Marriage, Receptivity and Wealth

Jesus has instructed his disciples to take up their cross, to give their lives for his sake and for the gospel (see 8:34-9:1), and on the necessity for receptivity and service (9:33-37). In 10:1-9 he debates with the Pharisees over divorce, and then speaks to the disciples "in the house" in vv. 10-12. After a passage where children are brought to Jesus (10:13-16), recalling the earlier message of receptivity (see 9:36-37), in 10:17-22 Jesus offers a wealthy man the possibility of eternal life, and subsequently speaks to his disciples in vv. 23-31 about wealth and possessions. Jesus' earlier instruction on the cross (see 8:34-9:1), service, and receptivity (see 9:35-50) operate *at the level of principle*, in secret discussions between Jesus and the disciples (see 9:30b). In 10:1-31, before moving to the final passion prediction (10:32-34), Jesus addresses the *lived experiences* of marriage and wealth in the life of a disciple. He draws *principle* into *every-day life*. In marriage and in the use of wealth the call to cross, service, and receptivity are at risk. Mark 10:1-31 is concerned with the *practice*, and not only the *theory*, of discipleship.

(a) Marriage and discipleship (vv. 1-12)

In 10:1 the scene is set for the encounter with the Pharisees. Its hostile nature is indicated by the fact that the Pharisees came to "test him" (v. 2a: πειράζοντες αὐτόν). They question him about the lawfulness of divorce (v. 2b). The well-known debate between Hillel and Shammai is not reflected in the Mark 10. The Pharisees ask for a judgment from Jesus on whether or not divorce should be allowed (v. 2b).[4] The

---

4. The Matthean report (Matt 19:3-12), asks whether the perspective of Hillel is lawful: to divorce one's wife "for any cause" (Matt 19:3). Rabbi Shammai and Rabbi Hillel interpreted the "shame of a thing" (*'erwat dabar*) of Deut 24:1, but Shammai, accentuating "shame," insisted that there be some moral defect. Hillel focussed upon "thing" and thus claimed that "any cause" was sufficient. See *m.*

question only touches upon *the rights of a man* to divorce his wife, but Jesus responds in a fashion that reflects the process of a rabbinic debate. He asks them about the command of Moses (v. 3).

They respond that according to Moses (see Deut 24:1-4) it is lawful to write a certificate of divorce, and in this way put a wife out of the man's house (v. 4). The debate appears to be based upon an awareness of Jesus' absolute prohibition of divorce. They have Moses on their side; how can Jesus take a different position? Jesus argues that Moses' teaching (v. 5) has crept into Jewish tradition, via Moses, *because of the hardness of the heart* of the Israel the Pharisees represent (v. 5). God's plan is found in his action "from the beginning of creation" (v. 6: ἀπὸ δὲ ἀρχῆς κτίσεως). Jesus comments upon the Genesis passages: "So they are no longer two but one flesh" (v. 8b). A woman and a man have been joined together in a loving and sexual union, as God designed.

In this debate, Torah has been used against Torah. For Jesus the legislation of Deuteronomy 24:1-4, established subsequent to creation as a concession to men who were unable to live as God had planned, was provisional.[5] *God has established* the union between a man and a woman (ὁ θεός συνέζειν). *No man has the authority* to tear that union apart (ἄνθρωπος μὴ χωριζέτω). The process used by Jesus has taken the Pharisees from an awareness of what was *commanded by Moses* (see v. 3) to what *God wills* (see vv. 6-9). Jesus' position is determined by *the design of God*.

Gittin 9:10; b. *Gittin* 90a; j. *Sotah* I:1.16b; *Numbers Rabbah* IX:30, and Francis J. Moloney, "Matthew 19,3-12 and Celibacy. A Redactional and Form Critical Study," *Journal for the Study of the New Testament* 2 (1979): 43. This issue, as we will see, becomes important in the ecumenical discussions of marriage and divorce. Recently, John P. Meier, *A Marginal Jew. Rethinking the Historical Jesus*, 5 vols., Anchor Yale Reference Library (New York/New Haven: Doubleday/Yale University Press, 1991-2016), 4:94-95, has argued strenuously against drawing the debate between Hillel and Shammai into New Testament interpretation, as the reports are too late.

5. See Morna D. Hooker, *The Gospel according to St. Mark*, Black's New Testament Commentary (London: A. & C. Black, 1991), 235: "It is significant that Mark does not suggest here that Jesus contradicted the Torah, but rather that he pointed to its true fulfilment." See further, Joel Marcus, *Mark*, 2 vols., The Anchor Yale Bible 27-27A (New York/New Haven: Doubleday/Yale University Press, 2000-2009), 2:710-711.

The story-teller focuses upon the disciples. For Mark, "the house" is the place for private teaching (see 3:20; 7:17-23; 9:28, 33). The disciples ask for further clarification on the debate they have just witnessed (v. 10). Jesus gives a God-directed motivation: men and women are equal, and equally responsible for their marital oneness (vv. 11-12). It is often pointed out that there is shift in the argument here. In vv. 2-9 the issue was divorce, while in vv. 11-12 Jesus speaks of the remarriage of the divorced as adultery.[6] There was long-standing and clear legislation against adultery (see Exodus 20:19; Deut 4:10; 5:21; Lev 20:10; Deut 22:22). Jesus' words to his disciples thus show how disobedience to his interpretation of Torah leads to the breaking of Torah. No disciple of Jesus, called to cross, humble service and receptivity, can contemplate such action.

The most intimate of human experiences, the union between a woman and a man, calls for loving self-gift. Jesus' new law in a new situation of God-human relationships, where the original creative design of God is re-established, can be costly. The teaching of Jesus on this matter is as idealistic, counter-cultural and difficult today as it was in the time of Jesus, but Mark has taken this element from Jesus' teaching and used it to tell disciples that cross, service and receptivity are not simple *theory*. They come into play in one of the fundamental structures of their day-to-day lives: in man-woman relationships.

The response of the Western Christian Churches to this teaching is fundamentally twofold.[7] In the first place, it is widely accepted that Jesus of Nazareth was not married, and that he prohibited divorce. This tradition is continued in the early Church. As well as Mark 10:5-9, an absolute prohibition of divorce is found in Q (Matt 5:32 [with an exception]; Luke 16:18). In 1 Cor 7.10-11, Paul speaks of the prohibition of divorce as "a word of the Lord."[8] The Roman Catholic Church

---

6. See, for example, Adela Y. Collins, *Mark*, Hermeneia (Minneapolis: Fortress, 2007), 469-70.
7. For a helpful survey, see David Instone-Brewer, *Divorce and Remarriage in the Bible. The Social and Literary Context* (Grand Rapids: Eerdmans, 2002), 238-67.
8. Jesus may not have been alone in this. Some suggest that he was part of a strain within first century Judaism that tended toward the prohibition of divorce (see Mal 2:13-16; *Damascus Document* 4,19-5,2 [for the text, see Florentino G. Martínez and Eibert J. Tigchelaar, *The Dead Sea Scrolls. Study Edition*, 2 vols. {Leiden: Brill, 1997-98}, 1:557]). See, among many, Joseph A. Fitzmyer, "The Matthean Divorce Texts and Some New Palestinian Evidence," *Theological Studies* 39 (1976): 221-23. Serious questions are posed to this by Meier, *A Marginal Jew*,

has adhered strictly to this teaching, prohibiting divorce among validly married Catholics, allowing a so-called "annulment" when a case can be made for the lack of preparation and unconditional consent *prior to the marriage contract*.⁹ This situation has led to a great deal of pain in unhappy and unsuccessful Catholic marriages. There is a widespread call for better pastoral care for these sometimes dramatic cases.¹⁰

Protestant Churches looked to the "exception clause" in Matthew 5:32 and 19:9: there is to be no divorce, "except in the case of unchastity (πορνεία)." The Greek word πορνεία can refer to a number of sexual misdemeanors.¹¹ The Protestant tradition has looked to the Matthean "dominical word" as offering the possibility of divorce for moral failure. Paul also allows for divorce within mixed marriages (see 1 Cor 7:12-16). Above all, the Protestant tradition insists upon "Jesus' spirit of unlimited forgiveness."¹² Ulrich Luz can even suggest "that the Catholic divorce law, close as it is to the substance of Matthew's position, does not do justice to the New Testament at an essential point."¹³ Taking seriously today's social and *psychological situation, and the increasing irrelevance of "established tradition" in a* secularized postmodern world, the issue of divorce, remarriage, and ongoing participation in a Christian communion, are urgent issues facing the Churches.

This New Testament reflection cannot enter the complex pastoral issues raised by the "Gospel message" in contemporary society. It must be said, however, that Mark presents Jesus' teaching as the

---

4:81-82, 87-93, who denies that Malachi 2:13-16 rejects divorce, and suggests that the situation at Qumran is not clear.

9. The Eastern Orthodox traditions equally defend the indissolubility of what they regard as a "sacramental marriage." But they allow "separation" and subsequent remarriage in situations where the relationship has broken down completely, accompanied by a confession of sinfulness, and the imposition of an appropriate penance.
10. The Synod on the Family, called by Pope Francis for October 2014 and October 2015, is one of the most important of these.
11. See Walter Bauer, William F. Arndt, and Frederick W. Gingrich, *A Greek-English Dictionary of the New Testament and Other Early Christian Literature*, 3rd ed., ed. Frederick W. Danker (Chicago: University of Chicago Press, 2000), 854, *sub voce* πορνεία.
12. Ulrich Luz, *Matthew*, trans. James E. Crouch, 3 vols., Hermeneia (Minneapolis: Fortress, 2001-2007), 2:496.
13. Luz, *Matthew*, 2:496.

reconstitution of God's original design (see Mark 10:6).[14] That reconstitution has been fully present only in the person of Jesus; it is otherwise "in process." The "ideal" of God's original creative plan is not present in the ambiguity of the human story. But much Church legislation presupposes that it is - from the first moment of the long journey of marriage. This is to confuse the "ideal" and the "real," with consequent complex results in the lives of "imperfect" people, striving (and sometimes failing) in their Christian lives.[15]

(b) Receiving the children (vv. 13-16)

Jesus and the disciples are still "in the house" (see v. 10), on the other side of the Jordan (see v. 1) as unidentified people bring children to Jesus, that he might touch them.[16] The choice of the expression παιδία (rather than τέκνα) for "children," indicates that they are past infancy, but still *dependent*.[17] Strategically located between Jesus' instructions on marriage (vv. 1-12) and possessions (vv. 17-31), the passage plays the same role as 9:35-37 within the larger context of 9:32-10:31. As 9:35-37 established the *theoretical basis* for Jesus' teaching on service and receptivity in 9:32-50, so does 10:13-16 within 10:1-31: discipleship is to be marked by service and receptivity.

The disciples rebuke (v. 13: ἐπιτίμησαν) those who led the children to Jesus, as Peter rebuked Jesus in his misunderstanding of the first passion prediction (8:32). As with Peter in 8:32, the disciples in 10:13 refuse to accept or understand Jesus' teaching on the way to Jerusalem. The disciples appear to have no recollection of Jesus' earlier words to them that had focused upon children (9:35-37). He asks

---

14. As Marcus, *Mark*, 2:710 puts it: "Jesus and the Markan Christians are people who rejoice in the dawning light of the new age – which is also the recaptured radiance of Eden."
15. See Hooker, *St Mark*, 237; and especially Francis J. Moloney, *A Body Broken for a Broken People. Divorce, Remarriage, and the Eucharist*, 3rd ed. (Melbourne: Garratt, 2015), 205-54, and Idem, "A New Testament Hermeneutic of Divorce and Remarriage in the Catholic Tradition," on pp. 283-307 of this volume.
16. Commentators regularly point out the appropriateness of the passage from marriage (vv. 1-12) to children (vv. 13-16). See, for example, Marcus, *Mark*, 2:713. Collins, *Mark*, 471, rightly points to the close link between the children who have nothing, but respond to the opportunity of entering the kingdom (vv. 13-16), and the rich man who has everything (vv. 17-31), and does not respond positively.
17. See Marcus, *Mark*, 2:714.

that the children be allowed to come to him, "for the Kingdom of God belongs to such as these." The gift of the Kingdom *of God* calls for receptivity. "The Kingdom belongs to such as these because they receive it as a gift."[18] Much is being offered to the disciples, but they are loth to accept it (v. 15).

Jesus takes the children in his arms, blessing them and laying his hands upon them. This action recalls what he offered the Twelve in 3:14. He appointed them so that they might be "with him." The children are used as a model of the true disciple, with Jesus and blessed by him. Taking the lowly and dependent (παιδία) in his arms, Jesus shows that the Kingdom *of God* reverses expected cultural absolutes (10:16. See 9:32-34).[19] Mark will not allow the reader to forget the *principles* that should determine the disciple's performance. "He has used a story which is linked to his basic theme of the meaning of discipleship."[20]

(c) Possessions and discipleship (vv. 17-31)

Jesus moves away from his location in the region beyond the Jordan (10:1), setting out on "the way" (ὁδόν) to Jerusalem (v. 17a). An unnamed man "runs" to Jesus and takes up the unusual position of kneeling before him. Addressing Jesus as "good teacher" (διδάσκαλε ἀγαθέ,), he asks what *he must do* (τί ποιήσω) to inherit eternal life (v. 17b). "What must *I* do?" is the wrong question. Jesus establishes that only God is good (see Deut 6:1-4), and points to a selection of the Decalogue as the way to eternal life (vv. 18-19). In affirming the goodness of God, Jesus provides the basis for his instructions to the man that he is to follow God's commandments, already known to him (v. 19). Jesus makes a selection of the commandments from the Decalogue (see Exod 20:12-16; Deut 5:16-20). Those chosen might be called social commandments, as they deal with a person's treatment of his neighbor: adultery, theft, false witness, defrauding and respect for parents (v. 19),[21] commandments that a rich man might

---

18. William L. Lane, *Commentary on the Gospel of Mark*, The New International Commentary on the New Testament (Grand Rapids: Eerdmans, 1974), 360.
19. On the background to the "relatively low state of children," see Collins, *Mark*, 472, and the further indications there.
20. Hooker, *St Mark*, 238. See also Marcus, *Mark*, 2:719.
21. The list given does not follow the biblical order of what is commonly called the "second table" (see the survey in Hooker, *St Mark*, 241-42; Marcus, *Mark*, 2:725-27). It is probably determined by the context: a rich man is likely to defraud.

be prone to offend. Ritual obligations towards God may be in place (see Exod 20:2-10; Deut 5:6-15), as one's weaker neighbor is dealt with sinfully. The man replies that he has always lived according to these commandments (v. 20). At this point Jesus' attitude to the man changes. He has shown Israel's way to God. The man who ran up to him and knelt before him (v. 17b) has dealt justly with his neighbor all his life (v. 20). He senses that Jesus has something more to offer for eternal life (v. 17c).[22] His problem lies in his belief that he can attain this "something more" *by his own efforts* (see v. 17b).

"Jesus looking upon him loved him" (v. 21). This is the first indication of a movement from Jesus toward the rich man. Capable of doing everything that he sets out to do, and having the means to do it, he asks Jesus' advice on *what he must do* to attain eternal life (v. 17b). Jesus' love for him (v. 21a) leads to an attempt to wrest the initiative from the man. There is only one thing that he lacks. He must rid himself of his possessions and his habitual determination of his own life. He must first sell everything he has and give it to the poor. Reduced to a situation of need and dependence he will have the opportunity to be *receptive* to the action of God in his life. He will not locate his treasure in this life, but with the only one who is good (see v. 18).

The invitation "Come, follow me" links this account to the earlier vocation stories (see 1:16-20; 2:13-17; 3:13-19).[23] Those accounts highlighted the initiative and authority of Jesus, followed by the immediate, wordless obedience of those called. The first disciples left their nets, boats, hired servants and their father (1:16-20), and Levi left his tax-house (2:13-15). *But Jesus does not command them to sell everything and give it to the poor.* Such a command is found *only in this story*. The earlier vocation stories show that a disciple must be *receptive* to the call of Jesus, manifesting unconditional trust in his person and word. "Jesus' demand is radical in character. He claims the man utterly and completely, and orders the removal of every other support which could interfere with an unconditional obedience."[24] The man fails, "for he had great possessions," and "went away" (ἀπῆλθεν)

---

22. The passage reflects the early Christian belief that, however valuable Torah was to find God's ways, following Jesus and his teaching went further.
23. See Collins, *Mark*, 480.
24. Lane, *Mark*, 368.

sorrowfully rejecting a vocation to discipleship (v. 22).[25] The theme of *receptivity* has been further developed by means of this story of a failed vocation to discipleship, and the every-day danger of allowing possessions to determine one's life. This is the reason for the man's failure to become a disciple. The link with discipleship, made clear in Jesus' calling him to follow in v. 21c, knits this episode into the wider context of 9:30-10:31.[26]

Jesus addresses the disciples, commenting upon the difficulty people with many possessions will have entering the kingdom of God (v. 23). The counter-cultural nature of Jesus' remarks is highlighted by the amazement of the disciples (v. 24a: ἐθαμβοῦντο). They lived in a world where wealth and possessions determined everything, from religion to politics, and everything in between.[27] Hard on the heels of a discussion over marriage and divorce (vv. 1-12), a second *practical* indication of what it means to serve and be receptive, leaves the disciples stunned. Jesus draws away from the case of the rich man. He speaks of the difficulty for *anyone* to enter the kingdom of God (v. 24).[28] Jesus compares the difficulties the rich have entering the kingdom with a camel passing through the eye of a needle (v. 25). This statement means what it says: it is impossible.[29] From the *difficulty* (δυσκόλως) those having possessions might have (v. 23), Jesus moves to an *impossibility* (v. 25. See v. 27: ἀδύνατον). The disciples are overwhelmed by his words on the impossibility experienced by the rich (v. 25. See v. 26a: "exceedingly astonished [περισσῶς ἐξεπλήσσαντο]). If for everyone it is difficult and for the rich impossible, the disciples'

---

25. Rather than following (ἀκολούθει μου [v. 21]), he went away (ἀπῆλθεν). The verbs indicate movement in opposite directions.
26. The tragic nature of this failure is shown by the narrator's comment that the man went away "sorrowful" (λυπούμενος).
27. Among many, see Lane, *Mark*, 369: "In Judaism it was inconceivable that riches should be a barrier to the Kingdom."
28. See the discussion of their attempts of early copyists to soften what Jesus says in Bruce M. Metzger, *A Textual Commentary on the Greek New Testament* (2nd ed. (Stuttgart: Deutsche Bibelgesellschaft, 1994), 90. For a survey of exegetical attempts to do the same, see Marcus, *Mark*, 2:730-32.
29. It is misleading to regard Jesus' words as "hyperbole." Jesus means exactly what he says. As Denis E. Nineham, *The Gospel of St Mark*, Pelican New Testament Commentaries (Harmondsworth: Penguin Books, 1963), 275, comments: "It would be a mistake to ignore the utterly serious truth it expresses." See also Craig A. Evans, *Mark 8:27-16:20*, Word Biblical Commentary 34B (Nashville: Thomas Nelson, 2001), 101, and the discussion of alternative suggestions there.

question makes sense: "Then who can be saved?" (v. 26b). "The disciples understood Jesus correctly. The application of this saying is not limited to the case of this rich man but is relevant for everyone."³⁰

The use of the passive voice in this question (τίς δύναται σωθῆναι;), shows that the disciples do not lack understanding. They recognize that people are saved by the action of God. It is not something that human beings are able to do by virtue of their possessions, strength, wisdom or authority. *God's ways are unlike human ways.* All human effort to enter the kingdom is like trying to get a camel through the eye of a needle. It cannot be done. For human beings, entry into the kingdom is absolutely impossible, but all things (πάντα) are possible with God (v. 27). The "all things" must be taken seriously. Both the rich man who has gone away sorrowful (v. 22) and the disciples who sink into misunderstanding and fear (vv. 25-26) can enter the Kingdom of God. God can make the impossible possible!³¹ What is asked of them, as the example of the restoration of God's order in love and marriage (vv. 1-12) and the rich man's inability to accept a vocation to discipleship have shown (vv. 17-31), is *receptivity* to the counter-cultural ways of God, made evident in the person and teaching of Jesus (vv. 13-16).

Peter looks back to the beginnings of the Gospel story (see 1:16-20; 2:14) and recalls that – in contrast to the man of vv. 17-22 - the disciples left everything, and unquestioningly followed Jesus (v. 28). Opening with a solemn "amen," Jesus praises and makes promises to those who have responded to the Gospel. Jesus lists the many possessions regarded as essential in the disciples' contemporary culture which they have put at risk: home, brothers and sisters, mother and father, children and lands.

Jesus' call to lose life for his sake and for the sake of the Gospel (see 8:35) has received a response. Peter's words (10:28) recall that this has already happened to people *in the story*, but 10:29-31 indicates that it has taken place in the lives of some who are readers *of the story* (10:29). They will be blessed abundantly even now, with the houses, the brothers and sisters and the mothers, children and land that come with belonging to a Christian community. They will lose

---

30. Eduard Schweitzer, *The Good News according to Mark*, trans. Donald H. Madvik (London: SPCK, 1971), 214.
31. As Marcus, *Mark*, 2:736, puts it: "the divine grace that transforms the impossible into the possible by creating new people of God out of hopeless human material."

nothing in their new family.³² The Markan community experiences persecutions. This must be accepted as part of "this time" (v. 30a: νῦν ἐν τῷ καιρῷ). Still addressing the community, but looking beyond it, disciples will be blessed with entry into the eternal life promised by the kingdom (v. 30b: ἐν τῷ αἰῶνι τῷ ἐρχονένῳ).³³ The agenda of Jesus turns the world upside down. A vocation to *service* and *receptivity*, now indicated as the *only* way to enter the kingdom (vv. 24-27), is a vocation to a reversal of values (v. 31), even the culturally accepted values that surround marriage, wealth, and possessions.

The reception of Jesus' demand that the man sell everything he has and give it to the poor as a prerequisite to following Jesus has long been a "thorn in the side" for the Christian Churches.³⁴ This has been made even more complex by the almost total lack of interest in Mark 10:17-22, given the dominant use of the Gospel of Matthew in the tradition, and Matthew's condition: "If you wish to be perfect" (19:21).³⁵

In the early centuries, despite Clement of Alexandria's contrary view, Origen, John Chrysostom and Basil insisted that Jesus' command (Mark 10:21//Matt 19:21) applied to everyone. One who retains anything more than what is needed for the necessities of life disobeys this commandment. The patristic period also developed allegorical readings of the text, in order to ease its severity (e.g., to be "rich" meant owning many evils), and this extended into the medieval period. On the basis of the Matthean "if you wish to be perfect" (19:21), the Catholic tradition has regarded the vow of poverty within the Monastic and Religious life as an "evangelical counsel," creating a two-tiered response to Jesus: the "perfect" and the rest.³⁶

The edge has been taken off the radical nature of Jesus' call. The Protestant tradition rightly rejected the vowed life as a superior

---

32. See Marcus, *Mark*, 737-40.
33. The contrast between "this time" and "the time to come" is widespread in apocalyptic thought, but this is the only place where Mark uses it. See the valuable commentary in Collins, *Mark*, 482-83.
34. For much of what follows, see Luz, *Matthew*, 3:518-23.
35. Regarded as an abbreviation of Matthew, no commentary on Mark appeared till the turn of the sixth century. From 650 to 1000 CE thirteen major commentaries were written on Matthew, and four on Mark. See the fine study of Brenda D. Schildgen, *Power and Prejudice. The Reception of the Gospel of Mark* (Detroit, MI: Wayne State University Press, 1999).
36. The Matthean notion of "perfection" has been added to Mark 10:21. See Luz, *Matthew*, 3:513-14.

vocation within the universal call to holiness. But it tended to adopt what Ulrich Luz describes as "Protestant middle-class domesticity."[37] Christian life within a financially secure and relatively comfortable social situation tends to regard this word of Jesus as hardly relevant. We have "thrown out the baby with the bathwater." Mark 10:17-22 does not direct all seeking discipleship to divest themselves of their possessions. Wealth and possessions were *this man's problem*. They stood between him and an unconditional self-gift to following the way of Jesus. This is the universal message that comes from Jesus' encounter with the rich man. In God's established order, wealth and possessions have their place, but they regularly obstruct a Christian's unconditional acceptance of the word and person of Jesus. Ulrich Luz insists that we need to take this problem seriously:

> [I]t is my opinion that any concrete suggestion that does not lead to changes in both personal and ecclesiastical finances simply ignores the text. … [A]ny present understanding of a biblical text must include practical application – that, in other words, a mere verbal, abstract understanding that excludes one's existence from the claims of the text is no genuine understanding.[38]

Conclusion

Across Mark 9:31-50 Jesus instructed failing disciples (9:32-34) on receptivity and service (vv. 35-50). Mark 10:1-31 tolled the same bell. But in this literary center-piece of the Markan journey to Jerusalem (8:22-10:52), Jesus has not only taught *principles*. He has pointed to

---

37. Luz, *Matthew*, 3:520. Luz rightly repeats the Protestant rejection of the idea of "evangelical counsels" and the creation of a two-tiered Church. Citing *The Catechism of the Catholic Church*, 2052-2054, he describes this as "Catholic doctrine" (p. 522). He misunderstands Catholic doctrine and the role of *The Catechism of the Catholic Church* as an articulation of that "doctrine." For a Catholic rejection of a two-tiered Church, see, among many, Francis J. Moloney, *Disciples and Prophets. A Biblical Model for the Religious Life* (London: Darton, Longman & Todd, 1980), 3-15. On the universal call to evangelical poverty, see Idem, *A Life of Promise: Poverty-Chastity-Obedience* (Wilmington: Michael Glazier, 1984), 18-73; Idem, *Reflections on Evangelical Consecration. Celebrating a Bicentenary* (Bolton, UK: Don Bosco Publications, 2015), 140-84.
38. Luz, *Matthew*, 3:522.

God's right-order in the lived reality of marriage and wealth. Jesus will shortly indicate that he asks them to follow a Son of Man who serves and lays down his life (10:45). Jesus' story challenges Christians to a reversal of the absolutes of "this world." The Christian reception of Mark 10:1-31 indicates that this "word of God" remains "living and active, a two-edged sword, piercing to the division of soul and spirit, of joints and marrow, and discerning the thoughts and intentions of the heart" (Heb 4:12).

5
Literary Strategies in the Markan Passion Narrative: Mark 14:1-15:47

The single most difficult fact the earliest Christians had to face was that Jesus of Nazareth, whom they believed was the Christ, had been ignominiously crucified. Some twenty years after the event of Jesus' crucifixion, Paul confesses: "We preach Christ crucified, a stumbling block to Jews and folly to Gentiles" (1 Cor 1:23). Paul was not a lone voice in the early Church, preaching the crucified Jesus of Nazareth as the Christ, the Son of God. Among many, the author of the Gospel of Mark shared that belief (see Mark 1:1, 11; 9:7; 14:62; 15:39). But the Markan storyteller's *narrative* had to describe the events presupposed by Paul's *epistolary* communications.[1] Like Paul and other early Christians, Mark was not primarily interested in simply recording the facts. He sought to convince his readers and listeners that Jesus was the Christ, the Son of God, in whom the Father was well pleased (1:11; 9:7). But in order to do that, he went back to *events* that marked Jesus' last days, assembling them in a "story" that communicates a *message* about the meaning of Jesus' suffering and death.[2]

---

1. See G. S. Sloyan, *Jesus on Trial. The Development of the Passion Narratives and Their Historical and Ecumenical Implications*, ed. J. Reumann (Philadelphia: Fortress, 1973), 1-3. As V. Taylor, *The Gospel According to St Mark*, 2nd ed. (London: Macmillan, 1966), 525 (paraphrasing K.-L. Schmidt) remarks: "The Passion Narrative ... is the oldest and most notable document in the garland of the acts of martyrs."
2. Contemporary literary critics coin the expressions "story" and "discourse" to describe the external succession of events that is reported (the story), and the message that the author of the account wishes to communicate to those who read and hear the story (the discourse). Perhaps the most influential work on this is from S. Chatman, *Story and Discourse: Narrative Structure in Fiction and Film* (Ithaca, NY: Cornell University Press, 1978).

Each of the four Gospels describes Jesus' final evening with his disciples, Gethsemane, an arrest, an interrogation before Jewish authorities, before the Roman authority of Pontius Pilate, a crucifixion and a burial.[3] Thus, Mark tells the traditional story of Jesus' passion and death, following this order of events, but he employs two techniques to insinuate his understanding of this climactic moment in the story of Jesus, the Christ and the Son of God.[4] In the first place, he continues his oft-used practice of "intercalation" into 14:1-15:47. Mark is well known for his use of intercalation, a literary strategy also called a "sandwich construction." It is found regularly through the Gospel.[5] Intercalation is generated by beginning the reporting of an event, but during the course of the narration inserting (or intercalating) the account of another event. Historical-critical analysis of the Gospel of Mark is not always certain of the origin of this practice. Some suggest that many of these intercalated stories were already told this way in the pre-Markan tradition. Others claim that the practice of intercalation is so widespread across the Gospel that they are most likely the result of Markan literary (and perhaps theological) creativity. There is no call for us to resolve the historical question here. The widespread presence of the use of intercalation across the Gospel indicates that it

---

3. Of course, each evangelist has told the story in an original fashion, even in the passion narrative. See the useful study of F. J. Matera, *Passion Narratives and Gospel Theologies. Interpreting the Synoptics Through Their Passion Stories* (New York: Paulist Press, 1986).
4. I am assuming Markan priority, aware that this is not the only option. See F. J. Moloney, *The Gospel of Mark: A Commentary* (Peabody: Hendrickson, 2002), 2-4. If, as is assumed, Mark was the first to write a narrative "gospel," then it could be claimed that the sequence of events was not traditional, but a Markan creation. As we will see, Mark is a very creative thinker, but bases his theological creation upon the traditional account of Jesus' passion and death.
5. For some good studies of Markan intercalation, see J. R. Donahue, *Are you the Christ? The Trial Narrative in the Gospel of Mark*, Society of Biblical Literature Dissertation Series 10 (Missoula: Society of Biblical Literature, 1973), 58-63; H. C. Kee, *Community of the New Age: Studies in Mark's Gospel* (London: SCM Press, 1977), 54-56; F. Kermode, *The Genesis of Secrecy: On the Interpretation of Narrative* (Cambridge: Harvard University Press, 1979), 128-31; R. M. Fowler, *Loaves and Fishes: The Function of the Feeding Stories in the Gospel of Mark*, Society of Biblical Literature Dissertation Series 54 (Chico: Scholars Press, 1981), 114-32; J. R. Edwards, "Marcan Sandwiches: The Significance of Interpolations in Marcan Narratives," *Novum Testamentum* 31 (1989): 193-216; T. Shepherd, "The Narrative Function of Marcan Intercalation," *New Testament Studies* 41 (1995): 522-40.

is one of Mark's favored literary strategies (see 2:1-12; 3:1-6; 3:20-35; 5:21-34; 6:6b-30; 11:12-25; 14:53-65; 15:6-32).[6]

Two well-known Markan examples of this practice can serve as good examples of the practice.

1. Jairus approaches Jesus, asking that he come to heal his ailing daughter (Mark 5:21-24a). While accompanying Jairus, in the midst of a large throng, a woman with a flow of blood approaches Jesus, touches him, and is healed (vv. 24b-34). As Jesus is still speaking to the healed woman, people from Jairus' house arrive. They announce that the girl is dead, and the story of Jesus' response to Jairus (see vv. 21-24a) is resumed, leading to Jesus' taking the girl by the hand and raising her (vv. 35-43).
2. The day after Jesus' arrival in Jerusalem, and his withdrawal to Bethany (11:1-11), he sets out to return to the city. On his way, he curses a fig tree (11:12-14). This episode is immediately followed by the so-called purification of the Temple (vv. 15-19). The following day, "they saw the fig tree withered" and Jesus points to a new approach to God: faith, prayer and forgiveness (vv. 20-25).

An analysis of these passages, and the several other passages in the narrative where Mark has used this literary strategy, indicates that the two different events that have been stitched together in this fashion *must be interpreted in the light of one another*. The woman with the flow and blood and the young girl are both restored to the fullness of their life and womanliness by means of Jesus' presence, word and touch.[7] The cultic life of the Temple, like the fig tree, has come to an end. In its place are faith, prayer and forgiveness, in a new Temple founded on the rejected cornerstone (see 12:10-11).[8]

The second feature of the Markan passion narrative that the following study will highlight is the use of "irony." Irony is "virtually as old as speech itself."[9] Mark's use of irony is simple and subtle, exploit-

---

6. For this list, see Kee, *Community*, 54. The following study will further develop Kee's claim that 14:53-72 and 15:6-32 are examples of Markan intercalation by suggesting that these intercalations are part of an even larger literary strategy.
7. For a more detailed treatment of this passage, see Moloney, *Mark*, 106-13.
8. For more detail, see Moloney, *Mark*, 221-28.
9. P. D. Duke, *Irony in the Fourth Gospel* (Atlanta: John Knox Press, 1985), 8. See the excellent summary of the use of irony in the history of language and literature on pp. 8-13.

ing two ways of understanding words or events. Direct speech and episodes can be reported factually, and taken on their face value. But the reader or listener is made aware that the real meaning of these reported words and events is in some kind of opposition to what is said or done. For example, people may insult the crucified Jesus by mocking his claims to rebuild the Temple in three days (15:29). But the reader knows that he will rise after three days, and become the foundation stone of a new Temple of God, a believing Christian community (see 12:10-11). The abuse hurled at Jesus in 15:29, can thus be called an "ironic" proclamation of the truth. As Camery-Hoggett as aptly commented:

Ironic narratives disrupt the superficialities of ordinary experience, opening up new and richer possibilities of understanding. In a sense, this is true of all narratives, since they are all in one sense or another interpretations of the experiences they convey. Irony, however, can carry that inherent tendency to an extreme, setting one interpretation of an event against another. In that sense the deeper reading of the narrative unmasks dimensions of the event to which its participants would have been fundamentally blind. Here, then, is the suggestion that in human experience "more is going on than meets the eye."[10]

Literary critics have traced various forms of irony,[11] but Mark's use of it is either verbal or dramatic. In "verbal irony," characters *say things* that at their face value are intended to have one meaning, but in reality convey a deeper truth that is the opposite to the meaning intended by the speakers. The above-mentioned example of the mocking request that Jesus rebuild the Temple in three days is a good example (15:29). In verbal irony, "The speaker ... stands protected behind the screen of ostensible meaning, while the silent intent of the word shoots beyond to do its piercing work."[12] "Dramatic irony" occurs when *certain events*, for example, Jesus' entry into Jerusalem (11:1-11), appear to have an obvious meaning, but in reality they point the reader elsewhere. The people and those following Jesus may appear to be welcoming the Messiah, but Jesus' entry into Jerusalem

---

10. J. Camery-Hoggatt, *Irony in Mark's Gospel. Text and Subject*, Society for New Testament Studies Monograph Series 72 (Cambridge: Cambridge University Press, 1992), 32.
11. For a fuller description of these forms of irony, see Duke, *Irony*, 18-27. On verbal irony, see Camery-Hoggatt, *Irony in Mark's Gospel*, 85.
12. Duke, *Irony*, 23.

ominously introduces a number of "endings," including the end of his own life. He will be the Messiah, but not in a way that matches the acclamation of Jesus as the long-awaited Son of David (see 11:10).[13] Mark weaves verbal and dramatic irony into his account of the passion and death of Jesus, making the tragic and cruel *words* and *events* that marked the end of the life of Jesus a *proclamation* of the fulfillment of God's design. Irony is a literary strategy used by Mark to guide the reader and the listener into and around the world of the story of the passion and death of Jesus, and thus into an awareness of its inner significance.[14]

The following reading of the Markan passion narrative, while not claiming to exhaust all the Markan use of literary strategies,[15] will focus upon the large-scale use of intercalation, and the regular use of irony, especially (but not only) verbal irony.

Mark 14:1-72: Jesus, the Disciples and the Leaders of Israel

Across 14:1-72 Mark leads the reader or listener through a series of eleven discrete scenes. The focus shifts from the disciples (these scenes are marked [A]), to a focus upon Jesus (marked [B]). The scenes, however, not only shift the storyteller's focus on the main characters within them. The [A] scenes indicate the steady progress of the plot against Jesus, and the disciples' unwitting (except in the case of Judas) association with it. The [B] scenes mark Jesus' acceptance of the darkness portrayed in the [A] scenes.[16] The storyteller,

---

13. For a helpful explanation of the irony of this episode, see Camery-Hoggatt, *Irony in Mark's Gospel*, 165-70.
14. Camery-Hoggatt, *Irony in Mark's Gospel*, 40. Camery-Hoggatt's study offers a helpful overview of the literary and social functions of irony in narrative, and uncovers some interesting ironies across the story of Mark. However, he devotes only a few pages (pp. 171-77) to the climax of the Markan use of irony in 14:1–16:8.
15. Much less does the following claim to be an exegetical study. My more detailed understanding of the Markan passion narrative can be found in Moloney, *Mark*, 275-336.
16. Donahue, *"Are you the Christ?"* 58-63, identified the importance of intercalation for the interpretation of 14:53-65. X. Léon-Dufour, *Sharing the Eucharistic Bread: The Witness of the New Testament*, trans. M. J. O'Connell (New York: Paulist Press, 1987), 187-88, identifies this pattern of intercalation as the "juxtaposition of light and darkness," but only applies it to 14:1-31. I have extended this suggestion across the whole of Mark 14-15.

unfolding his account of Jesus' passion in this way, develops and concludes a central feature of his understanding of what God has done in and through Jesus. Behind Jesus' journey to his death on the cross lies the will of God, and Jesus' unconditional acceptance of that will. The theme of the alternation between the darkness of failure and evil, and light of the majesty of Jesus' acceptance of its consequences as a revelation of God's design, enables Mark to state and restate this theme. In 14:21 Jesus will announce: "The Son of Man goes as it is written of him, but woe to that man by whom the Son of Man is betrayed." The Scriptures indicate God's plan for Jesus (καθὼς γέγραπται περὶ αὐτοῦ), but this does not take away the tragedy and evil that surround the fulfillment of that design. Mark returns to this theme in his report of Jesus' prayer at Gethsemane. Jesus prays: "Abba, Father, all things are possible to you; remove this cup from me; yet not what I will, but what you will" (14:36). Although God is never actively present in the drama, everything is in accordance with God's purposes.

Each of the eleven scenes used by Mark to construct 14:1-72 isolates a moment of darkness or light.[17] The individual scenes stand out clearly from one another, but together they form a powerful story that flows dramatically from one event to the other. What follows is a summary presentation of the eleven scenes that form 14:1-72, highlighting their intercalation, and drawing attention to the use of irony.

---

17. This is not the place to assess the scholarly discussion of the possible recovery of a pre-Markan passion narrative. Most would agree that Mark used sources. R. Pesch, *Das Markusevangelium*, 2 vols., Herders Theologische Kommentar Zum Neuen Testament II/1-2 (Freiburg: Herder, 1976-77), 1-27, argues that Mark is the conservative editor of a source that can be found behind much of Mark 8:27-16:8. For an excellent overview of research into the question, see M. L. Soards, "The Question of a PreMarcan Passion Narrative," Appendix IX in R. E. Brown, *The Death of the Messiah: From Gethsemane to the Grave: A Commentary on the Passion Narratives in the Four Gospels*, 2 vols., Anchor Bible Reference Library (New York: Doubleday, 1994), 2:1492-1524. Most would agree with Soards' conclusion: "We may safely conclude that Mark uses a source in writing his PN (passion narrative). We know that source, however, only as incorporated in Mark. The greatest challenge that lies before us is not the separation of tradition from Marcan redaction; for … that task may finally be an impossible one" (2:1523-24). Explanatory parenthesis mine.

[A] *The Jewish leaders plot to kill Jesus (vv. 1-2)*
Mark sets the story of Jesus' passion two days before the celebration of the Passover, the Feast of the Unleavened Bread (v. 14a).[18] Chief priests and scribes hatch a plan to slay Jesus, but are hesitant, as they fear an uprising from the people, who have so enthusiastically welcomed Jesus (see 11:1-11).[19] Their hesitation to act will be resolved when Judas, one of the Twelve, will join the plot (vv. 10-11), and this first moment of darkness will be a move from a plot to the possibility of immediate action against Jesus.

[B] *Jesus is anointed at Bethany (vv. 3-9)*
The discourse in which Jesus warns his disciples to "watch" (βλέπετε) and to be ready to respond to their call (γρηγορεῖτε) (13:1-37), is "framed" by the story of two women who give without reservation: the widow of 12:41-44 and the nameless woman of 14:3-9.[20] As the widow instructed the disciples by means of her unconditional gift of all she had, and her very self (12:44: ὅλον τὸν βίον αὐτῆς), the woman who anoints Jesus also steps forward as a moment of light in the increasing darkness. Mark tells her story here, as her unconditional self-gift to Jesus, symbolized by the smashing of the precious flask, and the pouring out of the oil, broaches the theme of Jesus' royal status (v. 3). The disciples are unhappy with such generosity,

---

18. Mark's chronology is difficult to follow. Most likely the "two days" of v. 1 would mean twenty-four hours, as a day was counted on each appearance of daylight. The evening of one day and the morning of the next would be "two days." The following *tentative* scheme is suggested by the narrative: plot and anointing (Wednesday), preparations and the Passover meal (Thursday), Gethsemane, arrest and Jewish hearing (during the night between Thursday and Friday), Roman hearing, crucifixion and burial (Friday). An empty tomb is thus discovered "after three days" (8:31; 9:31; 10:32-34) = end of daylight on Friday, daylight on Saturday, morning light on Sunday. See M. D. Hooker, *The Gospel according to St. Mark*, Black's New Testament Commentary (London: A. & C. Black, 1991), 325-26.
19. The Jewish historian, Josephus, records that the celebration of major feasts brought great tension during the time of Roman occupation. See Josephus, *Antiquities* 17.213-218; 20.1-5-112; *Jewish War* 2.255; 2.280-281; 5.244.
20. On the distinction between the use of βλέπω and γρηροpέω in Mark 13, with the latter insisting more upon the disciples' behaving as disciples should, see T. J. Geddert, *Watchwords: Mark 13 in Markan Eschatology*, Journal for the Study of the New Testament Supplement Series 26 (Sheffield: Sheffield Academic Press, 1989), 81-111.

reproach her, and miss the meaning of the gesture (vv. 4-5). Jesus corrects them, saying that she has anointed his body for burial, and that "wherever the gospel is preached in the whole world, what she has done will be told in memory of her" (v. 9). "The story is itself a proclamation of the good news."[21]

[A] *Judas, one of the Twelve, joins the plot of the Jewish leaders (vv. 10-11)*
The darkness deepens, as "one of the Twelve" turns against Jesus. In 3:14, Jesus appointed Judas to the Twelve. But in 3:19, Mark informed the readers that he would "hand him over" (παρέδωκεν αὐτὸν). The process begins here (v. 10) as the promise of money (v. 11) links Judas with a plot to kill Jesus that began in stealth (vv. 1-2), but now becomes possible. Jesus' executors have enlisted one of his intimate followers.[22]

[B] *Jesus attends to the preparations for a Passover meal (vv. 12-16)*
Mark brings Jesus back to the center of the action, not only accepting God's will, but also arranging for the events that follow. As the Passover is at hand, the disciples ask Jesus about the preparation for the meal (v. 12).[23] He gives them a series of commands (vv. 13-15). What he says will happen, does happen, and preparations are on the way for the meal that soon follows (v. 16). Despite what lies ahead, Jesus is master of the situation as he responds to God's will (see also 11:1-6).[24]

---

21. Hooker, *St Mark*, 330. This episode announces, at the beginning of the passion narrative, that Jesus is king, and his crucifixion, death and burial will point to that truth.
22. Paradoxically, there is a connection between Judas' action and God's design. In the passion predictions, Jesus has already said that he *must* (8:31: δεῖ) be "handed over" (9:31: παραδίδοται; 10:33: παραδωθήσεται). See D. Senior, *The Passion of Jesus in the Gospel of Mark*, The Passion Series 2 (Wilmington: Michael Glazier, 1984), 48-49.
23. There are problems with the chronology here, as the days outlined above in note 18 are hard to fit in with the information provided in v. 12. For more detail, which may not have bothered Mark as much as it does the modern interpreter, see Moloney, *Mark*, 283 n. 33.
24. As E. Lohmeyer, *Das Evangelium des Markus*, 17th ed., Meyers Kommentar (Göttingen: Vandenhoeck & Ruprecht, 1967), 300, comments on vv. 12-16: "It creates but an example for the thought that stands over the whole passion account."

The light of Jesus' response to God, in the midst of the surrounding darkness, continues to shine.

[A] *Jesus predicts his betrayal by Judas, one of the Twelve (vv. 17-21)*
In the three central passages (vv. 17-21, 22-25, 26-31) Jesus is with the disciples, and is the major actor. However, in vv. 17-21 and vv. 26-31 he predicts the future betrayals, denials, and flight *of the disciples*. All three scenes have Jesus at the center of the action. But in two of them (vv. 17-21, 26-31), he shows his awareness of the oncoming darkness of the betrayal, the denials and the flight of those he had chosen and appointed to be with him in a special way (see 3:14). In the first of these three scenes, Jesus sits at the meal "with the Twelve" (vv. 17-18), and predicts the horrible possibility that someone who shares his table-fellowship will betray him. Amid consternation, and the dramatic repetition of "Is it I?" as each person at the table asks that question (v. 19), the breach of table-fellowship by "one of the Twelve" is given as the sign (vv. 20). Yet, this terrible act is paradoxically part of God's design, in fulfillment of what was written of the Son of Man (v. 21a). But there can be no exonerating the betrayer (v. 21bc).[25]

[B] *Jesus shares the meal, giving bread and wine to the disciples (vv. 22-25)*
At the heart of 14:1-72 (the sixth of eleven scenes), dedicated to Jesus' never-failing presence to his disciples, Mark tells of his sharing the intimacy of a meal with them. Jesus takes bread, breaks and gives it *to the disciples* (v. 22). He takes a cup, gives thanks and shares the wine *with the disciples*. The broken bread and the shared wine point forward to the events of the following day. Jesus tells *his failing disciples* that his broken body and spilt blood will set up a new covenant, recalling the words of Moses, as he ratified the original covenant with Yhwh: "Behold the blood of the covenant which the Lord has made with you in accordance with all these words" (Exod 24:8). Mark's telling of his story of Jesus reaches one of its most poignant moments in

---

25. Judas' deliberate separation from Jesus (see 3:14, 19) is read by Mark, and by the early Church as a whole, as worthy only of the worst condemnation: it would be better if he had never been born (14:21bc). Yet, this tragic failure is part of God's design, fulfilling the Scriptures. The fundamental background of the unfolding of God's purposes across these intercalated passages must not be lost from sight.

a meal at which Jesus establishes a bond of loving self-gift with his disciples, who are about to betray, deny and abandon him.

Jesus sets up a new covenant through the sign of this broken bread and shared wine, a sign of his gift of self *for others*, establishing a covenant of freedom and oneness with God: "and they all drank of it" (v. 23b). The events of the following day will not bring this pact to an end. The word *until* rings out: "I shall not drink again of the fruit of the vine *until that day* when I drink it new in the kingdom of God" (v. 25). The readers must look beyond the coming death of Jesus. Mark has told this story of Jesus' final meal with his disciples to inform readers about his relationship with his disciples as well as his self-sacrifice in death, "seen as a new act of redemption, establishing a covenant between God and his people which supersedes the old covenant between God and Israel."[26] Mark's use of the story of the meal as the centerpiece of 14:1-72 allows him to highlight Jesus' unconditional response to the will of God in his gift of self for others (see 15:20b-25). Ironically, those to whom he gives himself will betray, deny, and abandon him (see vv. 17-21; 26-31).

[A] *Jesus predicts the denials of Peter and the flight of all the disciples (vv. 26-31)*

The meal itself concludes with a hymn, but the focus of the narrative remains with Jesus and the disciples as, together, they move to the Mount of Olives (v. 26). On arrival, oncoming darkness and failure return to Jesus' words with his disciples. He, the shepherd, will be struck, and they will all be scattered (v. 27). However, in the midst of these threatening words, he makes a further prediction: "But after I am raised up, I will go before you to Galilee" (v. 28). They may flee in fear, but Jesus will go before them. Peter will not hear of failure. He swears adhesion to Jesus, however weak everyone else might be. But he is warned that before the cock crows twice, he will deny Jesus three times (29-30). Peter swears allegiance unto death all the more vigorously (v. 31a), and so do all the others: "And they all said the same" (v. 31b). The readers of the story, who know more than the characters, in this case the disciples, sense the irony of these words of commitment to Jesus unto death. The readers and listeners know that Jesus will die

---

26. Hooker, *St Mark*, 340.

alone, and the disciples will have fled. They wait for Jesus' prophecy to come true.

[B] *Jesus prays in Gethsemane (vv. 32-42)*
The passion of Jesus begins with his experience in Gethsemane.[27] The storyteller assembles his description of this important moment with great care.[28] Jesus and the disciples gather in Gethsemane, as Jesus leaves them so that he might pray (v. 32). He takes Peter, James and John with him, instructing them to watch with him, in his moment of anguish (vv. 33-34). The storyteller gradually thins out the presence of the disciples as Jesus leaves the whole group, bringing only three of them with him. He prostrates himself before God in prayer, a prayer summed up in the words: "Abba, Father, all things are possible to you; remove this cup from me; yet not what I will, but what you will" (vv. 35-36). Returning to Peter, James and John, he finds that they are not able to watch one hour with him, as they have fallen asleep (vv. 27-38). Jesus is now totally alone. The irony of Jesus' command to his disciples to watch (βλέπετε; γρηγορεῖτε) in 13:33, 34, 35, 37 cuts deep, especially in the light of their recent vowing of adhesion to Jesus, even if this meant that they must die (14:29-31). They have been found asleep (see 13:36). He returns to his prayer again, repeating what he has already said, and laying himself open to all that lies ahead (14:39). He again returns to Peter, James and John, struggling against sleep and confusion (v. 40). The time for the action of the passion is in motion: "The hour has come; the Son of Man is betrayed into the hands of sinners. Rise, let us be going. See, my betrayer is at hand" (vv. 41-42). The light of Jesus' unconditional self-gift to the will of the Father turns toward the darkness of betrayal.

---

27. On the passage as a whole, see Brown, *Death*, 1:216-27. See also the excellent studies of D. M. Stanley, *Jesus in Gethsemane. The Early Church Reflects on the Suffering of Jesus* (New York: Paulist Press, 1980), 119-54, and R. Feldmeier, *Die Krisis des Gottessohnes: Die Gethsemaneerzählung als Schlüssel der Markuspassion*, Wissenschaftliche Untersuchungen zum Neuen Testament 2.21 (Tübingen: J. C. B. Mohr [Paul Siebeck], 1987).
28. Scholars have found tensions and contradictions in vv. 32-42. It is a finely crafted narrative, unfolding as follows: (a) Introduction (v. 32), (b) Jesus, Peter, James and John (vv. 33-34), (c) The prayer of Jesus (vv. 35-36), (d) Jesus, Peter, James and John (vv. 37-38), (c¹) The prayer of Jesus (v. 39), (b¹) Jesus, Peter, James and John, (a¹) Conclusion (vv. 41-42). For a detailed interpretation of the passage along these lines, see Moloney, *Mark*, 290-97.

[A] *Judas betrays Jesus, and all the disciples flee (vv. 43-52)*
Judas, *one of the Twelve*, comes with weapons of violence, and a crowd representing the Jewish leaders. Jesus' final words in Gethsemane (vv. 41-42) lead directly into the following scene. He accepts the darkness that follows the light of Jesus' acceptance of the Father's will (vv. 33-42). The hour has come (v. 43). Now called "the betrayer," Judas marks out Jesus with the title "Master," and a kiss, another breach of the intimacy established in 3:14 and in the shared meal (14:22-25). Jesus is taken by force (vv. 44-46). Violence surrounds the moment, as someone standing by takes a sword and cuts off the ear of the high priest's servant. But Jesus reminds them of his presence among them, teaching in the Temple (see 11:11-13:37). Ironically, the suffering of the righteous one, long predicted in the Scriptures of Israel, must be fulfilled.[29] The scene rushes to an end as Jesus' prophecy in 14:27 is fulfilled. The shepherd is struck, "and they all forsook him and fled" (v. 50).

The storyteller provides a commentary on what has just happened by adding a tiny parabolic action. Another young man "followed" Jesus, and his action comments upon the present situation of the disciples. Just as they fled in fear, so does this young man, but he leaves behind the linen cloth, his only article of clothing (vv. 51-52). He, like the disciples who have fled, is naked in the nothingness generated by separation from Jesus.[30]

[B] *Jesus reveals himself at the Jewish hearing (vv. 53-65)*
This passage is a moment of climax in the Gospel. Mark constructs it with great care, and his use of verbal irony turns this moment of accusation and condemnation into a moment when the truth about Jesus is revealed for the first time in the Gospel. Jesus, the leaders of Israel, Peter, and the guards assemble. Peter, who had followed him "at a distance" (ἀπὸ μακρόθεν), now draws ominously close to the guards. He is sitting with them, and the readers recall that Jesus has foretold that Peter will deny him (vv. 53-54; see v. 30). The process begins with a series of false charges, but there is no agreement in the

---

29. There is no specific "Scripture" referred to in v. 49c. On the background of the righteous sufferer for this passage, see Senior, *Passion*, 83-84.
30. On this enigmatic passage, see Brown, *Death*, 1294-95; H. Fledderman, "The Flight of the Naked Young Man (Mark 14:51-52)," *The Catholic Biblical Quarterly* 41 (1979): 412-17.

testimony brought against Jesus. At the center of the passage, the high priest rises and asks directly: "Are you the Christ, the Son of the Blessed" (v. 61). The reader recognizes the titles given to Jesus in 1:1: the Christ and the Son of God. For the first time in the narrative Jesus affirms his role in God's design. He accepts the charge as stated: "I am" (v. 62a), but adds another function that has been growing in importance across the narrative. The Son of Man who must suffer at the hands of his accusers (see 8:31; 9:31; 10:33-34) will be the same one who will be seated at the right hand of God, and will come with the clouds of heaven (v. 62b; see 13:24-27). The accused will become the final judge.

Jesus proclaims the truth. The storyteller's presentation of the person of Jesus is summed up in v. 62: Jesus is the Christ, the Son of God and the Son of Man. On these grounds, Jesus is condemned, but he is condemned falsely. The high priest asks: "What need have we of witnesses" (v. 63). Jesus is condemned for blasphemy, but on the basis of his own witness. Such a process is false,[31] but Jesus' physical suffering begins as some spit at him and strike him, crying out "prophesy!" (v. 65). Ironically, the reader has seen the prophecies of Jesus concerning both Judas' betrayal (see 14:17-21) and the disciples' flight (see 14:27) come true. He has just prophesied about the final coming of the Son of Man (v. 62). In the light of the very next episode, there is deep irony in the insults of his opponents.[32] What Jesus says will happen ... does happen! This must be the case, as the storyteller is shaping his tale to inform the reader that this is a story of the fulfillment of God's will. God will have the last word in and through the vindicated Son of Man who will return as judge.

[A] *Peter denies Jesus three times (vv. 66-72)*
Enigmatically, part of God's design is the failure of the disciples. Thus, the last of Jesus' prophecies uttered at the meal (14:17-31. See vv. 30-31) comes true. With increasing determination and vigor, Peter, now "with the guards" (v. 55), denies any knowledge of the maid's

---

31. On the falseness of the procedure here, see Moloney, *Mark*, 305-306, especially p. 306 n. 150.
32. Mark's careful writing is again evident. This scene is made up of (a) Introduction (vv. 53-54), (b) False charges (vv. 55-61a), (c) Jesus' self-revelation (vv. 61b-62), (b¹) False condemnation (vv. 63-64), (a¹) Conclusion (v. 66). This series of events is a blend of both verbal and dramatic irony.

suggestion that he was "with the Nazarene, Jesus" (vv. 66-68a). The truth concerning the person of Jesus has been ironically proclaimed in vv. 61-62, but, in a further use of irony, Peter has no knowledge of the Nazarene.[33] He moves closer to the gateway, but is trapped again as the maid makes more public that Peter was "one of them," and again he denies (v. 68b-70a). Now a matter of public discussion, one of the bystanders identifies Peter as a Galilean, and insists that he belonged to Jesus' followers. In his final denial, Peter rejects Jesus: "I do not know this man of whom you speak" (vv. 70b-71). As the cock crows, Peter has denied Jesus three times (see 14:30), and he broke down and wept (v. 72). The storyteller has thus told of the final appearance of a disciple in the Gospel. Although disciples have dominated 14:1-72, playing an active role in all the scenes marked [A], and shared a meal with Jesus in vv. 22-25, they will not appear again. Ironically, they have disappeared into the darker side of the fulfillment of God's design.

Mark 15:1-47: The Roman Trial, Crucifixion, Death and Burial of Jesus

A change of location marks another moment in the story of the passion of Jesus. In 15:1 he is led to Pilate. From there he will proceed to Golgotha (15:22), and eventually to a grave (15:46). The steady movement from a focus upon Jesus ([B]) to a focus upon other agents continues over nine brief scenes ([A]).[34] The major difference between the steady movement from one scene to another in 14:1-72 and 15:1-47 is that the characters who interact with Jesus is 14:1-72 are *always* disciples, while in 15:1-47 the group widens: the Romans, the Jewish leaders, and the crowd. As 14:1-72 closed with the Peter scene ([A]), 15:1-47 opens with a scene with Jesus at its center ([B]).

---

33. For a more detailed examination of the irony in Peter's performance, in the light of Jesus' prophecy and witness to the truth across 14:53-72, see Camery-Hoggatt, *Irony in Mark's Gospel*, 171-74.
34. The divisions into scenes in 15:1-47 are not as obvious as in 14:1-72, and at times subtle textual markers must be taken as indicating a move from one scene to another. I will highlight these details in what follows, but for a more detailed presentation of these scenes, see Moloney, *Mark*, 309-35.

[B] *Jesus reveals himself at the Roman hearing (vv. 1-5)*
The crowing cock indicates that it is morning. The action described with care by the storyteller links the Jewish and Roman trials. Jesus is led from the leaders of the Jews and the Sanhedrin, his chief antagonists in 14:1-72, and "handed over" (παρέδωκαν) to Pilate (15:1). It is the Romans who direct the action against Jesus from this point on. The Roman Procurator asks a Roman question: "Are you the King of the Jews" (v. 2a), and as in 14:62, Jesus accepts this ironic proclamation of the truth (v. 2b).[35] The chief priests continue to accuse Jesus (v. 3), but Jesus remains silent. Pilate is amazed (v. 5).

[A] *The question of Barabbas (vv. 6-11)*
Mark takes great care to allow neither Jesus nor Barabbas into the action as he informs the readers of Barabbas. He was a revolutionary and murderer (vv. 6-7). There is no need to inform the reader about Jesus. Although they are both discussed in vv. 6-11, neither Jesus nor Barabbas appears *in persona*. Thus vv. 6-11 is to be seen as an independent literary unity within the nine intercalated passages that form 15:1-47. When the crowd asks that Pilate release a prisoner, as was his custom,[36] Pilate ironically proclaims the truth. In an attempt to divide the crowd, he presents Jesus as "the King of the Jews" (v. 9). The dramatic irony cuts deeper as the leadership sways the people, and they ask for Barabbas (v. 11). The storyteller has presented two absent characters to the reader: Barrabas the murderer and Jesus the King. The crowd chooses the murderer.

[B] *Pilate proclaims Jesus innocent and also proclaims him king (vv. 12-15)*
Mark will not allow his understanding of Jesus as a suffering King slip away in the midst of this ironic tragedy. Pilate again presents Jesus

---

35. The parallel between the Jewish interrogation, leading to the ironic proclamation of Jesus as the Christ, the Son of God and the Son of Man (14:61-62) and the Roman interrogation, leading to the ironic proclamation of Jesus as King (15:2), should be noticed. These are all uses of verbal irony. Schweitzer remarks of Pilate's question: "It is a Greco-Roman formulation of the question which the high priest asked of Jesus in a Jewish version in 14:61" (*Mark*, 336).
36. It is difficult to find any support for this practice. For a full discussion, see Brown, *Death*, 1:793-95. Brown suspects that something akin to what Mark reports happened, but cannot be sure.

to the crowd as "the King of the Jews," asking what they want done to him (v. 14). Unlike vv. 6-11, in vv. 12-15 both Jesus and Barabbas appear *in persona*. The crowd demands that Jesus be crucified (vv. 13, 14), despite Pilate's insistence that he is innocent (v. 14). Mark reports Jesus' being handed over to death, despite the clear evidence that he is an innocent king. Ironically, these truths are met with rejection, as the crowd twice demands that Jesus be crucified. Both Jesus and Barabbas enter the scene as Pilate gives in: "So Pilate, wishing to satisfy the crowd, released for them Barabbas; and having scourged Jesus, he delivered him to be crucified" (v. 15). Jesus' opponents choose a violent revolutionary instead of the King of the Jews.[37] The simplicity, yet the depth, of the storyteller's use of irony is striking. The reader is aware that Jesus goes to the cross as an innocent king.

[A] *Roman soldiers ironically proclaim the truth (vv. 16-20a)*
Jesus is present, but entirely passive as the whole cohort of soldiers mockingly dress him as a king (vv. 16-17). The storyteller has the soldiers ironically proclaim the truth: "Hail, King of the Jews" (v. 18). They prostrate themselves fittingly, but they strike him and spit upon him. These actions indicate that, while they proclaim the truth, they reject what they are proclaiming (v. 19). To make this clear, he is stripped of the purple cloak (v. 20a). By means of mockery and insults, Jesus goes to the cross as a king. This is dramatic irony at its best.[38]

[B] *The crucifixion of Jesus (vv. 20b-25)*
A number of features single out vv. 20b-25 as a self-standing unit.[39] In terms of the overall literary structure, there are nine brief scenes across 15:1-47, and this climactic moment in the story, the crucifixion of Jesus, forms the fifth (and thus central) passage. However, a

---

37. This choice would have made a poignant impression on readers of the Gospel as Jerusalem fell, thanks to the implacable rage and violence of the Zealots.
38. For more detail, see R. Delbrueck, "Antiquarisches zu den Verspottung Jesu," *Zeitschrift für die Neutestamentliche Wissenschaft* 41 (1942): 124-45; Brown, *Death*, 1:873-77.
39. For a more detailed study, indicating this, see Francis J. Moloney, "The Centrality of the Cross: Literary and Theological Reflections on Mark 15:20b-25," *Pacifica* 21 (2008): 245-56.

close reading of the passage itself, set within this context, indicates that it bears all the marks of a deliberately contrived self-standing unit. The Romans continue to direct the action. As the passage opens we read: "And they led him out to crucify him" (v. 20b: ἵνα σταυρώσωσιν αὐτόν). It closes with the words: "they crucified him" (v. 25b ἐσταύρωσαν αὐτόν). The scenes before (vv. 16-20a) and after (vv. 26-32) are full of violence and the screaming of abuse. None of that is found in Mark's report of the crucifixion. Everything takes place in silence. There is no report of spoken words. Furthermore, every verb in the passage has "they" as the subject (meaning the soldiers), and tells of what the Romans do to Jesus: v. 20b: "they led," v. 21: "they compelled," v. 22: "they brought," v. 23: "they offered," v. 24: "they crucified," "they divided," v. 25: "they crucified." Almost all of these verbs report this past event by means of the "historic present" tense.[40] Mark has presented a unified and stark account of Jesus' crucifixion. As Jesus is led out (v. 20a), Simon of Cyrene, someone perhaps well known to the Markan community,[41] takes up the cross and follows Jesus (v. 21).

Usual Roman procedure is followed as Jesus is crucified at Golgotha, but the storyteller is interested in deeper themes. Jesus refuses anything that might lessen his unconditional response to the Father (v. 23). The division of his garments recalls Ps 22:19, and the reference to "the third hour" begins to mark the time frame for Jesus' agony. The storyteller's use of this time frame (see v. 33: "at the sixth hour;" v. 34: "at the ninth hour") shows "how carefully God took care of the events surrounding the death of his Son."[42] In a mysterious way, God's design is being worked out in this brutal murder (see 10:45; 14:36). The centerpiece of chap. 15, verses 20b-25, finally describe Jesus' unconditional response to the will of God in his unconditional gift

---

40. The verb is in the present tense, but it has a past meaning. It is used in narratives to create a dramatic effect. See Friedrich Blass, Albert Debrunner, and Robert W. Funk, *A Greek Grammar of the New Testament* (Chicago: Chicago University Press, 1961), 167 § 321: "The historical present can replace the aorist indicative in a vivid narrative at the events of which the narrator imagines himself to be present; the *Aktionsart* usually remains punctiliar in spite of the present tense form."
41. This is suggested by the mention of his sons Alexander and Rufus, who need no introduction to the readers.
42. Brown, *Death*, 2:960.

of self for others, repeating the message of 14:20b-25, the centerpiece of 14:1-72.[43] The skills of an uncomplicated but profound storyteller are evident.

[A] *Passersby and the Jewish leaders ironically proclaim the truth (vv. 26-32)*
Mark continues his carefully constructed narrative in vv. 26-32. This passage is dedicated to the ironic presentation of the crucified Jesus as King, savior and Christ. It opens with the proclamation of the kingship of Jesus in the title on the cross: "The King of the Jews" (v. 26) and the information that two robbers were crucified on either side of Jesus (v. 27). Two thieves have taken the positions of honor requested by the sons of Zebedee in 10:37, one on the left and one of the right of the crucified Christ. It closes with a development of v. 26 in another ironic proclamation: "the Christ, the King of Israel" (v. 32a), and a remark from the storyteller that returns to the two robbers mentioned as the passage opened. They joined in the abuse of Jesus (v. 32b). Between the frame of vv. 26-27 and v. 32 (the proclamation of Jesus' dignity and the presence of the two thieves), passersby recall the tradition on the construction of a new Temple of God (v. 29). They demand that Jesus show his authority by *coming down from the cross* (v. 30). The storyteller has already informed the readers that Jesus is the foundation stone of the new Temple of God (see 12:10-11, 22-25), and that only by *remaining on the cross* will he found the new community of God. The Jewish leaders acknowledge Jesus' saving presence among others, but answer the request of the passers-by by telling them that he cannot save himself (v. 31). They will only see and believe in Jesus' claim to be the Christ and the King of Israel (see 14:61-62a; 15:2) if he *comes down from the cross* (v. 31a). But the storyteller makes his point of view clear in this irony: it is only *on the cross*, abused and insulted, that Jesus is savior, Christ, and King of Israel. The crucifixion of the Messiah and Son of God, accompanied by the abuse of bystanders and Jewish leaders, is perhaps the most

---

43. For the parallel between 14:22-25 and 15:20b-25, I am grateful to Dr Noël Keller, RSM., who pointed this out to me during the course of the work of the Catholic Biblical Association Task force on "The Gospel of Mark in the 21st Century," at John Carroll University, Cleveland, OH, on August 5, 2002.

powerful combination of verbal and dramatic irony in the Gospel of Mark.[44]

[B] *The death of Jesus, Son of God (vv. 33-39)*
Mark makes another reference to time "and when the sixth hour had come" (15:33). These words introduce his dramatic report of the three hours that led to the death of Jesus "at the ninth hour" (15:34). Jesus is the focus of attention at all times, as he sinks into desolation, crying out in Aramaic, "My God, my God, why have you forsaken me" (v. 34). The use of Psalm 22, the lament par excellence of the righteous sufferer that has dominated the Markan passion story (see 14:17; 15:24, 29, 30-31), reaches its climax in these final words of Jesus in this cry from Psalm 22:1. The sense of abandonment, and the intensity of the question that Jesus asks in death, must be maintained to capture fully the storyteller's presentation of the crucified Christ.[45] The use of Psalm 22, and other OT texts related to the righteous sufferer, are the storyteller's way of indicating that God's design is being fulfilled. The cry of "My God" (ἐλωι) is misunderstood as a cry to Elijah, the helper of the helpless. The bystanders are still hoping that, at this last moment, Jesus will come down from this cross. His response is a further agonized scream, and he breathes his last (v. 37).

Only *after* his death do things begin to happen. The Holy of Holies, once hidden from the world by a curtain, is torn from top to bottom. The Temple is now available for the world to see. The centurion, who, facing Jesus, has witnessed Jesus' death, confesses: "Truly this man

---

44. The background of Ps 22 continues in this passage: "All who see me mock at me, they make mouths at me, they wag their heads" (Ps 22:7); "He hoped in the Lord, let him deliver him; let him save him because he wants him (Ps 22:9). On the chain of allusions to Ps 22 across vv. 29-31, see D. J. Moo, *The Old Testament in the Gospel Passion Narratives* (Sheffield: The Almond Press, 1983), 257-60.
45. Several attempts have been made to interpret Jesus' cry as an act of faith. See, for example, F. J. Matera, *The Kingship of Jesus: Composition and Theology in Mark 15*, Society of Biblical Literature Dissertation Series 66 (Chico: Scholars Press, 1982), 132-35; Senior, *Passion*, 123-24. In support of the above, see Brown, *Death*, 2:1045-47. After reviewing attempts to soften the sense of abandon, Brown comments: "I find no persuasive argument against attributing to the Jesus of Mark/Matt the literal sentiment of feeling forsaken expressed in the psalm quote" (*Death*, 2:1051).

was the Son of God" (v. 39).⁴⁶ Verbal and dramatic irony pervade the narrative as: "The death scene is the summit of Mark's narrative, the final resolution of the christological issues apparent throughout the Gospel."⁴⁷

[A] *The women at the cross (vv. 40-41)*
The narrator introduces a new set of characters in vv. 40-41. He names three women: Mary Magdalene, Mary the mother of James the younger and of Joses, and Salome (v. 40b).⁴⁸ He also introduces other, unnamed, women (v. 41b). Mark provides information about both the past and the present relationship between these women and Jesus. The three named women, and the larger group, have been associated with Jesus from his time in Galilee. This links the women with the earlier teaching and ministry of Jesus. They followed him (ἠκολούθουν αὐτῷ) and they ministered to him (διηκόνουν αὐτῷ) during that time (v. 41b).⁴⁹ The following, and the serving must be given their full Markan meaning. The storyteller wants the reader to associate the women's past activities with Jesus' teaching on discipleship.⁵⁰

But now, at the cross, they are described as "looking on from afar" (v. 40: ἀπὸ μακρόθεν). The language used for both the past and present activities of the women sets them in marked contrast with the other disciples, and especially the Twelve, who have abandoned, betrayed, and denied Jesus. The women are still portrayed as "with"

---

46. Again, both verbal and dramatic irony are present. Both these events are the subject of much debate. There is some doubt about which curtain is torn, and because the Greek for "was (the) Son of God" does not have the definite article (υἱὸς θεοῦ ἦν), some suggest that it does not have the full Markan sense of Jesus' being the Son of God. For a full discussion, and a defense of the positions taken above, see Moloney, *Mark*, 325-31, especially nn. 278, 279, 282.
47. Senior, *Passion*, 121.
48. The introduction of these names, and especially the reference to James and Joses, without explanation, could indicate that the Markan community knew the women and the two sons.
49. The use of the imperfect tense in the Greek verbs indicates the *durative* aspect of their following and serving.
50. See W. Munro, "Women Disciples in Mark?" *The Catholic Biblical Quarterly* 44 (1982): 225-41; E. S. Malbon, "Fallible Followers: Women and Men in the Gospel of Mark, in *In the Company of Jesus*, 57-67.

Jesus (see 3:14). But Mark's careful indication of their looking on "from afar" associates them with the vacillating Peter as Jesus began his passion. Peter also remained with Jesus after the arrest, but looked on from afar (see 14:54: ἀπὸ μακρόθεν). By means of this glance, back to Peter's earlier relationship to Jesus in 14:54, Mark has dropped a first hint that the women may not overcome the culminating irony of Jesus' death.

[B] *The burial of Jesus (vv. 42-47)*
Mark focuses strongly upon what happens to the body of Jesus in this episode. The arrival of the evening of preparation for the Sabbath generates the need for Jesus' body to be hastily buried. He must not be left hanging on the cross until after the Sabbath (v. 42). Joseph of Arimathea appears for the first time, a man of some influence. He has the courage to ask for the body, and after checking with the centurion whether or not Jesus was already dead, Pilate grants the body to Joseph (vv. 43-45). The body is hastily buried, without washing and anointing. Yet Joseph wraps the body in a freshly purchased linen shroud (σινδόνι), mentioned twice in v. 46a, lays it in a tomb hewn out of the rock. A stone is rolled across the entrance to seal the tomb (v. 46b). These details highlight Joseph's influence and care for the body of Jesus, but also prepare for the events that will take place "after three days" (see 8:31; 9:31; 10:32-34).

Two of the women who stood at the cross, Mary Magdalene and Mary the mother of Joses (see v. 40), see where Jesus was laid (v. 47). This is not the end of the story. The timing of the episode points the reader to the day after the Sabbath (v. 42. See 16:1). The body is not properly prepared for burial, and women who saw him die (vv. 40-41) have also watched to see where he was hurriedly buried (v. 47. See 16:1). Jesus is wrapped in a σινδών, the covering used in the description of the young man who fled from Gethsemane, a parabolic comment upon the flight of the disciples (14:51-52). The storyteller has led readers and listeners through the tale of the death of the Son of God and the burial of his dead body. They now wait for God's response to Jesus' question in 15:34. Ironically, this story of a cruel and ignominious death is told for a reader aware that God did not abandon the Christ, the Son of God (see 1:1).

Conclusion

The above outline of Mark 14:1-15:47 suggests that the Markan passion narrative is the result of a carefully wrought use of pre-Markan traditions to produce a unique narrative interpretation of the suffering and death of Jesus. Composed in two major sections, the first (14:1-72) is a continuous interplay between Jesus and the disciples. As Jesus moves steadily toward his ironic condemnation by the Jewish leaders, the disciples' failure intensifies. In the end, Jesus is proclaimed Christ, Son of God, whose suffering will be vindicated by the coming of the Son of Man (14:61-62). The disciples flee, fearful and naked in their separation from Jesus (14:50-52). Only Peter remains, following at a distance (14:54: ἀπὸ μακρόθεν). But he associates himself with Jesus' enemies and denies him three times (14:53-54, 66-72). Yet, at the center of 14:1-72, in the sixth of eleven scenes (vv. 22-25), Jesus shares a meal with his fragile and failing disciples. After their flight and fear in 14:50, the disciples do not reappear as active characters in the narrative. But at the meal-table they are promised that, despite their fear and flight, Jesus will go before them into Galilee. There they will see him (v. 28).

The second section (15:1-47) presents a further interplay of other characters with Jesus. Romans replace the disciples as Jesus' major dialogue partners throughout this section, although the Jewish leaders are never far away. The ironic proclamation of the Jewish trial (14:61-62) is extended into the Roman hearing and the crucifixion. Jesus is proclaimed "the King of the Jews" by Pilate (15:2, 9), by the crowd (15:12, indirectly), by the Roman soldiers (15:18), and in the title the Romans place upon the cross (15:26). Alone in his agony, he is proclaimed savior by the passersby (15:30) and by the Jewish leaders (15:31), and ironically recognized as the Christ, the king of Israel, as his enemies demand that he come down from the cross that they might see and believe (15:30, 32).

Crying out an anguished question of abandonment to his God (15:34), Jesus screams and expires (15:37). The christological highpoint of the Gospel arrives as a consequence of Jesus' agonizing death: the temple of Jerusalem is symbolically destroyed, and the sanctuary once reserved to the Jewish priests is laid open for all to see. A new temple, built upon the rejected cornerstone, is founded (see 12:10-11) and the Roman centurion, standing before Jesus and seeing the manner of his death, is the first of many to proclaim that Jesus is the

Son of God (15:38-39). The promise of the voice from heaven in 1:11 has been realized in 15:39. Women watch from a distance (15:40: ἀπὸ μακρόθεν), and Jesus is hurriedly buried in scenes which bring the traditional passion story to an end. But they point the reader toward the resurrection promised by Jesus during his journey to Jerusalem (8:31; 9:31; 10:33-34), and demanded by Jesus' question of God in the moment of his death (15:34). At the center of 15:1-47, the fifth of nine scenes, the account of the crucifixion of Jesus (vv. 20b-25) relates the silent and merciless execution, the event so long anticipated by the Gospel of Mark (see, as early as 2:20; 3:6).

As the first half of the passion narrative closed, the disciples moved tragically toward the denials of Peter (14:46-72). As the second half ends, the Romans' participation in Jesus' agony closes with one of them accepting that Jesus is the Son of God (15:39). The simplicity of the literary structure, combined with the depth of the verbal and dramatic irony used to proclaim the truth of Jesus Christ, King, Son of God and Savior on the cross, reflect a finely tuned Christian author. The figure that created the literary form "gospel" did more than edit the received tradition.[51]

The narrative has prepared the reader for the Gospel's climax: the much anticipated account of the resurrection of Jesus. There, one would expect, the failure of Jesus and the apparent failure of the disciples will be resolved. God will become the major actor in what follows, but there is a twist at the end of the tale. God will show that he has never abandoned his Son (see 15:34), but the expected restoration of discipleship to the fearful and frightened men who fled from Jesus at Gethsemane (14:50) will receive something of a setback. Even the women, who have remained with Jesus from Galilee to the cross (15:40-41) and the tomb (v. 47), will join the disciples in fear and flight (16:8). That "twist in the tail," however, is but further evidence of Mark's skilful narrative proclamation of the action of God in and through the life, teaching, death and resurrection of Jesus.[52]

---

51. This study indicates that Markan scholarship has come a long way from the days of Form Criticism, when R. Bultmann could confidently claim that "Mark is not sufficiently master of his material to be able to venture on a systematic construction himself" (*The History of the Synoptic Tradition*, trans. J. Marsh [Oxford: Basil Blackwell, 1968], 350).
52. On this, see Moloney, *Mark*, 349-54, and the essay "'He is going before you into Galilee.' Mark 16:6-8 and the Christian Community," on pp. 117-30 of this volume.

6
"He is going before you into Galilee." Mark 16:6-8 and the Christian Community

In Memory of Sebastian Karotemprel, SDB (1931-2014)

Scholarly debate over the ending of the Gospel of Mark must cover a number of critical questions. Did the Gospel originally end at 16:8? If not, do any of the other endings available in the manuscript traditions provide a possible original conclusion, or has it been lost? What is the relationship between 16:7, where the young man in the tomb tells the women that Jesus is going before them into Galilee and 14:28, where Jesus spoke almost these exact words to the disciples at the last meal? Most of all, however, if the Gospel ends at v. 8, why does Mark report that the women fled from the tomb, full of fear, and said nothing to anyone? Surely the promise of an encounter with the risen Lord, promised in 14:28 and 16:7 could not be thwarted by the silence of the women?[1] There is one truth, however, that cannot be contested, and where all scholars agree. This briefest, and probably earliest, of the Four Gospels was received by a Christian community late in the first Christian century. Only recently has its subtle power been recognized,[2] but the Gospel of Mark has been read, and is still read, within the context of the believing Christian Community. Without a community of Christian readers and listeners, over the centuries, this

---

1. This question is heightened by the fact that the very last word in v. 8 is γάρ ("for"), a most unusual ending for a complete document: ἐφοβοῦντο γάρ ("for they were afraid"). However, the strangeness of this ending is sometimes exaggerated. For a correction of this exaggeration see R. H. Lightfoot, *The Gospel Message of St Mark* (Oxford: Clarendon Press, 1950), 80-97. More recently, see Kelly R. Iverson, "A Further Word on the Final Γάρ (Mark 16:8)," *The Catholic Biblical Quarterly* 68 (2006): 79-94.
2. On the reception of the Gospel of Mark over the centuries, see B. D. Schildgen, *Power and Prejudice: The Reception of the Gospel of Mark* (Detroit: Wayne State University Press, 1999).

Gospel would have slipped off the shelves of Christian literature. It is upon this uncontested and obvious truth that I would like base my interpretation of Mark 16:6-8.

The study that follows will suggest that the literary utterance of the Gospel of Mark, for all its incongruence for modern Gospel scholarship, and a contemporary reader, was crafted to both comfort and provoke its readership.[3] One of the several reasons for the fascination of this Gospel is its *direct appeal* to a believing, yet struggling, community of Christian believers. The author of the Gospel closed his Gospel with an Easter message to the women at the tomb, and an enigmatic flight in silence and fear, to challenge and comfort the Christian community. It is a privilege that I offer this study to colleague, and fellow-Salesian, Sebastian Karotemprel, S.D.B (1931-2014). His life-long and often courageous labors, especially (but not only) in the area of inter-religious dialogue, were always at one with the intention of the Markan story-teller: to challenge and comfort the Christian community.

Mark 16:8 as the Original Ending

The problem we are facing emerged in the earliest days of Christian tradition. Once the written gospel texts were passed on from generation to generation, scribes began to provide more satisfactory endings to make the Gospel of Mark conform to the concluding stages of the Gospels of Matthew, Luke, and John. In Matthew and Luke, women receive the Easter message and report it to the disciples (Matt 18:1-10; Luke 24:1-12). In the Gospel of John, there is only one woman, Mary of Magdalene, but the story of the empty tomb is reported to Peter and the Beloved Disciple (John 20:1-3). Most English editions of the Gospel of Mark print either a longer ending (Mark 16:9-20) or a shorter ending (16:9-10). Some provide both. The imaginative gathering of a number of Easter appearance stories from the other Gospels, and the Acts of the Apostles generated the longer ending. The shorter ending merely affirms that the women reported the message, and from then

---

3. Significant evidence for this "incongruence" is found in the fact that in Year B of the Roman Catholic Sunday Lectionary, when Mark 16 is read at the Easter Vigil, only 16:1-7 is proclaimed, thus ending: "But go, tell his disciples and Peter that he is going before you to Galilee; there you will see him, just as he told you" (v. 7).

on salvation was proclaimed from east to west. However, these are only two of four major textual traditions that have come down to us, and none of them have any claim to authenticity. They are clearly the work of troubled scribes, unhappy with the silence of the woman in v. 8.[4] The *textual* problem was created by a *theological* problem. Is it possible that, for Mark, the Easter message was not proclaimed by the women, with the result that the relationship between Jesus and the faltering disciples was restored, as in Matthew, Luke and John?

Only one solution remains for those who would like to claim that the original Gospel of Mark did not end at 16:8: the ending was lost. Many have suggested that this was the case, unable to accept that Mark could change the tradition of the women's announcing of the Easter message.[5] It is so crucial to the Christian story, especially in the light of the promise of a future encounter in Galilee (v. 7), that there must have been a further page to resolve the tension created by vv. 7-8. However, the suggestion of a lost ending creates more difficulties than it resolves. The "lost ending" solution depends upon a number of well-nigh impossible hypotheses. The first hypothesis is that the original ending was contained in a self-standing page in what we call a codex. A codex is an ancient form of a book, with pages sewn together, as we bind a modern book. As even with modern books, with wear and tear, the first or last page might become detached. In the first place, it is unlikely that the Gospel of Mark was originally written in a codex. That form used for the preservation of texts came into Christian usage very early, but probably not for the original autographs of the New Testament texts.[6] It is thus more than likely

---

4. For a succinct treatment of the textual traditions, see B. M. Metzger, *A Textual Commentary on the Greek New Testament*, 2nd ed. (Stuttgart: Deutsche Bibelgesellschaft, 1994), 102-107.
5. See, for example, V. Taylor, *The Gospel According to St Mark* (London: Macmillan, 1966), 609-10; C. E. B. Cranfield, *The Gospel According to Saint Mark*, 2nd ed., The Cambridge Greek New Testament Commentary (Cambridge: Cambridge University Press, 1963), 470-71; E. Schweitzer, *The Good News According to Mark*, trans. D. H. Madvig (London: SPCK, 1971), 365-67; E. Linnemann, "Der (wiedergefundene) Markusschluss," *Zietschrift für Theologie und Kirche* 66 (1969): 255-87.
6. There is some discussion concerning the use of the scroll and the codex in the early Church. Most argue (as above) that the autographs would have been on scrolls, but that Christians used the codex very early, perhaps even toward the end of the first century. See, for example, B. M. Metzger, *The Text of the New Testament*.

that the very first "Gospel of Mark" have been written on a scroll, not a codex.[7] The use of the codex for transmitting the Gospels began as the need to preserve and facilitate the use of the early Church's emerging sacred texts increased.

Secondly, is it possible that the full resurrection account of the original manuscript was torn off, as the last page of a codex might have become detached? Although more difficult than losing the last page of a codex, wear and tear of a much-used scroll may have damaged its final several inches. It is certainly physically possible that this could happen. But we must then consider the possibility that the loss of the closing section of the scroll would have taken place *with the original autograph of the Gospel of Mark*. Would such a loss be regarded as so unimportant to the community which received the original scroll containing the Gospel of Mark that the ending was simply allowed to disappear? That is most unlikely. It is very difficult to imagine that before there existed even a single copied version of the original Gospel of Mark, the ending of that original was inadvertently torn off, and nothing was done to retrieve it. It would only take a few copies of the original Mark, containing the so-called "lost ending," to be in existence for something of that ending to be present in some ancient manuscripts. There is no such evidence, as our present endings all come from a later period, and are attempts to harmonize Mark 16:1-8 with the ending of Matthew, Luke and John.[8] A single conclusion imposes itself: the original Gospel of Mark ended at 16:8.

Its Transmission, Corruption, and Restoration, 2nd ed. (Oxford: Clarendon Press, 1968), 5-8; J. Finegan, *Encountering New Testament Manuscripts. A Working Introduction to Textual Criticism* (London: SPCK, 1975), 27-29. See, however, K. and B. Aland, *The Text of the New Testament. An Introduction to the Critical Editions and to the Theory and Practice of Modern Textual Criticism*, trans. E. F. Rhodes (Grand Rapids: Eerdmans, 1987), 75: "Apparently from the very beginning Christians did not use the scroll format for their writings, but rather the codex." See also pp. 101-102.

7. It was not called "The Gospel of Mark" at that stage. The titles ascribing authors to the Gospels is generally regarded as coming from the second century, although M. Hengel, *Studies in the Gospel of Mark*, trans. John Bowden (London: SPCK, 1985), 64-84, disputes this. He claims that once more than one "gospel" existed, they were attached to an author. Thus ""according to Mark" would have been attached to the title before the end of the first Christian century. However, even for Hengel, the Gospel titles did not belong to the original autographs.

8. As Taylor, *St Mark*, 610, admits: "How the original ending disappeared is … obscure."

If that is the case, then it is the responsibility of the interpreter to make sense of Mark's literary and theological reasons for closing his Gospel with the fear, flight and silence of the women (16:8).⁹

An Ending which Matches a Beginning

The story of Jesus, as we have it in the Gospel of Mark, is determined by a logic that leads inevitably toward the cross. The story opens with great promise (1:1-13), but the reader is led further into a story whose ending is known,¹⁰ yet is surprised on the way – and at the end. The plot is shot through with hints that look forward to the end of the story. The Gospel of Mark is unique among the Gospels because, unlike most narratives (including Matthew, Luke and John), the crises that emerge during the course of the narrative are not resolved through a *dénouement* at the end of the story (Mark 16:1-8). Much is resolved, but a further crisis emerges which cannot be resolved by the story itself. This suggests that it might be resolved in the lives of the people reading or hearing the story. We should recall that in a good story the reader/listener is told enough to be made curious, without ever being given all the answers. Narrative texts keep promis-

---

9. Many of the scholars who insist that there must have been a lost ending (see above, note 4) are reacting against the suggestions of E. Lohmeyer, *Das Evangelium des Markus*, 17th ed., Meyers Kommentar (Göttingen: Vandenhoeck & Ruprecht, 1967), 355-58, that the ending points to a Markan community waiting in Galilee for the parousia. This claim has been further developed by W. Marxsen, *Mark the Evangelist. Studies in Redaction Criticism*, trans. James Boyce and Others (Nashville: Abingdon Press, 1969), 75-92, and a number of more recent redaction critics in the USA who have accepted the conclusions of Lohmeyer and Marxsen (e.g., N. Perrin, T. J. Weeden, W. Kelber). This position, which stresses a community living in the absence of Jesus and waiting for the parousia, does not do justice to the message of the Gospel as a whole. See especially J. D. Kingsbury, *The Christology of Mark's Gospel* (Philadelphia: Fortress, 1983), and the summary of J. Marcus, *Mark 1-8*, Anchor Bible 27 (New York: Doubleday, 2000), 75-79. Although they reject the Lohmeyer proposal, Kingsbury and Marcus rightly insist that the original Gospel closed with 16:8.
10. Accepting that the Gospel was primarily written for a Christian community whose members knew that Jesus had been crucified, and who gathered because they believed that he had been raised. On this, see A. Y. Collins, *The Beginning of the Gospel. Probings of Mark in Context* (Minneapolis: Fortress, 1992), 1-38; Marcus, *Mark*, 25-28.

ing the great prize of understanding - later.[11] The "later" of the Gospel of Mark, I will suggest, is the "now" of the Christian reader.

The reader/listener meets a number of significant turning points in the story. The Gospel begins (1:1), Jesus opens his ministry in Galilee (1:14-15), he announces his forthcoming death and resurrection for the first time (8:31), he enters Jerusalem (11:1-11), a decision is made that Jesus must be arrested and killed (14:1-2), and women discover an empty tomb (16:1-4). As has been obvious since the days of Wilhelm Wrede, Karl-Ludwig Schmidt, Martin Dibelius, and Rudolf Bultmann, this "framework" was devised by the Evangelist Mark. It appearance as the "plot" of the first early Christian "gospel" was intentionally a theological statement.[12] *Whatever the first readers knew of the life-story of Jesus of Nazareth was subverted by the Markan story. Jesus' presence in Galilee, his single journey to Jerusalem to be rejected, tried and crucified, the resurrection and the surprising silence of the women was not familiar.* Such a "plot" saw the light of day *for the first time* when Mark invented it. It is this *radical newness* of the Markan story that must be kept in mind.[13] It is an original way of telling the story of Jesus, and its author must be credited with an equally original understanding of why he plotted the story in this way.

---

11. See S. Rimmon-Kenan, *Narrative Fiction: Contemporary Poetics*, New Accents (London: Methuen, 1983), 125.
12. In the middle of the nineteenth century, once scholars accepted that Mark was the earliest Gospel, many (especially H. J. Holzmann) concluded that the simple story-line of Mark provided what they called a "framework" for the life of the historical Jesus. This widely accepted "framework" was shown to be the theological creation of the Evangelist Mark by W. Wrede in 1901, and Wrede's work became a point of departure for the founders of Form Criticism, K.-L. Schmidt, M. Dibelius, and R. Bultmann from 1919-21. For a survey of this period, with full bibliographical details for the work of the above-mentioned scholarly giants, see F. J. Moloney, *Beginning the Good News. A narrative approach* (Collegeville: The Liturgical Press, 1992), 19-24.
13. See the important essay by E. Schweizer, "Mark's Theological Achievement," in *The Interpretation of Mark*, ed. W. Telford, Issues in Religion and Theology 7 (Philadelphia: Fortress Press, 1985), 42-63. W. H. Kelber, *The Oral and Written Gospel. The Hermeneutics of Speaking and Writing in the Synoptic Tradition, Mark, Paul and Q* (Philadelphia: Fortress, 1983), pushes this to the limit. He rightly argues that Mark took a vivacious and living oral tradition and created something quite different with his "writing" (see pp. 44-139). But he argues that the movement from oral tradition to written Gospel created a written text which was a contradiction of what went before. The thesis is overstated, but rightly highlights the radical newness of the Gospel of Mark.

Mark's plot is a God-designed sequence of time and events designed to lead the reader to a surprising re-telling of the story of death and resurrection of Jesus to which she or he could not remain indifferent. On the basis of the turning points we have identified, one can trace the following God-designed temporal and geographical strategies.

1. Mark 1:1-13 provides *the reader* with a great deal of information about God's beloved Son in a prologue to the Gospel.
2. Through Mark 1:14-8:30 the words and deeds of Jesus' ministry increasingly force the question: who is this man (see 1:27, 45; 2:12; 3:22; 4:41; 5:20; 6:2-3, 48-50; 7:37)? There are three parts to the first half of the narrative. Each section is made up of a summary (1:14-15; 3:7-12; 6:6a) followed by material on the disciples (1:16-20; 3:13-19; 6:6b-30) and narrative which leads to a decision (3:6: Jesus death is plotted; 6:1-6a: his home town reject him; 8:29-30: Peter confesses Jesus to be the Christ, but is warned). Across these three moments in his Galilean ministry, some accept Jesus, some are indifferent and many oppose him, but the question behind the story is: can he be the Messiah? In 8:29 Peter, in the name of the disciples, resolves the problem by confessing: "You are the Messiah." The guessing has come to an end. This section of the Gospel can be called "The Mystery of the Messiah," although it closes surprisingly with Jesus' warning Peter not to tell anyone of his confession of faith. This may not be the whole truth about Jesus.
3. Mark 8:31-15:47 is also made up of three sections. Mark 8:31-10:52 reports Jesus' journey to Jerusalem (8:22-52), largely focussed upon Jesus' teaching of his oncoming death and resurrection (8:31; 9:31; 10:32-33) and his instruction of increasingly recalcitrant disciples. He enters Jerusalem (11:1-11), brings all Temple practice to an end (11:12-24), encounters and silences Israel's religious authorities (11:27-12:44), and prophesies the end of the Holy City and the world (13:1-37). The ministry is over as Jesus enters his passion and death (14:1-15:47). Although the textual markers indicate that 8:31-15:47 is made up of three major sections, there is a sense in which the three sections work together to form a "second half" of Mark's literary and theological presentation of the story of Jesus. If 1:14-8:30 made it clear that Jesus is the Messiah (8:29),

but suggested that this may not be the whole truth (8:30). The reader/listener learns in the second half of the Gospel that Jesus is a suffering Messiah, the Son of Man (8:31; 9:31; 10:32-33). Jesus finally accepts that he is the Christ, the Son of God and the Son of Man in 14:62. In 15:37 a Roman centurion confesses: "Truly this man was God's Son!" The suffering Son of Man is truly the Son of God. The mystery has come to an end. Mark 8:31-15:47 can be called "The Mystery of the Son of Man".

4. Many questions raised by the story remain unresolved. The disciples have fled (see 14:50) and Jesus has cried out: "My God, my God, why have you forsaken me?" (15:34). Jesus' question is resolved in the concluding story of women visiting an empty tomb. In 16:1-8 the reader learns that God has not forsaken his Son. He has been raised (see 16:6). But a solution to the problem of failing disciples lies in the future. They are to go into Galilee, there they will see him (v. 7). The women, frightened by all that they have seen and heard, flee and say nothing to anyone (v. 8). Mark 16:1-8 asks questions of the experience of *the believing reader*.

The beginning (1:1-13) and the end (16:1-8) of the Gospel of Mark address the reader/listener. The prologue to the Gospel (1:1-13) is unashamedly full of confessions of faith in the person of Jesus of Nazareth. However, *the reader/listener* is the only one who hears these confessions. The characters from the story are not standing by, listening. The narrator tells *the reader/listener* that Jesus is the Christ, the Son of God (v. 1), the Lord (v. 3), the mightier one (v. 7), the one who will baptize with the Holy Spirit (v. 8), the beloved Son in whom God is well pleased (v. 11). Only the reader/listener recognizes that Jesus' presence in the wilderness, with the wild animals and served by angels, recalls God's original design for humankind, told in the story of Adam and Eve. God's original created order has been restored in the person of Jesus of Nazareth (vv. 12-13).[14]

By the time the reader has arrived at the end of the story, some doubts may have arisen about the confessions of faith that marked its beginnings. A feature of the Gospel of Mark is the disciples' steady movement away from an original enthusiastic following of Jesus (see 1:16-20), to their last appearance in the story in Gethsemane: "And

---

14. See Moloney, *Beginning the Good News*, 43-71.

they all forsook him and fled" (14:50). Only two disciples remain active: Judas who betrays Jesus (14:43-45) and Peter who denies him three times (14:66-72).[15] Jesus' cry of dereliction on the cross, "My God, my God, why have you abandoned me?" (15:34) rings in the reader's and the listener's mind and heart. If this is what happens to the Son of God, what sort of God and what sort of Son are we dealing with? The reader, aware of the Christian tradition, looks to the story of a glorious resurrection to resolve the question. But 16:1-8 proves to be something of a let down! The young man in the tomb announces an Easter message (v. 6), but there is no appearance of Jesus; only the promise of one (v. 7). The women deliver neither the Easter message of v. 6 nor the promise of v. 7. They join the disciples in fear and flight, as the Gospel comes to an end (v. 8).

Mark 16:6-8

A number of tensions exist in the Markan report of Easter day (Mark 16:1-8). They cannot detain us here, as we are concerned with vv. 6-8. However, some features must be noted. The women mentioned in v. 1 (Mary Magdalene, Mary the mother of James, and Salome) are the same women who stood looking upon the crucifixion from afar in 15:40-41. Although articulated differently, two of these women also appear in 15:47. Mary Magdalene and Mary the mother of Joses saw where the body of Jesus was laid.[16] Female followers of Jesus (see

---

15. The steady movement of the disciples away from Jesus, until they leave him, betray him and deny him, has been the subject of much research. For some (e.g. T. J. Weeden, *Mark – Traditions in Conflict* [Philadelphia: Fortress, 1971]), they represent an incorrect understanding of Jesus, the heresy that occasioned the writing of the Gospel of Mark. At the other end of the scale, others (the majority) see Mark's use of the disciples as an attempt to develop characters in the story who embody the failure of all disciples. See especially R. C. Tannehill, "The Disciples in Mark: the Function of a Narrative Role," in *The Interpretation of Mark*, ed. W. Telford, Issues in Religion and Theology 7 (Philadelphia: Fortress, 1985), 134-57.
16. This issue is somewhat clouded by the different names in 15:40 and 15:47. The confusion over the names need not detain us. It is the result Mark's respect for the traditions surrounding Jesus' death and resurrection that came to him. He accepts the tradition, but also wishes to show that women who had been with him in Galilee were at the cross, at the grave and then at the empty tomb. See J. Gnilka, *Das Evangelium nach Markus*, 5th ed., 2 vols., Evangelisch-Katholischer

15:40-41) remain with him at the cross, see where he is buried, and come to the empty tomb. There is a marked contrast between their performance and that of the disciples who have moved gradually into ignorance and failure to stay with Jesus, until the point where they flee in fear (14:50), betray and deny him (14: 43-45 [Judas], 66-72 [Peter]). The theme of the anointing of Jesus' body seems somewhat superfluous, after three days, and also after the symbolic anointing of Jesus body at Bethany by the unnamed women in 14:3-9. However, wonder is generated in the story as the women ask who will roll away the stone, which is very large ... only to find that it has been rolled away (ἀποκεκύλισται ὁ λίθος) (vv. 3-4).[17] The use of the passive voice ("had been rolled back") indicates that God has entered the story. An answer to the agonized question asked by Jesus of God in 15:34 is emerging. The answer becomes explicit in the appearance of the young man, seated on the right side of the tomb, dressed in a white robe.[18]

The Easter proclamation is carefully constructed, showing that the God of Jesus has never abandoned his Son (see 1:11; 9:7; 15:39). The young man tells the women that they are seeking "Jesus the Nazarene the crucified one" (v. 6a). The burial of Jesus was the last act in a series of seeming victories for Jesus' opponents, but the young man instructs them, "He is not here. See the place where *they* laid him" (v. 6c). The two affirmations cannot stand side by side. Jesus is

---

Kommentar zum Neuen Testament II/1-2 (Zürich/Neukirchen-Vluyn: Benziger Verlag/Neukirchener Verlag, 1999), 2:338.

17. Critics sometimes ask why the women did not think of these problems (anointing a body dead three days and the size of the stone) before they set out with their oils. See, for example, W. Grundmann, *Das Evangelium nach Markus*, 6th ed., Theologischer Handkommentar zum Neuen Testament 2 (Berlin: Evangelische Verlagsanstalt, 1973), 320-21.

18. This young man (νεανίσκος) is generally regarded as an angel, especially on the basis of the white clothing. See, for example, M. D. Hooker, *The Gospel According to St Mark*, Black's New Testament Commentaries (London: A. & C. Black, 1991), 584-85. But he also recalls the young man (νεανίσκος) of 14:51-52. In a tiny parable, commenting on the flight of the disciples in v. 50, the author tells of a young man who, like the disciples, fled when those who had come to take Jesus laid hands upon him. He leaves his linen cloth behind, and – a symbol of the disciples - flees naked. The appearance of a young man "clothed" (περιβεβλημένον [another passive]) is a symbolic first hint of the future restoration of the failed disciples. See, H. Fledderman, "The Flight of a Naked Young Man," *The Catholic Biblical Quarterly* 41 (1979): 412-18.

the crucified one (v. 6a), but he is not in the place where those who crucified him had lain the dead body (v. 6c). What has happened? The definitive answer to Jesus question to God in 15:34 is given in the passive verb of v. 6b: "He has been raised" (ἠγέρθη). God has entered the story of the crucified one, and raised him from death. His enemies (those who crucified him and laid him in the tomb) have been vanquished, and the empty tomb is a symbol of God's victory. The reader recalls Jesus' prophecies of his forthcoming death *and* resurrection as he journeyed with the increasingly obdurate disciples toward Jerusalem (see 8:31; 9:31; 10:33-34). *What Jesus said would happen, has happened.*

What of the disciples? The promise of the restoration of the failed disciples was first made by Jesus to his disciples as they walked away from their last meal: "After I am raised up, I will go before (future tense: προάξω) you into Galilee" (14:28). A hint that this promise was to be realized was found in the presence of a young man in the empty tomb (16:5), reversing the parabolic comment upon the fleeing disciples (see 14:50) in the episode of the young man who fled in fear, naked (14:51-52). The future tense of 14:28 is now rendered as a present tense in the young man's instruction to the women. They are to tell the disciples of Jesus ("his disciples") and Peter that "he is going (προάγει) before you into Galilee, as he told you" (v. 7). The stage is set for an encounter in Galilee where failure will be overcome and discipleship restored. They will see him there, as Jesus had promised (14:28).

But this is thwarted by the very last line of the Gospel: "And they went out and fled from the tomb; for trembling and astonishment had come upon them; and they said nothing to anyone, for they were afraid" (v. 8). Does this mean that there is, in Mark's view of things, no vision of the resurrected Jesus, and that the disciples are still waiting for his return?[19] Or is the fear and flight an indication of holy awe in the face of the wonder of the resurrection.[20]

---

19. This is the position of Lohmeyer, followed by a number of contemporary scholars. See above, note 9.
20. This is the traditional solution to the problem, generally with reference back to the fear of the disciples at the Transfiguration (see 9:6). See, for example, M.-J. Lagrange, *Évangile selon Marc*, Études Bibliques (Paris: Gabalda, 1920), 418; Taylor, *St Mark*, 609; W. L. Lane, *Commentary on the Gospel of Mark*, The New International Commentary on the New Testament (Grand Rapids: Eerdmans, 1974), 590-91.

The Christian Community

The ending of the Gospel of Mark must be understood in the light of the story as a whole. The reader was provided with all the information necessary to understand who Jesus was, and what he was doing for humankind in the prologue (1:1-13). Throughout the story the reader has followed the disciples, as they steadily fell further from the design God had for his Son, and for those who follow him (see 8:34-9:1). They have now abandoned him (14:50), betrayed him (14:43-45) and denied him (14:66-72). Only the women, who have been with him since his days in Galilee (see 15:41) have been present at the cross (15:40-41), at the burial (15:47) and at the empty tomb (16:1-7). But in the end, in the very last line of the Gospel, they too join the disciples in their trembling, astonishment, fear and flight (v. 8. See 14:50). Does this mean that the information provided in 1:1-13 is wrong?

Mark 16:8 is the masterstroke of a story-teller who has relentlessly presented the gradual movement to failure of all the male disciples. The evidence of the tradition (as reported by the Gospels of Matthew, Luke and John) indicates that, historically, women were the first witnesses of the Easter event, and reported an Easter message to the unbelieving and discouraged disciples.[21] This was well known by members of early Christian communities. In this, Matthew, Luke and John (each in their own way) have it right. *But Mark has changed the story.* Why has Mark taken a well-known tradition and altered it so radically? There is something profoundly Pauline in what Mark is trying to do.[22] As with the promises of Jesus' forthcoming death and resurrection (8:31; 9:31; 10:33-34), the promise of 16:7 will be fulfilled. *What Jesus said would happen, will happen.* But it does not take place within the limitations of the plot of the Markan story. It

---

21. See E. L. Bode, *The First Easter Morning: The Gospel Accounts of the Women's Visit to the Tomb of Jesus*, Analecta Biblica 45 (Rome: Biblical Institute Press, 1970).
22. Fundamental to Pauline thought is the belief that God has saved sinful humankind by his free gift of grace, made available in and through the death and resurrection of Jesus Christ (see Rom 3:21-26). It is not so much a question of how good the believer might be, or how well he or she performs (although a life modeled on that of Jesus is demanded [see the "ethical excursus" of Rom 5:1-8:39]). What ultimately changes the relationship between God and the human story, lost since the fall of Adam, is the boundless goodness of God (Rom 5:12-21), made visible in Jesus Christ (see Rom 8:31-39). For an excellent analysis of the similarities between Pauline and Markan thought, without suggesting literary dependence, see Marcus, *Mark*, 73-75.

cannot, because the women do not obey the word of the young man (vv. 7-8). They, like the disciples, fail. As with the disciples, they flee in fear (see 14:50-52).

When and how does Jesus' meeting with the failed disciples, women and men, take place? The answer to that question cannot be found *in the story*, but the very existence *of the story* tells the reader that *what Jesus said would happen, did happen*. The Gospel of Mark, with its faith-filled prologue (1:1-13) addressing a believing community, indicates that the disciples and Peter did see Jesus in Galilee, as he had said (14:28; 16:7). If the promise of 14:28 and 16:7 had been thwarted, there would be no Christian community, and thus no Gospel of Mark, read and heard within that community. The reason for the enigma of 16:8 lies in Mark's desire to teach his readers that the encounter between the risen Jesus and the failed disciples did not take place because of the success of the women. In the end, *all human beings fail* ... but God succeeds. God has raised Jesus from the dead (16:6). The Father has not abandoned the Son (15:34). The same God will also raise the disciples, men and women, from their failure. They will see the risen Lord in Galilee. That event took place because of the initiative of God, and not the success of the men *or the women*. The Christian community that produced and received the Gospel of Mark exists because of the initiative of God.

Conclusion

The unique conclusion to the Markan Gospel maintains its relevance. The Easter proclamation, the promise that Jesus was going before his disciples into Galilee, and the failure of the women to speak to anyone because they, like the disciples before them, fled in fear (16:6-8. See 14:50), point beyond the limitations of the Markan story to the existence of a believing Christian community. The Gospel of Mark has been read in such communities, despite their experiences of fear and flight, for 2,000 years. What Jesus said would happen (14:28; 16:7), has happened and continues to happen.

Christian communities and the Christian Church have their *raison d'être* in the attempt to follow Jesus. An honest reading of Christian history, and in a particular way the history of the encounter between European Christianity and the Christianity emerging in worlds where more ancient religions have determined culture, is instructive. Has the figure of the Son of Man who came to serve and not to be served, to lay down his life for all (see 10:45), been the guiding principle at all times? There has been much heroism, marked by fear and trembling (see 10:32), but this witness has at times been damaged by arrogance and sin. Yet, despite our ambiguity, like the many Christian communities which preceded us, we continue to celebrate Eucharist (see 6:31-44; 8:1-9). We continue our commitment to discipleship (see 8:22-10:52) aware that it is not the success stories of human beings, men or women, which make Christian discipleship and the Christian Church an effective presence of God and his word in the world. Mark 16:6-8 proclaims a message of fundamental importance for the Christian community: God always has and always will make sense of our nonsense.

7
God's Gift of Servant Discipleship in the Gospel of Mark

Each Gospel was written to proclaim the good news of Jesus Christ (see Mark 1:1; Matt 1:1; Luke 24:44-49; John 20:30-31). But Jesus is never a solitary figure. In each Gospel he calls followers and challenges them to learn from him as his disciples.[1] The disciples, present with Jesus at almost every turn, are major players in Mark's story. Jesus is certainly the most important character, but the disciples also play a vital role.[2] Surprisingly, however, the disciples of Jesus, despite a positive start to their relationship with him, fail their master as the story comes to an end. Indeed, unless one accepts the longer ending of Mark 16:9-20, the story closes without any resolution of their increasing fear and failure across the latter part of the Gospel. Their last appearance is marked by fear and flight, as the disciples abandon Jesus in the Garden of Gethsemane (14:50-52). Both Paul and the other Gospels tell of the presence of the risen Jesus to the disciples (see 1 Cor 15:3-11; Matt 28:16-20; Luke 24:36-49; John 20:18-23). This is not the case in the Gospel of Mark. Despite the command of the young man in the empty tomb to go to the disciples and Peter that Jesus is going before them into Galilee and that they will see him

---

1. In both Greek and Latin, the root of the word "disciple" means "to learn" (Greek: μαθηταί, from the verb μανθάνω, "to learn." Latin: from the verb "discere," also meaning "to learn").
2. For a survey of a variety of approaches and different interpretations of the role of the disciples in Mark, see C. Clifton Black, *The Disciples according to Mark: Markan Redaction in Current Debate*, Journal for the Study of the New Testament Supplement Series 27 (Sheffield: Sheffield Academic Press, 1989). For a briefer overview, see Francis J. Moloney, "The Vocation of the Disciples in the Gospel of Mark," in *"A Hard Saying." The Gospel and Culture* (Collegeville, MN: The Liturgical Press, 2001), 53-63.

there (v. 7), the women flee from the tomb, so full of fear that they do not say anything to anyone (16:8). The original Gospel of Mark came to an end at that point. There is no account of the appearances of the risen Jesus and the re-establishment of discipleship.[3]

Introduction

Mark told a Gospel-story. This means that his main purpose was to offer an interpretation of Jesus as the Christ, the Son of God (see 1:1). A major part of the literary technique he used to do this was to open his story of Jesus with a "Prologue" (1:1-13) and to close it with an "Epilogue" (16:1-8). I will conclude this paper by devoting my attention to the Epilogue, which contains Mark's unique and very brief account of the empty tomb and the Easter proclamation (16:1-8). It is a crucial element in understanding the victory of God over Jesus' death, and the victory of God over the failure of the disciples. For the moment, let us focus our attention, however briefly, upon the Prologue (1:1-13).

The Prologue of the Gospel introduces *the reader/listener* to the mystery of the person of Jesus in 1:1-13. The promise of "the beginning" in v. 1 (see Gen 1:1), and the coming of the creating presence of the Spirit of God in v. 10 (see Gen 1:3) indicate that the prologue to the Gospel of Mark is linked to the prologue to the human story, as it was told in Genesis 1-11. *God is the most active figure in vv. 1-13.* Jesus is *presented* to the reader. He is the Christ, the Son of God (v. 1), the Lord (v. 3), the Stronger One (v. 7); the one who will baptize with the Holy Spirit (v. 8).[4] God's voice has assured the reader that he is the

---

3. The tradition of the appearances of Jesus the disciples (especially in the light of 1 Cor 15:3-7) is older than the Gospel of Mark. Mark's original readers (as well as all subsequent readers) would have been surprised by the ending of Mark's Gospel at 16:8. They would be aware that he was not telling the story *as they knew it*. He is *re-interpreting* an established tradition. For an authoritative study of the development of the longer ending of the Gospel of Mark, now found in Bibles as Mark 16:9-20, see James A. Kelhoffer, *Miracle and Mission. The Authentication of Missionaries and Their Message in the Longer Ending of Mark*, Wissenschaftliche Untersuchungen zum Neuen Testament 2.112 (Tübingen: J. C. B. Mohr [Paul Siebeck], 2000).
4. Herman C. Waetjen, *A Reordering of Power: A socio-Political Reading of Mark's Gospel* (Minneapolis: Fortress Press, 1989), 22, speaks of Jesus in the prologue as "God's surrogate."

beloved Son of God, and that God is well pleased with him (v. 11). He is filled with the Spirit (v. 10), and driven into the desert to dwell with the wild beasts and to be served by the angels, thus reversing the tragedy of the Adam and Eve story, to re-establish God's original design (vv. 12-13).[5]

The story-teller has provided a dense Prologue for the reader/listener in which he provides a succinct summary of what *God has done* in and through Jesus, his beloved Son. There should be no doubt in the reader's mind about *who Jesus is*. Notice, however, that the disciples have not been party to what is said in the Prologue. They must work out the mystery of what God is doing in and through Jesus (and also in and through them) by participating in the mission and ministry of Jesus. There have been hints throughout the prologue that pointed to this ministry, if he is to baptize with a holy spirit (v. 8). There is perhaps even a hint that he will accept total and unconditional self-sacrifice as God's "beloved" (v. 11).

The reader comes to the end of the prologue well informed about *who* Jesus is, but as yet unaware of *how* Jesus is the Christ, the Son of God, the Lord, the Stronger One who baptizes with the Holy Spirit, and *how* in his person God's original creative design has been restored. The readers and hearers of this Gospel know that Jesus of Nazareth was crucified, and they may well wonder how such an end could be pleasing to God (see v. 11). The Prologue to the Gospel lays down this challenge. Now the reader/listener knows *who Jesus is*, and must be prepared to read through a story which will show *how Jesus pleases his Father*. The disciples of Jesus are an essential part of this story.

Even though they are not present in the prologue – and indeed they do not *know* what the reader has learnt about Jesus in the prologue – Mark is very focused upon the story of disciples, and the waxing and waning of their association with Jesus and his mission. We must follow their association with Jesus' person, his mission and his death and resurrection *within the story* better to understand Mark's portrait of them. As we will see, the Markan story of the disciples indicates, on the one hand, what they were called to and, on the

---

5. See Francis J, Moloney, *The Gospel of Mark. A Commentary* (Peabody, MA: Hendrickson, 2002), 27-41, for a detailed study of Mark 1:1-13. See also Idem, *The Living Voice of the Gospel. The Gospels Today* (Melbourne: John Garratt, 2006), 72-87.

other, who was ultimately responsible for a successful discipleship. This paper argues that they were called to a servant discipleship, but that God is the only source of what we now know as the success of disciples of Jesus. It had nothing to do with the talents, skills, and achievements of the disciples themselves. Mark's presentation of the performance of the disciples, and Jesus' teaching on the nature of discipleship is an *interpretation* that reaches beyond any attempt to report "how it was." Mark tells of disciples and discipleship with an eye to the Christian community, to interpret *their* story of following Jesus. The Markan presentation of Jesus *along with* his description of the role of the disciples sought to address the experience of being a follower of Jesus in his own post-70 Christian community. His message, however, can address all subsequent disciples who read the Gospel. While Mark was primarily interested in instructing his own community in the first century, the ongoing reading of the Gospel has continued to instruct Christian communities over two millennia. What Mark has said about disciples and discipleship late in the first century continues to address disciples early in the third millennium.

The Disciples

Some studies of Mark distinguish between "the Twelve" (οἱ δώδεκα), and the more generic description of "the disciples" (οἱ μαθηταί). In the life of Jesus, his choice of his first followers and the appointment of the inner circle of "the Twelve" was, historically, an important distinction.[6] However, for the purposes of the following reflection, they are considered together. Mark's interpretation of the Christian community depends upon the reader/listener's appreciation of his portrait of both "the Twelve" and "the disciples." Another, less clearly defined group, is simply called "those who follow" (οἱ ἀκολουθοῦντες). All three groups are called to follow, instructed on the requirements of true discipleship, and described as failing to understand and accept Jesus' demands. Though the Twelve were called to exercise a ministry of leadership, nevertheless, they belonged to the larger community, called "disciples" or "followers" of Jesus. Mark instructs his readers

---

6. On the historical "Twelve" and the more general group of followers or disciples of Jesus, see John P. Meier, *A Marginal Jew. Rethinking the Historical Jesus*, 5 vols., Anchor Bible Reference Library (New York: Doubleday, 1991-2016), 3:125-97.

on the blessings and challenges of living in a Christian community by means of his interpretation of all "the disciples": the twelve, the disciples, and those who followed.[7]

When one singles out the principal places across the Gospel where the disciples play a significant and active role, along with those passages where Jesus instructs them on the demands of discipleship, three themes emerge:

a) Initially disciples are called to follow Jesus and are associated with him (1:16-20; 2:13-14; 3:13-19; 6:7-13).
b) Gradually, the first signs of their inability or unwillingness to be true "followers" of Jesus becomes apparent (4:35-41; 6:30, 45-52; 8:22-10:52).
c) Finally they sink into total failure (14:50-52; 14:66-72; 16:8).

Strange as this movement into failure may at first appear, Mark's story of struggling and fragile disciples conveys his understanding of the role of their relationship with Jesus, and his care for them. Behind this portrayal of the disciples in the story of the Gospel lies Mark's teaching to his own community. He wants them to know that, in the end, authentic discipleship is a gift of God.

The call of the disciples and their sharing in Jesus' mission

Jesus' disciples share in a privileged way in Jesus' own person and mission. Jesus' first action, after his initial appearance and proclamation of the kingdom (1:14-15), is to call disciples to follow him. They respond to his call and take their place behind him. They leave all the signs of their earthly success and join him, to follow him down *his way* (1:16-20). He not only calls fishermen to become fishers of human beings, but he even summons a public sinner, the tax collector

---

7. It is nowadays generally accepted that these differently described disciples/followers of Jesus reflected the historical reality of Jesus' own entourage and supporters. A small group (including the Twelve and some women [see 15:40-41]) were itinerants, part of his wandering mission. Others (also "followers") remained in their homes and villagers, accepting and welcoming Jesus and his message about the Kingdom of God. On this, see Gerd Theissen, *The First Followers of Jesus. A Sociological Analysis of the Earliest Christianity* (London: SCM Press, Fortress, 1978), 8-23.

Levi, to become his follower. Like the fishermen, Levi responds without hesitation (2:13-14). Having called his first disciples, Jesus begins his ministry in Galilee. The disciples witness the wonders he does, and also receive private instruction from him (4:11, 34; 7:17). Across the early chapters of the Gospel, the disciples do not actually *do* anything, but they are his constant companions. The initial positive presentation of the disciples and their relationship with Jesus must not be lost from view. The disciples are called to follow Jesus, to be with him, and to share in his ministry. However much they may fail as the story proceeds, this understanding of discipleship retains its place in the Markan instruction of his early Christian community, called to be with Jesus and to continue his ministry in both word and deed.

Jesus is portrayed across the Gospel of Mark as forever on the move. Almost every episode begins with a verb of motion, generally closely associated with the adverb *immediately* (εὐθύς). He is forever going, coming, leading, entering, setting out, and so on. This way of telling the story creates the impression of a restless energy in Jesus, responding to a call of his own as he journeys on. While on this journey, Jesus can call his disciples to be fellow pilgrims, to follow him (ἀκολουθέω).[8] In the second half of the Gospel, this movement settles into a more regular pattern, as Jesus and the disciples, journey along the way to Jerusalem (see 8:27; 9:33, 34; 10:17, 32, 46, 52; 11:8). Jesus is not the master of his own destiny and this relentless and energetic movement, eventually leading to Jerusalem and the cross, is an indication of Jesus' unconditional response to the design of God.

After summoning a further larger group, he appoints from among them "the Twelve" (3:13-14). The appointment of "the Twelve" is an important moment in the Markan interpretation of discipleship He appoints them "to be with him" (v. 14a: ἵνα ὦσιν μετ'αὐτοῦ).[9] Jesus

---

8. This literary/theological aspect of the Markan story has been well caught by Paula Fredriksen, *From Jesus to Christ. The Origins of the New Testament Images of Jesus*, 2nd ed. (New Haven: Yale University Press, 2000), 44: "Mark's Jesus is a man in a hurry, dashing throughout the Galilee in rapid, almost random motion, from synagogue to invalid, from shore to grain field to sea, casting out demons and amazing those who witness him. The spare prose and the staccato cures create a mood of nervous anticipation. The times *must* be fulfilled. Who is this man, and what will he do next?"
9. For a detailed analysis of this passage, and the insistence that what is said of "the Twelve" is to be applied to followers of Jesus in general, especially the readers of the Gospel, see Moloney, *Mark*, 76-80.

establishes an intimacy between himself and his disciples, and this intimacy has its consequences. The "being with him" leads to the promise that they will share in Jesus' mission of spreading God's reign. They will be sent out, they will preach, and they will have authority to cast out demons (v. 14b-15). Up to this stage in the Gospel, Jesus has burst upon the scene; *he* has preached and *he* has cast out demons. What Jesus does, the disciples will now do, but only if they are *with* Jesus (14a). The action of the disciples flows from the disciples' *being with Jesus*. The intimate personal link between the disciple and Jesus must not be broken. Whatever the disciples are as followers of Jesus, and what they are able to do as his missionaries, depend upon being *with him*. This dependence is made clear by the construction of the Greek sentence, with a series of "so that" clauses following Jesus' establishment of the Twelve who are to be "with him."

The promise that they would share his ministry (1:17; 3:14b) becomes a fact when the Twelve are formally sent out on a mission (6:7-13). The disciples are to take Jesus as their model for mission; bereft of everything except a staff and sandals, like him they are sent on a wandering mission (6:7-9). They are not to seek comfort and security but to stay in the place where their message finds a home (vv. 10-11). They successfully preach repentance, cast out demons and heal the sick (vv. 12-13).[10]

These promising initial moments in the Markan use of his traditions are an important part of his interpretation of the role of disciples and the demands of discipleship. Mark presents Jesus' call to the disciples, and his close association with them so that they can join his mission: *disciples are models for all who are called to be followers of Jesus*. Mark wanted his original readers to develop a sense of oneness between the "disciples of Jesus" in the Gospel, and the "disciples of Jesus" reading the Gospel. The disciples in the Gospel formed an original community of "followers of Jesus." They were called by him, associated with him and granted a share of his mission to preach the gospel to the whole world (see 13:10). The successful creation of followers who left all (1:16-20), and shared successfully in Jesus' mission (6:7-13) was a fundamental message addressed to the original Markan community in the story of the Gospel. It retains its importance

---

10. See the essay, "Mark 6:6b-30: The Twelve, Mission, and Failure," on pp. 15-45 of this volume.

for today's Christian communities. However much the original readers, or hearers, of the Gospel of Mark may have been aware of their failure to live up to this summons to share in Jesus' life and mission, the voice of Jesus still issued the invitation: "Follow me" (1:17).

Signs of failure

What is surprising about the disciples in the Gospel of Mark is that they cut an increasingly poor figure the longer they are associated with Jesus. After the association of the Twelve with his mission (3:14-15), and even before he sends them out (6:7-13), Jesus chastises "those who were about him and the Twelve" (4:10) because they have not understood the parable of the scattered seed (4:3-9), suggesting that they will never be able to understand his teaching in parables (v. 13). After his teaching, Jesus and the disciples (see v. 34) set off in a boat to go to the other side of the lake. In the midst of a storm they are overcome by fear, an emotion that will become increasingly present among them. Rebuking the wind and the sea, as if they were personifications of evil and violence, Jesus calms the storm, but chastises his disciples for their fear and lack of faith (v. 40). But even this rebuke has little effect. The passage closes with his disciples filled with awe, saying to one another: "Who then is this, that even wind and sea obey him?" (v. 41). They are frightened, and unable to recognize the presence and authority of God in the one they are following.

The cost of discipleship is first made clear in the report of John the Baptist's fearless commitment to his mission, unto death (6:14-29). However, before this report, the Twelve were sent out on a successful mission (6:7-13). On their return, immediately following the account of the Baptist's death, they are eager to tell Jesus all the things they had said and done (6:30).[11] They are losing the sense of being the "sent ones" (ἀπόστολοι; see vv. 7, 30) of Jesus. They have reached a stage where they regard their successful mission as being the result of *their own* authority over sickness and the demonic. They forget

---

11. The passage that runs from 6:7-30 is an example of the Markan practice of "intercalation." The disciples are sent out (A: vv. 7-13), the cost of proclaiming the truth is reported in the death of the Baptist, which foreshadows the death of Jesus (B: vv. 14-29), those who were sent out return to Jesus (A¹: v. 30). On this Markan literary technique, among many, see Tom Shepherd, "The Narrative Function of Markan Intercalation," *New Testament Studies* 41 (1995): 522-40.

that what they *do* depends entirely upon their *being with* Jesus (3:14). Despite Jesus' two-fold feeding of the multitudes (6:31-44; 8:1-9), they are unable to understand his walking on the sea after the first miracle (6:51-52), and they do not understand what he means when he speaks of the leaven of the Pharisees and the Herodians after the second miracle (8:11-21). In 6:52 Mark reports, "For they did not understand about the loaves, but their hearts were hardened" (6:52). The same themes return in 8:11-21. Jesus accuses them of hard-heartedness and blindness (vv. 17-18), and frustratingly asks them, "Do you not yet understand?" (v. 21).

The disciples' blindness and inability to understand lead directly into the section of the Gospel that runs from 8:22 to 10:52 where Jesus predicts his passion and calls the disciples to the cross, to receptivity and to service. Jesus' challenging words are set between two miracles where blindness is transformed to sight (8:22-26; 10:46-52). These two miracles symbolically portray Jesus' accusation that the disciples may be blind (8:17-18), and their blindness becomes evident in the central section of the Gospel. Here, more than anywhere in the Gospel, Mark tells a story that makes clear the demands of discipleship. Repeatedly, Jesus draws his disciples to one side and instructs them (see, for example, 8:34-38; 9:33-50; 10:23-31, 35-45). As Jesus journeys toward Jerusalem, asking his disciples to follow him, he thrice announces his forthcoming passion (8:31; 9:31; 10:33-34). After each of these passion predictions the disciples show that they cannot or will not accept Jesus' "way," and are unwilling to follow him. With Peter as their representative they have their own idea of messiahship (8:32-33). They want to set up an exclusive discipleship, and are hostile to others who do not see things their way (9:38-41; 10:13-16). Even after the final passion prediction, full of the gruesome details of what will happen in Jerusalem (10:33-34), the sons of Zebedee are jockeying for positions of authority (10:35-37), and the other disciples are indignant that they might be beaten out of these honors (10:41). Remarkably, however, Jesus never fails the failing disciples. He instructs them on the need for the cross in 8:34-9:1, on the need for service and receptivity in 9:35-37, and draws cross, service and receptivity together as he instructs them on the need to forsake their search for human authority and political power in 10:38-44.

The earlier moments of close association between Jesus and disciples are attractive, and readers of the Gospel are prepared to accept the paradigm of the original disciples in their following of Jesus. However, on arrival at Mark 10:45, the fragility of the original disciples is becoming increasingly obvious, and a matter of concern. The disciples will not and cannot accept that to follow Jesus means to commit themselves to the cross (8:34-38; 10:39), to humble service and receptivity (9:33-37; 10:35-44), for the sake of Jesus and the Gospel. Despite these signs of failure, Jesus leads the way: "For the Son of Man came not to be served, but to serve, and to give his life as a ransom for many" (10:45). The first blind man stumbled from total blindness to partial sight to a fullness of vision (8:22-26); blind Bartimeus leaves all, and follows Jesus down his way toward Jerusalem (10:46-52).[12] But in the episodes between these two miracles, the disciples have not succeeded in such self-abandonment and enthusiastic preparedness to follow Jesus "down his way" (v. 52).[13]

What is surprising about this part of the story, as the disciples waver in their attachment to Jesus is that, despite the fact that they sink deeper into failure and an inability to understand what is being asked of them, Jesus perseveres with his instruction. This is not simply a sign of Jesus' persistence or patience. His teaching and journeying with his disciples "on the way" to Jerusalem is Mark's presentation of one of the central elements of his teaching on disciples and discipleship. *Jesus never abandons the fragile disciples.* He continues to summon his would-be "followers" to the cross (8:34-38; 10:39), to receptivity and service (9:33-50; 10:35-44). Jesus' message on discipleship still stands, despite the increasing failure of the disciples. The light in the darkness of their failures is the never-failing presence of Jesus to his fragile disciples. Here we are touching the heart of the Markan interpretation of the relationship between Jesus and the Christian community. Jesus' fidelity to failing disciples, originally articulated by this Gospel for the Markan community, offers comfort and inspiration to disciples of all time, wherever this Gospel is read.

---

12. For a detailed study of 8:22-10:52 that supports the sketch of the disciples offered in this paragraph, see Moloney, *Mark*, 171-214.
13. See the evocative treatment of this passage by R. Alan Culpepper, *Mark*, Smith & Helwys Bible Commentary (Macon: Smyth & Helwys, 2007), 344-49.

The ultimate failure

The failure of the disciples comes to a head in the passion story. Judas, "one of the Twelve," betrays Jesus (14:10-11), Peter denies him (14:66-72) and his most intimate followers, Peter, James and John, sleep through his hour of anguished prayer (14:32-42).[14] The final appearance of the group of disciples is found in 14:50: "And they all forsook him and fled." Following this lapidary statement of the flight of the disciples, Mark interprets their action with a brief parabolic narrative. There was also a young man "following." He too, at the threat of danger, fled, leaving in the hands of his assailants the only covering which he had on his body, a linen cloth. Like the disciples who have just fled, he is naked in his nothingness (vv. 51-52).[15] Apart from Judas, who betrays Jesus (14:43-46), and Peter who denies him (14:66-72), as Jesus had prophesied (14:10-11; 26-31), the disciples never again appear in Gospel. But, in their absence, they will be significantly mentioned by the young man at the tomb in 16:7.

We come now to the Epilogue of the Gospel (16:1-8). Just as the disciples were not addressed by the words and events of the Prologue (1:1-13), there are no disciples at the cross or at the resurrection of Jesus in Mark's Gospel (15:1-16:8). But the listener/reader is always present, and he or she is made aware of hints of an eventual restoration to their place "following" Jesus. The flight of the disciples is symbolized by the parallel flight of the young man, who leaves everything behind to forsake Jesus, but at the empty tomb the women find "a young man, sitting on the right side, dressed in a white robe" (16:5). The similarities between the parable of the naked young man, which describes the fleeing disciples in 14:51-52, and the presence of the young man whose clothing is described at the empty tomb at 16:5 are too close to be irrelevant. The reader/listener senses restoration.[16] The women are commissioned: "Go tell his disciples and Peter that he is going before you to Galilee; there you will see him, as he told you" (v. 7). These words from the young man recall earlier words of

---

14. Peter, James and John appear to have a special closeness to Jesus, (see 3:16-17; 5:37; 9:2; 13:3)
15. See Harry Fleddermann, "The Flight of as Naked Young Man (Mark 14:51-52)," *Catholic Biblical Quarterly* 41 (1979): 412-18; Moloney, *Mark*, 344-48.
16. See Neil Q. Hamilton, "Resurrection, Tradition and the Composition of Mark," *Journal of Biblical Literature* 84 (1965): 415-21; Moloney, *Mark*, 344-52.

Jesus. In the midst of his prophecies of their imminent failure Jesus had promised his disciples: "You will all fall away; for it is written, 'I will strike the shepherd, and the sheep will be scattered. But after I am raised up, I will go before you to Galilee'" (14:27-28). Nevertheless, the fear, silence and flight returns in v. 8, the last verse of the Gospel: "And they went out and fled from the tomb; for trembling and astonishment had come upon them; and they said nothing to anyone, for they were afraid." The story of failure is pushed to its limits. Mark is relentless in his interpretation of the fragility of the human response to the divine intervention that took place in the person of Jesus. The Father's voice from heaven that demanded disciples "listen to him" (9:7) seems to have fallen on deaf ears.

The Disciples, God, and the Christian community

Scholars have interpreted this negative portrait of the disciples in the Gospel of Mark in a variety of ways. Many claim that, for Mark, the disciples offer no paradigm for the Markan Church or for the Christian community of any age, as they fail so dismally. As one scholar puts it:

> I conclude that Mark is assiduously involved in a vendetta against the disciples. He paints them as obtuse, obdurate, recalcitrant men who at first are unperceptive of Jesus' messiahship, then oppose its style and character, and finally totally reject it. As a *coup de grace*, Mark closes his Gospel without rehabilitating the disciples.[17]

This widely held position throws into relief the failure, but underplays and misunderstands the importance of the positive side of the disciples' story in Mark's attempt to address his own community, and subsequently, the Christian communities down through the centuries who continue to read the Gospel of Mark. What is the reader to make of the earlier part of the narrative? In 10:32, as Jesus approaches Jerusalem, the disciples, despite all their fear and failure, are still called

---

17. T. J. Weeden, *Mark - Traditions in Conflict* (Philadelphia: Fortress, 1976), 50-51. For Weeden, the disciples are used in the story as the representatives of a false Christology. A similar negative reading of the role of the disciples is found in Richard A. Horsley, *Hearing the Whole Story: The Politics of Plot in Mark's Gospel* (Louisville: Westminster John Knox, 2001), 79-97.

"those who followed" (οἱ δὲ ἀκολουθοῦντες). The two sides of the disciples' response to Jesus must be held in tension, as there is a need to take into account both the positive and the negative in the story of the disciples, as it is the story of all disciples.[18] The Markan interpretation of the disciples *in the story* would have been strongly influenced by the Markan readers/hearers *of the story*. In other words, for Mark, the story of the disciples reached outside the boundaries of the story of the Gospel into the story of the Christian community for which he was writing his interpretation of the life of Jesus.[19] As God was the most important agent as the Prologue addressed the readers and listeners (1:1-13), God is again the most important agent in the Epilogue as the readers and listeners are again addressed (16:1-8).

The lived experience of failure and the ongoing presence of Jesus in the lives of the readers in the original Markan community determined Mark's interpretation of disciples and discipleship. There was little or no room for a *human success story* for Jesus, the Christ, the Son of God and the Son of Man. It appears that the same interpretation is continued into the Markan presentation of the disciples to the Christian community that he was addressing by means of his Gospel. Jesus was finally vindicated by God in the resurrection (see 16:6). Similarly, the disciples' experience of the never-failing presence of Jesus, even in their failure, will not be thwarted. He told them he would be struck and they would flee. At the same time, he promised he would go before them into Galilee (14:27-28). The women failed to communicate this Easter promise to the disciples and Peter (see 16:8), joining the other disciples who had fled in fear (see 14:50-52). *But the word of Jesus (see 14:28; 16:7) will not fail (see 13:31)!* The very existence of the Gospel of Mark, read and heard in the original Markan community about 70 CE, and all subsequent Christian communities, is proof that the word of Jesus did not fail. The promise of the young man returns to the earlier promise of Jesus, "He is going before you into Galilee. There you will see him," has come true (16:6; see 14:28). The Gospel of Mark tells the members of a struggling Christian community that human beings may fail, but God will not fail them. Fail-

---

18. See especially, Robert C. Tannehill, "The Disciples in Mark: The Function of a Narrative Role," *Journal of Religion* 57 (1977) 386-405. This important study is also available in William Telford, ed., *The Interpretation of Mark*, Issues in Religion and Theology 7 (Philadelphia: Fortress, 1985), 134-57.
19. See Moloney, *Mark*, 352-54.

ure will be overcome and discipleship restored, not because men or women understand and succeed, but because of God's graciousness.

The explanation of the enigma of the failure of the women in 16:8 lies in Mark's desire to instruct his readers that the encounter between the risen Jesus and the failed disciples did not take place because of the success of the women. As the disciples failed (14:50-52), so also the women failed (16:8). In the end, *all human beings fail* ... but God succeeds. God has raised Jesus from the dead (16:6); the Father has not abandoned the Son (15:34). The same God will also raise the disciples, men and women, from their failure. They will see the risen Lord in Galilee, but not because the disciples or the women succeed. The event that bridged the gap between the end of the Gospel of Mark and the community which heard it and read it took place because of the initiative of God, and not the success of men or women. The Christian community that produced and received the Gospel of Mark existed because of the initiative of God.[20] The promise of the Gospel's prologue (1:1-13) is fulfilled in the action of God described in its epilogue (16:1-8) and experienced by believing readers of the Markan story.

The Easter proclamation, "He has been raised" (v. 6),[21] the promise that Jesus was going before his disciples into Galilee (v. 7), and the failure of the women to speak to anyone because they, like the disciples

---

20. For an excellent synthesis of the ongoing relevance of the post-Easter Markan community, gleaned from a reading of the Gospel, see Klaus Scholtissek, "Nachfolge und Autorität nach dem Markusevangelium," *Trierer theologische Zeitschrift* 100 (1991): 56-74.
21. This is not the place to evaluate what might have been meant by "resurrection" in the earliest Church. Mark's terse narrative offers no help. For a survey, see Francis J. Moloney, "Faith in the Risen Jesus," *Salesianum* 43 (1981): 305-16. Scholarly opinion varies. See, by way of example: those who argue for the physical presence of the pre-Easter Jesus alive among his disciples (see, for example, Wolfhart Pannenberg, "Did Jesus Actually Rise from the Dead?" *Dialog* 4 [1965]: 18-35; Idem, *Grundzüge der Christologie* [Gutersloh: Gerd Mohn, 1964], 85-103); an experience among the disciples that they had been forgiven (see, for example Edward Schillebeeckx, *Jesus. An Experiment in Christology*, trans. John Bowden [London: Collins, 1979], 115-319.); a mysterious awareness that "the Jesus thing goes on" (see Willie Marxsen, *The Resurrection of Jesus of Nazareth*, trans. Margaret Kohl [London: SCM Press, 1970]); the expected fulfillment of the disciples' recognition of the pre-Easter Jesus as the Mosaic eschatological prophet (see, for example, Rudolf Pesch, "Zur Entstehung des Glaubens an die Auferstehung Jesu," *Theologische Quartalschrift* 153 [1973]: 201-228). See now, Francis J. Moloney, *The Resurrection of the Messiah. A Narrative Commentary on the Resurrection in the Four Gospels* (New York/Mahwah, NJ: Paulist, 2013), 137-82.

before them, fled in fear (16:6-8. See 14:50), point beyond the limitations of the Markan story to the existence of a believing Christian community. The prologue to the Gospel (1:1-13) informed the reader that Jesus was the Christ (1:1), the Lord (v. 3), the mightier one (v. 7), one who would baptize with the Holy Spirit (v. 8), the beloved Son of God (v. 11), restoring God's original creative design (vv. 12-13). The original Markan community accepted this confession of faith, and attempted to live as authentic disciples of Jesus, taking up their cross, receptive servants of all, in imitation of Jesus (see 8:31-10:44) who came to serve and not be served, and to lay down his life (10:45). Yet, in human terms, the disciples, both men and women, fail to follow Jesus through the cross to resurrection. In the same human terms, even Jesus failed, crying out in anguish from the cross (15:34). But Jesus' apparent failure is his victory. On the cross he is King, Messiah and Son of God (see 15:26, 31-32), and God has entered the story by raising his Son from the dead: "He has been raised" (16:6b: ἠγέρθη). He is no longer in the place where *they* laid him (v. 6c).

The author believes and wishes to communicate that the exalted christological claims of the prologue (1:1-13) have been vindicated by the story of the suffering and crucified Jesus, especially by means of the Easter proclamation of the epilogue (16:1-8). The affirmation of God's project by means of the prologue (1:1-13) and the epilogue (16:1-8) also points to God's vindication of failed disciples. The original readers of the Gospel of Mark, aware of their fragility, were encouraged by a story which told of the inability of the original disciples, men and women, to overcome their fear and follow Jesus through the cross to resurrection (14:50; 16:8). But as God has transformed the failure of Jesus by the resurrection (16:6), his promise to the failing disciples of a meeting in Galilee (14:28; 16:7) has also eventuated. God, and not human beings, generated the new Temple, built upon the rejected cornerstone (see 12:10-11; 14:57-58; 15:29, 38). The existence of the Gospel and its original intended readership are proof of that fact.[22]

---

22. On the perennial nature of the Markan message of the tension between success and failure among disciples, both women and men, see Hans-Joseph Klauck, "Die Erzählerische Rolle der Jünger im Markusevangelium. Eine narrative Analyse," *Novum Testamentum* 24 (1982): 1-26; Elizabeth S. Malbon, "Fallible Followers: Women and Men in the Gospel of Mark," *Semeia* 28 (1983): 29-48 (now available in Idem, *In the Company of Jesus. Characters in Mark's Gospel* [Louisville: Westminster John Knox, 2000], 41-69); Robert C. Tannehill, "The Disciples in Mark: The Function of a Narrative Role," 134-57.

The accomplishment of Jesus' promises is not found *in the text*. The existence of the Markan community and its story of Jesus indicate that it is taking place *among the readers of the text*, in the experience of the original readers (and hearers) of the Gospel of Mark. But that is not the end of the process. The proclamation of the Gospel of Mark in fragile Christian communities, experiencing their own versions of fear and flight, for almost 2,000 years, suggests that the accomplishment of the promise of 14:28 and 16:7 continues in the Christian experience of the subsequent readers (and hearers) of the Gospel. What Jesus promised (14:28; 16:7), happened for the Markan community, and continues to happen among generations of fragile followers of Jesus. As Christian disciples continue to fail and flee in fear, they are told that God's action in and through the risen Jesus overcomes all such failure.[23] Jesus is going before them into Galilee. There they will see him. The Epilogue, the conclusion to Mark's Gospel is not a message of failure, but a resounding affirmation of God's design to overcome all imaginable human failure (see 16:1-8) in and through the action of God's beloved Son (see 1:1-13). Words addressed to the struggling disciples at the transfiguration are addressed to all who take up this Gospel: "Listen to him" (see 9:7).

---

23. For similar suggestions, see Thomas Boomershine, "Mark 16:8 and the Apostolic Commission," *Journal of Biblical Literature* 100 (1981): 234-39; Robert C. Tannehill, "The Gospel of Mark as Narrative Christology," *Semeia* 16 (1980): 82-84; Susan R. Garrett, *The Temptations of Jesus in Mark's Gospel* (Grand Rapids: Eerdmans, 1998), 137-69.

8
Matthew 5:17-18 and the Matthean Use of "Righteousness"

In Honor of Frank J. Matera

One of the enigmas of the Gospel of Matthew is the apparent contradiction between Jesus' program not to abolish but to fulfill the law found at the beginning of the Gospel (5:17-18) and the risen Jesus' commission of the disciples to preach all that he has commanded to all nations (28:16-20). The closing scene in the Gospel appears to be a deliberate Christological re-reading of issues dear to the life and practice of the Judaism of the post-war period: all authority is given to Jesus (see Deut 6:4-9; Dan 7:14). He breaks through national and religious boundaries, as he invites his disciples to preach to all nations, replacing circumcision with baptism.[1] He teaches the observance of what Jesus has commanded them (πάντα ὅσα ἐνετειλάμεν ὑμῖν), as

---

1. This is widely, but not universally, accepted. See, for example, Michel-Joseph Lagrange, *Évangile selon Saint Matthieu*, Etudes Bibliques (Paris: Gabalda, 1927), 544-45: "On comprend très bien que la restriction au brébis d'Israel (Mt. X, 5s) ait été levée en ce moment." See also Wolfgang Trilling, *Das Wahre Israel. Studien zur Theologie des Matthäus-Evangelium*, 3d ed., Studien zum Alten und Neuen Testament 10 (München: Kösel Verlag, 1964), 21-51. For David C. Sim, *The Gospel of Matthew and Christian Judaism. The History and Social Setting of the Matthean Community*, Studies of the New Testament and Its World (Edinburgh: T. & T. Clark, 1998), 252-55, every aspect of the Law was still practised in the post-Easter Matthean community, including circumcision. Ulrich Luz, *Matthew*, 3 vols., Hermeneia (Minneapolis: Fortress, 2001-2007), 3:631-32, says that we do not know whether or not the practice of circumcision continued. William D. Davies and Dale C. Allison, *The Gospel According to Saint Matthew*, 3 vols., International Critical Commentary (Edinburgh: T. & T. Clark, 1988-1997), 3:685, argue "That he expected Jewish Christians to circumcise their male children is plausible; but he evidently did not think such necessary for Gentiles." As Davies, Allison and Luz all argue that 5:17-18 means that the law must be rigorously kept till the end of all time (see below), Sim, *The Gospel*, 252, is rightly critical of their lack of logic.

the law (see Exod 29:35).² This puzzle is intensified by Jesus' sending of his disciples only "to the lost sheep of the house of Israel" (10:5-6), and his explanation of his own mission as "only to the lost sheep of the house of Israel" (15:24).³ Jesus is actively involved with Gentiles in two miracles stories (8:5-13; 15:21-28). They are directed towards Gentiles, but they instruct Israel (see 8:10-12; 15:26-28).

This essay, offered with respect and gratitude to Frank Matera, scholar, colleague and dear friend, argues that the contradiction should not be regarded as an unresolvable tension in Matthew's narrative. It points to the situation of the Matthean Jewish-Christian community, struggling with its own identity vis-à-vis the Judaism of its time, and initiating a Gentile mission. This context determines the Evangelist's appreciation and presentation of Jesus, his mission and the mission of the Church.⁴

Time in Matthew's Narrative

Focusing our attention on the temporal element in the passages which highlight the contradiction between the accepted ways of Judaism and the new openness to "all the nations," we notice that the passages that limit Jesus' and his disciples' activities to Israel are located at the beginning, and then during the public ministry of Jesus (5:17-18; 10:5-6; 15:24). The mission to "all the nations" is the final scene of the Gospel (28:16-20).

---

2. This affirmation must be nuanced, as Matthew by no means regarded the Mosaic Law as abolished (see, for example, 9:14-17; 13:52), but it is Jesus' teaching as the interpretation of the Law that must be taught (28:20). See the excellent comment by Luz, *Matthew*, 3:633-34. See the annotated discussion of 28:16-20 in John P. Meier, *Law and History in Matthew's Gospel. A Redactional Study of Mt. 5:17-48*, Analecta Biblica 71 (Rome: Biblical Institute Press, 1976), 35-40.
3. Robert H. Gundry, *Matthew. A Commentary on His Literary and Theological Art* (Grand Rapids: Eerdmans, 1982), 8 eliminates the problem by claiming "in their numbers and in their following Jesus during his earthly ministry, the Jewish crowds symbolize the international Church, including the many Gentiles who were later to become disciples (4:25-5:1 with 7:28-8:1; 21:8-9, 11)."
4. This perspective, and much of the study that follows, depends upon Meier, *Law and History*, and Roland Deines, *Die Gerechtigkeit der Tora im Reich des Messias*, Wissenschaftliche Untersuchungen zum Neuen Testament 177 (Tübingen: Mohr Siebeck, 2004).

The temporal element of Jesus' words in 5:17-18 calls for a closer examination. These words open the Matthean Jesus' interaction with the law in vv. 21-48. They form part of one of Matthew's favorite themes: Jesus the teacher (see the summaries of 4:23; 9:35, and the discourses of 5:1-7:29; 10:1-11:1; 13:1-53; 18:1-35; 24:1-25:45). Although 5:17-18 comes early in Jesus' story, they contain words that look further into the narrative.

> Think not that I have come to abolish the law and the prophets; I have come not to abolish them but to fulfill them. For truly, I say to you, *till* (ἕως ἄν) *heaven and earth pass away*, not an iota, not a dot, will pass from the law *until* (ἕως ἄν) *all is accomplished*.

The two expressions of time in the passage refer to some future "time," using the same Greek words to point to the future: ἕως ἄν. There is the "now" of Jesus' preaching in his first discourse, but there is a time "yet to come" when the present order of things will be changed. These expressions refer to a time in the future when the perfection of the law will be completed: "till (ἕως ἄν) heaven and earth pass away ... until (ἕως ἄν) all is accomplished."[5] In the light of our understanding of Jesus' eschatological teaching beginning in the Christian narrative tradition in Mark 13 and importantly present Matthew 24, most scholars continue to read Matt 5:17-18 as a reference to the traditional Jewish notion of the end of time.[6]

This understanding of the future events referred to in 5:17-18 strengthens Jesus' limitation of his disciples' and his own preaching to the lost sheep of Israel (10:5-6; 15:24), and his hesitation before working two miracles for Gentiles (8:5-13; 15:21-28). However, in 28:16-20 Matthew reports words of the risen Jesus that reach outside the narrated events of the Gospel. The disciples are sent on a mission to the ends of the earth, and Jesus promises that he will be with them till the close of the age. If the future time of 5:17-18 referred to the end of all time, the command of Jesus that the law be observed,

---

5. See Meier, *Law and History*, 48: "It is important for the subsequent exegesis that 'until' is the *only* possible meaning. There are no solid grounds for changing the meaning to 'in order that.'"
6. See, for example, the authoritative interpretation of Davies and Allison, *Matthew*, 1:482-503, and Luz, *Matthew*, 1:213-219.

without changing even the tiniest detail, would still be in force in the post-Easter Matthean Community, and any subsequent Christian community using this document as Sacred Scripture, awaiting Jesus' final coming.⁷ But whatever one makes of Jesus' relationship to the law during his ministry, he abandons the perfect observance ("not an iota or a dot") of the law in 28:16-20 when he sends his disciples on a mission to all nations.⁸

For many exegetes these tensions reflect tensions already existing in pre-Matthean traditions. They remain within the narrative, once these traditions have been incorporated into Matthew's the story of Jesus' life, teaching, death and resurrection. In the end, we are left with ragged tensions that cannot/should not be resolved as they reflect the Matthean experience.⁹ This study takes a different methodological approach. The Gospel must be read as a single utterance that made sense to an author. Matthew did not leave these contradictory understandings of his community's relationship to Torah and its mission to the Gentiles, teaching what Jesus taught them, to stand unresolved in the Gospel.¹⁰

Between Jesus' insistence on the mission to Israel at the beginning and during the course of his public ministry (5:17-18; 10:5-6; 15:24), and his final commission as the risen Lord to the Matthean disciples to go out to the whole world (28:16-20), something happens which dramatically changes the future roles of both Jesus and his disciples. John Meier has drawn attention to the account of Jesus' death

---

7. This is argued by Luz, *Matthew*, 1:218: "If the Matthean Jesus had temporarily limited the validity of the Torah, that would have been a completely surprising message for the Jewish Christian readers of the Gospel. It would not at all have been in keeping with the one who wants to keep the same Torah down to its last iota."
8. There is some ambiguity over the meaning of τὰ ἔθνη in 28:19. Jews and Gentile are included in this expression. See, among many, the summary in Luz, *Matthew*, 3:628-31. For Deines, *Die Gerechtigkeit*, 183-256, Matt 5:13-16 is already a clear indication of Jesus' preparation of his disciples for a universal mission.
9. See the early study of Ulrich Luz, "The Fulfillment of the Law in Matthew (Matt 5:17-20)," in *Studies in Matthew* (Grand Rapids: Eerdmans, 2005), 185-218 (original German dates back to *ZTK* 75 [1978]: 398-435). Davies and Allison, *Matthew*, 3:707, give up on a theological synthesis: "He did not, however, explicitly reconcile 10:5 with 28:18-20. Perhaps exclusive attention to the accumulation of the implicit and explicit theological meanings of the text obfuscates the contradictory social realities behind Matthew."
10. See Meier, *Law and History*, 44; Deines, *Die Gerechtigkeit*, 28-30.

and resurrection. Two descriptions are found there - reported only in Matthew – of events that could be regarded as signs of "heaven and earth passing away" (see 5:17-18). The first of these moments is at the death of Jesus:

> From the sixth hour there was darkness all over the land until the ninth hour. ... The veil of the temple was torn in two from top to bottom; the earth quaked; the rocks were split; the tombs opened and the bodies of many holy men rose from the dead (27:45, 51-53).

The second of these moments is found in the Matthean description of the events surrounding the resurrection of Jesus:

> All at once there was a violent earthquake, for the angel of the Lord, descending from heaven, came and rolled away the stone and sat upon it. His face was like lightning, his robe white as snow. And for fear of him the guards trembled and became like dead men (28:2-4).

For Meier, the Matthean report of Jesus' death and resurrection indicate that *heaven and earth are passing away*. Matthew has taken some of his imagery and language from earlier Christian tradition concerning Jesus' death. It is found in Mark's report of the tearing of the veil, the darkness at the death of Jesus, and the whiteness of the robe of the figure at the tomb, although he was a "young man," not an angel (Mark 15:38; 16:5).[11] However, it is obvious that Matthew has changed the Markan scenario considerably. He has drawn upon some traditionally "apocalyptic" symbols from Jewish thought, but has shifted their timing. The events described: darkening of the skies, splitting of the rocks, earthquakes, lightning, the rising of the dead, the appearance of angels and men struck down as if dead are events that were expected at the end of all time when YHWH would return as Lord and Judge (see Amos 8:9; Joel 2:10; Hag 2:6; Zech 14:5; 1 Enoch 1:3-

---

11. It is regularly easily assumed that Mark's young man is an angel. For a different opinion, linking the young man in Mark 14:51-52 with the young man in 16:5, see Francis J. Moloney, *The Gospel of Mark. A Commentary* (Peabody: Hendrickson, 2002), 344-46. It is only the more apocalyptic Matthew who introduces an angel. Luke (24:4) has two men.

9; 71:1-2; Jer 15:9; Ezek 37:7, 12-13; Isa 26:19; Dan 7:9; 10:7-9, 16; 12:2; T. Levi 4:1). Matthew indicates that these events will not only take place at the end of history, as was held by Jewish traditions, well represented in Matthew 24. They have already happened at the death and resurrection of Jesus.[12]

Roland Deines agrees that the future time indicated in 5:17-20 is fulfilled in the death and resurrection of Jesus, but regards Meier's limitation of the fulfillment to the paschal events as too narrow. For Deines, everything that is said about Jesus (Son of God, Son of David, Messiah, the fulfillment of the Scriptures) and the Kingdom, from the beginning to the end of the Gospel, must come into play when the theme of "righteousness" emerges in the narrative. Jesus' coming (5:17), his fulfillment of the abiding validity of the Torah (v. 18), his instruction to the teachers (v. 19), establishes the righteousness that leads to heaven (v. 20). The disciples' righteousness as God's righteousness establishes the Kingdom of God (6:1, 33). Israel's traditional link between righteousness, the law and Davidic messianic expectation is maintained, but transformed and "fulfilled" in the life, teaching and ministry, climaxing in the eschatological events of the death and resurrection of Jesus, Son of David, son of God, Messiah.[13]

---

12. See Meier, *Law and History*, 30-35. Donald Senior, "The Death of Jesus and the Resurrection of the Holy Ones. Matthew 27:51-53," *The Catholic Biblical Quarterly* 38 (1976): 312-29, argues that the addition of these eschatological events are part of the Matthean redaction. Dale C. Allison, Jr., *The End of the Age has Come. An Early Interpretation of the Death and Resurrection of Jesus* (Philadelphia: Fortress, 1985), 40-50, against Senior, claims that Matthew is incorporating a pre-Christian eschatological tradition. Jesus' death and resurrection draw eschatological events into the human story. To use the language of Meier, this marks the "turning point of the ages." It is not the end of human history. The Matthean Christians were firmly located in a time and a place, living the "in between time," awaiting the final end of history (see Matt 24; 28:20). See Allison, *The End*, 49-50. For a recent very different reading of these apocalyptic elements as a figurative presentation of Jesus as the first born from the dead, corresponding to the birth of the believer, see Serge Wüthrich, "Naître de mourir: la mort de Jésus dans l'Évangile de Matthieu (Mt 27.51-56)," *New Testament Studies* 56 (2010): 313-25.

13. One cannot do justice to this remarkable study in a few lines. For his closing summary, see Deines, *Die Gerechtigkeit*, 639-54. In terms of "the turning point of the ages," see p. 449: "Matthäus beschreibt in seinem Evangelium die eine heilsgeschichtliche Wende, in der die Offenbarungsgeschichte Israels in Gestalt von Gesetz und Propheten in Jesus kulminiert und durch ihn einen neuen Anfang zu den Völkern der Welt nimmt." One of the strengths of Meier's position is his location of the death and resurrection of Jesus as the moment "when heaven and

Matthew shows that Jesus lived out the perfection of the Mosaic tradition, not only in what he does, but also in who he is. Before the story of Jesus begins, in the incontrovertible information provided for the reader in the Gospel's prologue (1:1-4:16), Jesus is portrayed as son of David and son of Abraham (1:1, further spelt out in 1:2-17), Messiah (1:16), King of Israel (2:1-6), and son of God (2:15; 4:1-11). The events of the birth and infancy of Jesus bridge the time between the former covenant into the days of Jesus. They are a fulfillment of the promises of the law and the prophets. Almost every scene in the Matthean prologue indicates that the events of Jesus' birth and infancy are "to fulfill what was said by the prophet ..." (see 1:22-23, 2:5-6, 15, 17-18, 23; 3:3; 4:6-7, 14-16).[14] The same theme also flows into the ministry of Jesus (see 8:17; 12:17; 13:35; 21:4; 26:54, 56).[15]

The members of Matthew's community are caught up (perhaps, for some, unwillingly?) in the Gentile mission (28:19). Nevertheless, Matthew makes it clear that they are products of the perfection of the law and the prophets in the person and teaching of Jesus, and that they are summoned to follow his way till the end of the age. Then, the Son of Man will come in final judgment (24:29-51). As this is the case, the Evangelist can claim that the followers of Jesus of Nazareth must still strive to live and teach what Jesus has taught them as they await, assured of the presence of their Risen Lord, the end of this age (24:1-25:46; 28:20). For Matthew, the synagogue-centered religion of post-war Judaism, which rejected and expelled the followers of Jesus, had said a definitive "no" to Jesus' teaching of God's law.[16]

---

earth pass away." See Deines acceptance of this in *Die Gerechtigkeit*, 359. For Deines' inclusion of Meier's thesis as a culmination of Jesus' life, teaching, death and resurrection, see *ibid.*, 278-79, 355-57.

14. On the formative role of the "prologues" in all four Gospels, see Francis J. Moloney, *Beginning the Good News. A narrative approach* (Collegeville: The Liturgical Press, 1992). On Matthew see pp. 73-100.

15. This is not the place to enter into an extended proof of this affirmation, but see Deines, *Die Gerechtigkeit*, 453-638, with extensive focus upon Jesus' fulfilment and transformation of Torah, righteousness and Davidic messianic expectation (pp. 469-500), as found the use of Torah and righteousness in the Prophets (pp. 501-74) and the Psalter as a Davidic Torah (574-638).

16. As Luz, *Matthew*, 1:55, succinctly and correctly points out: "The Gospel of Matthew is a response to the no of Israel's majority to Jesus. It is an attempt to come to terms with this no by defining the community's position and to contribute to forming and preserving its identity in a situation of crisis and transition."

The breakdown between Jesus and the leaders of Israel that dominates 11:2-16:12 and the harshness of the Matthean presentation of Jesus' Jewish accusers during the finals days in Jerusalem and his death and resurrection (21:1-28:15) are the major, but not the only, pointers to this truth. Only in Matthew's Gospel do we find the chilling words on the lips of "all the people" (πᾶς ὁ λαός): "His blood be upon us and on our children!" (27:25). Only in Matthew do the leaders of Israel pay those whom they set to guard to tomb, so that a lie could be spread abroad: Jesus was not raised; his disciples stole the body (27:62-66; 28:11-15). The Matthean Church was living out God's saving history, from Abraham to Jesus (see 1:1-17) into the Gentile mission (28:16-20).[17] I remain puzzled by the widespread rejection of any historical scheme behind Matthew's narrative.[18] It is generally coupled with a tortured attempt to understand how Matthew understood the role of the law, and the need for the Christian community to adhere to every detail until the end of all time. Every suggestion stumbles over several elements in Jesus' life and teaching that transcend the law. Outstanding, in this respect, is the almost total neglect of the extreme tension that exists between (at least) 5:17-20, 21-48, 10:5-6, 15:24 and 28:16-20.[19]

---

17. For a recent tracing of a saving history through Matthew, see Marvyn Eloff, "Ἀπό .. ἕως and Salvation History in Matthew's Gospel," in *Built upon the Rock. Studies in the Gospel of Matthew*, eds. Daniel M. Gurtner and John Nolland (Grand Rapids: Eerdmans, 2008), 85-107.

18. See unconvincing appendix of Davies and Allison on theology and salvation history in Matthew (*Matthew*, 3:704-07). I take it for granted that Matthew is *not* interested in the "stages of salvation history," so often identified in Luke. I suspect much of the rejection of a Matthean salvation history comes from a correct rejection of any attempt to impose a Lukan scheme upon Matthew.

19. See, for example, the two important works of David C. Sim, *Apocalyptic eschatology in the Gospel of Matthew*, Society for New Testament Study Monograph Series 88 (Cambridge: Cambridge University Press, 1996) and *The Gospel of Matthew*. Sim argues passionately for a Christian Jewish community unconditionally committed to the observance of Torah, bitterly opposed to a Gentile mission, living in a context of an imminent apocalyptic eschatology. No matter what 28:16-20 might suggest (e.g. baptism replaced circumcision), Sim claims that this was not happening in a community where "all parts of the law, both weighty and less weighty, are to be obeyed in full (cf. 23:23)" (*Gospel of Matthew*, 253). See also his *Apocalyptic Eschatology*, 208-09.

The Matthean Use of δικαιοσύνη

I was initially drawn to consider Matthean use of διακαιοσύνη by the encounter between John the Baptist and Jesus in 3:14-15: "John would have prevented him, saying, 'I need to be baptized by you, and do you come to me?' But Jesus answered him, 'Let it be so now (ἄφες ἄρτι) for thus it is fitting for us to fulfil all righteousness (πληρῶσαι πᾶσαν δικαιοσύνην).' Then he consented." This is the first time in the Gospel that the word δικαιοσύνη appears in the Gospel. These are *the very first words Jesus utters in the Gospel of Matthew*. They do not depend upon the Markan version of this encounter (as does Luke 3:21-22), there is no evidence that it may have come to Matthew from Q, and the passage thus represents a Matthean use of a time scheme of "now ... later."

Matthew uses the expression δικαισύνη seven times (3:15; 5:6, 10, 20; 6:1, 33; 21:32), and it is universally accepted that every usage reflects the Matthean redaction. The expression is deliberately chosen and used by Matthew.[20] Why he chose this expression and what it means, however, is open to debate. The discussion of this usage is clouded by two issues. Matthew is the most Jewish of the Gospels, and the interpreter leans naturally toward an interpretation of δικαισύνη within the broad semantic range of "law-righteousness." This interpretation is supported by Matthew's many uses of the adjective δικαίος, all of which, with different nuances, describe law-abiding characters (sometimes unfavourably) within the narrative (1:19; 5:45; 9:13; 10:41; 13:17, 43, 49; 20:4; 23:28, 29, 35; 25:37, 46; 27:19).

The shadow of the Pauline use of the expression δικαισύνη looms large. Current scholarship supports a blanket understanding of Matthew's use of "righteousness" as "moral conduct."[21] One of the driving principles of this interpretation is a distinction between Paul and Matthew. God's action (Pauline) must be eschewed in favour of human action (Matthew). "Hence 'righteousness' does not refer, even implicitly, to God's gift. The Pauline (forensic, eschatological) con-

---

20. See, among many, Luz, *Matthew*, 1:142.
21. My analysis will refer especially to the recent outstanding commentaries of William D. Davies, Dale Allison, and Ulrich Luz.

notation is absent."²² What follows attempts to show that this blanket exclusion of the action of God has narrowed interpretation too severely.

The temporal and spatial location of Matthew's use of δικαιοσύνη deserves attention. Five of the seven sayings appear in Jesus' first discourse, and are associated with the instruction of his disciples on the perfect living of the law (5:6, 10, 20; 6:1, 33). They are flanked the remaining two sayings, both of which are associated with John the Baptist (3:15; 21:31). Jesus *first words* are marked by the use of δικαιοσύνη in his discussion with John the Baptist, his *first discourse* is studded with its use, and his *final reference* to John the Baptist returns to the expression. The first two of these sayings (3:15; 5:6) are future orientated, while the remaining five address a "present" challenge or reality.²³

Matthew 3:15

Jesus' command to the Baptist: ἄφες ἄρτι, well translated by the RSV as "let it be for now," indicates to the reader (as well as to John the Baptist) that for "now" unexpected events must take place, and that the Baptist must be associated with God's design for Jesus in his response to this "now": "it is fitting for *us* (πρέπον ἐστὶν ἡμῖν). However, there will be a later time when all righteousness (πᾶσαν δικαιοσύνην) will be fulfilled (πληρῶσαι). Commentators are unwilling to read this passage as a reflection of Matthew's view of salvation history.²⁴ But is a

---

22. Davies and Allison, *Matthew*, 1:499. See also, among many, Gundry, *Matthew*, 70: "No evidence leads us to think that in a Pauline manner he means a sentence of justification when he uses the term. Ordinarily in his Gospel 'righteousness' refers to right conduct on the human side." As Georg Strecker, *The Sermon on the Mount. An Exegetical Commentary* (trans. O. C. Dean Jr.; Edinburgh: T. & T. Clark, 1988), 98, comments "the integrity of Jesus' disciples is expressly characterized as human doing (ποεῖν) and not as divine gift." For the discussion, see B. Przbylski, *Righteousness in Matthew and His World of Thought*, Society for New Testament Study Monograph Series 41 (Cambridge: Cambridge University Press, 1980), 1-8; Deines, *Die Gerechtigkeit*, 152-54.
23. For an introduction to the principles guiding literary readings of narrative passages, see Moloney, *Beginning the Good News*, 19-42.
24. See, for example, Davies and Allison, *Matthew*, 1:325-27. The crux of the issue lies in their following prejudice: "Because with the possible exception of 5.6, δικαιοσύνη seems in Matthew to be uniform in meaning – moral conduct in

time "now" when the Baptist must associate himself with Jesus as that is part of God's *present* design. There will be a later time, when God's intervention in the human story by means of his Son, Jesus, when such actions will no longer be needed. "John no longer simply points to the fulfiller, as did the Law and the prophets. Now, along with the fulfiller, John is also fulfilling God's prophesied plan for salvation."[25] A time will come when all righteousness will be fulfilled.

This passage comes *before* 5:17-18, and thus guides the reader better to understand the references to the "now" of the perfect living of the law and the prophets, and the "later" when the law and the prophets will be fulfilled (v. 17) and heaven and earth will pass away (v. 18). In the context of a discussion between Jesus and the Baptist, present practices are to continue - for now. When all righteousness is fulfilled this will no longer be the case. The same promise will be made later in the story when Jesus instructs his disciples, "This generation will not pass away till all these things take place (ἕως ἂν πάντα γένηται)"

---

accord with God's will – we are inclined to define the 'righteousness' of 3.15 as moral conduct." See also Luz, *Matthew*, 1:142-43; Strecker, *Sermon*, 36-38; Pierre Bonnard, *L'Évangile de Matthieu*, Commentaire du Nouveau Testament 1 (Neuchatel: Delachaux & Niestlé, 1963), 40: "soumission fidèle à la volonté de Dieu." This monochromatic interpretation of δικαιοσύνη in Matthew has its roots in the authoritative work of Georg Strecker, *Der Weg der Gerechtigkeit*, 3d ed. (Göttingen: Vandenhoeck & Ruprecht, 1971), 149-58, and Jacques Dupont, *Les Béatitudes*, 3 vols., Etudes Bibliques (Paris: Gabalda, 1969-1973), 3:211-384, especially pp. 383-84 (conclusions). It has been recently restated by Przybylski, *Righteousness*. For a Pauline reading of "righteousness" in 3:14-15, see John Nolland, *The Gospel of Matthew*, New International Greek Testament Commentary (Grand Rapids: Eerdmans, 2005), 153-54 ("that state of affairs which is all right between God and his world" [p. 154]). Donald A. Hagner, *Matthew*, 2 vols; Word Bible Commentary 33-33a (Dallas: Word Books, 1993-1995), 1:993-995, 55-57, sees the importance of the notion of fulfilling God's will, but argues that at least in 3:15 the salvation-historical perspective of how that happens is stated (especially p. 56).

25. John P. Meier, "John the Baptist in Matthew's Gospel," *Journal of Biblical Literature* 99 (1980): 392. See also Joachim Gnilka, *Das Matthäusevangelium*, 2 vols., Herders Theologische Kommentar zum Neuen Testament I:1-2 (Freiburg: Herder, 1986-88), 1:77; Deines, *Die Gerechtigkeit*, 127-32. Warren Carter, *Matthew and the Margins. A Sociopolitical and Religious Reading* (Maryknoll, NY: Orbis Books, 2000), 102, remarks, "God's saving action, previously stated by the scriptures, is being enacted in Jesus' and John's actions." Contrast David E. Garland, *Reading Matthew. A Literary and Theological Commentary* (Macon: Smyth & Helwys, 2001), 37: "It is simply the right thing to do."

(24:34). Jesus' first words immediately alert the reader that there will be a time when all righteousness will be fulfilled (3:15: πληρῶσαι πᾶσαν δικαιοσύνην), when the law and the prophets have reached their eschatological fulfilment (5:17: πληρῶσαι).[26] The reader is led by these words of Jesus, his first δικαιοσύνη-saying, to recognize on arrival at 5:17-18 that Jesus is not pointing forward to the final end of all time, but to the moment in the story of Jesus when all righteousness will be fulfilled.

This interpretation is strengthened by asking the question "when?" of some crucial Matthean texts. On three occasions during his ministry Jesus threatens Israel that the Kingdom will be taken away from them, and given to others (8:11-12; 21:42-43; 22:1-10): when? The Prologue to the Gospel (1:1-4:16) is framed by a reference to Abraham, the father of all nations (1:1) and Galilee of the Gentiles (4:16). Hope, nourishment and forgiveness of sins of is offered universally (3:13-19; 12:15-21; 14:13-21; 15:32-39; 26:28), and Jesus teaches that the Gospel will be preached to "throughout the whole world, as a testimony to all the nations" before the coming of the end of time. *When will all these things happen?* All these things (πάντα: 5:18; 24:34:) will be experienced in the life, teaching, death and resurrection of Jesus. For the *readers of the story* the fulfillment of all these things has already taken place.[27] They do not have to wait until the end of all time for the fulfillment of "divine expectation." Living in the presence of the risen Christ (28:20), it has already taken place in the life, teaching, death and resurrection of Jesus.[28] This "temporal" aspect in the reading process is central to an understanding of the shift from Jesus speaking of the fulfillment of righteousness in the future (3:6 and 5:6), and the present experience of the disciple (5:10, 20; 6:1, 33; 21:32), living in the period *after* that fulfillment.

This interpretation of 5:6 must be influenced by the meaning of δικαιοσύνη in 3:15. The beatitudes as a group, the fourth beatitude (5:6) among them, promise a future blessedness dependent upon a way of life. Within that context Jesus points to a future time when God *will satisfy* those who *now* hunger and thirst for righteousness. The "now" of those who hunger and thirst for righteousness who will

---

26. See Meier, *Law and History*, 41-89; Deines, *Die Gerechtigkeit*, 257-87.
27. On 5:18 and 24:34, see Meier, *Law and History*, 57-65.
28. See also Meier, *Law and History*, 77-80.

be blessed with a "future" satisfaction (χορτασθήσανται). As we will see, this "now and after" scheme is not found in the eighth beatitude (v. 10) where righteousness is attained in the "now" ("theirs *is* the kingdom of heaven) by enduring persecution (see also vv. 10-11). As Jesus asked John the Baptist to join him (3:15: πρέπον ἐστὶν ἡμῖν) in God's design "to fulfil all righteousness," the disciples are invited to a restless yearning and search (hunger and thirst) for righteousness that they may be eschatologically satisfied.

The first words that Jesus speaks in the Gospel of Matthew (3:15) generate a narrative tension that leads the reader to look beyond the immediate context for the meaning of διακιοσύνη, toward some future time in the story. Those who seek this eschatological gift of διακαιοσύνη are blessed (5:6) because their result of hungering and thirsting "now" for the righteousness that only Jesus can offer in its fullness (3:15), will eventually experience satisfaction.[29] At this stage in the story, the search for true righteousness marks the present experience of the listeners, while their satisfaction lies in the future. Those who hunger and thirst will come to final satiation in their search for the righteousness that God offers in and through Jesus. "The disciple, in effect, is to live now the life that is to be realized fully at the end of time, yet, through Jesus, is already breaking into the world."[30] From now on, however, as the disciples are drawn more deeply into the Kingdom by means of their association with Jesus, all the righteousness-sayings point to a present challenge or situation.

Matthew 5:10

Continuing to read the narrative in the light of the first use of δικαιοσύνη in 3:15, now reinforced by the promise of eschatological satisfaction in the immediate context of 5:6, this text hints at commitment to righteousness that will lead to persecution. For most inter-

---

29. See Donald Senior, *Matthew*, Abingdon New Testament Commentary (Nashville: Abingdon, 1998), 71; Carter, *Matthew*, 133-34.
30. Senior, *Matthew*, 73. See also Deines, *Die Gerechtigkeit*, 137-54. See p. 152: "Aber das 'gesättigt werden', d.h. das reichliche und ausreichende Empfangen dieser Gerechtigkeit ist denen verheißen, die danach hungern und dürsten. Wie das möglich ist? Weil Jesus gekommen ist, um 'alle Gerechtigkeit zu erfüllen' (3:15)." Craig L. Blomberg, *Matthew*, New American Commentary 22 (Nashville: Broadman, 1992), 95, speaks of "inaugurated eschatology."

preters, hamstrung with their limited understanding of the Matthean use of δικαιοσύνη, moral achievement is again at stake: "'Righteousness' here can only be something people have, namely their obedient, righteous conduct."[31] But the immediate and broader context suggests that Christology is involved. The fullness of righteousness is yet to be achieved in the story (see 5:17-48; 27:45, 51-53; 28:2-4, 16-20), but the Matthean disciples are promised that persecution for the sake of righteousness (ἕνεκεν διακαιοσύνης) brings (present tense: ἐστίν) the kingdom of heaven. A Christological reading of ἕνεκεν διακαιοσύνης is demanded by the expansion of what is meant by v. 10 in vv. 11-12. "Blessed are you when people revile you and persecute you ... because of me (ἕνεκεν ἐμοῦ)" (v. 11). The parallel between ἕνεκεν διακαιοσύνης (v. 10) and ἕνεκεν ἐμοῦ (v. 11), where vv. 10-11 are a Matthean addition to the tradition to relate v. 10 to the experience of the community, must be respected.[32]

The theme is repeated in Jesus' instructions to his community in 10:22: "You will be hated by all for my name's sake" (διὰ τὸ ὄνομα μοῦ). The suffering experience of the Matthean community was not primarily caused by their "obedient, righteous conduct." If persecution is the result of the Matthean disciples' living obediently, what distinguished them from their Jewish contemporaries? Were they also persecuted for their "obedient, righteous conduct"?[33] The immediate context spells out that Matthean disciples are reviled and persecuted because their commitment to Jesus renders the kingdom present "now" (5:11-12). In the next discourse (10:1–11:1: the community's

---

31. Davies and Allison, *Saint Matthew*, 1:459-60. See also Luz, *Matthew*, 1:242. Both make a close relationship between v. 6 and v. 10 as indicating moral performance.
32. As Luz, *Matthew*, 1:199, puts it: "Persecution for the sake of righteousness in v. 10 and the equally redactionally formulated persecution 'for my sake' in v. 11 mutually interpret one another." But he does not draw the Christological consequences, concluding: "Confessing Christ manifests itself in deeds (7:21-23; 25:31-46)." This, of course, is correct, but does not do full justice to the Christological possibilities of δικαιοσύνη. In response to Luz, see Deines, *Die Gerechtigkeit*, 179-80.
33. See the effort of Strecker, *Sermon*, 42-43, to respond to this question. 1 Peter 3:14a ("But even if you suffer for righteousness' sake, you will be blessed") is sometimes suggested as a parallel to Matt 5:10 (see Eduard Schweizer, *The Good News according to Matthew*, trans. David E. Green [London: SPCK, 1976], 95-96). This is helpful, as long as the whole context is taken into account: "Have no fear of them nor be troubled, but in your hearts reverence Christ as Lord" (v. 14b-15).

mission) this is further reinforced. Disciples are instructed that they will be hated for the sake of Jesus' name (10:22).[34]

Persecution for righteousness' sake (5:10) is the consequence of a commitment to God's design for the fulfilment of all righteousness (see 3:15), the yearning for the perfection of God's will and design (5:6), in imitation of Jesus who came to fulfil the law (see 5:17), and who called his disciples to follow him into a perfection of love that matches the perfection of God (5:48).[35] Rightly has David Garland commented on 5:10:

> It is one thing to pronounce blessed those who are persecuted because of righteousness or devotion to the law (2 Macc 7:9, 11, 23, 37; 4 Macc 6:24-30); it is something else to pronounce blessed those who are persecuted because of their relationship to Jesus, "for my sake" (see also 10:18, 39; 16:25; 19:29). This beatitude reflects the high christology of the Gospel.[36]

Matthew 5:20

Matthew 5:17-20 is generally regarded as an introduction to vv. 21-48. But it is a continuation of what has been said since 5:3, an argument that is not completed until 5:48, and beyond.[37] The exhortation of the disciples in the beatitudes, and especially in the parables of 5:13-16, continues to determine the argument. They are to be salt and light. God's righteousness must be manifested in them.

Meier has shown that vv. 17-18 are the result of Matthew's rewriting of the tradition, and that v. 19 probably came to Matthew from a prior reworking of Q. The association of the Matthean vv. 17-18 with the traditional v. 19 "resembles an undigested morsel in our text."[38] If everything in vv. 17-19 was meant by Matthew to indicate that each

---

34. See Gnilka, *Matthäusevangelium*, 1:127-29.
35. Rightly, Deines, *Die Gerechtigkeit*, 155-81. Meier argues for a variety of meanings for δικαιοσύνη in Matthew (*Law and History*, 76-7), but he accepts that in 5:10 "the meaning of Christian moral practice is clear" (p. 77).
36. Garland, *Reading Matthew*, 59. Nolland, *Matthew*, 206, on the other hand, suggests that Matthew's inspiration was the martyr tradition of the Maccabean period.
37. See Deines, *Die Gerechtigkeit*, 429-34.
38. Meier, *Law and History*, 104.

commandment (v. 19) of the law and the prophets (v. 17) was binding until the end of all time (v. 18), *as that event is described in Matthew 24*, and if anyone who dared to relax even the minutiae in life and teaching was to be least in the kingdom: Jesus stands among the least in the kingdom of heaven (v. 19). Obviously, Matthew did not want to say that!

While v. 19 continues the argument of vv. 17-18 by indicating the penalty ("least") or blessing ("great") flowing from one's observance of the various commandments that make up the law and the prophets, v. 19 looks forward to the series of reinterpretations of individual commandments (ἐντόλαι) that Jesus puts in place in the antitheses of vv. 21-48. It leads into v. 20. In the light of 3:15 and 5:6, the warning that compares the believers' righteousness with the righteousness of the Scribes and the Pharisees (v. 20) cannot *only* be a plea that the disciples be more moral than their Jewish contemporaries.[39] It has to do with the fulfilment of God's design, intimately associated with Jesus' understanding of the law, and his request that his disciples join him (5:3-13). The theme of righteousness that has appeared in this early section of the discourse has called followers of Jesus a qualitatively "different righteousness" (3:15; 5:6). The believer's righteousness "exceeds (περισσεύῃ) that of the Scribes and Pharisees" because its measure is the person of Jesus Christ. The disciple is to "exceed" the righteousness of the Scribes and the Pharisees, and exceed it πλεῖον. The comparison is a "qualitative" exceeding of the righteousness of the Scribes and the Pharisees, as it is to reflect the eschatological righteousness of God.[40]

Jesus' authoritative reinterpretation of Torah across vv. 21-48, stated categorically with the rhythmic repetition of ἐγὼ δὲ λέγω ὑμῖν (vv. 22, 28, 32, 34, 39, 44) maps out what it means to fulfil (πληρῶσαι) the law and the prophets. At the end of his reinterpretation of Torah, he turns to his disciples and informs them that they are to parallel his life and ministry in their performance of reinterpreted Torah. He commands them: "Be perfect, as your heavenly Father is perfect" (v. 48). Jesus claims that he has come to "fulfil" (πληρῶσαι) the law and the prophets. The "perfection" (τέλειοι) of the disciples, matching that of their heavenly Father, is the way in which they are to greatly

---

39. Major commentaries point to the comparison with the Scribes and the Pharisees as an indication v. 20 is about better moral performance. See Davies and Allison, *Matthew*, 1:499; Luz, *Matthew*, 1:221-22.
40. See Deines, *Die Gerechtigkeit*, 425-28.

exceed the righteousness of the Pharisees. It is this "perfect righteousness" that leads to the eschatological gift of the kingdom of heaven. The association of the disciples with a Christological principle is prepared in 5:3-16 and established in vv. 17-20. In Jesus' teaching on the practice of disciples, outlined vv. 21-48, the accent is upon the eschatological style of their living, determined by the fact that they are disciples of Jesus who do not abrogate the Mosaic law, but perfect it (v. 17).[41] "Despite appearances, despite all the eschatological sharpening and rescinding of the Law that goes on in the antitheses, Jesus' eschatological mission is not to do away with the Law and the prophets, but to give them their eschatological fullness."[42] Jesus' request that the righteousness of his disciples (v. 20) reflects the perfection of God (v. 48) draws them into this eschatological fullness.[43] In 6:1 and 6:33 the reader will learn that the disciples' righteousness is God's righteousness, and as such establishes the Kingdom of God.

Matthew 6:1[44]

A new section in the discourse opens with 6:1. The theme of authentic religious practice, over against the falsity of the "hypocrites," dominates 6:2-6 (ὑποκριταί: v. 5) and its parallel in 6:16-18 (ὑποκριταί: v. 16). The identity of the hypocrites who parade their virtue is not specified, but their association with the synagogue (see vv. 2, 5) links Jesus' instruction in 6:1 with his parallel instruction in 5:20.[45] The exhortation to δικαιοσύνη in 6:1 acts as a "hinge passage" between 5:21-48 and 6:2-28.[46] The formal link with 5:20, in the light of 3:15, 5:6,

---

41. See Meier, *Law and History*, 168: "The rule of life for the Christian is thus an 'umbrella concept': 'all things whatsoever I commanded you' – be that *secundum*, *praeter*, or *contra* the Mosaic Law."
42. Meier, *Law and History*, 69.
43. For a detailed analysis of vv. 17-20, set within its broader Matthean context, that supports this view, see Deines, *Die Gerechtigkeit*, 257-434.
44. There is some doubt about the originality of the first δέ, in 6:1. The textual evidence is evenly balanced. It makes no difference to the interpretation of δικαιοσύνη. See further, Deines, *Die Gerechtigkeit*, 435-46.
45. See Lagrange, *Matthieu*, 119: "Il est clair que la justice des disciples est celle de v. 20." See also Deines, *Die Gerechtigkeit*, 437-38.
46. Most commentators see 6:1 as "thematic" for 6:1-18. The presence of δικαιοσύνη in 5:6, 10, 20; 6:1, 33, leads Davies and Allison to claim that the term "expresses the essence of the sermon on the mount" (*Matthew*, 1:499).

10, warns against making light of this Matthean expression, used consistently to speak of the fulfillment of divine expectation. The "doing" (ποιεῖν) of "righteousness" looks to the future reward (μίσθον) from the Father in heaven. This is contrasted with those whose public parading of accepted practices "already" (ὅπως: vv. 2, 15, 16) have their reward. The Matthean Christology demands that the disciples being instructed must live as Jesus lived, "doing" the righteousness that he has already "fulfilled" (3:15; 5:6, 10, 17-20).[47] Although the expression "kingdom of heaven" is not explicit, the reward from the Father who is in heaven is not lost or gained only from right religious practice *before God* (5:20; 6:1); it is a participation in the life that is available to Jesus' disciples by means of their participation of the eschatological gift of a righteousness that comes *from God* (3:15).[48]

Matthew 6:33[49]

As 5:21-48 was introduced by describing its relationship to the fulfillment of the law and the prophets (5:17-20), 6:19-7:11 close with a description with the relationship that exists between right living and the law and the prophets (7:12).[50] Many regard 6:33 as an "end point" or a summary of the sermon on the mount (5:1-7:28).[51] The search for righteousness is intimately linked with the kingdom of God. The joining of τὴν βασιλείαν τοῦ θεοῦ and τὴν δικαιοσύνεν αὐτοῦ with καί can generate a hendiadys, "the co-ordination of two ideas, one

---

47. Deines, *Die Gerechtigkeit*, 439: "Sie 'erfüllen' die Gerechtigkeit nicht, sondern 'tun' bzw. 'verwirklichen' die durch Jesus erfüllte (und ihnen auf seinen Jüngern aufgetragene) Gerechtigkeit."
48. Deines, *Gerechtigkeit*, 440: "'Eure Gerechtigkeit' is darum keine andere als die, die Jesus erfüllt hat, es ist die Gerechtigkeit, die ihr Leben *von* Gott und *vor* Gott bestimmt. In 5,20 und 6,1 ist lediglich die Perspective eine jeweils andere, indem der Blick vom Jünger aus auf sein Tun geht."
49. There is some doubt about the presence of τοῦ θεοῦ in 6:33. A stronger textual tradition supports it and is a reading that would not have been easily omitted. However, Matthew almost always uses βασιλεία without a modifier. I am retaining it also because of the textual evidence, and the literary and grammatical balance that exists between the τοῦ θεοῦ (after "kingdom") and αὐτοῦ (after "righteousness"). There is no textual doubt about the latter which would have no antecedent noun if the former were omitted.
50. For this structure, see Luz, *Matthew*, 1:173.
51. For detail, see Deines, *Gerechtigkeit*, 441.

of which is dependent upon the other."⁵² It is impossible to equate the kingdom with moral performance. As Meier rightly observes "[D]ikaiosunē appears next to basileia as the co-equal object of the seeking."⁵³ Disciples are to seek, before everything else (ζητεῖτε δὲ πρῶτον), the righteousness that is kingdom of God (τὴν βασιλείαν τοῦ θεοῦ) in their lives. The kingdom is further described as *his* (i.e., God's) righteousness (τὴν δικαιοσύνεν αὐτοῦ). If "righteousness" in Matthew has "to be uniform in meaning – moral conduct according to God's will,"⁵⁴ how can this be said of God?⁵⁵ "No exegete would claim that the kingdom in Mt. is simply to be equated with Christian moral effort or the end result of that effort."⁵⁶

This final use of the expression in the sermon on the mount reinforces what Matthew has taught to this point: the imperative to search for the kingdom of God and his righteousness indicates that "the righteousness of God" describes the fulfillment of God's design in and through the life, teaching, and especially the death and resurrection of Jesus, that has fulfilled all righteousness (see 3:15). Disciples are not to seek "entry" into the kingdom, but to devote themselves assiduously to the spread and the strengthening of the kingdom in the world. It is an exhortation that they take seriously their universal mission as followers of Jesus.⁵⁷ The eschatological, beyond (but not excluding) the moral, aspect of the δικαιοσύνη-sayings in evidence throughout the discourse of 5:1-7:28, is summarized in 6:33.⁵⁸

---

52. Friedrich Blass, Albert Debrunner, and Robert W. Funk, *A Greek Grammar of the New Testament and Other Early Christian Literature* (Chicago: University of Chicago Press, 1961), 228 §442 (16). If not a hendiadys, recourse can be had to the use of the epexegetical καί where the second noun is an explanation of the first (para 42 [9]).
53. Meier, *Law and History*, 78. See also Hagner, *Matthew*, 1:166.
54. Davies and Allison, *Matthew*, 1:327.
55. This problem is well discussed in Nolland, *Matthew*, 314-15; Strecker, *Sermon*, 139-40.
56. Meier, *Law and History*, 78. However, exegetes do make this claim for 6:33.
57. Deines, *Gerechtigkeit*, 446: "Zusammenfassend ergibt sich für 6,33, dass der Imperativ ζητεῖτε nicht im Sinne von eingehen in die Basileia zu interpretieren ist, sondern als *sich bemühen um die Ausbreitung und Geltung der Basileia in der Welt*, d.h. er ist Aufruf zu einer missionarischen Existenz" (stress in original).
58. Uncomfortably, Davies and Allison, *Matthew*, 1:661, recognise this. They conclude their analysis of 6:33 with the comment: "Righteousness is the law of the realm, the law of eschatological rule one must strive for, the better righteousness of 5:20." This contradicts their earlier blanket assessment of righteousness as

Matthew 21:32

The final use of δικαιοσύνη in Matthew is found in 21:32. The first such saying appeared in a discussion with John the Baptist that asked the Baptist to accept the situation of Jesus' baptism, but to look forward to a time of the fulfillment of righteousness (3:15). This final saying, coming after a series of such sayings in 5:1-7:28, returns to a context that involves John the Baptist, and is Matthew's last reference to this figure.[59] It again associates the Baptist with righteousness. Located in the larger section of the story dedicated to the definitive breakdown between Jesus and Israel that leads to his death and resurrection (21:1-28:15), it is part of a bitter series of conflicts between Jesus and the leaders of Israel (21:12-23:39). As with 5:17-20 and 6:1, the expression δικαιοσύνη appears in a major introductory section of the narrative (21:12-33).

Following Jesus' action in the Temple (21:12-17) and the cursing of the fig tree (vv. 18-22), Jesus' authority is questioned by the chief priests and the elders of the people (vv. 23-27). He addresses this situation of unbelief by means of the parable of the two sons (vv. 28-31). Interpreting the parable, he attacks the leaders of Israel as having given lip-service to the commands of God, but doing what they want, while there are "outsiders" who have responded. This was also the case in the time of John the Baptist, described as one who came to them "in the way of righteousness" (v. 32: ἐν ὁδῷ δικαιοσύνης). This expression is a regarded as a traditional expression used to indicate a good life.[60] Matthew's use of "the way" (see 3:3; 4:15; 5:25; 8:28;

"moral conduct," and makes nonsense of their interpretation of 5:17-20 as the abiding command to observe the letter of the law until the end of time. On the other hand, Luz, *Matthew*, 1:344, is more consistent (and consequently less satisfactory) as he comments: "'Righteousness probably means, as in 3:15; 5:6, 10, 20; 6:1, the righteousness required of people, that is, the activity that God desires and that corresponds to the kingdom." His handling of the parallel between God's righteousness and God's kingdom is uncomfortable. He sees the parallel between this expression and the third and fourth petition of the Lord's Prayer, but must then comment, "Here the person's task is in the foreground, while there it is God's asked for action for and through the human person" (1:344-45). For a similar critique of Luz, see Deines, *Gerechtigkeit*, 443-45.

59. See Deines, *Gerechtigkeit*, 132-36. He refers to 3:15 and 21:32 as "der äußere Rahmen" of Matthew's use of "righteousness"
60. See the documentation in Davies and Allison, *Matthew*, 3: 170 n 42. It is never found in rabbinic sources. For a reading of these sources as the "Weg zur Gerechtigkeit," see Deines, *Gerechtigkeit*, 134-35.

10:10; 13:4, 19; 15:32; 20:17; 20:30; 21:8, 19; 22:16) is dependent upon Mark.[61]

The Baptist's coming "in the way of righteousness" brings Jesus' instruction to John the Baptist in 3:15 to closure. In their first encounter, the Baptist accepted his role as he waited for the fulfillment of righteousness. As with Jesus, so with the Baptist: both were rejected by a false Israel that claimed righteousness but did not live that way (see especially 15:10-20; 21:28-32, 33-41; 23:1-10, 11-36).[62] The consequence of this situation is that the "outsiders" (tax collectors and prostitutes) who join John and follow Jesus accept the fullness of righteousness present in Jesus (3:15). Israel will not repent and believe. This is already an initial fulfillment of Jesus' threats in 8:11-12, 21:42-43 and 22:1-10, and has been foreshadowed by Jesus' words on the reception of John the Baptist in 11:7-19. "Yet wisdom is justified (ἐδικαιώθη) by her deeds" (11:19). The situation will worsen from 21:33-28:16.

Given the complex of δικαιοσύνη-sayings, their arrangement across the Gospel narrative and the cumulative reading experience that leads to this final saying, understanding 21:32 as an indication that John the Baptist lived a morally upright life is unsatisfactory.[63] The Matthean uptake of the Markan theme of "the way" indicates that the dynamic sense of journeying, both physically and spiritually, is also congenial to Matthew.[64] John the Baptist, instructed by Jesus to attend to the fulfillment of righteousness (3:15) was ἐν ὁδῷ

---

61. There are a few uses in Matthean special material (2:12 [Magi]; 10:5 [the way of the Gentiles]; 22:9-10 [parable of the marriage feast]). We should not make too much of the remaining passages that come from Q (7:13-14 [see Luke 13:23-24: the narrow gate]; 11:10 [see Luke 5:27: citation of Mal 3:1, found in a different setting in Mark 1:2]). Matthew introduces ἡ ὁδός into the passage on the Q passage on narrow gate (7:13-14; Luke 13:23-24).
62. See Hagner, *Matthew*, 2:614; Meier, "John the Baptist," 383-405; Carter, *Matthew*, 425-26; Deines, *Gerechtigkeit*, 134.
63. Davies and Allison, *Matthew*, 3:170; Luz, *Matthew*, 3:31-32: "life that corresponds to the will of God" (p. 31). Nolland, *Matthew*, 863-64, rightly looks back to 3:15, but repeats the Pauline interpretation offered there ("that state of affairs in which all is right between God and his world" [p. 364]).
64. See Deines, *Die Gerechtigkeit*, 135-36. On the Markan theme, see Ermenegildo Manicardi, *Il cammino de Gesù nel Vangelo di Marco. Schema narrativo e tema cristologico*, Analecta Biblica 96 (Rome: Biblical Institute Press, 1986).

δικαιοσύνης, but the chief priests and the elders of the people (see v. 23) do not join him on this "way."

Israel's final rejection of the perfection of all righteousness that was first articulated during the Baptist's ministry (3:15) and further explained in Jesus' first discourse (5:6, 10, 20; 6:1, 33), is near at hand as Jesus turns towards the death and resurrection that will mark the turning point of the ages (21:32). Meier comments: "Both eschatological gift and man's moral effort may come together in 21:32."[65] The Matthean use of δικαιοσύνη marks both Jesus' first encounter with John the Baptist in 3:15, and his final comment on John's role in 21:32. This "location" of the sayings enhances the possibility that the theme of "eschatological gift," so prominent in 3:15, is also present in 21:32. This is further enhanced by the cumulative effect the sevenfold use of δικαιοσύνη has upon the reader. As Donald Hagner comments: "Probably this is to be understood as a reference to the process of the accomplishment of salvation in history through God's sending of John as the forerunner of Jesus."[66]

Conclusion

This study agrees that the Matthean δικαιοσύνη is not Pauline.[67] But it attempts to indicate that mainstream scholarship has over-reacted against possible Pauline interpretations of Matthew by insisting that *all* Matthean διακαιούνη-sayings are to be associated with human action, and *never* with God's design. This appears to be a straightjacketing of the Matthean text. Jesus is the fulfilment of all the promises made to Israel, as he obediently responds to all that God asks of him (5:17-18). In his final act of obedience and God's response, death and resurrection, Matthew makes it clear that a new era has dawned

---

65. Meier, *Law and History*, 79. See also Meier, "John the Baptist," 401.
66. Hagner, *Matthew*, 2:615, with reference to 3:15. See also Gnilka, *Matthäusevangelium*, 2:222.
67. Contrast what follows with Frank Matera, *New Testament Theology. Exploring Diversity in Unity* (Louisville: Westminster John Knox, 2007), 35-36. Even more trenchant is Sim, *The Gospel of Matthew*, 165-213. "Matthew openly and savagely attacks Paul and his law-free Gospel" (p. 213). These pages are reminiscent of Ferdinand Christian Bauer's understanding of the factions that determined early Christianity, and the development of the New Testament. See William Baird, *History of New Testament Research*, 3 vols. (Minneapolis: Fortress, 1992-2013), 1:258-69, esp. 263-69.

(27:45, 51-53; 28:2-4). Although, apart from δικαιοσύνη, Pauline language is not used (e.g., "in Christ," "grace," "sonship," new creation," etc.), Matthew tells of the establishment of an eschatological people (28:16-20. See also 16:13-19; 18:15-20).[68]

As he opens his ministry, Jesus points to the future fulfilment of righteousness (3:15). A future (eschatological) orientation is maintained in 5:6. But, from that point on, there is a righteous way of living "now" that reflects the fulfilment of all righteousness (5:10, 20, 6:1, 33). This "now" of the life of Jesus closes as he returns to John the Baptist, and shows that Israel has made its decision (21:32). From that point on in the story, Israel's no to the fullness of righteousness is played out. Jesus fulfils all righteousness. He is the perfection of the Davidic messianic promises, the son of God, the perfection of Torah and the prophets. A final "turning point of the ages" is revealed when heaven and earth pass away (5:17-18; 27:45, 51-53; 28:2-4).

The search for righteousness, for Matthew, is not primarily commitment to required moral response. It is a discipleship transformed by Jesus' fulfilment of righteousness through his life and teaching as the Son of David, Son of Abraham, Messiah and Son of God (1:1, 23; 4:1-11; 16:16-18), and climactically in and through his eschatological death and resurrection.

> In Matthew ... this age and the age to come seemingly overlap. Although the consummation lies ahead, although this age is still full of tribulation, and although the Christian casts his hope in the future coming of the Son of Man, saints have already been raised, the Son of Man has already been enthroned in the heavenly places, the resurrected Jesus is ever present with his followers (28:20). If we may so put it, Matthew's eschatology is, in some ways, more realized than that of Mark.[69]

---

68. Note the important closing comment of Deines, *Die Gerechtigkeit*, 654: "Das letzte Wort in dieser Sache haben aber weder Matthäus noch Paulus, sondern der auferstandene und wiederkommende Christus. Bis dahin wird die Christenheit gut daran tun, *beiden* Zeugen des Evangeliums mit ganzer Leidenschaft zuzuhören zu tun, was sie sagen" (stress in original).
69. Allison, *The End*, 49-50. See Meier, *Law and History*, 38: "There is much more 'realized eschatology' in Mt.'s theology than is usually admitted."

9
Luke 22:14-38: Eucharist and Mission[1]

Anyone reading through the four Gospels, even for the first time, senses that there is something special about the Gospel of John. It is very different from Mark, Matthew, and Luke, generally called the "synoptic" Gospels. They have been given that name because when placed on a page side-by-side they can be seen with one glance of the eye (*sun-opsis*: "with the eye"). But the Synoptic Gospels are not identical. Matthew is more loyal to Mark than Luke. Matthew changes very little, and follows Mark's sequence of events, adding words and episodes from the life of Jesus, especially an infancy story (Matt 1-2), long discourses where only Jesus speaks (e.g. 5:17-7:27: the Sermon on the Mount. See also 10:5-11:1; 13:1-53; 18:1-19:1; 23:1-24:46). He also records events only found in Matthew, and some of them reflect special interest in the leadership role of Simon Peter (e.g. 16:13-18: Peter's confession of faith and his appointment as "the rock").

Luke also depends upon the Gospel of Mark, but he is more creative and original than Matthew. As well as his very different infancy story (Luke 1-2), Luke is bolder in his rewriting of Mark, regularly refining his Greek, and some of the most memorable gospel parables and episodes are found only in Luke (e. g., the Good Samaritan [10:25-37]; the father with the two sons [15:11-32]; the walk to Emmaus [24:13-35]). As well as the Gospel of Mark, and their own

---

1. This is the only essay in this volume that has not appeared previously in a journal or a volume of collected essays. However, apart from the opening remarks on Luke's overall interest in mission, the setting for the reflection on Luke 22:14-38 depends heavily upon Francis J. Moloney, *A Body Broken for a Broken People. Divorce, Remarriage, and the Eucharist* (Melbourne: Garratt, 2015), 138-50, and is reproduced with the permission of the publishers.

traditions, Matthew and Luke sometimes share traditions not found in Mark. Commentators generally accept that both Matthew and Luke had independent access to another record of Jesus, especially his preaching, that Mark either did not know, or did not use. Although we do not have this record, it can be reconstructed by establishing the shape and contours of material found in both Luke and Matthew, but not in Mark. For convenience's sake, it is called "Q," the first letter of the German word for "source" (*Quelle*).[2]

The following reflection upon the Lukan version of the last meal that Jesus shared with his disciples (22:14-38) is important evidence of Luke's creative use of the traditions that came to him. A major theological and pastoral issue for Luke was the mission to the Gentile world. There are many indications in Luke's Gospel that point to the well-established conviction that it was written by a Gentile, somewhere in the Gentile mission. One of Luke's major concerns was to address the importance of mission as an essential aspect of God's design. This is sometimes described as the first systematic Christian presentation of God's salvation history.[3] In his first volume (the Gospel of Luke) he tells the story of the birth, life and teaching, death, resurrection and ascension of Jesus. That story was marked by a journey. Jesus is born by the road, as there is no "resting place" for him (Luke 2:7). Jesus opens his ministry in Nazareth, his home town (4:16-30). Rejected there moves on, never to come back to his origins. He wanders from village to village in Galilee, until "the days drew near for him to be taken up. He set his face to go to Jerusalem" (9:51).

From 9:52-19:44 he journeys to Jerusalem (see 9:57; 10:38; 13:22; 17:11; 18:31; 19:11, 28, 37, 41). Once there, he enters the temple (19:45), and all journeys cease, until Jesus' ascension into heaven

---

2. This rapid summary of the relationship between the Gospels accepts the so-called "two source hypothesis." The two sources are Mark and Q. Matthew used them, and material special to his traditions, as did Luke. It remains a majority hypothesis, and some wish to eliminate Q. For a very helpful assessment of the data, and defense of the "hypothesis," see John S. Kloppenborg, *Q, the Earliest Gospel. An Introduction to the Original Stories and Sayings of Jesus* (Louisville: Westminster John Knox, 2008), 1-40. For a critical reconstruction of Q, see James M. Robinson, Paul Hoffmann, and John S. Kloppenborg, *The Critical Edition of Q*, Hermeneia (Minneapolis: Fortress, 2000). A simpler reconstructed text is also available in Kloppenborg, *Q, the Earliest Gospel*, 123-44.

3. See François Bovon, *Luke the Theologian. Fifty-five Years of Research*, trans Ken McKinney, 2nd ed. (Waco, TX: Baylor University Press, 2006), 33-82.

(24:50-51). In Jerusalem, he takes possession of the temple, preaches there daily (21:37), until he is betrayed, suffers, dies, rises, and ascends, as the disciple praise God with joy in the temple (19:45-24:53). But before Jesus ascends to heaven, he instructs his apostles to *remain in the city* until they have been clothed with the power from on high. Only after that gift of God will they become witnesses to what God has done, proclaiming repentance and forgiveness of sins to all nations. They must begin their witnessing mission in Jerusalem (Luke 24:46-51). From there they will be witnesses to Jesus "in Jerusalem, in all Judea, in Samaria, and to the end of the earth" (Acts 1:8). Gifted with the Holy Spirit at Pentecost (2:1-13), they shape the earliest Christian community and its witnessing role in word and deed in Jerusalem (Acts 1-5), and then begin their missionary journey, described mainly through the journeys of Paul, until, at the end of the Acts of the Apostles, Paul is preaching the Gospel boldly, and without hindrance in Rome, the center of the world (28:31). The city of Jerusalem is the "fulcrum" of salvation history: everything from Moses, the Prophets, and the Psalms leads to it (see 24:17, 44), and everything in the Christian mission, reaching out to the ends of the earth (see 24:46-49; Acts 1:8), flows from what happened there.

In his opening words to both the Gospel and the Acts of the Apostles, he addresses a Gentile patron, Theophilus (Luke 1:1-4; Acts 1:1-2). The fruit of the missionary activity of the earliest Church, Theophilus represents the Gentile world.[4] The books are being written for him to assure him of the truth that God's design has been worked out through the events of a saving history that began in the Old Testament (Zechariah, Elizabeth, Simeon, and Anna in Luke 1-2).[5] It has been made evident in the life, teaching, death, resurrection, and ascension of Jesus, and is now available from the witnessing apostles at the ends of the earth. It comes as a surprise to many that among the Gospels *only Luke* regularly uses the word "apostle"

---

4. Commentators debate whether or not "Theophilus" was a historical person, or a symbol of the Gentile audience. Nowadays majority opinion is that there was a historical "Theophilus," a name which means a lover of God.
5. The words addressed to Theophilus say that Luke has written these books so that he might "know the truth concerning the things about which you have been instructed" (Luke 1:4. NRSV). The Greek word translated "truth" (ἀσφάλεια). Means more than intellectual truth. It indicates something in which you can have rock solid certitude.

(ἀπόστολος) to speak of Jesus' disciples. The word is used because of Luke's understanding of the role of the disciples; they are the *sent ones* (ἀπόστολλοι) who carry on the mission of witnessing Jesus to the ends of the earth (6:13; 9:10; 11:49; 17:5; 22:14; 24:10).[6] The Theology and the Christology of Luke-Acts are very rich, but this brief sketch indicates that the theme of "mission" lies behind much of it.[7] The following essay, focusing upon the encounter between Jesus and his apostles at the meal table in Luke 22:14-38, takes it for granted that Luke has a passionate interest in instructing his readers and listeners about the importance of mission, and the origins of the Christion mission in the life, teaching, and practices of Jesus of Nazareth.

One further introductory remark is called for. Our reflection upon 22:14-38 is part of the larger literary and theological context of Luke's account of Jesus passion, death, resurrection, and ascension. Luke's version of these events in 22:1-24:53 is *so different* from the account one finds in Mark, Matthew, and even John, that it was once thought that Luke's passion and resurrection account (22:1-24) must have come from a special source.[8] For example, after a very different interpretation of the women at the empty tomb (24:1-12), *everything else in Luke's resurrection account is unique to Luke*: the journey to Emmaus (vv. 13-35), Jesus appearance, sharing a meal and commissioning of his apostles (vv. 36-49), and his ascension (vv. 50-53).[9] Nowadays

---

6. The expression is also important for Paul, who saw his whole life as a person on mission, as the chosen "apostle" of Jesus Christ (see Rom 1:1; 1 Cor 1:1; 2: Cor 1:1; Gal 1:1; Col 1:1). The expression appears in Mark 6:30, but only in relating them to Jesus' having earlier "send them out" in 6:7. It is used only once by Matthew (10:2) to describe the Twelve. It is never found in John. See Hans Dieter Betz, "Apostle," in *The Anchor Bible Dictionary*, ed. David N. Freedman, 6 vols. (New York: Doubleday, 1992), 1:309-11.
7. On Lukan Theology as a whole, see the comprehensive study of Bovon, *Luke the Theologian*. For a detailed study of the theme of mission in Luke-Acts, see Stephen G. Wilson, *The Gentiles and the Gentile Mission in Luke-Acts*, Society for New Testament Studies Monograph Series 23 (Cambridge: Cambridge University Press, 1973).
8. Known as "proto-Luke." See, for example, Vincent Taylor, *The Passion Narrative of St Luke*, ed. Owen E. Evans, Society for New Testament Studies Monograph Series 19 (Cambridge: Cambridge University Press, 1972).
9. On the Lukan resurrection account, including a discussion of his sources, see Francis J. Moloney, *The Resurrection of the Messiah. A Narrative Commentary on the Resurrection Accounts of the Four Gospels* (New York/Mahwah, NJ: Paulist, 2013), 69-99. On the passion narrative, see pp. 69-76.

scholars are in almost universal agreement that the uniqueness of the Lukan narrative comes from the genius of the author. He does not have a special pre-Lukan account of the death and resurrection of Jesus. He has Mark, traditions that come to him from within his own Christian community and their experience, and his own genius. All of this is in evidence in the study of the Lukan association of the Eucharistic table and the mission of apostles of all ages.

The Last Supper in Luke's Gospel

The Gospel of Luke contains an account of the disciples' last meal with Jesus (22:14-38) that is strikingly different from that of Mark 14:17-31 and Matthew 26:14-35. Although, as we have seen, it is accepted that Luke's passion narrative was a creative rewriting of Mark's version, many suggest that his report of the Last Supper does not depend upon the Gospel of Mark, but reflects a creative reworking of his own sources.[10] Rather than a tracing a use of possible sources, contemporary scholarship focuses upon this narrative as a special example of Luke's literary skills. Two themes in particular seem to be intertwined in this account. The first is Luke's use of the theme of Jesus' eating with others. Throughout the Gospel of Luke there is a notable interest in food and meals.[11] This theme comes to a climax in the final meal celebrated with the twelve before Jesus dies (22:14-38), and in the meal which the risen Lord shares with those same apostles, less Judas (24:36-49). A further unique feature of the Lukan Last Supper

---

10. For a detailed analysis, see Joseph A. Fitzmyer, *The Gospel According to Luke*, 2 vols., The Anchor Bible 28-28A (New York: Doubleday, 1981-1985), 2:1385-1406. See also, more briefly, the recent commentaries of François Bovon, *Luke*, trans. Christine S. Thomas, Donald S. Deer, and James Crouch, 3 vols., Hermeneia (Minneapolis: Fortress, 2002-2012) 1:6-8; 3:153-56; John T. Carroll, *Luke: A Commentary*, The New Testament Library (Louisville: Westminster John Knox, 2012), 424-25, and the summary of the peculiarities of the Lukan text in Gerd Theissen and Annette Merz, *The Historical Figure of Jesus. A Comprehensive Guide*, trans. John Bowden (Minneapolis: Fortress, 1998), 417.
11. See the study of Robert J. Karris, *Luke: Artist and Theologian. Luke's Passion Account as Literature* (New York: Paulist Press, 1985), 47-78. See also Jerome Neyrey, *The Passion According to Luke. A Redaction Study of Luke's Soteriology* (New York: Paulist Press, 1985), 8-11; Markus Barth, *Rediscovering the Lord's Supper, Communion with Israel, with Christ, and Among the Guests* (Atlanta: John Knox Press, 1998), 71-74.

is its setting within a long "final discourse" which Jesus delivers to his disciples/apostles.[12]

Lukan Meals

The supper recorded in 22:14-38 climaxes of a long series of suppers through the Gospel. These suppers are consistently marked by Jesus' questioning the *status quo*. He shares the table with sinners; he radically questions the Pharisees on the numerous occasions where he is reported to have been invited to dine with them.[13]

Jesus shared a meal with Levi, the sinful tax collector. More than that, there were other sinners at the table who had been gathered by Levi to share fellowship with Jesus (5:27-32). Invited as "a prophet" (see 7:39) to share the table with another important religious figure, Simon the Pharisee, Jesus shows that his love cannot be contained within the limitations of conventional religion. He allows and even encourages the intimacy of a woman well-known for her sins (7:37). Her love has drawn her to the table and to Jesus' forgiveness (7:36-50). Again at table with the Pharisees, he challenges them to recognize their lack of true justice (11:37-54). He uses a further meal with the Pharisees to heal the disadvantaged man with dropsy on a Sabbath, to question the way the Pharisees "religiously" organized their meals, and to urge them to follow his example: "When you give a feast, invite the poor, the maimed, the lame, the blind, and you will be blessed because they cannot repay you" (14:14. See 14: 1-24).

The challenge which Jesus issues through the sharing of meals and his questioning of the *status quo* within the context of these meals is important for a proper understanding of the Lukan "point of view." As with all four Gospels, Luke tells of Jesus' words and actions in the

---

12. See especially Xavier Léon-Dufour, *Sharing the Eucharistic Bread: The Witness of the New Testament*, trans. Matthew J. O'Connell (New York: Paulist, 1987), 85-95, 230-247; Neyrey, *The Passion According to Luke*, 5-48. Bovon, *Luke*, 153 n. 2, accepts that the Lukan text belongs to the literary genre of a testament, but rightly insists that it "is not only a farewell speech." What follows will have occasion to show that this is the case.
13. For a detailed study of the significance of sharing one's table in Jewish thought and practice, see Philip Esler, *Community and Gospel in Luke-Acts: The Social and Political Motivations of Lucan Theology*, Society for New Testament Studies Monograph Series 57 (Cambridge: Cambridge University Press, 1987), 71-86.

"then" of what is technically called the "narrated time," that is, the Gospel's reporting of the life and times of Jesus, to question the "now" of current Christian practice. Commenting on Luke's parable of the great supper (14:16-24), John R. Donahue concludes:

> Within Christian communities, some of the most violent debates continue to rage over inclusiveness, often centered on the celebration of the Lord's Supper. Yet when Luke's Jesus told a parable about eating bread in the kingdom of God, he shattered his hearer's expectations of who would be the proper table companions. Can his parabolic word continue to challenge our expectations?[14]

The final eloquent witness to this important Lukan theme is found in 19:1-10. In an episode that both looks back across the rest of the Gospel for its meaning, and which points forward to the final days of Jesus' presence, Jesus' encounter and meal with Zacchaeus is a fitting climax to his journey towards the city of Jerusalem. This is the city from which Jesus will be "taken up" (see 9:31, 51), and equally the place from which the disciples will be sent out to the ends of the earth (see Acts 1:8; 28:31). As Jesus approaches Jerusalem he catches sight of Zacchaeus. Despite the murmuring opposition of the people standing by, Jesus publicly announces that he will stay and dine with Zacchaeus, a chief tax collector, a notorious sinner. In his own turn, Zacchaeus commits himself to the way of Jesus by promising to give half his possessions to the poor. Christology and discipleship blend in a reciprocal gift of self to the broken ones.[15]

Jerome Neyrey has commented on the function of Jesus' shared meals within the Lukan narrative strategy:

> Jesus' inclusive table fellowship mirrors the inclusive character of the Lukan Church: Gentiles, prostitutes, tax collectors,

---

14. John R. Donahue, *The Gospel in Parable* (Philadelphia: Fortress Press, 1988), 146.
15. For appreciations of the Zacchaeus story that indicate its strategic role within the Lukan narrative, see Gerhard Schneider, *Das Evangelium nach Lukas*, (2 vols., Ökumenischer Taschenbuch-Kommentar zum Neuen Teastament 3/1-2 (Gütersloh/Munich: Gerd Mohn/Echter, 1977), 2:376-78; Jean-Noël Aletti, *L'art de raconter Jésus Christ* (Paris: Seuil, 1989), 17-38. See also Robert C. Tannehill, *The Narrative Unity of Luke-Acts: A Literary Interpretation*, 2 vols., Foundations and Facets (Philadelphia: Fortress, 1986), 1:122-25; Bovon, *Luke*, 590-602.

sinners, as well as the blind, lame, maimed and the poor are welcome at his table and in his covenant.[16]

This Gospel permits no illusions about the composition of the Church of Jesus Christ. It is not made up of "perfect people." On the contrary, it is made up of people who have become Christians because they have been the recipients of the apostles' witnessing to the person and message of Jesus (see 24:45-48). The risen Christ commissions his apostles:

> Thus it is written that the Christ should suffer and on the third day rise from the dead, and that repentance and forgiveness of sins should be preached in his name to all nations, beginning from Jerusalem. You are witnesses of these things. And behold I send the promise of my Father upon you; but stay in the city until you are clothed with power from on high (24:46-49. See also Acts 1:8).

It is from this background of meals shared with sinners that we can best understand 22:14: "And when the hour came, he sat at table and the apostles with him."[17] Despite the importance for the overall argument of Luke-Acts that the apostles must play an essential and foundational role on the other side of the death and resurrection of Jesus, they too share this final meal with their Master as sinners and broken people. They are the last of a long group of broken and sinful people who have shared meals with Jesus during his life and ministry.

Luke understands "the broken" gathering at the table of the Lord more broadly and more boldly than Mark and Matthew. The products of a different setting, and a slightly different time, than the Gospel of Luke, Mark and Matthew have developed narratives that instruct the

---

16. Neyrey, *The Passion According to Luke*, 10. See the excellent synthesis of Jerome Kodell, *The Eucharist in the New Testament*, Zacchaeus New Testament (Wilmington, DE: Michael Glazier, 1989), 106-113. See also Josephine Massyngbaerde Ford, *Bonded with the Immortal. A Pastoral Introduction to the New Testament* (Wilmington, DE: Michael Glazier, 1987), 280-289. Karris, *Luke: Artist and Theologian*, 70, whimsically comments: "Jesus got himself crucified because of the way he ate."
17. Only the Gospel of Luke adds "and the apostles with him." Compare Mark 14:17: "He came with the twelve," and Matt 26:20: "He sat at table with the twelve disciples."

early Christians on the importance of Gentile and Jew sharing a table founded upon disciples who had failed Jesus. It appears that the Gentile mission was proving to be something of a difficulty for the early Christian Churches who told these stories of Jesus.[18] This not the case for the Gospel of Luke. The Gentile Church produced the Gospel of Luke. Thus, from the heart of a largely Gentile Church, Luke's Jesus-story has little interest in those questions. The third Gospel goes to some lengths to show that there are many ways in which one can be considered an "outsider." Indeed, for Luke, they are specially blessed (see 6:20-23). There are those who are guilty of sin, like the prostitute and the tax-collector, and there are Pharisees who suffer from their self-righteousness. There are disciples who fail Jesus, through the weakness of their faith and there are members of the twelve who deny him (Peter) and who betray him (Judas). Finally there are the Gentiles, the materially poor, and the physically maimed people from the highways and the byways who are all welcomed at the table of Jesus.[19]

Within this broad canvas of broken people who are offered the possibility of a real salvation through sharing meals with Jesus, the apostles will be able to give eloquent witness to repentance and forgiveness of sins to all the nations (24:47). Their own lives as followers and apostles of Jesus result from such an experience. They experience the repentance and forgiveness to which they eventually bear witness.[20] As Philip Esler has shown, Jesus' practice of sharing meals with outcasts will be continued by the apostles themselves in the second volume of these two "books" addressed to Theophilus (see Luke 1:3-4; Acts 1:1), the Acts of the Apostles. While the theme of Jesus' accep-

---

18. For more detailed readings of the Last Supper material in Matthew and Mark, see Moloney, *A Body Broken*, 82-97 (Mark), and 115-28 (Matthew).
19. For a thorough survey of scholarly discussion of the Lukan Church, see Bovon, *Luke the Theologian*, 329-463. For some studies of Luke's special interest in the marginalized, see Halvor Moxnes, *The Economy of the Kingdom. Social Conflict and Economic Relations in Luke's Gospel*, Overtures to Biblical Theology (Philadelphia: Fortress, 1988); Tannehill, *The Narrative Unity*, 1:103-39; Christopher F. Evans, *Saint Luke*, New Testament Commentaries (London: SCM Press, 1990), 99-104; Luke T. Johnson, *Prophetic Jesus, Prophetic Church. The Challenge of Luke-Acts to Contemporary Christians* (Grand Rapids: Eerdmans, 2011). See also the excursus on poverty and wealth in Carroll, *Luke*, 374-77.
20. See Francis J. Moloney, "Luke 24: To be Witnesses of the Forgiveness and Compassion of Jesus," in *Apostolic Passion "Give me Souls,"* eds. Rafael Vicent and Corrado Pastore (Bangalore: Kristu Jyoti Publications, 2010), 183-95.

tance and forgiveness of the broken highlights his table in the Gospel, the early Church's acceptance of the Gentiles marks the tables shared by the apostles in the Acts of the Apostles. Commenting on the conversion of Cornelius in Acts 10:1-11:18, Esler comments: "What matters to Luke is the legitimation of complete fellowship between Jew and Gentile in the Christian community, not just the admission of the Gentiles to those communities."[21] Apostles who have experienced forgiveness and admission to the table of the Lord are able to preach and practice such a mission to other "outsiders." *The very presence of the apostles at the table of Jesus broaches the theme of the Eucharist and mission.*

The Last Meal

The theme of Jesus' presence to the broken and the sinful throughout the Gospel, which stands at the basis of what the apostles will witness to the ends of the earth, reaches its high point at the Last Supper. "This final meal on the feast of Passover crowns the meals, both everyday and festive, which he has taken with his disciples and with sinners during his earthly life."[22] The theme of meals celebrated by Jesus is continued into the Last Meal. Mark used a pattern of alternating the actions of Jesus and the failure of the disciples in Mark 14:1-71.[23] Matthew follows Mark very closely at this stage of his narrative, and repeats that literary juxtapositioning of Jesus' presence and the failure of others in Matthew 26:3-75.[24] Those carefully arranged narratives told the story of the last moments of Jesus' unfailing presence to his failing disciples. Luke may have been aware of this literary pattern, but he develops a parallel alternation between Jesus' presence and the failure of the disciples in a different fashion in his construction of Luke 22:14-38.

In the Lukan account of the Last Supper there is an alternation between Jesus' teaching about the establishment of the Kingdom

---

21. Esler, *Community and Gospel in Luke-Acts*, p. 96. His excellent study of the sharing of the table in Acts is found on pp. 93-109. He has not considered the theme in the Gospel.
22. Léon-Dufour, *Sharing the Eucharistic Bread*, 233.
23. For detail, see the essay "Literary Strategies in the Markan Passion Narrative: Mark 14:1-15:47," on pp. 93-115 of this volume.
24. See Moloney, *A Body Broken*, 115-16.

through his death and resurrection, and the apostles' involvement in it on the one hand, and explicit indications of the future betrayal and denial of these same apostles on the other. The passage can be presented as follows:

> A] vv. 14-18: The sharing of the first cup, and the promise of the fulfilment of the Kingdom.
> > B] vv. 19-23: The account of the meal and the prediction of the betrayal of Judas.[25]
>
> A] vv. 24-30: The part that the disciples will play in the Kingdom.
> > B] vv. 31-34: The prayer of Jesus for Peter, but the prophecy that he will yet deny Jesus.
>
> A] vv. 35-38: The difficulties that will confront the disciples in their future mission.[26]

The alternation of themes is present, and this enables Luke to continue the tradition of a contrast between Jesus' gracious self-gift to his disciples, made up of a betrayer, a denier, and others who are unable to understand. In presenting the meal scene in this fashion, Luke continues this theme, also important for Mark and Matthew. However, another literary form lies behind in Luke 22:14-38. It is above all shaped as a discourse during which Jesus addresses his final words to his disciples. But Luke 22:14-38 is *not only* a farewell discourse, as it continues the primitive tradition of a Last Supper.[27] This blending of the tradition of the Last Supper and a farewell discourse enables Luke to develop an all-pervading sense of the imminent failure of the apostles. It is not only found in those passages dedicated specifically

---

25. There is difficulty with the original text here, as some ancient manuscripts omit the second word over the cup (22:19b-20). In defence of the longer reading, see Jeremias, *The Eucharistic Words of Jesus*, 139-159. For a briefer survey, also in defence of the longer text, see Fitzmyer, *Luke*, 2:1387-1389. Even if one were to accept the shorter reading, my structure would hold. More recently, Bovon, *Luke*, 3:154-56, who represents a majority position, defends of the longer reading, while Evans, *Saint Luke*, 788-89, and Carroll, *Luke*, 433-37, reject it. For a good summary of the evidence, concluding that vv. 19b-20 should be retained, see Bruce M. Metzger, *A Textual Commentary on the Greek New Testament*, 2nd ed. (Stuttgart: Deutsche Bibelgesellshaft, 1994), 148-50.
26. See, for example, Carroll, *Luke*, 433-34.
27. See Bovon, *Luke*, 3:152 n. 3.

to it (vv. 19-23, 31-34), but it appears in those passages dedicated more positively to the future role of the apostles in the kingdom (see vv. 24, 38).

Here one senses the skill of the story-teller. The sinners are strongly present. We read in v. 21: "the hand of him who betrays me is with me on the table." This ominous note sets the tone. The obtuseness and brokenness of the apostles in general are indicated through the report of a dispute in v. 24. Peter's betrayal is predicted v. 34. It is reported that the apostles will need "strengthening" (v. 32), implying that they are weak and frail. They seem, moreover, to misunderstand Jesus' missionary instructions in vv. 35-38. While Jesus hints of the trials, imprisonments, persecutions and death that await the apostolic mission, and which indeed take place in the Acts of the Apostles, they take his symbol of a "sword" literally. This leads to Jesus' comment to close all such discussion: "Enough!" (v. 38).[28] Thomas W. Manson has described this final reaction of Jesus to his failing disciples as "the utterance of a broken heart."[29]

Jesus' table includes Judas, his betrayer, Peter, who denied him, and the squabbling and obtuse apostles. Jesus eats with people who fail, even at the Last Supper. Although handled with more subtlety than Mark or Matthew, the presence of Jesus to his disciples at the Last Supper is even more markedly a presence to the broken. This theme, which has highlighted so many of the meal scenes throughout the Gospel, has been drawn to a fitting conclusion in 22:14-38. The disciples will be worthy candidates for the future mission, witnessing to repentance and the forgiveness of sins to all the nations (24:47).[30] They have personally experienced God's gift of forgiveness and sin, and thus can bring that experience to their mission.

The motley group which shares the table of the Lord, and which indicates how this table should be administered in the Church has been well described by Markus Barth:

---

28. For an excellent commentary upon Luke 22:35-38, which I have followed, see Neyrey, *The Passion According to Luke*, 37-43. Along the same lines, see Fitzmyer, *Luke*, 2:1428-1431.
29. Thomas W. Manson, *The Sayings of Jesus* (London: SCM Press, 1971), 341. See also Paul S. Minear, "A Note on Luke 22:36," *Novum Testamentum* 7 (1964-65): 128-134; Brendan Byrne, *The Hospitality of God: A Reading of Luke's Gospel*, 2nd ed. (Collegeville, MN: Liturgical Press, 2015), 174.
30. See Léon-Dufour, *Sharing the Eucharistic Bread*, 234.

Whoever sits at table with Jesus must also accept the other guests in Christ's company. Jesus is never without his elect, including especially the outcast. No one can have Jesus for oneself alone; Jesus is met with a strange entourage - the publicans and the sinners, the poor and the bums from the hedges and byways, a notorious woman whom Jesus permitted to touch his feet, the prodigal sons and such treacherous and cowardly disciples as Judas and Peter and the other disciples who partook of Jesus' last meal (none of whom loved him enough to arrange his funeral). Whoever considers those table companions of Jesus too bad, too base, too little, too far removed from salvation to be met at Jesus' side does not see, accept, and believe Jesus as he really is. Whoever feels too good and too noble to be found in that company cannot sit at the Lord's table. Only when the bums just mentioned have been received and waited upon is Jesus received, and only then does Jesus accept the service rendered to him.[31]

A Meal which is also a Farewell Discourse

The other important feature of Luke 22:14-38 noticed by recent scholarship, and mentioned above, is the presence of a literary form known as a "farewell speech." We have already noticed that the structured presentation of the text differs from the Markan use of a similar pattern of alternating themes. This is due, largely, to the fact that the Lukan report of the Last Supper is *not only* a narrative about a shared meal *but also* a final discourse. The deliberate use of this widely recognized literary form indicates that while early Christian Tradition of the Last Supper is being recalled, a unique literary form is utilized.[32]

---

31. Barth, *Rediscovering the Lord's Supper*, 73. See also Kodell, *The Eucharist in the New Testament*, 105: "The Last Supper is the final meal in a series during Jesus' ministry. There he teaches his disciples how they are to act after he is gone by his interpretation of the bread and wine, by his last instructions, and by sharing table fellowship with his betrayer." For similar sentiments, see Charles H. Talbert, *Reading Luke: a Literary and Theological Commentary on the Third Gospel* (New York: Crossroad, 1982), 206-211.
32. A number of commentators, recognizing this, comment upon 22:14-20 as a Christian adaptation of the Jewish Passover tradition, and then see vv. 21-38 as "instruction," or even a farewell discourse. See, for example, Schneider, *Lukas*, 443-56; Evans, *Saint Luke*, 779-82, 791-92; Luke T. Johnson, *The Gospel of Luke*,

But this literary form does not override the essential message of Jesus' presence to his fragile disciples revealed across all the New Testament accounts of the final meal. The form of a final testament, associated with the tradition of Jesus' unfailing presence to his fragile disciples, produces a narrative that is testamentary in literary form, but it is not *only* a final testament.[33]

In Mark 14:1-71 the account of Jesus' words and actions with the bread and wine at the final meal formed the center-piece of the passage (14:17-31). This is not the case in the Gospel of Luke. It forms part of the second section of the structure (22:19-23), dedicated to the prophecy of the betrayal of Judas. Luke 22:14-38 is not primarily about Jesus' eucharistic words. It is about the last testimony which Jesus left his disciples, within the context of a meal, as he parted from them. As Paul Minear has commented, "In this story the center of gravity lies not in the words of institution but, as at earlier tables, in the four key dialogues between Jesus and the disciples."[34]

The practice of placing a "farewell speech" on the lips of a great man as he goes to his death is a reasonably common practice in many religious writings from the first three centuries of the Christian era.[35] It is particularly widespread in the biblical literature.[36] In the

---

Sacra Pagina 3 (Collegeville, MN: The Liturgical Press, 1991), 336-50. Johnson is especially helpful on the "farewell discourse" genre on pp. 347-49.

33. See Tannehill, *Literary Unity*, 263: "Whether or not 22:14-38 technically belongs to a recognized genre which can be called 'farewell discourse' or 'farewell address,' Jesus' words are uttered in the light of his impending death and with awareness of the new situation which the apostles are entering, as appears in the command to 'do this for my memory,' the effort to prepare the apostles for their new role as leaders in 22:24-27, and a gift of a share in Jesus' royal power in 22:28-30." See his fine commentary on 22:14-38 on pp. 263-70.
34. Paul S. Minear, "Some Glimpses of Luke's Sacramental Theology," *Worship* 44 (1970): 326. I am following majority scholarly tradition, accepting that vv. 19b-20 are original to the Lukan text. See above, n. 25.
35. For the background, see Charles H. Dodd, *The Interpretation of the Fourth Gospel* (Cambridge: Cambridge University Press, 1953), 420-423.
36. For what follows I am depending on the work of Neyrey, *The Passion According to Luke*, 6-8. Although scholars have long been aware of the literary form of a farewell speech, the uncovering of a large number of "testaments" at Qumran, and especially significant parts of *The Testaments of the Twelve Patriarchs* has led to increased interest from Christian scholars. Originally pre-Christian, the present text of these testaments has numerous Christian interpolations, but they at least offer evidence of the early Christian use of a Hebrew scriptural tradition. See Robert A. Kugler, "Testaments," in *Encyclopedia of the Dead Sea Scrolls*,

Old Testament we find farewell speeches in Genesis 47-50 (Jacob), in Joshua 23-24 (Joshua) and in Deuteronomy 31-34 (Moses). In fact, the whole of the Book of Deuteronomy can be regarded as Moses' farewell speech. In the New Testament Paul gives a farewell speech at Miletus (Acts 20:17-35), and Peter is portrayed as giving a farewell speech (2 Peter 1:12-15). Jesus delivers a form of a farewell speech in Luke 22:14-38, and John 14:1-16:33. There is considerable interest on the part of New Testament scholars in a series of Jewish testamentary texts where this technique is used, especially *The Testaments of the Twelve Patriarchs* that has their origins in the second century BCE, modelled on Jacob's last words in Genesis 49.[37]

The main features of a farewell speech find correspondence in Luke 22:14-38. The Lukan report of Jesus' last meal with his disciples, as well as being a development of the tradition of Jesus' final meal with his disciples, can also be seen as a good example of the final discourse genre.[38] There are four elements fundamental to this form.

1. *Prediction of death.*
    The speech is understood by the patriarch, who is about to depart, as his "farewell" to his disciples. Thus there is some indication or prediction of his oncoming death in all of the testaments. In some cases, the death is unexpected (*Testament of Levi* 1:2; *Testament of Naphtali* 1:2-4; *Testament of Asher* 1:2). This prediction serves as the occasion for the speech. *In the Lukan Last Supper discourse*, this is found in 22:15: "I have earnestly desired to eat this passover with you before I suffer," and in 22:22: "For the Son of Man goes as it has been determined." Earlier references to the future suffering, death, and resurrection of the Son of Man (9:22, 44; 18:31-33) leave

---

ed. Lawrence H. Schiffman and James C. VanderKam, 2 vols. (Oxford/New York: Oxford University Press, 2000), 2:933-36, and Idem, "Twelve Patriarchs, Testaments of the," in *Encyclopedia of the Dead Sea Scrolls*, 2:952-53.

37. For an introduction and an annotated critical text of this document (prepared by Howard C. Kee), see James H. Charlesworth, ed., *The Old Testament Pseudepigrapha*, 2 vols. (London: Darton, Longman & Todd, 1983), 1:775-828.

38. Here I am following Neyrey, *The Passion According to Luke*, 7. See also Léon-Dufour, *Sharing the Eucharistic Bread*, 245-246; Johnson, *Luke*, 336-50. For a strong argument in defence of this position, see William S. Kurz, "Luke 22:14-38 and Greco-Roman and Biblical Farewell Addresses," *Journal of Biblical Literature* 104 (1985): 251-68.

no doubt in the audience's mind and heart that a departure through violent death is imminent.

2. *Predictions of future attacks upon the dying leader's disciples.*
    This feature of the farewell speech is also basic to its structure. One of the motivations for the speech is to forewarn disciples that they are in imminent danger. Most of the testaments portray this imminent danger as a sign of the end time. *In the Lukan Last Supper discourse* this feature is found in 22:31-34: "I have prayed for you that your faith may not fail; and when you have turned again, strengthen your brethren ... I tell you, Peter, the cock will not crow this day, until you three times deny that you know me." It is also present in 22:36: "Now let him who has a purse take it, and likewise a bag. And let him who has no sword sell his mantle and buy one." Here, as elsewhere, we find the blending of the widespread Christian traditions concerning the denials of Peter, and its use as a warning in the testament.

3. *An exhortation to ideal behavior.*
    The testaments devote a lot of attention to the difficulties to be endured in the future. They are to be met with a behavior which will both protect the members of the group from danger, and help them overcome their difficulties. *In the Lukan Last Supper discourse* there again the intrusion of the uniquely Lukan use of his meal theme, where failing disciples are the object of his exhortation. The meal tradition and the testamentary form blend. The instruction to ideal behavior of the "farewell discourse" is found within the context of disciples who squabble (22:24).[39] The exhortation then follows in vv. 25-26:

    > The kings of the Gentiles exercise lordship over them; and those in authority over them are called benefactors. But not so with you; rather let the greatest among you become

---

39. In the testaments there are frequent references to the future failings of the patriarchs sons, generally associated with the end time. See, for example, *Testament of Levi* 10:1-5; 14-16; *Testament of Isacchar* 6:1-4; *Testament of Dan* 5:7-8; *Testament of Naphtali* 4:1-5. On one occasion only there is a reference to present sinfulness, but the patriarch's exhortation quickly moves into a discussion of the evils of the end time. See *Testament of Judah* 23:1.

as the youngest, and the leader as one who serves (see the whole of vv. 24-27).

4. *A final commission.*
Instructions are given to the disciples of the departing patriarch concerning their reconstitution after his departure. *In the Lukan Last Supper discourse* the blending of the traditional theme of Jesus' presence to the broken at the meal table again intrudes, as it is within the context of a future denial that Peter is commissioned (vv. 33-34). Nevertheless, even though the commission is delivered to failing disciples, it still stands. The apostles are to continue what he has left with them, even after his departure. This is found in Luke 22:31-32: "Simon, Simon, behold Satan demanded to have you that he might sift you like wheat, but I have prayed for you that your faith may not fail; and when you have turned again, strengthen your brethren."[40]

Conclusion: Eucharist and Mission

The Lukan use of the theme of the meal has served to show that Jesus shared his Last Supper with broken disciples, while the use of the literary form of a farewell discourse establishes them as his legitimate successors. The legitimacy of those "apostles" who had formed the "bridge" as witnesses of Jesus to the ends of the earth was crucial for the self-identity of a Gentile Christian community. The crucial early Christian tradition about Jesus' final meal with his disciples, and its association with the Church's Eucharistic practice, is firmly embedded in a commissioning of his fragile disciples for mission. Both Eucharist and mission are central for Luke. His skillful narrative has enabled the blending of the traditional meal theme and the literary

---

40. Neyrey, *The Passion According to Luke*, 31-37 offers an excellent study of these verses. He shows convincingly that Jesus' words are a "commissioning" of Peter. He even suggests "that this verse (32b) contains a solemn commissioning of Peter comparable to Mt 16:17-19 and Jn 21:15-17" (p. 34). The theme of failure on the part of the commissioned future leader is also an important result of Luke's "blending" of his meal theme with the "farewell discourse." See, on this Léon-Dufour, *Sharing the Eucharistic Bread*, 241-242; Tannehill, *Narrative Unity*, 1:263-68.

pattern of a farewell speech.⁴¹ By intermingling both, Luke has been able to continue the tradition found in Mark and Matthew: the presence of Jesus to the broken and sinful disciples. But he has also been able to reinforce this important tradition within the Gentile settling of the Lukan Church: the disciples and apostles are the legitimate successors of Jesus of Nazareth. Celebrating Eucharist in the Lukan community also involved accepting Jesus' mandate for mission and service. One of the aims of the Lukan narrative of Luke-Acts is to overcome a tendency of self-sufficiency. There was a danger that the communities that received Luke-Acts may have regarded themselves as the "end of the journey." However fragile, they are exhorted to become missionaries, in their own turn.⁴²

Disciples are instructed and commissioned in the midst of failure (see especially vv. 31-38). Luke has produced a singular example of the farewell discourse form. Jesus' disciples, despite the brokenness of their table fellowship with the Lord, are also the apostles, the ones who will continue his presence "to all nations" (24:47; Acts 1:8).⁴³ A

---

41. This blending of the themes of failure and commissioning for a future brings its difficulties. The patriarch never gives his instructions to the sort of squabbling disciples found in Luke 22:24-27. Although the testaments do speak of a future sinfulness (see above, note 39), the "commissioning" never takes place within the context of a prophecy of future denial of the patriarch. See, on this, Léon-Dufour, *Sharing the Eucharistic Bread*, 236-239 and 243-245. He notes that "certain departures from the testamentary genre are significant" (243-244). They arise largely from the Lukan blending of the meal theme with the testamentary genre.

42. This affirmation could also be supported by a lengthy analysis of the text of Luke-Acts that is beyond the scope of this essay. It is often noticed that the most demanding of all requirements for discipleship of Jesus are found in the Lukan journey narrative (9:51-19:44. See, for example, 11:1-13, 37-52; 12:1-3; 13:24-25; 14:7-14, 26, 33; 18:15-17; 19:1-10). Disciples of all ages must recognize that the journey is not yet over! On this, see Francis J. Moloney, *Reading the New Testament in the Church. A Primer for Pastors, Religious Educators, and Believers* (Grand Rapids: Baker Academic, 2015), 126-28.

43. Here we find another marked difference between the Testaments of the Twelve Patriarchs and Luke 22:14-38. Many of the patriarchs speak at length of their sinful past, especially their sexual dalliances and their mistreatment of Joseph. See, for example, *Testament of Reuben* 1:6-10; 2:11-15; *Testament of Simon* 2:6-13; *Testament of Gad* 2:1-5. Obviously, there is no place for this theme in the Gospel of Luke, nor in a report of the events that took place on the night before Jesus died. Tannehill, *Narrative Unity*, 1:268, nevertheless writes: "The lawlessness of the apostles in the passion story fulfils scripture, and so it, too, has a place within God's purpose, which is able to make use of human failure and rejection."

departing Jesus commissions failing disciples in a farewell discourse delivered at the last of a long series of meals which Jesus has shared with broken people. The message is clear:

> Jesus will not distance himself from them because they fail him. The keynote of his ministry, and especially his table fellowship has been 'He was reckoned with transgressors' (Is 53:12; Lk 22:37), both by his own desire and the will of his persecutors (see 23:32). And he will continue to share his life with sinners in the kingdom meals of the time of the Church.[44]

---

44. Kodell, *The Eucharist in the New Testament*, 117.

10
When is John Talking About Sacraments?*

The Melbourne Scripture Seminar of 1981 was devoted to the theme: "The Sacraments: Celebrating Life." I had been invited to contribute in the area of Johannine scholarship, and the advertisement for the Seminar stated: "Johannine literature is perhaps regarded as the most explicitly sacramental of the New Testament collection." This is true. If one were to accept all the suggestions of scholars who have written on this issue in a positive sense, then one would finish with the following explicit sacramental teaching in the Fourth Gospel:[1]

Matrimony:
 – The marriage feast at Cana (John 2:1-11)

Sacrament of the Sick and Dying:
 – The anointing at Bethany (12:1-8)

---

* I have retained this title, despite its difficulties (see below, pp. 194-97 for clarifications on "John talking" and "Sacraments"), from the original setting of this paper, given at the Melbourne Scripture Seminar, Newman College, University of Melbourne, 24-31 August, 1981. The earliest essay in this collection, the text and the references have been updated, but it still represents what was published in 1982 (especially the four criteria). Interestingly, despite its age (and my naïvety in 1981), it is still regularly cited in the scholarly literature.
1. For this list, see R. E. Brown, "The Johannine Sacramentary," in *New Testament Essays* (London, Geoffrey Chapman, 1967), 75-76. Another good overview of scholarship up to the late 1960's, can be found in H. Klos, *Die Sakramente im Johannesevangelium. Vorkommen und Bedeutung von Taufe, Eucharistie und Buße im vierten Evangelium*, Stuttgarter Bibelstudien 46 (Stuttgart, Katholisches Bibelwerk, 1970).

Reconciliation:
- Lazarus (11:1-44)
- John 13:10: "He who has bathed does not need to wash, *except for his feet*"[2]
- John 20:23: "Whose sins you shall forgive, they are forgiven"

Baptism:
- Baptism of Jesus (1:32-33)
- The marriage feast at Cana (2:1-11)
- The cleansing of the Temple (2:13-22)
- The conversation with Nicodemus (3:1-21)
- The conversation with the Samaritan woman (4:1-30)
- The healing at Bethesda (5:1-9)
- The walking on the water (6:16-21)
- Source of living waters (7:38)
- Healing of the man born blind (9:1-38)
- The Good Shepherd (10:1-21)
- The raising of Lazarus (11:1-44)
- The foot washing (13:1-17)
- The miraculous draught of fishes (21:5-6)

Eucharist:
- The marriage feast at Cana (2:1-11)
- The cleansing of the Temple (2:13-22)
- "My food is to do the will of my Father" (4:31-34)
- The bread miracle and discourse (6:1-58)
- The foot washing (13:1-20)
- The vine and the branches (15:1-11)
- The meal of bread and fish (21:13)

Baptism and Eucharist:
- Blood and water from the pierced side of Jesus (19:34-35)
- Water and blood as witnesses (I John 5:8).

---

2. The words εἰ μὴ τοὺ ς πόδας νίψασθαι are textually doubtful, and may have been added by a copyist to solve the problem of sinfulness after Baptism. For a discussion, with bibliographical details (rejecting the insertion of washing the feet), see F. J. Moloney, *The Johannine Son of Man*, 2nd ed. (Eugene, OR: Wipf & Stock, 2007), 192-193.

This list is clearly "maximal," gathering the suggestions of *all* the scholars, and comes as something of a surprise to contemporary critics that all these episodes have been claimed, at one time or another, as explicit Johannine teachings on the Sacraments. Most of these claims are unacceptable. There are serious historical and theological questions associated with a number of the above proposals. I mention just a few here, as an example of the unlikely nature of many of the "maximalist" suggestions. How can the anointing of the feet of Jesus be an explicit reference to the Sacrament of the sick and the dying? Not only does this "Sacrament" appear very late in the development of the Roman Church's list of seven Sacraments (well after the Gospel of John!), but from the Johannine perspective, does the Johannine incarnate Logos of God (1:1-2, 14), Christ, and Son of God (20:30-31), need some form of "Sacrament" to see him through the passage of death? In a similar vein, is it helpful to look to the scene of the cleansing of the Temple to find links with Baptism? There are no references to any baptismal symbols or rituals (for example, water!). Nowadays, even the notion of "purification," long associated with this event in the Temple, is consistently challenged.[3] This is also another symbolic reading that reaches beyond the bounds of common sense and a critical reading of the Johannine text. The same could be said for most of the above proposed links between John and the sacramental life of the Catholic Church.

The unlikely list provided above serves as an example of how exaggerated claims about the Sacraments in John have been in the distant and recent past. Scholars who have made these various claims do not necessarily fall into clearly defined confessional groups. The defence of numerous explicit references to Sacraments is not the sole preserve of conservative Catholics, and the rejection of any sacramental teaching in the Fourth Gospel is not found only in schools of radical Protestant scholarship. I have no intention of discussing the many complications of the history of this long and unresolved debate, described Raymond Brown: "Perhaps on no other point of Johannine thought is there such division among scholars."[4] Anyone

---

3. The fundamental work on this issue is E. P. Sanders, *Jesus and Judaism* (Philadelphia: Fortress, 1985), 61-90. See also his *The Historical Figure of Jesus* (London: Penguin Press, 1993), 249-62.
4. R. E. Brown, *The Gospel According to John*, 2 vols., The Anchor Bible 29-29a (Garden City, NY, Doubleday, 1966-1970), 1:cxi.

interested in a fuller discussion should consult the surveys done by Raymond Brown, in his *New Testament Essays*, in his commentary on the Fourth Gospel, and the useful summary of Herbert Klos.[5] Scholars from all schools take up a variety of positions on the issue. A careful reading of this scholarship shows that, as always in approaching New Testament texts, what ultimately determines the answer to the question posed by the title of this paper, "When is John talking about Sacraments?" are the criteria each single scholar uses to approach the Johannine text in search of sacramental hints.

I will limit myself to a few contrasting positions in this debate, before setting out on my own discussion of possible criteria. However, further introductory remarks are called for.

1. *"When is John talking?"* It is naïve, in Johannine scholarship, to give the author(s) of this Gospel the name "John," nor is it justified to refer to his "talking" (although that may well have been part of the historical development of this Gospel). Detailed discussion of the authorship of the Gospel we know as "the Gospel of John" would take us well beyond the limitations required for this reflection. It is well and widely covered in the many fine introductions to this Gospel, including the introductions of the great contemporary commentators now all available in English: C. K. Barrett, B. Lindars, R. Schnackenburg, and R. E. Brown.[6] I have also discussed

---

5. Brown, "The Johannine Sacramentary," 51-56; Idem, *John*, 1:cxi-cxiv; Klos, *Die Sakramente*. Most recently, see F. J. Moloney, "'He loved them to the end': Eucharist in the Gospel of John," in *Johannine Studies 1975-2017*, Wissenschaftliche Untersuchungen zum Neuen Testament 372 (Tübingen: Mohr Siebeck, 2017), 427-49.

6. See C. K. Barrett, *The Gospel According to St. John. An Introduction with Commentary and Notes on the Greek Text* (2nd ed.; London, SPCK, 1978), 100-134; B. Lindars, *The Gospel of John*, New Century Bible (London, Oliphants, 1972), 28-34; R. Schnackenburg, *The Gospel According to St. John*, trans. Kevin Smyth and Others, 3 vols., Herder's Theological Commentary on the New Testament IV/1-3 (London/New York, Burns and Oates/Crossroad, 1968-1975), 1:75-104. It should be noticed that Schnackenburg, who hesitatingly opted for John, the Son of Zebedee, in the first volume of his great commentary, has since shifted to a position akin to the one adopted in this paper. See especially, Schnackenburg, *St John*, 3:375-88. Brown, *John*, 1:xxxvii-xcviii, also argued for apostolic authorship in the first volume of his commentary. However, like Schnackenburg, he has moved away from the identification of the Beloved Disciple with the Son of Zebedee (the position adopted in his commentary) to a position closer to the

this question, briefly in *The Word Became Flesh*.[7] The evidence of the Gospel itself, assuming that the link made between the author of the Gospel and the Beloved Disciple in the secondary 21:20-24 is correct, points to a tradition about Jesus, and a deepening and developing understanding of him, which took place in a Christian community, somewhere in Asia Minor (probably Ephesus) over a long period of time, through many trials and tribulations, caused by both external and internal difficulties.

It appears likely, then, that the community in which and for whom the Gospel was finally produced (in its present form) was gathered around an all-important figure who had a close contact with the historical Jesus, and most probably an ex-disciple of the Baptist (see 1:35-40). In the final stages of the physical writing of the Gospel this figure was deceased (see 21:22-23), and he was given a name of honour and respect: the Beloved Disciple. If this widely held hypothesis is correct, we cannot ask about "John talking." We must look deeper into the life and experience of faith of a particular Christian community. The Gospel of John, like all the other Gospels, is not the result of some single person "talking." No doubt a great deal of "talking" went on in the early stages of the life of the community and its Jesus-story. But this was no longer the case when the Gospel appeared in its final shape. Nor does someone "talk" to us today. Like all four Gospels, the Fourth Gospel is the fruit of a living community of first century Christians, communicating, through their own particular Spirit-filled journey, their journey of faith which is, especially in the Fourth Gospel, primarily theological and Christological.[8]

2. *"About Sacraments?"* The discussion of Johannine authorship is already complex, but the notion of "Sacrament," what they are, and how they function within Christian life is hotly contested,

---

one espoused here. See R. E. Brown, *The Community of the Beloved Disciple. The Life, Loves and Hates of an Individual Church in New Testament Times* (London, Geoffrey Chapman, 1979), 31-34.

7. F. J. Moloney, *The Word Became Flesh*, Theology Today 14 (Cork/Dublin, Mercier Press, 1979), 15-19. For developments since 1981, see my summary in "From History, into Narrative, and Beyond," in *Johannine Studies*, 23-27.

8. See, on this, the valuable contributions of R. E. Brown, "'And the Lord Said'? Biblical Reflections on Scripture as the Word of God," *Theological Studies* 42 (1981): 3-19; Idem, "The Meaning of the Bible," *Theology Digest* 28 (1980): 305-320.

and has been such since well before the Reformation. Our various ecclesial and theological traditions have wide-reaching differences in their understanding of "Sacrament," but I suggest that all would accept a general definition which argued that Sacraments are intimately associated with "life," and the communication of the divine life, an anticipated participation "in the triumphant eschatological salvation promised by God through Christ as the incarnate Son and mediator."[9] Obviously, this notion is never found explicitly stated in the New Testament, as the acceptance of "seven Sacraments" within the Roman Catholic tradition, and its associated sacramental theology took centuries to evolve.[10] Theological reflection upon the Sacraments continues to evolve, as it must in our pilgrim Church. The word "Sacrament" comes to us from the Pauline word μυστήριον, picked up by the second century Fathers in their attempts to forge a theology of the Sacraments,[11] and translated into the Latin version of the New Testament as "Sacramentum."[12] It is difficult for an interpreter to view the New Testament, and especially the highly symbolic

---

9. R. Schulte and B. Neunheuser, "Sacraments" in *Sacramentum Mundi. An Encyclopedia of Theology*, 6 vols. (New York/London: Herder & Herder/Burns & Oates, 1970), 5:378.
10. Especially problematic for the "seven" was the inclusion of marriage, long an important social reality, but seen as a socio-sexual reality, and not a situation where God' grace was communicated. The very influential teaching of Peter Lombard's *Four Books of Sentences* (1100-1160) can be credited with the institution of the seven Sacraments in the life of the Church. The *Sentences* was the basic book for theological formation in the universities for four centuries. Luther and Calvin refer to it with respect. Nevertheless, concern with the grace-giving effects of marriage continued, and the seven Sacraments (including marriage) were accepted for the first time at the Council of Florence (1439), and defined as part of Catholic doctrine at the Council of Trent (1543-1563), in response to the teaching of Martin Luther, who insisted that only those institutions that could be located in the New Testament should be accepted. Basically, this meant Baptism and Eucharist.
11. For full details, see G. W. H. Lampe, *A Patristic Greek Lexicon* (Oxford, Clarendon Press, 1961), 891-893, *sub voce* μυστήριον, especially under section F, where reference is made to Cyril, Theodotus, Clement of Alexandria, Dionysius, and Serapion from the early centuries, using the term μυστήριον in the sense of "*Sacramentum*, as revelation of divine activity."
12. The word "sacramentum" originally meant an oath, especially a soldier's oath of allegiance. This can still be traced in early Christian literature. See, for example, Tertullian, *Ad Martyres*, 3. On this, see "Sacrament" in F. L. Cross and E. A.

language of the Fourth Gospel, unburdened of a rich and long Christian tradition of sign and symbol, so closely associated with our sacramental life in the Church. One of my criteria for the investigation of sacramental material in the Fourth Gospel will look more closely at this difficulty. Yet we must be aware, from the outset, that for the Fourth Gospel, in one way all Jesus' activity and preaching, especially the whole notion of glory and glorification, so important to this Gospel (see, for example, 7:39; 8:54; 11:4; 12:23, 28; 13:31-32; 14:13; 15:8; 16:14; 17:1, 4, 5, 10), is the communication of a life-giving power, as Sandra Schneiders has insisted.[13] In this wider sense, a search for criteria is not needed: "Ultimately, the Sacramental principle in the Fourth Gospel is Jesus, manifesting himself in the Church, who experiences and bears witness in and by her own history to her divine filiation in the Spirit."[14] I will glance briefly at this issue as I conclude this reflection. However, as Sandra Schneiders fully appreciates,[15] this central Johannine belief in no way annuls the validity of our quest: are there moments in the story of the life of Jesus, as it is told by the Fourth Evangelist when there is a clear indication of the practice and the theology of an early Christian community that practised rituals that we would nowadays call a sacramental life, apart from their seeming conviction that their very existence as the continuing presence of Jesus' sonship in history made the community as such in some way sacramental?[16]

Livingstone, eds., *The Oxford Dictionary of the Christian Church* (2nd ed.; Oxford, Oxford University Press, 1974), 1218-1219.

13. See S. M. Schneiders, "History and Symbolism in the Fourth Gospel," in *L'Évangile de Jean. Sources, redaction, théologie*, M. de Jonge, ed., Bibliotheca Ephemeridum Theologicarum Lovaniensium 44 (Gembloux, Duculot, 1977), 71-76; Idem, "Symbolism and the sacramental principle in the Fourth Gospel," in *Segni e Sacramenti nel Vangelo di Giovanni*, ed. P.-R. Tragan, Studia Anselmiana 66, Sacramentum 3 (Rome, Editrice Anselmiana, 1977), 221-235; Idem, "The Foot Washing (John 13:1-20): An Experiment in Hermeneutics," *The Catholic Biblical Quarterly* 43 (1981): 76-92.

14. Schneiders, "Symbolism and the sacramental principle in the Fourth Gospel," 81-82.

15. See especially, Schneiders, "The Foot Washing (John 13:1-20)," 81-82.

16. Most recently X. Léon-Dufour has argued for a deeper appreciation of both levels of understanding for a proper evaluation of the Fourth Gospel. He interprets the cleansing and the sign of the Temple, the dialogue with Nicodemus, and John

There are many scholars who reply positively to that question. The departure point for a widespread understanding of sacramental references in John is that the early Church clearly had what we call sacramental practices. The Synoptic tradition and Paul carry words of institution. Although debated, it is generally held that across Paul, Mark, Matthew and Luke one can trace two basic traditions, these consistent reports of "final meal" events indicate that even before the writing of these New Testament documents, the communities in which and for which they were written had a history of a liturgical life and sacramental practice, however rudimentary they may have been. Liturgical and sacramental practices must have been part of the life of Christian communities well before passages that recall what happened between Jesus and his disciples "the night when he was betrayed" (1 Cor 11:23) were used in communications with them. The Pauline tradition, which seems to be represented in the Lukan account, carries a command which may have come from liturgical practices: "Do this in remembrance of me" (1 Cor 11:24-25 [twice]; Luke 22:19). This tradition preserves the original setting of a meal in Paul, as he is discussing the practice of Eucharistic meals with the Corinthians, and in Luke because it is associated with a farewell discourse.

There is no command to repeat the action and the setting within a meal is less accentuated in the Eucharistic practice behind the Markan tradition, paralleled by the Matthean account of Jesus' last evening with his disciples, contact with Eucharistic practice is clear (Mark 14:22-25; Matt. 26:26-29).[17] The practice of baptism in the pre-

---

6 at the level of Jesus in a non-Sacramental way, and then shows that the risen Lord present in the Spirit in his community, makes that *same text* Sacramental. See X. Léon-Dufour, "Towards a Symbolic Reading of the Fourth Gospel," *New Testament Studies* 27 (1980-81): 439-456. See especially p. 455: "The historical events call forth the mystery which sheds light upon it, but the mystery itself would peter out in pure imagination if it did not ceaselessly find its nourishment in the rich soil of time past." Interestingly, in his more recent commentary on the Gospel of John (*Lecture de l'Évangile selon Jean*, 4 vols., Parole de Dieu [Paris: Seuil, 1988-1996]), he makes little or no use of this hermeneutic.

17. For a lucid presentation of the case for two "traditions" (which he regards as from Antioch [Paul] and from Jerusalem [Mark and Matthew]), see J. Jeremias, "The Words of Institution," in *Understanding the Eucharist. Papers of the Maynooth Union Summer School 1968*, ed. P. McGoldrick (Dublin: Gill and Macmillan, 1969), 18-28. Still of classic dimensions is the same author's *The Eucharistic*

Johannine Churches is clearly indicated by Paul's regular reference to it as the ritual passage that introduces the Christian into a new life in the Spirit (see, for example, Gal 3:27-28), and his extensive reflection upon it in Romans 6:1-11. In the Gospels, the solemn closing words of the Matthean Jesus are also clear evidence of the practice of early Christian Baptism: "Go therefore and make disciples of all nations, baptising them in the name of the Father and of the Son and of the Holy Spirit" (Matt. 28:19).[18]

If pre-Johannine Christianity shows that *at least* Eucharist and Baptism were part of early Christian worship, then it seems logical that the author of the Fourth Gospel would recount narratives that suggested that Baptism and Eucharist had their bases in the words and works of Jesus.[19] To affirm this much is correct. I am in general agreement with those scholars who see allusions to the Sacraments in John. But to move from hidden references to the sacramental revelation of the μυστήριον of God at every turn as the *key* to an understanding of the Gospel as "sacramental" at every turn carries a correct insight too far.[20] To cite Raymond Brown's comment on Cullmann's

---

Words of Jesus (London, SCM Press, 1966). For recent developments on the study of Eucharist in the New Testament, see X. Léon-Dufour, *Sharing the Eucharistic Bread. The Witness of the New Testament*, trans. Matthew J. O'Connell (New York: Paulist, 1987), and F. J. Moloney, *A Body Broken for a Broken People. Marriage, Divorce, and the Eucharist* (Melbourne: Garratt, 2015). The Johannine tradition, found in John 6, 13, and 19, and perhaps even the hint of "words of Institution" in 6:51c, indicate that there were more than the two traditions identified by Jeremias in early Church practice.

18. There is almost universal agreement among contemporary scholars that Matt 28:16-20 is central to an understanding of the Matthean vision of his Church and its mission. See, for example, W. Trilling, *Das Wahre Israel. Studien zur Theologie des Matthäus-Evangelium*, 3rd ed.; Studien zum Alten und Neuen Testament 10 (München, Kösel, 1964), 21-51; J. P. Meier, *Law and History in Matthew's Gospel. A Redactional Study of Mt. 5, 17-49*, Analecta Biblica 71 (Rome, Biblical Institute Press, 1976), 25-40.

19. See, on this, X. Léon-Dufour, "Towards a Symbolic Reading." See above, n. 16.

20. See O. Cullmann, *Early Christian Worship*, Studies in Biblical Theology 10 (London, SCM Press, 1953), for a theological and exegetical defence of widespread allusion to sacramental practice in the Johannine Church, where he makes some valid points (see especially pp. 38-59), to which we shall return. His argument swivels around the important conclusion on p. 56: "The implicit assumption of this Gospel is that the historical events, as here presented, contain in themselves, besides what is immediately perceptible, references to further facts of salvation with which these once-for-all key events are bound up." There

position: "[H]e often seems to fall back on the principle that since a passage could have been understood sacramentally, it was intended sacramentally."[21]

This position, and the various scholars who follow it (e.g., Corell, Vawter, Niewalda, Bouyer, Stanley) has, as I have mentioned, a solidly-based point of departure: the positive indications of pre-Johannine literature that a form of what eventually came to be known as the sacramental life of a community was part of early Christian worship.[22] We should notice, however, that the only *firmly established evidence* which we have for pre-Johannine sacramental practices are concerned with Baptism and Eucharist.

Of course, those who discover a rich trove of sacramental hints in the Fourth Gospel have not had it all their own way. The most serious opposition has come from one of the most outstanding New Testament scholars of the twentieth-century: Rudolf Bultmann. Bultmann claimed that the Fourth Gospel was originally written as an anti-sacramental document. He can immediately point to the complete absence of words of Institution, and any command to baptise in this Gospel. He has a wide following from fellow German scholars (e.g., Schweitzer, Koester and Lohse) and also, in recent years, from North American scholars, although most do not necessarily claim that John is aggressively anti-sacramental.[23] For Bultmann, the notion of ritual and cult as a place of encounter with God is foreign to the Johannine world-view. He claims that the Gospel calls its audience to an encounter with God's revelation in and through Jesus Christ. It is not

---

is much to be said for this hermeneutical approach to the Gospel of John, and is part of Léon-Dufour's argument in his "Towards a Symbolic Reading." See above, n. 15. More recently Dorothy Lee has made a thorough study of the use of symbol in the Fourth study that eclipses the work of Cullmann and Léon-Dufour. See Dorothy A. Lee, *Flesh and Glory. Symbolism, Gender and Theology in the Gospel of John* (New York: Herder, 2002).

21. Brown, "The Johannine Sacramentary", p. 55.
22. For the bibliographical details of the scholars mentioned in parenthesis in this sentence, see above, nn. 4-5. See O. Cullmann, *Early Christian Worship*, 7-36 for his analysis of what he calls the "basic characteristics" of that worship. He is optimistic about the history he uncovers, but many scholars would argue against some of his firmly stated conclusions, as they seem to be based upon fragile evidence. For a better assessment, see F. Hahn, *The Worship of the Early Church*, trans. David E. Green (Philadelphia, Fortress, 1973).
23. For bibliography, see the summarising works provided in nn. 4-5.

concerned with *what* Jesus did or said, but *that* God is made known through the Word. The Word summons to a faith in God's that leads to a loss of self and "this-worldliness" in order to live an authenticity that can only come through faith.[24] The view, strongly influenced by the Existentialism of an early Martin Heidegger, allows no place for an encounter with God through a historical sacramental ritual, administered by a human intermediary.

Even Bultmann, however, would admit that there are three places in the final version of the Fourth Gospel where the Sacraments of Baptism and Eucharist are explicitly mentioned. He accepts that the practice of Baptism lies behind 3:5: Unless one is born of water and the Spirit, he cannot enter the Kingdom of God," and that there are clear Eucharistic references across the final section of Jesus discourse in John 6:51c-58, for example:

> v. 51c: "The bread which I shall give for the life of the world is my flesh".
> v. 53: "Unless you eat the flesh of the Son of Man and drink his blood, you have no life in you".
> v. 54: "He who eats (ὁ τρώγων) my flesh and drinks my blood has eternal life."[25]

Bultmann also accepts that there may be a eucharistic background to 19:34 where blood and water flow from the pierced side of the crucified Christ, especially when this text is read in the light of I John 5:8: "There are three witnesses, the Spirit, the water and the blood; and these three agree."

Bultmann, however, has no trouble with these so-called "sacramental" hints, as none of them belong to the Gospel, as the Evangelist originally compiled it. Despite the obviously sacramental hints in these passages, they cannot be taken into account as arguments against Bultmann's insistence that the Gospel of John was anti-sac-

---

24. See R. Bultmann, *Theology of the New Testament*, trans. G. Krodel; 2 vols. (London, SCM Press, 1955), 70-92.
25. There is a perfectly common verb available to speak of the human process of eating: ἔσθιω/φάγομαι. The verb τρώγω is normally used in contexts where some sort of stress is given to the physical "munching" or "crunching" of food. See, on this, C. Spicq, "τρώγειν est-il synonyme de φάγειν et de'ἔ σθιειν dans le Nouveau Testament?" *New Testament Studies* 26 (1979-80): 414-19.

ramental. For him, the Gospel developed in three stages, based upon three sources: (1) an original synoptic-like story of Jesus that contained the "signs" (miracles) worked by Jesus, (2) the great discourses that are a feature of the Gospel of John, coming from a Gnostic-like source of "revelatory discourses," and, (3) the creative final work of the Evangelist. However, at a later stage, given the radical departure of the Gospel of John from mainstream Christianity, it was further edited by what Bultmann calls an "Ecclesiastical Redactor."[26] He argues that clearly sacramental passages (and other more "mainstream" early Christian thought, like an end-time eschatology) have been added to an anti-sacramental Gospel at a later stage. The work of the Ecclesiastical Redactor was to make the Gospel of John conform more closely with the life and practice of the "greater Church."

Bultmann's brilliant analysis is based upon the fact that there are a large number of internal difficulties and tensions within this Gospel that call for a historical explanation. Taking John 6 as an example, he points to the apparent a contradiction in the positive use of the word "flesh" (σάρξ) which must be devoured for access to eternal life in vv. 51, 52, 53, 54, 55 and 56, and the negative use of the same word in v. 63: "It is the Spirit that gives life; the flesh (ἡ σάρξ) is of no avail." Bultmann's suggestions may not be the correct solution to a difficult problem, but they take us back to a point made earlier: this Gospel was not written overnight; it had a long history within the life and faith experience of a concrete Christian Community. It is quite possible that the sacramental passages of 3:5; 6:51c-58, and 19:34 came into the Johannine Gospel at a late stage in its development. But there is no call to omit them from an authentic Johannine Gospel. Such tensions must be explained, and not eliminated by a speculative theory of sources, however brilliant the theory may be. Raymond Brown has summarised this position when he wrote:

> "The recognition that some of the explicit Sacramental references belong to the final redaction does not mean any acceptance of the theory that the original Gospel was non-Sacramental or anti-Sacramental. It is a question of seeing

---

26. See Bultmann, *Theology of the New Testament*, 2:3-14; Idem, *The Gospel of John: A Commentary*, trans. G. R. Beasley-Murray (Oxford, Basil Blackwell, 1971), 138-140; 300; 324-325; 325-328; 677-678.

different degrees of sacramentality in the work of the evangelist and that of the final redactor".[27]

The two diametrically opposed positions just outlined show distinct methods of approach, and the use of different criteria to establish both history and meaning. From Oscar Cullmann we learn that the Gospel as a whole is the life story of Jesus, and that there is often a subtle use of that life-story *from the past* to address the community practice *of the present*. The Gospel of John is a post-Easter story of Jesus. It was written to address a post-Easter community. It has continued announced the Jesus' revelation of the δόξα of God to post-Easter Christian communities for almost 2000 years. There is also much to learn from Rudolf Bultmann: the Fourth Gospel may well reflect a long and troubled series of internal and external conflicts, producing a Gospel of theological, Christological, and ecclesiological complexity. Can we develop some criteria that might guide us in tracing sacramental teaching in the Gospel of John that respects the contributions of both of these important scholars, and the many who have adopted their approaches?

Internal Criteria

What follows is an attempt to steer a middle course, offering four criteria for the discovery of sacramental teaching in the Fourth Gospel. The first two of them are well established and widely used. They are can be classified as "internal," i.e.: they are an attempt to provide some

---

27. Brown, *John*, p. cxii. I would add to Brown's remark: the Spirit-filled journey of a community behind all the stages of development (see below). It is here that I differ from the suggestions of Léon-Dufour, "Towards a Symbolic Reading." Ignoring all the recent work done on the Johannine community and its journey of faith, he insists, for example, that 3:5 and 6:53-58 would make perfect sense to a Jewish audience as they stand, and that there are no indications in the text itself (e.g. the introduction of "water" into 3:5) to show a growing sacramental awareness within the Johannine community. See pp. 449-451; 452-454. I suggest that such additions were made, but they are not clumsy insertions of a later redactor who did not understand the Johannine argument, but evidence of a growing awareness of the sacramental potential without the developing Johannine community and its story. On this, see the recent commentary of E. Haenchen, *Das Johannesevangelium. Ein Kommentar* (Tübingen, J. C. B. Mohr, 1980), 218, 226-227.

reliable "rule of thumb" by which the exegete may work on the basis of the Johannine text itself. In many ways these are rather "negative" criteria, and there is a danger that some important material may be overlooked. However, I suspect that this is a sounder way to start an investigation, as once we establish a firmly based "minimum," on the basis of the Johannine text, then other material might come to light because of its close contacts with that "minimum."

First Criterion

The first criterion must be a rigorous search for elements in the text itself which indicate that the author is referring to some form of sacramental ritual and symbol. For example, in John 3:5 one finds explicit reference to a "rebirth," the use of the word "water" and the idea of "entering the Kingdom of God." The same cannot be said, for example, of the curing of the paralytic at the pool at Bethesda in John 5:1-8. In fact, the restoration of the man (a positive element in itself) is not effected through water, but independently of it - through the word of Jesus: "Rise, take up your pallet and walk" (v. 8). The sequel to the miracle shows no further understanding or life of faith in the cured man; in fact, he appears to be extraordinarily obtuse (see vv. 15-16). *Internal* evidence makes any baptismal understanding of John 5 most unlikely,[28] while contact with the ritual and theology of Baptism is clearly possible in 3:5.

This becomes clearer when one looks to the curing of the man born blind in John 9, a story in many ways parallel to the cure in John 5. Here the miracle is effected by contact with water, at the pool of Siloam, which the Evangelist then further explains as meaning "the sent one" (v. 7). The cure is followed by a gradual movement to theological sight and light, as the series of interrogations of the man lead him through a journey of confessions of faith:[29]

- To his friends he says: "The man called Jesus" worked a miracle (v. 11).
- To the Pharisees he says: "He is a prophet" (v. 17).

---

28. For a detailed study of John 5, with bibliographical detail, see Moloney, *Son of Man*, 68-86.
29. For further detail, see Moloney, *Son of Man*, 142-159.

- Under further interrogation from the Pharisees he retorts: "If this man were not *from* God" (v. 33).
- Finally, when Jesus himself meets him we find him arriving at the fullness of sight. "Do you believe in the Son of Man?" He answered, "And who is he, *sir,* that I may believe in him?" Jesus said to him, "You have seen him and it is he who speaks to you". He said, "*Lord*, I believe;" and he worshipped him (vv. 35-38).[30]

The same explicit internal evidence can be found in the texts which we have already mentioned several times: the Eucharistic section in John 6 and the blood and water flowing from the pierced side of the crucified Jesus, and there may be several others (the foot washing of 13:1-20; Jesus as the source of living waters in 7:38) which have this internal evidence that may point to an original sacramental meaning.[31]

Second Criterion

This criterion which must be used in close association with the first: the use of certain passages in the liturgical practice, the literature and the art of the early post-New Testament Church. The most significant use of this criterion came from a Protestant scholar, Paul Niewalda. He argued that, given the internal difficulties and the never-ending disputes among scholars, we should accept that when Johannine symbolism is used by the early Church for its sacramental life and reflection, then we have every right to push that meaning back into the intention of the Evangelist himself.[32] Care must be taken here. While this is a valid criterion, it is preferable to run the argument in the other direction. If we find that a passage has the internal qualities

---

30. The movement from κύριε ("sir") in v. 36 to Κύριε ("Lord") in v. 38 indicates a decisive step into a public confession of faith.
31. See, on this, the method advocated by R. Schnackenburg, "Die Sakramente im Johannesevangelium," in *Sacra Pagina. Miscellanea Biblica Congressus Biblicus Internationalis Catholicus de Re Biblica*, eds. J. Coppens and Others, 2 vols., (Gembloux, Duculot, 1959), 2:235-254. He suggests that we first study the clearly sacramental passages, and establish from them possible internal contacts with the more obscure texts.
32. P. Niewalda, *Sakramentssymbolik im Johannesevangelium. Eine exegetischhistorische Studie* (Limburg, Lahn-Verlag, 1958).

of a sacramental message, and then we find that the early Church has clearly used it in this way, then we have firmed the possible suggestions of the text itself. Great service has been done in this investigation by the remarkable commentary of Sir Edwyn Hoskyns, especially in his investigation of the early Church's use of John 9 and John 13.[33] This is an area where more research is needed, and a deeper association and awareness of the "reception" of the Fourth Gospel in the early Church is called for. Used in close connection with the hints and indications which come to us from our close study of the text itself, this criterion may offer surprising evidence for Johannine sacramentalism. Although the possibility is widely rejected by commentators, these first two criteria, used together, suggest that the sacramental life of the Johannine Church may have impacted on John 9:1-38 (the man born blind) and 13:1-20 (the foot-washing).

External Criteria

The two criteria or just outlined seek an answer to the question: why does John say these things? A careful study of the use of the language used and the context within which it is used can lead to a conclusion that John said these things because the community had a sacramental life. However, it is not enough to look to the words and context, asking: why does John say these things? A further step is required at this stage: why does John say these things *in this way*? Some of the Johannine sacramental material seems to be articulated in a singular fashion (third criterion), and in particular narrative contexts (fourth criterion). Contemporary literary studies are asking not only *why* certain things are said in narratives, but *how* they are said.

Third Criterion

One of the reasons given for the exclusion of the clearly sacramental passages of 3:5; 6:51c-58 and 19:34 is that the passages are powerfully anti-docetic, i.e, an affirmation that Jesus was a flesh and blood

---

33. E. C. Hoskyns, *The Fourth Gospel*, ed. F. N. Davey, 2nd ed. (London, Faber & Faber, 1947), 363-365; 443-446.

human being, and did not only "appear" to be human.[34] As the Gospel of John as a whole tends to stress the spiritual character of the faith commitment, the later redactors have added passages which insist upon the tangible, physical nature of the flesh and blood of Jesus, and the concrete reality of the ecclesial community. This can be sensed in all three passages, as they hint that they may have been shaped within polemical circumstances.

> 3:5: *Unless* one is born again of water and the spirit he *cannot* enter the kingdom of God.
> 6:53: *Unless* you eat the flesh of the Son of Man and drink his blood, you have *no life* in you.
> 19:34: The telling of the flow of blood and water from the side of Jesus (v. 34) is followed by a powerful insistence form the Evangelist: "He who saw it has borne witness - his testimony is true, and he knows that he tells the truth" (v. 35).

It has long been claimed that the Gospel of John is taking an early Christian community into Docetism. A brief but passionate study by Ernst Käsemann argued this case to great effect.[35] But in many ways, this outstanding student of Rudolf Bultmann (who differs from his master on this matter) brought to closure a long history of Johannine interpretation that situated the Johannine community on the margins of the early Christian phenomenon. The turning point was the work of J. Louis Martyn, a gifted scholar who drew attention to the possible "events" in the life of the Johannine community that may have led the Evangelist to tell his story *in this way*.[36] Although a lone voice is occasionally heard (often from German scholars), very few contemporary scholars would suggest that there was a basically docetic Gospel, into which anti-docetic elements have been inserted. A variety of sometimes apparently contrasting Christologies lie side-by-side in this

---

34. The word "docetic" and the noun Docetism is generated by the Greek verb δοκέω (*dokeō*) which means "to appear" to be something.
35. E. Käsemann, *The Testament of Jesus according to John 17*, trans. Gerhard Krodel (London: SCM Press, 1966).
36. See J. Louis Martyn, *History and Theology in the Fourth Gospel*, 2nd ed. (Nashville: Abingdon, 1969); Idem, *The Gospel of John in Christian History* (New York: Paulist Press, 1978).

Gospel, reflecting a long and conflicted history. A colleague of Louis Martyn at the Union Theological Seminary in New York, Raymond Brown, has developed the thesis of Martyn into a full-scale history of the Johannine Community in his provocative study: *The Community of the Beloved Disciple*.[37] This impressive work calls for some further explanation.

Brown's study makes full use of the Gospel, the Epistles, and the possible later "reception" of the Johannine Gospel and Letters to rediscover the life of the Johannine community, from birth to death. This fascinating reading experience, marked by careful scholarship and a close contact with contemporary literature, might tempt one to think that scholarship, after centuries of hypotheses, claims and counter claims, had at last found the answer. Brown himself is strongly aware of the speculative nature of his study, and asks that it be considered as yet another helpful hypothesis.[38]

Brown argues that four stages of development can be traced: before the Gospel, when the Gospel was written, when the Letters were written and finally, after the Letters. Through these four stages he rediscovers the following experiences of the community of the Beloved Disciple:

1. The original group, beginning within the circle of ex-disciples of John the Baptist, projected a typically early Christian "low" Christology. Important at this stage is the figure of the Beloved disciple, an ex-disciple of the Baptist, a follower of Jesus from the start, but *not* one of the Twelve. As I mentioned earlier, this is a change from the position on authorship that he took in the first volume of his Anchor Bible Commentary on the Gospel of John.[39] This outstanding historical personality, the father of the community serves as a link between the historical Jesus and the Johannine community.
2. After the admission of Samaritan and other "anti-Temple" groups, a conflict with "the Jews" is begun. This leads eventually to the

---

37. See above, n. 6, for the bibliographical details.
38. For some of my concerns, see F. J. Moloney, "Revisiting John," *Scripture Bulletin* II (1980): 11-13. For my understanding of the literary and theological "journey" of the Johannine community, see Moloney, "From History, into Narrative, and Beyond," *Johannine Studies*, 23-27.
39. See above, and especially note 6.

development of a "higher" Christology, especially in the use of ἐγώ εἰμι in an absolute sense as the revealing presence of God, and the idea of pre-existence.

3. As the Gospel is written, the community takes a final stance against those whom they would regard as non-believers: "the world," the Jews, the adherents of John the Baptist. Also included in the community's list of "non-believers" were some groups who, in other circles, would be regarded as believers. Brown call them crypto-Christians, indicating Jews who believed but remained in the synagogue. There may have even been Jewish Christian communities which would not confess the "high" Johannine Christology, and what could be termed "the greater Church," the Christians who followed the less charismatic line. Although never referred to as such in the Gospel and the Letters, from what we know of the "parties" in the early Church, this position would be reflected by the figure of James and the Jerusalem party (see, for example, Gal 2:11-14).

The Johannine community, having taken its stance to those "outside" their ranks, now began to experience serious internal struggles. These divisions grew entirely out of two possible but variant interpretations of the Johannine Gospel. A study of the Letters indicates that there are at least two groups involved, both seem to be using the Gospel, but they are at loggerheads without their original Gospel should be interpreted. In the areas of Christology, ethics, eschatology and pneumatology, the Epistles show a historicising, more conservative approach than the Gospel, moving generally in the direction of "the greater Church," while the "opponents" are being accused of de-historicising, eliminating all the obligations which ethics, eschatology and a true life in the Spirit must produce. They were moving in the direction of what was later known as docetic Gnosticism.

4. The final moment in the history of the community is its separation and dissolution. The group behind the Epistles merges with the greater Church, as can be seen from Ignatius of Antioch (c. 110): Johannine Christology has been accepted, but a Paraclete dominated ecclesiology and ethics has been lost. The "opponents"

take the Gospel and their interpretation of it into Gnosticism, as can be seen from the later use of the Fourth Gospel by the gnostic sects.

Stated so bluntly, the skill of Brown's analysis or, as he himself describes it, his "detective work" is lost. Whatever its strengths and weaknesses, building on the work of his colleague Louis Martyn, a new era began in Johannine scholarship. There is now more sensitivity to the lives, loves and experiences of the Community itself in any attempt to understand that community's Gospel. While discussing Brown's recent contribution I mentioned a group that he calls "crypto-Christians," describing them as Jews who believed, but remained in the Synagogue. There existed Jewish Christians who would not take the step "across the street" into the Johannine community. Here we may be in touch with the reason for the polemical nature of those so-called sacramental passage, mentioned above (sacramental passages: 3:5; 6:53; 19:34). Further reflection on *how* these divisions happened, and their consequences, may further guide us in identifying how this third criterion can test John's use of sacramental material.

John's consistent conflict with "the Jews" as the clearest indication of "when" the Gospel was written, and one of the main reasons "why" it was written.[40] Faced with the perseverance of a sect in its midst which confessed that Jesus of Nazareth was the Christ, the synagogue at Jamnia, which became the legal and intellectual centre of Rabbinic Judaism after the destruction of Jerusalem in A.D. 70, called upon all faithful Jews to condemn publicly the followers of Jesus. To do this, they inserted a "benediction" (called the *birkat ha-minim*, i.e.: "the blessing of the heretics") into one of their important synagogue prayers, the "Eighteen Benedictions" (the *shemoneh 'esreh*). It is impossible to be certain about the exact form of this "blessing,"

---

40. The following argument, briefly presented here, has been accepted, for example, by C. K. Barrett, *St. John*, pp. 127-128; R. E. Brown, *John*, pp. lxxiv-lxxv; E. C. Hoskyns, *The Fourth Gospel*, pp. 360-362; R. Schnackenburg, *St John*, 2:248-52; B. Lindars, *John*, p. 147; S. Schulz, *Das Evangelium nach Johannes*, Das Neue Testament Deutsch 4 (Göttingen, Vandenhoeck und Ruprecht, 1972), 144-145. It has been rejected by J. A. T. Robinson, *Redating the New Testament* (London, SCM Press, 1976) pp. 292-298. See, on this discussion, Moloney, "The Fourth Gospel's Presentation of Jesus as 'the Christ' and J. A. T. Robinson's 'Redating'," *Johannine Studies*, 169-83.

(called such because most of the prayer is formed by positive blessings) but it ran something like this: "For apostates may there be no hope, and may the Nazarenes and the heretics suddenly perish."[41] It is difficult to determine the exact date of this decision taken at Jamnia, but the Eighteen Benedictions, their order and the *birkat ha-minim* are associated with Rabbi Gamaliel II; thus some time after 85 seems to be most likely. It is also difficult to determine just how rapidly this practice was implemented by the synagogues of the diaspora. Earlier studies of this process were too optimistic about its date and its location. The situation of separation from the Synagogue reflected in the Gospel of John may have been an extremely local affair. There is evidence for ongoing good relationships between Jews and Christians well into the second century.[42] Nevertheless, for the Johannine Christians, it was the point of no return. A declaration of faith in Jesus as the Christ led them out of the Synagogue and a lively, positive relationship with their Jewish neighbours.

It is often argued that John 9 reflects the drama of the Jewish-Christian Church subsequent to the decision of the synagogue at Jamnia.[43] The parents of the man born blind refused to answer the questions of the Jewish authorities about how their son was given his sight "because they feared the Jews, for the Jews had already agreed that if anyone should confess him to the Christ, he was to be put out of the synagogue" (9:22). The Greek for "to be put out of the synagogue" is ἀποσυνάγωγος γένεται. The term ἀποσυνάγωγος is found *only* in John (see also 12:42 and 16:2). When the man himself encounters the Jews, he claims: "If this man were not from God he could do nothing"

---

41. The original wording of this "blessing" cannot be exactly determined, as it has understandably come down to us in various corrupted forms. For the recensions (Palestinian and Babylonian), see H. Strack and P. Billerbeck, *Kommentar zum Neuen Testament aus Talmud und Midrasch*, 5 vols. (München, C. H. Beck, 1922-61) 4:211-214. On the question of the expulsion from the Synagogue, see pp. 293-333. For the history of the Benedictions and the conflict which the insertion of the Benediction against the heretics (*birkat ha-minim*) caused, see G. F. Moore, *Judaism in the First Centuries of the Christian Era*, 2 vols. (Cambridge, MA: Harvard University Press, 1958) 1:289-296. For his reconstruction of the twelfth Benediction, which I have followed, see p. 292, n. 8.
42. See J. Lieu, *Image and Reality. The Jews in the World of Christians in the Second Century* (Edinburgh: T. & T. Clark, 1996).
43. See, for example, Martyn, *History and Theology*, 24-62; Brown, *John*, 1:380; Schnackenburg, *St John*, 2:249-50; Lindars, *John*, 347.

(9:33), and they is "cast him out" (v. 34: ἐξέβαλον αὐτὸν ἔχω). Once a link is made between this event reported in John 9 and the decisive break between this event reported in John 9 and the decisive break between Judaism and Christianity caused by the *birkat ha-minim*, then other passages in the Gospel take on a new sense:

> 12:42: Many even of the authorities believed in him but for fear of the Pharisees they did not confess it, lest they should be put out of the synagogue (ἵνα μὴ ἀποσυνάγωνται).
> 16:2: They will put you out of the synagogues (ἀποσυναγώγους ποιήσουσιν ὑμᾶς); indeed the hour is coming when whoever kills you will think he is offering a service to God.

In both of these passages the term ἀποσυνάγωγος, found only in the Fourth Gospel in the whole of Greek literature, again appears. This language indicating a link between belief in Jesus as the Christ and distancing from the Synagogue is something unique to John, and must reflect lived experience. Barnabas Lindars has described the situation well when he claims that John "speaks of discipleship in terms of the conditions with which his readers were familiar."[44]

We are now better able to articulate why the third criterion for tracing sacramental material in the Johannine Gospel can be found in its polemic tone (see 3:5; 6:53; 19:34). The Johannine community strongly affirms that belief in Jesus meant more than an acceptance that he was the Messiah. Those former members of the local Synagogue who had come to such belief then acted accordingly. They "crossed the road" from their Synagogue, to publicly insert themselves into a new community. This public gesture was an entrance into "the kingdom of heaven," a rebirth from above, indicated by a process of passing through water and receiving the Holy Spirit (3:3-5). This led to a further public act: the participation in a Eucharistic celebrations within the Christian community. John W. Miller, in an unpublished Princeton doctoral dissertation, has put it well:

---

44. Lindars, *John*, 347.

"The observance of baptism and eucharist suggest a worshipping community sharing in a cultic life. In view of John's understanding of the unity of the Church as a visible unity and his criticism of secret disciples, it is likely that the sacraments were important as a means by which believers identified themselves with the visible community of the Church."[45]

In this way, what one generation of scholars has taken as anti-docetic because of its polemic tone may not be "anti" anything. On the one hand, it reflects the gradual growth of a Christological consciousness within the developing Christian community. As we have seen, this element in the process of understanding why sacramental material is presented in this fashion applied to all Johannine Christians, Greeks and Jews. On the other, at a more local level, and in contrast to the Synagogue and perhaps the "crypto-Christians," it reflects an aggressive affirmation of entry in a new community, based on faith that Jesus is the Christ, the Son of God (20:30-31), where Baptism and Eucharist played an important role.[46]

Fourth Criterion

We come now to our final suggestion. I regard this criterion, even though only briefly treated here, as very important. It is again an "external criterion," calling for focus upon the situation and experience of the Johannine community which may account for *the way in which* John reflects upon potentially sacramental material. Through all of the complexities of this Gospel, one can trace a central Chris-

---

45. J. W. Miller, *The Concept of the Church in the Gospel according to John* (Unpublished Doctoral Dissertation, Princeton University, 1976), 103. See also p. 98. Miller's suggestion, which I have developed here, needs more attention in this discussion.
46. Most recently exactly the *opposite* suggestion has been made by K. Matsunaga, "Is John's Gospel Anti-Sacramental?" *New Testament Studies* 27 (1980-81) 516-24. Matsunaga also bases his contribution on the recent suggestions of R. E. Brown and J. L. Martyn. He argues that the Fourth Evangelist has eliminated certain synoptic passages (baptism of Jesus and the words of institution) in a spiritualising process. He did this so that the "drop-outs" from the Johannine community would see that, above all, they should have been primarily committed to the high Christology developed within the community, and the subsequent "Word" of Jesus.

tological and ecclesiological message which is consistent. A God who is love (1 John 4:8, 16) loves the world so much that he sent his only Son (3:16-17). This Son, Jesus Christ, has a task (ἔργον) to bring to its completion (see especially 4:34 and 17:4, along with the many passages in the Gospel which use words coming from τὸ τέλος [the end]). That task is to make God known, so that all can come to eternal life (17:2-3). He performs this task in many ways, through his discourses (λόγοι and ῥήματα), through his "signs" (σημεῖα), and consummately through the supreme act of love, when he is "lifted up" (ὑψωθῆναι δεῖ: "must be lifted up") on the Cross (see 3:13-14; 8:28; 12:32; 13:1; 15:13; 19:30). Jesus not only "speaks" and "gives signs" of his oneness with a Father who is love (see 10:30), but he actually loves in a consummate fashion.[47] Because this is the case, Jesus is the unique revealer of God (see especially 1:18; 3:13; 6:46; 8:38), and thus the Fourth Evangelist demands that the believers "look upon" Jesus to see the revelation of the Father. This is promised in the programmatic 1:51: "You *will see* heavens opened, and the angels of God ascending and descending upon the Son of Man," and repeated like an antiphon through the whole Gospel (see 1:18; 4:45; 5:37; 6:2, 36; 8:38, 57; 9:37; 11:40; 14:7, 9; 15:24; 16:16, 17; 19:22, 35), climaxing in the final words of the scene at the Cross: "They shall *look on* him whom they have pierced" (19:37).[48]

But for the Johannine community, as the first century drew to a close, Jesus was no longer present! How were they to "see" him, to "gaze upon" him. The "absence" of the physical revelation of the glory of God in the person of Jesus must have posed a problem for the community. The Evangelist handles the problem in a variety of ways, through the teaching on the Paraclete (14:16-17, 25, 26; 15:26;

---

[47]. This is clearly involved in John's continual use of verbs and nouns which go back to the expression τὸ τέλος. Especially significant are 13:1 (εἰς τέλος) and 19:30 (τετέλεσται). See now, for an extensive development of this theme, central to the Theology and Christology of the Fourth Gospel, F. J. Moloney, *Love in the Gospel of John. An Exegetical, Theological, and Literary Study* (Grand Rapids: Baker Academic, 2013). Sandra Schneiders has insisted that we look more closely at this feature of the Gospel. See especially her article, "Symbolism and the sacramental principle in the Fourth Gospel," 221-235. See above, n. 13.

[48]. See C. Traets, *Voir Jésus et le Père en Lui selon l'Évangile de saint Jean*, Analecta Gregoriana 159 (Rome, Gregorian University Press, 1967), and Moloney, *Son of Man*, 155. Further bibliographical indications are given in n. 77 of that page.

16:7-11, 13-15),⁴⁹ Jesus' assurance of his continued presence and care throughout the last discourse (especially 13:31-14:31), and in his final prayer (especially 17:9-19).

This theme was noticed and discussed in a brief study by C. Charlier almost thirty years ago. I paraphrase the title of his article as the final suggested criterion for the presence of sacramental material in the Fourth Gospel: "The presence of the absent one."⁵⁰ The proposals of Oscar Cullmann regain importance in the light of this criterion. Cullmann had noticed that a central issue in this Gospel was to indicate that what was happening in the community's cult was a special sort of "remembering" (see 12:16; 16:12).⁵¹ While recognising the value of this insight, I would like to pursue it in a slightly different direction. As one reads through the discourse of John 6:25-51b one hears again and again a theme spelt out most clearly in 6:40: "For this is the will of my Father, that everyone who sees the Son and believes in him should have eternal life," and repeated in 6:46-48: "Not that anyone has seen the Father except him who is from God; he has seen the Father. Truly, truly, I say to you, he who believes has eternal life." A possible reaction from a Christian audience listening to these words of Jesus at the end of the first Christian century might well be: "Where is he, that we may see him, and thus come to know the Father

---

49. See, on this, the fine work of F. Porsch, *Pneuma und Wort. Ein exegetischer Beitrag zur Pneumatologie des Johannesevangeliums*, Frankfurter Theologische Studien 16 (Frankfurt, Josef Knecht, 1974). Recently John Painter has taken up the suggestions of Brown and Martyn to show a developing understanding of the Paraclete, evidenced in the development of the farewell discourse's use of the concept. See J. Painter, "Glimpses of the Johannine Community in the Farewell Discourses," *Australian Biblical Review* 28 (1980): 21-38. He has developed his argument further in a more recent article, "The Farewell Discourses and the History of Johannine Christianity," *New Testament Studies* 27 (1980-81): 525-43.
50. C. Charlier, "La presence dans l'absence (Jn 13,31-14,31)," *Bible et Vie Chrétienne* 2 (1953): 61-75. It is interesting to note that the same title has been taken up in a recent study by S. Migliasso, *La presenza dell'Assente. Saggio di analisi letterario - struttutale e di sintisi teologica di Gv. 13, 31-14, 31* (Rome, Pontificia Università Gregoriana, 1979). These two studies are not concerned with sacramental material in the Gospel as an indication of "the presence of the absent one," but focus upon the articulation of this theme in John 13-14, widely accepted as the first part of Jesus' Last Discourse. However, although it is a major question that the Johannine Jesus must face in the final discourse, where he speaks openly of his departure, the question surely hangs over the whole of the narrative.
51. See Cullmann, *Early Christian Worship*, 47-50.

and possess eternal life?" In this particular context, the response is given in 6:51c-58. The revelation of the absent Jesus can be found in the broken bread and the spilt wine of their Eucharistic celebrations. The Eucharist, for the Johannine community, was the presence of the absent one.[52]

The same literary technique is being used in 19:34. The Johannine passion account has culminated with the exaltation of Jesus as King upon his Cross (19:17-21). There he has founded his Church (19:25-27) and brought to perfection the task which his Father had given him (19:28-30).[53] That is the Johannine reinterpretation of a horrific past event, read in the light of Easter. But how is that ecclesial reading of the passion of Jesus to become part of the experience of the Church at a later period? The answer is found in 19:34: as the blood and water, the life-giving Sacraments of Eucharist and Baptism, are described as flowing down upon the nascent Church from the King, lifted up upon his throne.[54] Again it is in the Sacraments of Baptism and Eucharist that the Johannine Church can find the presence of the absent one. Can a parallel reading of John 3, 9, 13, and perhaps other passages be unfolded with this post-Easter perspective: the sacramental life of the community provides "the presence of the absent one" for the members of the Christian community?

Conclusion

The length of these reflections are but one indication of the complexity of the question, and the widely differing points of view that surround the identification of the Johannine use of sacramental material, or hints at Johannine sacramental practices.[55] Although promising

---

52. See, on this, Moloney, *Son of Man*, pp. 87-107, Idem, "John 6 and the Celebration of the Eucharist," in *Johannine Studies*, 375-83.
53. On this, see Moloney, "The Johannine Passion and the Christian Community," in *Johannine Studies*, 467-503.
54. See E. Malatesta, "Blood and water from the pierced side of Christ", in *Segni e Sacramenti nel Vangelo di Giovanni*, pp. 164-181. This is a well-documented study, with a fine appendix on the Patristic use of John 19:34 (see our second criterion) on pp. 179-181. See also S. Carnazzo, *Seeing Blood and Water. A Narrative-Critical Study of John 19:34* (Eugene, OR: Pickwick Publications, 2012).
55. The origins of the paper in the 1981 Melbourne Scripture Seminar also occasioned its length. Background information to such significant figures as Rudolf Bultmann, J. Louis Martyn, and Raymond Brown had to be provided for

that the systematic application of the four criteria outlined above may introduce some fresh ways of looking at the Johannine material, leading to clearer decisions both for an against sacramentalism in John, they have only introduced a possible methodology.

By this I mean that I have done nothing more than apply these four criteria to the widely (but by no means universally) accepted Sacramental passages of 3:5; 6:51c-58 and 19:34. Thus, in terms of broadening the identification of Johannine sacramental material, this paper has contributed very little, except to suggest, on the basis of the first two criteria, that John 9 and John 13 may contain sacramental teaching.[56] Its purpose, however, is to start with established material, to test the criteria there. If they bear fruit, and it appears to me that they do, then interpreters may be able to move into areas which are not so clear.[57] That task must be faced by myself and others on other occasions, and in other places.

---

an intelligent and passionately interested audience, many of whom had little or no formation in Gospel studies.

56. For my recent claims for sacramental links with Baptism and Eucharist in 13:1-38, see Moloney, "'He loved them to the end,'" 427-49.

57. A method advocated some years ago by Schnackenburg, "Die Sakramente im Johannesevangelium," 235-254. See above, n. 31.

Christian Life

11
Sacred Scripture and the Magisterium: A Restless Relationship?

In Honour of Archbishop Joseph Doré (Strasbourg)

The teaching of Vatican II, that the Scriptures and the sacred Tradition form "a single sacred deposit of the Word of God" (*Dei Verbum* 10) is well known. The precise nature of the relationship between them, however, can be difficult to determine. The Council itself, after much deliberation, simply stated that they flow together from the same well-spring and "come together in some fashion (*in unum quodammodo coalescunt*)" (*Dei Verbum* 9). The deliberate vagueness of this description leaves a delicate balance, necessarily calling for the ongoing interpretation of biblical text and sacred Tradition "under the watchful eye of the Magisterium" (*Dei Verbum* 23). Yet, the Council insists, "this Magisterium is not superior to the word of God, but is its servant" (*Dei Verbum* 10).[1] Subsequent to the Council, and especially under the direction of Pope John Paul II, the Church's leadership has shown increasing interest in the question of the many cultures and the overwhelming challenge, in an increasingly secular world, for "the inculturation of the Gospel, and the evangelization of the cultures."[2] The relationship between Sacred Scripture and the sacred Tradition, and the role of the Magisterium in an increasingly complex period of rapid cultural change, guiding "the Church, during

---

1. For a careful exegesis of *Dei Verbum* 10, see F. A. Sullivan, *Magisterium. Teaching Authority in the Catholic Church* (New York/Mahwah, NJ: Paulist Press, 1983), 31-33.
2. This "slogan" contains a massive challenge. It demands, above all, a preparedness to listen and learn from the many cultures in that part of the equation: "the inculturation of the Gospel." It is here, as I will mention below, that the post-Vatican II Church leadership has had great difficulty. "The evangelization of the cultures" takes pride of place. In the recent past the Catholic Magisterium has not shown (differently to Pope Francis) a great ability to listen to alternative voices.

its pilgrim journey here on earth … until such time as she is brought to see him face to face as he really is (cf. Jn. 3:2)" (*Dei Verbum* 7), is fraught with difficulty.[3]

Biblical Truths

Subsequent to Pius XII's *Divino Afflante Spiritu* (1943) gifted and hard-working scholars gave much to see that historical-critical scholarship took its rightful place in the Catholic tradition of biblical interpretation (see also *Dei Verbum* 12). The Council's discussions of the role of the Bible in the Church reflects an acceptance of this achievement (see especially, *Dei Verbum* 7). But since that time biblical interpretation has developed further, in its own turn devoting attention to culturally determined ways of interpreting the Bible and Tradition (see The Pontifical Biblical Commission, *The Interpretation of the Bible in the Church*, 34-72).[4] A respectful application of historical-critical methods to both text and tradition benefited the Magisterium's constant concern to affirm the "truths" of the Catholic belief system. Less subjective, historical critics were confident that they could uncover "the meaning which the sacred writers really had in mind" (*Dei Verbum* 12. See *Divino Afflante Spiritu* 23: "let the Catholic exegete undertake the task, of all those imposed on him the greatest, that namely of discovering and expounding the genuine meaning of the Sacred Books").

The relentless application of the criterion of *objectivity*, so important to historical-critical methods, is dissipating as contemporary biblical criticism recognizes the "worlds" involved in the process of (a) the original production, (b) the ongoing relevance and (c) the interpretation of the Sacred Text. This can create further difficulty for the Magisterium's oversight of the ongoing interpretation of "the

---

3. On the evolution of the current (relatively recent) understanding of "Magisterium" as a distinct and authoritative mode of Church teaching, see Sullivan, *Magisterium*, 24-34, and especially R. R. Gaillardetz, *Witness to the Faith. Community, Infallibility, and the Ordinary Magisterium of Bishops* (New York/Mahwah, NJ: Paulist, 1992), 9-145.
4. The document, The Pontifical Biblical Commission, *The Interpretation of the Bible in the Church* (Vatican City: Libreria Editrice Vaticana, 1993), has no paragraph numbers. I will refer to it throughout by means of the page numbers of the above edition.

things (God) had once revealed for the salvation of all peoples" as it is "transmitted to all generations" (*Dei Verbum* 7). There are worlds "behind," "within," and "in front of" the text. Thus, the Bible, one of the great classical texts of all time, must be approached as a window through which one can look to discover what lies behind it, a portrait with a world of its own, and a mirror in which one may or may not find one's own reflection.[5] Interpretation of the Bible must attempt to create a "horizon" which respects all three elements generated by the world behind, within, and in front of the text. This should not discourage, but lead to a great sense of humility in interpretation. As a contemporary literary critic has written: "The meaning of a text is inexhaustible because no context can provide all the keys to all its possibilities."[6] It can thus rightly be claimed that there has never been an objective reading of any text. The patristic and reformation traditions focussed upon *the world in the text*, but unashamedly read their own worlds and their own texts into it. The Form Critics focussed upon *the world behind the text*, but their reconstruction of that world is now seen to have been often influenced by their own worlds, especially the world of post-Enlightenment Europe. The Redaction Critics claimed to have returned, in a more scientific fashion, to *the world in the text*. But their dependence upon form critical conclusions concerning *the world behind the text*,[7] and the risk that they render the Evangelists in their own image, makes their work open to the criticism leveled against both Form Criticism and Patristic-Medieval exegesis. The Magisterium now exercises its ministry in and for a Church faced with biblical interpretations that are more focussed upon the subjective and culturally conditioned nature of all interpretation, including that of the Magisterium itself.

---

5. For this image, see M. Krieger, *A Window to Criticism* (Princeton, NJ: Princeton University Press, 1974), 3-70. To my knowledge, it was first applied to the New Testament literature by N. R. Petersen, *Literary Criticism for New Testament Critics*, Guides to Biblical Scholarship NT Series (Philadelphia: Fortress Press, 1978), 24-48.
6. E. V. McKnight, *Post-Modern Use of the Bible: The Emergence of Reader Oriented Criticism* (Nashville: Abingdon, 1988), 241.
7. See, for example, H. Conzelmann, *The Theology of St Luke*, trans. Geoffrey Busswell (London: Faber & Faber, 1961), 9: "The analysis of the sources renders the *necessary service* of helping distinguish what comes from the source from what belongs to the author" (stress mine).

Contemporary Approaches to Biblical Interpretation

Following the larger world of literary criticism, contemporary biblical scholars are focussing more and more upon *the world in front of the text* (see *The Interpretation of the Bible*, 41-69). But this shift of focus presents its own problems. There are many "worlds," cultures, individuals, faith communities and interpretative traditions in front of the text. The emergence of narrative critical and reader-response criticism in the late 1980's initiated a process in which more attention was given to the multiplicity of readers and cultures, and to an increasingly sophisticated literary critique of a the biblical text.[8] In an attempt to devote greater attention to *the world in the text*, narrative critics trace implied authors and readers within a text that maintains its status as Divine Revelation. However, many of them have exaggeratedly claimed that the only issue that deserves attention is the text itself, and questions concerning *the world behind the text* are irrelevant. A detachment of the biblical text from its historical setting, and an interest in the reader(s) of the text has led into increasingly subversive readings where the reader and her or his contexts are the determining factors in interpretation. Even in these more subversive readings, the text can be regarded as ideologically offensive, but still part of a revealing tradition.[9] Some, however, see it as irrelevant to the multiplicity of post-colonial, feminist, agnostic, postmodern readers.[10] Between these two extremes there are many other interpretations, produced by readers reading "from their place."[11]

One of the most significant axioms behind these contemporary so-called postmodern methods of reading a biblical text can hardly

---

8. See F. J. Moloney, "Narrative Criticism of the Gospels," *Pacifica* 4 (1991): 181-201.
9. See, for example, S. M. Schneiders, *The Revelatory Text. Interpreting the New Testament as Sacred Scripture*, 2nd ed. (Collegeville, MN: The Liturgical Press, 1999).
10. See The Bible and Culture Collective, *The Postmodern Bible* (New Haven: Yale University Press, 1996); S. D. Moore, *Poststructuralism and the New Testament. Derrida and Foucault at the Foot of the Cross* (Minneapolis: Fortress, 1990). Ironically, many of these scholars hold academic positions in Universities that exist because of the Christian (and thus in some way biblical) tradition. See my review of *The Postmodern Bible* in *Pacifica* 9 (1996): 98-101.
11. See F. F. Segovia and M. A. Tolbert, eds., *Reading from This Place*, 2 vols. (Minneapolis: Fortress, 1995-96).

be challenged: every interpreter inscribes his or herself in interpretation. On the basis of this axiom a wave of newer scholars suggests that we be honest at all times, admitting that the story I read into my interpretation is my story. But must one accept that biblical interpretation can be no more than a multiplicity of never-ending possible interpretations, reflecting the fragmented story of the reader, the highly mobile result of intertextuality, with no place for a time-honored canon? Some scholars are developing what is known as autobiographical criticism, claiming that the most honest way to interpret a biblical text I still regard as revelatory is to read it as neither his- or her-story, but as my-story.[12]

How is the Magisterium to respond to the contemporary insistence that no interpretation of a given text can lay claim to ultimate authority? It must be admitted that no contemporary religious, historical or cultural context can claim to understand *all the possibilities* of an ancient text, especially one which has remained alive in a reading public, across many cultures and historical eras, for 2,000 years. Paul Ricoeur has done much to indicate that once the act of interpretation has come to its conclusion, there is always a significant "remainder" which lies beyond the limits of the completed interpretation, "the residue of the literal interpretation."[13] However, this same philosopher has also insisted that *many* interpretations are possible, but not *any* interpretation.[14] The contemporary interpreter of the biblical text must create a horizon where the worlds meet, behind, within and in front of the text. The role of the Magisterium is to guide the contemporary Catholic interpreter as he or she locates this horizon within the faith-tradition of the Catholic Church which reveres the Bible as part of Divine Revelation (*Dei Verbum* 11-12, 23). This is no small task, and it calls for inquiring minds and open hearts.

---

12. See J. L. Staley, *Reading with a Passion. Rhetoric, Autobiography, and the American West in the Gospel of John* (New York: Continuum, 1995); J. Capel Anderson and J. L. Staley, eds., "Taking it Personally," *Semeia* 72 (1995); I.-R. Kitzberger, ed., *The Personal Voice in Biblical Interpretation* (London: Routledge, 1998).
13. P. Ricoeur, *Interpretation Theory: Discourse and the Surplus of Meaning* (Fort Worth: Texas Christian University Press, 1976), 55.
14. See, for example, P. Ricoeur, *Hermeneutics and the Human Sciences*, ed. J. B. Thompson (Cambridge: Cambridge University Press, 1981), 210-213.

Text and Context

So-called postmodern criticism lays claim to "point the way toward a more rigorously self-reflective and contextualized biblical criticism."[15] But such claims have a certain arrogance. At the beginning of the third Christian millenium, after several decades of intense ecumenical activity and scholarly communion, biblical scholars are aware of the motivating principles, scholarly, cultural and ecclesial, of their various (and sometimes conflicting) interpretations. Some contemporary biblical scholars may use methods that start from the presupposition that the Bible is an oppressive and corrupt text, asking to be subverted by a variety of postmodern readings. Jews and Christians demand that such scholars respect the rights of the believing biblical scholars to inscribe their stories in Jewish and Christian interpretations which situate themselves creatively, but comfortably, within the Jewish or Christian Tradition. The limited comprehension created by context is not detrimental until one pretends to be free from it.

How is the Magisterium of the Catholic Church, based upon two thousand years' experience of reading and responding to the biblical text as Divine Revelation, given its rightful role in the process of interpreting the Bible within the Church (see *The Interpretation of the Bible* 41-50)? Much culturally driven interpretation invites the reader into the text, giving *primacy* to cultures and a multiplicity of possible reading experiences. Such interpretations correctly point to the subjective nature of any interpretation, but they ignore an even more important hermeneutical principle. Read within the Christian Tradition, not only does the reader shape the text. As any observer of the Christian story can point out, *the text has shaped the reader, obvious in the Christian practice of reading and listening to the word of the Bible, for almost two thousand years.*[16] *Primacy* must be given to the text and its literary, historical and theological context, not to the socio-cultural context of the contemporary reader, however important the latter may be.

If everything is "intertext," the product of a highly volatile number of possibilities which happened to come together at one particu-

---

15. Anderson and Staley, "Taking It Personally," 16.
16. Artistic and musical expression, every-day language and practices across all the cultures where the Bible is read are eloquent proof of the formative power of the biblical text.

lar, but passing, point in time, then why bother involve oneself in the process of interpreting a text which exists because of a tradition? Why subject to analysis a cultural, historical and religious moment "frozen" in the past to generate (and subsequently impose) a normative "canon," if all that matters is the enculturated reader? From this perspective, it must also be noted that every potential reader is also "intertext": the product of an infinite number of possibilities that have come together in one particular reading experience. As this *reductio ad absurdum* indicates, to displace the primacy of the biblical text in the act of interpretation and to replace it with a closed focus upon the cultural context of the reader and the reading community would be a tragic loss. Christians would be faced with the giddy possibility of spiraling through a never-ending whirlwind of interpretative possibilities, accepted today and discarded tomorrow.

No human community, especially one watched over by the Magisterium of a Christian community that accepts the Bible as Divine Revelation, can survive in such a whirlwind. But the Magisterium must also be warned against falling into the same error. The Magisterium may also "displace the primacy of the biblical text in the act of interpretation and replace it with the cultural context of the reader and the reading community." In this case, the reader and the reading community would be the culturally conditioned perspective of a particular Catholic authority or community. Within the complexity of contemporary society and cultures, this danger has not been avoided over the decades since the Second Vatican Council. The Catholic Church and its magisterial activity still has much to learn, as it listens very little to alternative voices, and has issued major doctrinal and disciplinary statements that are very much the work of elements in Catholic leadership that seem to have "deaf ears."[17]

---

17. There are a number of examples of this, especially under the pontificates of John Paul II and (to a lesser extent) Benedict XVI. Two that merit particular attention are *Dominus Jesus*, insisting on the uniqueness of the Roman Catholic tradition, rejecting that the Anglican and Protestant communities can be regarded as "sister Churches" (doctrine), and *Liturgiam Authenticam* that imposed a direct translation of the Latin *Editio Princeps* of the Roman Missal and the Latin Vulgate translation for all vernacular celebrations of the Roman Liturgy *everywhere in the Catholic world* (discipline). These documents, the former from the Congregation of the Doctrine of the Faith, and the other from the Congregation for Divine Worship and the Sacraments, are unrelentingly mono-cultural. They came as a complete surprise to the larger Catholic world.

A Contemporary Catholic Approach

Contemporary cultural, postmodern, and biographical interpretations focus more intensely upon the cultural situations of the interpreters and their reading and hearing communities. Catholic biblical scholarship accepts that agenda, but submits that the process must run in two directions. *Biblical exegesis is not only shaped by culture and the cultures. Culture and the cultures have been profoundly shaped by the biblical revelation.* This essential interplay between text *and* reader and reader *and* text affirms the ongoing importance, and indeed the priority, of the text transmitted in the Tradition above the culturally situated reader.

At least two factors lie behind the Catholic insistence upon the priority of the text over the situated reader, individual or communitarian. The first is the tradition, which has its beginnings in Israel's recognition that *Torah, Nebi'im* and *Ketubim* provided an authoritative word of God determining all aspects of the life and practice of the individual Israelite and the nation. This, of course, was particularly the case with *Torah*, but the commentary upon *Torah* provided by the Prophets and the Writings also gave them an exalted status as *Tanak*. This sense of "Scripture" (γραφή) passed rapidly into the early writings of the Christian communities. Already partially recognized as Sacred Scripture late in the Second Century, there are indications from the very beginnings of a Christian literature, that a Christian Sacred Scripture was emerging. This can be sensed in the Lukan and Matthean use of Old Testament texts and literary forms in their narrative, and in the explicit Johannine claim to be γραφή (see John 20:9: οὐδέπω γὰρ ᾔδεισαν τὴν γραφήν; 20:30-31: ἃ οὐκ ἔστιν γεγραμμένα ἐν τῷ βιβλίῳ τούτῳ ταῦτα δὲ γέγραπται ἵνα πιστεύσετε).[18] The same impression is created for the Pauline Corpus in 2 Peter 3:14-16.

The second factor is the evidence that culture, especially – but not only – European culture, has been shaped by the biblical tra-

---

18. On this, see F. J. Moloney, "The Gospel of John as Scripture." Pages 333-347 in *The Gospel of John. Text and Context*, Biblical Interpretation Series 72 (Boston/Leiden: Brill, 2005), 333-347, and Idem, "'For as yet they did not know the Scriptures' (John 20:9): A Study in Narrative Time," in *Johannine Studies 1975-2017*, Wissenschaftliche Untersuchungen zum Neuen Testament 372 (Tübingen: Mohr Siebeck, 2017), 505-19.

dition. Language, art, music, architecture, literature, ethical traditions, national constitutions and modes of government bear its imprint. To use the language of contemporary literary criticism, the biblical text is the essential intertext for much contemporary culture. As the English poet, William Blake, said of the biblical text, it is our "great code."[19] A rejection of the formative nature of what Jews and Christians regard as the Word of God is the rejection of 4,000 years of human endeavor. Such a rejection, present in some contemporary philosophical and hermeneutical schools, in unacceptable in our Catholic community. Our Catholic life depends upon a history that, despite its ambivalence, reflects the unfolding of God's design.

The Catholic community and its leadership, of course, must accept that it is no longer able to dictate terms to a culture, as it has done for many centuries, especially after the necessary reforms of Gregory VII in the eleventh century, in the struggle in Europe between the authority of the Pope, and the emerging, powerful, Christian political powers.[20] That era has passed, and there is every possibility that the European culture that reflected the biblical tradition so profoundly for two thousand years is waning quickly. There is no longer widespread adhesion to Catholic values and practice. In some places the birth-rate has dropped below zero, and the massive influx of refugees, many deeply committed to the faith and practice of Islam, is changing the face of Europe and the cultures in other parts of the world that derive from it. In this very rapidly developing situation, the Catholic community and its magisterial leadership must become an ever better "listener," an ever more caring institution, aware that it now stands

---

19. See N. Frye, *The Great Code. The Bible and Literature* (London: Routledge & Kegan Paul, 1982).
20. The development of a more juridically structured Church goes back to the reforms of Pope Gregory VII (1073-1085). The authority of the Pope over the secular Princes was dramatically acted out in the submission of Henry VII (Holy Roman Emperor) to Gregory VII at Canossa in 1077. As the issue of authority took center-stage, reflection on the Word of God, the Liturgy, and the great Patristic tradition waned. For a brief summary of this period, and its effects upon the Catholic Church's self-understanding, see Richard Gaillardetz, *The Church in the Making*, Rediscovering Vatican II Series (New York/Mahwah, NJ: Paulist, 2006), 145-47.

on the peripheries of cultural formation.[21] We have come a long way from Gregory VII, but perhaps this is a "graced" moment for the history of the Catholic Tradition. A Catholic Church speaking from the peripheries of a culture it once dominated can be more Christ-like, and perhaps raise a prophetic voice, rooted in Gospel values, rather than pretending that it is still an institution that wields the authority of the "two swords."[22]

Almost every element in the Christian Creeds reflects the mutuality between the biblical texts and the cultural contexts that generated the Creeds. That, of course, is the way the great Creeds grew. In the earliest centuries of the Church there was no fixed body of doctrine. The great councils had to articulate them on the basis of the Word of God, their liturgical traditions, and the accumulated wisdom that went before them and provided them with the beginnings of "the Tradition." As one of the elements in this dynamic interaction between traditions and cultures (shifting an original Jewish belief in Jesus as the Christ, the Son of God into the categories of the Greco-Roman world), the biblical text shaped the Church's creedal formulations.

One example of the interface between the biblical story and the articulation of Christian faith must suffice, taken from a passage in the Gospel of John (John 3:1-21).[23] Such examples could be multiplied to form a sizeable volume. *The text* of the encounter between

---

21. In this respect, Pope Francis leads the contemporary Catholic community in an exemplary fashion, despite some strong opposition (e.g. the Polish Bishops, Cardinals Burke, Pell, and Sarah, and Archbishop Chaput of Philadelphia). Whatever Pope Francis says rings with "Gospel truth," however embarrassing it sometimes is to other Catholic leaders.
22. The expression "the two swords" was absorbed from Luke 22:38 ("They said, 'Lord, look, here are two swords.' He replied, 'It is enough'") to refer to the religious and secular authority of the Roman Church. This issue was at the center of the conflicts between Gregory VII and the Holy Roman Emperor, Henry VII, at Canossa in 1077.
23. For this example, I have deliberately chosen a narrative that suits my purposes well. Not all are as straight-forward as this (e.g. violent passages from the Hebrew Bible, never-ending genealogies, or such puzzling passages as Jesus' parable on the cunning steward [Luke 16:1-13], or Jesus' instructions to Peter on paying the Temple tax with a coin from a fish's mouth [Matt 17:24-27]!). On the other hand, there are Gospel passages that play immediately into doctrinal formulations, as with the Johannine Prologue (John 1:1-18). Indeed, reflection on the implications of that passage played a critical role in the great Trinitarian and Christological councils from Nicea (325 CE) till Chalcedon (451 CE).

Jesus and Nicodemus recorded in the Fourth Gospel (John 3:1-21) provides formative articulations of a number of fundamental elements of the *Christian belief system*. It is not only here that we find these claims, but we learn the Christian Tradition was born within Judaism (3:1-2), and summoned those who wished to adhere to that Tradition to allow the impulse of the Spirit to draw them beyond rituals, accepting the divine origins of their beginning and their end (vv. 3-10). We are instructed that in both past and present times, many claim to speak authoritatively of God, but there is only one who has come from God, and has made God known (vv. 11-12). Jesus of Nazareth, the Son of Man, has been lifted up on a cross to show in his flesh the love of God, so that all who gaze upon this unique revelation of a unique God will have life (vv. 13-15). In this God's love has been made known; God sent Jesus, his Son, not to judge us but to give us life (vv. 16-17). Christianity is life, not judgment, but we are shapers of our own destiny. Johannine "realized eschatology" is not just a technical term dear to Charles Harold Dodd, Joachim Jeremias and Rudolf Bultmann. It speaks to those of us who need to be taught that we are responsible for our words and deeds (vv. 18-21).[24]

From this brief example, one can see that the list of Christian "truth-claims" that flow naturally from a critical acceptance of the biblical text is potentially very lengthy. These claims have an impressive history in the confessed and lived faith of the Church, watched over by a Magisterium that certainly has the task to teach authoritatively, but which is always subject to the Word of God (*Dei Verbum* 10).

Despite its long hesitation to do so, the contemporary Roman Catholic Magisterium must allow a multiplicity of possible readings of the biblical text and a multiplicity of interpretations resulting from such readings. The biblical text has shaped and continues to shape a Catholic Community and a Catholic Tradition which recognize Jesus as Son of God, Son of Man, the unique revelation of God in the human story (*Dei Verbum* 2). But there is more. The person of Jesus Christ gives the text authority, not the text itself. Christian Tradition pre-existed the text, and gave us the βίβλια of the New Testament to grant access for their own and later generations to the person of

---

24. For more detail, see F. J. Moloney, *The Gospel of John*, Sacra Pagina 4 (Collegeville, MN: The Liturgical Press, 1998), 88-103.

Jesus Christ. We continue to read the story of Jesus within that Tradition.[25] Not only is there a narrative world behind, within and in front of the text, but there is also a Christian Tradition which pre-dated the text, generated the text, and which continues to give it life within the many contemporary cultures. The relationship between Tradition and Scripture, however, is never stable; much less "frozen." The Tradition gave birth and continues to enliven the Scriptures in a Christian community, but the Scriptures perform the prophetic role of keeping the Tradition honest when it falls to the temptation of absolutizing, through accommodation, any age, culture or particular religious practice (*Dei Verbum* 9-10).[26] Not all will accept this view, but within a postmodern world, where "différance" is so important, Catholics affirm our "difference."[27] Within this highly volatile interaction of Scripture, Tradition, and the many, increasingly fragmented, cultures addressed by the one Word of God, the Magisterium exercises its difficult ministry.

Conclusion

The narrator in Arundhati Roy's Booker Prize winning novel, *The God of Small Things* (1997), has a reflection appropriate for this setting:

> The Great Stories are the ones you have heard and want to hear again. The ones you can enter anywhere and inhabit comfortably. They don't deceive you with thrills and trick endings. They don't surprise you with the unforeseen. They are as familiar as the house you live in. Or the smell of your lover's skin. You know how they end, yet you listen as though you don't. In the way that although you know that one day you will die, you live as though you won't. In the Great Stories you

---

25. Parallel affirmations could (and should) be made concerning the place of *Torah*, *Nebi'im* and *Ketubim* within the Jewish Tradition. It is beyond the scope of this paper to do so.
26. For further development of this point, see F. J. Moloney, "Jesus Christ: The Question to Cultures," *Pacifica* 1 (1988): 15-43.
27. This play on words refers to the practice, developed by Jacques Derrida, of continually deferring meaning, and thus never locating a "metaphysic" behind text or in words. To describe this practice he invented the neologism "différer/différance."

know who lives, who dies, who finds love, who doesn't. And yet you want to know again.[28]

It is important for Catholic Christians that there be a Catholic community where both the text *of the Bible* and the interpretation *of the Bible* are treasured. For the Catholic Tradition, the Bible is one of the ways God is made known, it is our Great Story. It is the house we live in ... the smell of our lover's skin. It has given us the fixed points that support the silken threads upon which the many possible tapestries of Jewish and Catholic responses to that belief can be woven. We know, and yet we want to know again. Our interpretation of the text is not determined by a dogmatic tradition, itself interpretation of text, but inspired by its beauty and the Tradition giving it life.

The Magisterium watches carefully over "the house we live in," "not superior to the Word of God, but its servant" (*Dei Verbum* 10).[29] Herein lies the tension, the "restless relationship" mentioned in the title of this study. The Magisterium, as an institution of human beings grappling with the timeless mysteries of God's action in and through Jesus Christ, always runs the risk of distorting the Word of God by demanding that the interpretation of Scripture correspond to the demands of a particular time, place or culture.[30] Such distortions are understandable, and were wisely commented upon by Joseph Ratzinger in his commentary upon *Dei Verbum*. Addressing the problem of the relationship between Scripture and Tradition described as "*in unum quodammodo coalescunt*" (*Dei Verbum* 9), the then Profes-

---

28. Arundhati Roy, *The God of Small Things* (London: Flamingo, 1997), 229.
29. On this, see R. R. Gaillardetz, *Teaching with Authority: A Theology of the Magisterium of the Church* (Collegeville: The Liturgical Press, 1997), 69-100.
30. A more theological and less negative statement of the limitations of the Magisterium's interventions can be found in Gaillardetz, *Teaching with Authority*, pp. 98-99: "To speak of the normative character of doctrine is not to suggest that Church doctrines serve as a kind of punctuation mark ending discussion or reflection on the particular belief in question. In fact, a doctrinal statement's often terse, conceptual character virtually demands more developed theological formulations. ... A doctrine can norm Christian belief, but it does not and cannot exhaust it." *Mutatis mutandis*, the same applies to the relationship between the Magisterium and contemporary Scripture studies. See further the application of these principles in R. R. Gaillardetz, "*Ad tuendam fidem*: An Emerging Pattern in current Papal Teaching," *New Theology Review* 12 (1999): 42-51, especially pp. 48-51.

sor of Systematic Theology at the University of Regensburg rightly remarked:

> We shall have to acknowledge the truth of the criticism that there is, in fact, no explicit mention of the possibility of a distorting tradition and the place of Scripture as an element in the church that is also critical of tradition, which means that a most important side of the problem, as shown by the history of the church – and perhaps the real crux of the *ecclesia semper reformanda* – has been overlooked. … That this opportunity has been missed can only be regarded as an unfortunate omission.[31]

In a later article, in the same volume, commenting on *Dei Verbum* 23 and the use of the Scriptures in the Church, Ratzinger again correctly focuses upon the necessity of the "restless relationship" which must exist between Sacred Scripture and the Magisterium:

> A reference to the ecclesial nature of exegesis on the one hand, and to its methodological correctness on the other, again expresses the inner tension of church exegesis, which can no longer be removed, *but must simply be accepted as tension*.[32]

The interpretation of Sacred Scripture within the Catholic Tradition, and the ever caring, but watchful role of the Magisterium, necessarily belong to this tension. Neither exegete nor Magisterium has the right to ease the pain of this tension by a rigid and unbending dogmatism or an uncritical and ungrounded "change for the sake of change" approach.[33] In the end, neither the exegete nor the Magisterium can resolve this restless relationship. It is a tension that the Catholic

---

31. J. Ratzinger, "The Transmission of Divine Revelation," in *Commentary on the Documents of Vatican II*, ed. H. Vorgrimler, 5 vols. (London: Burns & Oates/Herder & Herder, 1967-69), 3:192-93.
32. Ratzinger, "Sacred Scripture in the Life of the Church, in Vorgrimler, ed., *Commentary*, 3:268. Stress mine.
33. See the remarks of R. E. Brown, "Critical Biblical Exegesis and the Development of Doctrine," in *Biblical Exegesis and Church Doctrine* (New York: Paulist Press, 1985) 52: "Neither a fundamentalist interpretation of the NT, which finds later dogmas with great clarity in the NT era, nor a liberal view, which rejects anything that goes beyond Jesus, is faithful to Catholic history."

Church embraces willingly, under the guidance of the Holy Spirit, and directed by its teaching authority. It is yet another indication of the mystery and messiness of the Incarnation, and situates the teaching authority of the Catholic Church within the mystery and messiness of contemporary culture(s). It is for one such teaching authority, Archbishop Joseph Doré, colleague and friend, that I gladly dedicate this reflection. It comes with an awareness of his need for faith and courage to live in his flesh the "restless relationship" between Sacred Scripture and the Magisterium as he exercises his episcopal ministry in the Archdiocese of Strasbourg. It is easier for a scholar to ponder these issues at his desk, and in his library, than for a leading figure in the Church's Magisterium to put them into action, while the scholar looks on!

The mystery of the Catholic Church, local and universal, itself a "world" within and yet beyond the cultures, cannot freeze the Christian response to the biblical revelation, ever attentive to "the living voice of the Gospel" (*Dei Verbum* 8), into an irrelevant past. Nor should it attempt to create for the Catholic believer of any particular time a comfortable house to live in. The proclamation of the Kingdom and is a never-ending summons to conversion: "The Kingdom is at hand. Repent and believe in the Gospel" (Mark 1:15. See *Lumen Gentium* 8). The interpreters of Sacred Scripture and the Magisterium must accept and live their restless relationship that this summons be heard and re-heard until the Lord comes again.[34] It will call for love, humility, and not a little patient pain, from both parties.

---

34. A serious problem, closely allied to the question of the relationship between Scripture and the Magisterium, is the widespread ignorance of the Word of God in the Catholic Church, including many in leadership, despite the effort of Popes (Leo XIII: *Providentissimus Deus* [1893], Pius XII: *Divino Afflante Spiritu* [1993], and Benedict XVI, *Verbum Domini* [2009]). For more detailed reflection of this phenomenon within the Catholic Church, see F. J. Moloney, *Reading the New Testament in the Church. A Primer for Pastors, Religious Educators, and Believers* (Grand Rapids, MI: Baker Academic, 2015), 1-21.

12
Sacred Scripture at Vatican II

Some 50 years after the promulgation of the most important document on the Sacred Scriptures from the Second Vatican Council (Vatican II), *Dei Verbum*, it is time to look back and assess what emerged from that critical moment in Catholic Church history.[1] Current reflection on Vatican II often debates whether "the word" of the Council be followed, rather than its "spirit."[2] This reflection attempts to affirm the ongoing importance of the "word" of the Council, as its "spirit" inevitably impacts upon the life, teaching and practice of the Catholic Church.

The Fathers of Vatican II asked that the Sacred Scripture be returned to the centre of the life and practice of the Catholic Church:

---

1. The Dogmatic Constitution on Divine Revelation (*Dei Verbum*) was promulgated on 18 November, 1965. The Latin title for *Dei Verbum* and *Sacrosanctum Concilium* will be provided in the text, but paragraph references will use the abbreviations *DV* and *SC*. All citations are taken from Austin Flannery, ed., *The Basic Sixteen Documents. Vatican Council II. Constitutions, Decrees, Declarations. A Completely Revised Translation in Inclusive Language* (Northport, NY/Dublin: Costello Publishing Company/Dominican Publications, 1995).
2. Those who ask for more attention to "the word" of the Council suggest that what was actually *said* at the Church at Vatican II is not known. See the influential comments of Joseph Ratzinger, *The Ratzinger Report* (San Francisco: Ignatius Press, 1985), 29-42; Henri de Lubac, *A Brief Catechism on Nature and Grace* (San Francisco: Ignatius Press, 1984), 235-60. Others regards this approach as freezing the Council in the "world and words" of the 1960's, and thus ask that "the spirit" of the Council guide its interpretation and implementation in the third millennium. For further reflections on this current rift among post-Conciliar Catholics, see Neil Ormerod, "Vatican II-Continuity or Discontinuity? Toward an Ontology of Meaning," *Theological Studies* 71 (2010): 609-36, and Richard R. Gaillardetz, *The Church in the Making*, Rediscovering Vatican II Series (New York/Mahwah, NJ: Paulist Press, 2006), 145-47.

> It (the Church) has always regarded and continues to regard the scriptures, taken together with sacred tradition, as the supreme rule of its faith (*DV* 21).
> Access to sacred Scripture ought to be widely available to the Christian faithful (*DV* 22).
> Taught by the holy spirit, the spouse of the incarnate Word, which is the church, strives to reach an increasingly more profound understanding of the sacred scriptures, in order to nourish its children with God's words (*DV* 23).

This dream is yet to be realized.[3] An opening sketch plots a potted history from the eleventh century to the pre-Conciliar Catholic community. Two documents from the Council that attended to the issue of the place and role of the Sacred Scriptures in the Church, *Sacrosanctum Concilium* and *Dei Verbum*, are then surveyed. An assessment of the reception and implementation of this teaching will follow, concluding with some speculation about the future. "The crucial process of reception, that all-important part of any church council, can take several generations. It continues today."[4]

Some History

A decisive turning point in the history of the Church was the reform carried out by Pope Gregory VII (1028-1085), in the eleventh century.[5] In order to protect the proper autonomy of the Church and its mission, Gregory insisted that the Pope had authority over all ecclesiastical offices, and also over the authority of the secular princes.[6]

---

3. For further reflection on this difficult post-Conciliar period, and some suggestions for a way forward, see Francis J. Moloney, "The Word in the World: Then and Now," on pp. 349-69 of this volume. For a negative evaluation of the post-Conciliar Church, see Hans Küng, *Disputed Truth. Memoirs*, trans. John Bowden; (London: Continuum, 2008). This informative book is marred by overindulgent self-promotion and a bitter rejection of the agenda of Benedict XVI, the former Tübingen colleague of Küng, Joseph Ratzinger.
4. Cardinal Franz König, cited by Gerald O'Collins, *Living Vatican II. The 21st Council for the 21st Century* (New York/Mahwah, NJ: Paulist Press, 2006), vii.
5. See Yves Congar, *L'Église de saint Augustin à l'époque modern* (Paris: Cerf, 1970), 102-12. For the summary that follows, see Gaillardetz, *The Church*, 41-42.
6. Spectacularly symbolised by the submission of Henry VII (Emperor of the Holy Roman Empire) to Gregory VII at Canossa in 1077.

Gregory set in motion a gradual yet inexorable shift away from a Church whose foundation lay in the Scriptures, theological tradition and sacramental practice to a Church whose foundation lay in law. Gregory's reforms preserved the autonomy and the freedom of the Church from secular authority at a difficult time in European history. However, as one commentator has observed:

> One may wonder whether the juridical means used to achieve this end may not have overshadowed the desired effect. The desired freedom was won, but the fundamental "sacramentalism" of the church was somewhat forgotten in the face of the overriding insistence that the church is a juridically structured society.[7]

The response to the Reformation at the Council of Trent (1545-1563) introduced significant reform, but it was accompanied by an increasing pattern of ecclesiastical defensiveness.[8] The Protestants attacked the visible and institutional Church (e.g., Papacy, Priesthood, Sacraments) and this had to be defended. During the following century the Church was presented as a *societas perfecta*, a "perfect society." This did not mean that the Church was morally perfect, but that it was completely self-sufficient. In a stress of its institutional features, too little attention was given to the investigation of the Church's origins in the life and teaching of Jesus, its spiritual nature, in association with Jesus' preaching of the reigning presence of God, and its mission as an expression of the Trinitarian missions of the Son and Holy Spirit from the Father.

The Enlightenment, an intellectual movement that has produced so much that is good for the modern era, rejected as false what could not be proved and was very sceptical about a revealed religion. Revolutions in the United States of America (1775-1783), France (1789, 1848), Germany (1848), Italy (1848-1849) and Russia (1905, 1917-1918) often aimed their anger against the Catholic Church. The Church belonged to the *ancien régime*. In many ways, it had con-

---

7. William Henn, *The Honor of my Brothers. A Brief History of the Relationship between the Pope and the Bishops* (New York: Crossroad, 2000), 107-108.
8. For a fine, readable, study of the achievements of the Council of Trent, see John W. O'Malley, *Trent: What Happened at the Council* (Cambridge, MA: Harvard University Press, 2013).

structed it and had received many privileges from those political and social arrangements. The more modern movements promised much to an oppressed people asking for democracy. The Catholic Church responded by centralizing all authority on the Papacy, culminating in the declaration of the infallibility of the Pope at Vatican I in 1870. Most twentieth century Roman Catholics lived "the spirit" of Vatican I that took teaching on Papal infallibility further than the intentions of the Council.[9] Associated with this, the Church's leadership did little to instruct the practising Catholics on the treasures of their faith, and their concomitant responsibilities. This led, inevitably, to a form of abdication of responsibility among Catholic lay people that persists.

It is crucial, however, to recall the more charismatic movements that emerged in the life of the Church in the nineteenth and twentieth centuries. They produced Vatican II. This period was marked by a great growth of religious congregations that broke from the monastic traditions to turn to the urgent needs of the people, especially the service of the poor and the missionary activity of the Church.[10] This was matched by the steady increase of lay participation in the Church's mission. A renewed appreciation of the passion for the Scriptures that dominated the teaching and writing of the Fathers of the Church (e.g., Origen [c. 184-c. 254], Augustine [354-430], Athanasius [296-373], and Cyril of Alexandria [378-444]), and the leadership of the Popes in difficult times, especially Leo the Great (440-461) and Gregory the Great (590-604) entered the Catholic academy. These figures, among others, had been extremely formative of recent reflection upon the Catholic Tradition.

After an initial hesitation to accept the critical approach to the Bible that had its beginnings in the Enlightenment and the English Deist movement, in 1893, Pope Leo XIII issued *Providentissimus Deus*, urging Catholic scholars, with due caution, to embrace a critical reading

---

9. Recourse to increasingly totalitarian form of government in the face of conflicting ideologies is complex. Simplistic historical analysis should be avoided. Some 50 years after Vatican I, for example, Germany and Italy readily accepted the regimes of Adolf Hitler and Benito Mussolini.
10. As a result of the request from Vatican II that religious communities undertake a process of renewal by carefully examining their academic origins (see *Perfectae Caritatis* 2), many studies of the religious congregations founded in the eighteenth and nineteenth centuries have appeared. See, for example, the outstanding work of Arthur Lenti, *Don Bosco. History and Spirit*, 7 vols. (Rome: LAS, 2007-2010).

of the Word of God, which, he insisted, was the very soul of Theology. To mark the fiftieth anniversary of that epoch-making Encyclical, in 1943 Pius XII invited all Catholic scholars to embrace more critical methods in his Encyclical *Divino Afflante Spiritu*.[11] Silently, and often "behind closed doors," work on the biblical, liturgical and patristic sources of Catholic life and faith had been increasing in depth and breadth across the latter half of the nineteenth and the first half of the twentieth Century. Biblical and liturgical renewal. Dom Gueranger, OSB, the Abbot of Solesmes (1837-75), set in motion a re-birth in interest in liturgical Theology and practice. Marie-Joseph Lagrange, OP, an outstanding Catholic biblical scholar, was the foundational figure of the now world-famous *Ecole Biblique et Archéologique de Jérusalem*.[12] On the basis of these, and other scholars and institutions, the giants of Vatican II were poised for the opportunity rethink the Scriptural basis for all aspects of theology, liturgical life and the mystery of the Church itself, rooted in the mystery of the Trinity.

Bubbling away below the surface of the life and practice of the pre-Conciliar Catholic Church were movements asking for intellectual, liturgical, theological and structural change. It would take Vatican II to bring these two aspects of the Catholic Church of the twentieth century together in a manner that saw an emergence of enthusiastic reformers. But they did not emerge from a vacuum. Naturally, the more legal, and less biblically founded traditions, continued. Biblical and liturgical renewal met steady opposition from those who saw the Church as a perfect society, juridical in nature and governed by

---

11. Given the context of the late nineteenth century, Leo XIII's openness to the centrality of the word of God to the life of the Church is remarkable. The claim of *Dei Verbum* 24 that the study of the sacred page "should be the very soul of sacred theology" was first articulated in *Providentissimus Deus* 16. On these two Encyclicals, see Francis J. Moloney, *Reading the New Testament in the Church. A Primer for Pastors, Religious Educators, and Believers* (Grand Rapids: Baker Academic, 2015), 9-12.
12. Lagrange began his publishing career in the *Ecole's* famous journal, the *Revue Biblique*, with studies of the Hebrew Bible. He published a study suggesting that the Pentateuch has been composed over a period of time on the basis of sources. As the accepted position was that Moses wrote all five books of the Pentateuch, he was given a *monitum* (warning) from Rome, forbidding him to publish on such matters. Thankfully, he then turned his brilliant mind, and love for the Word of God to the New Testament. He wrote commentaries on Matthew, Mark, Luke, and John, still regarded as classics, and continually consulted by contemporary scholars. His cause for beatification and canonisation has been introduced.

an infallible Pope.[13] For the first time in the Church's history, Vatican II saw the emergence of a previously silent group: Bishops from the third world, and strong figures from beyond the then "iron curtain." Since then, they have begun to raise a "new voice," no one more so than for former Archbishop of Krakow, Poland, who was to become Pope John Paul II. This "voice" is hard to identify. One cannot speak of a single voice. Some (especially the African and former Communist regime Bishops) tend stoutly to defend traditional practices. However, given the tribal and complex religious backgrounds of some of these Catholic leaders (Africans, Indians and Asians), many are open to dialogue and diversity, especially in the area of liturgical diversity.

The Teaching and Recommendations of Vatican II

The Constitution on the Sacred Liturgy, *Sacrosanctum Concilium*, was one of the first Conciliar documents to appear, promulgated at the end of the second session on December 4, 1963. Ideological struggles within the Council had begun to appear during the first session in 1962. A feature of this conflict between what has been called the conservative and the progressive elements in the Council was the rejection of the Preparatory Commission's schemes *De Ecclesia* and *De Fontibus Revelationis*, in the first session (November, 1962).[14] The fruit of bitter debates that ran through the course of the Council, the Dogmatic Constitution on Divine Revelation, *Dei Verbum*, was finally promulgated as the Council came to an end after the fourth session. Paul VI promulgated it on November 18, 1965. A process of theological and pastoral maturation took place between the promulgation of *Sacrosanctum Concilium* (1963) and *Dei Verbum* (1965). Factions and ideological differences played into the formulation of documents.

---

13. On these reflections, see Gaillardetz, *The Church*, 1-6, and especially the outstanding study of John W. O'Malley, *What Happened at Vatican II* (Cambridge & London: Harvard University Press, 2008), 36-52.
14. This terminology was widely used inside and outside the Council Hall, to refer to the ideological stances taken by different Council Fathers. O'Malley, *What Happened*, 292-93 recognises this, but prefers to refer to the groups as "minority" (conservatives) and "majority" (progressives). A remarkable first-hand witness to these tensions, that did not ease as the Council progressed, is now available in the sprawling and highly personal Yves Congar, *My Journal of the Council*, trans. Denis Minns, and Others (Adelaide: ATF Theology, 2012).

They are the result of compromise, even though all documents were accepted with huge majorities prior to their Papal promulgation.

Sacrosanctum Concilium

When the Conciliar document on the Sacred Liturgy was promulgated in late 1963 the entire Catholic Church was amazed by its boldness. Principles were stated in the document that promised to make the Liturgy, so crucial to Catholic faith and practice (see SC 1-2), understandable to all peoples and cultures. The introduction of the vernacular into liturgical celebrations, the renewal of the liturgical year, renewal of liturgical books, including the Lectionary, permission for clergy to concelebrate, respect for local cultures, their music and their rites, an increased respect for differing forms of art and architecture, were unexpected. These practices were only a dream for a handful of Catholics in the pre-Conciliar period. However, the document still protects many pre-Conciliar traditions: the primacy of the Latin Mass, the single celebrant, control of the Holy See, the control of a "competent territorial ecclesiastical authority" or a local Ordinary over all change, no matter how insignificant some of it may appear to us today.

A positive feature of this first Constitution to emerge from Vatican II is its language, a new "literary form" for Church documents never seen before. Almost every affirmation, either theological or pastoral, is inspired or supported by the use of biblical texts. This characteristic is an indication of the decision of the Fathers of the Council, responding to a desire of Pope John XXIII,[15] to turn away from a juridical approach, to speak to the whole Church in more biblical, patristic and liturgical language. This practice continued and strengthened as the Council unfolded. It is not a direct exhortation for the Church to devote more attention to the Sacred Scriptures, but demonstrates what happens when the riches of the biblical text are well used in theological and pastoral discourse.

Sacrosanctum Concilium recognises the central importance of Sacred Scripture in the readings, the Psalms, the hymns and the preaching, and recommends "that warm and lively appreciation of

---

15. On the calling of Vatican II by Pope John XXIII and his hopes for the Council, see O'Malley, *What Happened*, 15-18.

sacred scripture to which the venerable tradition of both eastern and western rites gives testimony" (*SC* 24). Living in the Catholic Church of the 1940's till the 1960's, my contemporaries have no memory of a "warm and lively appreciation for sacred scripture." Biblical texts, following a one year cycle, were read during Mass in Latin and were seldom the basis of a homily. Catholics popularly regarded the Bible as a Protestant book. In paragraph 35, the Council gives a number of directives about the use of Sacred Scripture that alter that practice and understanding: there must be a richer selection of texts, preaching is to be more biblical, and Bible services are to be encouraged as vigils for important feasts, especially in those places where a Priest is unavailable. A shadow of what will be said three years later in *Dei Verbum* appears in paragraph 48. An instruction is given concerning the participants in the Liturgy: "They should be formed by God's word, and be nourished at the table of the Lord's Body." This is some distance from the "one table of the word of God and the Body of Christ" (*DV* 21), but it is an early indication of things to come. Finally, among the norms, there is a further repetition of the need for more Scripture in celebrations, and adoption of a practice that will make a major impact on the post-Conciliar liturgical practice of the Church: the request for a more representative portion of the Sacred Scriptures in the Lectionary (*SC* 51).

The bulk of the document is made up of norms, carefully legislating who will be responsible for the new initiatives, many of which have subsequently developed beyond anything the Council had in mind.[16] One lost opportunity is the Chapter dedicated to the renewal of the celebration of the Divine Office (*SC* 83-101). There is no recognition that the Office is a continuous and cyclic praying of the Sacred Scriptures, reflecting an ancient Jewish practice adopted by Chris-

---

16. For example, concelebration is only permitted for the Masses of Holy Thursday, during councils, synods and bishops' conferences, for the Blessing of an abbot, conventual Mass and at Priests' meetings, regulated by the local Bishop (par 57). Although heavily reworked and rewritten, *Sacrosanctum Concilium* is the only document from the Preparatory Commission, chaired by Cardinal Ottaviani, which survived the first session of the Council. Its schemas on Revelation and on the Church were rejected in November, 1961. Congar, *My Journal of the Council*, 829-30, witnesses his respect for Ottaviani: "Now the laws are being changed. He will have to change his norms. That will be difficult for him, but he will give himself to the new rules, and will see to their observance. There is a certain nobility of the faithful old servant" (recorded on Saturday, 30 October, 1965).

tian monasticism. Instruction on the renewed "Prayer of the Church" bringing the Psalter, the biblical prayer of Israel, into the Church's prayer, would have been helpful to Catholics who have little knowledge of the role of the Psalms in the life of God's people. Instead, attention is focussed upon such matters as the obligation to recite the office (*SC* 95), the need to read from the lives of the Saints (*SC* 97) and the need to recite the Office in Latin (*SC* 101).[17] *Sacrosanctum Concilium* gives more space to the liturgical year (*SC* 102-111), sacred music (*SC* 112-121) and sacred art and furnishings (*SC* 122-129) than to the use of Scripture in the life and Liturgy of the Church.

Nevertheless, coming as the first document to emerge from the Council, *Sacrosanctam Concilium* breathed remarkable fresh air into the Catholic world and its practices. It also brought the Sacred Scriptures to center-stage. Given the centuries-long history of solid resistance to change within the Catholic tradition, it ushered in dramatic developments that irrevocably marked the post-Conciliar Church and changed the face of the liturgical practice of the Roman Church in a way not intended by the majority of the Council Fathers.[18]

Dei Verbum

The Dogmatic Constitution on Divine Revelation was one of the great battlefields of the Council. The final document is an epoch-making statement on the communication that takes place between God and the human condition by means of Scripture and Tradition. This is not the place to rehearse all the debates and difficulties. The Constitution

---

17. Benedict XVI remedies this in his *Post Synodal Apostolic Exhortation* Verbum Domini *of the Holy Father Benedict XVI to the Bishops, Clergy, Consecrated Persons and the Lay Faithful on the Word of God in the Life and Mission of the Church* (Vatican City: Libreria Editrice Vaticana, 2010), 52, 62.
18. This is but one example of the tension within contemporary Catholicism between those who wish to interpret the Council literally, asking for obedience to its "written word" and those who wish to take the "spirit of the Council" further in order to make the Church and its practices more relevant to passing times (see above, and note 2). Those who point to what *Sacrosanctum Concilium* actually "said," claim that many contemporary practices are aberrations neither mentioned nor approved by the Council. This approach legitimates the current return to many pre-Conciliar liturgical practices.

still reflects unresolved tensions.[19] Nevertheless, great progress had taken place in the Conciliar agenda between *Sacrosanctum Concilium* and *Dei Verbum*. The preface to the document states unequivocally that the Council wishes "to set forth the authentic teaching on divine revelation and its transmission. For it wants the whole world to hear its summons to salvation, so that through hearing it may believe, through belief it may hope, through hope it may come to love" (*DV* 1).[20] The intimate link between revelation and the Christian commitment to faith, hope and love is established in a way unheard of in earlier teaching on Revelation.

Throughout the document Scripture and Tradition are intimately linked. Both serve "to make the people of God live their lives in holiness and increase their faith" and "converse with the spouse of his beloved Son" (*DV* 8). The two different sources for revelation are now regarded as one. The theological principal is stated unequivocally in paragraph 9: "Sacred tradition and sacred scripture, then, are bound closely together, and communicate one with the other. Flowing from the same divine well-spring, both of them merge, in a sense, and move towards the same goal." This is a major contribution to the history of Roman Catholic thought.[21] Chapters dealing with Scripture, its inspiration and interpretation (*DV* 11-13), the Old Testament (*DV* 14-16) and the New Testament (*DV* 17-20) follow. The Council follows Pius XII's *Divino Afflante Spiritu* in endorsing the use of critical methods to interpret the Scriptures (*DV* 12), but cautiously insists

---

19. For a description of these conflicts that continued through all four sessions of the Council, see O'Malley, *What Happened*, 144-52, 162, 226-229, 277-280, 291-301. See also, with respect to debates surrounding *Dei Verbum* in the fourth session, Congar, *My Journal of the Council*, 773-828.
20. As with much of the Council's language, this moving expression comes from the Patristic tradition. It is based upon Augustine, *De Catechizandis Rudibus* 4.8 (PL 40, 316).
21. An unresolved tension is found in the words 'both of them merge, in a sense' (Latin original: *in unum quommodo coalescent*). In the light of the differences of opinion (some seeking a restatement of "two sources" and others "one source") the Fathers of the Council wisely decided not to attempt a description of how the two merge into one. This is providential. We are dealing with the divine communication with the human. We do not know *how* this functions, but we are able to state *that* it happens, as in *DV* 9. See further, Joseph Ratzinger, 'The Transmission of Divine Revelation,' in *Commentary on the Documents of Vatican II*, ed. Herbert Vorgrimler, 5 vols. (London: Burns & Oates/Herder & Herder, 1967-69), 3:190-96. See also, *Verbum Domini*, 6-21, esp. 17-19.

on the essential historicity of the Gospels and their apostolic origins (*DV* 18-19).²² It also asks for interpretation of the biblical text in the light of the Fathers of West and East and the Sacred Liturgy (*DV* 23). Correctly, the Council Fathers insist that "no less attention must be devoted to the content and the unity of the whole of scripture, taking into account the tradition of the entire church and the analogy of faith" (*DV* 12).

This teaching of *Dei Verbum* has led many to insist that the Catholic scholar should never push at the boundaries of interpretation, but work only under the guidance of the teaching office of the Church. *Dei Verbum* 10 indicates that this need not always be the case:

> But the task of giving an authentic interpretation of the word of God, whether in its written form or in the form of tradition, has been entrusted to the living teaching office of the Church alone. Its authority in this matter is exercised in the name of Jesus Christ. *The magisterium is not superior to the word of God, but is rather its servant. It teaches only what has been handed on to it.* At the divine command and with the help of the holy Spirit, it listens to this devoutly, guards it reverently and expounds it faithfully.²³

This passage needs careful exegesis and depends a great deal upon the distinction made between "the word of God" and "the Magisterium." The teaching office of the Church has come to be known

---

22. Between the lines one senses a concern with European and USA New Testament scholarship, especially in the immediate post-Bultmannian period of the early 1960's. On these issues, see the careful assessment of Raymond E. Brown, "Historical-Critical Exegesis of the Bible in Roman Catholicism," in *Biblical Exegesis and Church Doctrine* (New York/Mahwah, NJ: Paulist Press, 1985), 10-25, and especially Ormond Rush, *The Eyes of Faith. The Sense of the Faithful and the Church's Reception of Revelation* (Washington, DC: The Catholic University of America Press, 2009), 116-52.
23. Italics mine. Conciliar tensions hide behind this affirmation. No one has explained them better than Joseph Ratzinger, "Sacred Scripture in the Life of the Church," in Vorgrimler, ed., *Commentary on the Documents of Vatican II*, 3:268: "A reference to the ecclesial nature of exegesis, on the one hand, and to its methodological correctness on the other, again expresses the inner tension of church exegesis, which can no longer be removed, *but must be simply accepted as tension.*" Italics mine. For a somewhat different approach, see *Verbum Domini*, 29-49. See also Rush, *The Eyes of Faith*, 261-68.

(relatively recently) as the Magisterium. It is important to understand that what is said in *Dei Verbum* 10 does not disrupt the unity that exists between the word of God and the Scriptures in paragraph 9. The Magisterium is a *third element*: the interpretative ministry of the Church's leadership, "exercised in the name of Jesus Christ." This is evident in the structure of *Dei Verbum* itself when it deals with the issue of the transmission of revelation. It first presents Scripture (*DV* 7), then the dual role of Tradition in forming Scripture and handing it on (*DV* 8), followed by the union between Scripture and Tradition in a Revelation that flows "from the same divine wellspring" (*DV* 9). Finally, *Dei Verbum* 10 explains the role of the Magisterium: listening humbly to the word of God that comes to it in *both* Scripture and Tradition (*DV* 7-9). The Magisterium is *not* Revelation, but humbly serves God's self-revelation.

The Council Fathers dedicated the final chapter of *Dei Verbum* to "Sacred Scripture in the Life of the Church" (*DV* 21-26). This section of the document opens with one of the most memorable statements from Vatican II: 'The Church has always venerated the divine Scriptures as it has venerated the Body of the Lord, in that it never ceases, above all in the sacred liturgy, to partake of the bread of life and to offer it to the faithful from the table of the word of God word and the Body of Christ" (*DV* 21). The parallel between the reception of the Eucharist and the reception of God's word from the same table strikes the Catholic mind and heart forcibly. There may have been a time when the Scriptures and the Eucharist have been equally "venerated," but it was not the case in the pre-Conciliar Church. *Dei Verbum* asked that a series of initiatives and practices to be put in place to see that the Scriptures be restored to their place of veneration, side by side with traditional Catholic veneration of the Eucharist.

- Provide access to the biblical text through accurate and correct translations (*DV* 22).
- Come to a deeper understanding of the Scriptures by reading them in the light of the Patristic interpretations and the Liturgy (*DV* 23).
- Make the Scriptures a source for theological reflection, and not just a tool: "The study of the sacred page is, as it were, the soul of sacred theology" (*DV* 24).

- Form all clergy in an adequate understanding of the Scriptures to enrich their preaching and pastoral ministry (*DV* 25a).
- Commission the Bishops to ensure that these norms are put into place (*DV* 25b).

This rich section of *Dei Verbum* closes in *DV* 26 in a way that parallels its opening: "Just as from constant attendance at the eucharistic mystery the life of the church draws increase, a new impulse of spiritual life may be expected from an increased veneration of the word of God, which 'stands forever' (Is. 40:8; see 1 Peter 1:23-25)."[24]

The long process of gestation that ran from the Council's beginnings in 1962 till its closing moments in 1965 enabled the Fathers of the Council to come to a greater awareness of the centrality of the Sacred Scriptures, and to repeat the words of Saint Jerome: "Ignorance of the scriptures is ignorance of Christ."[25] Their hope was that this Conciliar document, assisted by the liturgical renewal initiated by *Sacrosanctum Concilium*, would set in motion a renewal of Catholic focus on the word of God.

Reception and Implementation

We may be too close to Vatican II to record its lasting fruits, and doubtless different parts of the Catholic world have responded differently. The South American, Asian, and African Churches appear to be healthier than the traditionally powerful and wealthy Churches of the West. I am only able to record my own personal experiences, gained from my life in the Catholic Church on two continents, my native Australia, and in the USA, where I taught from 1999-2005 at the Catholic University of America, Washington, DC. However, on this limited basis, keenly aware of those limitations, some impressions can be shared. We must also be aware, especially in these exciting times, under the prophetic leadership of Pope Francis, that fifty

---

24. In *Verbum Domini*, 56, Benedict XVI cites the striking words of Saint Jerome: "When we approach the Mystery, if a crumb falls to the ground we are troubled. Yet when we are listening to the word of God, and God's word and Christ's flesh are being poured into our ears we pay no heed" (Jerome, *In Psalmum*: CCL 78.337-338).
25. Cited in paragraph 25, from the Prologue to Jerome's *Commentary on Isaiah* (PL 24.17).

years from now the following observations may show themselves to be provisional, and only passing. Fifty years is a short period of time in the Church's story!

Practising Catholics in the USA and in the Australian Catholic Church have not been significantly proactive in the biblical and liturgical renewal.[26] Pre-Conciliar American and Australian Catholics were loyal to their Parish, their Priests, and unquestioningly accepted the decisions of their Bishops, not to mention an infallible Pope.[27] Not much was expected of Vatican II. After the first session a senior Australian Bishop (Bishop Muldoon of Sydney) announced that nothing had changed and nothing would change. As we have seen, this assessment was challenged by the publication of *Sacrosanctum Concilium* at the end of the second session.

The Council's document on the Liturgy was fundamental in developing a deep interest in the role of the word of God in the life and practice of the Church. The gradual introduction of English into the celebration of Eucharist and the Sacraments, and especially the eventual production of the post-Conciliar Lectionary, stirred the minds and imaginations of many. The first twenty years after the Council were marked by great excitement, and a growth of interest in the Scriptures. Practising Catholics began to hear, for the first time, from the historical, wisdom and legislative texts of the Old Testament. Who were the Prophets? When did they live and what was their role in the life and faith of Israel? How come there are four Gospels? What is the difference between Matthew, Mark, Luke and John? Who was

---

26. This is not to say that the Australian, and especially the United States Catholic Churches, have not produced outstanding Catholic biblical and theological leaders. Some preceded the work of the Council, and played a role there, and much of it flourished in the post-conciliar period. In biblical scholarship, the names of the Canadians, David Stanley and Roderick McKenzie, and the Americans, Raymond Brown, Joseph Fitzmyer, and Roland Murphy come immediately to mind.
27. There were some impressive "alternative voices" in the USA. One thinks, for example, of Dorothy Day (1897-1980) and *The Catholic Worker* group. However prophetic she and the movement may have been, they did not "shape" American Catholicism in the pre-Conciliar period. Her nemesis, Cardinal Spellman (1889-1967) did that more effectively in his period of ecclesiastical leadership as the Cardinal-Archbishop of New York (1939-1967). On the Australian Church, see John N. Molony, *The Roman Mould of the Australian Church* (Carlton: Melbourne University Press, 1967).

Paul? Why is he so important? By the time *Dei Verbum* was promulgated in late 1965 these questions were emerging. The idea that "going to Mass" was now a privileged moment when the Church "receives and offers to the faithful the bread of life from the table both of God's word and Christ's body" (*DV* 21) led to an enthusiastic and excited response from the bulk of practising Catholics. It must be noted that such novelties were – at all times, as at the Council itself - strongly rejected by a small but vociferous minority.

These early days led to a number of important initiatives from the Bishops, the leaders of Religious Congregations, and many lay groups. The biblical education provided by the seminaries was entirely reviewed. This was supported by groups of Catholic Religious leaders, supported by the Bishops, to unite what had previously been very small "houses of formation" into a single (originally) Catholic theological institution, drawing rich resources from across the earlier independent bodies. The Chicago Theological Union, the Washington Theological Union, and Catholic participation in the Graduate Theological Union in Berkeley had their beginnings in these days, and very quickly introduced important ecumenical relationships into biblical and theological education. Over the 1960's and 1970's the academic formation of a number of Catholic scholars in the best European and American universities reached a peak, and a number of internationally significant North American and Australian Catholic biblical scholars emerged.[28]

In Australia, Religious Congregations also gathered to form the Yarra Theological Union, largely based upon the structure and curriculum of the Chicago Theological Union. A smaller Catholic union, the association of a smaller group of Religious with local seminarians, directly dependent upon the Bishops was founded in Melbourne: Catholic Theological College. As in the USA and Canada, the

---

28. The names and numbers of such scholars from Canada and the United states are impressive. Their dominance of the 1990 publication of Raymond E. Brown, Joseph A. Fitzmyer and Roland E. Murphy, *The New Jerome Biblical Commentary* (Englewood Cliffs: Prentice Hall, 1990) is a good indication of their preparation and skill. Sixty-eight of the seventy-four contributors to this volume were from the USA or Canada. Of the remaining six, four were Australians: Antony F. Campbell, SJ, Brendan Byrne, SJ, William J. Dalton, SJ and Francis J. Moloney, SDB. The remaining non-North Americans were Jerome Murphy-O'Connor, OP, of the *École biblique et Archéologique de Jérusalem*, Israel, and Frans Neirynck, of the Catholic University of Leuven, Belgium.

ecumenical association of these theological institutions with larger formerly Protestant academic degree-giving bodies, such as the Melbourne College of Divinity, first founded in 1910, and the newer ecumenical centres founded for similar purposes (Brisbane College of Divinity, Sydney College of Divinity, Adelaide College of Divinity) were a further challenge to excellence. The Protestant Churches relied heavily on the expert and passionate use of the Scriptures in their life and practice. This "rubbed off" onto their new Catholic partners.

The increasing expertise spilled out to the people and to the ongoing formation of Bishops and Priests. Bishops, Religious and lay groups invited significant international biblical scholars to run seminars that were heavily attended. The Religious Education curricula were rewritten in almost every Diocese, focussing more intensely on the Scriptures. Many lay groups sprang up, from small Bible groups in the Parishes, looking ahead to the Lectionary readings of the following Sunday, to larger groups that followed biblical study programmes like the *Little Rock* program. Those who had received formal training were in great demand, and gave of themselves generously to gatherings of Bishops, Priests, Religious, educators, and people from all parts of the country. Well-informed popular commentaries were provided by the scholars in Parish newsletters, and a number of books were published to guide both Priests and people through the Lectionary.[29] It was not all plain sailing. Some Catholics objected to this Protestant-like enthusiasm for the Scriptures that shifted doctrine from centre-stage, and groups sprang up to oppose the renewal of Religious Education in the schools.[30]

The initial fervour has run into hard times, as Christian practice has run into hard times in the developed world. It is difficult to pinpoint just when and where this enthusiasm ran out of steam. It was not a dramatic process, but the result of gradual cultural change that has touched all aspects of life in the developed world. However out-

---

29. Although not alone, outstanding in this respect has been the long commitment to supporting liturgical and biblical reform by The Liturgical Press in Collegeville, Minnesota, associated with the St John's Benedictine community and University.
30. As one example, during a lecture I was giving to a broad public audience on a Gospel portrait of Mary, a group gathered at the back of the lecture theatre and recited the rosary out loud throughout the course of the lecture. They represented a Melbourne group called "Catholics united for the faith" (CUFF). Similar groups have emerged in both the United States and Canada.

standing the intellectual giftedness and holiness of Pope John Paul II (1978-2005) and Pope Benedict XVI (2005-2013), Church leadership encouraged a slowing down of enthusiasm and a strong focus upon decisions and directions determined by the Holy Father and other Vatican authorities. The startling newness that has accompanied the administration of Pope Francis is clear evidence of that historical reality. It must be said that for thirty-five years attention shifted from the renewal initiated by Vatican II, to a leadership more attentive to a central authority, accompanied by ritual correctness. The singular most obvious sign of this return to "centralisation" was the imposition of a new translation of the English Mass, more faithful to the Latin, upon all English speaking Catholic communities in the world.[31] The inappropriateness of this clumsy, and sometimes despairingly opaque, translation is universally recognized.

The Lectionary is under review, as Priests and people find the readings too long, and without apparent internal logic. This could be a good opportunity for a resumption of some of the principles enunciated by *Sacrosanctum Concilium* and *Dei Verbum*, but the signs of the more broadly based biblical renewal requested by the Council (see *DV* 25) are lacking. National and local seminars devoted to biblical questions have all but come to an end, and regular exchange of international biblical scholars is waning. Among some that have come to Australia, a few have been banned from speaking in various Dioceses.

The lay-directed biblical centres still operating are prone to use Evangelical texts and practices for their seminars, meetings and publications. In Australia, the scholars trained in the 1960's and 1970's, now in their seventies, are still required to do their best, but their energies are diminishing. The situation is better in the United States and Canada, where many Universities run major research centres and doctoral programs in Biblical Studies. However, even with these rich resources, in my years in the Biblical Studies Department at the Catholic University of America, the majority of the students came from Protestant backgrounds. The presence of Priests and Religious was minimal. I suspect that that the dramatic shortage of candidates

---

31. The *Editio Typica* was approved by the Congregation for Divine Worship and Sacraments on 27 June, 2010, and the publication of the Roman Missal approved on 25 March, 2011. Episcopal Conferences in the various English-speaking regions determined the exact date of its implementation. In Australia, it took make on the First Sunday of Advent, 2011.

for the Priesthood and the Religious life is a major reason for this phenomenon.

This is certainly the case in Australia. We experience an almost complete absence of young Priests and Religious doing further studies and research in biblical studies. There is a small trickle of well-prepared Catholic lay people, trained overseas and now in the Faculty of Theology and Philosophy at Australian Catholic University, the University of Divinity and other theological schools. But it is difficult to find employment in traditional seminaries and theological institutions that do not have the funds to pay a professional salary to a lay person with a family, or to support post-doctoral research programs. Finding an academic position once one has a qualification is almost impossible in Australia, and increasingly difficult in North America.

The challenge of placing the Scriptures at the heart of the life of the Church articulated in *Sacrosanctum Concilium* and *Dei Verbum* was the fruit of considerable conflict at the Council. Now, almost fifty years after the Council began, strange forces are at play within the Catholic community. Conflict is again in place, as at the Council. The group described as 'minority,' whose agenda was regularly defeated at the Council, have had a firm hand on the helm of the Catholic Church at most levels of governance for thirty-five years. It will take time and courageous leadership to change this direction, and perhaps Pope Francis and his successors will provide it. An Ecumenical Council is the highest level of the Church's magisterium, and must not be ignored.

Two significant publications from the Holy See show that the Council's teaching on the centrality of the Scriptures in the life of the Church has not been received and implemented. The first of these is the 1993 document of the Pontifical Biblical Commission, *The Interpretation of the Bible in the Church*.[32] Secondly, Benedict XVI entrusted the 2008 Synod of Bishops with the theme: *The Word of God in the Life and Mission of the Church*. He subsequently released his fine post-Synodal Exhortation, *Verbum Domini*.[33] Both of these documents, very different in scope and content, respond to the

---

32. Pontifical Biblical Commission, *The Interpretation of the Bible in the Church* (Rome: Editrice Vaticana, 1993).
33. See above, n. 17.

request of the agenda initiated by *Dei Vebum* 21-26.[34] The *need* for Benedict XVI to state his aim "to point out fundamental approaches to a rediscovery of God's word in the life of the Church as a wellspring of constant renewal" (*Verbum Domini*, 1) indicates that, more than fifty years after the promulgation of *Sacrosanctum Concilium*, this rediscovery and renewal is yet to be achieved.

Recent Catholic leadership has strongly urged a return to ritual and mystery, an insistence on unified dress, often asking for the ornate rather than the practical, unified words and actions, ignoring the requests of Episcopal Conferences for inculturated Eucharistic celebrations, and so forth. The same leadership responds to conflicts that emerge in an increasingly complex world with sometimes highhanded and poorly motivated magisterial pronouncements. This is happening while the practising Catholic population is dwindling dramatically. It is claimed that the largest Christian denomination in the United States is made up of former Catholics.[35] In a recently-conducted Survey of Religious Institutes in Australia, it has been calculated that 6,000 young baptised Catholics reject Catholicism every year.[36]

---

34. The document from the Biblical Commission offers expert instruction on the various ways in which the biblical text can be interpreted, and applied to life in the Church. *Verbum Domini* is a lengthy theological/patristic/spiritual and pastoral application, worked out as a protracted application of John 1:1-18 (see *Verbum Domini*, 5), to the word of God itself (*Verbum Dei*), the Word in the Church (*Verbum in Ecclesia*) and the Word in the World (*Verbum Mundo*). The sections that deal explicitly with Scripture in the life of the Church (pars 72-89 ["The Word of God in the Life of the Church"], pars 90-124 ["*Verbum Mundo*"]) are challenging, but out of the reach of most contemporary Catholic and even many contemporary Priests and Bishops, for a number of reasons.
35. In an article in *National Catholic Reporter* (April 18, 2011), Thomas Reese reports the conclusions of recent research indicating that one third of USA Catholics have left the Church and that one out of every ten Americans is an ex-Catholic. Many of them have gone to Protestant Churches. The research shows that the reasons for this shift in allegiance are "spiritual sustenance, worship services and the Bible" (http://ncronline.org, 4).
36. Stephen Reid, Robert Dixon and Noel Connolly, *Catholic Religious Institutes in Australia. A Report on the 2009 survey of Religious Institutes in Australia* (Fitzroy/Annandale: Pastoral Projects Office/Catholic Religious of Australia, 2010), 44. For some reflections on the cultural shifts that have generated this situation, among both young and the not-so-young, see Moloney, "The Word in the World," on pp. 349-69 of this volume.

One could suggest that, despite all the hopes of the Council Fathers and an initial exciting reception and implementation of the teaching of Vatican II on Scripture, a long-term, co-ordinated and committed engagement of the Catholic Church with the word of God, is either not happening, or has not borne fruit. Perhaps the initiative of Benedict XVI's *Verbum Domini* may elicit a response. It has been strongly supported by Pope Francis' lengthy treatment of the word of God and the homily in the life of the Church in *Evangelii Gaudium* 110-174.[37] However, I suspect Bishops, Priests, Religious and active Catholics are worried by matters they consider more urgent for the ongoing life of the Church than the Scriptures.[38] But we must not give up hope. As I wrote above, 50 years is a short time in the history of the Catholic Church. Like the great Council of Trent, which took centuries to generate the Church dreamt of by those Catholic leaders who had to grapple with the shock of the Protestant Reform, so will it also be with the great Vatican Council II.

Conclusion

For the moment, perhaps the word of God must be "caught not taught."[39] All four Gospels, and the Pauline tradition, *tell the story of Jesus*, albeit in their different ways. A return to the Gospel is a good place to start reading Jesus' story, but *reading* is not enough. Without too much fear of contradiction, it can be claimed that the radical living of Gospel values has *never* been practised by the great Churches.[40] Measured according to this standard, we have failed as followers of Jesus: "For the Son of Man also came not to be served but to serve, and to give his life as a ransom for many" (Mark 10:45).[41]

---

37. Pope Francis, *Evangelii Gaudium. Apostolic Exhortation on the Proclamation of the Gospel in Today's World* (Vatican City: Libreria Editrice Vaticana, 2013).
38. Would that the energy and financial resources dedicated to the horror of the clerical abuse of minors be also devoted to re-establishing the word of God at the heart of the life and practice of the Church.
39. For much of what follows, see Moloney, "The Word in the World," on pp. 349-69 of this volume.
40. The never-ending debate whether the Sermon on the Mount (Matt 5:1-7:27) is a way of life, something unachievable but to be strived after, or an impossible dream, could be extended to all the Gospels.
41. Vincent Taylor, *The Gospel According to St. Mark*, 2nd ed. (London: Macmillan, 1966), 444, claims that "This saying is one of the most important in the Gospels."

It is his story that gave birth to the Christian tradition, and the ongoing telling of the Scriptural story is essential to the ongoing life and relevance of that tradition. As Yann Martel wrote in *Beatrice and Virgil*: "Stories – individual stories, family stories, national stories – are what stitch together the disparate elements of human existence into a coherent whole. We are story animals."[42] Mystery and ritual have their place, they are central to the *internal* ongoing life and practice of the Church. To tell Jesus' story effectively, more is called for. We must "put on Christ" (Gal 3:27) or, as the author of 1 John would put it, "walk in the same way in which he walked" (1 John 2:6). Paul inserts a hymn into his letter to the Philippians, most likely used by the Philippians themselves in their liturgies. He uses the hymn to instruct them on what it means to "have this mind among yourselves, which is yours in Christ Jesus," telling of Jesus' loving self-gift in Philippians 2:5-11.[43] The Christians in Philippi are asked to put their lives where their words are. Once this process, the driving agenda of Pope Francis, is firmly in place *within* the Catholic Church, then the creative and life-giving power of the word of God will be visible to those *outside the Church*.

Regular practice of the Catholic faith is waning in the Western world. Some are pinning their hopes upon what is called "the Francis effect," claiming that the present papacy is drawing former Catholics back to the Church, and generating interest in the Church from non-Catholics. I regard this as a "passing fad," as (despite some signs of hope) major leaders in the Catholic hierarchy continue a winning battle *against* Francis' agenda. Two crucial figures, the Cardinal Prefect of the Congregation for the Doctrine and the Faith (Cardinal Gerhard Müller) and the Cardinal Prefect of the Congregation for Divine Worship and Sacraments (Cardinal Robert Sarah) are outstanding in this. The former, an appointment of Benedict XVI, was confirmed by Francis and the latter Francis' appointment. In two crucial areas that touch upon the daily life of the Catholic Church these two men continue to lead the Church in ways that reject Francis' agenda. They devote little or no attention to the sensitivities of the Church at large. Conservative

---

42. Yann Martel, *Beatrice and Virgil* (Edinburgh: Canongate Books, 2010), 7.
43. The same rhetorical strategy is adopted by Paul when he inserts his tradition of Jesus' final meal with his disciples (1 Cor 11:23-25) into his critique of the selfish practices of the Corinthian community. They are exhorted to "live" what they "celebrate" (see esp. v. 26). On this, see Francis J. Moloney, *A Body Broken for a Broken People. Divorce, Remarriage, and the Eucharist* (New York/Mahwah: Paulist Press, 2016), 41-69.

Bishops continue to be appointed all over the world.[44] The prophetic gestures of Francis are stimulating, but the day-to-day administration of the Catholic Church shows little interest in "the Francis effect."

As this is the reality we must face, I suggest that the word of God should not primarily be a spoken word, but something that is *seen and experienced* in the way we live and love, inspired by our being nourished at the one table of the word of God and the body and blood of Christ (*DV* 21, 26). We cannot be Catholics unless we preach the Gospel at all times (see 1 Cor 9:16; Rom 1:14; 2 Tim 4:2), but we are struggling to make that Word live in a world that those who constructed Vatican II never imagined possible. There is a serious disjuncture between Catholicism of the 1960's and that of the early Third Millennium that we must recognise. An important contribution of Vatican II to the Catholic Church of the late 1960's was *The Church in the Modern World* (*Gaudium et Spes*).[45] But that document addressed the world of the 1960's. We now face the dilemma of "the Church in the post-modern world" of the third Millennium. Is it possible that we might bring Scripture back into the life and practice of the Church by "telling the story" of Jesus better in our preaching, in our behaviour, in our commitment to our earth, and to education that is "sourced by the Gospel"?[46] We might thus better reflect the presence of Christ in the life and practice of our Catholic Church.[47] It was the dream of the Fathers of Vatican II, and it is time we returned to the dream.

---

44. Among a number of instances, I refer to Cardinal Müller's strong resistance to the challenge of the Encyclical *Amoris Laetitia*, especially around the question of the divorced and the remarried, and Cardinal Sarah's recent request (July, 2016), that all Priests return to the celebration of Mass *ad orientem* (i.e., back to the people). Readers will recall Cardinal Sarah's rejection of Francis' instruction that the feet of women could be washed at the foot-washing on Holy Thursday. The appointment of Bishops is more difficult. The Prefect of the Congregation of Bishops (Cardinal Marc Ouellet) is a well-known conservative, determined to maintain the *status quo*, even though he has now been joined by Archbishop Blaise Cupich. The latter will be one among many, including such powerful ultra-conservative figures as Cardinal George Pell, on the Congregation for Bishops.
45. Promulgated on 7 December, 1965.
46. In this, Pope Francis, *Encyclical Letter* Laudato Si' *of the Holy Father Francis on Care for Our Common Home* (Vatican City: Libreria Editrice Vaticana, 2015), leads the way.
47. *Catechism of the Catholic Church* (Homebush: St Paul Publications, 1994), 752, looking back to *Dei Verbum*, 21, 26, describes the Church: 'She draws her life from the word and body of Christ and so herself becomes Christ's body.' I would add 'and so herself becomes Christ's word.'

13
The Gospel of Creation
A Biblical Response to *Laudato Si'*

Pope Francis' *Laudato Si'* is driven by the conviction that creation is "good news," and thus "gospel."[1] Only the first (paras. 65-75) and final (paras. 96-100) sections of Chapter Two focus directly upon the Word of God.[2] It is not my task to review the ecological science

---

1. All references to the text of the Encyclical will follow the paragraph numbers in Pope Francis, *Encyclical Letter* Laudato Si' *of the Holy Father Francis on Care for our Common Home* (Vatican City: Editrice Vaticana, 2015). For an attractive study of the potential intimate link between the environment and Christian faith and experience, see Denis Edwards, *Ecology at the Heart of Faith* (Maryknoll, NY: Orbis Books, 2006).
2. I indicate, in the name of my professional guild, examples of traditional defects in the pontifical use of the Scriptures that continue in *Laudato Si'*. No doubt experts were consulted, and the majority of associations between the argument of the Encyclical and the use of the biblical text are appropriate. Some are "appropriations" that call for some imagination, but that is acceptable in a document like *Laudato Si'*. However, there are places where one would expect better, given the high quality of contemporary Catholic biblical scholarship. When referring to words of Jesus from the Synoptic tradition, the Matthean text is invariably used (see, for example, the use of Matthew 20:25-26 in paragraph 82; Matthew 13:31-32 in paragraph 97, and Matthew 8:27 in paragraph 98). It is almost universally accepted that Matthew (written in the late 80's CE) is dependent upon Mark (written about 70 CE). The Markan text should be used (in this case, Mark 10:42-43; 4:30-32, and 4:41, respectively). See the clear summary of this widely accepted position in John S. Kloppenborg, *Q, the Earliest Gospel: An Introduction to the Original Stories and Sayings of Jesus* (Louisville: Westminster John Knox, 2008), 1-40. More serious is the uncritical application of the "woman clothed with the sun" of Revelation 12:1 to Mary as "the Mother and Queen of all creation" (*Laudato Si'*, 241). The image has many possible interpretations, from the original state of sinless humanity to a figure for the Church. But it does *not* refer to Mary of Nazareth. For a survey and critical evaluation of the suggestions made over the centuries, see Charles Brütsch, *La Clarté de l'Apocalypse*, 5th ed.

that lies behind the Holy Father's explicit use of the biblical text, or the many occasional references scattered throughout the Encyclical. However, as a professional Catholic biblical scholar, it is a relief to have Pontifical support to abandon once and for all a fundamentalist "seven days of creation" view (see, for example, *Laudato Si'*, 2 and 9).[3]

The Use of the Bible in Laudato Si'

The papal use of biblical texts and traditions in the Encyclical is easily traced in the document, especially paragraphs 65-97 and 96-100. What follows will offer a sketch of that material, but its main focus – in a second and more novel fashion - is to raise a question in response to *Laudato Si'* asking if, despite the abundance of biblical reference, more could and should be said.

The Wisdom of the Biblical Accounts (Laudato Si', 65-97)

In dialogue with contemporary biblical scholarship, *Laudato Si'* insists that Genesis 1:1-2:4a and 2:4b-3:24, ancient stories eventually shaped to form part of Israel's Sacred Scriptures, communicate *profound*

(Geneva: Labor et Fides, 1966), 199-203. More broadly, see Bruce Chilton, *Visions of the Apocalypse. Receptions of John's Revelation in Western Imagination* (Waco, TX: Baylor University Press, 2013). On Rev 12:1, see pp. 105, 115, 144. This response will later deal extensively with the Book of Revelation. The Encyclical cites it on only two further occasions: in paragraph 74 (Rev 15:3, again wrongly, in my estimation [see below, n. 21]), and in paragraph 243 (Rev 21:5). For a study of the problem of the serious lack of biblical awareness in the Catholic tradition despite more than a century from the Church's leadership (from Leo XIII's *Providentissumus Deus* [1893] to Benedict XVI's *Post-Synodal Exhortation Verbum Domini* [2010]), see Francis J. Moloney, *Reading the New Testament in the Church. A Primer for Pastors, Religious Educators, and Believers* (Grand Rapids: Baker Academic, 2015), 1-21, 191-201.

3. The association of the Magisterium of the Catholic Church with the contemporary sciences of evolution and ecology did not begin with Pope Francis' *Laudato Si'*. It can be traced back to Pius XII's *Humani Generis*, and was strongly present in the teaching of John Paul II and Benedict XVI. See *Laudato Si'*, 3-6, and the more wide-ranging surveys of Denis Edwards, *Jesus and the Natural World. Exploring a Christian Approach to Ecology* (Melbourne: Garratt, 2012), 71-77; Idem, *Partaking of God. Trinity, Evolution, and Ecology* (Collegeville, MN: The Liturgical Press, 2014), 121-24. See also Pope Benedict XVI, *The Environment*, ed. Jacqueline Lindsey (Huntington, IN: Our Sunday Visitor, 2012).

religious truth (*Laudato Si'*, 65, 66, 67, 70, 71). The story-tellers told of relationships "with God, with our neighbour and with the earth itself" (*Laudato Si'*, 66).[4] At the apex of God's creative activity, human beings, male and female, are made in the image of God (1:26-27). According to the Bible, humans are interpersonal creatures,[5] including personal relationship with the living God. "Humans are created in such a way that their very existence is intended to be their relationship with God."[6] Dominion over other creatures (v. 28) does not justify ecological destruction. Human beings, made in the image of God, are asked to cooperate with the creator, ensuring that the whole world be "good" (*tōb*), that the natural world, despite its challenges, be the good creation that God made it to be "in the beginning" (1:1).[7] This view is made very clear in the Eden story, where God takes the newly created human (*'adam*) into the Garden of Eden in order "to till and keep it." The Hebrew word we translate as "till" (*'abad*) has the basic meaning of "serve" (see *Laudato Si'*, 66-67, 124). God's final rest, on the seventh day, aetiologically rooted in the Jewish practice of Sabbath, is a sign of God's covenant blessing (*Laudato Si'*, 71).[8] God is present to *everything* as its source, and its ongoing existence (*Laudato Si'*, 12, 68, 69, 72, 77, 94, 124).[9] Nothing is imperfect before God, as

---

4. For more on what follows, see Edwards, *Jesus and the Natural World*, 10-15.
5. Claus Westermann, *Genesis. A Commentary*, trans John J. Scullion, 3 vols. (Minneapolis: Augsburg, 1984-1986), 1:156-57, points out that the "singularity" of the creation of man and woman is influenced by the origins of this saying. It "had its origin in an independent narrative about the creation of human beings which in its present form has been completely integrated into a narrative about the creation of the world." Once in its new context, it must be interpreted within that context.
6. Claus Westermann, *Genesis*, 1:158.
7. The Hebrew word *tōb*, is translated regularly (especially in Genesis 1:1-2:4), as "good." This is correct, but it carries with it a further meaning: what is described as "good" is exactly as God created it to me. On this, see Brendan Byrne, *Inheriting the Earth. The Pauline basis of a spirituality for our time* (Homebush: St Paul Publications, 1990), 14-19.
8. The word "aetiology" describes a narrative that looks back from an existing practice or experience, in this case, the practice of Sabbath within Israelite religion, and explains its "origins" in its mythic past. As a "myth," one cannot trace its historical origins, but one finds there the theological and religious significance of the *current* celebration.
9. A glance at these indications in *Laudato Si'* shows a use of important themes in Israel's Wisdom traditions (see Wisdom 6:7; 11:24; 13:5 [Romans 1:20], Proverbs 22:2; Ben Sirach 38:34; Psalms 104, 136, 148).

everything is "good" (*Laudato Si'*, 65). Humans have a "caring" role of their fellow creatures in the community of God's creation. Male and female are the basis of the social nature of the human person; human sexuality is "good," and women are equal before God.[10] God's rest on the Sabbath is aetiologically rooted in the Jewish practice of Sabbath, but it is more: a sign of God's covenant blessing, and an invitation to take time for rest, for celebration, for joy in family, friends and community life (see *Laudato Si'*, 71).[11]

Genesis unfolds into insights on human sin, rooted in disobedience to the word of God, bringing alienation from God, tensions between man and woman, violence among human beings, and from the natural world, including the animals which become hostile, and the earth which must be dug with the sweat of one's brow (3:1-24) (*Laudato Si'*, 70-71). Pope Francis draws a number of interesting reflections from the ambiguous narratives of sin and grace that fill Genesis 4-11 to indicate that God never withdrew his promise of salvation. In the midst of the wickedness that covered all the earth (see Genesis 6:5), the just man Noah emerges. Through him, "God decided to open a path to salvation. ... All it takes is one good person to restore hope!" (*Laudato Si'*, 71. See Gen 8:20-9:17).

Francis' optimism is pervasive. After the account of the Tower of Babel in Genesis 11, we come to learn more of the enduring promise of salvation from God. As human beings scatter across the face of the earth, divided by their languages (Gen 11:1-9), God calls Abraham, in whom all nations will be blessed (12:1-3; 22:15-18; 28:14 [promise renewed to Jacob]). A long biblical history begins in which human beings bear responsibility before God to respect and care for the integrity of other creatures. We have "our place" in God's creation, and it is not one of "dominion" (*Laudato Si'*, 67, 67, 68).[12]

The Holy Father uses biblical traditions to insist that humans are part of a community: e.g., Proverbs 3:19; Psalms 104 and 148; Isaiah

---

10. This is another important aetiological narrative (see above, n. 8) that retains its crucial importance for contemporary society and culture.
11. *Laudato Si'*, 71, develops this theme of rest very well. Pope Francis not only uses the narrative texts from Genesis (Gen 2:2-3) and Exodus (Exod 16:23; 23:10), but also turns to the legislation of the Sabbath rest found in Leviticus (see Lev 19:9-10; 25:1-4, 4-6, 10).
12. As Pope Francis closes the Encyclical, he prays: "God of love, show us our place in this world as channels of your love for all the creatures of this earth."

40:28b-29 (*Laudato Si'*, 68, 69, 72, 73).[13] The Word of God communicates these truths directly to human beings, made in the image of God. Human beings, able to enter into communion with God, are called by these biblical passages to rejoice with God in the whole world of creation, *of which we are members and not masters*. This is to think biblically, to see ourselves in the community of creation. It calls for conversion, away from anthropocentric and exploitive attitudes, towards profound respect for the integrity of our fellow creatures before God.[14]

The gaze of Jesus (Laudato Si', 96-100)

Surprisingly, the Holy Father largely limits his New Testament reflections to the experience of Jesus, his awareness of God as his Father, and the father of all (*Laudato Si'*, 96), shaped by the world in which he grew up and ministered, using images from the world that surrounded him and his audience (*Laudato Si'*, 96-97). He refers to Jesus' experience of the world of human labour (*Laudato Si'*, 98).[15] More could be taken from the Gospels. For example, as Mark tells briefly of Jesus' encounter with Satan at the beginning of his ministry (Mark 1:12-13), once Satan is overcome, Jesus, in the desert, "was with the wild beasts, and the angels ministered to him" (v. 13). When read as an allusion to the Roman persecution of the Markan Christians, this interpretation misses an important element of Mark's message. Having overcome Satan, the situation of Eden is re-established, eliminating the animosity of the wild beasts generated by the presence of sin when it first entered the world (see Gen 3:14). The idyllic perfection of human oneness with the wild beast, dreamt of in the messianic passage of Isaiah 11:1-9 (when the wolf dwells with the lamb, and the child plays over the hole of the asp), is restored. An early Jewish tradition asked what Adam and Eve ate in the Garden. Mark responds:

---

13. One misses reference to the splendid affirmation of God's lordship and the unique relationship he has with creation found in Job 38:1-39:2. On this, see Edwards, *Jesus and the Natural World*, 19-21.
14. See Edwards, *Partaking of God*, 147-82.
15. See also Edwards, *Jesus and the Natural World*, 26-31.

"the angels ministered to him." The advent of Jesus restores creation to the way God made it "at the beginning" (see Mark 1:1; Gen 1:1).[16]

One might also have expected more on the great texts from New Testament that link the pre-existent Logos, Lord, and Christ with creation. Colossians 1:16, 19-20 and John 1:1-18 are briefly mentioned (*Laudato Si'*, 99-100). Paul's eloquent reference to the yearning and the birth pangs of the whole of creation, including the baptized, of Romans 8:18-25 (side-by-side with Genesis 2:7) is cited in paragraph 2. The Holy Father draws attention to "[t]his is why the earth herself, burdened and laid waste, is the most abandoned and maltreated of our poor; she 'groans in travail'" (Rom 8:22). Paul no doubt had another purpose in mind when he wrote those words, but it "works" for Pope Francis. As the title of this section of the Encyclical ("The gaze of Jesus") indicates, the Holy Father wishes to focus his attention upon Jesus of Nazareth.[17] He insists that "[t]he very flowers of the field and the birds which his human eyes contemplated and admired are now imbued with his radiant presence" (*Laudato Si'*, 100). The great cosmological texts from the Christian biblical tradition are less relevant in that setting.[18]

---

16. For the importance of "the desert" in Mark 1:1-13, and the theme of the "new creation" in v. 23, with documentation of the non-biblical Jewish background, see Francis J. Moloney, *The Gospel of Mark. A Commentary* (Grand Rapids: Baker Academic, 2012), 30-32, 39-40. Commenting on another passage of the Gospel of Mark (10:6), Joel Marcus, *Mark*, 2 vols., The Anchor Yale Bible 27-27A (New York/New Haven: Doubleday/Yale University Press, 2000-2009), 2:710, writes: "Jesus and the Markan Christians are people who rejoice in the dawning light of the new age – which is also the recaptured radiance of Eden."
17. A deliberate focus upon the experience of the historical Jesus is indicated by the choice of the term "Jesus," rather than "Christ" in the sub-title.
18. The Papal use of Romans 8:22 is but one example of what I described above in n. 2 as an "appropriation that calls for imagination." The biblical *text* suits the Holy Father's *context* very well, however much it reflects (or does not reflect) what Paul wanted to say when he penned (or dictated: see Rom 16:22) the letter in c. 58 CE. Pope Francis passingly cites passages from John 1:1-18 and Colossians 1:15-20, but what of Philippians 2:5-11, and Ephesians 1:3-5? For further reflections on John 1:1-18 and Romans 8:18-25, see Edwards, *Jesus and the Natural World*, 33-39. Pauline scholars will be disappointed by the absence of reference to the Pauline and post-Pauline tradition. See, for example, Brendan Byrne, "A Pauline Complement to *Laudato Si*," *Theological Studies* 77 (2016): 308-27. Some Johannine scholars, who see creation as an all-pervading theme across the Gospel, a view I do not share, will also be disappointed. See especially, the work of Mary Coloe (e.g., "Creation in the Gospel of John," in *Creation is*

The Lamb that Was Slain "Before the Foundation of the World" (Rev 13:8)

Within this exciting environment generated by Pope Francis' prophetic response to the new cosmology, a further biblical theme from the Book of Revelation calls for attention. This inspired, but puzzling, text from our Christian tradition is the subject of vast erudition, and sometimes unfounded speculation.[19] I take my cue for what follows from the largely ignored interpretation of Eugenio Corsini.[20] For Corsini, John the Seer does not write to encourage late-first century Christians to persevere, or to resist, in the presence of the imperial power, or in the face of persecution. Such lived realities may well

---

Groaning: Biblical and Theological Perspectives, ed. Mary Coloe (Collegeville: The Liturgical Press, 2013], 71-90; "The Garden as a New Creation in John," *The Bible Today* 53 [2015]: 159-64). For my rejection of the popular "seven days of a new creation" in John 1:19-2:12, see Francis J. Moloney, *The Gospel of John*, Sacra Pagina 4 (Collegeville, MN: The Liturgical Press, 1998), 50-63, and my rejection of the "creation-recreation" theme in 18:1-11 and 19:38-42, in *ibid.*, 484, 513.

19. A good indication of this is the massive "selected" bibliography, arranged historically, in Craig A. Koester, *Revelation*, Anchor Yale Bible 38A (New Haven: Yale University Press, 2014), 113-206.

20. My reading of the Book of Revelation is guided by the remarkable, but little known, work of this Italian emeritus Professor of Early Christian Literature at the University of Turin. In brief, the book is not dedicated to the encouragement of persecuted Christians at the end of the first century (although that can also be involved), but a statement and re-statement of the perennial revelation of God's saving activity in the death and resurrection of Jesus "from the foundation of the world." After the decisive heavenly liturgy of Rev 4-5, the conclusion of each "seven" announces the saving event of Jesus' death and resurrection (8:1 [seals]; 11:15-19 [trumpets]; 16:17-22:5 [bowls]). See the English version of his 1980 study (*Apocalisse prima e dopo*) in Eugenio Corsini, *The Apocalypse: The Perennial Revelation of Jesus Christ*, trans. Francis J. Moloney, Good News Studies 5 (Wilmington, DE: Michael Glazier, 1983). See now, Eugenio Corsini, *Apocalisse di Gesù secondo Giovanni* (Torino: Società Editrice, Internazionale, 2002). For a summary of his argument, see Moloney, *Reading the New Testament in the Church*, 180-89. The most exhaustive contemporary commentary on Revelation in English is David E. Aune, *Revelation*, 3 vols.; Word Biblical Commentary 52a-52c (Dallas, TX: Word, 1997-1998). In more than 1300 pages, Aune mentions Corsini twice, in association with his identification of the 144,000 in 7:4-8 (pp. 440, 447). The highly regarded most recent commentary by Koester, *Revelation*, never mentions Corsini's interpretation, not even in the 93 page general bibliography (see above, n. 19), even though it has been available in English since 1983. I acknowledge the support of my colleague Stuart Moran, well-versed in the work of Corsini, for the following reflections.

have formed part of the *Sitz im Leben* that produced the book. But its driving theological motivation is to communicate belief that the saving effects of the crucified and risen Christ have *already* assured victory over the corrupt powers of this world in both the former (pre-Christian) covenant, and in the Christian era.[21] John the Seer articulates this belief by means of carefully arranged statements and re-statements of that fundamental Christian truth through the opening of seven seals, the sounding of seven trumpets, and the pouring out of seven bowls.[22]

The Perennial Relevance of the Death and Resurrection of Jesus

In brief, Corsini sees the book as based upon a series of "sevens." After the introduction (1:1-8), there are letters to seven Churches (Rev 1:9-3:22), seven seals to the scroll (4:1-8:1), and seven trumpets (8:2-11:19). An interlude looks back upon the teaching of the seals and the trumpets (12:1-14:20). The cosmic drama of the pouring out of the seven bowls follows. The bowls are poured out (15:1-16:21), and a long section is dedicated to a description of the effects of the events accompanying the pouring out of the bowls (17:1-22:5). The book closes with an epilogue (22:6-21). Crucially, the scenes and events associated with the opening of the seals, the blowing of the trumpets, and the pouring out of the bowls, each tell of the saving effect of the Lamb, slain and risen before all time. This saving effect is applied initially to the faithful of the period prior to the historical presence of Jesus, the so-called "old economy," and then to the current Christians, reading or hearing the message of this document in the era after Jesus' death and resurrection.

---

21. I thus regard the association of Rev 15:3 with Roman persecution in *Laudato Si'*, 74, as at best questionable. Aune, *Revelation*, and Koester, *Revelation*, are fine examples of an interpretation that asks persecuted Christians to face persecution with faith and hope. Loren L. Johns, *The Lamb Christology of the Apocalypse*, Wissenschaftliche Untersuchungen zum Neuen Testament 2.167 (Tübingen: Mohr Siebeck, 2007), questions this with her fine study of the possibility that the work asks Christians to resist the cult of emperor worship passively.
22. I acknowledge that my attention was drawn to the potential contribution of the biblical image of Revelation's slain and risen Lamb to current theological reflection upon ecological issues by my friend and colleague at Australian Catholic University, Rev. Professor Anthony J. Kelly, C.Ss.R.

Rejecting contemporary commentary, Corsini insists that there is no literary and theological tension building up across the various visionary experiences, waiting for a final "end time" intervention in the pouring out of the final bowl and its aftermath. On the contrary, each "seven" repeats the story of the saving effect of the Lamb from a different perspective and with varying intensity. The conclusion of each "seven" announces the saving event of Jesus' death and resurrection.

- In 8:1, at the opening of the seventh seal: "there was silence in heaven for about half an hour," reminiscent of the darkness over the earth that precedes Jesus' death in Mark 14:33.
- The sounding of the seventh trumpet leads to a resounding acclamation of the victory of God in and through Jesus' death and resurrection: "The kingdom of the world has become the kingdom of God and of his Messiah" (11:15). It closes with a report of events, reminiscent of the Gospel accounts, especially, but not only, Matthew 27:51-54, of the death of Jesus: "Then God's temple in heaven was opened and the ark of the covenant was seen within his temple; and there were flashes of lightning, rumblings, peals of thunder, an earthquake, and heavy hail" (see also Mark 15:33-39; Luke 23:44-46).
- A theme familiar from the moment of Jesus' death in John 19:30 reappears as the seventh bowl is poured out: "It is done" (11:17).[23]

The bulk of contemporary interpretation reads the puzzling use of apocalyptic imagery and thought-patterns as a divinely sanctioned destruction of the universe, to be replaced by the new heaven and the new earth (21:1), a holy city that comes down out of the heaven of God (v. 2). In the light of that interpretation, little wonder that *Laudato Si'* almost entirely ignores the Book of Revelation, citing only three passages (15:3 [para. 74], 12:1 [para. 241], and 21:5 [para. 243]).

---

23. This is the most important contribution of Corsini. *Each* septet reaches a Christological climax, proclaiming the saving event of the death and resurrection. But each septet has also indicated that this "saving event" also acts for the faithful Hebrew people of the old dispensation. This is possible because of the pre-existence of the slain and risen Lamb whose influence affects the whole of history. For more precision on the so-called "reminiscences" indicated in the dot points above, see further, nn. 29, 30, and 32.

Such a destructive vision is of little help in ecological thinking. The interpretation presented here, following Corsini, summons Christians to enjoy the life of the new earth and the new Jerusalem *now*. It is *already* in place because Jesus' death and resurrection has been present to the universe from before the foundation of the world. The image of life in the new Jerusalem, centred on the river of life-giving waters and the tree of life (22:1-5), is that of a pristine creation that gives life and healing to all creatures. The symbol of the city not only images a return to the ideal situation of Genesis 1-2, but depicts a pristine creation in harmony with human civilisation represented by "the city." It does not advocate social primitivism, but affirms that the values of economics, culture, artistic creativity, and ecology are not irreconcilable.[24] The Book of Revelation is not an encouragement to wait and suffer with patience and hope for the coming of the Lord.[25] The words of Jesus at the very beginning of the book state that the opposite is the case: "Do not be afraid, I am the first and the last, and the living one. I was dead, and see, I am alive forever and ever; and I have the keys of death and Hades" (1:18).

The Role of the Lamb

A pre-existent slain Lamb plays a major role in the Book of Revelation. The Lamb appears for the first time as major player across the events associated with the opening of the seven seals (4:1-8:1).[26] Within the liturgical setting of the heavenly court in Revelation 4-5,

---

24. The conclusion of Revelation is determined by an ideal vision of the city of Jerusalem, but the biblical saga begins in a God-given "garden" ("the Lord God planted a garden in Eden" [Gen 2:8]), and closes in a God-given "city" ("coming down out of heaven from God" [Rev 21:10]). This is not a summons to the dream-world of Jean-Jacques Rousseau.
25. It could be claimed that such a view is hardly Christian. The insistence that God will finally ease the suffering and death of persecuted Christians gives too little attention to the salvific effects of the death and resurrection of Jesus *now*.
26. For a recent study of the role of the Lamb in Revelation, especially against a near-Eastern background that would have influenced first century readers, see Johns, *The Lamb Christology of the Apocalypse*, 40-149. As mentioned above (n. 20), she locates the rhetoric of Revelation as a non-violent resistance to the Emperor cult: "The Apocalypse is a subversive resistance manual" (p. 153). For a survey of those who regard the Lamb as the "central image" that serves to control and interpret other major themes, see p. 151 n. 4.

as the question of the opening of the seven seals of the scroll emerges, the pre-existent Lamb appears for the first time: "Then I saw between the throne and the four living creatures and among the elders a Lamb *standing* as if it had been *slaughtered*" (Rev 5:6).[27] The twenty-four elders recognize the slain Lamb, and only he is worthy to open the seven seals (vv. 7-8). The angels surrounding the throne sing with full voice: "Worthy is the lamb that was slaughtered" (vv. 11-12). The scroll symbolizes the revelation of God.[28] At the opening of the sixth seal, accompanied by cosmic phenomena, the great multitude that no one can count because it is so numerous proclaims that salvation belongs to God and to the pre-existent Lamb (7:9-11).[29] The blood of the Lamb has washed clean all who have been through the great ordeal, and the slain Lamb will be their shepherd (vv. 13-17). Thus the seals climax with an indication of what God did for the Hebrew people (the former dispensation), and what was done in Jesus Christ (the establishment of the new covenant). "There was silence in heaven for about half an hour" (8:1).[30] All creation waits for a new access to

---

27. On the throne-scene and all that accompanies it in 4:1-5:14 as a symbol of the original creation, and the establishment of cosmic order, see Corsini, *Apocalisse*, 126-34; Idem, *Apocalypse*, 125-31. The slain Lamb is not "created," but is already "present" as God establishes cosmic order. The close, but strange, association of "standing" (ἑστηκός) and "slain" (ἐσφαγμένον) in 5:6 presents the crucified and risen Christ as alive, exercising plenipotentiary authority. See also Johns, *The Lamb Christology*, 168. See also pp. 160-61.
28. See Corsini, *Apocalisse*, 135-37. Johns, *The Lamb Christology*, has an ambitious title. The section of the book devoted to an analysis of the text of Revelation (pp. 150-205) is largely based upon a study of Rev 5. From this point, on the basis of her work with near-Eastern uses of lamb-symbolism, she develops her interesting proposal of the use of the Lamb (rather than the lion) as a symbol of peaceful, but necessary resistance to the Empire. The use of the Lamb is "paradigmatic for human ethical response."
29. The earthquake, the darkening of the sun, and other cosmic phenomena recall the Synoptic, and especially the Matthean, accounts of Jesus' death (see Mark 15:33, 37; Matt 26:51-54; Luke 23:41-42 [somewhat muted]).
30. This "silence" is reminiscent of Jesus' presence in Jerusalem in Mark 11:1-13:36, marking the end of one era and the beginning of another. He brings temple worship to an end (11:1-25), silences the voices of the leaders of Israel (11:26-12:44; see 12:34: "After that no one dared ask him any question"), and tells of the end of Jerusalem (13:1-23), and the end of the world (vv. 24-37). See Moloney, *Gospel of Mark*, 215-73.

God, made possible by the death and resurrection of Jesus, the slain Lamb who has unsealed the revelation of God's design (the scroll).³¹

The Lamb plays no role in the effects of the sounding of the seven trumpets (8:2-11:19), that closes by announcing the death of Jesus Christ and the results of that event: the "fulfilment of the mystery of God" (10:7). The death of the Messiah and his enthronement open the Temple, and the old economy and its cult come to an end (11:15-19).³² It is not an anxious suffering group of persecuted Christians that hears the message of the seventh angel that the kingdom of this world has become the kingdom of our Lord and his messiah (11:12), or the song of the twenty-four elders on thrones before God announcing: "We give thanks, Lord God Almighty, who are and who were, for you have taken your great power and begun to reign" (11: 17).

Most of the second half of the Book of Revelation is dedicated to the pouring out of the seven bowls (15:1-22:5). But before the pouring out of the bowls begins, Revelation 12:1-14:20 recapitulates and deepens what has been revealed to John the Seer to this point. This "interim section" has three parts:

> 12:1-17: The creation and fall of humankind.³³
> 13:1-18: The corruption of religious and political authority.
> 14:1-20: The old economy as God's first salvific intervention.³⁴

Following the ambiguity of the woman, cast down from heaven to earth, and pursued there by the ancient serpent, the role of the Lamb is restated. All who have "come to the salvation and the power and the kingdom of God" have done so because "they have conquered him by the blood of the Lamb" (12:11).³⁵ Those who choose evil (the beast of

---

31. For detail on the slain Lamb and the seven seals, culminating in the new order established by the opening of the seventh seal, see Corsini, *Apocalisse*, 135-68; Idem, *Apocalypse*, 133-63.
32. The theme of the opening of the Temple at the death of Jesus is found across the Synoptic tradition (see Mark 15:38; Matt 27:51; Luke 23:45).
33. The "woman," recalling Genesis 3 is a symbol of innocent humanity. She falls to earth, and is pursued there by the serpent, recalling Genesis 3. Pope Francis' Marian use of Rev 12:1 in *Laudato Si'*, 241, has no place in contemporary interpretation of the passage. See above, n. 2.
34. See Corsini, *Apocalisse*, 220-97; Idem, *Apocalypse*, 206-78.
35. Although she does not adopt Corsini's overall view of the Lamb and those who have come to salvation as the faithful of the first dispensation (pre-Jesus

13:1) are described as those "whose name has not been written in the book of the life of the Lamb that was slaughtered from the foundation of the world" (13:8: AT).[36] The Lamb and his blameless followers from the time prior to the event of Jesus Christ are "the first fruits for God and the Lamb." They gather on Mount Zion (14:1-4). But those who have worshipped the beast (see 13:1) are punished in the presence of the Lamb (14:10).

As the pouring out of the bowls opens, those who have already conquered the beast sing a hymn in praise of God and the Lamb (15:2-4). The successive pouring out of the bowls, modelled on the plagues of Exodus (see Exod 15:1-16:21) is used to show various aspects of the one event, the death of Christ, especially judgment and condemnation of the wicked powers.[37] As the seventh bowl is poured the accomplishment of the mystery of God in the death of Jesus is proclaimed for the third time: "It is done" (16:17).[38] A sequence of cosmic and historical events follow the pouring out of the seventh bowl, symbolic of the death and resurrection of Jesus.

Christ), Johns, *The Lamb Christology*, 154, points out that those in view are not necessarily martyrs, but those who have resisted and remained faithful.

36. An exegetical note is called for. Corsini, *Apocalisse*, 256-59; Idem, *Apocalypse*, 240-46, argues convincingly for the association of "from the foundation of the world" (ἀπὸ καταβολῆς κόσμου) with "the Lamb" in 13:8. Others would argue that the expression should be associated with "whose name has not been written." As throughout, I am following Corsini. For the widespread reading of "whose name had not been written from the foundation of the world," see Aune, *Revelation*, 746-48; Koester, *Revelation*, 575. Johns, *The Lamb Christology*, 137-40, tends to accept that the Lamb has existed "from the foundation of the world," and sees this as possibly related the *aqedah* tradition (see Gen. 22), evidenced by a parallel use of the idea in 1 Peter 1:19-20.

37. For a summary, see Corsini, *Apocalypse*, 279-86. See also, on the plagues, Johns, *The Lamb Christology*, 131-32.

38. Although the verbs are different, this cry of the voice from the Temple as the seventh bowl is poured matches Jesus' final word from the cross in the Gospel of John: "It is finished." Rev 16:17 has γέγονεν, while John 19:30 has τετέλεσται. Despite the different verbs, the Gospel traditions surrounding the death of Jesus continue to play into John the Seer's three-fold presentation of the salvific death of Christ, associated with the final seals, trumpets, and bowls. See above, nn. 30-32. This position rejects the widely held claim that 4:1-18:24 reveals "the time between the present and the end," and 19:1-22:5 describes "The end: the future victory." See, for example, Robert A. Spivey, D. Moody Smith and C. Clifton Black, *Anatomy of the New Testament. A Guide to Its Structure and Meaning* (Minneapolis: Fortress, 2013), 440.

Ambiguity continues, and must be defeated (17:1-22:5). False political and religious authorities continue to make war on the Lamb, but the Lamb will conquer them, because he is already established as "Lord of lords and King of Kings" (17:14). The marriage of the Lamb and the Holy Ones can take place amidst joy and celebration (19:7-9). The symbolic presentation of the old economy and its end in the death of Christ (see 19:11-14: the Word of God whose robe is dipped in his own blood) is told again in 19:11-20:15. The "thousand year reign" (20:4-6) represents the heavenly reign of the martyrs of the old economy. Ultimately, all evil authority is destroyed (20:7-15). The new Jerusalem, a bride adorned for her husband, comes down from heaven. She is the people of God, the wife of the Lamb, the city of God, with twelve gates: the twelve apostles of the Lamb. There is no need for the Temple in the new Jerusalem, as the Lord God and the Lamb dwell there: they are the divine presence. God is its light, and the Lamb is its lantern (21:22), and only those whose names are written in the book of the Lamb can enter (v. 27). The new Jerusalem, like the Lamb, already exists for believers. They are not waiting for the "end time" but living the fruits of the death and resurrection of Jesus (see 1:6).[39] From the throne of God and the Lamb flow the waters of life, producing the fruits that nourish a people worshipping God and the Lamb in an endless day (22:1-5).

---

39. The programmatic statement of the Seer in Rev 1:6 is crucial: Christ by his blood has *already* made us a kingdom of priests, serving his God and Father. See Corsini, *Apocalisse*, 73-75; Idem, *Apocalypse*, 68-71. The eschatology of Revelation is largely realised, but not totally. The Gospel of John, also dominated by a realised eschatology (see, for example, John 3:15-21; 5:21-26; 11:26), also retains a traditional end-time view (see, for example, 5:28-29; 6:39-40, 44). The closing prayer of Revelation: "Come, Lord Jesus!" (Rev. 22:20) is still an imperative that speaks into the future. Corsini is especially clear on this issue in the second edition of his work (*Apocalisse*, 414-17). As throughout the New Testament, the graced presence of the "now" does not eliminate the "not yet" aspect of sacred history. Johns, *The Lamb Christology*, recognises this tension, and associates it with the liturgical elements of the document. They "proclaim and experience salvation proleptically as part of the believing community's resistance to the empire" (p. 155. See also pp. 160-61). This is helpful, but not as convincing as Corsini's thoroughgoing reading of the whole document as a proclamation of the saving effects of the death and resurrection of Jesus from before the foundation of the world (13:8).

The Slain Lamb and the agōnia *of the Cosmos.*

Whatever one makes of the many symbols and apocalyptic visions that appear across these pages, the image of "the Lamb that was slaughtered" (see 5:6, 7-8, 11-12; 7:13-17; 12:11; 13:8) and whose blood has touched and given life to all generations from "before the foundation of the world" (13:8), is dominant. John the Seer is not encouraging suffering Christians to persevere in hope, or to non-violent resistance to the Empire. He tells his audience that the saving death of Christ has always been present to them, from before all time.[40] It has touched and saved all those faithful to God's covenant within the old economy, and generates a new "city of God": the Christian Church to which the document is addressed (see 1:1-3; 22:21).

The literary and theological process of drawing various aspects of Jesus' person and role into pre-existence is found in a number of places in the New Testament. There are several well-known examples. The earliest is Paul's affirmation that Christ Jesus emptied himself of "the form of God," to take on the form of a slave (Phil 2:5-7).[41] The post-Pauline literature develops this further, as the author of the Let-

---

40. In n. 2, above, I commented briefly on the shortcomings of the Encyclical from a biblical perspective. There is scarce reference to Revelation in *Laudato Si'*. The book is widely interpreted as a divinely sanctioned destruction of the universe, and of little help in ecological thinking. The interpretation presented here summons Christians to enjoy the life of the new earth and the new Jerusalem *now*. Rev 11:18, a passage closely associated with the seventh trumpet and the death and resurrection of Jesus, plays directly into the theme of *Laudato Si'*, if one accepts the interpretation suggested by this essay. The kingdom of the world has become the kingdom of our Lord (v. 15), and the twenty-four elders sing their praise, as the time of judgment has come: "for rewarding your servants," and "for destroying those that destroy the earth" (v. 18). At the blowing of the seventh trumpet the reign of Jesus as Messiah is *already* in place because of Jesus' death and resurrection (v. 19). The image of life in the new Jerusalem, centred on the river of life-giving waters and the tree of life (22:1-5) is that of a pristine creation that gives life and healing to all creatures, because the destroyers of the earth have been destroyed (11:18). Rev 11:15-19 expresses the hope of Pope Francis. I am grateful to Professor Ian Boxall of the Catholic University of America for this suggestion.
41. Some contemporary Pauline scholars claim that being "in the form of God" (Phil 2:6) is a reference to Adam, and not to pre-existence. For a convincing exegetical and theological argument in favour of pre-existence, see Brendan Byrne, "Christ's Pre-Existence in Pauline Soteriology," *Theological Studies* 58 (1997): 308-30. See also Larry W. Hurtado, *How on Earth Did Jesus Become God. Historical Questions about Earliest Devotion to Jesus* (Grand Rapids: Eerdmans, 2005), 83-107.

ter to the Colossians describes the Lord Jesus Christ as "the image of the invisible God, the first born of all creation. ... He himself is before all things, and in him all things hold together" (Col 1:15, 17). The author of the Letter to the Ephesians proclaims: "He chose us in him before the foundation of the world to be holy and blameless before him in love" (Eph 1:4). Foundational to Johannine Christology is the intimate union between the *Logos* with God that pre-existed "the beginning" (John 1:1-2). During his final prayer, the Johannine Jesus prays to his Father that he might return to the glory which was his in God's presence "before the world existed" (17:5, 24).[42] However strange such notions may appear to us, they form an essential part of the early Church's developing Christology.

David Aune ignores this "process" when he claims, against the possibility that Revelation 13:8 speaks of the Lamb slain from the foundation of the world, that: "It is logically and theologically impossible to make sense of the statement that the Lamb 'was slaughtered *before* the foundation of the world.'"[43] On the contrary, John the Seer is "logically and theologically" part of a growing tendency within the literature of the New Testament. For John the Seer, the crucified and risen one existed before all time. In typical apocalyptic fashion, the natural sequences of history have been collapsed. The reality of the slaughtered and risen lamb is constitutive of all history "from the foundation of the world" (5:6; 13:8). This early Christian insight can serve as a biblical contribution to contemporary Christian ecological and evolutionary thought: Jesus Christ, the pre-existent *slain and risen Lamb*, stands before all time in the heavenly court (Rev 5:6).[44]

---

42. The incarnate *Logos*, known as "Jesus Christ" (1:14-17), is the key to the mystery of the Johannine Jesus. This theme is present across the story, but most clearly expressed in the words of the Pharisees to the man who had been born blind: "We know that God has spoken to Moses, but as for this man, we do not know where he comes from" (9:29). That, of course, is the problem!
43. Aune, *Revelation*, 2:747.
44. This practice is not unique to early Christianity. It has its precedents in Israel's teaching on the pre-existence of Wisdom (see Sirach 1:1-5; 15:1; 24:1-12; 34:8; Proverbs 8:22-31), and its parallel in a Jewish understanding of the pre-existence of Torah (see *Genesis Rabbah* 1:4; 28:4; *Leviticus Rabbah* 19:1; *bPesahim* 54a; *jShebuot* 6:1, 499; *Tanḥuma Bereshit* 2). See Warren Harvey, "Torah: Origin and Pre-Existence," *Encyclopaedia Judaica*, 16 vols. (Jerusalem: Keter Publishing House, 1971-72), 15:1236-1238, and the remarkable essay of Daniel Boyarin,

It has been rightly said that side-by-side with the cosmic cooperation that enables the evolutionary process, "competition, pain, and death (are) intrinsic to evolutionary processes."[45] Catherine Vincie poses the question sharply:

> Our growing knowledge of an evolutionary cosmos complete with its explosive propensities and upheavals on a massive scale presses the theist to ask why there is such pain, predation, suffering, and death in the evolutionary process and what this says about the creator of such a World.[46]

The power of Jesus' death and resurrection suffuses these processes from their beginning. The evocative image of the Lamb slain and risen before the foundation of the world plays into that essential aspect of the evolutionary *agōnia* of the cosmos.[47] We cannot ask the

---

"The Gospel of the *Memra*: Jewish Binitarianism and the Prologue to John," *Harvard Theological Review* 94 (2001): 243-84.

45. Edwards, *Partaking of God*, 88. See further, pp. 130-46, where Edwards discusses "Evolution, Cooperation, and the Theology of Original Sin." See also Idem., *How God Acts*, 11-14, 129-42. In these latter pages, Edwards adopts Girardian "scapegoat" theory, and necessarily speaks of the lamb, but without reference to the Book of Revelation.

46. Catherine Vincie, *Worship and the New Cosmology. Liturgical and Theological Challenges* (Collegeville, MN: The Liturgical Press, 2014), 48. Vincie takes this question very seriously, and on pp. 37-80 surveys a number of scholars who, among other questions, attempt to respond to the problem of the agony of the cosmos (John Haught, Denis Edwards, Arthur Peacocke, Elizabeth Johnson, Ilia Delio).

47. Revelation's presentation of the sheer grace of Jesus' death and resurrection "from before all time," in a way parallel to the Pauline understanding of Jesus as the pre-existent one, equal to and image of an invisible God (Philippi and Colossians), and the Johannine understanding of the eternal union between God and the *Logos*, could be a significant contribution to Christian ecological thought. It is also possible that Colossians 1:15-20 links Christ as "the image of the invisible God, the firstborn of all creation" (v. 15), "through him God was pleased to reconcile all things, whether on earth or in heaven, by making peace through the blood of his cross" (v. 20), locates the efficacy of Jesus' death and resurrection "before all time," although this is unlikely. See Eduard Schweitzer, *The Letter to the Colossians. A Commentary*, trans. Andrew Chester (London, SPCK, 1976), 79-88. This thought is passingly caught in Pope Francis' prayer at the end of *Laudato Si'*. In addressing the Spirit he prays: "By your light you guide the world towards the Father's love and accompany creation as it groans in travail."

biblical Word of God for solutions to all the questions that are put to the theist by a cosmology and a contemporary scientific awareness that are totally foreign to the biblical world. The search for such solutions is the task of the theologian, hand-in-hand with the scientist. But perhaps the biblical image of the Lamb slain and risen "before the foundation of the world" (Rev 5:6; 13:8) may guide them when they come to consider the pain that is a necessary part of the evolutionary process.[48]

The Word of God, understood in the light of the redemptive agony of Jesus Christ, does not sidestep the agony of the universe, and of the world.[49] Jesus' death has been variously interpreted. Paul's rich Theology of the Cross presents Jesus' unconditional obedience to God that reversed the disobedience that generated sin in the world (Romans 5:12-21). But it has its roots in the bloody event that took place on Calvary (see, among many places, Phil 2:7-8). Mark the Evangelist saw the Cross as the lowest point in Jesus' human experience, embracing the depths of all possible humiliation (Mark 15:33-39). John the Evangelist reverses this view: Jesus' death is the high point in the revelation of God's love (John 19:17-37).[50]

But John the Seer locates that agony "before the foundation of the world." The ambiguities of creation, from the beginnings of all time and space, can be washed clean by the blood of the Lamb (Rev 7:13-17). Contemporary thinkers correctly point out that the destructive

---

48. Most Christian theologians correctly have recourse to the unlimited love of God, manifested in the unconditional free-gift of Jesus Christ, allowing the cosmos to run its course freely. See the references to Edwards' work in n. 45, and the survey available in Vincie, *Worship and the New Cosmology*, 43-80 (see n. 46). Edwards, *Jesus and the Natural World*, 44, states the conundrum well: "We certainly know that we are the products of this evolutionary history and that we and all other creatures of our planet are inconceivable without this evolutionary history and all that it involves. But theology does not have any kind of full, rational answer as to why God creates in an evolutionary and emergent way. Our question stands before a God of incomprehensible mystery." The pre-existent slain and risen Lamb may play a role in these ponderings.
49. See Moloney, *Reading the New Testament in the Church*, 55-56: "*Everything is written in the light of Jesus' death and resurrection. There is not a letter, a phrase, a sentence, a paragraph, a document, that does not come from belief that the crucified Jesus had been raised by God*" (stress in original).
50. On these different interpretations of the cross, see Moloney, *Love in the Gospel of John*, 135-60.

Darwinian "preservation of the fittest" neglects important principles of collaboration in evolutionary processes.[51] Nevertheless, we recognise the inevitable pain and struggle that are an essential part of the ongoing story of the ecological and evolutionary processes. John the Seer suggests that part of the divine interface with that story, from "before the foundation of the world," has been the never-ending presence of the crucified and risen one: "Do not be afraid; I am the first and the last, and the living one. I was dead, and see, I am alive forever and ever; and I have the keys of Death and Hades" (Rev. 1:17b-18).

It is naïve to adopt an unconditionally positive reading of science, theology, and spirituality.[52] Our scientists tell us the evolutionary process is necessarily marked by violence and pain. The human story, and subsequent theological reflection upon it, tells the same story of violence and pain, generated by what Denis Edwards calls "the evolutionary tendencies toward insider-outsider attitudes."[53] John the Seer introduces the crucified into that process, bringing God's healing, in and through his pre-existent Son, a Lamb slain before all time. "The Christian community carries the message of the Gospel of Jesus and embodies the transforming, liberating Spirit, but does this as a human community still subject to tendencies to exclude others and make them into scapegoats and enemies."[54] Thus, that community faces its ambiguous reality with a hope founded in an awareness that it has been cleansed by the blood of the slain Lamb since "before the foundation of the world."

---

51. See, for example, Martin A. Nowak and Sarah Coakley, eds. *Evolution, Games, and God. The Principle of Cooperation* (Cambridge, MA: Harvard University Press, 2013). In a variety of ways, this collection of studies explores how cooperation, *working alongside mutation and natural selection,* plays a critical role in populations from microbes to human society. Inheriting a tendency to cooperate may be as beneficial as the self-preserving instinct usually thought to be decisive in evolutionary dynamics.
52. For a reflection on this ultimately unanswerable enigma, see Edwards, *Partaking of God*, 88-103. Christianity must not fall into the freedom of any form of "new age" religion, nor uncritically accept Gaia theory.
53. Edwards, *Partaking of God*, 146.
54. Edwards, *Partaking of God*, 144.

Conclusion

I close with some concerns over the laudable good cheer of an optimistic Pope.[55] He is motivated by his desire to "encourage an honest and open debate so that particular interests or ideologies will not prejudice the common good" (*Laudato Si'*, 188). He asks all peoples of good will: "Is it realistic to hope that those who are obsessed with maximizing profits will stop to reflect upon the environmental damage which they will leave for generations?" (*Laudato Si'*, 190). I would also claim to be born with an optimistic streak, but my response to that question must be that such a hope is unrealistic. All developed countries are dominated by anthropologies, sociologies, and economic theories that have become their spirituality, determined by their Gross Domestic Product. Productivity determines everything and drives the national *ethos*, cost what it may to the more fragile in the community.[56] A minority group of Catholic Cardinals, Bishops, and Priests, and influential conservative Catholic intellectuals,[57] reject the questioning of "maximizing profits."

---

55. Neither in his citation of the *Canticle* in *Laudato Si'*, 87, nor in his final prayers following paragraph 246, continuing the tradition of Francis of Assisi's *Canticle* after which the Encyclical is named, does Pope Francis match Francis of Assisi's recognition of the importance of death. Francis closes his *Canticle* with the words: "Praised be you, my Lord through our Sister Bodily Death, from whom no one living can escape. Woe to those who die in mortal sin! Blessed are those whom death will find in Your most holy will, for the second death shall do them no harm. Praise and bless my Lord and give him thanks, and serve him with great humility" ("Canticle of the Creatures," in *Francis of Assisi: early documents* (eds. Regis J. Armstrong, J. A. Wayne Hellmann, and William J. Short; 3 vols. [Hyde Park, NY: New City Press, 1999-2001], 1:114.). For a fine reflection on "Integral Ecology and Sister Death," see Anthony J. Kelly, *Laudato Si'. An Integral Ecology and the Catholic Vision* (Adelaide: ATF Theology, 2016), 139-66.
56. In Pope Francis, *Evangelii Gaudium. The Joy of the Gospel. Apostolic Exhortation on the Proclamation of the Gospel in Today's World* (Vatican City: Libreria Editrice Vaticana, 2013), paras. 52-60, the Holy Father had already criticised this economic theory that claims that the best way to help the poor is by means of what is called the "trickle down" effect. If the rich become richer, some of that wealth "trickles down" to the poor. Our current history of human selfishness, and the widening of the gap between the wealthy and the poor, shows that this "economic system" simply does not deliver sufficient "trickle down."
57. This group is well represented in the USA, in the work of such figures as Michael Novak and, more recently, George Weigel. See the report "Pope's popularity declines in US ahead of visit," *The Tablet. The International Weekly* (1 August 2015): 29: "Many conservative Americans do not attribute climate change to

The Holy Father offers as one of his motives for hope: "The majority of people living on our planet profess to be believers" (*Laudato Si'*, 201).[58] But what does that mean in real terms? I was born and live in one of the most resource-blessed nations in the world. The bulk of its leadership, the Prime Minister, his predecessor, the Deputy Prime Minister, several leading ministers, and the Leader of the Opposition are, or were, all Catholics, educated at some of the most significant Catholic schools in the country. They are unilaterally opposed to offering any support to the thousands of refugees floating abandoned in seas to our north, without food or water.[59] When asked if this dire situation would lead the Government to rethink its policy of "turn back the boats," the former Prime Minister responded: "Nope, Nope, Nope." That attitude has only hardened in what is a bi-partisan policy since then. Side-by-side with this seriously sinful attitude to our fellow-humans, Government policy supports the increase of the use of fossil fuels, which generate productivity and income, and a cut back on the less wealth-productive renewable energy sources.[60]

Faced with complaints from the younger generation that they are being priced out of the housing market by a small number of very wealthy investors, the Federal Treasurer has advised the young to get a good job, and make more money. All of this is covered with

---

human activity and Americans of all political stripes are reluctant to question contemporary capitalism."

58. See also *Laudato Si'*, 205-208, which opens confidently: "Yet all is not lost. Human beings, while capable of the worst, are also capable of rising above themselves, choosing again what is good, and making a new start, despite their mental and social conditioning" (para. 205).
59. See *Laudato Si'*, 25: "There has been a tragic rise in the number of migrants seeking to flee from the growing poverty caused by environmental degradation. They are not recognised by international conventions as refugees; they bear the loss of the lives they have left behind, without enjoying any legal protection whatsoever. Sadly, there is widespread indifference to such suffering, which is even now taking place throughout our world. Our lack of response to these tragedies involving our brothers and sisters points to the loss of that sense of responsibility for our fellow men and women upon which all civil society is founded."
60. See *Laudato Si'*, 165: "We know that technology based on the use of highly polluting fossil fuels – especially coal, but also oil, and to a lesser degree, gas – needs to be progressively replaced without delay."

thinly-veiled rhetoric: the need to stop the evil of people smuggling and the jobs and productivity generated by the fossil fuel industry.[61] But few are convinced. The Australian Government wishes to protect its mining interests and control its population, in order to continue the growth of its GDP.[62] There is a profound hiatus (the Italian *distacco* says it better!) between "belief" and ecological commitment. This hiatus may eventually be touched by ecological tragedy, and that will be too late, "leaving to coming generations debris, desolation, and filth" (*Laudato Si'*, 161).[63]

The Holy Father is exactly right in pointing out that the incredible design of God, long ago described in a variety of ways in the Judeo-Christian biblical tradition, has been deepened and unimaginably enriched by modern research and discoveries. We can now bet-

---

61. In a Parliamentary session that introduced legislation to block public intervention over the increase of mining for fossil fuels, generated by a challenge to the immense development of the Asani Carmichael coal mine in central Queensland, the Prime Minister commented: "I regret to say, Mr Speaker, that some green groups are doing their best to sabotage jobs and investment in Australia" (*The Age*, Wednesday, August 19, 2015, page 1). I suspect that Pope Francis would belong to those "green groups."
62. The above comments were written prior to 16 September, 2015, when the governing Liberal Party's parliamentary representatives changed their leader. Consequently, the Prime Minister of Australia changed and a number of ministers have also changed. However, at this stage, there has been no hint of major change in the above policies, and the new Prime Minister is a Catholic.
63. The Holy Father calls it "the globalisation of indifference" (*Laudato Si'*, 52). This hiatus is widely reflected in both political and religious leaders (especially in the USA) greeting the publication of *Laudato Si'* with the comment that the Pope should look after the problems of the Roman Catholic Church, and not worldwide, and universe-wide, ecological questions. An emeritus professor of Political Science at the Australian National University, Canberra, John Warhurst, has indicated the mood of Australians in this matter as follows: "The Catholic Church can appear to wedge many Catholic political leaders in all sorts of policies. If that really mattered, it would make life impossible for leading Catholics in politics. But it rarely does. They feel free to disagree with their spiritual leader and probably are applauded by the wider community by being free agents. It can be a bonus for them." Warhurst refers to pontifical statements that raise political consciousness as an "unwelcome irritation." Downloaded on June 25 from "Was Tony Abbott wedged by Pope Francis on climate change?"(www.WAtoday.com.au, June 24, 2015). I regard the current "privatisation" of a belief system that makes no impact on public performance an issue with *at least* the same seriousness as the contemporary ecological crisis.

ter understand that we are part of a wonderful universe, in which "our very bodies are made up of her elements" (*Laudato Si'*, 2). He is also correct in dramatically pointing to the truth that human behaviour and human sinfulness are responsible for putting "our common home" at great risk.

In conclusion I pose a biblical question not raised by *Laudato Si'*. Do the environmental risks courageously addressed by Pope Francis, impacting upon our world, our relationships as peoples, nations, ethnic groups, political alliances, sexual beings, and our relationships with the whole of creation, fall under the shadow of the Lamb, slaughtered before the foundation of all time? The Christian Scriptures address the mystery of pain, death, and human failure without hesitation. The foundation of Christianity in the death and resurrection of Jesus of Nazareth, makes this necessary. They make it clear that resurrection and new life are achieved only through the process of death and burial (see 1 Cor 15:3-19). Might this not also be the case for the earth and our place in it?[64] "Do not be afraid, I am the first and the last, and the living one. I was dead, and see, I am alive forever and ever; and I have the keys of death and Hades" (Rev 1:18).

There is timely wisdom in Francis' prophetic, but optimistic, voice. Perhaps society, and especially its leaders, need to hear this clarion call. Francis writes: "The universe unfolds in God, who fills it completely. Hence there is a mystical meaning to be found in a leaf, in a mountain trail, in a dewdrop, in a poor person's face. The ideal is to pass not only from the exterior to the interior to discover the action of God in the soul, but also to discover God in all things" (*Laudato Si'*, 233). This discovery of God in all things has traditionally been

---

64. My primary concern with the above question is a reminder that Pope Francis' desired rebirth of our endangered earth will demand pain and sacrifice from many. But it also carries the innuendo that the future of the earth as we know it is not guaranteed. A tiny speck on the fringes of our known universe, it may have arrived at a stage where only death and destruction lies ahead: the end of the earth as we know it. Such a possibility is not God's responsibility, but the result of humankind's abuse of God's loving gift of unconditional freedom to those who dwell on this planet. At this stage of scientific investigation, we have no idea what has happened, is happening, and will happen, elsewhere in God's universe. But we who dwell on the earth have no inalienable right to continue our present use and abuse of God's gracious gifts.

seen as tracing the *vestigia Dei*. May this courageous, optimistic, yet prophetic intervention of Pope Francis be evidence that *vestigia Dei* continue to be found in the caring minds and hearts of women and men of our time.[65]

---

65. On the notion of the *"vestigia Dei"* as privileged insights and experiences of the "footmark" of God's presence in creation according to the Christian tradition, see Anthony J. Kelly, *An Expanding Theology. Faith in a world of Connections* (Sydney: E. J. Dwyer, 1993), 157-68.

14
A New Testament Hermeneutic for Divorce and Remarriage in the Catholic Tradition

Jesus' teaching on divorce is a question of central importance to the Christian churches.[1] The ministry of Pope Francis, and the agenda of the Synod of Bishops on the Family, has again drawn attention to the issue. Given the paucity of material on marriage and divorce in the entre Bible, it is not surprising that very little material in the New Testament is dedicated to Jesus' attitude to the issue.[2] But what is found in Paul, Mark, Matthew, and Luke is confronting to contemporary sensitivities, and calls for clear analysis. An uncritical affirmation that Jesus prohibited divorce does not do justice to what is recalled in our inspired Scriptures. The fact that he did so must be given its due importance, but Jesus' prohibition of divorce and remarriage is not the only word on marriage and divorce in the pages of the New Testament.[3] A neglect of the subtleties expressed across the pastoral and

---

1. John P. Meier, *A Marginal Jew. Rethinking the Historical Jesus*, Anchor Yale Bible Reference Library, 5 vols. (New York/New Haven: Doubleday/Yale University Press, 1991-2016), 4:128 39 provides twelve densely printed pages of "sample of representative works." I will limit my consultation of secondary literature to the detailed work of Meier, Raymond F. Collins, *Divorce in the New Testament*, Good News Studies 38 (Collegeville, MN: The Liturgical Press, 1992), and David Instone-Brewer, *Divorce and Remarriage in the Bible* (Grand Rapids: Eerdmans, 2002), as well as classical and recent commentaries on 1 Corinthians, Mark, and Matthew.
2. This essay is a reworked version of the final chapter of my recent *A Body Broken for a Broken People. Divorce, Remarriage, and the Eucharist* (Melbourne: John Garratt, 2015)
3. The recent study of William R. G. Loader, "Did Adultery Mandate Divorce? A Reassessment of Jesus' Divorce Logia," *New Testament Studies* 61 (2015): 67-78, raises a doubt about Jesus' prohibition of divorce. For Loader, Jesus' prohibition of divorce may only appear to be absolute. As a person of his time and tradition,

theological re-interpretations of Paul, Mark, and Matthew, accepted by the Church as the inspired Word of God, call for close attention.

In terms of the texts, Jesus' teaching on divorce and remarriage appears in 1 Corinthians 7:10-11; Mark 10:1-12; Matthew 5:32; 19:1-12, and Luke 16:18. The material itself, however, comes from three sources:

1. Paul (1 Corinthians 7:10-11)
2. "Q" (Matt 5:32 and Luke 16:18)
3. Mark (Mark 10:11-12// Matthew 19:9).

On the basis of these three sources the following reflection on the teaching of the New Testament on divorce and remarriage responds to four questions:

1. Can we claim with certainty what Jesus said about marriage and divorce, on the basis of our earliest traditions: Paul, "Q," and Mark 10:11-12?
2. Using that tradition, what does Paul say about the question in 54 CE, as he speaks to the situation of the Greco-Roman Christian community at Corinth in 1 Corinthians 7:8-16?
3. How does Mark use that same Jesus-tradition, in the context of the Roman Empire about 70 CE, as he reports Jesus' debate with the Pharisees, and in his subsequent discussion with his disciples in Mark 10:1-12?
4. Finally, how does Matthew use it, both in his adaptation of his "Q" source, and in his rewriting of Mark 10:1-12 in Matthew 19:3-12, in the latter half of the 80's CE?

A New Testament Hermeneutic

The Gospels bear witness to what Jesus did and said during his lifetime; they also reflect the pastoral and theological agenda of the inspired Scriptures that have been accepted by the Church as its New Testament. The earliest Christian writers looked back to Jesus and

---

Jesus took it for granted, on the basis of Genesis 2:24, that adultery *necessarily* led to divorce. He did not need to say it. As Loader recognises, the weakness of suggestion is its argument from silence.

inform their audience about Jesus of Nazareth; but they go further.[4] They also instruct a Christian audience about what God has achieved for humankind in and through the event of Jesus. One leads to the other, but the latter very regularly develops the traditions that come from Jesus to speak to the needs of the community for which any single author is writing. These "writings" subsequently became part of the Christian Sacred Scriptures because they were recognized as speaking to the ongoing history of the Church as a "Word of God" (see *Dei Verbum* 11-13).

This simple affirmation hides a very important principle of interpretation for a Church that takes the New Testament as part of its inspired Scriptures (see *Dei Verbum* 17-20). The Word of God in the New Testament is not *only* to be identified with the words of Jesus that we can confidently find within its pages. The Word of God is *also* the ongoing interpretation and application of those words developed within the teaching of the earliest and inspired Christian authors to address the Church.

It is universally accepted that the Gospel of John, that appeared about 100 CE, is the most theologically developed document in the New Testament. Without hesitation, it proclaims that Jesus of Nazareth was the Christ, the pre-existent Logos of God (John 1:1-2), the only begotten Son of God (1:14), I AM HE (8:24, 28, 58; 13:19, etc.), the Son of Man (1:51; 3:13-14, 5:27; 6:27, 53; 8:28, etc.) and the Messiah (20:30-31), who was always aware of his oneness with God, and thus made God known in an authoritative and unique fashion (6:25-59, etc.). Having come from a oneness with God that the Logos has occupied since before all time (John 1:1-2, 14), Jesus returns to the Father (17:5; 20:18), to send the gift of the Paraclete (14:15-17, 25-26; 15:26-27; 16:7-11, 12-15; 19:30; 20:21-23). The Christology of John's Gospel became the backbone for the eventual articulation of the

---

4. No document called "Q" is found in the New Testament. It is a sigla used by critics to indicate early material, common to Matthew and Luke, but not found in Mark, that would have been earlier than Mark. See John S. Kloppenborg, *Q, the Earliest Gospel: An Introduction to the Original Stories and Sayings of Jesus* (Louisville, KY: Westminster John Knox, 2008), 1-40, and Ivan Havener, *Q: The Sayings of Jesus*, Good News Studies 19 (Wilmington, DE: Michael Glazier, 1987). The most complete treatment of "Q," is James M. Robinson, Paul Hoffmann, and John S. Kloppenborg, *The Critical Edition of Q. Synopsis including the Gospels of Matthew and Luke, Mark and Thomas with English, German, and French Translations of Q and Thomas*, Hermeneia (Minneapolis: Fortress, 2000).

Christian Church's faith at the Councils of Nicea (325 CE), Constantinople (381 CE), Ephesus (431 CE), Chalcedon (451 CE), and again at Constantinople (553 CE).[5] As Christians make their confessions of faith, they do so in a language that has been shaped by the Gospel of John, not by what we can be determine about what Jesus of Nazareth *actually said* between 28-30 CE.

The same must be said for the formative role of the Letters of Paul, written in the 50's of the first Christian century, in the development of the later Christian Tradition. Jesus understood his forthcoming death as in some way "for others," but the inspired writings of Paul the Apostle make the saving significance of the death and resurrection of Jesus Christ so central to his thought and teaching that it has shaped all subsequent Christian teaching – and practice.[6] The revelation of God to the world is not found in *either* the Word of God in the Bible, *or* the formal teaching of the Councils. It is found in *both*. Indeed, without John and Paul, there would be very little in the teaching of the Councils. Scripture and Tradition "flow from the same divine well-spring" (*Dei Verbum* 9). "Tradition and scripture make up a single sacred deposit of the word of God, which is entrusted to the Church" (*Dei Verbum* 10).

Obviously, therefore, God's revelation is not only found in those words of Jesus that can be reliably traced to the life and teaching of Jesus and Nazareth. What follows will initially trace what Jesus of Nazareth taught about divorce and remarriage. Once that is in place, we must examine what the earliest Church (Paul, Mark, and Matthew) passed on to their own communities in their letters and gospels, accepted as an integral part of the Word of God to the Church. As with the example of the use of the Christologies of the Gospel of John and the Letters of Paul for the eventual formation of the Catholic Tradition, so also with the Church's understanding and practice of marriage and divorce, we must *see the entire picture*.

---

5. Most, but not all, mainstream Christian Churches have continued the use of the pre-Reformation Creeds, originally forged through vigorous debate at the early Councils, as an essential statement of what they believe.
6. On Jesus' approach to his death, see Dale C. Allison, Jr., *Constructing Jesus. Memory, Imagination, and History* (Grand Rapids: Baker Academic, 201), 387-433. On the centrality of the saving effects of Jesus' death and resurrection in Paul, among many, see James D. G. Dunn, *The Theology of the Apostle Paul* (Grand Rapids: Eerdmans, 1998), 207-65.

Jesus of Nazareth and Divorce

Jesus of Nazareth was a product of traditional Palestinian Jewish thought and practice. He would have been shaped by the teaching of the Mosaic Torah.[7] Adultery was a capital crime. According to Leviticus 20:10 and Deuteronomy 22:22 both offending parties involved must die, and its prohibition is found in the Decalogue (Exodus 20:19; Deuteronomy 4:10; 5:20-21).[8] Surprisingly, however, the question of divorce and remarriage was not a major concern for the Jewish legal tradition. It was taken for granted that divorce and remarriage would take place. The tradition ensured that the male partner was always in command of the situation. There is only one passage in the Torah that deals with the question in any detail: Deuteronomy 24:1-4.[9] The text itself is one long single Hebrew sentence. Its major concern is to ensure that a woman who is dismissed from the household by the male, not be permitted to return to the intimate situation of man and wife by returning to the husband who dismissed her. This is regarded as bringing "sin upon the land" (v. 4). "That, remarkably, is the extent of the divorce laws in the Pentateuch."[10] The same basic approach to the question is found in the Prophets (already part of Israel's Sacred Scripture) and the Wisdom literature (an important pseudo-philosophical reflection reflecting Israel's gradual integration with its surrounding Hellenistic world, but with ancient roots in Israel's tradition).[11]

---

7. For much of what follows, I am indebted to the work of Meier, *A Marginal Jew*, 4:74-181.
8. See the discussion in Elaine A. Goodfriend, "Adultery," in *The Anchor Bible Dictionary*, ed. David N. Freedman, 6 vols. (New York: Doubleday, 1992), 1:82-86.
9. See Collins, *Divorce*, 89-91.
10. Meier, *A Marginal Jew*, 4:80.
11. See Meier, *A Marginal Jew*, 4:81-86; Instone-Brewer, *Divorce and Remarriage*, 34-58. One anomaly needs attention. Archaeologists have uncovered documents from a Jewish community in Elephantine in Egypt that reflects the thought and practice of a diaspora Jewish military community from the 5th century BCE. The practice of divorce is taken for granted, but the documents indicate, for the first time, that a "bill of divorce" had to be prepared, and that it was not only possible for the man to divorce the woman, but also for the women to divorce the man. This was a quite unique diaspora situation, and should not be given too much weight in trying to establish divorce practices in first century Palestinian Judaism. See Meier, *A Marginal Jew*, 4:83-84.

Recourse is often had, by Christian scholars, to the prophet Malachi 2:10-16. The RSV renders v. 16: "For I hate divorce, says the Lord the God of Israel." It has come down to us in a corrupted Hebrew text, and does not make sense the way it stands. Using an image found elsewhere in the prophets (e. g., Isaiah, Jeremiah, Ezekiel, and Hosea),[12] Malachi 2:10-16 criticizes Jerusalem and Judah for their unfaithfulness to God by paralleling their behaviour with husbands unfaithful to their wives. After careful consideration of the Hebrew of v. 16, however, John Meier states categorically that the text does not say: "I hate divorce." The closest he can come to generating a confusing English translation for the confused Hebrew is "For [or: 'if'; or 'when'; or 'indeed'] he hated [or possibly: 'hating'], send away! [or possibly "to send away"].[13] The same confusion is found in the Greek translations, and the Latin Vulgate for 2:16 is "cum odio habueris dimitte" ("when [or: since] you hate [her], send [her] away." Later Christian interpreters and Rabbinic thought have turned to Malachi 2:16 for biblical support for the absolute prohibition of divorce. But this is a misuse of the original text (which remains confused), and would not have influenced Jesus of Nazareth in any way. When Jesus comes to discuss divorce, he turns to the Torah texts of Deuteronomy and Genesis. He never mentions Malachi.

There are other witnesses to Jewish thought that come from the same period, notably Philo of Alexandria (20 BCE – 40 CE), a Jew who worked strenuously to make Jewish traditions relevant to a Hellenistic world, and Josephus (37-100 CE), a Jewish historian who wrote significant commentaries on the Jewish War and the history of Jewish life and practice. They both demonstrate minimal interest in the matter of marriage and divorce, and repeat the legislation of Deuteronomy 24:1-4.[14]

The texts found at the Dead Sea raise further questions about the attitude of a first century Jewish sect that produced those documents, generally recognized as the Essenes. Much has been made of two texts that suggest a prohibition of divorce, the Damascus Document (CD 4:20-21) and the Temple Scroll (11QTemple 57:15-19). The for-

---

12. See Instone-Brewer, *Divorce and Remarriage*, 34-58.
13. Meier, *A Marginal Jew*, 2:82. For the discussion, see pp. 81-82, and the associated footnotes on pp. 144-49. The options in the square parentheses generate a translation: "Indeed he hated to send away."
14. See Meier, *A Marginal Jew*, 4:84-87.

mer is a difficult text to interpret. It has been widely translated as a condemnation of those who take two wives in their lifetime, but it may be better understood as the prohibition of multiple wives. The second envisions the way things will be when the ideal king rules in the near future. One of the telling arguments against the prohibition of divorce at Qumran is that there is no suggestion of any such practice in the Community Rule (1QS). The Damascus Document was written for Essene communities at large; the Community Rule determines the life of the Essene community at Qumran.[15] Regularly regarded as a minority sectarian group that advocated the prohibition of divorce, reflecting a sectarian strain within Judaism to which Jesus also belonged,[16] recent detailed analysis of the situation at Qumran is more reserved. While such a view of divorce and remarriage at Qumran is not ruled out, majority position is nowadays that "[t]he Essenes did forbid polygamy; their position on divorce remains a question mark."[17]

This is the cultural, religious, and legal setting for Jesus' teaching on divorce. Our earliest witness is 1 Corinthians 7:10-11. Addressing this enthusiastic community, Paul regularly opens his reflections with the expression "now concerning ..." (περὶ δέ: 7:1, 25; 8:1; 12:1; 16:1). He responds to queries concerning the Corinthians' state of life, now that they live in new existence generated by the death and resurrection of Jesus.[18] His general principle is that they should stay as they

---

15. For excellent treatments of CD 4:20-21 and 11QTemple 57:15-19, and wide-ranging scholarship that surround the interpretation of these texts, see Meier, *A Marginal Jew*, 4:87-93, and the associated notes on pp. 155-62.
16. See, for example, Joseph A. Fitzmyer, "The Matthean Divorce Texts and Some New Palestinian Evidence," *Theological Studies* 39 (1976): 221-23.
17. Meier, *A Marginal Jew*, 4:93. But see Joseph A. Fitzmyer, "Marriage and Divorce," in *Encyclopedia of the Dead Sea Scrolls*, ed. Lawrence H. Schiffman and James C. VanderKam, 2 vols. (Oxford/New York: Oxford University Press, 2000), 1:512, who interprets these same documents as the prohibition of divorce, and not only polygamy. Meier's uncertainty is shared by Ulrich Luz, *Matthew*, Hemeneia, 3 vols. (Minneapolis, MN: Fortress, 2001-2007), 2:494. William R. G. Loader, *The Dead Sea Scrolls on Sexuality in Sectarian and Related Literature at Qumran* (Grand Rapids: Eerdmans, 2009), 107-19, argues that the availability of all the Qumran material now makes it clear that " the cited prohibition is best taken as referring not to divorce but to polygamy."
18. See Benjamin A. Edsall, *Paul's Witness to Formative Early Christian Instruction*, Wissenschaftliche Untersuchungen zum Neuen Testament 2.365 (Tübingen: Mohr Siebeck, 2014), 99-109; Collins, *Divorce*, 11-13.

are,[19] and this is what he tells them to do concerning their marital state in 7:1-9. To this point in his argument he is expressing his own opinion. He will resume giving advice on these ground in vv. 12-16 (see v. 12: "I say, not the Lord"). However, in vv. 10-11 he leaves his own opinion to one side, and gives a word of Jesus on divorce:

> To the married I give charge, not I but the Lord, that the wife should not separate from her husband (but if she does, let her remain single or else be reconciled to her husband) – and that the husband should not divorce the wife.

There are two remarkable aspects to these words that Paul claims come from Jesus. Most significantly, Paul reports that Jesus forbad divorce. The wife was not to leave her husband (v. 10), and if she does, she must return to him (v. 11a). No husband should divorce his wife (v. 11b). Secondly, unlike anything we find in Jewish tradition, Paul takes it for granted that a woman could leave her husband on her own initiative.

There may be a number of possible explanations for the latter element from the teaching of Jesus (the initiative of the woman),[20] but our concern is with the former. We have no verbatim use of the words of Jesus of Nazareth. But Paul's consistent claim that he is teaching on his own authority (vv. 1-9 and vv. 12-16), and the dramatic change to a "charge" that comes from the Lord (v. 10) when he prohibits divorce, is early evidence of Jesus' prohibition of divorce and remarriage.[21] Paul has not provided a setting for this "word of the Lord." The early evidence of Matthew 5:32, paralleled in Luke 16:18 (thus "Q" material), provides two different narrative settings for a tradition that looks back to the words of Jesus.[22]

---

19. On this principle, see Joseph A. Fitzmyer, *First Corinthians*, The Anchor Yale Bible 32 (New Haven: Yale University Press, 2008), 305-307.
20. The possible remembrance in the tradition of the new world that Jesus created for women could be one of the motivations. Most explain it by indicating the Corinthian situation in the Roman colony of Corinth. See Richard A. Horsley, *1 Corinthians*, Abingdon New Testament Commentaries (Nashville: Abingdon Press, 1998), 98-99; Collins, *Divorce*, 13-22; Meier, *A Marginal Jew*, 4:165-66 note 92.
21. See Collins, *Divorce*, 29-39; Idem, *First Corinthians*, Sacra Pagina 7 (Collegeville, MN: The Liturgical Press, 1999), 263-65.
22. For the discussion of possible links between 1 Corinthians 7:10-11 and Synoptic sayings, see Collins, *Divorce*, 32-38.

In the Gospel of Luke, Jesus addresses the question of divorce only once: in Luke 16:18. These words are found in a rather loosely connected series of teachings poised between Jesus' parable on the dishonest steward (16:1-9) and the parable on the rich man and Lazarus (vv. 19-30). Most of these teachings are connected in some way with the theme of wealth and possessions that is present in the two parables (see vv. 10-13, 14-15), while vv. 16-17 touches upon important Lukan concerns: the place of John the Baptist, and the law and the prophets in God's design. Oddly, v. 18 follows: "Everyone who divorces his wife and marries another commits adultery, and he who marries a woman divorced from her husband commits adultery."[23]

The issue of divorce appears twice in Matthew.[24] In 19:1-12 Matthew reports, in his own way, an encounter between Jesus and the Pharisees originally found in Mark 10:1-12. Although Matthew reports this discussion of divorce between Jesus and the Pharisees by using Mark 10:1-12 as his source, he does so in his own way. In a fashion that fits its narrative context more coherently than Luke 16:18, Matthew deals with the question of divorce in 5:32, in the series of ethical instructions located in the antitheses of 5:17-48. Commenting on the words of Decalogue forbidding divorce (Exodus 20:14 and Deuteronomy 5:18), Jesus extends his commentary to the legislation of Deuteronomy 24:1-4. He comments: *"But I say to you that* every-

---

23. For a discussion of the problems surrounding Luke's narrative composition at this point of his Gospel, see Collins, *Divorce*, 175-79.
24. In fact, as Dale C. Allison, Jr, "Divorce, Celibacy and Joseph (Matthew 1.18 25 and 19.1-12)," *Journal for the Study of the New Testament* 49 (1993): 3-10, points out, Matthew raises the issue of divorce *three times*: Joseph's decision to divorce his wife "quietly" is recorded in 1:19. Allison's main concern is to show that πορνεία in 19:9 means adultery, and that Joseph's celibacy in 1:24-25 clarifies what is meant by the eunuch saying in 19:10-12. However, he makes an important point when he suggests that the description of Joseph as a "righteous man" (Greek: δίκαιος) demands that there be an exception to Jesus' absolute prohibition of divorce. It is "righteous" to divorce the unfaithful wife. Not to do so would bring "sin upon the land" (see Deut 24:4). Joseph "is to be regarded as a model of behaviour in accord with God's will" (p. 5). Coherently, therefore, Matthew *must* add the exception clauses to Matthew 5:32 and 19:9. If divorce was necessary for Joseph, the just man, it must be fine for the followers of Jesus. Loader, "Did Adultery Mandate Divorce?" 68-69, understands Joseph's "righteousness" as a judgment of his decision to divorce Mary, rather than execute her. But he agrees that this decision is closely linked to the addition of the exception clauses in 5:32 and 19:9.

one who divorces his wife, *except on the ground of unchastity*, makes her an adulteress; and whoever marries a divorced woman commits adultery" (Matt 5:32).

The closeness between the two teachings is clear. Once the Matthean redactional additions, "But I say to you that," and "except on the ground of adultery," are removed, then the possibility that Luke 16:18 and Matthew 5:32 come from the same source ("Q") is very real.

Matthew 5:32	**Luke 16:18**
(a) Everyone who divorces his wife *except on the ground of unchastity*	Everyone who divorces his wife and marries another
(b) makes her an adulteress	commits adultery
(a) and whoever marries a divorced woman	and the one who marries a woman divorced by her husband
(b) commits adultery.	commits adultery.

Allowing for stylistic and slight changes of content made by the two authors using the same source (Luke clarifies, while Matthew takes the details of divorce between a husband and a wife for granted), the literary structure and the message of this passage indicates that Matthew and Luke are using the same source. The passage (from "Q") points back to a very early record of a word from Jesus that prohibited divorce, prior to Matthew and Luke, but not found in Mark. Unlike Paul's words, "from the Lord," the "Q" passage makes no allowances for the initiative of the woman. At least in that respect, it continues Jewish tradition.

Calling upon the data provided by 1 Corinthians 7:10-11, where Paul appears to be paraphrasing a word of Jesus, Matthew 5:32, and Luke 16:18 ("Q"), scholars are able to suggest the probable "primitive form" of this word of Jesus that had its origins on the lips of Jesus of Nazareth during the course of his ministry. Reflecting a Semitic balance, intricacy, and a density worthy of the importance of the subject being dealt with, a two part saying emerges:

Part 1a: Everyone who divorces his wife and marries another
Part 1b: commits adultery.
Part 2a: And the one who marries a divorced woman
Part 2b: commits adultery.[25]

Whether or not one accepts this "reconstruction" as words of Jesus himself, there is no doubt that Jesus of Nazareth forbad divorce and remarriage.[26] Our glance at the society and religious practice of Jesus' time and Jewish society, indicates that such teaching stands alone. "Jesus the Jew clashes with the Mosaic Torah as it was understood and practiced by mainstream Judaism before, during, and after his time."[27]

Although centuries and worlds apart, there is a certain parallel between the challenge of Jesus' teaching then and now. Modern society is structured, legally and socially, to accept and even encourage (in certain circumstances) the practice of divorce and remarriage. Although the practice of divorce and remarriage was not as widespread at the time of Jesus, Deuteronomy 24:1-4 indicated that a man could dismiss his wife and marry another (see Mark 10:3-4; Matt 19:7).[28] Jesus contradicted this teaching and practice.

John Meier indicates how Jesus' prohibition of divorce and remarriage must have appeared to his contemporaries.

---

25. See Meier, *A Marginal Jew*, 4:107-108 for the reconstructed text, and reflections upon its structure and meaning. This is also the reconstruction of Robinson, Hoffmann, and Kloppenborg, *The Critical Edition of Q*, 470.
26. See also Collins, *Divorce*, 214; Fitzmyer, *First Corinthians*, 290-91. However Loader, "Did Adultery Mandate Divorce?" 67-78, has indicated his serious doubt. He claims that, on the basis of Genesis 2:24 (see pp. 75-76), Jesus took it for granted that divorce would follow adultery. "[T]he exception now found in Matt 5.32 and 19.9 was already presupposed in Mark 10.11-12, Luke 16.18 and 1 Cor 7.10-11. Matthew, rather than uncharacteristically softening Jesus' demand, simply spelled out what has always been assumed" (p. 74).
27. For an application of the usual "criteria" used by historians to detect the historicity of material found in such sayings, see Meier, *A Marginal Jew*, 4:112-19. The citation comes from p. 114. Not all would be so clear-cut. See, among many, Collins, *Divorce*, 178, who suggests that Moses did not mandate divorce, so therefore there is some "room" for Jesus' hard line in these debates. Most recently, see Gerhard Lohfink, *Jesus of Nazareth. What He Wanted, Who He Was*, trans. Linda M. Maloney (Collegeville, MN: The Liturgical Press, 2012), 202-204.
28. A huge social and legal chasm exists between the time of Jesus and modern society and practice in the acceptance of "partners" (heterosexual or homosexual) rather than wives and husbands.

Jesus consciously presented himself to his fellow Jews as the eschatological prophet, performing Elijah's task of beginning the regathering of Israel in the end time while also performing miracles like Elijah's. These miracles were interpreted as signs of the kingdom that was coming and yet that, in a way, was already present in Jesus' ministry. In this highly charged context of future-yet-realized eschatology, the eschatological prophet named Jesus may have inculcated as already binding certain types of behaviour that pointed forward, as did his whole ministry, to the final period of Israel's restoration as God's holy people.[29]

1 Corinthians 7:8-16: God has called us to peace

In 1 Corinthians 7:1 Paul turns his attention to a number of issues related to marriage, with his usual indication of "now concerning these matters ..." (περὶ δέ ...). Writing to his over-enthusiastic new Christians, in vv. 1-7 he informs them that there should not be anything "new" in the way husband and wives should relate, although expressing his personal support for his own way of life, most likely celibate, admitting that not all have this gift from God (v. 7).[30] He then addresses, in sequence, the issues face by the unmarried and the widows (vv. 8-9), the married (vv. 10-11), and the situation of a woman married to an unbeliever (vv. 12-16). On the first and the third question he provides his own opinion: "I say" (v. 8); "I say, not the Lord" (v. 12). In dealing with the married, he indicates: "I give charge, but not I but the Lord" (v. 10), taking us back to our earliest record of Jesus' prohibition of divorce.

As he has done in his general discussion of matters sexual (vv. 1-7), in vv. 8-9 he asks that people maintain their current status. But in vv. 12-16 he moves on to discuss what must have been a common enough reality in Pauline Corinth: a man (v. 12) or a woman (v. 13)

---

29. Meier, *A Marginal Jew*, 4:127. See also Collins, *Divorce*, 218-22.
30. The likely background to Paul's insertion of this thought is that some of the Corinthians, who were not able to live such a life (see v. 9), aspire to live as Paul lives. This would not be appropriate. See Pheme Perkins, *First Corinthians*, Paideia Commentaries on the New Testament (Grand Rapids: Baker Academic, 2012), 109-110.

married to an unbeliever.³¹ Paul recommends that they too remain in their current sexual situation. He provides reason for this recommendation: the potential for mutual consecration of a couple through marriage, and the subsequent consecration of the children (see v. 14).³² Critically, however, "if the unbelieving partner desires to separate, let it be so; in such a case your brother or sister is not bound" (v. 15abc). He again provides reason for this decision: there can be no certainty that such a mixed marriage will lead to salvation (v. 16).³³ The fundamental principle of human relationships must be maintained: "for God has called us to peace" (v. 15d). Immediately after reporting Jesus' word that there be no separation between married couples, Paul addresses the difficult situation of couples and families in Corinth where the union of a believer and an unbeliever is damaging an essential elements in God's calling (see the Greek of v. 15d: κέκληκεν) the Christians tηo live in peace (Greek: ἐν δὲ εἰρήνῃ).³⁴ He reads that situation in the light of God's call of the Christian to peace and salvation, and instructs the Christians in Corinth that a separation should take place.

---

31. It was only natural that adult conversion to Christianity (which was the norm in this founding period) brought women and men into Christianity who already had non-Christian spouses.
32. On the idea of the mutual "sanctification" of spouses and children in the biblical and Jewish tradition, see Collins, *First Corinthians*, 266-67. See also Fitzmyer, *First Corinthians*, 299-301. See p. 301: "God's sanctifying power is greater than any unbelief."
33. The interpretation of v. 16 concerning a wife or a husband's knowledge of the eventual salvation of their respective partner is divided. A positive interpretation supports the permanence of the union, in the hope that the partner might come to salvation. A negative interpretation suggests that there is no point staying in the marriage hoping that salvation will come to one's spouse. That is beyond anyone's knowledge of control; it belongs to God. See Collins, *First Corinthians*, 272, for the discussion.
34. I have drawn attention to the Greek verb "to call" (Greek: καλέω) as this became a technical expression in early Christianity for God's initiative in calling people to the following of Jesus Christ: "vocation." See Collins, *First Corinthians*, 267. Following the RSV, I have used the first-person plural pronoun; "us" (ἡμᾶς). This is textually doubtful. The original may be the second person plural: "you" (Greek: ὑμᾶς). Although the "us" is more clearly associated with the inner-group of the Christian community, the use of "you" does not alter the argument. The reference to "any brother" (Greek: τις ἀδελφός) in v. 12 makes it clear that Paul is addressing the inner-dynamics of a Christian community.

Paul sees the necessity to *accommodate* the special circumstances of a mixed marriage between a pagan and a Christian, and *reverses* Jesus' decision to prohibit divorce. However, Paul does not permit the believing partner, no doubt instructed and committed to the word of the Lord recalled in vv. 10-11, to initiate the process of separation.[35] Jesus has *reversed* the traditional Jewish understanding of the possibility of divorce; Paul now does the same thing with the teaching of Jesus (vv. 10-11) in *allowing* separation between Christian and non-Christian partners. There were no doubt outstanding pastoral reasons for making this decision in support of the God-given peace of Corinthian community.[36] Paul does not appear to be in any anguish over this decision. Juxtaposed with the word of the Lord (vv. 10-11), in vv. 12-16 he gives instructions that are not consistent with vv. 10-11, but which clearly *accommodate* the situation of the Church in Corinth.[37] There is no indication from Paul whether or not the Christian spouse would be permitted to remarry; what he said about remarriage in v. 11 ("remain single") may well continue to apply.[38] Pheme Perkins wisely suggests that Paul might expect them to be guided by v. 7: "I wish that all were as I myself am. But each one has his own special gift from God, one of one kind and one of another."[39]

There are a number of puzzles associated with the interpretation of 1 Corinthians 7:12-16.[40] What is crucial for this essay, however, is that *within the Sacred Scriptures of Christianity* we find an accommodation of Jesus' absolute prohibition of divorce.[41] But Paul is not alone in instituting an exception.

---

35. See, among many, Horsley, *1 Corinthians*, 99.
36. Perkins, *First Corinthians*, 110, points out that Paul is speaking to "the social goal of harmony within the household is the divine intent for all marriages."
37. For a awareness of the sharpness of the contrast, see Fitzmyer, *First Corinthians*, 301-302.
38. Collins, *Divorce*, 63-64, rightly claims that there is a lack of clarity in what Paul thinks about remarriage. Meier, *A Marginal Jew*, 174 note 126, suggests that the texts reflect Paul's own lack of certainty as to "what the Christian caught in this difficult situation can or should do." Fitzmyer, *First Corinthians*, 301-302 is more optimistic: "Paul says nothing against further marriages" (p. 302).
39. Perkins, *First Corinthians*, 110.
40. They are expertly dealt with by Collins, *Divorce*, 40-64.
41. The Catholic Church recognizes this "exception" in its law. Naming Paul, it claims that it has the authority to "dissolve" a marriage between two non-believers (not baptized), when one of the parties subsequently becomes a Catholic. This so-called *privilegium paulinum* (the Pauline privilege), is carefully legislated in

Mark 10:1-12//Matthew 19:1-12 (Matthew 5:32 again)

Matthew regularly uses Mark as one of his major sources. But he generally has something of his own to say, and does not re-write Mark *verbatim*. The reporting of Jesus' debate with the Pharisees over divorce is a good example of this.[42]

Mark 10:1-12	Matthew 19:1-12
¹ And he left there and went to the region of Judea and beyond the Jordan,	¹ Now when Jesus had finished these sayings, he went away from Galilee and entered the region of Judea beyond the Jordan;
and crowds gathered to him again; and again, as his custom was, he taught them.	² and large crowds followed him, and he healed them there.
² And Pharisees came up and in order to test him asked, "Is it lawful for a man to divorce his wife?"	³ And Pharisees came up to him and tested him by asking, "Is it lawful to divorce one's wife for any cause?"
³ He answered them, "What did Moses command you?"	
⁴ They said, "Moses allowed a man to write a certificate of divorce, and to put her away."	[**Transposed:** *⁷ They said to him, "Why then did Moses command one to give a certificate of divorce, and to put her away?"*
⁵ But Jesus said to them, "For your hardness of heart he wrote you this commandment.	*⁸ He said to them, "For your hardness of heart Moses allowed you to divorce your wives,*

Canons 1143-1150. Fitzmyer, *First Corinthians*, 302-302, comments: "That is a development in Canon Law that goes beyond the limits of the case envisaged by Paul."

42. The following parallel presentation of the Markan and Matthean texts provides the order of the Markan text. Both texts are presented in full, in regular type. However, passages that Matthew has relocated are presented in *italics*, so that the reader will more easily be able to follow the parallels. They also show Matthew's creative freedom with his source.

⁶ But from the beginning of creation, 'God made them male and female.'	but from the beginning it was not so.] ⁴ He answered, "Have you not read that he who made them from the beginning made them male and female,
⁷ 'For this reason a man shall leave his father and mother and be joined to his wife, ⁸ and the two shall become one flesh.' So they are no longer two but one flesh.	⁵ and said, 'For this reason a man shall leave his father and mother and be joined to his wife, and the two shall become one flesh'? ⁶ So they are no longer two but one flesh.
⁹ What therefore God has joined together, let not man put asunder."	What therefore God has joined together, let not man put asunder." ⁷ They said to him, "Why then did Moses command one to give a certificate of divorce, and to put her away?" ⁸ He said to them, "For your hardness of heart Moses allowed you to divorce your wives, but from the beginning it was not so.
[**Transposed**: ¹¹ *And he said to them,* "Whoever divorces his wife and marries another, commits adultery against her; 12 and if she divorces her husband and marries another, she commits adultery."]	⁹ And I say to you: whoever divorces his wife, *except for unchastity* (Greek: *mē epi porneia*), and marries another, commits adultery."
¹⁰ And in the house the disciples asked him again about this matter.	The disciples said to him, "If such is the case of a man with his wife, it is not expedient to marry."

¹¹ And he said to them, "Whoever divorces his wife and marries another, commits adultery against her; ¹² and if she divorces her husband and marries another, she commits adultery."	¹¹ But he said to them, "Not all men can receive this saying, but only those to whom it is given. ¹² For there are eunuchs who have been so from birth, and there are eunuchs who have been made eunuchs by men, and there are eunuchs who have made themselves eunuchs for the sake of the kingdom of heaven. He who is able to receive this, let him receive it."

Mark 10:1-9 is shaped like a traditional rabbinic discussion. The question of divorce is posed. Mark indicates the hostility of the Pharisees; they asked the question "in order to test him" (v. 2). Jesus responds with a further question, asking the Pharisees to locate their query within the teaching of the Law (v. 3). They respond by citing the general meaning of Deuteronomy 24:1-4 (v. 4), but Jesus counters with a correction of the Pharisees' understanding of Torah by showing that this was not God's original design. It was allowed, through Moses, only because of the hardness of hearts in Israel. The *original* design of God, *from the beginning of creation*, is found in Genesis 1:27 and 2:24 (vv. 5-8). It provides his response to the original question (see v. 2) with the words, "What therefore what God has joined together, let no man put asunder" (v. 9).[43] Jesus has answered Torah with Torah, and the Pharisees fall silent. But "in the house" as the disciples who ask him about this matter, he shifts the argument from divorce to adultery.[44] Mark regularly uses "the house" as the location for teaching the disciples (see 3:20; 7:17-23; 9:28, 33). A man or a woman who divorces and remarries "commits adultery" (vv. 11-12). Although adultery has been introduced in Jesus' discussion with the disciples, there is a logical link with what Jesus has taught the Pharisees. The Torah legislates against adultery (Exod 20:19; Deut 4:10; 22:22; Lev

---

43. A crucial distinction is drawn between what God (ὁ θεός) has done, and what "man" (ἄνθρωπος) attempts to undo in v. 9.
44. See, for example, Adela Y. Collins, *Mark*, Hermeneia (Minneapolis: Fortress, 2007), 469-70.

20:10). Jesus teaches his disciples (and they are the object of all that is found across 10:1-31) that the practice of the Pharisees leads to a breach of Torah, as divorce and remarriage is adultery.[45] Jesus' absolute prohibition of divorce in Mark 10:1-12, echoes the earlier record of 1 Corinthians 7:10-11. Writing in the Roman world, Mark addresses the possibility of divorce and remarriage (and subsequent adultery) on the part of both the man and the woman.

Matthew does not have the parrying back-and-forth that shapes rabbinic discussion. The Pharisees test Jesus by asking if it is lawful to divorce one's wife *for any cause* (v. 3).[46] Matthew has Jesus respond immediately in terms of Genesis 1:27 and 2:24 (vv. 5-6). Only when the Pharisees are cornered by Jesus' use of the Torah do they turn to Deuteronomy 24:1-4 (v. 7). Jesus replies in terms of Israel's hardness of heart, catching up his earlier response from Genesis by telling them that "from the beginning it was not so" (v. 8). Mark's location of the link between divorce and adultery (Mark 10:11-12) is used to end the Matthean encounter between Jesus and the Pharisees (v. 9), rather than to the disciples (Mark 10:11-12). Matthew, reflecting a more Jewish tradition, regards the man as the one who might initiate divorce, and thus commit adultery. The woman is not considered. As in Mark (10:10-12), Matthew closes the episode with an explanation to the disciples in 19:10-12, but the discussions are very different. Matthew uses his own special traditions, not found anywhere else in the New Testament.[47] The disciples cannot imagine how such a prohibition could work. If one cannot divorce, then the institution of marriage is to be avoided (v. 10). Jesus' responds that the never-failing gift of loyalty in marriage is "a special gift from God" (v. 11; recalling

---

45. On the focus upon teaching the disciples across 10:1-31, see Francis J. Moloney, *The Gospel of Mark. A Commentary* (Grand Rapids: Baker Academic, 2012), 192-203.
46. It has long been argued that Matthew's addition of "for any cause" reflects the difference of opinion between the school of Shammai, who only allowed divorce on the basis of moral disorder on the part of the woman, and the school of Hillel, who allowed divorce "for any cause." This debate is widely recorded in Rabbinic documents. See, among most, Fitzmyer, "The Matthean Divorce Texts," 197-226. This position is strenuously opposed by Meier, *A Marginal Jew*, 94-95, 163 note 80. He claims the Rabbinic texts are too late (written early in the third century) to be used in the interpretation of a first century document.
47. See Collins, *Divorce*, 119-20.

1 Cor 7:1), and closes with the famous saying about being a eunuch because of the kingdom of heaven (v. 12).[48]

Within these parallel narratives in Mark and Matthew, there are two significant issues that call for closer attention:

1. Matthew's report of Jesus' prohibiting divorce, "except for unchastity" in his encounter with the Pharisees (19:9: μὴ ἐπὶ πορνείῃ). This exception must have been important for Matthew and his Christian community. It was not present in Mark 10:11-12, that Matthew is using as a source. He also inserts the same sentiment, "except for unchastity" in 5:32 (παρεκτὸς λόγου πορνείας), where the original "Q" passage (see Luke 16:18) did not allow any such possibility (see Luke 16:18).
2. Jesus' use of Genesis in both accounts, and his explanation that the prohibition of divorce is based upon God's design "from the beginning of creation" (Mark 10:6a) and "from the beginning" (Matthew 19:4b, 8c).

1. *"Except for Unchastity" (Matthew 5:32; 19:9)*

When Matthew uses two of his major sources, "Q" (see Luke 16:18) and the Gospel of Mark (see Mark 10:1-12), he *accommodates* the absolute prohibition of divorce found in both of them. What is perhaps more remarkable, for the contemporary interpreter of the New Testament, he uses exactly the same expression to describe the motivation for this exception. The Greek word used, πορνεία, is a notoriously difficult word to translate with any precision. This is so because a number of different Greek expressions are used with reference to specific sexually immoral acts, but πορνεία is a more generic word that can refer to any one of them, or to all of them.[49] In his use of "Q" he softens Jesus' absolute prohibition by adding "except in the case of πορνεία," and his rewriting of Mark is similarly softened by the words "except for πορνεία."

---

48. It is beyond our scope to discuss the history and meaning of Matthew 19:10-12. For more detail, see Francis J. Moloney, "Matthew 19,3-12 and Celibacy: A Redactional and Form Critical Study," *Journal for the Study of the New Testament* 2(1979): 42-60.
49. For a very good survey, see William R. G. Loader, *The New Testament on Sexuality* (Grand Rapids: Eerdmans, 2012), 244-50.

Understandably, given the importance of these two exceptions, what Matthew meant by his use of πορνεία has long been the source of debate and discussion.⁵⁰ A decision need not be made here, and what I am about to suggest is one possibility among many. The situation of the early Christian community addressed by the Gospel of Matthew would have been marked by the presence of both Jews and Gentiles. No doubt the inner-community marital situation addressed by Paul in 1 Corinthians 7:12-16 would have again been present, even though the cultural and religious settings of Corinth and Antioch were different. In the newly founded Christian community, there would have been marriages that had been entered into by the pre-Christian *Gentile* members of some of the new Christians. For the Christian community, and especially for the Matthean community where an observance of the Law was required (see 5:17-19), some of these pagan marriages were regarded as πορνεία.

We need not decide precisely what that meant, and the generic word used by the RSV, "unchastity," serves well. I suspect that Paul's use of the expression πορνεία to refer to the incestuous relationship between a man and his father's wife in 1 Corinthians 5:1 is a pointer to its meaning in Matthew 5:32 and 19:9.⁵¹ Whatever one makes of that suggestion, Matthew asks that marriages marked by what the Christian community considered πορνεία be ended. In rewriting Mark 10:1-12, he adds vv. 10-12, found only in Matthew, to his Markan source instructing his disciples (again in a way that echoes 1 Corinthians 7:8-9) that, once freed from this unacceptable marriage situation, they should remain single.⁵² Such a request, however, is recognized as extremely difficult. It is not possible for everyone to live that way, and only those gifted for such a life-style should practice it (v. 12d. See 1 Cor 7:7-9).⁵³

---

50. For a survey of this discussion see Ulrich Luz, *Matthew*, Hermeneia, 3 vols. (Minneapolis: Fortress, 2001-2007), 1:250-59.
51. As we have seen, Loader, "Did Adultery Mandate Divorce?" 67-78, challenges this suggestion. He claims that *porneia* certainly meant adultery, and that it was taken for granted, even by Jesus, that divorce would follow adultery.
52. This case is argued at length in Moloney, "Matthew 19:3-12 and Celibacy," 44-60. In support of the meaning of "incestuous relationship," see also Fitzmyer, "Matthean Divorce Texts," 221.
53. The verb used by Matthew in 19:12d, translated in the RSV in the command "He who is able to *receive* this, let him *receive* it," is χωρέω. Its primary meaning is not

Whatever the precise situation addressed by Matthew, and whatever the exact meaning he wishes to give to the word πορνεία, the decisive matter is that he uses two sources that record the memory of Jesus' absolute prohibition of divorce and remarriage ("Q" and Mark), and he modifies *both* of them (Matt 5:32; 19:9). We are dealing with another moment in the developing theological and pastoral consciousness of the earliest Church that quite freely *and consistently* accommodates a teaching of Jesus. This is a further indication *within the inspired pages of our Christian Sacred Scriptures* that shows the need for the Church to rethink Jesus' fiercely eschatological teaching, in the light of the long-term pastoral situation of the developing Christian Church. As Craig Keener has pointed out: "In practice, the early Christians immediately began to qualify Jesus' divorce saying; other principles of Jesus, such as not condemning the innocent (12:7) or the principle of mercy (23:23), would have forced them to do so in some circumstances. ... Paul and Matthew's exceptions (Mt 5:32; 19:9; 1 Cor 7:15, 27-28) constitute two-thirds of the extant first-century Christian references to divorce."[54]

2. *From the Beginning (Mark 10:6; Matthew 19:4, 8)*

The dispute between Jesus and the Pharisees over divorce and remarriage in Mark 10:1-12 swings upon the use Jesus makes of the Torah texts of Genesis 1:27 and 2:24 to overcome their use of the Torah text of Deuteronomy 24:1-4 as the reason for allowing divorce. Whether or not this use of a text that comes "before" the legislation handed down through Moses in Deuteronomy 24:1-4 because of the hardness of heart of Israel closes the issue, Jesus' explanation of why the Genesis texts close the discussion is provided with words "from the beginning of creation" (ἀπὸ δὲ ἀρχῆς κτίσεως) that open his citations from Genesis (Mark 10:6. See also Matt 19:8). A crucial theological point needs to be made here: Mark (followed by Matthew) presents Jesus' teaching as the reconstitution of God's original design: "from the beginning (ἀρχῇ) of creation" (Mark), "from the beginning" (ἀρχῇ) (twice in Matthew).

"receive," but "make space" (see Mark 2:2). It carries the idea of being open to a gift, and thus "accept."

54. Craig S. Keener, *A Commentary on the Gospel of Matthew* (Grand Rapids: Eerdmans, 1999), 191.

Jesus' appeal to texts from Genesis, and his explicit reference to "the beginning," situates Jesus description of the situation between a woman and a man in the Garden of Eden! Genesis 1:27 and 2:24 describe the situation between a man (Adam) and a woman (Eve) *before* the introduction of sin into the human story (see Gen 3:1-24). As Joel Marcus has correctly commented, "Jesus and the Markan Christians are people who rejoice in the dawning light of the new age – which is also the recaptured radiance of Eden."[55] But sin has entered the world, and we now claim that only Jesus of Nazareth has embodied the perfect human condition designed by God for the human condition. That perfection has been represented in the biblical account of Adam and Eve, but such perfection has been lost to the human condition (Genesis 3). The loss of the glory of these beginnings through the sin and disobedience of Adam has been overcome by the universal significance of the obedience of Jesus, revealed in his death and resurrection. But the story of Adam and the story of Jesus Christ continue to run side by side throughout the human story. Nowhere has this been more eloquently stated than in the close contrasting parallels that Paul draws between Adam and Christ in Romans 5:12-21. The Christian must live the in-between-time, called to join the Christ story and reject the Adam story.[56] As history eloquently demonstrates, humankind is "in process": the ideal of God's original creative plan has never been fully present in the ambiguity of that history.[57]

The introduction of Pauline thought on the "new creation" (see Gal 2:15; 2 Corinthians 5:17) raises a further question. Reflecting upon Jesus' bold rejection of Torah in forbidding the practice of divorce, we earlier saw John Meier arguing that Jesus understood himself and was understood by his followers as the eschatological prophet.

---

55. Joel Marcus, *Mark*, The Anchor Yale Bible 27-27A, 2 vols. (New York/New Haven: Doubleday/Yale University Press, 2000-2009), 2:710
56. On Paul's concept of the Adam story, and the "new creation" of Jesus' death and resurrection, see Moloney, *Reading the New Testament in the Church*, 97-102.
57. Some may query this statement in the light of the saints, and especially the Mother of Jesus, in Catholic teaching. Such holiness, which is a restoration of God's original design, is only possible because of a positive response to the gift of God's grace. It is not *natural*.

> In this highly charged context of future-yet-realized eschatology, the eschatological prophet named Jesus may have inculcated as already binding certain types of behaviour that pointed forward, as did his whole ministry, to the final period of Israel's restoration as God's holy people.[58]

Both Paul (in the 50's CE) and Mark (about 70 CE) continue to portray Jesus in this fashion. However, they not only continue Jesus' teaching by looking to "the end" as the explanation for the uniqueness of Jesus and his teaching.[59] They reach back to the beginnings of all creation. This tendency develops as the early Church developed an ever-deepening understanding of Jesus' significance.[60] Paul refers to a pre-existent Christ in Philippians 2:6-11, but this development finds its highest expression in the Prologue to the Gospel of John, where Jesus is described as the Logos of God, who dwelt in a unique oneness of time "in the beginning" (John 1:1-2: ἐν ἀρχῇ).

Mark 10:1-12 and Matthew 19:1-12 are bearers of this theological tradition. The strength of Jesus' prohibition of divorce comes from his indication that there was no divorce in the Garden of Eden. Christians do not live in the Garden of Eden, but within the ambiguity of the contemporary human story. Contemporary Catholic legislation prohibits divorce on the basis of the fact that Jesus did so. This position misses an important theological truth in its presupposition that the "ideal" of God's original creation is in place from the very first moment of the long, and often complex, "real" journey of Christian marriage. It transfers what was primarily a christological intuition of the early Church into an essential element of its marriage legislation (Canon 1141). The confusion of the "ideal" with the "real" in the lives of imperfect people, striving (and sometimes failing) in their Christian lives, calls for re-examination by the Church's highest authority.

---

58. Meier, *A Marginal Jew*, 4:127.
59. Jesus' looking to "the end" as the basis for an understanding of his person and message has been splendidly shown by Allison, *Constructing Jesus*.
60. There is considerable contemporary interest in the relationship between Pauline and Markan theology, initiated by Joel Marcus, "Mark – Interpreter of Paul," *New Testament Studies* 46 (2000): 473-87

Conclusion

The Christian Church does not base its teaching and practice only on what can be shown as the authentic teaching and practice of the historical Jesus. The foundational Councils that produced much of the Christian Tradition ranged widely across *everything in the New Testament*, especially the Gospel of John and the Letters of Paul, to establish its rule of faith, and to articulate it in the Creeds. There should be no "picking and choosing" with the Word of God. These debates are often coloured by the suggestion that the Church is selective in what it chooses from the teaching of Jesus, and point to such requirements as cutting off the hand, the foot, and plucking out the eye (see Mark 9:43-47). They are not legislated in Canon law, but Jesus' prohibition of divorce (found only in 1 Cor 7.10-11 and Mark 10:1-12) is found there (see Canon 1055). Such debates can sometimes be superficial, but they contain a challenge. Martin Hengel has devoted detailed attention to a saying of Jesus, found in "Q," that he argues lies at the heart of Jesus' personal sense of his charism: "Leave the dead to bury their own dead; but as for you, go and proclaim the kingdom of God" (Luke 9:60//Matt 8:22).[61] Living the Word of God in the Christian Church is no easy matter.[62]

An important hermeneutic has always been at play in the development of Christian tradition, and in the Church's necessary commitment to play an effective role in an increasingly informed world. It has never been a simple process. It generates tension and misunderstanding, as the story of the Ecumenical Councils, from Nicea (325 CE) to Vatican II (1962-65 CE), indicate.[63] But the Church does not simply look back to the identifiable words of Jesus to establish its doctrinal and moral bedrock truths; it reflects upon its biblical and eccle-

---

61. Martin Hengel, *The Charismatic Leader and His Followers*, trans. James C. G. Greig, Studies of the New Testament and Its World (Edinburgh: T. & T. Clark, 1981). This study rightly points to the importance of Jesus' intense eschatological understanding of his mission, shared by his followers.
62. This statement could lead to a discussion of the need for all the Christian Churches to reflect a "shared wisdom and experience" when they face such difficult questions. This is not the place for such a debate, but the Catholic Church stands alone among Christian Churches that also look to the Word of God for their founding and formative Traditions in the matter of divorce and remarriage. This calls for some self-examination.
63. The tensions surrounding Vatican II have been graphically documented by Yves Congar, *My Journal of the Council*, trans. Dennis Minns, and Others (Adelaide: ATF Theology, 2012).

sial tradition in dialogue with an ever-expanding body of knowledge and experience.

The Church's treatment of the divorced and the remarried must take into account *the entire picture*. As the early Church recognized that Jesus had begun a "new creation," it challenged believers to resist and overcome sin, guided by the example of Jesus, enlivened by the pardoning and life-giving grace generated by his death and resurrection (see Rom 5:12-21; Mark 10:6; Matt 19:4, 8). The earliest Tradition recognized that only Jesus incarnated the "new creation." The rest of humankind strives to live a Christian life caught in the ambiguity of the ongoing presence of both the Adam and the Christ story (see Rom 5:12-21), confident that "where sin increased, grace abounded all the more" (Rom 5:20). Consequently Paul and Matthew, without compunction, accommodated Jesus' absolute prohibition of divorce for its fragile members (1 Cor 7:14-16; Matt. 5:32; 19:9).

This is the *authentic Tradition* generated within the Spirit-filled formative decades of Christianity. It should direct us as we read the *entire New Testament*, seeking the guidance that is found there.[64] No one has stated this more authoritatively than Joseph Fitzmyer:

> If Matthew under inspiration could have been moved to add an exceptive phrase to the saying of Jesus about divorce that he found in an absolute form in either his Marcan source or in 'Q,' of if Paul likewise under inspiration could introduce into his writing an exception on his own authority, then why cannot the Spirit-guided institutional Church of a later generation make a similar exception in view of problems confronting Christian married life of its day or so-called broken marriage?[65]

Recognizing this *authentic Tradition*, the Church's leadership should see that its current legislation is based on a late, biblically unfounded, *tradition*. The Church must face the confusing challenges of contemporary society through an examination of its Tradition, and not purely on the basis of mercy and compassion - however precious these hallmarks of Francis' papacy might be.

---

64. This hermeneutic was hesitatingly proposed to the teaching authority of the Church 35 years ago by Pierre Benoit, "Christian Marriage according to Saint Paul," *The Clergy Review* 65 (1980): 309-321. See especially pp. 320-21.
65. Fitzmyer, *First Corinthians*, 298. Fitzmyer first made this suggestion in 1976 ("The Matthean Divorce Texts," 224-26).

15
On the Writing of *The Gospel According to Judas:* Some Theological and Pastoral Reflections

My association as a Catholic Priest and New Testament scholar with a notorious British novelist to produce a work with the title *The Gospel According to Judas* has created mixed reactions across the world, especially the conservative Catholic world.[1] But on the whole, people who have taken the time to read the book have found that, with the aid of Jeffrey Archer's story-telling skills, *The Gospel According to Judas* is an attractive and nuanced story of Jesus. For many, this reading has sent them back to the canonical Gospels. More than that, it indicates that there is goodness and hope in even the worst of villains. I am grateful to have this opportunity to speak at greater length to the genesis of the book, and some of the issues that arise from such a publication.

The Genesis of The Gospel According to Judas

Jeffrey Archer claims to have been interested in the figure of Judas, as presented in the canonical Gospels, for some years. He was aware of the apparent contradictions in the Gospel portraits of Judas. Peter and the other ten disciples also failed, but only Judas is depicted as one of the greatest villains of history. However, on approaching his publisher he was told that they did not want a Jeffrey Archer attempt to upstage Dan Brown. The publisher suggested that he seek scholarly assistance for the project to have historical credibility. Archer approached Cardinal Carlo Maria Martini, and he suggested that I may be the best person to speak to. All this happened without my knowledge. When I eventually I received a letter from Archer, asking

---

1. J. Archer and F. J. Moloney, *The Gospel According to Judas by Benjamin Iscariot* (London: Macmillan, 2007).

for my collaboration I thought that he was seeking some background research for yet another of his well-told novels. Shortly after accepting that role I had to go to Rome for a meeting of the Superiors of my Religious Congregation, the Salesians of Don Bosco. Archer flew from London to Rome to meet with me. It quickly became apparent that he wanted more from me than the occasional consultation on historical background for a novel about Judas.

Archer had already decided that he wanted a "gospel." He did not understand the full implications of that request. He was more concerned with the *form* of a Gospel, a book, with chapter and verses, about the length of the Gospel of Luke. I was quick to tell him that the word "gospel" meant more than a literary form. If we were to write a "gospel," it had to be a proclamation of the good news of what God had done for us in and through the life, teaching, death and resurrection of Jesus. Indeed, this was the most difficult challenge in our collaboration. From the start I told Archer that we would have to use the traditions that come to us from the canonical Gospels, and that the main character had to be Jesus. The figure of Judas could only emerge as the person who told the story of Jesus. This is not an account of the life of Judas, but Judas' telling the life of Jesus. As all gospels are second or third generation documents, and not biographies (see Luke 1:1-4), Judas' son, Benjamin, was created.

On Sunday, October 18, 2006, Pope Benedict XVI devoted his Angelus address to the pilgrims in St Peter's Square to Judas. During the course of that address he said: "To understand the life of Judas means to understand decisive aspects of the mystery of man's relationship with God." My prayer was that the Archer-Moloney story of Jesus and Judas might make some contribution to such an understanding.

The Nature of The Gospel According to Judas

Once we had agreed that not only *the form* of this document was to be that of a "gospel," but also *the content*, the writing process could begin. I initiated the story-telling by adopting the time-frame and the geography of the Synoptic Gospels, especially that of Mark. I developed the narrative of a chapter, depending heavily upon the four-fold Gospel tradition, and sent it to Archer. He would then work through that material, shaping it into something of a page-turner. This process was painstaking. As those of you who have read any of his novels are aware, Archer has a fertile imagination. I had to insist at all times that while I was prepared to allow him to develop narrative sequences that might be improbable, they had to be possible. For example, the death of Judas by crucifixion at the hands of the Romans is highly improbable, but the crucifixion of any Jewish resistance by Titus and his forces during and after the Jewish War of 70 CE is well documented (see Josephus, *Jewish War* 5.449-451). Judas *most likely did not* die this way, but he *could have* (see *Judas* 25:52-59).

The canonical Gospels, and the many other "gospels" that appeared in the early Christian centuries were never intended to be a day-by-day eye-witness report of Jesus' life story.[2] Each story teller, and the Evangelists for the Canonical Gospels, assembled traditions that came to them from the memory of Jesus and from the teaching and praying that flowed from that memory. From among those traditions, they chose those which best suited their purpose, to bring people into the Christian community, or to instruct, support and encourage those who were already Christians. Nowhere is this more clearly articulated than at the close of the Gospel of John, where the evangelist turns to his readers and announces:

> Now Jesus did many other signs in the presence of his disciples *which are not written in this book*. But *these are written* so that you may go on believing that Jesus is the Christ, the Son of God, and that by means of this belief, you may have life in his name (John 20:30-31).

The Evangelist has *made a selection* from the many traditions that he knew existed, and he told them so that people might go on believing, and have life in the name of Jesus, the Christ and the Son of God.[3]

---

2. For a very useful critical collection of the non-canonical Gospels, with an introduction to each apocryphal text, see the first volume of E. Hennecke and W. Schneemelcher, eds., *New Testament Apocrypha*, ttrans. R. McL. Wilson, 2 vols. (London: SCM Press, 1963). This volume runs into 531 pages.
3. For a more detailed introduction to the formation of the Gospels, see F. J. Moloney, *The Living Voice of the Gospel. The Gospels Today* (Melbourne: John Garratt, 2006), 13-42. On John 20:30-31, see F. J. Moloney, *The Gospel of John*, Sacra Pagina 4 (Collegeville: The Liturgical Press, 1998 [updated and corrected reprint, 2005]), 542-45. The same declaration of intention is found in Luke 1:1-4. After telling Theophilus that there had been eyewitnesses to the life and teaching

I would not be so brash as to claim that our efforts matched that of the authors of the canonical Gospels. But I suspect that we have done better with *The Gospel of Judas* than some writers from the Church's early centuries who created narratives that remain with us in the non-canonical gospels. Our sources are all too obvious. We have published them in red, with the exact references or allusions indicated in the margins, so that our readers will be aware of what we are up to. It is obvious to a Christian who knows Jesus' story well where we have departed from our received traditions and where Archer's imagination runs loose. But even here, remember, he was allowed to generate narratives that may not be probable; but they had to be possible.

To my mind, the greatest weakness of my association with a professional storyteller is Archer's self-confessed desire to create a "linear story." The canonical Gospels have a literary form of their own that is certainly not "linear." As Michael McGirr wrote in a perceptive review of the book: "It does not create moments of wonder or stillness. It can't reduce, or raise, a reader to speechlessness in the way the original Gospels do. There are too few gaps. This book wants to explain everything; it doesn't seem to understand the difference between information and wisdom."[4] This is true, but as I will ask below, how many of our contemporaries are being reduced to speechlessness as they commit themselves *en masse* to a reading of the original Gospels? As many as are committing themselves *en masse* to Dan Brown's *The da Vinci Code* and Richard Dawkin's *The God Delusion*?[5] Is it worth taking the risk to provide some *information* that might draw people back to the *wisdom* of the original Gospels? For better or for worse, I thought that was a risk worth taking.

The text went through eleven editions before we let it go. There were two critical moments that almost brought the process to a stand-

---

of Jesus in a first generation (v. 2), and then that many (second generation) had "undertaken to set down an orderly account" (v. 1), the author of the Third Gospel informs him that he (third generation) has also decided to produce a written "orderly account" (v. 3): "so that you may know the truth about which you have been instructed" (v. 4). This NRSV translation misses the weight of the statement with the noun "truth" (Greek: ἀσφάλειαν). The word carries the notion of "reliability, soundness."

4. M. McGirr, "When four gospels just aren't enough," *The Age* (Saturday, April 7), Section A2, 22.
5. D. Brown, *The da Vinci Code* (New York: Random House, 2003); R. Dawkins, *The God Delusion* (London: Bantam Press, 2006).

still. Archer had written a long and interesting development of the thirty pieces of silver (see Matt 26:15; 27:3-5). The fact that the detail of the thirty pieces of silver is only found in Matthew, and is obviously taken directly from Zechariah 11:12-13, led me to warn him that he was making too much of something that was important in the Christian tradition, but which most likely did not happen. It is possible – but not certain – that money changed hands. Mark mentions it (Mark 14:11), and John suggests that Judas was pilfering money from the common purse (John 12:6). In the end, this chapter was dropped, but only after lengthy argument and debate. That debate generated what can now be found, in a condensed form, in the Glossary note xli.[6]

However important that debate may have been – and there were many lesser skirmishes - the ending proved to be the critical issue. Archer is used to bringing his stories to a comfortable *dénouement*, he demanded that a further resurrection appearance be added to the Gospel traditions. He wanted Judas to have an experience of the risen Lord, and come to belief before he died. *For me, as a credible critic and historian, such an ending was unacceptable.* Archer could not understand why not. Untrained in the critical use of the tradition, he found it hard to accept my total rejection of such an ending. It took some time – and almost the total abandoning of the project – to convince him that if Judas had experienced some form of conversion, then it would be found *somewhere in the tradition*. It might be possible to accept that the canonical Gospels did not record such an event, but somewhere – even in the non-canonical tradition – there would be some mention of such an experience. It is not found anywhere. In the end, Archer capitulated. In my opinion, the improbable but possible ending he eventually produced is far more poignant than a conver-

---

6. For more detail on the development of traditions around the figure of Judas, see the work of the Catholic scholar (with an imprimatur given on May 17, 2006), J. P. Meier, *A Marginal Jew*, 5 vols., Anchor Yale Bible Reference Library (New York/New Haven: Doubleday/Yale University Press, 1991-2016), 3:142-46, 208-11. On the use of Zechariah 11 in the formation of Matthew's story of Judas, see another Catholic scholar, D. Senior, *Matthew*, Abingdon New Testament Commentaries (Nashville: Abingdon Press, 1998), 293-94, and the detailed analysis of B. Lindars, *New Testament Apologetic. The Doctrinal Significance of the Old Testament Quotations* (London: SCM Press, 1961), 116-22. Another Catholic scholar, D. Harrington, *The Gospel of Matthew*, Sacra Pagina 1 (Collegeville. MN: The Liturgical Press, 1991), 364, adds the background of Exod 21:32: thirty pieces of silver is the value of a slave gored by an ox.

sion story that never happened. This was an outstanding application of the criterion that I applied to Archer's imaginative developments of the received tradition: he was allowed to develop a narrative that may not be probable, but it had to be possible. The conversion of Judas was impossible, but the crucifixion of a pious and enthusiastic Jew by the forces of Trajan in 70AD was very possible.

On two occasions we had day-long sessions together, one in London and another in Sydney. The bulk of our communications, several times a week across twelve months, was by means of email and attachments. That correspondence alone could fill a large volume, I suspect. Archer and I had also discussed how we would like the book to appear. For centuries gospel books have been presented in small booklets, with gilt edges and a cloth marker. We asked if our work could be presented in the same way. Macmillan responded to our suggestions with alacrity and skill. Thus we have an elegant little volume.

The Gospel According to Judas *and* the Gnostic Gospel of Judas

It is unfortunate that Archer's long desire to work on the theme of Judas came to fruition in the midst of a flurry of interest in the person of Judas, generated by what has been called "The Gospel of Judas," a small text found in a larger Coptic codex (Codex Tchacos), made available in 1997. This is a valuable text, but it is not a "Gospel of Judas," a narrative telling of the life of Jesus through the eyes of Judas. It is a third century Coptic translation of an original Greek text that may be dated as early as 180-190 A.D.[7] It reflects a form of second century Gnosticism called "Sethism." One of the features of this form of Gnostic Christianity is that it regards the human condition as an experience of enslavement. The human being is captured in a fleshly dwelling. In this text, after experiencing a revelation, Judas finds that he is destined to betray Jesus. Jesus tells Judas that he is the one ordained by God to hand him over to his executors so that Jesus may be loosed from his flesh to attain true illumination. Judas, therefore, is not a villain, even though he betrays Jesus. He is a part of God's design, and therefore a hero.

---

7. For an excellent edition of the text, see R. Kasser, M. Mayer and G. Wurst, eds., *The Gospel of Judas* (Washington, DC: National Geographic, 2006).

Recent "Judas books" approach this Gnostic text in a number of ways. Some attempt to reconstruct the damaged ancient Coptic manuscript. Some work to identify the social and religious setting that might have produced such a Greek text late in the second century, and led to its preservation in Coptic. More sensationally, a small group of scholars attempts to show that these traditions about Judas are more authentic that those found in Matthew, Mark, Luke and John. This scholarly position, the fruit of the so-called "Jesus Seminar," plays to the widespread desire in the Western world to debunk the Christian tradition as it has come down to us, and to replace the canonical tradition with the non-canonical and Gnostic traditions. Whatever one makes of these "Judas books," they belong to a world other than Archer-Moloney, *The Gospel According to Judas*. Their concerns are not our concerns. As a Roman Catholic Priest and theologian, their agenda is not my agenda![8]

Theological Reflections

Let me turn to a few details in the book that may bother traditional Christian readers. I have already stated and restated the criteria used in the relationship between the storyteller and the biblical scholar. Not everything in this book can be regarded as probable. But everything must be possible. This covers a number of issues that might make people wonder. Did Judas have a son named Benjamin? If Judas did not commit suicide immediately after the death of Jesus, did he wander off to Qumran? Was Judas slain by Titus' Romans at the destruction of the so-called monastery at Khirbet Qumran? Is it possible – even though he could not accept that Jesus was the Messiah, or that he had been raised by God from the dead – that he admired Jesus so much that he thanked the God of Israel for a death that repeated Jesus' crucifixion? None of this can be shown to be factual. Most of it is improbable, but none of it – in my judgment – is impossible. There is ample evidence from the first century that Jewish males were

---

8. For a popular discussion of the Coptic *Gospel of Judas*, see T. Wright, *Judas and the Gospel of Jesus* (London: SPCK, 2006). I would agree entirely with Bishop Wright's assessment of the Coptic text, and the literature that has developed since its publication in 1997. For a more positive assessment of the Gnostic document, and the place of Gnostic traditions in Christian history, see B. D. Ehrmann, *The Lost Gospel of Judas Iscariot. A New Look at Betrayer and Betrayed* (New York: Oxford University Press, 2006).

expected to have sons, out of obedience to Genesis 1:28: "Be fruitful and multiply." Rejected by his fellow disciples of Jesus and betrayed by Jewish leadership, it would have been logical for this passionate believer to join a community of similarly-minded Jews at Qumran, passionate about traditional Judaism, and opposed to Jewish leadership. We have first-hand archeological and literary evidence that the armies of Titus destroyed the so-called monastery at Qumran, and that crucifixion was the form of execution used to punish those Jews who continued to resist the Romans. Most of these episodes in the *Gospel According to Judas* come from the fertile imagination of Jeffrey Archer, but they were closely monitored, and checked against historical records, before they were allowed to appear in the text only because they were "possible."

Readers will experience that these elements in the story give power and deeper meaning to the puzzle of the person of Judas. In the end, after all my scholarly pondering, it was Archer's powerful story that led me to accept these "possible" and powerful moments in the *Gospel*. But I must insist that – however improbable they may be – they are all possible.

But there are other places where I have taken the lead, and these are the elements in the book that have created difficulties for some Roman Catholics, especially in the USA. What must be accepted in reading *The Gospel According to Judas* is that it is a re-telling of the story of Jesus *from the point of view of Judas*. Thus, for example, it is Judas who cannot accept the tradition of the virgin birth. The Jewish Messiah has to be the legitimate child of Jewish parents. Indeed, so that there would be no doubt about my own sentiments on this issue, I added a glossary note to *Judas* 2:6-8 stating: "Judas' understanding of the birth of Jesus is not the Roman Catholic interpretation, as expressed in the Marian doctrines, especially that of Mary's perpetual virginity."[9] Similarly, as Benjamin tells his father many of the stories that are circulating about Jesus, stories that we have in the canonical Gospels, Judas remains unconvinced that Jesus was the Messiah, the founder of a new community of God. His death demonstrates his deep affection for Jesus, but there is no commitment in faith that God has done anything special for humankind in and through the life, teaching, death and resurrection of Jesus of Nazareth. He is also,

---

9. *Judas*, 93 (glossary note v).

therefore, similarly unconvinced by some of the "memories" from the life of Jesus that his son recounted to him at Qumran (see *Judas* 25:25-43). Judas was not part of the early Christian community, born at the resurrection of Jesus and fired by the Pentecostal gift of the Spirit. He remains "outside" all the faith-filled storytelling that went on in the first decades of Christian history.

He becomes angry when he hears rumors that he died by his own hand (see Matt 27:5), especially when another story-teller claims that he burst asunder (see Luke 1:18). He had no memory of the changing of 120 gallons of water into wine, or of Jesus walking on the water. I could have simply left it at that, hinting that there were traditions about Jesus that Judas had neither witnessed nor heard. However, in my desire to represent a critical reading of the Gospel traditions, I pointed out in a glossary note that the so-called "nature miracles" may have grown in the Church's telling of the story of Jesus, and thus were not abroad while Judas was associated with the Jesus movement.[10] The bulk of Gospel critics, both Catholic and non-Catholic, take it for granted that such stories grew in the telling, as the early Church, full of the Spirit, began to articulate stories that made Jesus' presence among us more akin to the presence of God to Israel, especially as it is told in the Old Testament.

For example, the outstanding Catholic commentators on the Gospel of John from the 20th century, Rudolf Schnackenburg and Raymond E. Brown, argue that the miracle at Cana is more theological than historical.[11] John Meier, the eminent Catholic authority on the reconstruction of the life of the historical Jesus whose work has received the *Imprimatur* of the Catholic Archdiocese of New York (December 10, 1993, in this case), after a lengthy study of all the evidence, concludes:

> When one adds these historical difficulties to the massive amount of Johannine literary and theological traits permeating the whole story, it is difficult to identify any "historical kernel" or "core event" that might have a claim to go back to the

---

10. See *Judas*, 99 (glossary note xxxviii).
11. See R. Schnackenburg, *The Gospel according to St John*, trans. K. Smyth, C. Hastings, F. McDonough, D. Smith and R. Foley, 3 vols., Herders Theological Commentary on the New Testament IV/1-3; (London/New York: Burns & Oates/Crossroad, 1968-82), 1:337-40; R. E. Brown, *The Gospel According to John*, 2 vols., The Anchor Bible 29-29A (Garden City: Doubleday, 1966-70), 1:101-10.

historical Jesus. Put another way: if we subtract from the eleven verses of the first Cana miracle every element that is likely to have come from the creative mind of John or his Johannine "school" and every element that raises historical problems, the entire pericope vanishes before our eyes verse by verse.[12]

Similarly, after a painstaking review of all the accounts of Jesus' walking on water found in the New Testament (Mark 6:45-52; Matt 14:22-33; John 6:16-21),[13] Meier concludes:

> The walking on the water does not cohere with the miracle stories that have a good chance of going back to some event in Jesus' ministry. Indeed, this miracle story is emphatically discontinuous with them. Instead, it is continuous with the Christology of the early church, especially with an early thrust toward high Christology that tended to associate Jesus with Yahweh or to make Jesus the functional equivalent of Yahweh. … I think that the walking on the water is from start to finish a creation of the early church, a Christological confession in narrative form.[14]

I have already raised the matter of the historicity of the thirty pieces of silver. On the basis of the silence of Mark, Luke, and John, I suspect that, while money may have been involved (see Mark 14:11; John 12:6), we really do not know. The payment of the thirty pieces of silver obviously came into Matthew's account through his use of Zechariah 11. Similar doubts about the historicity of Judas' suicide arise from the fact that again it is only Matthew who reports it (Matt 27:3-10). Luke tells of his death in the Acts of the Apostles, but it is not by his own hand (Acts 1:18). I am further drawn to suspect Matthew's version of the events when I find that he has leant heavily upon the Old Testament as background, in this case Jeremiah 32:6-15 and 18:2-3.

I was aware at all times that these suggestions were not the common fare of the average Christian reader of the Bible, and that many might be surprised to find a Catholic scholar pursuing such views. They are, of course, mainstream New Testament scholarly positions. I wanted to produce a story that represented Judas' experience of the

---

12. Meier, *A Marginal Jew*, 2:949. His study of John 2:1-11 runs from pp. 934-50.
13. Meier, *A Marginal Jew*, 2:905-24.
14. Meier, *A Marginal Jew*, 2:921

events that took place in the life of Jesus. He was not present in the Christian community as the early Church's understanding of Jesus and belief in God's action for us in and through Jesus began to be articulated in terms of the fulfillment of the Old Testament. In order to guide the readers of *The Gospel According to* Judas through such subtleties, each of these issues – which are minor moments in the whole story - is dealt with in greater detail in the glossary that closes the book but that must be read in close association with the text itself.

Pastoral Reflections

Let me now turn to an issue that my fellow Christians and many of my scholarly colleagues have raised. These are not easy days for a recognized Catholic scholar to go into the world of mass media airing some of the issues just mentioned, and some of the reviewers reflect this. I refer, for example, to the review in *The Tablet* by Christopher Howse. His judgment of the book closes: "To read *The Gospel According to Judas* is an exercise in embarrassment on behalf of its authors."[15] But my colleagues discuss these matters with poise and confidence in journals and scholarly books. I wonder if Christopher Howse is aware of that scholarship. As a highly educated Catholic, what does he think of the historicity of the Cana miracle, and the nature miracles? Has he ever pondered the regular use of the expression "gospel values" in the Catholic Church, where very few practicing Catholics even know that a "gospel" is, much less what can be found in Matthew, Mark, Luke, and John. An awareness of the background to my contribution to *The Gospel According to Judas* is far more important than my mistaken understanding Tom Wright's Episcopal status at Durham, which merits serious mention in his review.[16] I think especially of John P.

---

15. C. Howse, Review of *The Gospel According to Judas* in *The Tablet* (24 March, 2007), 24. Anecdotally, the former editor of *The Tablet*, John Wilcken, attended the launch of the book at Westminster Cathedral on Wednesday, March 21. He was excited by what we were trying to do, and went out of his way to make that clear to me.
16. My reference to Wright as an "Archbishop" comes from my Catholic upbringing. I took it for granted that all Bishops in major Anglican Sees (like Durham, with its famous Cathedral) were "Archbishops," as in the Catholic tradition. Christopher Howse went to some length to inform the world of my ignorance: there is only a Bishop at Durham.

Meier's unfinished multi-volume study of the historical Jesus, *A Marginal Jew*, already cited, but earlier much-respected Catholic scholars whom I admire greatly, like Joachim Gnilka and Rudolf Schnackenburg from Germany, Xavier Léon-Dufour and Marie-Émile Boismard from France, Raymond Brown and Joseph Fitzmyer from the United States, who have educated my generation of Catholic scholars. Yet I can still hear the question: "Why did you, a respected Catholic New Testament scholar, accept Lord Archer's request to work with him on *The Gospel According to Judas*?"[17] All authors have reasons for writing a book, of whatever genre, and this is a good occasion for me to lay bare mine.

My motivation comes from who I am and what I do. I am a person deeply convinced by the relevance of the authentic Christian message, lived and proclaimed now for 2,000 years. I - like many of my contemporaries - have difficulties with the "public face of the Christian Church." But despite its sometimes ugly face, it holds a treasure … despite the earthenware vessels! The greatest treasure is the Gospel message of Jesus of Nazareth. I have spent more than 40 years of my life plumbing this message and it continues to fascinate me. I have done my best to overcome ignorance and prejudice among Christians by teaching and writing about these matters, at every level. I am the author of almost 60 books, scholarly, popular, catechetical, etc., and innumerable articles in journals both popular and scholarly.

My work has always been "in the Church," and has made little impact on the skepticism surrounding the Christian Church (and, increasingly, within the Christian Church). In the meantime deeply flawed and uninformed works like Dan Brown's *The da Vinci Code* and Richard Dawkins' *The God Delusion* have become best sellers. People are so willingly convinced that at last the truth is being told. A "best seller" from Frank Moloney may be read by about 5,000 already converted people across the entire globe. Are we to stand by silently, and allow the Gospel message of Jesus of Nazareth to be trivialized (Brown) and ridiculed (Dawkins), *and read by millions*? A dear friend wrote to me from the United Kingdom: "Can your fans look forward to a work of solid scholarship such as we've come to expect and admire." Yes, the whole 5,000 of them! Two thousand years of

---

17. See, as an example, Howse, *ibid.*, 24: "Why Professor Francis J. Moloney, the biblical scholar, got mixed up in this, I can't imagine."

Christian tradition and thought have provided us with sufficient intellectual strength to address the trivialization and insults of Dan Brown and Richard Dawkins. But who will imaginatively communicate this message to the audiences so easily convinced by Brown and Dawkins. Will a Papal Encyclical do it? I doubt that very much. How many have actually read Francis Encyclical *Laudato Si'* and his post-Synodal Exhortation *Amoris Laetitiae*?

By associating myself with Archer to write *The Gospel According to Judas* I wanted to achieve at least four goals:

1. To reach out to a world impacted and easily swayed by the mass media, and not just the small world that generally receives my work. I am a well-known scholar and author in an extremely limited circle of committed Christian readers. But Archer, Brown and Dawkins are in another league. After a "combative" (her word) interview with Elena Curti of *The Tablet*, she told me that there was need for another explanatory book to accompany *The Gospel According to Judas*.[18] There is one, my recent *The Living Voice of the Gospel. The Gospels Today*, published in Australia, Ireland and the UK in 2006, and in the USA in 2007.[19] But I wonder if Elena Curti – or others from the world of mass media (Christopher Howse?) – will ever open it, much less read it. I took the risk and joined Archer, Brown and Dawkins in the hope more readers might turn back to the Gospels of Matthew, Mark, Luke and John. I clearly failed to realize this hope.
2. To be involved in writing a text that shows what a "Gospel" is all about. It is not *primarily* a narrative history, but a use of recollections from the past, told from a specific "point of view" to communicate truths about what God has done for us in and through Jesus Christ. The Gospels of Matthew, Mark, Luke and John are never read in that way by the bulk of even assiduous Christian Bible readers. Despite 150 years of critical scholarship, and the formation of clergy in the seminaries to read the Gospels

---

18. E. Curti, "The Tablet Interview: Judas the Obscure," *The Tablet* (31 March, 2007): 8-9.
19. This book, which introduces the general reader to gospel study, and then devotes two chapters to each of the Four Gospels, was published in Australia by John Garratt, in the UK and Ireland by Columba Press, and in the USA by Baker Academic.

for what they are: narrative proclamations of what God has done for us in and through Jesus, they are read like history books, despite the tensions that such a reading generates (e.g. who has the birth stories right: Matthew 1-2 or Luke 1-2?). *The Gospel of Judas* attempts to show its readership "how a Gospel works." I hoped to lead people back to the canonical Gospels with different eyes. This has been another unrealized hope.
3. The message of *The Gospel of Judas* never betrays the teachings of Jesus Christ, as they are recorded in the Gospels. An important message, at the heart of the mission and message of Jesus and subsequently of the Christian Church, is compassion for the broken. *The portrait of Jesus* in *The Gospel of Judas* attempts to communicate that core message of the Christian tradition. Readers of *The Gospel of Judas* will recognize that – although it is Judas' story – the hero of the story is Jesus of Nazareth. Here, at least, I have the support of Pope Francis, and his recently concluded Holy Year of Mercy and Compassion.
4. To tell a story of Judas in which every reader can find her or himself. Failure lies at the core of human experience, and both human and Christian maturity emerges from an ability to handle failure. Judas' story in *The Gospel of Judas* is about handling failure. I hope to speak to everyone, myself included, through the story of Judas. Success or failure in this is not for me to judge, except for myself.

The Gospel According to Judas suggests that the traditional popular portrait of Judas, the result of a pastiche of the negative portraits of him found in the Four Gospels, is open to reinterpretation. The texts in the Gospels are the result of the early Church's attempt to explain why someone Jesus loved and called had failed so badly. Maybe there is another "point of view": the way Judas himself may have seen things. Since the time of the Renaissance and the Reformation the artistic presentations of Judas have always portrayed him as the archetypal Jew, a dark figure with the large, hooked nose that has long caricatured "the Jew." Only recently have I had the chance to see the Dublin Caravaggio of the arrest of Jesus. The evil Jew, Judas/Judah, dominates the painting, emerging from a darkness that only Caravaggio can create.

Is it problematic to do some imaginative thinking and writing – on the basis of a critical reading of the four Gospels – that suggests that this portrait is open to reinterpretation? Perhaps the point of view that emerges by telling Jesus' story through the inner eye of Judas makes a small contribution to the Holy Father's link between the story of Judas and "decisive aspects of the mystery of man's relationship to God." At the moment, we are only hearing one end of a telephone conversation.

Conclusion

One of the most subversive documents to come out of the Council was the Dogmatic Constitution on Divine Revelation (*Dei Verbum*).[20] The pre-conciliar Church was a deeply Eucharistic Church, but an Ecumenical Council, the supreme teaching authority of the Roman Catholic Church, now told us that there was a new player on the block:

> Just as from constant attendance at the Eucharistic mystery the life of the Church draws increase, so a new impulse of spiritual life may be expected from increased veneration of the word of God, which "stands forever" (Isa 40:8; 1 Peter 1:23-25) (*Dei Verbum* 26).

Nowhere have the principles guiding critical biblical scholarship been better stated than in *Dei Verbum* 13:

> Indeed the words of God, expressed in the words of men, are in every way like human language, just as the Word of the eternal Father, when he took on himself the flesh of human weakness, became like men.

The interest in the restoration of the Liturgy joined hands with an emerging biblical movement to restore the Word of God to its rightful place at the heart of the life of the Church. The very life-blood of the

---

20. For a very recent and readable presentation of *Dei Verbum*, especially valuable because it takes into account much that has happened since the Council, see R. D. Witherup, *Scripture. Dei Verbum*, Rediscovering Vatican II Series (New York/Mahwah, NJ: Paulist Press, 2007).

Catholic Tradition, the Eucharist, was seen to be inextricably associated with the living presence of the Word of God in the community. These sentiments were succinctly articulated in *Dei Verbum* 21:

> The Church has always venerated the divine Scriptures as she venerated the Body of the Lord, in so far as she never ceases, particularly in the sacred liturgy, to partake of the bread of life and to offer it to the faithful from the one table of the Word of God and the Body of Christ.

In my experience, some of which is reflected in the angry response of some Catholics to *The Gospel According to Judas*, this major element in the teaching of the Church's highest teaching authority has not taken root among believers. Shock still descends in some circles when the original intentions of the various authors of Genesis 1-11 are uncovered. There is more to these stories than Adam and Eve, a snake and an apple. Even more serious is the problem of the historicity of the events reported in the infancy narratives of Matthew 1-2 and Luke 1-2. Was Mary the hero? Did the events unfold as in Luke: annunciation, visitation, birth of our Lord, presentation and the finding of the child Jesus in the Temple, readily recognised as the Joyful Mysteries of the Rosary? Or was Joseph the hero, and did the events unfold as in Matthew: a genealogy, the suspicion of an illegitimate birth, the lurking Herod surrounding the visit of the Wise Men from the East, the flight into Egypt, the slaying of the Innocents, the return from Egypt and the need for a further flight to Nazareth? This sequence hardly serves as Joyful Mysteries!

No doubt there was a great deal of naivety among teachers and scholars in those early decades after the Council, and many mistakes were made. There was a moment of "stumbling in the dark," often not recognised as we were buoyed up by the excitement of those heady days. There was the occasional abuse of the new freedom we had been given. These exceptional cases stood in the limelight, and added fuel to a growing "slowing down" of the original enthusiasm, often initiated or encouraged by Church leaders.

As a professional biblical scholar of more than 40 years' experience, I have had the mixed blessing of living through the pre-conciliar experience to our present moment in the life of the Church when, in my experience, the "slowing down" has almost become a full stop. There is an increasing lack of confidence in a critical reading of the Bible. Many, including important Church leaders and Catholic lay leaders, see biblical scholarship as a danger to the simple faith of the ordinary people. Our contemporaries can be exposed to every subtlety of their particular profession or trade, and critically educated that way at both School and University. However, they are not to be challenged to look critically at the source that nourishes our faith: the Word of God. We are facing a time in the life of the Christian Church when the Word of God is seen as legitimately expressed only in the word of the teaching Church. Many of those teachers are untrained, and thus strenuously resist the richness uncovered by 150 years of critical biblical and theological scholarship, endorsed by Pope Pius XII and the Second Vatican Council.

In 1973, the outstanding Catholic biblical scholar, Raymond Brown, wrote a caricature of a phenomenon that he regarded as a thing of the past:

> If the biblical scholar was going to insist on the freedom to play with his new-fangled toys of language and literary form, he was to be kept in a playpen and not let out to disturb the good order of the theological household.[21]

It is my sense that this desire to curb the role of the exegete within the life of the Church is not a thing of the past. Indeed, there are many indications that the golden era of biblical enthusiasm in the Catholic Church that followed the Second Vatican Council and the publication of *Dei Verbum* is on the wane.[22] The esteem for Catholic biblical scholarship among non-Catholics remains high, but its function within the life of the Church no longer occupies the place it had in the decades following the Council. As the Professor of New

---

21. R. E. Brown, *The Virginal Conception and the Bodily Resurrection of Jesus* (London: Geoffrey Chapman, 1973), 6.
22. Since the publication of *The Gospel According to Judas*, and the original delivery of the lecture that generated this publication, I have done my best to help by resorting to more traditional means. See F. J. Moloney, *A Friendly Guide to the New Testament* (Melbourne: Garratt, 2012); Idem, *A Friendly Guide to the Gospel of Mark* (Melbourne: Garratt, 2013); Idem, *Reading the New Testament in the Church. A Primer for Pastors, Religious Educators, and Believers* (Grand Rapids, MI: Baker Academic, 2015); Idem, *A Friendly Guide to the Resurrection of Jesus* (Melbourne: Garratt, 2016).

Testament at the Catholic University of America, I was fortunate to teach in an internationally significant Department of Biblical Studies. But non-Catholic students far outnumbered the Catholics, and there were virtually no Priests or Religious in the programme. The beautiful document produced by the Pontifical Biblical Commission in 1993, *The Interpretation of the Bible in the Church* has been largely ignored or, at best, kept alive within its playpen.[23]

But I remain encouraged by the constant teaching of Benedict XVI on these matters. Long an attentive critical reader of biblical texts, he dedicated the 2008 Synod of Bishops to the theme of the Word of God in the Life and Mission of the Church. His 2010 post-Synodal Exhortation, *Verbum Domini* is a masterly work from a skilled interpreter of the Word, and someone deeply immersed in the great traditions of the Church.[24] In *Verbum Domini* 56, he cites the striking words of Saint Jerome: "When we approach the Mystery, if a crumb falls to the ground we are troubled. Yet when we are listening to the Word of God, and God's word and Christ's flesh are being poured into our ears we pay no heed." In an earlier address to delegation of the Theology Faculty of the University of Tübingen, he insisted:

> An exegete, an interpreter of Sacred Scripture, must explain it as a historical work "secundum artem," that is, with the scientific rigour that we know is in accordance with all the historical elements that require it and with the necessary methodology.
> This alone, however, does not suffice for him to be a theologian. If he were to limit himself to doing this, then theology, or at any rate the interpretation of the Bible, would be something similar to Egyptology or Assyriology, or any other specialization.
> To be a theologian and to carry out this service for the University, and I dare say for humanity ... he must go further and ask: but what is said there true? And if it is true, does it

---

23. The Pontifical Biblical Commission, *The Interpretation of the Bible in the Church* (Rome: Libreria Editrice Vaticana, 1993).
24. Benedict XVI, *Post-Synodal Exhortation* Verbum Domini *to the Bishops, Clergy, Consecrated Persons, and the Lay Faithful on the Word of God in the Life and Mission of the Church* (Vatican City: Libreria Editrice Vaticana, 2009).

concern us? And how does it concern us? And how can we recognize that it is true and concerns us.²⁵

This is not the time to be discouraged, but to develop our sense of history, and a proper understanding of the significance of an Ecumenical Council that has asked those of us trained to serve the Church as scholars to do all we can to recognise what is true and how it concerns us. Most major events in world history are followed by a desire to restore the security of a time prior to those events. A similar historical experience is evident in our post-conciliar period. This can be painful and confusing, especially for those of us who have been part of the authentic Catholic tradition before, during and after the experience of the Council, and who have given our lives to its agenda. Many would like to restore us to our playpens.

In a moment of supreme teaching authority, the Church has stated:

> But the task of giving an authentic interpretation of the Word of God, whether in its written form or in the form of Tradition, has been entrusted to the living teaching office of the Church alone. Its authority in this matter is exercised in the name of Christ. *Yet this Magisterium is not superior to the Word of God, but is its servant. It teaches only what has been handed on to it* (*Dei Verbum* 10. Stress mine).²⁶

These are not easy times for the Catholic Church – neither for its leadership nor for its faithful - as 90% of Australian Catholics no longer practice their faith.

But I believe it is a time of painful growth that cannot be denied by the "restoration" of an idealised past made possible by the sometimes passionate repression of any attempt to raise a critical voice. The growth unleashed by the Second Vatican Council let loose a hunger for things unseen, and this hope will not be thwarted. "Now hope that is seen is not hope. For who hopes for what he sees? But if we hope for what we do not see, we wait for it with patience" (Rom 8:24-25).

---

25. As published in *Zenit.org* (April 29, 2007).
26. For an excellent presentation of the complex consequences of the Church's attempt to practice what is taught in *Dei Verbum* 10, see Witherup, *Scripture*, 87-132. See also the essay "Sacred Scripture and the Magisterium: A Restless Relationship?" on pp. 221-35 of this volume.

For better or for worse, one of the authors who produced Archer-Moloney, *The Gospel According to Judas* was motivated by this dream. Maybe I still suffer from a hangover, the result of the heady days of the period immediately following the Second Vatican Council, but only time and the integrity of the Church itself, responding to the authentic Magisterium articulated at the Council, will be the judge.

The book is now in the public arena, in the hands of its readers. From this point on it will have its own life. What Jeffrey Archer and Frank Moloney may have wanted to do by writing it is of minor importance. I suspect that our motives were very different. I cannot speak for Lord Archer, but I have now spoken for myself, for what that is worth. How our readers, across many cultures and languages, will respond to the book is up to them. My ongoing hope is that *reading The Gospel According to Judas* might bring the increased excitement and fascination with the person of Jesus that *writing* it has brought into mine.

16
The Word of God, Jesus Christ, and the Eucharist: Christian Hope in a Secularized World[1]

In 1996 the American Sociologist, Rodney Stark, published a provocative sociological study, called *The Rise of Christianity*.[2] He wrote this book because his reading of the work of the historians of early Christianity showed that their history was good, but their sociology was non-existent. He minimalized many theories about the rise of Christianity. Theologians and the Church historians regularly point to the transforming effect of the purity of the doctrine, the teaching of the resurrection, the blood of the martyrs, a sacramental life, and other such central Christian beliefs and phenomena as the reasons for its rapid spread in the Roman Empire. Stark questions this, insisting that the fundamental motivation for the phenomenon was that the Christians cared for one another, especially their women.

By "caring" he means that they refused the widely-practiced infanticide by exposing unwanted children, especially unwanted infant girls; they looked after the elderly and the fragile; they rejected abortion, so crude in those days that it generally led to the death of the mother. They attended to the basic needs of others in a way that was unheard of in the Roman Empire. As Stark puts it: "What Christians did was take care of one another. Their apartments were as smoky as the pagan apartments, since neither had chimneys, and they were cold and wet and they stank. But Christians loved one another and when they got sick they took care of one another. Someone brought

---

1. This paper was delivered, as a contribution to the International Eucharistic Congress in Cebu, The Philippines, on January 25, 2016.
2. Rodney Stark, *The Rise of Christianity* (Princeton, NJ: Princeton University Press, 1996).

you soup. You can do an enormous amount to relieve those miseries if you look after each other."[3]

Stark suggested that early Christianity was an alternative voice in the society of the time. Its care for the needy generated energy and attracted the interest of Roman society, led by its appeal to the pagan women and through them won the hearts of families and eventually society as a whole. This is a helpful starting reflection for a Christian Church's mission to bring hope to a secularized world. As an Australian, I attempt to live my Christian life in a comfortable, self-sufficient, and very secular society. We have no determining Christian past, as do the Americas, including the United States. We were founded by eleven shiploads of criminals, accompanied by a cohort of soldiers.[4] I must take my own background and formation as my starting point, aware that a process of secularization determines a great deal of what is said and done, at every level, in developed societies, but not only there. What follows does not pretend to resolve this dilemma for the contemporary Christian. I wish to turn to themes dear to Pope Francis to add further reflection to his prophetic voice.

All of us must recognize that we are called to be bearers of an alternative voice within contemporary society. Christianity is an increasingly counter-cultural form of life, celebrating the life and death of Jesus Christ, who loved the world so much (see John 3:16). For better or for worse, we acknowledge that we live in a world that has changed very rapidly in two generations. The bulk of any population, no matter what their belief, and also those without a religious bent, were once able to claim adhesion to an external form of life marked by regularity and time-tested practices and a life-style underpinned by great truths. It was taken for granted we lived good lives by means

---

3. "A Double Take on Early Christianity. An Interview with Rodney Stark." Stark was originally interviewed by Michael Aquilina for *Our Sunday Visitor*. The text of the interview, posted July 22, 2004, can be found on http://www.jknirp.com/stark3.htm, 1-6. The above citation can be found on p. 2. Accessed on August 10, 2014.
4. A reflection of the secular nature of the current Australian Catholic situation is found in the fact that an International Eucharistic Congress held in the neighbouring Philippines that drew 15,000 registrations, among them many Australian pilgrims and Australian Bishops, opened to a public Eucharist in the presence of more than 300,000 people, and closed with a *Statio Orbis* attended by almost 1,000,000 people, was almost entirely neglected by Australian Catholic media outlets.

of the time-honored, regular and consistent practice of a good life. This is much less the case today, and especially so in contemporary youth culture. We live in an increasingly fragmented world in which the value of regularity, time-tested practices, ways of life, and adhesion to time honored truths is often not recognized. As Phyllis Tickle reports in her important book, *God-Talk in America*: "When my contemporaries and I closed the doors of our mothers' houses behind us, we locked ourselves out of five hundred years of human habits and entered into disjuncture."[5]

As I attempt to live my Christianity in Australia, and other parts of the secularized world, I find that the most difficult encounters with that world do not come from those who have never seriously embraced Christianity, but from what we might call *post-Christians*. By that expression I mean those millions of people who have been born, brought up, and educated Christians, but have now energetically rejected it. They appear to nurture an aggressive opposition to a Christian God, revealed in and through Jesus Christ, and the lifestyle that it should have nurtured. Among other issues, this suggests that there was something seriously wrong with the way we communicated our faith to the past two generations.

Many look at the world with increasing uncertainty.[6] Not only the young, but also their parents and more and more of their grandparents, are developing a distrust of "great truths." The young look upon them as we would consider hair growth medications for balding men: if one medication had proved effective, then all others would have disappeared from the market place. Rather than surrender themselves to one meaningful tradition, life-style or fashion, they com-

---

5. Phyllis A. Tickle, *God-Talk in America* (New York: Crossroads, 1997), 25.
6. Equally important, and deserving of more than this passing reference, is the exact opposite phenomenon: a current generation that locks itself into a world of blind certainty about everything. All religiously driven cultures, but especially Christianity and Islam, are marked by an increasing *fundamentalism*. This is very evident in the fascination that ISIS holds for many young Muslims, and the attraction that pre-Conciliar thought and especially liturgical practice holds for a number of young Catholics. Many of them are attracted to the Priesthood and the Religious Life, but ignore the challenges of a secular world. In my opinion, this move to fundamentalism is largely generated by a secularism that mocks people who wish to pray, fast, hold public religious functions, etc. A strong voice comes from young Muslims in Australia: "In this country it is impossible to practise Islam."

bine fragments of an ever incomplete and temporary fashion into an unfinished whole – a collage identity. Perhaps the most outstanding symbol of this "collage" is the widespread use of Christian symbols, especially the cross, and the rosary-beads, but also others, in fashions and body-marking.

There is an understandable tendency for some of us from my generation to look back to our past, see how we responded to these and similar symptoms, and to insist that we go on repeating the same processes. That is the path to certain failure. There is so much that is very good in society that is *new and different*, not simply a continuation of the "good things" of our past. We are called to recognize that we are living an experience of disjuncture, and act accordingly. If there is no longer a prevailing sense of religion or adherence to core beliefs and practices among at least the immediate past three generations (Generation X, Y, Z, and beyond), what lies at the heart of this potentially creative "disjuncture"?

My contemporaries were *instructed* in the great truths and the moral principles that determined our lives. We have done our best – no doubt with some failure - to live the rest of their lives following these *principles*. That was a *head-process*. Nowadays, we move in the opposite direction. Many young people today, and indeed a generation or two ahead of them, perhaps a high percentage of those present at this lecture, journey through life in search of a number of different, and sometimes contrasting, *experiences* that might eventually establish the principles that will mark the future. In the past we moved from *head* to *heart*. Nowadays, and in the recent past, we tend to move from *heart* to *head*. This can be exciting and challenging, but it has a down side: slaughter on the roads, promiscuous sexual activity, starting at a very young age, slavery to the omnipresent social media, recreational drugs widely available and used, often leading to a death-dealing involvement with serious drugs. On all sides we witness family breakups and dysfunctional young people, racism, abuse of alcohol, and physical violence in the streets.

But this list of woes does not recognize that much of our secular society is *not like this*. Indeed, there are many fine people, living quality family, social, and politically involved lives that are not like this. It is here that we must look to the model of optimism, mercy, and hope for the world at large that is embodied in Pope Francis. Indeed, his message to the whole Church, and to the world, rings true. In his as yet brief Papacy, he has asked us to look *beyond ourselves*, to abandon the widespread trashing of "our common home," to reconsider the challenges of marriage, family, and human sexuality, and to live a Holy Year of Mercy and Compassion.[7] In the world envisioned by Pope Francis, we believers are summoned to generate a culture in which people, and especially young people, arrive at life-determining decisions through positive experiences that begin with *the heart*, eventually to arrive at *the head*. As he puts it:

> How much I desire that the year to come will be steeped in mercy, so that we can go out to every man and woman, bringing the goodness and tenderness of God! May the balm of mercy reach everyone, both believers and those far away, as a sign that the Kingdom of God is already present in our midst (*Misericordiae Vultus*, 5).

Here we can go back to Rodney Stark, and take his guidance on what made the earliest Christians such an effective presence in a pagan world. He argued, correctly in my opinion, that early Christians developed an *alternative experience* in pagan Roman society. Can we generate an *alternative Christian and Catholic experience* that does not start in the head and eventually go to the heart, as my generation did, but that begins with the heart, and only through an *experience* of what it means to live, love and serve arrives at the head. You are all aware of the contemporary search for goodness, justice and well-being among so many good people, not all of whom are Christian. Our trust in God and commitment to the way of Jesus Christ must defend us against any loss of hope. Our desire to respond to the Gospel by means of our unconditional gift of self for the good of others,

---

7. These three issues are only the outstanding aspects of Pope Francis' ministry, made clear in his *Encyclical Letter* Laudato Si' *of the Holy Father Francis on Care for Our Common Home* (Vatican City: Libreria Editrice Vaticana, 2015), the Episcopal Synod on marriage and family life, followed by the *Post-Synodal Apostolic Exhortation* Amoris Laetitia *of the Holy Father Francis to Bishops, Priests and Deacons, Consecrated Persons, Christian Married Couples and all the Lay Faithful on Love in the Family* (Vatican City: Libreria Editrice Vaticana, 2016), and in his Misericordiae Vultus. *Bull of Indiction of the Extraordinary Jubilee of Mercy* (Vatican City: Libreria Editrice Vaticana, 2015). His concern for the universal presence of an experience of the mercy and compassion of God and Jesus Christ can be found in almost everything he says and writes.

in the way of the Good Shepherd, cannot be lost. As Pope Francis would put it, our ongoing hope in a secularized world calls for an "education of the heart."

In order to do this, however, we do not have to "reinvent the wheel." The education of the heart is found in our Great Christian Tradition: hearing and responding to the Word of God in the Scriptures, a deeper understanding and love for the person of Jesus Christ, and the practice of a Eucharistic lifestyle, which means more than "going to Mass."

My concern will thus be threefold:

1. A reflection upon the centrality of the Word of God. Have we responded to the consistent insistence of the Church, from Leo XIII's *Providentissimus Deus* to Pius XII *Divino Afflante Spiritu* to the Synod of Bishops on the Word of God in the life of the Church of 2008, followed by Benedict XVI's post-Synodal Exhortation *Verbum Domini*?
2. From the beginnings we have been called "Christians" (see Acts 11:26) because we confess that Jesus of Nazareth is the Christ, the Son of God and that he saved us (John 9:22; 12:42; 20:30-31). How central is our focus upon what God has done for us in and through Jesus, and his command that we "follow" him (see Mark 1:16-20; John 21:15-20). Is our spirituality based upon the God revealed to us by Jesus Christ in the Scriptures? Does that Spirituality make any impact upon our surrounding secularized world.
3. This leads us necessarily, especially in this context, to a reflection upon the Eucharist, the "place" where we have most intimate contact with our crucified and risen Lord.

I will close these thoughts with a reflection upon the Walk to Emmaus, a stunning Gospel narrative that encapsulates all three concerns: Word of God, the person of Jesus, Eucharist and Reconciliation.

The Centrality of the Word of God

In the earliest Church the authors of the New Testament books looked back to the Old Testament as their "Scripture," as they began to articulate what the God of Israel had done for humankind through the life, teaching, death and resurrection of Jesus.[8] Their inspired interpretation of what God had done for humankind in and through Jesus of Nazareth has come down to us in the Christian "Sacred Scripture" of the New Testament. In the time of the so-called Apostolic Fathers, Christian authors continued to use the Old Testament as their "Scripture," and steadily began to recognize many early Christian writings as authoritative. The Apostolic Fathers of the second century strained to articulate the message of the Bible, and especially the message of Jesus Christ, in a new world that had little or no understanding of the Jewish matrix that had given birth to Jesus, and the subsequent early reflection upon what God had done in and through him. The New Testament Scriptures were formally accepted as part of the inspired Word of God in the third century.

The great Fathers of the Church constantly used these Scriptures to develop and understand the Christian mysteries, and the life and practice of the Church. There was *no single interpretation* of the Bible in these periods. Different methods of interpretation were used in the West and in the East, and in the East between Antioch and Alexandria. The great Councils that determined the Christian community's teaching and practice (Nicea [325], Constantinople I [381], Ephesus [431], Chalcedon [451], Constantinople II [553]) are awash with reflections upon the Word of God. The richness of this founding heritage is found in the writings of such figures in the West as Tertullian (c. 160 – c. 225), St Ambrose (340-397), St Jerome (347-420), St Augustine (354-430), Leo the Great (c. 391-461), and St Gregory the Great (540-604), and in the East, Origen (184-254), St Athanasius (c. 296-373), St John Chrysostom (347-407), St Basil (329-379), and St Gregory of Nyssa (335-395), only to mention a few of the giants from that era.

Many of these biblically inspired traditions were forced into the background in the eleventh century, as Papal authority struggled with the secular princes. A more juridical, and less biblical, theological and sacramental self-understanding of Christianity began to develop. The development of a more structured Church, following the models of the society of the time, goes back to the much-needed

---

8. For a more detailed study of the issued raised in this section of the present reflection, see Francis J. Moloney, *Reading the New Testament in the Church. A Primer for Pastors, Religious Educators, and Believers* (Grand Rapids: Baker Academic, 2015), 1-21.

reforms of Pope Gregory VII (1073-1085). The authority of the Pope over the secular Princes was dramatically acted out in the submission of Henry VII (Holy Roman Emperor) to Gregory VII at Canossa in 1077. The conflicts between the two most powerful authorities, the Church and the Princes, needed to be addressed.[9] However, a more juridical and hierarchical Catholicism emerged, accompanied by an insistence on what was right and wrong, and disciplinary processes that kept the people subservient to ecclesiastical hierarchy. Great achievements continued in the medieval period with scholars, saints and artists. Its richness can be *read* in representatives like Thomas Aquinas, *heard* in the splendor of the musical rendition of biblical texts in Gregorian chant, and *seen* in the glass windows of the great medieval Churches of Europe.[10]

The Council of Trent (1545-1563) was called to guide the Roman tradition in its response to the Protestant Reform. There were many Catholic doctrines and practices that could not be found in the Bible. The Reformers rejected such beliefs and practices as the institution of the Priesthood, many Marian teachings, the seven Sacraments, the Papacy, and the real presence of the crucified and risen Jesus in the celebration of the Eucharist. These doctrines were not found in the Word of God of the Old and New Testaments. The Council responded by teaching that there were two sources of Revelation: Tradition and Scripture. It was true that many doctrines and practices of the Catholic Church could not be found in the Bible, but they could be found in the Tradition. If a belief or a practice of the Catholic Church could not be found in the Bible, only one of the sources of Revelation, the authentic Tradition of the Church could be called upon as the other source of Revelation. The dominant opinion was that the Revelation found in the Catholic Tradition was superior to the Revelation found in the Bible. This assessment of Tradition and

---

9. Anyone who has read the novels or watched the filmed versions of Ken Follett's renditions on this period, focussed upon the conflict between the Church, the State, and the suffering people trapped in these conflicts, in *Pillars of the Earth* and *World Without End*, will catch some idea of why this reform was necessary.
10. Interestingly, it was precisely this aspect of twelfth century Catholicism that led Ken Follett, who had been raised in a puritan background, to write his two novels that focus upon the emergence of gothic architecture and the context of the rich liturgical settings of Medieval England.

Scripture was repeated in 1870, in the Constitution on Revelation (*Dei Filius*) at Vatican I.[11]

Familiarity with the Word of God as it is found in the Bible had waned. Subsequently, passing "traditions," generated by a given time and place, became dearer to Catholics than the Word of God. The acceptance and observance of these "traditions" can sometimes become the touch-stone of Catholic orthodoxy, but a faith-filled reading of the Bible is uncommon, and often regarded as irrelevant to Catholics. Vatican II, in its all-determining agenda of returning to the sources of the faith (using the French word *ressourcement*), asked all Catholics to rediscover the original "sources" of their faith and practice.[12] This necessarily summons the whole Church to return to the Scriptures. This renewal began in an Encyclical of Leo XIII in 1893: *Providentissimus Deus*, and a further biblical Encyclical from Pius XII, *Divino Afflante Spiritu*, written in 1943 to commemorate the fiftieth anniversary of *Providentissimus Deus*. Both documents come from troubled times. The first, written in a period of rationalist rejection of the Bible as the Word of God, insisted on its role in the life and ministry of the Church. Pius XII's Encyclical, published in 1943, as the Allied forces struck back in Europe and the War in the Pacific extended, is a watershed in the history of Catholic biblical interpretation. The Holy Father insisted that Catholics must enter the world arena of critical scholarship, to provide greater nourishment to the life and practice of the Church. Catholic scholars are now among the best in the world, precisely because of their *catholicity*: we listen to, and speak to *everyone*.

The teaching of Vatican II made a unique contribution to the history of Catholic Theology. Breaking the stranglehold of those who argued for *two sources*, *Dei Verbum* 9 teaches: "Sacred tradition and sacred scripture, then, are bound closely together, and communicate one with the other. Flowing from the same divine well-spring, both of them merge, in a sense, and move towards the same goal." The theological and spiritual consequences of this development in Catholic doctrine from a *two source* to a *unified source* understanding of Rev-

---

11. For a balanced assessment of the history and importance of the Council of Trent, see John W. O'Malley, *Trent: What Happened at the Council* (Cambridge, MA: Harvard University Press, 2013).
12. On this, see John W. O'Malley, *What Happened at Vatican II* (Cambridge, MA: Harvard University Press, 2008), 40-43, 300-302.

elation are manifold. There is a further intervention from *Dei Verbum* that is not "new," but for Catholics, it is "novel." The section of the document dealing with Sacred Scripture in the Life of the Church (paras 21-24), opens and closes by affirming:

> The church has always venerated the divine scriptures as it has venerated the body of the Lord, in that it never ceases, above all in the sacred liturgy, to partake of the bread of life and to offer it to the faithful from the one table of the Word of God and the Body of Christ (*Dei Verbum* 21)

> Just as from constant attendance at the Eucharistic mystery the life of the church draws increase, so a new impulse of spiritual life may be expected from increased veneration of the Word of God which "stands forever" (Is 40:8; see 1 Pet 1:23-25) (*Dei Verbum* 24).

While the unification of Scripture and tradition, flowing from the same divine well-spring is new, the teaching on the one table of the Word of God and the Body of Christ is ancient … but forgotten.

In an attempt to bring the Church back to the Word of God, Benedict XVI called a Synod of Bishops on the Word of God in the Life of the Church in 2008. Like most such attempts – from Councils, Popes, Bishops, and Major Religious Superiors – the Synod made little impact on the day-to-day life of the Church. Bishops and Religious Superiors have more important things to do than lead us through an intense biblical renewal. In the very first paragraph of his post-Synodal exhortation, *Verbum Domini* (2009), almost 50 years after the proclamation of *Dei Verbum*, Benedict XVI still had to point out "fundamental approaches to a rediscovery of God's Word in the life of the Church as a wellspring of constant renewal."

During the course of his exhortation, the Holy Father was thus moved to look back to striking words from St Jerome (347-420): "When we approach the Mystery, if a crumb falls to the ground we are troubled. Yet when we are listening to the Word of God, and God's word and Christ's flesh are being poured into our ears we pay no heed."[13]

---

13. Benedict XVI, *Post-Synodal Apostolic Exhortation* Verbum Domini *of the Holy Father Benedict XVI to the Bishops, Clergy, Consecrated Persons and the Lay*

A Spirituality Based upon the God revealed to us by Jesus Christ

Starting with the heart, we should recognize that what is deepest within us is formative of us, making or breaking us as human beings, yet somehow beyond our control. To use philosophical language, it "transcends" us. It is bigger than us, and yet so real: it overwhelms us, but determines us. This covers the whole gamut of possible human experiences, from the good to the bad, from extraordinary and unconditional love to the frustration that results from unresolved anger and jealousy. These all-determining and formative elements within the human spirit can be read as *experienced* signs of the divine within us. On the basis of these experiences of the heart, we sense that we are radically open to, and determined by, the transcendent. *This is the key to a Christ-centered spirituality.* Once we begin to see things this way ... we are opening the doors to the possibility that all human beings share in the divine. We are touching the so-called theme of "deification," so important to earliest Christian tradition, but lost in the steady juridical shaping of the Tradition since the late Middle Ages. A Christian spirituality is built upon a personal and communitarian acceptance of the God revealed to us by Jesus Christ. *But here our lack of a biblical culture becomes a problem.* When asked about the Word of God, we have no self-confidence: it is all too hard. A personal and communitarian relationship with Jesus and a lifestyle directed by Gospel values are obviously intimately related, but without any real familiarity with the Gospels, we turn to religious authority, or popular culture.[14]

We are all irrevocably marked by the divine; we yearn for the divine home, for which we were created. The well-known words of St Augustine continue to ring true: "You have made us for yourself, and our heart is restless until it rests in you" (*Confessions* I, 1). It is in our humanity that we are in touch with our divine, because in Jesus of Nazareth humanity has been lived as it should be lived. This is something many of us cannot accept: that Jesus was unconditionally

---

Faithful on the Word of God in the Life and Mission of the Church (Vatican City: Libreria Editrice Vaticana, 2009), paragraph 56, citing Jerome's *Commentary on the Psalms*, 147 (Corpus Christianorum Latinorum 78, 337-338).

14. Anecdotal evidence for this affirmation was articulated at a meeting of Religious Educators at Australian Catholic University. A senior figure honestly stated: "We keep on talking about Gospel values, but what are they?"

human, like us in all things but sin (see Heb 4:15). We nod acceptance to the *doctrinal* truth that Jesus was both human and divine, but we do not identify with his humanity. It was as a human being that Jesus loved, hoped, sang, danced, prayed, interacted with other human beings in creative ways, and suffered. We share all that with Jesus: love, hope, song, dance, prayer, interaction with others, and suffering. We sin when we do not respond properly to the presence of that which is most sublime in our humanity, and we begin to act selfishly, arrogantly, jealously, proudly, satisfying the hungers of our basic urges. These responses are not "human." They are less than human, and played no role in the life of Jesus. To sin means to reject the experience of the divine within us that yearns for fulfilment.

A relationship with Jesus means sharing in the communion of the human and the divine *that is both his and ours*. We are to live and love as he lived and loved. As the author of the First Letter of John puts it: "Whoever says 'I abide in him' ought to walk just as he walked" (1 John 2:6). But Jesus never rejected the experience of the divine that yearns for fulfilment. As the Letter to the Hebrews says: "We have not a high priest who is unable to sympathize with our weaknesses, but one who *in every respect* has been tempted has as we are, *yet without sin*" (Heb 4:15). There are three essential elements that lie at the heart of an understanding of the Gospel portrait of Jesus.[15] He related to God as his Father. During his life he experienced was a oneness of purpose between Jesus and God so profound that he was able to cry out "*Abba*, father" in his prayer (see Mark 14:36). This oneness led to Jesus' unswerving commitment to preaching, especially via his unforgettable parables, establishing and living the presence of God as king (the Kingdom of God). Israel had spoken of God as "father," but not as a father who sets his children free, and who seeks them out in the failure, finding them in the darkness, telling them "all that I have is yours" (Luke 15:11-32). Jesus not only *told* parables about such a father, but he lived as the Father asked, praying from the Cross that they be forgiven, as they did not know what they were doing (Luke 23:34), and welcomed the repentant criminal into paradise (23:43).

---

15. For a more detailed analysis of the Gospels that produces the "portrait" of Jesus sketched in the following paragraphs, see Moloney, *Reading the New Testament in the Church*, 64-90.

But Jesus' unswerving openness to God, his bold proclamation of God's way and the establishment of the Kingdom led to his rejection, suffering and death. He could see the clouds darkening on the horizon, but he did not sidestep suffering and death. He used an expression taken from the Book of Daniel (Dan 7:13-14), "the Son of Man," that indicated that he followed down this conflicted way in the conviction that God would have the last word. Suffering and death were accepted by Jesus, not without fear, as he took on the role of the suffering Son of Man, confident that good would come from it. The resurrection, then, is God's "yes" to Jesus' lifelong "yes" to God, whom he called his Father, cost him what it may.

In Jesus of Nazareth, and only in him, humankind realized its full potential. In Jesus of Nazareth there is an "upward" exaltation of the human condition: the human breaks into the divine. The Gospels lead us to suggest that in Jesus the full potential of humankind has been totally realized. In and through Jesus of Nazareth, *the human invaded the divine*. Our humanity is something which Jesus shared with us, and where we too can experience the presence of the divine in us.

Jesus brought in the reigning presence of God. As Son, he responded unconditionally to God, costing the Son of Man no less than everything. But he did not do this simply because he was a good human being who realized his potential. While there is truth in claiming: "One of us made it!" ... it is not the whole truth. Jesus realized the fullness of the divine possibilities of all human beings *because he was Son*. It is his being the Son of God that engenders his response to God. This does not mean that we can never hope to do the same because we are not *born* incarnate children of God. We are all capable of repeating the life-style of Jesus and, in our own time and in our own way, realizing our "divineness" in its fullness. However, we do this, not because we *are* sons and daughters, but because we are *made* sons and daughters by means of our Baptism. We have been *graced* with discipleship. To say it in somewhat technical language: Jesus was son of God *by nature*; we are sons and daughters of God *by grace*. This was what Paul was trying to convey to the Galatians and the Romans when he told them how blessed they were to be able to cry out in the Spirit, as a result of God's saving action in the death and resurrection of Jesus: *Abba* Father! (Gal 4:4-7; Rom 8:14-15). We are potentially "another Christ," but, for a variety of reasons, we betray our true selves and fall short of our potential deification. But the process of deification is there for us, if we recognize our dignity. Already in the second century Irenaeus wrote: "He revealed God to us and raised us to God" (*Adversus Haereses* IV, 20,5-7).[16]

All that is noble in us: our loving, our laughter, our play, our dancing, our eating and drinking, our praying, alone or with others, our search for justice and peace, and the many other things that we do in response to that which is deepest within us, is part of our journey to be as Jesus Christ was (see Phil 2:5-11; 4:8-9). Like Jesus, we reach beyond ourselves into the mystery of the divinity that is, at one and the same time, constitutive of our being, yet the object of our search. As Karl Rahner puts it:

> I encounter myself when I find myself in the world and when I ask about God; and when I ask about my essence, I always find myself already in the world and on the way to God. I am both of these at once, and cannot be one without the other.[17]

Our secularized world would never put it like that! But today we are called to reflect more deeply on the opportunity we have, as convinced Christians, to present the face of God, made known to us in and through Jesus, in our confused and confusing world.

Eucharist and Reconciliation

As Karl Rahner puts it, we are "in the world and on the way to God." This journey, which we travel as individuals, and in communities, is marked by ambiguity. In this situation we must reflect upon the Sacraments of Eucharist and Reconciliation. In their preparation for the second session of the Synod on the Family, on 22 December, 2014, the German Bishops issued a statement in which they rightly declared:

---

16. The theme of the "deification," now possible for the human condition because of what God has done for us in and through Jesus Christ, was a central theme in early Christian tradition, especially (but not only) in the Greek Fathers of the Church. For a very clear description of this process, based in the tradition, and still central to Christian life, see Denis Edwards, *Partaking of God. Trinity, Evolution, and Ecology* (Collegeville, MN: The Liturgical Press, 2014), 27-53.
17. Karl Rahner, *Spirit in the World*, trans. William Dych (London: Sheed & Ward, 1968), 406.

"The Eucharist is not a reward for the perfect but a magnanimous remedy and nourishment for the weak."[18]

The writings of the New Testament, without fail, indicate that such is the case.[19] The Gospels of Mark (14:17-31) and Matthew (26:20-35) locate Jesus' final meal with his disciples within a narrative "frame" that tells the audience that he breaks his body and spills his blood for them: betrayers and deniers. Matthew heightens this message by adding to Jesus' words over the cup from his Markan source clear indication of the purpose of Jesus' self-gift: "the blood of the covenant poured out for many *for the forgiveness of sins*" (Matt 26:28). Luke's account of the final meal is more complex, but interlaced with the same sentiments, shaped as a farewell discourse as the Lord leaves behind fragile disciples to continue his mission (Luke 22:14-38). In a poignant use of Psalm 41:9 the Lukan Jesus states: "The hand of him who betrays me is with me on the table" (Luke 22:21). For John, the gift of the foot washing, a symbol of Baptism, and the gift of the morsel, a symbol of Eucharist, is the sign of Jesus' revelation of God's incredible love for his failing disciples. He loves his own "to the end" (John 13:1). Judas will betray him, Peter will deny him, none of the other disciples, not even the Beloved Disciple, understands what Jesus is doing for them. He tells them why he manifests such love: "I am telling you these things before they happen, so that when they happen, *then you may believe that I AM HE*" (13:18). It is precisely in this crazy self-gift in love to others who do not love him in the same way that he makes God known.[20]

Paul is often used to defend the tradition that only the worthy are allowed at the table. But it is not the worthy who are privileged in 1 Corinthians 11:17-34. Paul is attacking those who would prevent the poor and the marginalized from sharing the meal, while they eat their fill and drink to inebriation: "Do you show contempt for the church

---

18. See the report of Christa Pongraz-Lippert, *The National Catholic Reporter*, December 29 (2014), 1. This sentiment has been repeated by Pope Francis, in different ways, since then.
19. For a detailed study of the Eucharistic texts in the Gospels, see Francis J. Moloney, *A Body Broken for a Broken People. Divorce, Remarriage, and the Eucharist*, (Melbourne: Garratt Publications, 2015), 71-203.
20. For a fuller study of John 13, see Francis J. Moloney, *Love in the Gospel of John. An Exegetical, Theological, and Literary Study* (Grand Rapids: Baker Academic, 2013). See also Idem, *A Body Broken for a Broken People*, 175-88.

of God and humiliate those who have nothing?" (11:22). It is to these "holier than thou" people at Corinth that Paul warns: "Examine yourselves, and only then eat the bread and drink of the cup. For all who eat and drink without discerning the body eat and drink judgment to themselves" (vv. 28-29). "The body" certainly means discerning the presence of Jesus, but it also means the "body" of the community of the weak and poor, which they are tearing apart with their sense of superiority.[21]

Whatever riches of Eucharistic theology we have developed over the centuries, this is the biblical bedrock upon which all such theology must be built. "The Word of God stands forever" (Isaiah 40:8). Theological and juridical opinion will necessarily come and go as history evolves with its own inner dynamic. Eucharist and Reconciliation are deeply intertwined. The move away from regular reception of Sacramental Reconciliation increases each year. Perhaps this is a way back: an understanding and practice of Eucharist in the light of the Word of God will lead us to accept that the Eucharistic mystery also brings Reconciliation.[22] A claim that we no longer need to experience never-ending conversion and recognition of our sinfulness, cripples our association with God, and a development of a healthy spirituality. However it is celebrated, we must accept our sinfulness, our drift away from the dynamic process of being one with Jesus. Without such honesty and genuine trust in God's saving presence among us in the gift of his Son, the divine within us shrinks and dies.

A Story: By Way of Conclusion

A feature of Luke's resurrection account is his insistence that everything took place *on the one day* (see Luke 24:1, 13, 29, 36, 51). The whole of Luke's Gospel has been directed towards this "day." As Jesus began his journey towards Jerusalem in 9:51, the narrator commented, "When the days drew near for him to be received up, he set his face to go to Jerusalem." On this resurrection "day" we sense that we are at the end of a long journey. The Lukan use of this theme is at the center

---

21. For a detailed study of the Pauline Eucharistic material (1 Corinthians 10-11), see Moloney, *A Body Broken for a Broken People*, 41-69.
22. For a fuller development of this theme, see Francis J. Moloney, *Eucharist as a Celebration of Forgiveness* (New York/Mahwah, NJ: Paulist Press, 2017).

of his account of the journey of two disciples to Emmaus (24:13-35), which will serve as our conclusion. Here we will find the face of God in the compassion of Jesus, the fulfillment of the Scriptures, the forgiveness of sin, and the breaking of the Eucharistic bread.[23]

The opening remarks of the journey to Emmaus are an indication of the wrong choice made by two disciples. "That very day" - in the midst of the paschal events – two disciples were going to Emmaus, "about sixty stadia away from Jerusalem" (24:13). They are walking *away from Jerusalem*, the central point of God's story; away from God's journey, making himself known in his Son, from Nazareth (Luke 1-2) to the ends of the earth (Acts 1:8; 28:16-31). The paschal events are in the forefront of the disciples' minds, and the subject of their conversation, as they walk (v. 14), and as the risen Jesus joins them, and "went with them" (v. 15). As the risen one, he "walks with" two disciples who are abandoning God's saving story. God is behind this encounter. Luke does not say that they were unable to recognize Jesus, but that "their eyes were kept from recognizing him" (v. 16). There is a mysterious "other" directing the presence of Jesus with disciples, indicated by the use of the divine passive voice of the verb. Jesus opens the conversation by asking them what they were discussing with one another as they walked. At Jesus' question, they stop (v. 16).

A hint of something new has entered the story but it does not last, as one of them, named Cleopas, responds to Jesus' question. He wonders how Jesus could even ask such a question. Surely, every visitor to Jerusalem would know "the things that have happened there in these days" (v. 18). This is incredible irony, as Cleopas asks Jesus, indeed a visitor to Jerusalem who had journeyed from Galilee to the city, to bring to a climax part of God's saving design. This journey has been under way since 9:51, when Jesus set his face for Jerusalem, "as the days drew near for him to be received up." He asks the very "visitor," to whom these events happened, why he does not know about them. Jesus, who has been at the center of the events, is also the measure of their significance. But the two disciples know only of the "events," not what God has done through them. Indeed, "their eyes were kept from recognizing him" (v. 16).

---

23. For a more detailed study of Luke 24:13-25, upon which the following is based, see Francis J. Moloney, *The Resurrection of the Messiah. A Narrative Commentary of the Resurrection Accounts in the Four Gospels* (New York/Mahwah, NJ: Paulist Press, 2013), 81-86. See also, Idem, *A Body Broken for a Broken People*, 144-50.

A catechetical-liturgical process begins in v. 19 where, in response to Jesus' further query about the events, they show their extent of their knowledge of "what has happened" in Jerusalem. Crucial to their response to Jesus is their explanation of their expectations of Jesus: "We had hoped that he was the one to redeem Israel" (v. 21). They have not understood the significance of the life, teaching, death and resurrection of Jesus. His way of responding to the Father has not fulfilled their hopes for the one who would redeem Israel. But they do know of *the facts* his life, teaching, death and resurrection.

- They know of his life, teaching and miraculous ministry: Jesus of Nazareth, a prophet mighty in word and deed (v. 19).
- They know of his death: "Our chief priests and rulers delivered him up to be condemned to death, and crucified him" (v. 20).
- They know of the events at the tomb: "it is now the third day" (v. 21), women have been at the tomb early in the morning, but "they did not find his body" (v. 23).
- They have even heard the Easter proclamation: there has been a vision of angels who said: "He is alive!" (v. 23).
- If, perhaps the witness of the women was not enough, "some of those who were with us" have been to the tomb, and found it empty. "But him they did not see" (v. 24).

The two disciples on the way to Emmaus know everything ... but him they did not see (vv. 15-17). Thus they do not understand the *significance* of these *events*, and they continue their walk away from Jerusalem.

Jesus chides them for their foolishness. He opens the Scriptures for them, explaining that it was necessary that the Christ should suffer many things to enter his glory (vv. 25-26). He "interpreted to them in all the scriptures the things concerning himself" (v. 27). Jesus journeys with these disciples who have abandoned God's journey, and on the way a "liturgy of the Word" takes place. He calls to their memory the necessity for the Christ to suffer in order to enter into his glory (v. 26). Not only did Jesus teach these truths (see 9:22, 44; 18:31-33), but it was the true meaning of "all the Scriptures," beginning with Moses and the prophets (24:27).

The narrative has reached a turning point. Initiative must come from the erring disciples themselves. Has the word of Jesus made any impact upon them? The Greek of v. 28 reads: "He pretended to be going further." Jesus has opened the Word of God for them. The disciples must now take some initiative in response to Jesus' explanation of the Word. They do so generously: "Stay with us for it is toward evening, and the day is now far spent" (v. 29). As the evening of the Easter "day" draws in, the littleness of faith which led them to leave Jerusalem and the eleven is being overcome by the presence of the risen Lord (v. 15) and his opening of the Word (vv. 25-27). A process of repentance and forgiveness is under way, generated by the action of Jesus who walks with his fragile disciples.

At the meal the disciples recognize him in the breaking of the bread (vv. 30-31). He is recognized in the breaking of the bread. The memory of the many meals that Jesus has shared with them, and especially the meal he shared on the night before he died (22:14-38) opens their eyes, and anticipates the many meals that will be celebrated in the future. Touched by Jesus' word and presence in their failure, the failing disciples turn back on their journey: "And they rose that same hour and returned to Jerusalem" (v. 33). The journey "away from Jerusalem" (v. 13) has been reversed as they turn back "to Jerusalem" (v. 33). Once they arrive back to the place they should never have abandoned and the eleven apostles upon whom the community is founded, before they can even utter a word about their experience, they find that Easter faith is already alive. They are told: "The Lord has risen indeed and has appeared to Simon" (v. 34). Easter faith has already been born in Jerusalem.

As the Gospel opens, the reader/listener comes to know of a man called "Simon" (4:38). Within the context of a miraculous catch of fish he is called to be a disciple of Jesus and Jesus introduces a new name for him "Peter" (see 5:8). The reader/hearer is reminded of this transformation in the Lukan list of the twelve apostles: "Simon, whom he named Peter" (6:14). From that point on, throughout the whole of the Gospel, he is called "Peter" (see 8:45, 51; 9:20, 28, 32-33; 12:41; 18:28). At the Last Supper, where the mingling of the themes of Jesus' sharing his table with the broken and the commissioning of his future apostles is found, he is still "Peter" (22:8, 34, 54, 55, 58, 60-61). Only in foretelling his future denials does Jesus emphatically revert to the name he had before he became a disciple: "Simon, Simon, behold, Satan demanded to have you that he might sift you like wheat" (22:31). It is to the failed "Simon" that the risen Lord has appeared, to restore him to his apostolic role (24:34). The name "Simon," without any link with the apostolic name "Peter" appears only before this man's call to be a follower of Jesus (4:18) and at the end of the Emmaus story, when two failing disciples are restored to God's saving story which is taking place in Jerusalem. The failed disciples have returned to another disciple who had failed his Lord. This return home, however, has happened because the risen Lord reached out to them in their brokenness, and made himself known to them in the breaking of the bread.

This unforgettable story, the subject of imaginative art, poetry and dramatic representation across the centuries, captures our agenda for hope in a secularized world: contemplate God in Jesus Christ and the Scriptures, recognize our need for God, welcoming his reconciling and nourishing presence in his Sacraments across our journey. We do not walk alone. Jesus of Nazareth is with us. Even in our failures, he leads us home.

17
The Word in the World: Then and Now

It is fitting that an event marking the Centenary of the Melbourne College of Divinity features a Roman Catholic scholar speaking to a topic that has been, up till recent times, a pillar of many manifestations of the Protestant tradition: "The Word in the World." It is but one sign of the effective ecumenical maturation of Melbourne's theological world that has been in place for half a century. Since the mid-sixties, with the advent of the Society of Jesus to Melbourne, its association with the Uniting Faculty of Theology in the form of the Jesuit Theological College, superbly located in Parkville, the Melbourne College of Divinity has been outspokenly ecumenical. Following the leadership of the Society of Jesus, a wide cross-section of the Christian Churches have become part of the Melbourne College of Divinity, either as fully Recognised Teaching Institutes, or as participating members of one or other of those Teaching Institutes.[1]

For a person of my vintage, the theme "the Word in the world" jolts me back to the Christian and theological formation I received in the parallel burgeoning of ecumenical theological formation in the latter half of the twentieth century. It recalls my exciting immersion into the debates that emerged from the Second Vatican Council, aided and abetted by the contributions of the two Twentieth Century giants, Karl Barth (1886-1968) and Rudolf Bultmann (1884-1976).

---

1. This essay was originally delivered in 2010 as a lecture at Trinity College, the University of Melbourne, at an event marking the centenary of the foundation of the Melbourne College of Divinity in 1910. The theme of the event was "The Word in the World." See the brief sketch of the history of the MCD in Paul Beirne, "The Melbourne College of Divinity: A Selective Historical Overview," *Pacifica* 23 (2010): 123-36. The origins of this paper explain the sometimes "local" references, but the questions raised are broader than Melbourne, Australia.

My formal education culminated in Oxford in 1975, the year before Bultmann's death. The shadows of the Council and these two great figures were never far away in all theological and exegetical activity conducted in that era. As I think about the Word in the world for a reflection delivered in 2010, I remain strongly influenced by my religious and professional formation *"then,"* healthily influenced by the Council, Karl Barth and Rudolf Bultmann, especially the latter, given my interest in the Gospel of John and New Testament Theology.[2] But, armed with that intellectual and ecclesial faith formation, I find myself somewhat at a loss *"now"* in a highly secularised western society and a struggling Christian Church.

Dominant as these figures and these debates were in my formative years as a scholar ("then"), I must nowadays face the fact that we live in a different era, and I invite you to face that fact with me ("now"). The context of theological and biblical reflection today, I will argue, is light years away from where we were in the second half of the immediately past century. In the autumn of my own life, and certainly in the autumn of my years as a serious contributor to biblical and theological learning and debate, I sometimes hanker regretfully for the ecclesial and theological context of my youth. But if we are serious about "the Word in the world," we need to reassess where we are currently placed within our society and culture, our *world*, and *go elsewhere*. I wonder if, in theological education in Australia, we have the capacity to take the risk of *going elsewhere*. What follows is a request that we should make the effort – or become increasingly irrelevant.

The first part of this paper is dedicated to major twentieth century challenges to the Christian Church to revitalise the presence of the Word in the world. The Roman Catholic story is well known, stung into action by the surprising John XXIII and the Second Vatican Council. Within the Protestant tradition it was not a Council, or a revisiting of the Castle Church of Wittenberg to post theses. It was the unforgettable understanding of the Word in the world by Karl Barth and Rudolf Bultmann. Both men understood their work to be a return to Martin Luther. As I look back over it today, I am still thrilled by their ground breaking courage and preparedness to stand on the

---

2. See Rudolf Bultmann, *The Gospel of John*, trans. George R. Beasley-Murray (Oxford: Blackwell, 1971 [original German in 1943]); Idem, *Theology of the New Testament*, trans. Kedrick Grobel (2 vols. London: SCM Press, 1952-55).

margins of their Church, especially in the time of National Socialism in Germany, *to proclaim the Word boldly*.³ No doubt the context of *their world* was part of their eventual text, their understanding of the crucial centrality of *the Word*. However, even though only 50 years ago, that was "then."

What of our "now"? Our world is not without social, political and religious issues that are troubling. Subtle and not so subtle reciprocal misunderstanding and division exists in an increasingly religiously indifferent, but traditionally Christian, Western world and its steady islamisation. Indeed, violence can explode from either side as some commit acts that others call "terrorism," while others enact laws that attempt to curtail the religious influence of Islam. The current situation is more and more highlighted by an aggressive insistence that any belief in God is destructive, and impoverishes the human spirit. This year even Melbourne, Australia, managed to assemble 2,500 people for the Global Atheist Convention. The established Churches, and especially the Catholic Church, are steadily losing moral authority as a result of the sexual abuse accusations that are even pounding heavily on the Bronze Doors of the Vatican City. We live in interesting times, to say the least!

Beyond the Western world, but often because of the interests of the Western world, wars are still waged in nations deeply divided by religious affiliation and the various interpretations of those affiliations, or by the rift between the rich and the poor. This Western world watches the world burn – including the destruction of our very habitat - as it delights in the freedoms generated by our "postmodern" situation, whatever that may mean. I will return to a brief reflection on that "now" in the second major section of my paper.

Text is always determined and shaped by context. No doubt the Second Vatican Council, Karl Barth and Rudolf Bultmann and the schools of thought that depended upon their understanding of the Word in the world were shaped by their "world," the turmoil of Euro-

---

3. Karl Barth had to relinquish his teaching post at the University of Bonn (Germany) when he refused to take an oath of allegiance to Hitler. He returned to his native Switzerland, and continued to teach at the University of Basel. Rudolf Bultmann held his professorial position at the University of Marburg from 1921-1951. However, during the war years this was under threat as he publicly supported *The Confessing Church*, a group of Lutheran leaders (among them Dietrich Bonhoeffer) who rejected Hitler's nationalisation of that communion.

pean social and religious contexts and perhaps the inevitable "turn to God" generated by two World Wars. The issue is always "the Word in the world," but there is a "then and now" of the world that must be respected. The Word of God may stand forever (see Isaiah 40:8; John 1:14), but it stands in very different worlds. A rapid (and no doubt superficial) description of "then" and "now" will lead me to draw some suggestions about the Word in the world today, by way of conclusion.

"Then": the Twentieth Century "Word in the World"

The following brief presentation of some Twentieth Century Christian thought and practice is necessarily limited, given the nature of this commemorative reflection. However, for our purposes, it touches the bases that interest us most: western Catholicism and Protestantism in the recent past. Much in the theological scene that was already on the march in the latter decades of the Twentieth Century is not discussed: the emergence of liberation theology in the Americas and Asia, feminist and womanist theologies that have their roots in the USA, but have become world-wide approaches to the presence of the Word in the world, the emergence of Pentecostal Churches and the charismatic movement, the literary and increasingly postmodern interpretations of the Scriptures, the exciting encounters with the great world religions, especially – but not only - Islam, Buddhism and Hinduism. But one cannot do everything!

The Catholic Tradition

I was brought up to accept that it is the Mass that matters. That remains a core belief of many practising Catholics to this day, and is regularly used as the yardstick for the assessment of the catholicity of anyone who was baptised Catholic. In those days, before the Second Vatican Council, ritual dominated Catholic life. The Mass was in Latin, and even the biblical texts read during the celebration were proclaimed in Latin. Eventually they came to be read in translation, but only after they had been formally read in Latin. Homilies did not have much to build on. They often focussed on doctrinal and moral questions, and – all too regularly – on acceptable political parties or personalities. People were baptised, married and buried to the tune of a ritual in Latin, and where possible, the accompanying music was the unforgettable Gregorian chant.

There was little or no reading of the Bible, in private or in public, but the biblical world was present – sometimes powerfully – in the various devotions, and certainly in the annual cycle of the liturgical year. We knew what we were doing as we moved from Lent to Easter and Pentecost, and then through the Sundays after Pentecost until we met Advent and the Christmas season. Despite the sectarian nature of pre-Conciliar Catholicism – a "them versus us" mentality – a sense of the living presence of God and the love of his Son, Jesus Christ, was very present to Catholic believers. The weekly participation in the Lord's Supper, the experience of sacramental reconciliation, and devotions such as the Sacred Heart and the Marian Novena, were not without meaning. The Word, therefore, was very present in what one might call "mystery." The obscure rituals, the little known language of the liturgy, and a strong sense of "belonging" must not be denied their value: the Word was very present, even though somewhat divorced from "the world," even of that era.

The Second Vatican Council (1962-65) was a remarkable event that attempted to bring the Catholic Church as a whole into the world, and dedicated one of its most significant documents, *The Church in the Modern World* (*Gaudium et Spes*) to this very question. The theological issues of the Word of God present in the Sacred Scriptures was faced with courage in the *Dogmatic Constitution on Divine Revelation* (*Dei Verbum*), as was the presence of the Word in the Liturgical life of the Church in the *Constitution on the Sacred Liturgy* (*Sacrosanctum Concilium*). Understandably, the debates were marked by considerable conflict among those present at the Council.[4] It is only as an "older Catholic" that one can appreciate the radical newness of the Conciliar teaching on the intimate link that exists between the Eucharist, the Church's central act of cult, and the Word:

---

4. For an excellent presentation of the sometimes conflictual processes that led to the eventual promulgation of *Sacrosanctum Concilium* and *Dei Verbum*, see John W. O'Malley, *What Happened at Vatican II* (Cambridge, MA: Harvard University Press, 2008), 126-59, and for *Gaudium et Spes*, pp. 247-89. For a feisty personal view of Vatican II, see now Yves Congar, *My Journal of the Council*, trans. Denis Minns and Others (Adelaide: ATF Theology, 2012).

> The Church has always venerated the divine Scriptures as it has venerated the Body of the Lord, in so far as it never ceases, above all in the sacred liturgy, to partake of the bread of life and to offer it to the faithful from the one table of the word of God and the Body of Christ (*Dei Verbum* 21. See also *Sacrosanctum Concilium* 48).[5]

Now, almost fifty years after the Council began, strange forces are at play within the Catholic community that defy analysis here because I have neither the time nor the skills to do so. Since the Council there have been valiant attempts to return to the issue of the Word of God in the life of the Catholic Church.[6] But the problem remains unresolved. Catholic leadership is strongly urging a return to ritual and mystery, and responds to conflicts that emerge in an increasingly complex world with sometimes high-handed and poorly motivated magisterial interventions,[7] while the practising Catholic population is dwindling dramatically. One could say that the bulk of *practising* Catholics (with all that means) are those who accept those magisterial interventions without question. All others are sidelined or, at best, viewed with suspicion. One could suggest that, despite all the hopes of the Council Fathers, the more serious engagement of the Catholic Church with the world, is not happening, or has not as yet

---

5. All citations from Vatican II are taken from Austin Flannery, ed., *Vatican Council II: Constitutions, Decrees, Declarations: A Completely Revised Translation in Inclusive Language* (Northport, NY: Costello, 1995).
6. I think, especially, of the document prepared by the Pontifical Biblical Commission and signed off by the then Cardinal Prefect of the Congregation for the Doctrine of the Faith, Cardinal Joseph Ratzinger, *The Interpretation of the Bible in the Church* (Rome: Editrice Vaticana, 1993), and the 2008 Synod of Bishops with the title *The Word of God in the Life and Mission of the Church*. Benedict XVI's Post-Synodal Exhortation Verbum Domini *of the Holy Father Benedict XVI to Bishops, Clergy, Consecrated Persons and the Lay Faith on the Word of God in the Life and Mission of the Church* (Vatican City: Editrice Vaticana, 2010) is outstanding, but has been largely ignored. The work of the Biblical Commission and the Synod of Bishops responds to the request of the Second Vatican Council's *Dei Verbum*, 21-26 ("Sacred Scripture in the Life of the Church"), promulgated in 1962!
7. One looks back nostalgically to *Dei Verbum* 10: "This Magisterium is not superior to the word of God, but rather its servant. It teaches only what has been handed on to it. At the divine command and with the help of the holy Spirit, it listens to this devoutly, guards it reverently and expounds it faithfully."

born fruit.[8] Indeed, in a recently conducted Survey of Religious Institutes in Australia, it has been calculated that 6,000 young baptised Catholics reject Catholicism every year.[9]

The Protestant Tradition

As I did not live a "life in the pews" of a Twentieth Century Protestant Church, my view of that era is influenced by the contributions of Barth and Bultmann, and their intense focus upon the Word.[10] However much their contribution reached "the pews" is something that I cannot judge, but I refuse to accept that my understanding of them was "bookish." What they said and did impinged upon my Christian life at least as much as the Council; perhaps even more, as I tended to read the Council through their spectacles.[11] They stood at centre-stage of Protestant Theology for much of the final century of the second millennium. Summaries, in a few paragraphs, can never do justice to anyone's work; and this is especially true for what follows. I have been greatly influenced by Rudolf Bultmann whom I still regard as the greatest biblical scholar of the twentieth century. That estimation is not based upon my acceptance of his exegetical and theological conclusions, but upon my acceptance of his courage to read the biblical text *as a theological document*, and courageously to apply an existentialist reading of the text, especially Paul and John, to summon

---

8. This rather bleak assessment of the situation of the Roman Catholic Tradition in 2010 has been challenged by the Papacy of Francis I. Elected in 2014, he has begun a reform agenda that addresses many of the issues raised here, always driven by his passion for the poor and the marginalised. As is well known, however, he is meeting considerable opposition from many senior Catholic leaders and Catholic laity who see him as a threat to the "status quo," and regard his teaching as a threat to Catholic faith and morals.
9. Stephen Reid, Robert Dixon and Noel Connolly, *Catholic Religious Institutes in Australia. Results of the 2009 survey of Religious Institutes in Australia* (Fitzroy/Annandale: Pastoral Projects Office/Catholic Religious of Australia, 2010), 33.
10. It is also influenced by some remarkable Australians whom I came to know through my association with the Melbourne College of Divinity. Chief among these was Athol Gill.
11. In my first presentation to the International Theological Commission to the Holy See in 1986, a study of "Jesus and Culture" (see Francis J. Moloney, "Jesus Christ: The Question to Cultures," *Pacifica* 1 [1988]: 15-43), Hans Urs von Bathasar and Christoph von Schönborn, OP, commented in the subsequent debate that it was "too Protestant."

"the modern man" to a decision for authenticity or inauthenticity.[12] However learned his exegetic work and his biblical Theology may have been, his restless concern was always "the Word in the world." As we will see below, the same must also be said for the contribution of Karl Barth, but his work has not impinged on my life as a biblical scholar in the same way as that of Rudolf Bultmann.

Karl Barth responded to his understanding of the liberal tradition represented most importantly by Friedrich Schleiermacher.[13] In an attempt to re-establish the credibility of the Christian message in the post-Enlightenment period, Schleiermacher argued that religion had to be regarded as belonging to an autonomous sphere within human experience. He attributes to the structure of the human self-consciousness an experience of absolute dependence upon God, a "God consciousness." He would then claim that "Christian doctrines are accounts of the Christian religious affections set forth in speech."[14] Barth rails against any such mediation between God and the human condition.

Barth distrusts formal methods that mediate the content of the Logos. He comments upon the Scriptures, using traditional methods. The task of Theology is reflection on the Word of God as it is found in Scripture, and is accountable to no other human discipline. It is based upon God's objective Word to us. This Word reveals God's perspective on things, and allows of no appeal to human experience. The direction of God's Word is from the authority of Scripture and God's word, from above. We do not discover God's Word; it addresses us, and Jesus Christ is the absolute centre of all history. There is no authentic knowledge of God apart from Jesus Christ. God is envisioned as coming down from above and entering the human condition in stark judgment as the first moment of salvation. Barth's theology reads like pure assertion, as he eschews explanation as an attempt on the part

---

12. On Bultmann's understanding of "the modern man," see Walter Schmithals, *An Introduction to the Theology of Rudolf Bultmann*, trans. John Bowden (London: SCM, 1968), 49-70; André Malet, *The Thought of Rudolf Bultmann*, trans. Richard Strachan (Garden City, NY: Doubleday, 1971), 22-31.
13. I say "his understanding" because many would regard Barth's view of Schleiermacher as partial and biased, playing into his denial of all human mediation of the content of revelation.
14. Friedrich Schleiermacher, *The Christian Faith* (New York: Harper Torchbooks, 1963), 76.

of human mediation to distort the purity of God's direct access to the human condition. God is understood as over against sinful human existence. Barth loves to offend human reasoning, and consequently his theology is profoundly prophetic and counter-cultural.

> It is precisely the hidden things, inaccessible to human perception, that are displayed by the Spirit of God. He promises eternal life – to those who are dead. He speaks of the blessedness of resurrection – to those who are compassed about with corruption. He pronounces those in whom sin dwells – to be righteous. He calls those oppressed with ceaseless tribulation – blessed. He promises abundance of riches – to those abounding only in hunger and thirst. God cries out to us that he is coming quickly to our aid – and yet He seems deaf to every human cry for help. What, then, would be our fate, if we were not powerful in hope, were we not hurrying through the darkness of the world along the road which is enlightened by the Spirit and by the Word of God?[15]

The attractiveness of such an approach to the mystery of God and the communication of that mystery through the unadulterated in break of the Word into the sinfulness of the human condition is obvious. The condemned mass that was Martin Luther's understanding of the condition of the human race, following the lead of Augustine, is given hope. There is nothing we can to do to mediate the Word of God. It comes to us as pure and unadulterated gift from above. Barth is thrilling to read, and he touches the deepest senses of the believer in a way that Luther had done some four hundred years earlier. Indeed, Barth favourably cites a Catholic reviewer of his work (Erich Przywara, SJ) who regards his theological contribution as a "genuine rebirth of Protestantism."[16] He himself, however, is aware of the immensity of the task. In 1926, in writing his Preface to the fifth edition of the *Römerbrief*, he remarks that "it does mark the moment

---

15. Karl Barth, *The Epistle to the Romans* (trans. Edwyn C. Hoskyns; 6th ed.; Oxford: Oxford University Press, 1933), 20. The above caricature of Barth's theological and exegetical stance was guided by the synthesis of Roger Haight, *Jesus Symbol of God* (Maryknoll, NY: Orbis Books, 1999), 309-310.
16. Barth, *Romans*, 21.

when a breach, however small, has been made in the inner and outer afflictions of Protestantism."[17]

Almost Barth's exact contemporary, Rudolf Bultmann worked brilliantly and tirelessly for an unconditional acceptance of Martin Luther's principle of *sola fide*.[18] It is more difficult to synthesise Bultmann's contribution for two reasons. In the first place, he was primarily an exegete. His doctoral dissertation was on the rhetoric of the Pauline letters, and he burst onto the scholarly scene with his epoch-making contribution to the foundation of Form Criticism in his *Die Geschichte der Synoptischen Tradition* in 1921.[19] Secondly, both his exegesis and his subsequent theological contributions were very influenced by the early Martin Heidegger, his fellow-academic at the University of Marburg.[20] Bultmann's exegetical expertise led him to a relentless search for what he regarded as the heart of the proclamation, what he would call *die Sache*. His existentialist philosophical approach demanded that he focussed upon the essential "thing" (*die Sache*) as the relentless challenge of the Word, day in and day out. Before the revelation of the truth that comes each day in proclamation of the Word, the human being can decide for that truth as salvific (and thus merit the Heideggerian assessment of *authentic*) or reject it (and thus remain *inauthentic*). Bultmann's program of demythologisation was driven by his belief that "modern man" was no longer persuaded by the "myth" that may have spoken to the world in which the New Testament first appeared, but made no sense today (angels, walking on water, empty tombs, etc.).[21]

---

17. Barth, *Romans*, 23.
18. For a very helpful recent biography of Bultmann, see Konrad Hammann, *Rudolf Bultmann. A Biography*, (trans. Philip E. Devenish; Salem, OR: Polebridge Press, 2013).
19. Available in English as Rudolf Bultmann, *The History of the Synoptic Tradition* (trans. John Marsh; Oxford: Blackwell, 1968).
20. For excellent presentations of these issues, see Schmithals, *An Introduction*, 1-21; John Painter, *Theology as Hermeneutics. Rudolf Bultmann's Interpretation of the History of Jesus* (Sheffield: The Almond Press, 1987).
21. For a very clear presentation of this agenda, see, among many, Rudolf Bultmann, "New Testament and Mythology," in R. Bultmann and Five Critics, *Kerygma and Myth* (ed. Hans Werner Bartsch; trans. Reginald H. Fuller 2 vols.; New York: Harper & Row, 1961), 1:1-44, and subsequently, "On the Problem of Demythologizing," in *New Testament and Mythology and Other Basic Writings*, (rans. and ed. Schubert M. Ogden; Philadelphia: Fortress, 1984), 95-130.

The theological traditions that attempt to objectify God make God into an idol. What is essential is the acceptance of God's *action*. We can only discover God's action in the proclamation. To go to the heart of the matter, what singles out Jesus' crucifixion as unique among the many people who were crucified by the Romans? If the Gospels' reporting of Jesus' life, his teaching, his miracles, his death and resurrection, need to be demythologised, how is it that Bultmann can argue that the saving event occurs in and through Jesus Christ? Bultmann's response is that there is only one answer: because it is proclaimed as such. "Christ meets us in the preaching as one crucified and risen. He meets us in the word of preaching and nowhere else. The faith of Easter is just this – faith in the word of preaching."[22] Bultmann's view of the cross is that "it may no longer be considered as just the historical event of Jesus' crucifixion on Golgotha ... Removed from all temporal limitation, it continues to take place in any present moment, both in the proclaiming word and in the sacraments. The apostle bears about in his body the dying of Jesus and is stamped with the *stigmata* of Jesus (II Cor. 4:10f.; Gal. 6:17); the sufferings of Christ overflow abundantly upon him."[23] Christianity stands or falls on the presence of the Word in the world, and its acceptance or rejection.[24]

There is a place for the Church, but it must be kept in its place. The Church is where the Word is found. As is often said, but not with Bultmann's intensity, without the Word there would be no Church or saving community, but without the Church there would be no word as proclamation of God's action. "The *ecclesia* is just as ambiguous a

---

22. Bultmann, "New Testament and Mythology," 1:41.
23. Bultmann, *Theology*, 303.
24. Bultmann's insistence upon the presence of the crucified and risen Christ "in the proclamation" has often been ridiculed, suggesting that the presence of the Lord depends upon the skill of a preacher. This is a serious misunderstanding of Bultmann. He simply claims that we do not know *what actually happened*, and that this lack of objective historical certitude should not concern us. Easter faith is not generated by stories of empty tombs. Bultmann may overstate his case, but when contemporary Greek Christians greet one another at Easter time with the joyful salutation: χριστόςανήστι and receive the affirmative response: αληθώςανήστι, Jesus Christ, crucified and risen, is alive "in the proclamation." On this, and the many related hermeneutical issues surrounding the reception of Bultmann's work, see John Painter, "The Fourth Gospel and the founder of Christianity. The place of historical tradition in the work of C. H. Dodd," in *Engaging with C. H. Dodd on the Gospel of John* (eds. Tom Thatcher and Catrin H. Williams; Cambridge: Cambridge University Press, 2013), 257-84.

phenomenon as the cross of Christ: visible as a worldly fact, invisible – yet to the eye of faith also visible – as a thing of the world to come."[25] Bultmann also asks the question about the possibility of other events, as well as the Jesus-event, as being a place where God's saving act can be experienced. He cannot deny this possibility, but wonders why the question is even asked. Anyone who has experienced the event of the love of God in the Word of Jesus Christ will not speculate about other possibilities which God might have had as instituting his "word of life."[26]

Obviously, Barth and Bultmann had occasion to differ. In 1952 Barth published a short work, *Rudolf Bultmann – Ein Versuch, ihn zu verstehen*.[27] Barth accuses Bultmann of putting at risk the objective nature of revelation. His demythologising, his existentialism and his focus upon the human response led Barth to complain that Bultmann humanises and objectifies revelation, but subsequent reflection has shown how Barthian Bultmann could be.[28] Let me close this section of the paper with a citation from Bultmann which, I suggest, might have rested comfortably with Barth.

> [I] am at pains to talk about the living God in whose hands our time is held and who encounters each of us in our time. But insofar as anything more is to be said, it can be put in the single statement that God encounters us in the word, namely, in a specific word, in the proclamation established with Jesus Christ. Of course, it can be said that God encounters us always and everywhere, but we do not see God everywhere unless – as Luther often said – God's word is added and enables us to understand the particular moment in its light.[29]

Very few believing Christians, from either the Protestant or the Catholic tradition, remain unmoved by the single-minded and courageously systematic attempt on the part of these two giants to place

---

25. Bultmann, *Theology*, 2:308.
26. See Schmithals, *An Introduction*, 193-94.
27. Available in English as Karl Barth, "Rudolf Bultmann: An Attempt to Understand Him," in Bartsch, ed., *Kerygma and Myth*, 2:82-132.
28. For an excellent presentation of this debate, and an insistence that Bultmann may well be the best of all Barthians, see Malet, *The Thought*, 376-426.
29. Bultmann, "On the Problem of Demythologizing," 119.

the Word at the centre of our world. But have we all "moved on" from this "rebirth of Protestantism" (Przywara), just as we all seem to have "moved on" from John XXIII's dream, expressed in his personal diary for January 20, 1962 of a great Council "as an invitation to the spiritual renewal for the church and for the world?"[30]

If the Roman Catholic Church struggled and – at least by a current assessment of its situation – failed to embrace the Second Vatican Council, the shocked reaction of established churches to a taste of Barth and Bultmann in 1963 indicates that not all were ready for their call to let go of the trappings of Twentieth Century Protestantism, and accept the radical Lutheran challenge of an aggressive presence of the Word in the world. An Anglican Bishop, John A. T. Robinson, translated current German theology, especially as it was being articulated by the Barthian Christian martyr, Dietrich Bonhoeffer, who was not entirely free from the influence of Bultmann, as *Honest to God*.[31] The good order of the ecclesiastical household was disturbed by scholars and teachers who dared to step out of the confines of the playpen within which their radical speculations could be safely entertained![32]

For the purposes of this schematic analysis of the "then" of the Twentieth Century, allow me to draw a parallel that may or may not work. It is worth trying all the same. If the rock solid and unified "closed shop" of Catholic Christianity was questioned in the 1960's by the Second Vatican Council, a longer process had been under way within the Protestant tradition from much earlier in the century, beginning with the second edition of Barth's *Römerbrief* published in 1922,[33] and argued thoroughly for several decades in the steady

---

30. As cited in O'Malley, *What Happened at Vatican II*, 18.
31. John A. T. Robinson, *Honest to God* (London: SCM Press, 1963). The lasting impact of the book, described by Robinson himself as "not radical enough" (p. 10), can be seen in the 40th anniversary reprint (Louisville: Westminster John Knox, 2002), with essays by Douglas John Hall (on the response to the book in the USA) and Rowan Williams (on the response to the book in Great Britain).
32. I take this image from a telling remark by Raymond E. Brown on the emergence of critical New Testament scholarship in the Catholic Church: "If the biblical scholar was going to play with his new-fangled tools of language and literary form, he was to be kept in a playpen and not let out to disturb the good order of the theological household" (*The Virginal Conception and Bodily Resurrection of Jesus* [New York: Paulist Press, 1973], 6).
33. Available in English as Barth, *Romans* (see above, footnote 12).

publication of his *Kirkliche Dogmatik*.[34] Bultmann's work covered much the same period. Could it be suggested that, as with the Second Vatican Council, the Twentieth Century challenge to Protestantism dominated by Barth and Bultmann to be "Word in the world" has run out of steam?

If that is the case, and I would very happy to be proved wrong, then we should at least begin to ask the question "why?" The problem, to my mind, does not lie so much in the never-failing and powerful presence of the Word (see Isaiah 40:8; John 1:14), but in the inability of the established churches to receive and communicate that Word in the contemporary world in a way that at least matches the courage of John XXIII and his Council, Karl Barth and Rudolf Bultmann.

"Now": The Twenty-First Century "Word in the World"

For all the ridicule that we might heap upon the term "postmodern," we live and attempt to live as Christians in a postmodern world. Perhaps the best way to describe the postmodern world is to point to its most obvious sacramental sign: the Personal Computer. The written word, once so sacred and firmly fixed upon the page, comes and goes with a few key-strokes. What was for centuries transmitted through the painstaking work of the scribes was made more available by the printing press. Indeed, there are some who claim that the widespread availability of the Word as a result of Gutenberg was one of the catalysts for the Reformation. But nowadays, by means of the Internet and a few good search engines you can move swiftly from the daily newspapers, breaking news, the latest sports results, the New York Metropolitan Museum, to hard pornography, and so on. We correspond by instant e-mail contact. This collapsible vision of any number of worlds is on the desk in today's offices, homes, studies and bedrooms. Which Word is the one that matters? The Word has been collapsed into an infinite number of possibilities. What does this do to "the Word in the world"?

We were once able to claim adhesion to an external form of life marked by regularity and time-tested practices and life-style underpinned by never-changing truths into which the Word was pro-

---

34. Available in English as Karl Barth, *Church Dogmatics* (eds. Geoffrey W. Bromily and Thomas F. Torrence; Edinburgh: T. & T. Clark, 1975).

claimed. It was taken for granted that Catholics encountered the Word in their regular and consistent practice of a traditional life of faith, along with its devotions and its seven Sacraments. It was taken for granted by Barth and Bultmann that Christians were consistently exposed to the Word by well-researched and well delivered proclamation that, like Paul, focussed upon the new creation initiated by God's action in the death and resurrection of Jesus. This is no longer the case. Contemporary believers and preachers of the Word in the world live in an increasingly fragmented world in which all such regularity, time-tested practices, ways of life, and universal adhesion to never-changing truths are not recognized. Indeed, they are ridiculed.

Today's western society is marked by high mobility, a fracturing of previously sacred barriers and a seeming relativisation of all that was once regarded as permanent and sacred. As Phyllis A. Tickle reports in her important recent book, *God-Talk in America*: "When my contemporaries and I closed the doors of our mothers' houses behind us, we locked ourselves out of five hundred years of human habits and entered into disjuncture."[35] We must accept this as a given to be responded to creatively. This is not a simple task. It would be easier to wring our hands in disgust over the loss of the past and tremble with fear for the future, and many of us are doing just that. But the tradition we belong to – in its richest manifestations – tells us to "be of good cheer, I have conquered the world" (John 16:33).

Although there is no longer a prevailing sense of religion or adherence to a belief system among at least the immediate past three generations (Generation X, Y and Z),[36] this does not mean that there is *no religion*. We are living through a period of transition from adherence to traditional religion to a non-tradition bound religiosity sometimes referred to as "popular religion." Young people look at the world with increasing uncertainty. No traditional value system or life perspective is unshakeable. This applies to *both* the young *and* their parents and teachers in our contemporary world, and certainly in Australian society. There is less generation conflict because there is no clearly

---

35. P. A. Tickle, *God-Talk in America* (New York: Crossroad, 1997), 25.
36. I have been guided in these few remarks by the work of Denis Rochford, "Postmodernity, Religion and Youth," *Compass* 32 (1998): 33-37. See now the massive and critically important assessment of the history of the secularization of Western social and cultural order, and what it means to live "religiously" in this world: Charles Taylor, *A Secular Age* (Cambridge, MA: Belknap Press, 2007).

defined crisis among more recent generations. There is only a search for an identity which is unavailable – each one has her or his truth.[37]

Many of our contemporaries cherish a deep distrust of the "great truths." They look upon these as they would consider hair growth medications for balding men: if a medication would have proven effective, then all the others would have disappeared from the market place. Rather than surrender themselves to one meaningful tradition, life-style or fashion, they combine fragments of an ever incomplete and temporary fashion into an unfinished whole – a collage identity. Perhaps the most outstanding symbol of this "collage" is the widespread use of Christian symbols, especially the cross, but also others, in fashions and body-marking.

Painting the broad picture, one would have to admit that there is a severe breakdown between traditional Christian faith and practice in western contemporary society. This is particularly clear in the areas of both sexual ethics and adherence to creeds. To ask that Bultmann's "modern man" limit sexual activity to one partner, and only after marriage, and for unconditional intellectual commitment to a man who is also divine, and a God who is three in one and one in three, is to ask the impossible. More often than not, even serious people cannot agree with one or other teaching of the Church, especially its moral teaching, and thus detach themselves from all of them. A further serious and widespread problem, among the young and the not so young, is the heavy use of alcohol, and the widespread use of recreational drugs. To ask for a life-long commit to a life of conjugal chastity, especially when the Church is plagued by the problem of clerical and religious sexual abuse, is – for many - to ask the even more impossible. Major role models are footballers, Kylie Minogue, Paris Hilton and the Posh Girls or, for the more sophisticated, Cate Blanchette and Nicole Kidman. The Word most listened to today has shifted its focus, and the death and resurrection of Jesus are not in sight.

Yet if postmodernity is marked by a freedom which makes everything possible, there are – as was powerfully exemplified among Catholics in the recent Sydney celebration of World Youth Day, either in person or via the media - many young people for whom Jesus

---

37. For a penetrating description of this "religious" phenomenon in North America, see Tickle, *God-Talk in America*, 81-175.

Christ and some form of adhesion to a Church remains important. However, a crucial *difference* between our contemporary world and my generation is that *people are not Christians by birth*. Many of them were born into Christian families. Leading figures in our postmodern world are products of prosperous families, educated at Xavier College, Methodist Ladies College, Melbourne Grammar, Carey Baptist College, Presbyterian Ladies College, Scotch College, and so forth.[38] But birth context no longer determines adhesion to Christianity, or a preparedness to listen to the Word. I have close and dear friends who are born and baptised Catholics, but who no longer have adherence to any Church, and send their children to Carey Baptist College. Interestingly, one of those children, now beginning her adult life in the work-force, has never been baptised.

Where you were born and to whom you were born does not mean much nowadays. Non-practising parents often have their children baptised to ensure their eventual admission to a private college that is supposedly inspired by a Christian tradition, and supported by a Christian Church. But there is no sign of their preparedness to listen to "the Word" that is proclaimed by Baptism. Recently, at the request of the non-baptised bride who had been to school at Camberwell Grammar, I witnessed a marriage between this fine young lady and a past-pupil of Xavier College. The quality of the couple, their families and the guests was outstanding. The speeches from bride and groom and from the best man were wonderful testimony to the quality of their families and their educational background: but God, Christ and Church were nowhere to be found. The presence of the Catholic Priest was, at best, "quaint."

This bleak description applies to *the majority of Australian Christians*, young and not so young. Yet there remains a minority that manifests an enthusiastic adhesion to the Christian Church. They *are not Christians by birth, but by conversion*. They are who and what they are because they want to be. Many of them, after years somewhat distant from Christian institutions, have come back to *their own understanding* and practice of their faith *through conversion*. For centuries Christian principles and practice were "taught." This was the way "the

---

38. The educational establishments listed are the most prestigious and successful private secondary schools in the city of Melbourne. They are all closely associated with their founding Christian tradition: Roman Catholic, Methodist, Anglican, Baptist, and Presbyterian.

Word" was communicated. The Roman Catholic Magisterium, the Protestant preacher and the educational systems founded on Christian principles played their crucial role. The Word was delivered and we listened. We heard the Word and accepted it. As the years went by we attempted to have the Word shape our life-style. We began with the head, as we heard and accepted the Word. We accepted the principles associated with the acceptance of the Word of God. Over a lifetime, we gradually attempted to allow these principles determine our experience and our hearts. We had mixed success, and we understood our failures as "sin." We had a strong sense of what was right or wrong, true or false, because the notions we had heard and accepted as we received the Word that had been passed on to us.

This process has now been reversed. Young people will not simply accept principles ("a Word") *as such*. They do not start with their heads, but with their hearts. They must *experience* first. Gradually, on the basis of experience, they may come to develop a set of principles which are born from experience. This can sometimes be a rough ride, and lives are broken as the experience goes wrong. There are industries that thrive on the lives they break. It can also be a wonderful ride, as many young Christians witness daily. This is the challenge that the Church must face. Perhaps we need to first of all hear the Word from the young. The experience of World Youth Day was one of joy, of a great community across the nations of young people who celebrated together, of well-prepared liturgies and catechetical sessions in the Parishes. Is this what young people find in their local Christian communities, and in their families? How can we best promote an experience of faith and joy, generating a conversion that makes for an experience of wholeness and belonging?

Conclusion

In the light of all the above, it appears to me that the Word will be present in today's world in an appeal to contemporary *experience*. How is that Word to be made available, and impinge upon contemporary society? It is our experience of God which will be "caught not taught" and may touch hearts and may initiate a process of *conversion*. Our young people might ask, "What makes practising Christians different?" If there is no difference, we have a problem. Our difference must be located in our following the Pauline command to put on Christ. But which Christ? In my opinion, it is the Son of Man Christ who lays down his life in love and service. There would be, of course, other points of view, but allow me to sketch mine. All four Gospels, and the Pauline tradition, *tell the same story of Jesus*, albeit in their different ways.

There have been a number of "servant Christologies" developed over recent times, but we cannot do better than go back to the Gospel for a departure point.[39] What follows is a brief example of what happens when we read Jesus' story as *narrative*. As the sons of Zebedee are told that they must be prepared to share in Jesus' baptism rather than taker places on his left and the right, the other ten are annoyed (Mark 10:35-41). They suspect that these two pushy "sons of thunder" are jockeying themselves into future positions of authority and power when Jesus comes to his glory in Jerusalem (v. 37). Jesus' response is as shattering to the contemporary Church as it was to those first disciples. Indeed it is even more challenging, as we have collected so much baggage over the centuries.

> You know that those who are supposed to rule over the Gentiles lord his over them, and their great men exercise authority over them. *But it shall not be so among you*; but whoever would be great among you must be your servant, and whoever would be first among you must be slave of all (vv. 42-44).

These words, reaching back to Jesus himself,[40] have *never* been practised by the great Churches, and we wonder why we have become irrelevant now that a Church-less society is quite capable of looking after itself. In the end, we have failed as followers of Jesus: "For the Son of Man also came not to be served but to serve, and to give his

---

39. For more detail on what follows, see Francis J. Moloney, *The Gospel of Mark. A Commentary* (Peabody: Hendrickson, 2002), 203-08.
40. The application of the criteria for "historicity" lends strong support for these words as belonging to Jesus' way of speaking to his disciples. On the criteria, see John P. Meier, *A Marginal Jew: Rethinking the Historical Jesus*, 5 vols., Anchor Tale Biblical Reference Library (New York/New Haven: Doubleday/Yale University Press, 1991-2016), 1:167-95.

life as a ransom for many" (v. 45).⁴¹ We should try to tell the story of Jesus more often, and better. As Yann Martel has recently written in his *Beatrice and Virgil*: "Stories – individual stories, family stories, national stories – are what stitch together the disparate elements of human existence into a coherent whole. We are story animals."⁴²

And once we have told the story, we must "put on Christ," or, as the author of 1 John would put it "walk in the same way in which he walked" (1 John 2:6). Among other locations, Paul has turned this narrative into his sublime insertion of a hymn into his letter to the Philippians, most likely used by the Philippians themselves in their liturgies, to instruct them on what it means to "have this mind among yourselves, which is yours in Christ Jesus," in his instruction on the importance of mutual love and service in Philippians 2:5-11.⁴³

Our *practising* Christians are widely caricatured as elderly, stodgy, lacking in joy and an ability to take a few risks, much less serve and lay down their lives for others. We know that this is a caricature, but "the world" does not. I suggest that the Word in this world will not be a spoken word, but something that is seen and experienced in the way we live and love. Except for a small but strong number of conservative young people searching for ultimate security in the Church, the Word will not be found in Latin liturgies and vestments that smack of the Constantinian era, nor in an uncompromising Barthian or Bultmannian proclamation of the biblical Word.⁴⁴ For all their grandeur, that era is lost to us.

The Christian population is dwindling, but theological educational institutions multiply. Each of them lays claim to a uniqueness that leads to under-paid and sometimes poorly trained teaching,

---

41. For an excursus on Mark 10:45, see Moloney, *Mark*, 213-14. Vincent Taylor, *The Gospel according to St. Mark*, 2d ed. (London: Macmillan, 1966), 444, claims that "This saying is one of the most important in the Gospels."
42. Yann Martel, *Beatrice* and *Virgil* (Edinburgh: Canongate Books, 2010), 7. Martel, of course, was the winner of the Man Booker Prize with his *Life of Pi*.
43. Among many, see Francis J. Moloney, *In the Footsteps of Paul*, Catholic Education Week Address (Melbourne: Catholic Education Office, 2009), 14-19.
44. There are some who are very much attracted to the more solemn and formal face of the Church, commonly called in the Catholic tradition "sacristy Priests." For my reflections on that contemporary phenomenon, see Francis J. Moloney, "Young People and the Future of Religious and Priestly Vocations," *The Swag* 17/4 (Summer 2009): 10-13.

poor administration, and everyone dipping their hands into the same Federal Government pot of gold. Is this saying something about the Word in the world? How well are we "telling the story of Jesus"?

We cannot be Christians unless we preach the Gospel at all times (see 1 Cor 9:16; Rom 1:14; 2 Tim 4:2), but we are struggling to make that Word live in a world that those who constructed the Second Vatican Council, Karl Barth and Rudolf Bultmann never imagined possible. There is a serious disjuncture between Christianity of the 1960's and that of the early Third Millennium that we must take seriously. Our Christian future is at stake, but there are good signs of joy, hope and faith. A significant non-Catholic Australian media figure, Andrew Denton described World Youth Day as the Olympic Games without the drugs. Half a million young people from all over the world affirmed one another: it is OK to love God and Jesus Christ, and to love one another. This is part of their "telling the story of Jesus," and thus communicating the Word to us.

However, as we are all aware, there were many millions of young people who would go down in a census as belonging to one of the Christian Churches who *were not* in Sydney. Add to that, millions of adults who would also regard such activity as a waste of time. They will continue to regard the half a million who celebrated World Youth Day as having "lost it." They are happy to sink more deeply into a culture that is a success-oriented, individual-focused, too often alcohol and drug supported, unconditionally committed to a consumer society – and a growth in the Gross Domestic Product - that either does not think about or denies that they are destroying the earth that welcomes and nourishes us. As we celebrate a centenary, what are we going to do about making the Word present to that particular world? Maryanne Confoy's outstanding recent essay in the most recent number of *Pacifica*, basing herself upon the dreams of the principles for founding the Melbourne College of Divinity in 1910, argues this case passionately:

> The prophetic voice of the Church must be heard at all levels of ministerial life so that the message is vital, generative and sourced in the gospel. With such ministerial vitality Christian

Church communities will be integral to the healing of the broken body of humanity and that of the planet as a whole.[45]

Is it possible that we might "tell the story" of Jesus better in our preaching, in our behaviour, in our commitment to our earth, and in our theological education, and thus better reflect our Christian vocation?

---

45. This admirable centenary challenge to the MCD can be found in the essay: Maryanne Confoy, "'Consider, Take Counsel, and Speak Out' (Judges 19:30). Contemplative, Dialogical and Prophetic Dimensions of Christian Ministry," *Pacifica* 23 (2010): 212-32. For the citation, see p. 231.

BIBLIOGRAPHY

Commentaries

Anderson, Hugh. *The Gospel of Mark*. New Century Bible. London: Oliphants, 1976.

Aune, David E. *Revelation*. 3 vols. Word Biblical Commentary 52a-52c. Dallas, TX: Word, 1997-1998.

Barrett, C. Kingsley. *The Gospel According to St. John. An Introduction with Commentary and Notes on the Greek Text*. 2nd ed. London: SPCK, 1978.

Blomberg, Craig L. *Matthew*. New American Commentary 22. Nashville: Broadman, 1992.

Bonnard, Pierre. *L'Évangile de Matthieu*. Commentaire du Nouveau Testament 1. Neuchatel: Delachaux & Niestlé, 1963.

Bovon, François. *Luke*. Translated by Christine S. Thomas, Donald S. Deer, and James Crouch. Hermeneia. 3 vols. Minneapolis: Fortress, 2002-2012.

Branscomb, B. H. *The Gospel of Mark*. The Moffatt New Testament Commentary. London: Hodder & Stoughton, 1937.

Brown, Raymond E. *The Gospel According to John*. 2 vols. The Anchor Bible 28-28A. Garden City, NY: Doubleday. 1966-70.

Bultmann, Rudolf. *The Gospel of John: A Commentary*. Translated by G. R. Beasley-Murray. Oxford: Basil Blackwell, 1971.

Byrne, Brendan. *The Hospitality of God. A Reading of Luke's Gospel*. 2nd ed. Collegeville, MN: Liturgical Press, 2015.

Carroll, John T. *Luke: A Commentary*. The New Testament Library. Louisville: Westminster John Knox, 2012.

Carter, Warren. *Matthew and the Margins. A Sociopolitical and Religious Reading.* Maryknoll, NY: Orbis Books, 2000.

Collins, Adele Y. *Mark.* Hermeneia. Minneapolis: Fortress, 2007.

Collins, Raymond F. *First Corinthians.* Sacra Pagina 7. Collegeville, MN: The Liturgical Press, 1999.

Corsini, Eugenio. *Apocalisse di Gesù secondo Giovanni.* Torino: Società Editrice Internazionale, 2002.

_____. *Apocalisse prima e dopo.* Torino: Società Editrice Internazionale, 1980.

_____. *The Apocalypse. The Perennial Revelation of Jesus Christ.* Translated by Francis J. Moloney. Good News Studies 5. Wilmington, DE: Michael Glazier, 1983.

Cranfield, C. E. B. *The Gospel According to Saint Mark.* 2nd ed. The Cambridge Greek New Testament Commentary. Cambridge: Cambridge University Press, 1963.

Culpepper, R. Alan. *Mark.* Smith & Helwys Bible Commentary. Macon: Smith & Helwys, 2007.

Davies, William D. and Dale C. Allison, *The Gospel According to Saint Matrthew.* 3 vols. International Critical Commentary. Edinburgh: T. & T. Clark, 1988-1997.

Evans, Christopher F. *Saint Luke.* New Testament Commentaries. London: SCM Press, 1990.

Evans, Craig A. *Mark 8:27-16:20.* Word Biblical Commentary 34B. Nashville: Thomas Nelson, 2001.

Fitzmyer, Joseph A. *First Corinthians.* The Anchor Yale Bible 32. New Haven: Yale University Press, 2008.

_____. *The Gospel According to Luke.* 2 vols. The Anchor Bible 28-28A. New York: Doubleday, 1981-1988.

Garland, David E. *Reading Matthew. A Literary and Theological Commentary.* Macon: Smyth & Helwys, 2001.

Gnilka, Joachim. *Das Evangelium nach Markus.* 5th ed. 2 vols. Evangelisch-Katholischer Kommentar zum Neuen Testament II/1-2. Zürich/Neukirchen-Vluyn: Benzinger Verlag/Neukirchener Verlag, 1999.

_____. *Das Matthäusevangelium.* 2 vols. Herders Theologische Kommentar zum Neuen Testament I/1-2. Freiburg: Herder, 1986-1988.

Grundmann, W. *Das Evangelium nach Markus*. 6th ed. Theologischer Handkommentar zum Neuen Testament 2. Berlin: Evangelische Verlagsanstalt, 1973.

Guelich, Robert. *Mark 1-8:26*. Word Biblical Commentary 34a. Dallas: Word Books, 1989.

Gundry, Robert H. *Matthew. A Commentary on His Literary and Theological Art*. Grand Rapids: Eerdmans, 1982.

Haenchen, Ernst. *Das Johanesevangelium. Ein Kommentar*. Tübingen: J. C. B. Mohr (Paul Siebeck, 1980.

Hagner, Donald. A. *Matthew*. 2 vols. Word Bible Commentary 33-33a. Dallas: Word Books, 1993-1995.

Harrington, Daniel. *The Gospel of Matthew*. Sacra Pagina 1. Collegeville, MN: The Liturgical Press, 1991.

Hooker, Morna D. *The Gospel According to St Mark*. Black's New Testament Commentaries. London: A. & C. Black, 1991.

Horsley, Richard A. *1 Corinthians*. Abingdon New Testament Commentaries. Nashville: Abingdon Press, 1998.

Hoskyns, Edward C. *The Fourth Gospel*. Edited by F. N. Davey. 2nd ed. London: Faber & Faber, 1947.

Johnson, Luke T. *The Gospel of Luke*. Sacra Pagina 3. Collegeville, MN: The Liturgical Press, 1991.

_____. *The Letter of James*. Anchor Bible 37a. New York: Doubleday, 1995.

Keener, Craig S. *A Commentary on the Gospel of Matthew*. Grand Rapids: Eerdmans, 1999.

Koester, Craig. *Revelation*. Anchor Yale Bible 38A. New Haven: Yale University Press, 2014.

_____. *Évangile selon Matthieu*, Études Bibliques. Paris: Gabalda. 1927.

La Verdiere, Eugene. *The Beginning of the Gospel. Introducing the Gospel According to Mark*. 2 vols. Collegeville, MN: The Liturgical Press, 1999.

Lagrange, M.-J. *Évangile selon Marc*. Études Bibliques. Paris: Gabalda, 1920.

Lane, William L. *Commentary on the Gospel of Mark*. The New International Commentary on the New Testament. Grand Rapids: Eerdmans, 1974.

Léon-Dufour, Xavier. *Lecture de l'Évangile selon Jean*. 4 vols. Parole de Dieu. Paris: Seuil, 1988-1996.

Lindars, Barnabas. *The Gospel of John*. New Century Bible. London: Oliphants, 1972.

Lohmeyer, Ernst. *Das Evangelium des Markus*. 17th ed. Meyers Kommentar 1/2. (Göttingen: Vandenhoeck & Ruprecht, 1967.

Luz, Ulrich. *Matthew*. 3 vols. Hermeneia. Minneapolis: Fortress, 2001-2007.

Marcus, Joel. *Mark*. 2 vols. Anchor Yale Bible 27-27A. New York/New Haven: Doubleday/Yale University Press, 2000-2009.

Moloney, Francis J. *A Body Broken for a Broken People. Divorce, Remarriage, and the Eucharist*. 3rd ed. Melbourne: Garratt, 2015.

_____. *Belief in the Word. Reading John 1-4*. Minneapolis: Fortress, 1992.

_____. *Glory **not** Dishonor. Reading John 13-21*. Minneapolis: Fortress, 1998.

_____. *Johannine Studies 1975-2017*. Wissenschaftliche Untersuchungen zum Neuen Testament 372. Tübingen: Mohr Siebeck, 2017.

_____. *Signs and Shadows. Reading John 5-12*. Minneapolis: Fortress, 1996.

_____. *The Gospel of John*. Sacra Pagina 4. Collegeville, MN: The Liturgical Press, 1998.

_____. *The Gospel of John. Text and Context*. Biblical Interpretation Series 72. Boston/Leiden: Brill, 2005.

_____. *The Gospel of Mark. A Commentary*. Grand Rapids: Baker Academic, 2012.

Nineham, D. E. *The Gospel of St Mark*. Pelican Gospel Commentaries. Harmondsworth: Penguin Books, 1963.

Nolland, John. *The Gospel of Matthew*. New International Greek Testament Commentary. Grand Rapids: Eerdmans, 2005.

Painter, John. *Mark's Gospel*. New Testament Readings. London: Routledge, 1997.

Perkins, Pheme. *First Corinthians*. Paideia Commentaries on the New Testament. Grand Rapids: Baker Academic, 2012.

Pesch, Rudolf. *Das Markusevangelium*. 2 vols. Herders theologischer Kommentar zum Neuen Testament II/1-2. Freiburg: Herder, 1977.

Schnackenburg, Rudolf. *The Gospel According to St. John*. Translated by Kevin Smyth and Others. Herder's Theological Commentary on the New Testament IV/1-3. London/New York: Burns & Oates/Crossroad, 1968-1975

Schneider, Gerhard. *Das Evangelium nach Lukas*. 2 vols. Ökumenischer Taschenbuch-Kommentar zum Neuen Testament 3/1-2. Gütersloh/Munich: Gerd Mohn/Echter, 1977.

Schulz, S. *Das Evangelium nach Johannes*. Das Neue Testament Deutsch 4. Göttingen: Vandenhoeck & Ruprecht, 1972.

Schweitzer, Eduard. *The Good News According to Mark*. Translated by Donald H. Madvig. London: SPCK, 1971.

_____. *The Good News According to Matthew*. Translated by David E. Green. London: SPCK, 1976.

_____. *The Letter to the Colossians. A Commentary*. Translated by Andrew Chester. London: SPCK, 1976.

Senior, Donald. *Matthew*. Abingdon New Testament Commentary. Nashville: Abingdon, 1998.

Strack, H., and P. Billerbeck. *Kommentar zum Neuen Testament aus Talmud und Midrasch*. 5 vols. München: C. H. Beck, 1922-1961.

Talbert, Charles H. *Reading Luke: a Literary and Theological Commentary on the Third Gospel*. New York: Crossroad, 1982.

Taylor, Vincent. *The Gospel According to St Mark*. London: Macmillan, 1966.

Westermann, Claus. *Genesis. A Commentary*. Translated by John J. Scullion. 3 vols. Minneapolis: Augsburg, 1984-1986.

Other Cited Literature

Aland, K. and B. *The Text of the New Testament. An Introduction to the Critical Editions and the Theory and Practice of Modern Textual Criticism*. Translated by E. F. Rhodes. Grand Rapids: Eerdmans, 1987.

Aletti, Jean-Noël. *L'art de raconteur Jésus Christ*. Paris: Seuil, 1989.

Allison, Dale C., Jr. *Constructing Jesus. Memory, Imagination, and History*. Grand Rapids: Baker Academic, 2010.

_____. "Divorce, Celibacy and Joseph (Matthew 1.18-25 and 19.1-12)." *Journal for the Study of the New Testament* 49 (1993): 3-10.

_____. *The End of the Age is Come. An Early Interpretation of the Death and Resurrection of Jesus*. Philadelphia: Fortress, 1985.

Archer, Jeffrey and Francis J. Moloney, *The Gospel according to Judas*. London: Macmillan, 2007.

Armstrong, Regis J., J. A. Wayne Hellmann and William J. Short, eds. *Francis of Assisi: early documents*. 3 vols. Hyde Park, NY: New City Press, 1999-2001.

Baird, William. *History of New Testament Research*. 3 vols. Minneapolis: Fortress, 1992-2013.

Barth, Karl. *Church Dogmatics*. Edited by Geoffrey W. Bromily and Thomas F. Torrence. Edinburgh, T. & T. Clark, 1975.

_____. "Rudolf Bultmann: An Attempt to Understand Him." Pages 82-132 in *Kerygma and Myth*. Edited by Hans Werner Bartsch. Translated by Reginald H. Fuller. 2 vols. New York: Harper & Row, 1961.

_____. *The Epistle to the Romans*. Translated by Edwyn C. Hoskyns. 6th ed. Oxford: Oxford University Press, 1933.

Barth, Markus. *Rediscovering the Lord's Supper. Communion with Israel, with Christ, and Among the Guests*. Atlanta: John Knox Press, 1998.

Bauer, Walter, William F. Arndt, and Frederick W. Gingrich, *A Greek-English Dictionary of the New Testament and Other Early Christian Literature*, 3rd ed. Edited by Frederick W. Danker. Chicago: University of Chicago Press, 2000.

Beirne, Paul. "The Melbourne College of Divinity: A Selective Historical Overview." *Pacifica* 23 (2010): 123-36.

Benedict XVI, Pope. *Post-Synodal Apostolic Exhortation* Verbum Domini *of the Holy Father Benedict XVI to the Bishops, Clergy, Consecrated Persons and the Lay Faithful on the Word of God in the Life and Mission of the Church*. Vatican City: Libreria Editrice Vaticana, 2010.

Benedict XVI, Pope. *The Environment*. Edited by Jacqueline Lindsey. Huntington, IN: Our Sunday Visitor, 2012.

Benoit, Pierre. "Christian Marriage according to Saint Paul." *The Clergy Review* 65 (1980): 309-321.

Berger, Klaus. *Die Auferstehung des Propheten und die Erhöhung des Menschensohnes. Traditionsgeschichtliche Untersuchungen zu Deutung des Geschickes Jesu in frühchristlichen Texten*. Studien zur Umwelt des Neuen Testaments 13. Göttingen: Vandenhoeck & Ruprecht, 1976.

Best, E. *Following Jesus. Discipleship in the Gospel of Mark*. Journal for the Study of the New Testament Supplement Series 4. Sheffield: JSOT Press, 1981.

_____. *The Temptation and the Passion: The Markan Soteriology*. Society for New Testament Studies 2. 2nd ed. Cambridge: Cambridge University Press, 1990.

Betz, Hans Dieter. "Apostle." Volume 1, pages 309-311 in *The Anchor Bible Dictionary*. Edited by David N. Freedman. 6 vols. New York: Doubleday, 1992.

Black, C. Clifton. *The Disciples according to Mark: Markan Redaction in Current Debate*. Supplements to the Journal for the Study of the New Testament 27. Sheffield: Sheffield Academic Press, 1989.

Blass, F., A. Debrunner and R. W. Funk. *A Greek Grammar of the New Testament and Other Early Christian Literature*. Chicago: The University of Chicago Press, 1967.

Bode, E. L. *The First Easter Morning: The Gospel Accounts of the Women's Visit to the Tomb of Jesus*. Analecta Biblica. Rome: Biblical Institute Press, 1970.

Boomershine, Thomas. "Mark 16:8 and the Apostolic Commission." *Journal of Biblical Literature* 100 (1981): 225-39.

Bovon, François. *Luke the Theologian. Fifty-five Years of Research*. Translated by Ken McKinney. 2nd ed. Waco, TX: Baylor University Press, 2006.

Boyarin, Daniel. "The Gospel of the *Memra*: Jewish Binitarianism and the Prologue to John." *Harvard Theological Review* 91 (2001): 243-84.

Brown, Dan. *The da Vinci Code*. New York: Random House, 2003.

Brown, Raymond E. "'And the Lord Said'? Biblical Reflections on Scripture as the Word of God." *Theological Studies* 42 (1981): 3-19.

_____. "Critical Biblical Exegesis and the Development of Doctrine." Pages 26-53 in *Biblical Exegesis and Church Doctrine*. New York: Paulist Press, 1985.

_____. "Historical-Critical Exegesis of the Bible in Roman Catholicism." Pages 10-25 in *Biblical Exegesis and Church Doctrine*. New York/Mahwah, NJ: Paulist Pressm 1985.

_____. *The Community of the Beloved Disciple. The Life, Loves and Hates of an Individual Church in New Testament Times*. London: Geoffrey Chapman, 1979.

_____. *The Death of the Messiah: From Gethsemane to the Grave: A Commentary on the Passion Narratives in the Four Gospels*. 2 vols. Anchor Bible Reference Library. New York: Doubleday, 1994.

_____. "The Johannine Sacramentary." Pages 51-76 in *New Testament Essays*. London: Geoffrey Chapman, 1967.

_____. "The Meaning of the Bible." *Theology Digest* 28 (1980): 305-320.

_____. *The Virginal Conception and the Bodily Resurrection of Jesus*. London: Geoffrey Chapman, 1973.

Brown, Raymond E., Joseph A. Fitzmyer and Roland E. Murphy, eds. *The New Jerome Biblical Commentary*. Englewood Cliffs: Prentice Hall, 1990.

Brütsch, Charles. *La Clarté de l'Apocalypse*. 5th ed. Geneva: Labor et Fides, 1966.

Bühner, Jan-A. "ἀποστέλλω/ἀπόστολος." Volume 1, pages 141-46 in *Exegetical Dictionary of the New Testament*. Edited by H. Balz and G. Schneider. 3 vols. Grand Rapids: Eerdmans, 1990.

Bultmann, Rudolf, and Five Critics. *Kerygma and Myth*. Edited by Hans Werner Bartsch. Translated by Reginald H. Fuller. 2 vols. New York: Harper & Row, 1961.

_____. *The History of the Synoptic Tradition*. Translated by John Marsh. Oxford: Basil Blackwell, 1968.

_____. *Theology of the New Testament*. Translated by G. Krodel. 2 vols. London: SCM Press, 1955.

Bultmann, Rudolf. *New Testament and Mythology and Other Basic Writings*. Translated and Edited by Schubert M. Ogden. Philadelphia: Fortress, 1984.

Byrne, Brendan. "A Pauline Complement to *Laudato Si'*." *Theological Studies* 77 (2016): 308-317.

——————. "Christ's Pre-Existence in Pauline Soteriology." *Theological Studies* 58 (1997): 308-330.

——————. *Inheriting the Earth. The Pauline Basis of a spirituality for our time*. Homebush: St Paul Publications, 1990.

Camery-Hoggatt, J. *Irony in Mark's Gospel. Text and Subject*. Society for New Testament Studies 72. Cambridge: Cambridge University Press, 1992.

Capel Anderson, J., and J. L. Staley, eds. "Taking it Personally." *Semeia* 72 (1995).

Carnazzo, Sebastian. *Seeing Blood and Water. A Narrative Critical Study of John 19:34*. Eugene, OR: Pickwick Publications, 2012.

Catechism of the Catholic Church. Homebush: St Paul Publications, 1994.

Charlesworth, James H., ed. *The Old Testament Pseudepigrapha*. 2 vols. London: Darton, Longman & Todd, 1983.

Charlier, C. "La presence dans l'absence (Jn 13,31-14,31)." *Bible et Vie Chrétienne* 2 (1953): 61-75.

Chatman, Seymour. *Story and Discourse: Narrative Structure in Fiction and Film*. Ithaca, NY: Cornell University Press, 1978.

Chennattu, Rekha M. *Johannine Discipleship as a Covenant Relationship*. Peabody, MA: Hendrickson, 2006.

Chilton, Bruce. *Visions of the Apocalypse. Receptions of John's Revelation in Western Imagination*. Waco, TX: Baylor University Press, 2013.

Collins, Adele Y. *The Beginning of the Gospel. Probings of Mark in Context*. Minneapolis: Fortress, 1992.

Collins, Raymond F. *Divorce in the New Testament*. Good News Studies 38. Collegeville, MN: The Liturgical Press, 1992.

Coloe, Mary. "Creation in the Gospel of John." Pages 71-90 in *Creation is Groaning: Biblical and Theological Perspectives*. Edited by Mary Coloe. Collegeville, MN: The Liturgical Press, 2013.

_____. "The Garden as a New Creation in John." *The Bible Today* 53 (2015): 159-64.

Confoy, Maryanne. "'Consider, Take Counsel, and Speak Out' (Judges 19:30). Contemplative, Dialogical and Prophetic Dimensions of Christian Ministry." *Pacifica* 23 (2010): 212-32.

Congar, Yves. *L'Église de saint Augustin à l'époque modern*. Paris: Cerf, 1970.

_____. *My Journal of the Council*. Translated by Denis Minns and Others. Adelaide: ATF Theology, 2012.

Congregation for the Doctrine of the Faith. *Declaration "Dominus Iesus" on the Unicity and Salvific Universality of Jesus Christ and the Church*. Rome: Congregation for the Doctrine of the Faith, 2000.

Conzelmann, Hans. *The Theology of St Luke*. Translated by Geoffrey Busswell. London: Faber & Faber, 1961.

Cross, F. L., and E. A. Livingstone, eds. *The Oxford Dictionary of the Christian Church*. 2nd ed. Oxford: Oxford University Press, 1974.

Cullmann, Oscar. *Early Christian Worship*. Studies in Biblical Theology 10. London: SCM Press, 1953.

Curti, E. "The Tablet Interview: Jude the Obscure." *The Tablet* (31 March, 2007): 8-9.

Dawkins, Richard. *The God Delusion*. London: Bantam Press, 2006.

de Jonge, Marinus. *Stranger from Heaven and Son of God: Jesus Christ and the Christians in the Johannine Perspective*. Translated by J. E. Steely. Missoula, MT: Scholars Press, 1977.

de Lubac, Henri. *A Brief Catechism on Nature and Grace*. San Francisco: Ignatius Press, 1984.

Deines, Roland. *Der Gerechtigkeit der Tora im Reich des Messias*. Wissenschaftliche Untersuchungen zum Neuen Testament 177. Tübingen: Mohr Siebeck, 2004.

Delbrueck, R. "Antiquärisches zu den Verspottung Jesu." *Zeitschriftg für die Neutestamentliche Wissenschaft* 41 (1942): 124-45.

Depuis, Jacques. *Towards a Christian Theology of Religious Pluralism*. Maryknoll, NY: Orbis Books, 1997.

Dodd. Charles H. *The Interpretation of the Fourth Gospel*. Cambridge: Cambridge University Press, 1953.

Donahue, John R. *Are You the Christ? The Trial Narrative in the Gospel of Mark.* Society of Biblical Literature Dissertation Series 10. Missoula, MT: Society of Biblical Literature, 1973.

_____. *The Gospel in Parable.* Philadelphia: Fortress, 1988.

Doré, Joseph. *A cause de Jésus.* Paris: Éditions Plon, 2011.

_____. *Peut-on vraiment rester catholique?* Paris: Éditions Bayard Culture, 2012.

Duffy, Eamon. *Ten Popes who Shook the World.* New Haven: Yale University Press, 2011.

Duke, P. D. *Irony in the Fourth Gospel.* Atlanta: John Knox Press, 1985.

Dunn, James D. G. *The Theology of the Apostle Paul.* Grand Rapids: Eerdmans, 1998.

Dupont, Jacques. *Les Béatitudes.* 3 vols. Etudes Bibliques. Paris: Gabalda, 1969-73.

Edsall, Benjamin A. *Paul's Witness to Formative Early Christian Instruction.* Wissenschaftliche Untersuchungen zum Neuen Testament 2.365. Tübingen: Mohr Siebeck, 2014.

Edwards, Denis. *Ecology at the Heart of Faith.* Maryknoll, NY: Orbis Books, 2006.

_____. *Jesus and the Natural World. Exploring a Christian Approach to Ecology.* Melbourne: Garratt, 2012.

_____. *Partaking of God. Trinity, Evolution, and Ecology.* Collegeville, MN: The Liturgical Press, 2014.

Edwards, J. R. "Markan Sandwiches. The Significance of Interpolations in Markan Narratives." *Novum Testamentum* 31 (1989): 193-216.

Ehrmann, Bart D. *The Lost Gospel of Judas Iscariot. A New Look at Betrayer and Betrayed.* New York: Oxford University Press, 2006.

Eloff, Marvyn. "Ἀπό .. ἕως and Salvation History in Matthew's Gospel." Pages 85-107 in *Built upon the Rock. Studies in Matthew's Gospel.* Edited by Daniel M. Gurtner and John Nolland. Grand Rapids: Eerdmans, 2008.

Esler, Philip. *Community and Gospel in Luke-Acts. The Social and Political Motivation of Luke's Theology.* Society for New Testament Studies Monograph Series 57. Cambridge: Cambridge University Press, 1987.

Feldmeier, Richard. *Die Krisis des Gottessohnes: Gethsemaneerzählung als Schlüssel der Markuspassion*. Wissenschaftliche Untersuchungen zum Neuen Testament 2.21. Tübingen: J. C. B. Mohr (Paul Siebeck), 1987.

Finegan, J. *Encountering New Testament Manuscripts. A Working Introduction to Textual Criticism*. London: SPCK, 1975.

Fitzmyer, Joseph A. "Marriage and Divorce." Volume 1, pages 511-15 in *The Encyclopedia of the Dead Sea Scrolls*. Edited by Lawrence H. Schiffmann and James VanderKam. 2 vols. Oxford/New York: Oxford University Press, 2000.

_____. "The Matthean Divorce Texts and Some New Palestinian Evidence." *Theological Studies* 39 (1976): 197-226.

Flanagan, Patrick J. *The Gospel of Mark Made Easy*. New York: Paulist Press, 1997.

Flannery, Austin, ed. *The Basic Sixteen Documents. Vatican II. Decrees, Declarations. A Completely Revised Translation in Inclusive Language*. Northport, NY/Dublin: Costello Publishing Company/Dominican Publications, 1995.

Fledderman, H. "The Flight of a Naked Young Man." *The Catholic Biblical Quarterly* 41 (1979): 312-18.

Fowler, Robert M. *Let the Reader Understand. Reader-Response Criticism and the Gospel of Mark*. Minneapolis: Fortress, 1991.

_____. *Loaves and Fishes. The Function of the Feeding Stories in the Gospel of Mark*. Society of Biblical Literature Dissertation Series 54. Chico, CA: Scholars Press, 1981.

Francis, Pope. Encyclical Letter Laudato Si' *of the Holy Father Francis on Care for our Common Home*. Vatican City. Libreria Editrice Vaticana, 2015.

_____. *Evangelii Gaudium. Apostolic Exhortation on the Proclamation of the Gospel in Today's World*. Vatican City: Libreria Editrice Vaticana, 2013.

_____. Misericordia Vultus. *Bull of Indiction of the Extraordinary Jubilee of Mercy*. Vatican City: Libreria Editrice Vaticana, 2015.

_____. Post-Synodal Apostolic Exhortation Amoris Laetitia *of the Holy Father Francis to Bishops, Priests and Deacons, Consecrated Persons, Christian Married Couples, and all the Lay Faithful*. Vatican City: Editrice Libreria Vaticana, 2016.

Fredriksen, Paula. *From Jesus to Christ. The Origins of the New Testament Images of Jesus*. 2nd ed. New Haven: Yale University Press, 2000.

Frye, N. *The Great Code. The Bible and Literature*. London: Routledge & Kegan Paul, 1982.

Gaillardetz, Richard R. *Ad tuendam fidem*: An Emerging Pattern in current Papal Teaching." *New Theology Review* 12 (1999): 42-51.

_____. *Teaching with Authority. A Theology of the Magisterium of the Church*. Collegeville, MN: The Liturgical Press, 1997.

_____. *The Church in the Making*. Rediscovering Vatican II Series. New York/Mahwah, NJ: Paulist Press, 2006.

_____. *Witness to the Faith. Community, Infallibility, and the Ordinary Magisterium of the Bishops*. New York/Mahwah, NJ: Paulist Press, 1992.

Garrett, Susan R. *The Temptations of Jesus ibn Mark's Gospel*. Grand Rapids: Eerdmans, 1998.

Geddert, T. J. *Watchwords: Mark 13 in Markan Eschatology*. Journal for the Study of the New Testament Supplement Series 26. Sheffield: Sheffield Academic Press, 1989.

Gill, Athol. *Life on the Road: The Gospel Basis for a Messianic Lifestyle*. Homebush, NSW: Lancer Books, 1992.

_____. *The Fringes of Freedom: Following Jesus, Living Together, Working for Justice*. Homebush, NSW: Lancer Books, 1990.

Goodfriend, Elaine A. "Adultery." Volume 1, pages 82 86 in *The Anchor Bible Dictionary*. 6 vols. New York: Doubleday, 1992.

Hahn, Ferdinand. *The Worship of the Early Church*. Translated by David E. Green. Philadelphia: Fortress, 1973.

Haight, Roger. *Jesus Symbol of God*. Maryknoll, NY: Orbis Books, 1999.

Hamilton, Neil Q. "Resurrection, Tradition and the Composition of Mark." *Journal of Biblical Literature* 84 (1965): 415-21.

Hammann, Konrad. *Rudolf Bultmann. A Biography*. Translated by Philip E. Devenish. Salem, OR: Polebridge Press, 2013.

Harvey, Warren. "Torah: Origin and Pre-Existence." Volume 15, pages 1236-1238 in *Encyclopaedia Judaica*. 16 vols. Jerusalem: Keter Publishing House, 1971-1972.

Havener, Ivan. *Q: The Sayings of Jesus*. Good News Studies 19. Wilmington, DE: Michael Glazier, 1987.

Hengel, Martin. *Studies in the Gospel of Mark*. London: SCM Press, 1985.

_____. *The Charismatic Leader and His Followers*. Translated by C. G. Grieg. Studies of the New Testament and Its World. Edinburgh: T. & T. Clark, 1981.

Henn, William. *The Honor of my Brothers. A Brief History of the Relationship between the Pope and the Bishops*. New York: Crossroad, 2000.

Hennecke, E., and W. Schneemelcher, eds. *New Testament Apocrypha*. Translated by R. McL. Wilson. 2 vols. London: SCM Press, 1963.

Hoehner, H. W. *Herod Antipas. A Contemporary of Jesus Christ*. Grand Rapids: Zondervan, 1980.

Horsley, Richard A. *Hearing the Whole Story: The Politics of the Plot of Mark's Gospel*. Louisville: Westminster John Knox, 2001.

Hurtado, Larry W. *How on Earth Did Jesus Become God. Historical Questions about Earliest Devotion to Jesus*. Grand Rapids: Eerdmans, 2005.

Instone-Brewer, David. *Divorce and Remarriage in the Bible. The Social And Literary Context*. Grand Rapids: Eerdmans, 2002.

Iverson, Kelly R. "Incongruity, Humor and Mark: Performance and the Use of Laughter in the Second Gospel." *New Testament Studies* 59 (2013): 2-19.

_____. "Performance Criticism." Volume 2, pages 97-105 in *The Oxford Encyclopedia of Biblical Interpretation*. Edited by Steven McKenzie. 2 vols. New York/Oxford: Oxford University Press, 2013.

Iverson, Kelly R. and Christopher W. Skinner, eds. *Mark as Story. Retrospect and Prospect*. Society for Biblical Literature Resources for Biblical Study 64. Atlanta: Society for Biblical Literature, 2011.

Jeremias, Joachim. *The Eucharistic Words of Jesus*. London: SCM Press, 1966.

_____. "The Words of Institution." Pages 18-28 in *Understanding the Eucharist. Papers in the Maynooth Union Summer School 1968*. Edited by P. McGoldrick. Dublin: Gill and Macmillan, 1969.

Johns, Loren L. *The Lamb Christology of the Apocalypse.* Wissenschaftliche Monographien zum Neuen Testament 2.167. Tübingen: Mohr Siebeck, 2007.

Johnson, Luke T. *Prophetic Jesus, Prophetic Church. The Challenge of Luke-Acts to Contemporary Christians.* Grand Rapids: Eerdmans, 2011.

_____. *Religious Experience in Earliest Christianity.* Minneapolis: Fortress, 1998.

Karotemprel, Sebastian. *Albizuri among the Lyngams. A Brief History of the Catholic Church among the Lyngams.* Shillong: Vendrame Institute Publiucations, 1985.

Karris, Robert J. *Luke: Artist and Theologian. Luke's Passion Account as Literature.* New York: Paulist Press, 1985.

Käsemann, Ernst, *The Testament of Jesus according to John 17.* London: SCM Press, 1966.

_____. *Meeting Christ on the Indian Road.* Shillong: Don Bosco Centre for Indigenous Cultures, 2000.

_____. *Volti Africani, Latinoamericani e Asiatici dello Stesso Signore.* Bologna: EMI, 1997.

Kasser, R., M. Mayer and G. Wurst, eds. *The Gospel of Judas* (Washington, DC: National Geographic, 2006.

Kee, Howard C. *The Community of the New Age. Studies in Mark's Gospel.* London: SCM Press, 1977.

Kelber, Werner. *The Oral and Written Gospel. The Hermeneutics of Speaking and Writing in the Synoptic Tradition.* Philadelphia: Fortress, 1983.

Kelhoffer, James A. *Miracle and Mission. The Authentication of Missionaries and their Message in the Longer Ending of Mark.* Wissenschaftliche Untersuchungen zum Neuen Testament 2.112. Tübingen: J. C. B. Mohr (Paul Siebeck), 2000.

Kelly, Anthony J. *An Expanding Theology. Faith in a world of Connections.* Sydney: E. J. Dwyer, 1993.

_____. *Laudato Si'. An Integral Ecology and the Catholic Vision.* Adelaide: ATF Theology, 2016.

Kermode, Frank. *The Genesis of Secrecy. On the Interpretation of Narrative.* Cambridge: MA: Harvard University Press, 1979.

Kingsbury, Jack D. *Conflict in Mark. Jesus, Authority, Disciples*. Minneapolis: Fortress, 1989.

_____. *The Christology of Mark's Gospel*. Philadelphia: Fortress, 1983.

Kitzberger, Ingrid-Rosa, ed. *The Personal Voice in Biblical Interpretation*. London: Routledge, 1998.

Klauck, Hans-Joseph. "Die Erzählerische Rolle der Jünger im Markusevangelium. Eine narrative Analyse." *Novum Testamentum* 24 (1982): 1-26.

Kloppenborg, John S. Q, *The Earliest Gospel. An Introduction to the Earliest Stories and Sayings of Jesus*. Louisville: Westminster John Knox, 2008.

Klos, H. *Die Sakramente im Johannesevangelium. Vorkommen und Bedeutung von Taufe, Eucharistie und Busse im vierten Evangelium*. Stuttgarter Bibelstudien 46. Stuttgart: Katholisches Bibelwerk, 1970.

Kodell, Jerome. *The Eucharist in the New Testament*. Zacchaeus New Testament. Wilmington, DE: Michael Glazier, 1989.

Krieger, M. *A Window to Criticism*. Princeton, NJ: Princeton University Press, 1974.

Kugler, Robert A. "Testaments." Volume 2, pages 933-36 in *Encyclopedia of the Dead Sea Scrolls*. Edited by Lawrence H. Schiffmann and James C. VanderKam. 2 vols. Oxford/New York: Oxford University Press, 2000.

Küng, Hans. *Disputed Truth. Memoirs*. Translated by John Bowden. London: Continuum, 2008.

_____. "Twelve Patriarchs, Testaments of the." Volume 2, pages 952-52 in *Encyclopedia of the Dead Sea Scrolls*. Edited by Lawrence H. Schiffmann and James C. VanderKam. 2 vols. Oxford/New York: Oxford University Press, 2000.

Kurz, William. "Luke 22:14-38 and Greco-Roman and Biblical Farewell Addresses." *Journal of Biblical Literature* 104 (1985): 251-68.

Lampe, G. W. H. *A Patristic Greek Lexicon*. Oxford: Clarendon Press, 1961.

Lee, Dorothy A. *Flesh and Glory. Symbolism, Gender and Theology in the Gospel of John*. New York: Herder, 2002.

_____. *Transfiguration*. New Century Theology. London/New York: Continuum, 2004.

Lenti, Arthur. *Don Bosco. History and Spirit*. 7 vols. Rome: LAS, 2007-2010.

Léon-Dufour, Xavier. *Sharing the Eucharistic Bread. The Witness of the New Testament*. Translated by Matthew J. O'Connell. New York: Paulist Press, 1987.

_____. "Towards a Symbolic Reading of the Fourth Gospel." *New Testament Studies* 27 (1980-81): 439-56.

Lieu, Judith. *Image and Reality. The Jews in the World of the Christians in the Second Century*. Edinburgh: T. & T. Clark, 1996.

Lightfoot, R. H. *History and Interpretation in the Gospels*. The Bampton Lectures 1934. London: Hodder and Stoughton, 1935.

_____. *The Gospel Message of St Mark*. Oxford: Clarendon Press, 1950.

Lindars, Barnabas. *New Testament Apologetic. The Doctrinal Significance of the Old Testament Quotations*. London: SCM Press, 1961.

Linnemann, E. "Der (wiedergefundene) Markusschluss." *Zeitschrift für Theologie und Kirche* 66 (1969): 255-87.

Loader, William R. G. "Did Adultery Mandate Divorce? A Reassessment of Jesus' Divorce Logia." *New Testament Studies* 61 (2015): 67-78.

_____. *The Dead Sea Scrolls on Sexuality in Sectarian and Related Literature at Qumran*. Grand Rapids: Eerdmans, 2009.

_____. *The New Testament on Sexuality*. Grand Rapids: Eerdmans, 2012.

Lohfink, Gerhard. *Jesus of Nazareth. What He Wanted, Who He Was*. Translated by Linda Maloney. Collegeville, MN: The Liturgical Press, 2012.

Luz, Ulrich. "The Fulfillment of the Law in Matthew (Matt 5:17-20)." Pages 398-435 of *Studies in Matthew*. Grand Rapids: Eerdmans, 2005.

Malatesta, Edward. "Blood and water from the pierced side of Christ." Pages 164-81 in *Segni e Sacramenti nel Vangelo di Giovanni*. Edited by Pius-Ramon Tragan. Studia Anselmiana 66, Sacramentuim 3. Rome: Editrice Anselmiana, 1977.

Malbon, Elizabeth S. "Disciples/Crowds/Whoever. Markan Characters and the Readers." Pages 70-99 in *In the Company of Jesus. Characters in Mark's Gospel*. Louisville: Westminster John Knox, 2000.

_____. "Fallible Followers: Women and Men in the Gospel of Mark." Pages 57-67 in *In the Company of Jesus. Characters in Mark's Gospel*. Louisville: Westminster John Knox, 2000.

Malet, André. *The Thought of Rudolf Bultmann*. Translated by Richard Strachan. Garden City, NY: Doubleday, 1971.

Manicardi, Ermenegildo. *Il cammino di Gesù nel Vangelo di Marco. Schema narrative e tema cristologico*. Analecta Biblica 96. Rome: Biblical Institute Press, 1986.

Manson, Thomas W. *The Sayings of Jesus*. London: SCM Press, 1971.

Marcus, Joel. "Mark – Interpreter of Paul." *New Testament Studies* 46 (2000): 473-87.

Marshall, Christopher D. *Faith as a Theme in Mark's Gospel*. Society for New Testament Studies Monograph Series 64. Cambridge: Cambridge University Press, 1989.

Martel, Yann. *Beatrice and Virgil*. Edinburgh: Canongate Books, 2010.

Martinez, Florentino G. and Eibert J. Tigchelaar, *The Dead Sea Scrolls. Study Edition*. 2 vols. Leiden: Brill, 1997-1998.

Martyn, J. Louis. *History and Theology in the Fourth Gospel*. 2nd ed. Nashville: Abingdon, 1969.

_____. *The Gospel of John in Christian History*. New York: Paulist Press, 1978.

Marxsen, Willi. *Mark the Evangelist. Studies in Redaction Criticism*. Translated by Roy A. Harrisville. Nashville: Abingdon Press, 1969.

_____. *The Resurrection of Jesus of Nazareth*. Translated by Margaret Kohl. London: SCM Press, 1970.

Massingbaerde Ford, Josephine. *Bonded with the Immortal. A Pastoral Introduction to the New Testament*. Wilmington, DE: Michael Glazier, 1987.

Matera, Frank J. *Galatians*. Sacra Pagina 9. Collegeville, MN: The Liturgical Press, 1992.

_____. *New Testament Christology*. Louisville: Westminster John Knox, 1999.

_____. *New Testament Ethics. The Legacies of Jesus and Paul.* Louisville: Westminster John Knox, 1996.

_____. *New Testament Theology. Exploring Diversity and Unity.* Louisville: Westminster John Knox, 2007.

_____. *Passion Narratives and Gospel Theologies. Interpreting the Synoptics Through Their Passion Stories.* New York: Paulist Press, 1986.

_____. *Romans.* Paideia Commentaries on the New Testament. Grand Rapids: Baker Academic, 2010.

_____. *The Kingship of Jesus: Composition and Theology in Mark 15.* Society of Biblical Literature Dissertation Series 66. Chico, CA: Scholars Press, 1982.

Matsunaga, K. "Is John's Gospel Anti-Sacramental?" *New Testament Studies* 27 (1980-81): 516-24.

McKnight, E. V. *Post-Modern Use of the Bible: The Emergence of Reader Oriented Criticism.* Nashville: Abingdon, 1988.

Meier, John P. *A Marginal Jew. Rethinking the Historical Jesus.* 5 vols. The Anchor Yale Bible Reference Library. Doubleday/New Haven: Doubleday/Yale University Press, 1991-2016.

_____. "John the Baptist in Matthew's Gospel." *Journal of Biblical Literature* 99 (1980): 383-405.

_____. *Law and History in Matthew's Gospel. A Redactional Study of Mt. 5:17-48.* Analecta Biblica 71. Rome: Biblical Institute Press, 1976.

Metzger, Bruce M. *A Textual Commentary on the Greek New Testament.* 2nd ed. Stuttgart: Deutsche Bibelgesellshaft, 1994.

_____. *The Text of the New Testament. Its Transmission, Corruption, and Restoration.* 2nd ed. Oxford: Clarendon Press, 1968.

Migliasso, S. *La presemnza dell'Assente. Saggio di analisi letterario-strutturale e di sintisi teologica de Gv. 13,31-14,31.* Roma: Pontificia Università Gregoriana, 1979.

Miller, J. W. *The Concept of the Church in the Gospel of John.* Unpublished Doctoral Dissertation, Princeton University, 1976.

Minear, Paul S. "A Note on Luke 22:36." *Novum Testamentum* 7 (1964-65): 128-34.

_____. "Some Glimpses of Luke's Sacramental Theology." *Worship* 44 (1970): 322-31.

Moloney, Francis J. *A Body Broken for a Broken People. Divorce, Remarriage, and the Eucharist*. 3rd ed. Melbourne: Garratt, 2015.

_____. *A Friendly Guide to the Gospel of Mark*. Melbourne: Garratt, 2012.

_____. *A Friendly Guide to the New Testament*. Melbourne: Garratt, 2010.

_____. *A Friendly Guide to the Resurrection of Jesus Christ*. Melbourne: Garratt, 2016.

_____. *A Life of Promise: Poverty-Chastity-Obedience*. Wilmington: Michael Glazier, 1984.

_____. *Beginning the Good News. A narrative approach*. Collegeville, MN: The Liturgical Press, 1992.

_____. "*Constructing Jesus* and the Son of Man." *The Catholic Biblical Quarterly* 75 (2013): 719-38.

_____. *Disciples and Prophets. A Biblical Model for the Religious Life*. London: Darton, Longman & Todd, 1980.

_____. *Eucharist as a Celebration of Forgiveness*. New York/Mahwah, NJ. Paulist Press, 2017.

_____. "Faith in the Risen Jesus." *Salesianum* 43 (1981): 305-16.

_____. *In the Footsteps of Paul*. Catholic Education Week Address. Melbourne: Catholic Education Office, 2009.

_____. "Jesus Christ: The Question to Cultures." *Pacifica* 1 (1988): 15-43.

_____. *Johannine Studies 1975-2017*. Wissenschaftliche Untersuchungen zum Neuen Testament. Tübingen: Mohr Siebeck, 2017.

_____. *Love in the Gospel of John. An Exegetical, Theological, and Literary Study*. Grand Rapids: Baker Academic, 2013.

_____. *Mark: Storyteller, Interpreter, Evangelist*. Peabody, MA: Hendrickson, 2004.

_____. "Matthew 19,3-12 and Celibacy. A Redactional and Form Critical Study." *Journal for the Study of the New Testament* 2 (1979): 42-60.

_____. "Narrative Criticism of the Gospels." *Pacifica* 4 (1991): 181-201.

_____. *Reading the New Testament in the Church. A Primer for Pastors, Religious Educators, and Believers.* Grand Rapids: Baker Academic, 2015.

_____. *Reflections on Evangelical Consecration. Celebrating a Bicentenary.* Bolton, UK: Don Bosco Publications, 2015.

_____. "Resurrection and Accepted Exegetical Opinion." *The Australasian Catholic Record* 58 (1981): 191-202.

_____. "Revisiting John." *Scripture Bulletin* II (1980): 11-13.

_____. "The Fourth Gospel and the Jesus of History." *New Testament Studies* 45 (1999): 42-58.

_____. "The Gospel of John as Scripture." Pages 333-47 in *The Gospel of John. Text and Context.* Biblical Interpretation Series 72. Leiden/Boston: Brill, 2005.

_____. *The Gospel of John. Text and Context.* Biblical Interpretation Series 75. Boston/Leiden: Brill, 2005.

_____. *The Johannine Son of Man.* 2nd ed. Eugene, OR: Wipf & Stock, 2007.

_____. *The Living Voice of the Gospel. The Gospels Today.* 2nd ed. Melbourne: Garratt, 2006.

_____. *The Resurrection of the Messiah. A Narrative Commentary on the Resurrection Accounts of the Four Gospels.* New York/Mahwah, NJ: Paulist Press, 2013.

_____."The Vocation of the Disciples in the Gospel of Mark." Pages 53-63 in *"A Hard Saying." The Gospel and Culture.* Collegeville, MN: The Liturgical Press, 2001.

_____. *The Word Became Flesh.* Theology Today 14. Cork/Dublin: Mercier Press, 1979.

_____. "To be Witnesses of the Forgiveness and Compassion of Jesus." Pages 183-95 in *Apostolic Passion "Give me Souls."* Edited by Rafael Vicent and Corrado Pastore. Bangalore: Kristu Jyoti Publications, 2010.

_____. "Young People and the Future of Religious and Priestly Vocations." *The Swag* 17/4 (Summer 2009): 10-13.

Molony, John N. *The Roman Mould of the Australian Church*. Carlton: Melbourne University Press, 1967.

Moo, D. J. *The Old Testament in the Gospel Passion Narratives*. Sheffield: The Almond Press, 1983.

Moore, George F. *Judaism in the First Centuries of the Christian Era*. 2 vols. Cambridge, MA: Harvard University Press, 1958.

Moore, Stephen D. *Poststructuralism and the New Testament. Derrida and Foucault at the Foot of the Cross*. Minneapolis: Fortress, 1990.

Morrison, Gregg. *The Turning Point in the Gospel of Mark. A Study in Markan Christology*. Eugene, OR. Pickwick Publications, 2014.

Moxnes, Halvor. *The Economy of the Kingdom. Social Conflict and Economic Relations in Luke's Gospel*. Overtures to Biblical Theology. Overtures to Biblical Theology. Philadelphia: Fortress, 1988.

Munro, W. "Women Disciples in Mark?" *The Catholic Biblical Quarterly* 44 (1982): 225-41.

Myers, Chad. *Binding the Strong Man. A political Reading of Mark's Story of Jesus*. Maryknoll, NY: Orbis Books, 1990.

Neyrey, Jerome. *The Passion According to Luke. A Redaction Study of Luke's Soteriology*. New York: Paulist Press, 1985.

Niewalda, P. *Sakramentssymbolik im Johannesevangelium. Ein exegetischhistorische Studie*. Limburg: Lahn-Verlag, 1958.

Nowak, Martin A., and Sarah Coakley, eds. *Evolution, Games, and God. The Principle of Cooperation*. Cambridge, MA: Harvard University Press, 2013.

O'Collins, Gerald. *Living Vatican II. The 21st Council for the 21st Century*. New York/Mahwah, NJ: Paulist Press, 2006.

O'Malley, John W. *Trent: What Happened at the Council*. Cambridge, MA: Harvard University Press, 2013.

_____. *What Happened at Vatican II*. Cambridge, MA: Harvard University Press, 2008.

Ormorod, Neil. "Vatican II – Continuity or Discontinuity? Towards and Ontology of Meaning." *Theological Studies* 71 (2010): 609-36.

Painter, John. "Glimpses of the Johannine Community in the Farewell Discourses." *Australian Biblical Review* 28 (1980): 21-38.

_____. "The Farewell Discourses and the History of Johannine Christianity." *New Testament Studies* 27 (1980-81): 525-43.

----------. "The Fourth Gospel and the Founder of Christianity. The place of historical tradition in the work of C. H. Dodd." Pages 257-84 in *Engaging with C. H. Dodd on the Gospel of John*. Edited by Tom Thatcher and Catrin Williams. Cambridge: Cambridge University Press, 2013.

----------. *Theology as Hermeneutics. Rudolf Bultmann's Interpretation of the History of Jesus*. Sheffield: The Almond Press, 1987.

Pannenberg, Wolfhart. "Did Jesus Actually Rise from the Dead?" *Dialog* 4 (1965): 18-35.

----------. *Grundzüge der Christologie*. Gutersloh: Gerd Mohn, 1964.

Peron, Gian Paolo. *Sequitimi! Vi faro diventare pescatori di uomini*. Biblioteca di Scienze Religiose 162. Rome: LAS, 2000.

Perrin, Norman. "The Christology of Mark. A Study in Methodology." *Journal of Religion* 51 (1971): 173-87.

Pesch, Rudolf. "Zur Entstehung des Galubens an die Auferstehung Jesu." *Theologische Quartelschrift* 153 (1973): 201-28.

Petersen, N. R. *Literary Criticism for New Testament Critics*. Guides to Biblical Scholarship NT Series. Philadelphia: Fortress, 1978.

Porsch, Felix. *Pneuma und Wort. Ein exegetische Beitrag zu Pneumatologie des Johannesevangeliums*. Frankfurter Theologische Studien 16. Frankfurt: Joseph Knecht, 1974.

Przbylski, B. *Righteousness in Matthew and His World of Thought*. Society for New Testament Studies Monograph Series 41. Cambridge: Cambridge University Press, 1980.

Rahner, Karl. *Spirit in the World*. Translated by William Dych. London: Sheed and Ward, 1968.

Ratzinger, Joseph. "Sacred Scripture in the Life of the Church." Volume 3, pages 262-272 in *Commentary on the Documents of Vatican II*. Edited by H. Vorgrimler. 5 vols. London/New York: Burns & Oates/Herder & Herder, 1967-69.

----------. *The Ratzinger Report*. San Francisco: Ignatius Press, 1984.

----------. "The Transmission of Divine Revelation." Volume 3, pages 181-198 in *Commentary on the Documents of Vatican II*. Edited by H. Vorgrimler. 5 vols. London/New York: Burns & Oates/Herder & Herder, 1967-69.

Reid, Stephen, Robert Dixon and Noel Connolly, *Catholic Religious Institutes in Australia. A Report on the 2009 survey of Religious Institutes in Australia*. Fitzroy/Annandale: Pastoral Projects Office/Catholic Religious of Australia, 2010.

Rhoads, D., J. Dewey, and D. Michie, *Mark as Story. An Introduction to the Narrative of a Gospel*. 2nd ed. Minneapolis: Fortress, 1999.

Ricoeur, Paul. *Hermeneutics and the Human Sciences*. Edited by J. B. Thompson. Cambridge: Cambridge University Press, 1981.

_____. *Interpretation Theory: Discourse and the Surplus of Meaning*. Fort Worth: Texas Christian University Press, 1976.

Rimmon-Kenan, S. *Narrative Fiction: Contemporary Poetics*. New Accents. London: Methuen, 1983.

Robinson, J. A. T. *Honest to God*. Fortieth Anniversary Reprint. Louisville: Westminster John Knox, 2002.

_____. *Redating the New Testament*. London: SCM Press, 1976.

Robinson, James M., Paul Hoffmann, and John S. Kloppenborg, *The Critical Edition of Q. Synopsis including the Gospels of Matthew and Luke, Mark and Thomas, with English, German, and French Translations of Q and Thomas*. Hermeneia. Minneapolis: Fortress, 2000.

Rochford, Denis. "Postmodernity, Religion and Youth." *Compass* 32 (1998): 33-37.

Roy, Arundhati. *The God of Small Things*. London: Flamingo, 1997.

Rush, Ormond. *The Eyes of Faith. The Sense of the Faithful and the Church's Reception of Revelation*. Washington, DC: The Catholic University of America Press, 2009.

Sanders, Ed P. *Jesus and Judaism*. Philadelphia: Fortress, 1985.

_____. *The Historical Figure of Jesus*. London: Penguin Press, 1993.

Schildgen, B. D. *Power and Prejudice: The Reception of the Gospel of Mark*. Detroit: Wayne State University Press, 1999.

Schillebeeckx, Edward. *Jesus. An Experiment in Christology*. Translated by John Bowden. London: Collins, 1979.

Schleiermacher, Friedrich. *The Christian Faith*. Translated and Edited by H. R. Mackintosh and J. S. Stewart. New York: Harper Torchbooks, 1963.

Schmithals, Walter. *An Introduction to the Theology of Rudolf Bultmann*. Translated by John Bowden. London: SCM Press, 1968.

Schnackenburg, Rudolf, "Die Sakramente im Johannesevangelium." Volume 2, pages 235-54 in *Sacra Pagina. Miscellanea Biblica Congressus Biblicus Internationalis Catholicus de Re Biblica*. Edited by Joseph Coppens and Others. 2 vols. Gembloux: Duculot, 1959.

Schneiders, Sandra M. "History and Symbolism in the Fourth Gospel." Pages 71-76 in *L'Évangile de Jean. Sources, redaction, théologie*. Edited by Marinus de Jonge. Bibliotheca Ephemeridum Theologicarum Lovaniensium 44. Gembloux: Duculot, 1977.

——————. "Symbolism and sacramental principle in the Fourth Gospel." Pages 221-35 in *Segni e Sacramenti nel Vangelo di Giovanni*. Edited by Pius-Ramon Tragan. Studia Anselmiana 66, Sacramentuim 3. Rome: Editrice Anselmiana, 1977.

——————. "The Footwashing (John 13:1-20). An Experiment in Hermeneutics." *The Catholic Biblical Quarterly* 43 (1981): 76-92.

——————. *The Revelatory Text. Interpreting the New Testament as Sacred Scripture*. 2nd ed. Collegeville, MN: The Liturgical Press, 1999.

Scholtissek, Klaus. "Nachfolge und Autorität nach dem Markusevangelium." *Trierer Theologische Zeitschrift* 100 (1991): 56-74.

Schulte, Raphael and Burkhard Neunheuser. "Sacraments." Volume 5, pages 378-87 in *Sacramentum Mundi. An Encyclopedia of Theology*. 6 vols. New York/London: Herder & Herder/Burns & Oates, 1970.

Schweitzer, A. *The Quest of the Historical Jesus*. Translated by W. Montgomery. London: A. & C. Black, 1910.

Schweitzer, E. "Mark's Theological Achievement." Pages 42-63 in *The Interpretation of Mark*. Edited by W. Telford. Issues in Religion and Theology 7. Philadelphia: Fortress.

Segovia, F. F., and M. A. Tolbert, eds. *Reading from this Place*. 2 vols. Minneapolis: Fortress, 1995-1996.

Senior, Donald. "The Death of Jesus and the Resurrection of the Holy Ones. Matthew 27:51-53." *The Catholic Biblical Quarterly* 38 (1976): 312-29.

——————. *The Passion of Jesus in the Gospel of Mark*. The Passion Series 2. Wilmington, DE: Michael Glazier, 1984.

Shepherd, T. "The Narrative Function of Markan Intercalation." *New Testament Studies* 41 (1995): 522-40.

Sim, David. *Apocalyptic Eschatology in the Gospel of Matthew*. Society for New Testament Studies Monograph Series 88. Cambridge: Cambridge University Press, 1996.

_____. *The Gospel of Matthew and Christian Judaism. The History and Social Setting of the Matthean Community*. Studies of the New Testament and Its World. Edinburgh: T. & T. Clark, 1998.

Sloyan, Gerard S. *Jesus on Trial. The Development of the Passion Narratives and their Historical and Ecumenical Implications*. Edited by John Reumann. Philadelphia: Fortress, 1973.

Soards, Marion L. "The Question of a PreMarcan Passion Narrative." Volume 2, pages 1492-1524 in Raymond E. Brown, *The Death of the Messiah: From Gethsemane to the Grave: A Commentary on the Passion Narratives in the Four Gospels*. 2 vols. Anchor Bible Reference Library. New York: Doubleday, 1994.

Spicq, Ceslas. "τρώγειν est-il synonyme de φάγειν et d'ἔσθιειν dans le Nouveau Testament?" *New Testasment Studies* 26 (1979-80): 414-19.

Spivey, Robert A., D. Moody Smith and C. Clifton Black. *Anatomy of the New Testament. A Guide to Its Structure and Meaning*. Minneapolis: Fortress, 2013.

Staley, J. L. *Reading with a Passion. Rhetoric, Autobiography, and the American West in the Gospel of John*. New York: Continuum, 1995.

Standaert, B. *L'Évangile selon Marc. Composition et Genre Littéraire*. Brugge: Sint-Andreisabdij, 1978.

Stanley, David. *Jesus in Gethsemane. The Early Church Reflects on the Suffering of Jesus*. New York: Paulist Press, 1980.

Stark, Rodney. *The Rise of Christianity*. Princeton, NJ: Princeton University Press, 1996.

Stock, A. *Call to Discipleship. A Literary Study of Mark's Gospel*. Good News Studies 1. Wilmington, DE: Michael Glazier, 1982.

Stock, K. *Boten aus dem Mit-Ihm-Sein. Das Verhältnis zwischen Jesus und den Zwölf nach Markus*. Analecta Biblica 70. Rome: Biblical Institute Press, 1975.

Strecker, Georg. *Der Weg der Gerechtigkeit*. 3rd ed. Göttingen: Vandenhoeck & Ruprecht, 1971.

_____. *The Sermon on the Mount. An Exegetical Commentary.* Translated by O. C. Dean, Jr. Edinburgh: T. & T. Clark, 1988.

Sullivan, Francis. *Magisterium. Teaching Authority in the Catholic Church.* New York/Mahwah, NJ: Paulist, 1983.

Tannehill, Robert C. "The Disciples in Mark: The Function of a Narrative Role." Pages 134-57 in *The Interpretation of Mark.* Edited by William Telford. Issues in Religion and Theology 7. Philadelphia: Fortress, 1985.

_____. "The Gospel of Mark as Narrative Christology." *Semeia* 16 (1980): 137-69.

_____. *The Narrative Unity of Luke-Acts: A Literary Interpretation.* 2 vols. Foundations and Facets. Philadelphia: Fortress, 1986.

Taylor, Charles. *A Secular Age.* Cambridge, MA: Belknap Press, 2007.

Taylor, Vincent. *The Passion Narrative of St Luke.* Edited by Owen E. Evans. Society for New Testament Studies Monograph Series 23. Cambridge: Cambridge University Press, 1972.

The Bible and Culture Collective. *The Postmodern Bible.* New Haven: Yale University Press, 1996.

The Pontifical Biblical Commission. *The Interpretation of the Bible in the Church.* Vatican City: Libreria Editrice Vaticana, 1993.

Theissen, Gerd, and Annette Merz. *The Historical Figure of Jesus. A Comprehensive Guide.* Translated by John Bowden. Minneapolis: Fortress, 1998.

Theissen, Gerd. *The First Followers of Jesus. A Sociological Analysis of the Earliest Christianity.* Translated by John Bowden. London: SCM Press, 1978.

Tickle, Phyllis A. *God-Talk in America.* New York: Crossroads, 1997.

Traets, C. *Voir Jésus et le Père in Lui selon l'Évangile de saint Jean.* Analecta Gregoriana 159. Rome: Gregorian University Press, 1967.

Trilling, Wolfgang. *Das Wahre Israel. Studien zur Theologie des Matthäus-Evangeliums.* 3rd ed. Studien zum Alten und Neuen Testament 10. München: Kösel Verlag, 1964.

van Iersel, B. *Reading Mark.* Collegeville, MN: The Liturgical Press, 1999.

Vincie, Catherine. *Worship and the New Cosmology. Liturgical and Theological Challenges.* Collegeville, MN: The Liturgical Press, 2014

Waetjen, H. C. *A Reordering of Power. A Socio-Political Reading of Mark's Gospel*. Minneapolis: Fortress, 1989.

Weeden, T. J. *Mark – Traditions in Conflict*. Philadelphia: Fortress, 1971.

Wilson, Stephen G. *The Gentiles and the Gentile Mission in Luke-Acts*. Society for New Testament Studies Supplement Series 19. Cambridge: Cambridge University Press, 1973.

Witherup, Ronald D. *Scripture*. Dei Verbum. Rediscovering Vatican II Series. New York/Mahwah, NJ: Paulist Press, 2007.

Wrede, W. *The Messianic Secret*. Translated by J. C. G. Greig. Cambridge and London: James Clark, 1971.

Wright, T. *Judas and the Gospel of Judas*. London: SPCK, 2006.

Wüthrich, Serge. "Naître de mourir: la mort de Jésus dans l'Évangile de Matthieu." *New Testament Studies* 56 (2010): 313-25.

Index of Authors

A
Aland, B.: 120
Aland, K.: 120
Aletti, Jean-Noël: 177
Allison, Dale C.: 147, 149–150, 152, 154–156, 160, 162–163, 165–167, 169, 286, 291, 305
Anderson, Hugh: 24, 26
Aquilina, Michael: 330
Archer, Jeffrey: 12, 309–316, 320–321, 328
Arndt, William F.: 83
Aune, David E.: 265–266, 271, 274

B
Baird, William: 168
Barrett, C. Kingsley: 194, 210
Barth, Karl: 349–351, 355–358, 360–363, 369
Barth, Markus: 175, 182–183
Bauer, Walter: 83
Beirne, Paul: 349
Benedict XVI, Pope: 227, 235, 245, 249, 254–256, 260, 310, 326, 334, 338, 354
Benoit, Pierre: 307
Berger, Klaus: 39
Best, E.: 21, 29
Betz, Hans Dieter: 174
Billerbeck, P.: 211
Black, C. Clifton: 18, 271
Blass, F.: 30, 109, 165

Blomberg, Craig L.: 159
Bode, E. L.: 128
Bonnard, Pierre: 157
Boomershine, Thomas: 146
Bovon, François: 172, 174–179, 181
Boyarin, Daniel: 274
Branscomb, B. H.: 24
Brown, Dan: 309, 312, 320–321
Brown, Raymond E.: 98, 103–104, 107–109, 111, 191, 193–195, 199, 200, 202–203, 208–211, 213, 215–216, 234, 247, 250–251, 317, 320, 325, 361
Brütsch, Charles: 259
Bühner, J.–A.: 26
Bultmann, Rudolf: 115, 122, 200–203, 207, 216, 231, 247, 349–351, 355–356, 358–364, 368–369
Byrne, Brendan: 182, 251, 261, 264, 273

C
Camery-Hoggatt, J.: 96–97, 106
Capel Anderson, J.: 225–226
Carnazzo, Sebastian: 216
Carroll, John T.: 175, 179, 181
Carter, Warren: 157, 159, 167
Charlesworth, James H.: 59
Charlier, C.: 215
Chatman, Seymour: 93
Chennattu, Rekha M.: 47
Chilton, Bruce: 260
Collins, Adele Y.: 82, 84–86, 89, 121, 299

Collins, Raymond F.: 4, 283, 287, 289–291, 293–296, 300
Coloe, Mary: 264
Confoy, Maryanne: 369–370
Congar, Yves: 238, 242, 244, 246, 306, 353
Connolly, Noel: 255, 355
Conzelmann, Hans: 223
Corsini, Eugenio: 265–272
Cranfield, C. E. B.: 27, 119
Cullmann, Oscar: 199–200, 203, 215
Culpepper, R. Alan: 140
Curti, E.: 321

D

Davies, William D.: 147, 149–150, 154–156, 160, 162–163, 165–167
Dawkins, Richard: 312, 320–321
de Jonge, Marinus: 47, 197
de Lubac, Henri: 237
Debrunner, A.: 30, 109, 165
Deines, Roland: 148, 150, 152–153, 156–167, 169
Delbrueck, R.: 108
Depuis, Jacques: 11
Dewey, J.: 16
Dibelius, M.: 122
Dixon, Robert: 255, 355
Dodd, Charles H.: 184, 231, 359
Donahue, John R.: 23, 27, 94, 97, 177
Doré, Joseph: 8, 10–12, 235
Duffy, Eamon: 77
Duke, P. D.: 95–96
Dunn, James D. G.: 286
Dupont, Jacques: 157

E

Edsall, Benjamin A.: 289
Edwards, Denis: 259–261, 263–264, 275–277, 342
Edwards, J. R.: 23–24, 27, 38, 41, 94
Ehrmann, Bart D.: 315
Eloff, Marvyn: 154

Esler, Philip: 176, 179–180
Evans, Christopher F.: 179, 181, 183
Evans, Craig A.: 87

F

Feldmeier, Richard: 103
Finegan, J: 120
Fitzmyer, Joseph A.: 4, 82, 175, 181–182, 250–251, 289–290, 293, 295–297, 300, 302, 307, 320
Flanagan, Patrick J.: 43
Fledderman, H.: 104, 126, 141
Follett, Ken: 336
Fowler, Robert M.: 16–17, 24, 27–28, 30, 44, 94
Francis, Pope: 83, 230, 256–267, 270, 273, 275, 278–282, 321, 323, 333–334
Fredriksen, Paula: 59, 136
Frye, N.: 229
Funk, R. W.: 30, 109, 165

G

Gaillardetz, Richard R.: 222, 229, 233, 237–238, 242
Garland, David E.: 157, 161
Garrett, Susan R.: 146
Geddert, T. J.: 99
Gill, Athol: 9, 15
Gingrich, Fredrick W.: 83
Gnilka, Joachim: 24, 29, 35, 38–39, 41, 43–44, 125, 157, 161, 168, 320
Goodfriend, Elaine A.: 287
Grundmann, W.: 126
Guelich, Robert: 24, 29, 31, 40, 53
Gundry, Robert H.: 148, 156

H

Haenchen, Ernst: 203
Hagner, Donald. A.: 157, 165, 167–168
Hahn, Ferdinand: 200
Haight, Roger: 357
Hall, Douglas John: 361

Hamilton, Neil Q.: 141
Hammann, Konrad: 358
Harrington, Daniel: 313
Harvey, Warren: 274
Havener, Ivan: 285
Hengel, Martin: 120, 306
Henn, William: 239
Hoehner, H. W.: 40
Hoffmann, Paul: 172, 285, 293
Holzmann, H. J.: 122
Hooker, Morna D.: 25, 33, 35, 37–39, 43, 66, 73, 81, 84–85, 99–100, 102, 126
Horsley, Richard A.: 142, 290, 296
Hoskyns, Edward C.: 206, 210, 357
Howse, C.: 319–320
Hurtado, Larry W.: 273

I

Instone-Brewer, David: 82, 283, 287–288
Iverson, Kelly R.: 17, 53, 117

J

Jeremias, Joachim: 181, 198–199, 231
Johns, Loren L.: 266, 268–269, 271–272
Johnson, Luke T.: 37, 39, 179, 183–185

K

Karotemprel, Sebastian: 8, 10–11
Karris, Robert J.: 175, 178
Käsemann, Ernst: 207
Kee, Howard C.: 23, 27, 94–95, 185
Keener, Craig S.: 303
Kelber, Werner: 17–18, 121–122
Kelhoffer, James A.: 132
Kelly, Anthony J.: 8–9, 278, 282
Kermode, Frank: 16, 23, 27, 94
Kingsbury, Jack D.: 16, 121
Klauck, Hans-Joseph: 145
Kloppenborg, John S.: 48, 172, 259, 285, 293
Klos, H.: 191, 194
Kodell, Jerome: 178, 183, 189

Koester, Craig: 200, 265–266, 271
Krieger, M.: 223
Kugler, Robert A.: 184
Küng, Hans: 238
Kurz, William: 185

L

La Verdiere, Eugene: 25, 29, 33–34, 38–39, 41, 44
Lagrange, M.-J.: 24, 29, 31, 33, 39, 127, 147, 163, 241
Lampe, G. W. H.: 196
Lane, William L.: 24, 85–87, 127
Lee, Dorothy A.: 66, 200
Lenti, Arthur: 240
Leo XIII, Pope: 260, 334, 337
Léon-Dufour, Xavier: 97, 176, 180, 182, 185, 187–188, 197–200, 203, 320
Lieu, Judith: 211
Lightfoot, R. H.: 58, 66, 117
Lindars, Barnabas: 194, 210–212, 313
Linnemann, E.: 119
Loader, William R. G.: 283–284, 289, 291, 293, 301–302
Lohfink, Gerhard: 293
Lohmeyer, Ernst: 24, 29, 32–33, 39–40, 100, 121, 127
Luz, Ulrich: 83, 89–90, 147–150, 153, 155, 157, 160, 162, 164, 166–167, 289, 302

M

Malatesta, Edward: 216
Malbon, Elizabeth S.: 63, 112, 145
Malet, André: 356, 360
Manicardi, Ermenegildo: 167
Manson, Thomas W.: 182
Marcus, Joel: 52, 81, 84–85, 87–89, 121, 128, 264, 304–305
Marshall, Christopher D.: 72
Martel, Yann: 257, 368
Martinez, Florentino G.: 82
Martyn, J. Louis: 207, 211, 213

Marxsen, Willi: 121, 144
Massyngbaerde Ford, Josephine: 178
Matera, Frank J.: 9–10, 94, 111, 168
Matsunaga, K.: 213
McGirr, M: 312
McKnight, E. V.: 223
Meier, John P.: 38–40, 48, 71, 81–82, 134, 148–153, 157–158, 161, 163, 165, 167–169, 199, 283, 287–290, 293–294, 296, 300, 304–305, 313, 317–320, 367
Merz, Annette: 175
Metzger, Bruce M.: 87, 119, 181
Michie, D.: 16
Migliasso, S.: 215
Miller, J. W.: 212–213
Minear, Paul S.: 182, 184
Moloney, Francis J.: 5–9, 12, 18, 20, 28, 39, 45, 47, 51, 56, 60, 70, 77–78, 81, 84, 90, 94–95, 100, 103, 105–106, 108, 112, 115, 122, 124, 131, 133, 136, 140–141, 143–144, 151, 153, 156, 171, 174, 179–180, 188, 192, 195, 199, 204, 208, 210, 214, 216–217, 224, 228, 231–232, 235, 238, 241, 255–257, 260, 264–265, 269, 276, 300–302, 304, 309, 311, 320, 325, 328, 335, 340, 343–345, 355, 367–368
Molony, John N.: 250
Moo, D. J.: 111
Moore, George F.: 211
Moore, Stephen D.: 224
Morrison, Gregg: 50
Moxnes, Halvor: 179
Munro, W.: 112
Murphy, Roland E.: 251
Myers, Chad: 18, 21, 41

N

Neunheuser, Burkhard: 196
Neyrey, Jerome: 175–178, 182, 184–185, 187
Niewalda, P.: 205
Nineham, D. E.: 24, 43–44, 87
Nolland, John: 154, 157, 161, 165, 167

O

O'Collins, Gerald: 238
O'Malley, John W.: 239, 242–243, 246, 337, 353, 361
Ormerod, Niel: 237

P

Painter, John: 25, 38, 215, 358–359
Pannenberg, Wolfhart: 144
Perkins, Pheme: 294, 296
Peron, Gian Paolo: 49
Perrin, Norman: 50, 121
Pesch, Rudolf: 24, 29, 31, 33–35, 38–39, 98, 144
Petersen, N. R.: 223
Pius XII, Pope: 334, 337
Pongraz-Lippert, Christa: 343
Porsch, Felix: 215
Przybylski, B.: 156–157
Przywara, Erich: 357

R

Rahner, Karl: 342
Ratzinger, Joseph: 233–234, 237–238, 246–247, 354
Reese, Thomas: 253
Reid, Stephen: 253, 355
Rhoads, D.: 16
Ricoeur, P.: 225
Rimmon-Kenan, S.: 17, 122
Robinson, J. A. T.: 210, 361
Robinson, James M.: 172, 285, 293
Rochford, Denis: 363
Roy, Arundhati: 232–233
Rush, Ormond: 247

S

Sanders, Ed P.: 193
Schildgen, B. D.: 89, 117
Schillebeeckx, Edward: 144

Schleiermacher, Friedrich: 356
Schmidt, K. -L.: 18, 122
Schmithals, Walter: 356, 358, 360
Schnackenburg, Rudolf: 194, 205, 210–211, 217, 317, 320
Schneider, Gerhard: 26, 177, 183
Schneiders, Sandra M.: 197, 214, 224
Scholtissek, Klaus: 144
Schulte, Raphael: 196
Schulz, S.: 210
Schweitzer, A.: 18
Schweitzer, Eduard: 17–18, 24, 26, 33–34, 88, 107, 119, 122, 160, 275
Senior, Donald: 100, 104, 111–112, 152, 159, 313
Shepherd, T.: 24, 27, 94, 138
Shildgen, D. E.: 16
Sim, David: 147, 154, 168
Sloyan, Gerard S.: 93
Smith, D. Moody: 271, 317
Soards, Marion L.: 98
Spicq, Ceslas: 201
Spivey, Robert A.: 271
Staley, J. L.: 225–226
Standaert, B.: 18
Stanley, David M.: 103
Stark, Rodney: 329–330, 333
Stock, A.: 18
Stock, K.: 25, 29, 31–32, 34, 37, 42, 44
Strack, H.: 211
Strecker, Georg: 156–157, 160, 165
Sullivan, Francis: 221–222

T

Talbert, Charles H.: 183
Tannehill, Robert C.: 125, 143, 145–146, 177, 179, 184, 187–188
Taylor, Charles: 363
Taylor, Vincent: 24, 26, 93, 119–120, 127, 174, 256, 368
Theissen, Gerd: 135, 175
Tickle, Phyllis A.: 331, 363–364
Tigchelaar, Eibert J.: 82
Traets, C.: 214
Trilling, Wolfgang: 147, 199

V

van Iersel, B.: 18
Vincie, Catherine: 275–276

W

Waetjen, H. C.: 25, 132
Weeden, T. J.: 45, 121, 125, 142
Westermann, Claus: 261
Williams, Rowan: 361
Wilson, Stephen G.: 174
Witherup, Ronald D.: 323, 327
Wrede, W.: 17, 122
Wright, T.: 315, 319
Wüthrich, Serge: 152

Index of Biblical References

Old Testament

Genesis
1–2	268
1–11	324
1:1	132, 261, 264
1:1–11	132
1:1–2:4	260–261
1:3	132
1:18	268
1:26–27	261
1:27	299–300, 303–304
1:28	261, 316
2:2–3	262
2:4–3:24	260
2:7	264
2:8	268
2:18–20	51
2:24	284, 293, 299–300, 303–304
3	270, 304
3:1–24	262, 304
3:14	263
4–11	262
6:5	262
8:20–9:17	262
11:1–9	262
12:1–3	262
19	185
22	271
22:2	68
22:12	68
22:15–18	262
22:16	68
28:14	262
47–50	185

Exodus
12:11	33
13:21–22	68
15:1–16:21	271
16:23	262
19:16–25	67
20:2–10	86
20:12–16	85
20:14	291
20:19	82, 287, 299
21:32	313
23:10	262
24:8	101
24:16	65, 68
29:35	148
33:7–11	68
34:5	68
40:34–35	68

Leviticus
19:9–10	262
20:10	82, 287, 299–300
25:1–4	262
25:4–6	262
25:10	262

Deuteronomy

4:10	82, 287, 299
5:6–15	86
5:16–20	85
5:18	291
5:20–21	287
5:21	82
6:1–4	85
6:4–9	147
17:6	32
18:15	68
18:15–18	67
18:18	39, 58, 68
19:15	32
22:22	82, 287, 299
24:1–4	81, 287–288, 291, 293, 299–300, 303
24:4	287, 291
31–34	185
34:5–8	67

Joshua

23–24	185

1 Kings

19:11–18	67

2 Kings

3:9–12	67

Job

38:1–39:2	263

Psalms

2:7	68
22	111
22:19	109
41:9	343
104	261–262
136	261
148	261–262

Proverbs

3:19	262
8:22–31	274
22:2	261

Isaiah

11:1–9	263
11:6–9	51
26:19	152
35:5–6	53
40:8	249, 323, 344, 352, 362
40:28–29	263
53:12	189

Jeremiah

5:21	53
15:9	152
18:2–3	318
32:6–15	318

Ezekiel

1:28	68
11:23	68
12:2	53
37:7	152
37:12–13	152

Daniel

7	70
7:9	66, 152
7:13	70
7:13–14	341
7:14	147
7:15–27	70
10:7–9	152
10:16	152
12:2	152

Joel

2:10	151

Amos
8:9	151

Haggai
2:6	151

Zechariah
11	313
14:5	151

Malachi
2:10–16	288
2:13–16	82–83
3:1	167
3:1–2	69
4:5	58
4:5–6	39, 69

2 Esdras
2:18	58

1 Maccabees
2:38	67

2 Maccabees
6:18–31	40

Wisdom
6:7	261
11:24	261
13:5	261

Sirach
1:1–5	274
15:1	274
24:1–12	274
34:8	274
38:34	261
48:9	67

New Testament

Matthew
1–2	322, 324, 171
1:1	131, 153, 158, 169
1:1–17	154
1:1–4:16	153, 158
1:2–17	153
1:16	153
1:19	155, 291
1:22–23	153
1:23	169
1:24–25	291
2:1–6	153
2:5–6	153
2:12	167
2:15	153
2:17–18	153
2:23	153
3:3	153, 166
3:6	158
3:13–19	158
3:14–15	155
3:15	155–159, 161–169
4:1–11	153, 169
4:6–7	153
4:14–16	153
4:15	166
4:16	158
4:23	149
4:23–24	31
4:25–5:1	148
4:30–32	259
4:41	259
5:1–7:27	256
5:1–7:28	164–166
5:1–7:29	149
5:3	161
5:3–13	162
5:3–16	163
5:6	155–156, 158–159, 161–164, 166, 168–169

5:10	155–156, 158–161, 163–164, 166, 168–169	10:1	31
		10:1–11:1	31, 149, 160
		10:2	174
5:10–11	159–160	10:5	167
5:11–12	160	10:5–6	148–150, 154
5:13–16	150, 161	10:5–10	31
5:17–18	147–169	10:8–10	30
5:17–19	302	10:10	32, 167
5:17–20	152, 154, 161, 163–164, 166	10:11–15	34
		10:22	160–161
5:17–48	160	10:41	155
5:18	158	10:42–43	259
5:20	155–156, 158, 161–166, 168–169	11:2–16:12	154
		11:7–19	167
5:21–48	149, 154, 161–164	11:10	167
5:25	166	12:7	303
5:32	82–83, 284, 290–293, 297, 301–303, 307	12:15–21	158
		12:17	153
		13:1–53	149
5:45	155	13:4	167
5:48	161, 163	13:17	155
6:1	152, 155–156, 158, 163–164, 166, 168–169	13:19	167
		13:31–32	259
		13:35	153
6:1–18	163	13:43	155
6:2–6	163–164	13:49	155
6:2–28	163	13:52	148
6:15	164	14:3–12	40
6:16	164	14:13–21	158
6:16–18	163	14:22–33	318
6:19–7:11	164	15:1–16:20	55
6:33	152, 155–156, 158, 163–165, 168–169	15:10–20	167
		15:21–28	148–149
7:12	164	15:24	148–150, 154
7:13–14	167	15:26–28	148
7:21–23	160	15:28	154
7:28–8:1	148	15:32	167
8:5–13	148–149	15:32–39	158
8:10–12	148	16:13–19	169
8:11–12	158, 167	16:15	48
8:17	153	16:16–18	169
8:22	306	16:17–19	187
8:27	259	16:23	62
8:28	166	16:24–28	48
9:13	155	17:24–27	230
9:14–17	148	18:1–10	118
9:35	31, 149	18:1–35	149

18:15–20	169	23:35	155
19:1–12	284, 291, 297–299, 305	24	149, 152
		24:1–25:45	149
19:3	300	24:1–25:46	153
19:3–12	284	24:29–51	153
19:4	301, 303, 307	24:34	158
19:5–6	300	25:31–46	160
19:7	293, 300	25:37	155
19:8	300–301, 303, 307	25:46	155
19:9	83, 284, 291, 293, 300–303, 307	26	7
		26:3–75	180
19:10	300	26:14–35	175
19:10–12	291, 300–301	26:20	178
19:11	300	26:20–35	343
19:12	301–302	26:26–29	198
19:21	89	26:28	158, 343
20:4	155	26:51–54	269
20:17	167	26:54	153
20:25–26	259	26:56	153
20:30	167	27:3–10	318
21:1–28:15	154, 166	27:5	317
21:4	153	27:19	155
21:8	167	27:25	154
21:8–9	148	27:45	151, 160, 169
21:11	148	27:51	270
21:12–17	166	27:51–53	151, 160, 169
21:12–33	166	27:51–54	267
21:12–23:39	166	27:62–66	154
21:18–22	166	28:2–4	151, 158, 169
21:19	167	28:11–15	154
21:23	168	28:16–20	131, 147–150, 154, 158, 169, 199
21:23–27	166		
21:28–31	166	28:19	153, 199
21:28–32	167	28:20	152–153, 158, 169
21:31	156		
21:32	155, 158, 166–169	**Mark**	
21:33–41	167	1:1	5, 17, 21–22, 51, 59, 66, 74–75, 93, 105, 113, 122, 131–132, 264
21:33–28:16	167		
21:42–43	158, 167		
22:1–10	158, 167		
22:9–10	167	1:1–3	66
22:16	167	1:1–13	19, 39, 50–51, 58–59, 74, 121, 123–124, 128–129, 132–133, 141, 143–146, 264
23:1–10	167		
23:11–36	167		
23:23	303		
23:28	155		
23:29	155		

Reference	Pages	Reference	Pages
1:1–6:6	28	1:29	32
1:1–8:13	50	1:29–31	36
1:1–8:30	21, 28	1:32–34	31
1:1–16:8	45	1:34	36
1:2	167	1:35	32
1:2–3	41, 58, 66	1:35–39	74, 75
1:3	51	1:38	29
1:4	40, 41	1:38–39	29
1:4–6	70	1:39	21, 31
1:4–8	66	1:40–45	36
1:4–13	66	1:45	19, 21, 57, 123
1:7	51	2:1	32
1:7–8	58	2:1–12	36, 95
1:8	51	2:2	31, 303
1:9–11	66	2:10	64
1:10	51	2:12	19, 57, 123
1:11	51, 59, 68, 74–75, 93, 115, 126	2:13	31–32
1:12	32	2:13–14	33, 37, 41, 44–45, 62, 75, 135–136
1:12–13	51, 62, 263	2:13–15	86
1:14	22, 32, 58	2:13–17	36, 86
1:14–15	17, 21, 28, 31, 36–37, 50, 63, 74, 122–123, 135	2:14	88
		2:14–15	75
		2:20	59, 115
1:14–3:6	22, 28–29	2:26	73
1:14–8:21	57	2:28	64
1:14–8:30	19, 20–23, 28, 56, 61, 78, 123	3:1–6	36, 95
		3:5	53
1:14–16:8	50	3:6	21–22, 28, 52, 59, 64, 115, 123
1:15	235		
1:16	32	3:7–12	21–22, 28, 123
1:16–20	21, 32–33, 36–37, 41, 43–45, 57, 62, 75, 86, 88, 123–124, 135, 137, 334	3:7–6:6	22, 29
		3:7–6:13	27
		3:10	36
		3:10–12	22
		3:11–12	31
		3:12	59
1:17	137, 138	3:13	33, 36–37, 44
1:17–18	277	3:13–14	25, 33, 42, 136
1:17–4:34	44	3:13–19	21–22, 29, 41, 43–45, 57, 62, 86, 123, 135
1:19	32		
1:21	32		
1:21–28	31		
1:21–3:6	21	3:14	26, 31–33, 36–37, 42, 76, 85, 100–101, 104, 113, 137, 139
1:24	72		
1:25	59		
1:27	19, 31, 57, 123		

3:14–15	31–32, 34, 36–37, 42, 44, 72–73, 75, 137–138	5:32	291
		5:35–43	23, 95
		5:37	141
3:14–19	44	5:39	73
3:15	31, 42	6:1–6	21, 29, 35–37, 123
3:16	32	6:2	36, 44, 74–75
3:16–17	65, 141	6:2–3	19, 57, 123
3:19	32, 65, 100–101	6:3	22, 44
3:20	74, 82, 299	6:5	36–37
3:20–21	29	6:6	21–22, 26, 28–29, 39, 43, 52, 123
3:20–35	22–23, 41, 95		
3:22	19, 57, 123	6:6–7	44
3:22–30	29	6:6–13	21–22, 24–26, 29, 30, 38, 44–45, 135
3:28–29	74–75		
3:31–35	29	6:6–16	25
3:34–35	29, 36, 44	6:6–30	15–45, 75, 95, 123
4:1–32	23	6:6–8:30	23
4:1–34	22, 29, 52	6:7	26–27, 29, 32, 36, 42, 138, 174
4:3–9	138		
4:10	57, 138	6:7–8	41
4:10–11	41	6:7–9	30–36, 42
4:10–12	74	6:7–13	15, 22, 26–27, 29–37, 41–44, 75, 137–138
4:10–25	69		
4:11	59, 136		
4:12	53	6:7–30	52, 57, 73, 138
4:13	57, 138	6:8	32
4:23	57	6:8–9	26, 30, 32
4:33–34	21, 41, 74	6:10–11	26, 34–36
4:34	136, 138	6:12	27, 29
4:35–41	41, 52, 135	6:12–13	26, 36–37
4:35–5:43	22, 29	6:13	27, 73
4:40	44, 138	6:13–30	54
4:40–41	57	6:14	27
4:41	19, 44–45, 57, 68, 75, 123, 138	6:14–19	45, 54
		6:14–29	15, 23, 26–27, 37–43, 52, 67, 70, 138
5:1–43	44		
5:7–10	72		
5:14	42	6:14–8:26	27
5:16	52, 57	6:15	58
5:17–48	291	6:16	58
5:19	42	6:17–19	40
5:20	19, 57, 123	6:21–35	23
5:21–24	23, 95	6:30	15, 24–27, 29, 38, 41–45, 73, 75, 135, 138, 174
5:21–34	95		
5:24–34	23, 95		
5:25–34	36	6:30–44	22, 28
5:31	52, 57	6:31	27, 28

6:31–44	24, 50–55, 130, 139	7:37	19, 57, 123
6:31–8:21	54	8:1–4	28
6:32	27	8:1–9	50–55, 78, 130, 139
6:33–34	28	8:1–10	20, 22, 28
6:33–8:21	28	8:3–4	54
6:35–36	52, 54	8:4	52, 57
6:36–44	28	8:5	51
6:37	54, 57	8:5–7	44
6:37–38	44	8:6	54
6:38	51	8:8	54
6:41	54	8:11–12	54
6:43	54	8:11–13	52
6:44	28	8:11–21	28, 57, 139
6:45–52	52, 54, 135, 318	8:12	72
6:48–50	19, 57, 123	8:14	53
6:50	68	8:14–21	28, 50–55, 68–69
6:51–52	139	8:14–26	21
6:52	53–55, 75, 139	8:14–9:19	51
6:53–56	21	8:14–9:29	47–76
6:54–56	28	8:15	52, 72
7:1–23	22, 28, 51–52, 54	8:17–18	54–55, 68, 75, 79, 139
7:2	52, 54		
7:2–5	28	8:17–21	57
7:2–13	65	8:18	21, 53, 55–56, 58–59
7:3	52, 54		
7:4	52, 54	8:22	58
7:5	52, 54	8:22–26	20, 49, 55–58, 61, 76, 78, 139–140
7:14	53		
7:14–15	28, 52	8:22–30	61
7:15	54	8:22–52	123
7:17	74, 136	8:22–9:29	49–50
7:17–18	52	8:22–10:52	49–50, 53, 78–80, 90, 130, 135, 139
7:17–23	69, 82, 299		
7:18	52, 54	8:23–24	59
7:18–19	52	8:24	71
7:18–20	28	8:27	22, 49, 58, 62, 136
7:19	54	8:27–28	61
7:24–30	28, 51–52, 73	8:27–30	56–60, 78
7:24–37	28	8:27–9:1	65
7:25–37	54	8:27–9:13	50
7:26–28	28, 73	8:27–9:29	49, 74
7:27	54	8:27–10:45	79
7:28	54	8:27–16:8	98
7:29–30	73	8:28	22, 67
7:31–37	28, 53, 55	8:29	19–22, 48, 61–64, 68–70, 75, 123
7:35	53		

8:29–30	56, 123	9:14–19	75
8:30	19–20, 23, 61–62, 124	9:14–27	79
		9:14–28	76
8:31	17, 19–21, 49, 52, 56, 61–64, 67–71, 75, 78, 99–100, 105, 113, 115, 122–124, 127–128, 139	9:14–29	71–74, 79
		9:18	75
		9:19	74, 76
		9:19–27	76
		9:28	75, 82, 299
		9:29	75–76
8:31–32	61	9:30	58, 80
8:31–9:1	41, 70	9:30–31	21
8:31–9:29	61–63	9:30–10:29	49
8:31–10:44	145	9:30–10:31	49–50, 79, 87
8:31–10:52	19, 123	9:31	19–20, 49, 56, 78, 99–100, 105, 113, 115, 123–124, 127–128, 139
8:31–15:47	19, 21, 56, 61, 70, 123–124		
8:32	61–62, 75, 84		
8:32–33	20, 49, 62–63, 68–69, 73, 76, 139	9:31–50	90
		9:32–34	49, 85, 90
8:32–9:29	71	9:32–50	84
8:33	74	9:32–10:31	84
8:34	76	9:33	49, 58, 82, 136, 299
8:34–35	41	9:34	49, 58–59, 136
8:34–38	75, 139–140	9:33–37	20, 80, 140
8:34–9:1	48, 63–65, 67–69, 74, 80, 128, 139	9:33–50	139–140
		9:35–37	84, 139
8:34–9:29	50	9:35–50	80, 90
8:35	76, 88	9:35–10:31	50
8:38	67, 69–70, 72, 76	9:36–37	80
9:1	5, 76	9:37	35
9:1–4	65	9:38–41	139
9:1–8	69	9:43–47	306
9:2	71, 141	10	80
9:2–4	76	10:1	21, 58, 84, 85
9:2–7	76	10:1–9	80, 299
9:2–8	70	10:1–12	79–84, 87–88, 284, 291, 297–303, 305–306
9:2–13	65–70		
9:5–6	68–69, 74, 76		
9:7	68–69, 75–76, 93, 142, 146	10:1–31	77–91, 300
		10:2–9	79
9:8–13	76	10:3–4	293
9:9	69, 71	10:5–9	82
9:10–11	74	10:6	264, 301, 303, 307
9:11	76	10:10	84
9:11–13	39, 67	10:10–12	80, 300, 302
9:12–13	76	10:11–12	284, 293, 299–301

10:13–16	80, 84–85, 139	11:10	97
10:15	35	11:11–13:37	104
10:17	49, 58, 136	11:12–14	23, 95
10:17–22	79–80	11:12–24	19, 123
10:17–31	79, 84–90	11:12–25	95
10:21	89	11:15–19	23, 95
10:23–31	80, 139	11:20–21	23
10:27	74	11:20–25	95
10:28	88	11:24	42
10:29–31	88	11:26–12:44	269
10:30–45	49	11:27–12:44	19, 123
10:32	49, 58, 130, 136, 142	12:10–11	95–96, 110, 114, 145
10:32–33	19, 123–124	12:14	58
10:32–34	19, 49, 56, 78, 80, 99, 113	12:22–25	110
		12:34	269
10:32–35	20	12:41–44	99
10:32–52	49–50	12:44	42
10:33	100	13	99, 149
10:33–34	105, 115, 127–128, 139	13:1–23	269
		13:1–37	19, 99, 123
10:35–37	49, 139	13:3	141
10:35–41	367	13:9–13	5
10:35–44	140	13:10	137
10:35–45	139	13:24–27	105
10:36–45	20	13:24–37	269
10:37	59, 110, 367	13:31	143
10:38–40	50	13:33	103
10:38–44	139	13:34	103
10:39	140	13:35	103
10:41	49, 139	13:36	103
10:42–44	367	13:37	103
10:42–45	50	14	7
10:45	49, 91, 109, 130, 140, 145, 256, 368	14–15	97
		14:1–2	17, 21, 99–100, 122
10:46	49, 58, 136	14:1–31	97
10:46–52	20, 49, 56, 78, 139, 140	14:1–72	97–106, 114, 180, 184
10:52	49, 58, 136	14:1–15:47	19, 94, 114, 123
11:1–6	100	14:1–16:8	97
11:1–11	17, 19, 21, 23, 95–96, 99, 122–123	14:3–9	99–100, 126
		14:10–11	99–100, 141
		14:11	318
11:1–25	269	14:12–16	100–101
11:1–13:36	269	14:14	99
11:8	58, 136	14:17	111, 178

14:17–21	101–102, 105	14:63–64	105
14:17–31	23, 105, 175, 184, 343	14:66	105
		14:66–72	105–106, 114, 125–126, 128, 135, 141
14:20–25	110		
14:21	98		
14:22–25	101–102, 104, 106, 110, 114, 198	15:1	106
		15:1–5	107
14:26–31	101–103, 141	15:1–47	106–115
14:26–32	110–111	15:1–16:8	141
14:27	104–105	15:2	107, 110, 114
14:27–28	142–143	15:6–11	107–108
14:27–38	103	15:6–32	95
14:28	20, 45, 60, 114, 117, 127, 129, 143, 145–146	15:9	114
		15:9–10	41
		15:10	41
14:29–31	103	15:12	41, 114
14:30	104, 106	15:12–15	107–108
14:30–31	105	15:14	41
14:32–42	103, 141	15:14–15	41
14:33	267	15:16–20	108–109
14:33–42	104	15:18	114
14:36	98, 109, 340	15:20–25	102, 108–110, 115
14:39	103	15:22	106
14:41–42	104	15:24	111
14:43–45	125–126, 128	15:26	114, 145
14:43–46	141	15:26–32	57
14:43–52	104	15:29	96, 111, 145
14:46–72	115	15:30	114
14:50	5, 19, 60, 114–115, 124–129, 141, 145	15:30–31	111
		15:31	114
14:50–52	114, 129, 131, 135, 143–144	15:31–39	69
		15:32	114
14:51–52	113, 126–127, 141, 151	15:33	109, 269
		15:33–39	111–112, 267, 276
14:53–54	105, 114	15:34	19, 109, 113–115, 124–127, 129, 144–145
14:53–65	95, 104–105		
14:53–72	23, 106		
14:54	113–114	15:37	19, 114, 124, 269
14:55	105	15:38	145, 151, 270
14:55–61	105	15:38–39	115
14:57–58	145	15:39	5, 57, 93, 115, 126
14:58	41	15:40	113, 115, 125
14:60–62	41	15:40–41	112–113, 115, 125–126, 128, 135
14:61–62	57, 64, 69, 105–107, 110, 114	15:41	128
		15:42–47	113
14:62	5, 93, 107, 124		

15:46	106	7:39	176
15:47	45, 115, 125, 128	8:45	347
16	118	8:51	347
16:1	113	9:10	174
16:1–4	17, 21, 45, 122	9:10–36	55
16:1–7	118, 128	9:20	48, 347
16:1–8	16, 19, 41, 120–121, 124–126, 132, 141, 143–146	9:22	185, 346
		9:23–27	48
		9:28	347
16:5	127, 141, 151	9:32–33	347
16:6	19, 129, 143–145	9:44	185, 346
16:6–8	117–130	9:51	172, 344–345
16:7	20, 45, 60, 117, 128–129, 132, 141, 143, 146	9:51–19:44	188
		9:52–19:44	172
		9:57	172
16:7–8	16, 119, 129	9:60	306
16:8	5, 20, 45, 68, 115, 117–121, 128–129, 132, 135, 142–144	10:4	30, 32
		10:5–12	34
		10:5–11:1	171
16:9–10	118	10:10–11	35
16:9–20	118, 131–132	10:25–37	171
16:10	42	10:34	37
16:13	42	10:38	172
		11:1–13	188
Luke		11:37–52	188
1–2	171, 173, 322, 324, 345	11:37–54	176
		11:49	174
1:1–4	173, 310–311	12:1–3	188
1:3–4	179	12:41	347
1:4	173	13:1–53	171
1:18	317	13:22	172
2:7	172	13:23–24	167
3:19–20	40	13:24–25	188
3:21–22	155	14:1–24	176
4:16–30	172	14:7–14	188
4:18	348	14:14	176
4:38	347	14:16–24	177
5:8	347	14:26	188
5:17–7:27	171	14:33	188
5:27	167	15:11–32	171, 340
5:27–32	176	16:1–9	291
6:13	174	16:1–13	230
6:14	347	16:10–13	291
6:20–23	179	16:13–18	171
7:36–50	176	16:14–15	291
7:37	176	16:16–17	291

16:18	82, 284, 290–293, 301	22:35–38	181–182
		22:36	186
16:19–30	291	22:37	189
17:5	174	22:38	182, 230
17:11	172	22:44–49	131
18:1–19:1	171	22:54	347
18:15–17	188	22:55	347
18:28	347	22:58	347
18:31	172	22:60–61	347
18:31–33	185, 346	23:1–24:46	171
19:1–10	177, 188	23:32	189
19:11	172	23:34	340
19:28	172	23:41–42	269
19:31	177	23:43	340
19:37	172	23:44–46	267
19:41	172	23:45	270
19:45	172	24:1	344
19:45–24:53	173	24:1–12	118, 174
19:51	177	24:4	151
21:37	173	24:10	174
22	7	24:13	344–345, 347
22:1–24	174	24:13–25	345
22:1–24:53	174	24:13–35	171, 174, 345
22:8	347	24:14	345
22:14	174, 178	24:15	345, 347
22:14–18	181	24:15–17	346
22:14–20	183	24:16	345
22:14–38	171–189, 343, 347	24:17	173
22:15	185	24:18	345
22:19	198	24:19	346
22:19–20	181	24:20	346
22:19–23	181–182, 184	24:21	346
22:21	182, 343	24:23	346
22:21–38	183	24:24	346
22:22	185	24:25–26	346
22:24	182, 186	24:25–27	347
22:24–27	187–188	24:27	346
22:24–30	181	24:28	347
22:25–26	186	24:29	344, 347
22:31	347	24:30–31	347
22:31–32	187	24:33	347
22:31–34	181–182, 186	24:34	347–348
22:31–38	188	24:36	344
22:32	182	24:36–49	131, 174–175
22:33–34	187	24:44	173
22:34	347	24:45–48	178

24:46–49	173, 178	6:16–21	192, 318
24:46–51	173	6:25–51	215
24:47	179, 188	6:25–59	285
24:50–51	173	6:27	285
24:50–53	174	6:36	214
24:51	344	6:39–40	272
		6:40	215
		6:44	272

John

1:1–2	193, 274, 285, 305	6:46–48	215
1:1–18	230, 255, 264	6:51	202
1:14	193, 285, 352, 362	6:51–58	7, 201–202, 206, 216–217
1:18	214		
1:19–2:12	265	6:52	202
1:32–33	192	6:53	202, 207, 210, 212, 285
1:35–40	195		
1:51	214, 285	6:53–58	203
2:1–11	191–192	6:54	202
2:13–22	192	6:55	202
3	216	6:56	202
3:1–21	192, 230–231	6:63	202
3:3–5	212	7:38	192, 205
3:5	201–204, 206–207, 210, 212, 217	7:39	197
		8:24	285
3:13	214	8:28	214, 285
3:13–14	214, 285	8:38	214
3:15–21	272	8:54	197
3:16	330	8:57	214
3:16–17	214	8:58	285
3:66	214	9	204, 206, 212, 216–217
4:1–30	192		
4:31–34	192	9:1–38	192, 206
4:34	214	9:7	204
4:45	214	9:11	204
5	204	9:17	204
5:1–8	204	9:22	334
5:1–9	192	9:33	205, 212
5:8	204	9:34	212
5:21–26	272	9:35–38	205
5:27	285	9:36	205
5:28–29	272	9:37	214
5:37	214	9:38	205
6	202, 205	10:1–21	192
6:1–15	7	10:30	214
6:1–58	192	11:1–44	192
6:2	214	11:4	197
6:15–16	204	11:26	272

11:40	214	16:17	214
12:1–8	191	16:33	363
12:6	318	17:1	197
12:16	215	17:2–3	47, 214
12:23	197	17:4	197, 214
12:28	197	17:5	197, 285
12:32	214	17:9–19	215
12:42	212, 334	17:10	197
13	206, 216–217, 343	17:18–20	47
13:1	214, 343	17:21	47
13:1–17	192	17:23	47
13:1–20	192, 205–206	18:1–11	265
13:1–38	217	19:17–21	216
13:10	192	19:17–37	276
13:16	26	19:22	214
13:18	343	19:25–27	216
13:19	285	19:28–30	216
13:21–38	7	19:30	214, 267, 271, 285
13:31–32	197	19:34	201–202, 206–207, 210, 212, 216–217
13:31–14:31	215		
13:34–35	47	19:34–35	7, 192
14:1–16:33	185	19:35	207, 214
14:7	214	19:37	214
14:9	214	19:38–42	265
14:13	197	20:1–3	118
14:15–17	285	20:9	228
14:16–17	214	20:18	285
14:25	214	20:18–23	131
14:25–26	285	20:21–23	47, 285
14:26	214	20:23	192
15:1–11	192	20:30–31	131, 193, 213, 228, 285, 311, 334
15:5	32, 37		
15:8	197	21:5–6	192
15:12	47	21:15–17	187
15:13	214	21:15–20	334
15:17	47	21:13	192
15:24	214	21:20–24	195
15:26	214	21:22–23	195
15:26–27	285		
16:2	212	**Acts**	
16:7–11	215, 285	1–5	173
16:12	215	1:1	179
16:12–15	285	1:1–2	173
16:13–15	215	1:8	173, 177–178, 188, 345
16:14	197		
16:16	214	1:18	318

2:1–13	173	11	7
10:1–11:18	180	11:17–34	343
11:26	334	11:22	344
20:17–35	185	11:23	198
28:16–31	345	11:23–25	257
28:31	173, 177	11:24–25	198
		11:26	257
		11:28–29	344

Romans

1:1	174	12:1	289
1:14	258, 369	15:3–7	132
1:20	261	15:3–11	131
3:21–26	128	15:3–19	281
5:1–8:39	128	16:1	289
5:12–21	128, 276, 304, 307		
5:20	307		

2 Corinthians

1:1	174
5:17	304

6:1–11	199
8:14–15	341
8:18–25	264
8:22	264
8:24–25	327
8:31–39	128
16:22	264

Galatians

1:1	174
2:11–14	209
2:11–21	55
2:15	304
3:27	257
3:27–28	199
4:4–7	341
6:17	359

1 Corinthians

1:1	174
1:23	93
4:10	359
5:1	302
7:1	289, 301
7:1–7	294
7:1–9	290
7:7	296
7:7–9	302
7:8–9	302
7:8–16	284, 294–296
7:10–11	82, 284, 289, 292–293, 300, 306
7:12–16	83, 289–290, 296, 302
7:14–16	307
7:15	303
7:25	289
7:27–28	303
8:1	289
9:16	258, 369
10–11	344

Ephesians

1:3–5	264
1:4	274

Philippians

2:5–7	273
2:5–11	257, 264, 342, 368
2:6–11	305
2:7–8	276
4:8–9	342

Colossians

1:1	174
1:15	274
1:15–20	264, 275
1:16	264
1:17	274

1:19–20	264	8:1	265, 267, 269
		8:2–11:19	266, 270
2 Timothy		9:29	274
4:2	258, 369	10:7	270
		11:12	270
Hebrews		11:15	267, 273
4:12	91	11:15–19	265, 270, 273
4:15	340	11:17	267, 270
		11:18	273
James		11:19	273
5:14	37	12:1	259–260, 267, 270
		12:1–17	270
1 Peter		12:1–14:20	266, 270
1:19–20	271	12:11	270, 273
1:23–25	249, 323	13:1	271
3:14–15	160	13:1–18	270
		13:8	265, 271–274, 276
2 Peter		14:1–4	271
1:12–15	185	14:1–20	270
3:14–16	228	14:10	271
		15:1–16:21	266
1 John		15:1–22:5	270
2:6	257, 340, 368	15:2–4	271
4:8	214	15:3	260, 266–267
4:16	214	16:17	271
5:8	192, 201	16:17–22:5	265
		17:1–22:5	266, 272
Revelation		17:5	274
1:1–3	273	17:14	272
1:1–8	266	17:24	272
1:6	272	19:1–22:5	271
1:9–3:22	266	19:7–9	272
1:14–17	274	19:11–14	272
1:18	281	19:11–20:15	272
4–5	265, 268	20:4–6	272
4:1–5:14	269	20:7–15	272
4:1–8:1	266, 268	21:1	267
4:1–18:24	271	21:2	267
5	269	21:5	260, 267
5:6	269, 273–274, 276	21:22	272
5:7–8	269, 273	21:27	272
5:11–12	269, 273	22:1–5	268, 272–273
7:9–11	269	21:10	268
7:13–17	269, 273, 276	22:6–21	266
		22:20	272
		22:21	273

www.ingramcontent.com/pod-product-compliance
Ingram Content Group UK Ltd.
Pitfield, Milton Keynes, MK11 3LW, UK
UKHW041304180426
11947UKWH00009B/674